Introduction to Operations Research Techniques

HANS G. DAELLENBACH

JOHN A. GEORGE

University of Canterbury
Christchurch, New Zealand

Allyn and Bacon, Inc.

Boston • London • Sydney • Toronto

Introduction to Operations Research Techniques

Library of Congress Cataloging in Publication Data

Daellenbach, Hans G

   Introduction to operations research techniques.

   Bibliography: p.
   Includes index.
   1. Operations research. I. George, John A., joint author. II. Title.
T57.6.D3   658.4'034   77-7626
ISBN 0-205-05755-1

Contents

2 LINEAR PROGRAMMING—A GRAPHICAL INTRODUCTION   42

3 THE SIMPLEX METHOD   88

4 DUALITY AND POSTOPTIMAL ANALYSIS 116

5 NETWORKS AND THE TRANSPORTATION PROBLEM 148

9 MARKOVIAN DECISION PROCESSES   286

10 INTRODUCTION TO WAITING LINE MODELS   312

Preface

This text is an attempt to provide a survey of the major quantitative tools and techniques used by operations researchers. We make no pretense that it is a complete treatment of any of these tools, rather we see it as a springboard to more advanced study, either practical or theoretical. For this reason it stresses only those aspects and properties that are crucial for a fundamental understanding and use of each tool. The finer points that make a tool computationally efficient, and the mathematical niceties that attract the theoretician are largely ignored for the sake of brevity and simplicity. To keep the level of mathematical sophistication needed to a low level, proofs—mostly heuristic in nature—are only given if they enhance the understanding and the application of a tool. For each model or technique the questions foremost in our minds were: "What are its assumptions? How is a real life problem translated to fit into it? What are the basic ideas underlying its solution method? What are its strengths and weaknesses?"

We have attempted to keep the mathematical prerequisites to a minimum. However, the text assumes that the reader has been exposed to the material taught in elementary college algebra, differential calculus, and introductory statistics courses, as is commonly required of students in business administration, economics, and industrial engineering. Chapters 3, 4, 5, 8, 9, 12, 13, and 14 require some linear algebra—the concepts of vectors, bases, and systems of linear equations—though no matrix algebra, except for Chapter 8 which uses matrix multiplication. Appendix A on linear algebra briefly reviews, with examples, all concepts and operations used, and it has an optional section covering a matrix algebra treatment of linear programming. Chapters 11, 13, and 14 use elementary differential calculus, such as first and second order derivatives and partial derivatives of simple polynomial and exponential functions. One section of Chapter 6, Chapters 7 to 11, and Chapters 15 and 16 include stochastic aspects for which Appendix B on probability provides the necessary background. Starred sections of Chapters 4 to 11 require a higher level of mathematical maturity than other parts. These sections cover optional material and can be skipped without loss of continuity. Similarly, Chapters 12 to 14 are, by the

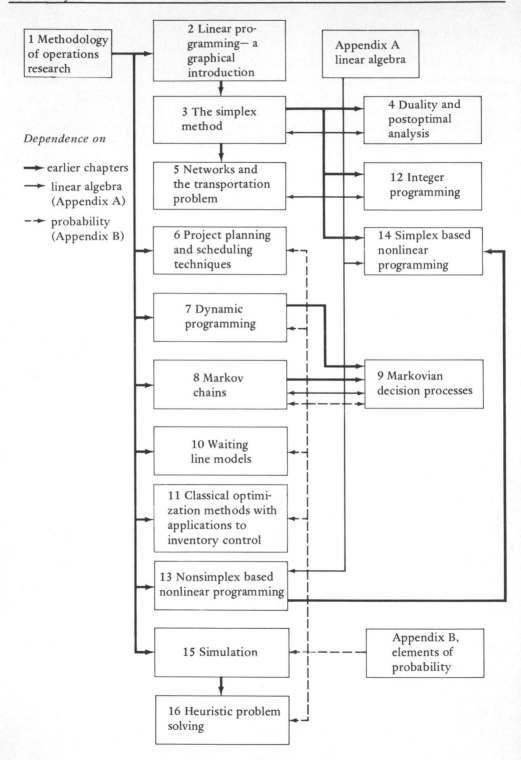

very nature of the subjects treated, at a more advanced level than the other parts of the text.

Although the mathematical sophistication of the text is not demanding, the subtle logic often used in operations research tools is far from simple. The translation process from a behavioral situation to a valid mathematical model calls for a facility to think quantitatively. This is particularly true for the inventory control models presented in Chapter 11. Some basic understanding of computer programming would prove helpful for a number of chapters, particularly Chapter 15 on simulation and Chapter 16 on heuristic problem solving.

A complete list of English language journals and bibliographies in operations research, as well as a selection of some general introductory texts in operations research appear in the Bibliography.

The text is suited for introductory and intermediate courses in operations research at a junior, senior or first-year graduate level in almost any field, and especially business, economics, and engineering. While readers are not assumed to have an in-depth knowledge in any of these fields, they should not be completely naive in these subjects, especially the most basic principles of managerial economics. Many of the basic ideas in operations research are akin to economic thinking.

Whenever possible, the various chapters or sets of chapters have been made self-sufficient, in the sense that they do not rely on the material covered earlier, except for starred sections. All chapters assume that the reader is familiar with the basic philosophy and methodology of operations research expounded in Chapter 1 since this forms the framework within which all techniques are applied. The dependence relations between chapters are depicted in the chart on the facing page.

The instructor has considerable scope in choosing the collection and sequence of topics, and may fit the text to either a half-year or a full-year course. For instance, Chapters 2 through 6 provide sufficient material for a half-year course, dealing exclusively with linear models. Alternatively, Chapters 1, 2, 3, 5, 6, 7, 11, and 15 given at lesser depth could be used to cover a broader spectrum of topics in a half-year course. Except at the graduate level, the text contains more material than can be covered adequately in a full-year course.

ACKNOWLEDGEMENTS

This text is an outgrowth of teaching operations research for several years. Both undergraduate and graduate students have contributed to it by suggesting improvements in the presentation of the material as well as by diligently combing the manuscript for errors. Chapter 16, Heuristic Problem Solving, was written by John Rodgers, who guides us on a delightful excursion to the land of the hobbits.

Introduction
to Operations
Research Techniques

1

Methodology
of
Operations
Research

What is operations research? The name is of little help in explaining what it is all about. A product of World War II, its name reflects its first applications—the analysis and research of military operations. Although operations research problems are concerned with control of operations of all types, it is not scientific research into the control of operations as the term *research* is used today, with its connotation of advancing knowledge in some science.

Operations research is the systematic application of quantitative methods, techniques, and tools to the analysis of problems involving the operation of systems. The aim is the evaluation of probable consequences of decision choices, usually under conditions requiring the allocation of scarce resources—funds, manpower, time, or raw materials. The objective is to improve the effectiveness of the system as a whole, with emphasis on the last three words. We shall return to this point. Thus, most operations research projects involve the optimization of some operation of a system, such as minimizing production costs, maximizing profits, maximizing the capacity of a flow (of goods or information) through some network, or minimizing the cost of achieving certain technical properties for some engineering entity or operation.

It is fair to say that operations research is not a science, for it is not about any well defined physical, biological, or social phenomena. While chemists know about atoms and molecules and have theories about their interactions, and biologists know about living organisms and have theories about vital processes, operations researchers do not claim to know or have theories about operations. Operations research is essentially a collection of mathematical techniques and tools which, in conjunction with a systems approach, are applied to solve practical decision problems of an economic or engineering nature. Although this text is aimed mainly at business or industrial applications, operations research techniques are being used in such diverse fields as medicine; ecology; forestry; urban planning; architecture; civil, mechanical, electrical, and chemical engineering; space exploration; law enforcement; and logistics.

In this chapter we will explore how operations research projects are dealt with. We will demonstrate some of the philosophy underlying operations research. As you read through these pages, you will become increasingly aware of the fact that the complexities of reality call for great flexibility in how operations research projects are tackled. There exists no one correct approach. The "best" approaches to be followed not only depend on the nature of the problem and the amount of time and funds available, but also on the training and personality of the operations researcher. Therefore, all we can do is to highlight the most important aspects of the methodology, give some illustrations, and point out the various pitfalls that will invariably crop up along the crooked way to the successful completion of a project.

While writing this chapter we found that it is not really possible to discuss the methodology of operations research without assuming at least some familiarity with operations research techniques. Thus, should we expose you to the most basic operations research techniques first? On the other hand, it does not make much sense to study individual techniques without a framework of methodology and the philosophy of operations research. Discussing techniques in a "vacuum" tends to convey a completely wrong picture of the true nature of operations research. We chose to consider methodology first, accepting the risk that some concepts will remain fuzzy on first reading. In fact, Chapter 1 should be studied once more when you have become familiar with some of the techniques in the following chapters.

1-1 THE PHASES OF AN OPERATIONS RESEARCH PROJECT

Any operations research project that has a happy ending goes through five major steps or phases:

1. formulating the problem;
2. constructing a mathematical model to represent the operation studied;
3. deriving a solution to the model;
4. testing the model and evaluating the solution;
5. implementing and maintaining the solution.

The remaining chapters of this text will be devoted to Steps 2 and 3, namely the translation of the empirical and theoretical observations made during the formulation of the problem into formal mathematical models consisting of functions, equations and/or inequalities and the techniques available to find optimal solutions to such models.

Although the phases are normally initiated in this order they do not necessarily terminate in the same order. In fact, each phase usually continues until the project is successfully implemented. All phases overlap subsequent as well as preceding phases. For example, the successful formulation of the problem depends on having at least tentatively considered each of the other four phases. Why? Interrelationships between various aspects of the operation may suggest a form of model, which in turn may dictate what data are needed for problem formulation, testing, and implementation. The complexity of the solution to a model may call for additional simplifications to be introduced into the model. The form of the solution used must be suitable for implementation. Testing the model and consideration of the implementation may reveal obstacles that lead to a reformulation of the original problem. So, even if we must discuss each phase separately, it should be borne in mind that they overlap.

As pointed out earlier, the objective of an operations research project is to improve the effectiveness of the system as a whole. This improvement can, however, only be secured if the solution to the problem is fully implemented. Securing the implementation of the solution is thus the prime concern underlying the first four phases. All measures that enhance the chances of implementation have to be initiated and planned for from the very outset of the project. In fact, Professor C. W. Churchman—one of the wise men of operations research—states that "securing implementation is the first phase of any operations research project."

During all phases, it is crucial to record for future reference: all assumptions made (e.g., the basis for all simplifications introduced into the model); all data used and their sources; and a complete description of the various steps of the analysis made, including any weaknesses and uncertainties in the assumptions and in the data. This point cannot be stressed enough. As the operations researcher gets more familiar with the problem and as a project progresses through its various phases it invariably will undergo minor and major revisions and corrections. Assumptions, simplifications, and shortcuts in the logic introduced a few weeks or months earlier are easily forgotten unless they have been documented in detail. It is also a prerequisite to establish effective maintenance procedures for the solution. As is true for most technical professions, proper documentation for the project is part of the professional ethics of any operations researcher.

Most operations research projects are not the sole effort of a single analyst, but the fruit of a team effort where team members complement each other with specialized knowledge. The composition of the team may change as the project progresses. However, the team should include at least one person intimately involved with the operation being studied, to provide the necessary physical and technical know-how about the operation, as well as the likes and dislikes of the people affected by the project. This may be the decision maker, a close assistant, or one of the persons who will actually be in charge of using the solution of the model. Not only will this person serve as the liaison between the operations research team and the sponsor of the project, but also as a sounding board for the other members of the team. His or her participation throughout the project will improve the chances of successful implementation.

Although there are numerous possibilities for using some of the operations research techniques for small projects that can be completed within a few days, most operations research projects that have a major impact on the operations of any organization require a few months to several years from project initiation to a successful conclusion. The total manpower invested may easily be a multiple of the total time span. Even a routine inventory control problem may involve 2 to 3 man months of problem formulation and model construction, followed by 3 to 9 man months of computer programming and data collection, and take several months to be properly implemented. The sponsor of a project should be made aware from the outset of these realities. He should be warned that unforeseen factors (such as missing, or bad data, or unexpectedly complex relationships) will invariably result in deadlines being overshot. The discussion in the following sections is relevant mainly for projects of such scope.

1-2 FORMULATION OF THE PROBLEM

The formulation of the problem is a sequential process—the initial and often tentative formulation goes through a series of progressive reformulations and refinements as the project proceeds and more and better insight is obtained into the problem. It may only end when the project has been properly implemented and has proved itself successful in actual operation. It is this phase where the ultimate success, or failure, of a project usually has its roots!

What is a problem?

For a problem to exist:

1. There must be an individual (or group of individuals)—referred to as the *decision maker(s)*—who has a felt-need to be satisfied or an *objective* to be achieved.
2. The decision maker must have at least two *alternative courses of actions* available, i.e., the decision maker must have a choice of behavior.
3. There must be some doubt as to which course of action is best in terms of the decision maker's objective. (All problems eventually boil down to an evaluation and a comparison of alternative courses of action.)
4. There must be an *environment* to which the problem pertains, i.e., to which it is relevant. For operations research projects, this environment is usually part or all of an organized system, such as a firm, a governmental agency, an economic market, or an engineering entity.

In short, a decision maker is said to have a problem if he or she wants something within a real context, has alternative ways of obtaining it, and is in doubt as to which alternative is best in terms of the objectives.

The components of a problem are thus: (1) the decision maker, (2) the objectives, (3) the alternative courses of action, and (4) the environment. To formulate the problem, we have to first identify these components and analyze the relationships between them.

1-3 THE COMPONENTS OF A DECISION PROBLEM

The decision maker is the individual or group who has control over the choice of actions to be taken. In many instances, there are several levels of decision makers: those who actually make the day-to-day decisions for the operation studied, those who have the power to initiate and change policies governing how decisions are to be made, and those who have delegated the power of decision making.   The operations researcher should have a thorough understanding of the span of control vested with each level.   This is important in order to define the scope of a project—those aspects of the decision problem that can be changed and those that are "off limits."   Organization charts help to provide part of the information.   But a complete picture can be obtained only by interviewing and questioning the people within an organization.

A decision maker usually has multiple objectives, some of which are acquisitive—something to be achieved such as maximizing profits or maximizing output—and some of which are retentive—retaining certain achievements at a specified level, such as keeping a given share of the market or maintaining a certain degree of customer goodwill.   Direct questioning of the decision maker may not reveal all the objectives; retentive objectives may be hidden or implicit in the policies currently pursued.

If there are conflicts in the objectives of different levels of decision makers, they must be resolved before the study proceeds any further.

C. W. Churchman, in *The Systems Approach* (Dell, 1968), asks the following two questions: "Can I [the decision maker] do anything about it?" and "Does it matter relative to my objectives?"   If the answer to both questions is yes, this particular aspect is part of the alternative courses of actions relevant to the problem. If the answer to the first is no but yes to the second, then the problem is part of the environment.   If the answer to both is no, then this aspect is not relevant to the problem.   Therefore, the alternative courses of action are those aspects of the system which are under the direct control of the decision maker and which contribute towards achieving his or her objectives.   Identification of alternative courses of action is best accomplished by analyzing the system or the environment in which the decisions are made.

The environment consists of those aspects of the system that are not controllable by the decision maker, such as the available financial resources, manpower, and machine capacity; constraints on alternative courses of action; costs and returns associated with alternative courses of action; and those aspects that are external to the organization, such as demand and supply patterns, legal constraints and possible counteractions that can be taken by competitors or labor unions, as well as the interrelationships between the various components.

The distinction between controllable and uncontrollable aspects may not be clear-cut or may even be somewhat arbitrary.   Some examples may help to clarify this point.   In many instances, the decision maker considers the demand for a product or service as uncontrollable (as part of the environment) in spite of the fact that if the firm chooses, it can affect the volume and pattern of demand in various ways, such as by granting quantity discounts and engaging in a variety of promotional activities.

Similarly, the length of a firm's manufacturing cycle (i.e., the production lead-time) can often be affected, within limits, by procedural changes such as the way in which the various documents are processed and channeled through the production department.   However, the production manager—our assumed decision maker—may decide for certain reasons that changes in such aspects are off-limits for the operations research practitioner.

It also happens that aspects are erroneously perceived as uncontrollable. The analysis of an inventory control problem showed that a number of products produced by a batch process had to be cooked in a pressure cooker. The quantity produced had always been equal to the full capacity of the cooker. When the operations researcher asked whether smaller quantities could be made, the answer was no. Probing into the technical reasons for this revealed that, in fact, it was only twenty years of tradition that determined the production quantities. "Why?" and "What happens if this is changed?" are undoubtedly the most frequent questions asked by operations researchers.

Analysis of the environment will reveal whether the data base, such as detailed records for sales or demand and cost factors, is adequate enough for proceeding with the project. If it is not, then procedures for collecting the required data must be initiated without further delay so that later, when solutions are to be computed and tested, the project is not jeopardized by missing or bad data. For instance, if the contemplated mathematical model requires daily demand data in the form of probability distributions and only summary records for monthly sales are presently kept, steps to collect such data may have to be undertaken immediately. Likewise, few firms have a record of the demand for their products; they only maintain sales records. However, sales records may underestimate demand due to lost sales, particularly large orders. (Why?) Furthermore, actual demand patterns may be distorted regarding timing and fluctuations if orders come in as a trickle but shipments are accumulated to fill truck loads.

1-4 STATE OF NATURE OR ENVIRONMENT

Most decision problems involve some elements of uncertainty. It may not be possible to completely identify all relevant aspects of the current or the future environment in which the decision has to be made because the state of the environment, or what in decision theory is referred to as the *state of nature*, may not be known exactly. In many problems, the effects of uncertainty may be so small that they can be ignored for purposes of analysis. We then talk about *decision making under certainty*. Each action leads to one and only one known outcome. There is only one state of nature relevant for the decision problem. See Figure 1-1. This does not necessarily mean that such problems are easy to solve. Consider the problem of the traveling salesman who has to visit a number of cities and would like to find an itinerary that minimizes the total distance traveled. Theoretically, problems of this sort can be solved by enumerating all possible itineraries (actions). From a practical point of view, such enumeration may not be economically feasible. If there are only ten cities, the number of possible itineraries is 3,628,800. For twenty cities, it is 2,432,902,008,176,640,000— clearly an impossible task. More powerful methods of evaluation are needed.

If a given action may lead to one of a number of possible outcomes, and the outcome is only known after the action has been taken, then we are dealing with *decision making under uncertainty*. As depicted in Figure 1-1, there are then several possible future states of nature for each action.

Decision problems under uncertainty may be graduated further according to

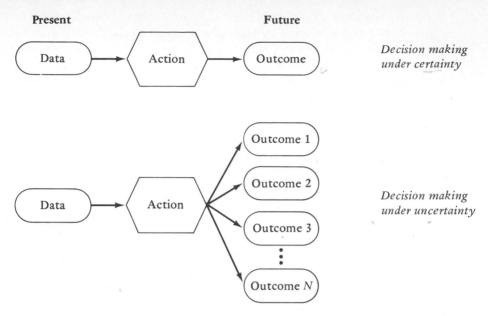

Present

Future

Data → Action → Outcome

Decision making under certainty

Data → Action → Outcome 1, Outcome 2, Outcome 3, ⋮ Outcome N

Decision making under uncertainty

Figure 1-1. *Decision making under certainty and uncertainty.*

the degree of uncertainty. If it is possible to specify a probability distribution over the outcomes for each action, the problem is classified as a *decision problem under risk,* whereas the label *decision making under uncertainty* is then reserved for those problems for which no objective information about the likelihood of the various outcomes is available. For example, from past experience, a newspaper vendor may have a fair idea of the chances of selling more than 50, 60, or 70 copies of the Saturday edition of the local paper. Thus, he faces a decision problem under risk. On the other hand, a firm contemplating whether or not to finance a given research project that, if successful, may lead to development of a new product usually will have no hard information about the chances of success, but only the personal judgments of the biased researchers. If the analyst is willing to make subjective probability judgments about the various outcomes, he or she may have recourse to the methods of *statistical decision theory*—a subject too vast for even cursory treatment in this text. (See H. Raiffa, *Decision Analysis,* Addison Wesley, 1968, for a delightful elementary introduction!)

Similarly, in adversary situations where two or more competitors try to outguess the opponents, little or nothing may be known about the likelihood or the various strategies that the competitors may take. *Game theory,* a subject not covered in this text, is an attempt to deal with such problems. (See J. D. Williams, *The Compleat Strategyst,* McGraw-Hill, 1965.)

Although interesting in theory, in practice these fine distinctions are not really helpful. The boundary between objective and subjective probabilities is rather fuzzy. The method finally chosen by the operations researcher will depend on many other elements, such as the time and amount of funds available to complete the project or the accuracy required, rather than on the classification of the problem.

تَوْجِيه (م.ب)

1-5 THE SYSTEMS ORIENTATION OF OPERATIONS RESEARCH

How does the operations researcher approach the task of identifying the components of a problem? Most projects start with an *orientation period* which involves visits to the facilities, interviews with the personnel involved, and, very early in the project, establishing lines of communication and procedural rules for obtaining the various bits and pieces of information and data needed during the formulation of the problem. This orientation period also has the important function of allowing the operations researcher to make a preliminary assessment of whether the project looks promising before spending large amounts of money and effort.

For the actual identification of the components of the problem, a *systems approach* or even formal *systems analysis* is used. Briefly, a systems analysis consists of the following steps.

1. Determine whose needs or desires the organization tries to satisfy and the nature of the needs and desires. For a business firm this means that the type of customers (including age groups and social strata), the geographical distribution for each type of goods or service offered, and the substitutability or complementarity of goods and services must be identified.
2. Determine how these needs and desires are communicated to the organization. For instance: How are orders communicated to the firm? What is the number of accounts? What are the patterns and sizes of orders? How are they affected by exogenous factors, such as seasonality, competition, etc.?
3. Determine how the information is recorded and transmitted within the organization. For instance, how are orders received and processed? How is each copy of any document used and filed? How are materials received and processed? How are goods prepared and shipped to customers? This is done by creating charts for the flow of documents and materials, and charts depicting various decision processes.

Such descriptive models are systematic approaches for identifying points where decisions are made, where they could be made, constraints on the decision-making process, and most aspects of the environment in which the decisions are made.

But what is a system? A system consists of a set of parts which in turn may be subsystems that interact with each other. Each part is in charge of some mission, task, or homogeneous set of activities. Some or all of the output of these missions become input into other parts. These missions contribute toward achieving some organizational goals, and their contribution is measurable in terms of their effectiveness toward achieving these goals.

Consider a firm where the various tasks are assigned to several functional departments, such as procurement of raw materials, production, warehousing and distribution, marketing, finance and credit management, and personnel.

Let us say that the production department considers changing the mode of producing a number of products from a batch method to a continuous production

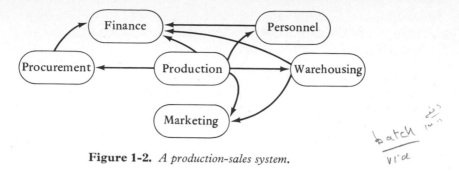

Figure 1-2. *A production-sales system.*

process. This would allow them to increase the *efficiency* of the operation by reducing unit production costs substantially. Should such a decision be made by considering the production department alone?

To answer this question we have to trace all possible direct and indirect effects of the proposed change on all other parts of the system, such as procurement, warehousing, and finance. Under a batch process, raw materials can be purchased in lots equal to the batch size. Delivery of the raw materials can be scheduled in such a way that they arrive at the factory just in time for the batch to be initiated. Hence, no raw material inventories have to be kept. Under a continuous production process, raw materials will still have to be procured in lots, though maybe different size lots. But they will have to be stored and used up gradually by the continuous production process. As a consequence, warehouse space has to be provided for raw materials, and they have to be handled twice before entering the production process. The creation of raw material inventories may also require additional financing.

Similarly, under a batch method, finished goods are received at the warehouse in big production lots. Assuming randomly fluctuating sales, finished goods inventories are depleted gradually until a new production lot arrives. Thus, finished goods inventories fluctuate in a regular saw tooth fashion. Under the continuous production process, finished goods will arrive at the warehouse in small (maybe daily) quantities and for the same pattern of sales, inventories will fluctuate in an irregular fashion—increasing when sales lag, decreasing or even running short when sales are above average. This will affect the amount of warehouse space needed, the frequency of shortages, and the required protection against such shortages. Note that shortages may occur under a batch method too!

The quality of the finished goods may be different under the two methods, affecting marketing via sales. The number of production workers needed may be different, affecting personnel. Some of these effects may be beneficial, others may be detrimental. Before a final decision is made, the net effect and accompanying indirect changes will have to be assessed as part of the overall savings produced by the project. In other words, we have to determine the *effectiveness* of the proposed change in terms of the performance of the system as a whole.

In brief, the essence of the systems approach is to trace, for each proposed change, all significant direct and indirect effects on all parts of the system, and to evaluate each action in terms of the effect for the system as a whole. (An excellent description of an actual case study of the systems approach in operations research is given in Churchman *et al.* in *Introduction to Operations Research*, chapter 2.)

Unfortunately, the boundaries of a system are often rather fuzzy. For instance, a firm's customers are usually regarded as exogenous to the system although, in fact, the decision maker may be able to influence them through advertising. Similarly, the government and the law are considered as outside the system. But the first may be influenced through lobbying, the second through changes in interpretation by the courts. Clearly, each system is in some way embedded in a larger system.

The operations researcher is usually asked to study a specific problem that may involve only one part (such as a department of an operation) or a group of parts or subsystem (such as production and procurement). For example, the problem may involve finding the "best" or optimal itinerary for the daily pick-up of checks and cash from suburban branch bank offices for processing at the head office (optimization of one operation), or it may deal with finding the optimal inventory control policy that minimizes total inventory and production costs (optimization of the operations of a subsystem). In rare instances the operations researcher may be given the unique opportunity to study the system as a whole in view of improving its overall effectiveness. An example of this sort is the development of a corporate planning model.

Any optimization problem that covers less than the whole system, where significant interactions with other parts are ignored, is referred to as *suboptimization*. If it covers the system as a whole we talk about *optimization*.

Most operations research projects involve suboptimization. There are many reasons why the operations researcher looks at less than the total system. There are technological reasons: the total system may be too complex to be properly included within the constraints of time and money imposed upon the project. There are practical reasons: the project is often restricted to cover only those parts that are under the direct control of the sponsor of the project, or the sponsor arbitrarily restricts the scope of the project to some specific operation. In such instances, the operations researcher should always question whether this may not severely jeopardize the success of the project and whether the project should be undertaken under such conditions. There may be political reasons: the project may be a door-opener for future projects. It may be politically more expedient to take only a small "bite" that can be handled successfully within a relatively short time, and then go on to more ambitious projects. This is particularly advisable for a novice operations researcher. Let us immediately add a word of caution. These restrictions on the scope of a project should not be used as an excuse to simply increase the efficiency of an operation at the expense of other parts of the system. It is the net contribution to increasing the effectiveness of the system as a whole that counts.

1-6 THE SEPARABILITY OF SYSTEMS

The determination of the scope of a project, i.e., the search of which parts and elements of a system should be included, becomes an integral part of the project itself. In general, the larger the portion of the system explicitly covered by the project, the

Scope

more expensive the project will be in terms of manpower and money, not only for the formulation of the problem and its mathematical solution, but also for data collection and implementation.   However, the larger the scope of a project, the larger are the benefits that can be gained from its implementation.   Thus, there exists the strategic problem of balancing the additional costs of enlarging the scope of the project with the additional benefits to be derived.   Economic theory would view this problem as a problem of equating marginal costs with marginal benefits.   Unfortunately, in the present state of operations research, we rarely have the means or information to perform such an analysis for finding the best scope of the project.   This aspect of operations research still remains largely a matter of judgment, experience or expediency, and the personality of the operations researcher, rather than of science.

Let us look at other avenues that may be helpful.   We said that a system consists of parts, each part contributing toward achieving the objectives of the system as a whole.   If the state of all parts but one is held fixed, then the effectiveness of the system may increase as that part is made more efficient.   Were it not for the interaction between parts, one could thus achieve an optimal system by improving each part, one by one.   But the path to the optimal system may not consist of optimizing each part individually, because once a given part is optimal for a given state of all other parts, it may lose this property as another part is changed.   For instance, a given set of bus routes for a public urban transportation system may be optimal for the existing road network, but may become inefficient with the introduction of a system of one-way streets.

However, if a part is independent of the rest of the system (e.g., the method of hiring and training bus drivers seems to be independent of the road network and bus routes), then changes in other parts of the system will not affect that part's efficiency.

A part or subsystem is said to be *separable* if its contribution towards the effectiveness of the system as a whole is independent of the state of all other parts. A system is completely separable if all its parts are separable.   A group of mail-workers, assigned to sort and distribute the mail in a given community may be a separable system.   The efficiency of each worker can usually be improved without affecting the efficiency of all others.   The work each worker completes simply adds to the total.   On the other hand, most production systems are not separable.   The optimal procurement policy depends on the mode and schedule of production, the optimal production set-up depends on the quality of the raw materials purchased, and all parts depend on the investment budget of the firm as a whole.

Any separable part can be optimized independently of all other parts.   A system can be optimized as a whole by optimizing each part individually only if the system is completely separable.

In practice, a few systems are truly separable; but some systems may have parts that have only weak interactions with other parts, whereas others are highly inter-dependent.   It is, therefore, more useful to talk about *degree of separability*.   If the interactions of a given part with all other parts of the system are relatively weak or insignificant, then this part exhibits a high degree of separability.   If such is the case, it may be safe to proceed as if the part were truly separable.

A new question now arises. When is the degree of separability sufficiently high so that any residual interactions can be ignored? No hard and fast rules exist. Again, the answer is largely a matter of judgment and experience.

In an optimization project that only covers a nonseparable part or subsystem of a system, the operations researcher explicitly or implicitly assumes that one of the following three propositions holds.

1. The modes of operation of the ignored parts of the system are not subject to being changed during the productive life of the project.
2. The states of the ignored parts are already optimal with respect to the optimum mode of operation of the part studied.
3. Although the states of the ignored parts are not optimal yet with respect to the optimum mode of operation of the part studied, the system as a whole will move toward an overall optimum by successive rounds of changes and adjustments of individual parts or subsystems.

Point 3 assumes that the system as a whole can be optimized by suboptimizing individual parts, one at a time. If a given part loses its optimality with respect to the state of all other parts as a result of changes in these parts, its optimal solution is updated accordingly. As a result, the system as a whole tends to move gradually toward an overall optimum. Point 3 assumes that the system is "well behaved."

1-7 SOME FURTHER IMPLICATIONS OF THE SYSTEMS APPROACH

Analysis of the environment of a decision problem is usually done on the basis of past records. Take for instance the problem of identifying and determining the relevant cost factors and demand situation for a production and inventory control problem. Most of the relevant cost factors are either obtained from cost accounting data or by actual observation on the production floor. Similarly, a picture of the demand situation for the various products is extracted from past sales records. These records and the observations made on the production floor reflect the present organizational structure and the present mode of operation of the system studied.

The parameters extracted from these data are then used to derive new "optimal" policies for the system. These new policies may involve changes in the mode of operation. But any parameters extracted from data prior to these changes may become out-of-date and may not be valid for the new mode of operation. For instance, under the current mode of operation, stock runouts may occur quite regularly. If demand for the products has to be estimated from sales, predictions derived from past sales may underestimate future demand considerably. Suppose the proposed mode of operation promises to reduce such shortages to a small fraction of the present rate. As a result, total sales will increase. Parameters derived from past sales records, without appropriate adjustments for lost sales, are, therefore, not relevant. Similarly, cost accounting data may cover a rate of pilferage and obsolescence reflecting the present inventory set-up, but these costs may change under the new mode of operation.   Thus, it is clear that **the values of all environmental parameters relevant for the derivation of "optimal" policies are those that reflect the proposed mode of operation once the project has been implemented and not the current mode of operation.**

In conclusion, although operations research is said to have certain qualities of scientific methods, in particular that it is objective (i.e., independent of the analyst), it becomes obvious that its objectivity is somewhat of an illusion.   The formulation of the problem involves a large element of more or less subjective judgment on the part of the operations researcher.   In particular, the observations concerning the environment are always based on strong systemic assumptions and simplifications about the behavior of the system.

1-8 SHOULD THE PROJECT CONTINUE?

As the formulation of the problem progresses, the operations researcher will have fairly definite ideas about the form of the mathematical model contemplated for the problem.   Before plunging fully into the next phase he or she should pause and attempt to evaluate the economic feasibility of the project.   The operations researcher should estimate the total manpower and funds required to complete the project. This must include the costs of implementation.   Approximate potential benefits should be evaluated as well.   Then, all the information should be submitted to the sponsor of the project who, on the basis of such information, will decide whether the project should be continued or abandoned.   More ambitious and innovative projects have to be treated largely like research and development projects, where final judgment may have to be postponed until the project has gone well into the actual mathematical modeling phase.

1-9 AN ABBREVIATED CASE STUDY

The manager of the lubricating oil division of a large oil company approaches the supervisor of the company's operations research section with a request for a preliminary study of the division's inventory control system: "Could operations research techniques help them in any way?"   This is the first time any division manager had approached the operations research section with an inventory control problem. Following the sound advice of Churchman *et al.* (*Introduction to Operations Research*), on how to attack such a project, the operations researcher assigned to the project arranges for a guided tour of the offices, plant, and warehouse of the lubricating oil division.   The tour is followed by a long and frank talk with the division manager. This reveals some of the reasons for the request.   The main reason is a statement in the company auditors' report that inventories seem excessively high—a remark passed on by the company comptroller to the vice-president of manufacturing, the immediate boss of the division manager and the man in charge of the whole refinery complex where the facilities of the division are located.   He also has to O.K. any project proposal involving funds in excess of $1,000. This factor immediately indicates that any proposal has to be written with the vice-president of manufacturing in mind.

Physically, the division consists of four parts:

1. a lubricating oil mixing plant where various base oils stocked in tanks outside the plant are mixed in large vats of different sizes;
2. a filling plant where the finished lubricating oils are packed, by one of several machines according to the type of container, in 50 gallon drums, gallon, quart, and pint cans;
3. the finished goods warehouse, where the filled containers are stored until they are shipped by rail or truck to customers;
4. a reconditioning plant, where drums returned from customers are cleaned and reconditioned for reuse.

A fairly large office staff processes customer orders, prepares bills of lading for shipment of the goods to customers, and prepares invoices. In that office there is an inventory clerk who for the last 20 years has been in charge of replenishing the finished goods inventories. His activities are of prime interest to the operations researcher.

The tour is followed up over the next two weeks by more thorough analysis of the various operations performed in the division on the basis of interviews with the people responsible and detailed observation in the plants and offices.

Leaving out most technological aspects, which in practice are important, the following picture emerges. The customers of the division consist of about 500 company-owned regional wholesale distributors, who sell to company-owned service stations and other retailers, and a small number of large industrial firms and governmental institutions that purchase on a wholesale basis. The warehouse also serves as the wholesale distributor for the region in which it is located. Sales are not solicited by the division itself, but by the company's marketing department.

Wholesale orders are always executed in a four-day cycle. Wholesale orders received on day n are processed in the offices on day $n+1$, where shipping documents are prepared. Each order usually covers an assortment of different products in various containers. The entire order is assembled for shipment during day $n+3$ and shipped on day $n+4$. Assembling an order consists of picking the correct amount of each product from the stocks in the warehouse and preparing it for shipment in an assigned area on the shipping docks. On the other hand, retail orders are executed on the same day that they are received. Retail sales (in physical quantity) amount to approximately 10 percent of the total sales.

Under the present inventory control procedures, the inventory clerk daily reviews the current inventory position for each of the approximately 800 different products stocked in the warehouse. Every morning he receives an inventory file—a computer printout listing each product, its current inventory at the end of the preceding business day (day n) and reflecting any customer orders received on day n. Table 1-1 is an excerpt of a typical inventory file.

Table 1-1. *Inventory File.*

Product Code	Name	Package Code	Stock on Hand	Sold but not yet Shipped	Replenishments in Process	Open Balance	Reorder Point	Order Quantity
0101	SUPER	001	108	26	0	82	24	144
0101	SUPER	011	440	84	0	356	120	720
0101	SUPER	101	636	112	0	524	150	700
0102	SPEC	001	18	32	120	106	20	120
0102	SPEC	011	64	42	0	22	60	360
0102	SPEC	101	212	72	0	140	80	480
…	…	…	…	…	…	…	…	…
			+	−	+	=		

Whenever the open balance is less than or equal to the critical level called the *reorder point*, a replenishment request for an amount equal to the *order quantity* shown in the last column of the file is issued. For product 0102 SPEC 001 the open balance was less than the reorder point of 20 already on the day $n-1$ inventory file and a replenishment request for 120 drums was issued on day n. For 0102 SPEC 011 customer orders received during day n reduced the open balance at the end of day n below the reorder point. Hence the inventory clerk will issue a replenishment request for 360 cartons (each containing eight 1-gallon cans) on day $n+1$. The number 360 will appear under the column *replenishments in process* on the updated inventory file, as of the end of day $n+1$, reviewed on day $n+2$. Once the replenishment has been physically added to the inventory, this amount will automatically be added to the number shown under *stock on hand* and the column for *replenishments in process* will again be zero. On the average about 30 replenishment requests are issued every working day.

The reorder points and order quantities are reviewed annually. They are set to an equivalent of one and six weeks average sales, respectively, resulting in an average inventory turnover of about $8\frac{2}{3}$ times per year (52 weeks/6 weeks).

The replenishment request is forwarded on the same day to the foreman of the mixing plant who prepares a batch specification sheet, listing exactly the quantities of base oils and additives to be mixed. On the basis of the batch specification sheet an operator makes the actual mixing run either on the same day or the following day, day $n+2$. Prior to releasing a batch for filling, it is tested by a laboratory technician. If it fails the test it is upgraded appropriately. When a batch has passed the test, it is released for filling.

A second copy of the inventory replenishment request is forwarded to the foreman of the filling plant, who orders the required amount of empty containers to be delivered to the plant on day $n+2$. Drums come from the reconditioning plant, other containers from the stock of empty containers. Once he receives the release notice from the operator of the mixing plant he schedules a filling run to be made either on day $n+2$ or day $n+3$. Therefore, the replenishment is added to the stock no later than day $n+3$. The *replenishment lead time*, i.e., the time between placing a replenishment request and the time the goods are received in inventory is thus less than the time available to execute a wholesale customer order of 4 days.

Figure 1-3 shows a flow chart for the present inventory replenishment process.

According to the foreman of the warehouse, floor space is presently at a premium. In fact, he estimates that the division needs additional warehouse space equivalent to 4000 square feet. Temporary storage areas have been created on some of the shipping docks, resulting in increased pilferage.

First, let us identify the various components of the problem. There are three levels of decision makers involved: the vice-president of manufacturing whose approval is required for any nonroutine expenditures in excess of $1000, and who has delegated the day-to-day management of the division to the division manager; the division manager who is in charge of introducing any operational changes subject to the approval of the vice-president of manufacturing under specified conditions; and the inventory clerk who actually makes the decisions on inventory control according to the policy laid down by the division manager. Clearly, the inventory clerk has little say in any policy matters. The crucial man and prime decision maker is the division manager.

What are his objectives? They include the acquisitive objective of (1) minimizing operation costs, and the retentive objectives of (2) maintaining the smooth operation of his division, (3) maintaining prompt service to the marketing department, (4) avoiding shortages, and (5) keeping the levels of inventory within the available space limits. None of these objectives seems to be in conflict with the board of directors' principal objective—profit maximization. Further probing for hidden objectives reveals that the division manager will not implement any recommendation to shorten or lengthen the present 4-day cycle to execute wholesale customer orders, nor does he wish to make any substantial changes to the time allotted for inventory replenishments. Both time periods were established as a result of a recent lengthy study by the company's department of methods and procedures and both have been very satisfactory. Since the project is viewed as a door-opener by the operations research section, no attempt is made to remove these restrictions on the scope of the project.

Identifying all controllable aspects is the next step. However, this cannot be done without clearly defining the limits of the subsystem to be studied—the scope of the project. Essentially the lubricating oil division forms the first part of a complex inventory system where inventories are kept at several different levels and in different forms: base oils in storage tanks; oil additives in small bulk quantities; empty containers and packaged finished goods in the warehouse; finished goods by a large number of company-owned wholesale distributors; and finally, finished goods by an even larger number of company-owned retail outlets. See Figure 1-4.

The span of control of the decision maker covers levels 1 and 2, whereas levels 3 and 4 are controlled by the marketing department. After some discussions with the division manager, it is agreed that this first project should not go beyond his span of control. In order to assure that the project can be completed within a reasonable length of time (one to two years), it is further restricted to packaged finished goods only. The last restriction assumes that base oils, additives, and empty containers

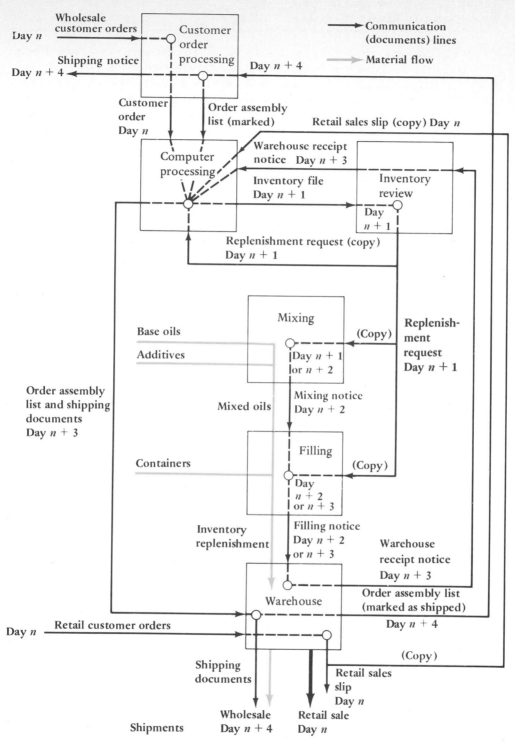

Figure 1-3. *Inventory replenishment process.*

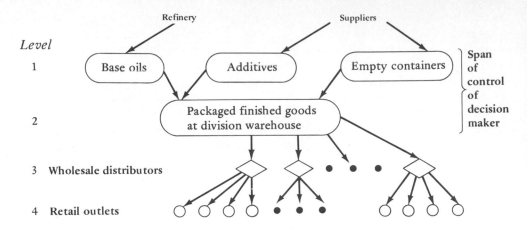

Figure 1-4. *Multi-stage inventory system.*

are always available in sufficient quantities. The decision as to whether the project might be extended to include inventories at level 1 also is postponed for the present time.

It is clear that control of finished goods at the division warehouse is by no means a highly separable part of the system. There exists a fair degree of separation between level 2 and levels 3 and 4, since deliveries from the warehouse to wholesale distributors do not depend on the inventory levels at the warehouse. Any product can be mixed and filled within the 4-day cycle available to execute wholesale orders. On the other hand, a sufficient degree of separability of levels 1 and 2 is more questionable, since a shortage of base oils, additives, or empty containers could delay replenishments of finished goods. Such delays could affect levels 3 and 4. In spite of this, it is agreed by all concerned that for a first project these restrictions of the scope are desirable.

With these restrictions, the controllable aspects of the problem are reduced to (1) the time of placing an inventory replenishment, and (2) the amount of inventory replenishments for each product. Analysis of the production process and the nature of the products points to additional aspects that are controllable within the scope of the project, and that opens up the possibility of developing new alternative courses of action. Most lubricating oils are packaged in 3 or 4 different size containers. Should some or all sizes be replenished jointly whenever the inventory of one size has to be replenished or should they all be replenished individually? A second set of possibilities is given by the fact that the replenishment lead time is shorter than the 4-day cycle for executing wholesale orders. This means that there actually exists the possibility of mixing and filling a product and then shipping it directly to wholesale customers, bypassing the inventory stage. Finished goods are then handled only once rather than twice. (Why?) Under what conditions is this course of action advantageous? (The answer to this question will be found in Chapter 11.)

The environment of the problem consists of (1) the technological aspects of the mixing, filling, and warehousing operations; (2) the costs associated with each operation as a function of changes in the controllable aspects; (3) technological constraints on the controllable aspects, such as the minimum and maximum feasible batch sizes for mixing oils; and (4) the demand pattern for the products. Some information, particularly the cost factors, has to be obtained from cost accounting data. In some instances, particularly the time needed for mixing or filling, the data needed can be obtained only by actual observation of the operations. Annual sales summaries, by product, are compiled periodically. More detailed demand data can be extracted either from sales records or directly from the original customer orders. Although the latter source is more representative of the demand pattern than past sales records, the effort of collecting information for more than 800 products would be staggering. Individual sales records, on the other hand, are available on computer cards which only require sorting by product—also a substantial amount of work to get the data reduced to a usable form. (This analysis indicates that, depending on the model used, formal procedures should immediately be set in motion to collect demand data in the required form for future use.) This largely completes the formulation of the problem. We shall pick up the thread later on as we proceed through the remaining phases of operations research.

1-10 CONSTRUCTION OF A MATHEMATICAL MODEL

A model is a partial representation of some entity of reality, such as an object, a process, an operation, or a system. The kinds of models of interest to operations researchers are those that allow manipulation of the entity modeled. The manipulation is aimed at answering certain questions about this entity, such as, "What is the effect of a change in some aspect or some property of this entity in terms of its effectiveness towards achieving some set of objectives?" The purpose of a model is either to explain, predict, or control the behavior of the entity modeled.

Mathematical models are the essence of the operations research approach to problem solving. In a mathematical model, the controllable properties of the entity modeled usually take the form of *decision variables* whose values can be chosen by the decision maker from a specified set of values. The uncontrollable aspects are represented by uncontrollable variables, such as *random variables*, or by *parameters* and *constants*, such as the parameters of a probability distribution or technological and cost constants. The technological and behavioral relationships between these variables are expressed in the form of *functional relations*, such as *functions, equations,* or *constraint inequalities*.

Consider the inventory control problem in the preceding section. The time of placing an inventory replenishment—one of the controllable aspects—is equivalent to specifying a critical number of the inventory level which, whenever the inventory falls below this number, triggers an inventory replenishment to be initiated. This is nothing else but the reorder point—the number listed in the inventory file. Let S_i denote this number for product i. Similarly, the second controllable aspect gives rise to another decision variable, say Q_i, where Q_i is the inventory replenishment quantity.

The demand for each product fluctuates randomly and is expressed in the form of a random variable. Let X_i denote the random variable for the daily demand.

Its probability distribution may be approximated by a theoretical probability distribution, such as the normal distribution defined by its two parameters—the mean daily demand and the variance of the daily demand—or we may use the empirical frequency distribution derived directly from past sales data. Other uncontrollable aspects give rise to cost factors c_{ik} (the cost factor of type k for product i) such as the product value for product i, or technological coefficients, a_{ik}, such as the amount of warehouse space required for product i.

A mathematical model is called *deterministic* if it represents a problem of decision making under certainty. It is termed *probabilistic* or *stochastic* if it deals with a problem of decision making under uncertainty (or risk) and the probabilities of the alternative states of nature are known.

A mathematical model is a *general purpose model* if any problem that satisfies certain assumptions as to the form of the decision variables and the nature of the functional relationships between them can be cast into the structure of this model. It is a *special purpose model* if its structure is peculiar to a given problem. Most models and the associated solution methods discussed in this text are general purpose models.

With most general purpose models we associate one or several specialized techniques to find the optimal solution. For this reason, general purpose models are often simply referred to as *techniques*. Many problems can be solved by several techniques, each offering certain advantages. Familiarity with all essential features of the various techniques is a must, therefore, in order to choose the technique that best fits the special aspects of the problem studied.

1-11 THE MEASURE OF EFFECTIVENESS

The contributions of the alternative courses of action towards acquisitive objectives of the decision maker are usually expressed in the form of a function, called a *measure of effectiveness* or an *objective function*. Unless the problem is a one-shot deal, the measure of effectiveness is defined for some specific interval of time or a specific *planning horizon*, e.g., one year.

If the number of alternative actions is finite, the measure of effectiveness may be expressed in the form of a *payoff table* or *payoff matrix*. The entries in the table represent the (monetary or utility) value of the outcomes (payoffs) for each combination of state of nature and action. Thus, the table has one row for each action and one column for each state of nature.

$$
\begin{array}{c}
\text{States of Nature, } s_j \\[4pt]
\begin{array}{cccccc}
 & 1 & 2 & 3 & \cdots & N \\
\end{array} \\
\text{Actions, } a_i
\begin{array}{c}
1 \\ 2 \\ 3 \\ \vdots \\ K
\end{array}
\left[
\begin{array}{ccccc}
r_{11} & r_{12} & r_{13} & \cdots & r_{1N} \\
r_{21} & r_{22} & r_{23} & \cdots & r_{2N} \\
r_{31} & r_{32} & r_{33} & \cdots & r_{3N} \\
\vdots & \vdots & \vdots & \vdots & \vdots \\
r_{K1} & r_{K2} & r_{K3} & \cdots & r_{KN}
\end{array}
\right]
\end{array}
$$

A decision problem under certainty has only one column, since there is only one possible state of nature. For a decision problem under uncertainty, there will be two or more alternative states of nature. With each state s_j we may associate a probability p_j, where $\sum_{j=1}^{N} p_j = p_1 + p_2 + \cdots + p_N = 1$. The worth of each action a_i can then be expressed as the expected value of the payoffs over all alternative states:

$$\begin{bmatrix} \text{Expected outcome} \\ \text{of action } a_i \end{bmatrix} = E_i(\text{payoff}) = \sum_{j=1}^{N} r_{ij}\, p_j$$

If the number of alternative courses of action is large or even infinite—such as for continuous decision variables—the measure of effectiveness is more conveniently expressed in analytical form as a functional relationship of the decision variables.

Say that the objective of the division manager in our inventory problem is to minimize operating costs and that we use one year as the base period. The measure of effectiveness has to cover only those costs that change if the values of the decision variables change. All other costs are irrelevant for the problem.

What type of costs are incurred in an inventory operation? There are material costs, labor costs, machine costs, financial charges, and overhead. To determine which of these costs are relevant, we have to study how each is affected by changes in the decision variables. To simplify the discussion let us consider changes in the order quantity only. A change in the order quantity of product i will affect its average inventory level and the number of replenishments that have to be made per year to satisfy a given annual demand of, say, R_i units.

To determine the average inventory level, assume that a replenishment is issued for product i whenever its inventory has been reduced to zero. Such a policy is feasible if replenishments are *instantaneous* (i.e., the replenishment lead time is zero) or the time available to execute a customer order is longer than the replenishment lead time. In either case, no shortages can occur. If we ignore retail sales, the second condition is satisfied for our example. Just prior to a replenishment, the inventory level is therefore zero, and just after a replenishment it is Q_i. Assuming that demand occurs at a constant rate (which is not true here), inventories will reduce as the straight line shown in Figure 1-5. The time between replenishments will be a fraction of Q_i/R_i of a year. (Explain why!)

From Figure 1-5 it follows immediately that the average inventory is $Q_i/2$.

Inventories tie up funds, a scarce resource. The cost of investing funds in inventories is the *opportunity cost* equal to the return that the company could earn on an investment of equal risk. For governmental organizations this cost may coincide with the bank loan rate whereas for commercial enterprises it is more likely to be close to the average cost of capital. Let c_1 stand for this cost, expressed as a fraction per dollar invested per year. Let V_i be the value per unit (a drum, a carton of cans) of product i once it is on the warehouse floor. V_i is assumed to be constant regardless of the size of Q_i. Then $V_i Q_i/2$ is the average inventory investment for product i, and

(1-1) $$c_1 V_i Q_i/2$$

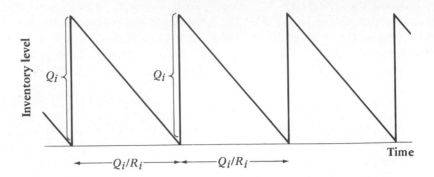

Figure 1-5. *Inventory level over time for batch replenishments.*

is the annual cost of holding this product in inventory, referred to as the *inventory holding cost*. There could be other costs of a similar nature associated with holding goods in inventory, such as insurance, inventory taxes, warehouse space rental, and pilferage. If so, c_1 would be adjusted appropriately.

The number of inventory replenishments per year required to satisfy a demand of size R_i if each replenishment is of size Q_i is equal to the ratio R_i/Q_i. Every time a replenishment is made two types of costs are incurred: a fixed cost independent of the replenishment size Q_i, covering clerical costs and equipment set-up costs (on mixers and filling machines, including cleaning costs); and variable costs, such as the cost of raw materials, additives, and containers used, variable equipment operating costs, and handling costs of storing the goods in inventory. The variable costs are usually proportional to the replenishment size. Let V_i denote the total variable cost per unit. (This is obviously the same as the value per unit of the goods on the warehouse floor.) Let c_{2i} be the fixed cost per replenishment (referred to as the *ordering* or *set-up cost*). Then, for each replenishment for product i, a cost of $c_{2i}+V_iQ_i$ is incurred. For a total of R_i/Q_i replenishments per year the total annual ordering and product cost amounts to

(1-2) $$(c_{2i}+V_iQ_i)R_i/Q_i = (c_{2i}R_i/Q_i) + V_iR_i$$

As expected the annual product cost is a constant regardless of the value of Q_i. It is not affected by changes in the decision variable Q_i, and can therefore be ignored as irrelevant.

The relevant total annual cost for product i, denoted by $T_i(Q_i)$ (a function of Q_i), is equal to the sum of expressions (1-1) and (1-2), excluding V_iR_i:

(1-3) $$T_i(Q_i) = c_1V_iQ_i/2 + (c_{2i}R_i/Q_i)$$

The relevant total annual cost for all products (say there are N of them) is given by expression (1-3) summed over all N products.

(1-4) $$T(Q_1,Q_2,...,Q_N) = \sum_{i=1}^{N} T_i(Q_i)$$

Ignoring any costs associated with the reorder points S_i, expression (1-4) is the measure of effectiveness for this simplified version of our inventory control problem. The decision maker's objective is to find those values of $Q_1, Q_2, ..., Q_N$ that minimize expression (1-4).

1-12 MULTIPLE OBJECTIVES   *here?*

As we have seen, decision makers may have multiple objectives, some of which are acquisitive and some of which are retentive.   Expression (1-4) represents the measure of effectiveness for one acquisitive objective associated with the problem, of minimizing operating costs.   How can we deal with several acquisitive objectives, such as maximizing profits and maximizing sales, which may be in conflict with each other. Maximizing profits may imply sacrificing some sales, maximizing sales may imply reduced profits.

Two ways to deal with such conflicts are:

1. Determine the most important objective and express all other objectives as firm constraints on the decision variables.   For instance, we could decide that maximizing profits is the most important objective and substitute, for maximizing sales, a constraint that states sales cannot drop below a certain minimum level or minimum share of the market.
2. Construct *trade-off functions* that translate all objectives to some common measure, such as costs and returns, or to units of the most important objective. A trade-off function shows how much successive changes in one objective are worth in terms of another objective.   For instance, how much each successive decrease in sales by 1 percent is worth in terms of successive increments in profits.   (For more detailed analysis of this approach, the reader is referred to Churchman *et al.*, *Introduction to Operations Research*.)

Retentive objectives naturally lend themselves to being expressed in the form of constraints on the decision variables.   For instance, the retentive objective of keeping inventory levels within the available warehouse space would be expressed as a constraint on the Q_i-values as follows: if each unit of product i requires an area of a_i square feet of warehouse space and warehouse space is allocated proportionately to the maximum inventory level (Q_i in our case) then each product requires an area of $a_i Q_i$ square feet.   The total area required for all N products cannot exceed the presently available space of A square feet, or

(1-5)
$$\sum_{i=1}^{i=N} a_i Q_i \leqslant A$$

Although such constraints are derived by policy decisions and are thus not absolute but relative constraints, they are treated from a mathematical point of view in exactly the same way as those representing physical conditions.   However, in the analysis of the optimal solution, the operations researcher has to examine carefully how changes in these constraints reflecting alternative policy decisions affect the solution.

Sometimes, the various objectives can be expressed in the form of target levels to be achieved as closely as possible. If the objectives are highly conflicting, it may not be possible to reach each target level exactly. In such instances, the decision maker may wish to choose an objective function that minimizes an appropriately weighted sum of the deviations from the target levels. In other instances, the objectives may be ranked in order of priority. The solution procedure would then attempt to satisfy the objectives in that order. No attempt to satisfy any lower order objective would be made until all higher order objectives have been reached. Such approaches have been formalized in what has become known as *goal programming*. Section 2-14 of Chapter 2 gives a simple example of goal programming where all relationships are linear.

1-13 MODELS AS APPROXIMATIONS

An operations researcher is confronted with conflicting goals. On the one hand, he wants to have the model sufficiently simple to remain tractable, and on the other hand, it should be elaborate enough to be a close representation of reality. A simple model facilitates its manipulation and makes finding a solution easier. Often, the solution will be intuitively appealing to the decision maker, which increases the chances of a successful implementation. However, simplicity in a model can be achieved only by making suitable approximations of the entity modeled.

Striking a proper balance between the conflicting goals of detail and tractability is a delicate matter of weighing the cost of constructing the model, collecting the required data, implementing and operating the model versus the expected benefits that can be gained from its implementation—all increasing functions of the sophistication and accuracy of the model, though rarely quantifiable in practice. Finding a proper balance remains a matter of trial and error. Figure 1-6 depicts the likely shape of the costs and benefits, with marginal benefits rapidly falling. What is your conclusion?

What type of approximations can be made?

(A) Omitting relevant variables. Often variables that have relatively small effects or that tend to behave in a similar fashion to other variables that have been included in the model are omitted. For instance, inventories for goods-in-process are often ignored, particularly if their impact on total costs is small, as is the case if production lead times are short, or they tend to be proportional to the inventory replenishment quantities. However, if the production process is lengthy, then they may have to be incorporated explicitly.

To determine whether a variable has a significant effect on the measure of effectiveness, the operations researcher will have recourse to various statistical techniques and tests, such as *correlation* and *regression analysis*, *analysis of variance* and *covariance*, and *tests of significance*. Knowledge of these tools, their capabilities and limitations, such as the assumption of normality of error terms made by most of

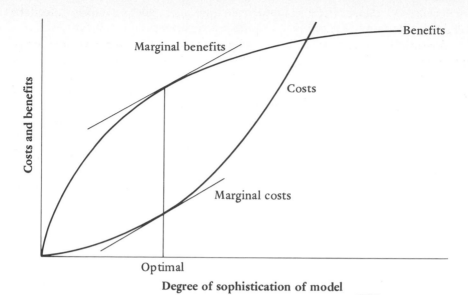

Figure 1-6. *Costs and benefits as a function of a model's sophistication.*

these techniques, is part of the required bag of tools of any operations researcher. We refer the reader to texts such as R. L. Ackoff, *The Design of Social Research* (University of Chicago Press, 1953); or G. W. Snedecor and W. G. Cochran, *Statistical Methods* (Iowa State University Press, 1967).

(B) Aggregating variables. Rather than omit relevant variables, variables are aggregated or standardized, particularly if there is a large number of fairly homogenous variables and their individual impact is small (e.g., in terms of benefits gained). In inventory models covering thousands of different products, products might be grouped into (1) high usage/high cost, (2) high usage/low cost, (3) low usage/high cost, and (4) low usage/low cost items. Only for products in group 1 would individual cost and demand factors be collected to determine optimal control parameters, whereas all others are dealt with completely or partially in groups, using a simpler model and substituting an average group cost for some of the cost factors. Similarly, in large corporate models depicting an entire sector of an organization activities are grouped together and expressed in a common standard activity, and by-products are aggregated with the main products.

(C) Changing the nature of variables. Variables may be treated as constant. For instance, replenishment lead times may fluctuate. Rather than represent them by a random variable we use an average. Discrete variables are treated as continuous and vice-versa to simplify the solution procedure. Similarly, the probability distribution of random variables is approximated by a known theoretical distribution, such as the normal distribution.

(D) Changing the relationship between variables. The true functional relationship between variables is approximated by a form that is simpler to manipulate, such as substituting *linear* or *quadratic* functions for *nonlinear* functions.

(E) Omitting constraints. Constraints may render the solution of a model more difficult. Therefore, they may be ignored initially and only those violated by the solution introduced subsequently. Sometimes constraints are more easily worked in backwards, for instance, by the use of *marginal analysis*.

(F) Disaggregating the model. One single model that covers the entire system or subsystem studied may be highly complex and difficult to solve. It may also require increased centralization of decision making that is undesirable and unwieldy. Instead, the problem is broken into sufficiently small and partially self-contained subproblems, each of which is represented by a separate model that may be relatively simple. The output of each model becomes an input into other models. For example, a multilevel inventory system may be handled by a sequence of models dealing separately with base stocks, empty containers, finished goods in the plant warehouse, and finished goods at each wholesale warehouse. Such disaggregation may even be desirable if the various subproblems are controlled by different departments.

(G) Sequential models. Problems that require a sequence of decisions to be made at different points in time are solved sequentially. This is particularly attractive if the outcomes of earlier decisions are uncertain. A first decision is made and the result observed. On the basis of the new state of the system, a new decision is taken, etc. Sequential random sampling is a well-known example of this approach.

Let us briefly hint at the various approximations made in the inventory problem that led to expressions (1-4) and (1-5). The products are sold in discrete units—we treated them as continuous and would simply round the solution to the nearest integer. The daily demand is a random variable—we treated the demand rate as a constant. This is justified since individual sales are in small lots of a few packages per customer, and tend to occur at a fairly even trickle. We assumed that mixing and filling set-up costs are independent of the sequence in which products are produced which in fact is not true, although the cost differences are small due to sequence. If we build a separate model to determine the reorder points, then we use a multiple-model approach. Again this may be justified since a positive reorder point is only required to allow retail sales to be executed immediately during the replenishment lead time. However, retail sales are a small portion of total sales, and the interaction between the reorder point and the replenishment size is, therefore, negligible.

1-14 DERIVING A SOLUTION TO THE MODEL

The solution may be analytic, using the classical methods of algebra and calculus. For instance, disregarding the constraint (1-5) on the decision variables, the optimal values of $Q_1, Q_2, ..., Q_N$ that minimize the measure of effectiveness (1-4) can be obtained by the use of differential calculus, as we shall see in Chapter 11. The optimal solution has the form of

$$(1\text{-}6) \qquad\qquad Q_i{}^* = \sqrt{\frac{2R_i c_{2i}}{c_1 V_i}}, \qquad i = 1, 2, ..., N$$

If no constraint on the values of Q_i is present, then each optimal Q_i obtained only depends on the demand and cost parameters directly associated with product i and is independent of all other products. Expression (1-6) can therefore be obtained from the relevant total annual cost for product i as given by expression (1-3) directly. Expression (1-6) is known as the *economic order quantity* or the *EOQ formula* and is the most basic model in inventory control theory.

More often than not the optimal solution to a model has to be computed by numeric methods. This is even so for models where, theoretically, algebra or calculus apply. Many numeric methods are sophisticated variations of trial and error. The most powerful numeric methods are based on an *algorithm*—a set of logical and mathematical operations performed in a specific sequence. Starting from a given initial solution to the problem, the algorithm is applied to derive a new and better solution. The sequence of operations that lead to the new solution is called an *iteration*. The new solution is now substituted as the starting point, and the process is repeated repetitively until certain conditions—referred to as *stopping rules*—are satisfied, indicating that an optimal solution has been reached or the current solution deviates from the previous solution by less than prespecified tolerances, or no feasible or no bounded solution exists to the problem.

For an algorithm to be a practical solution method, the algorithm has to have certain properties: (1) each successive solution has to be an improvement over the preceding one; (2) successive solutions have to converge to the optimal solution; (3) convergence arbitrarily close to the optimal solution has to occur in a finite number of iterations; and (4) the computational requirements at each iteration have to be sufficiently small to remain economically feasible.

Numeric methods applied to any real problem invariably require access to high-speed electronic computers. In fact, it was the availability of more and more sophisticated computers that made the development and use of algorithmic methods possible.

If neither analytic nor algorithmic methods exist for a given model, then other search procedures may have to be used, such as systematic search on a finite *grid of points* over the entire domain of the decision variables with possibly successive refinements of the grid points, around the area where the optimal solution seems to be located, or the use of *simulation* to evaluate various heuristically derived decision rules to find a "good" policy rather than the "best" policy. To simulate means to duplicate the operation of a system on paper using either past data or artificially created data and recording, step by step, the detailed performance of the system over a sufficient length of operation. Chapter 15 will deal with this topic.

1-15 SENSITIVITY ANALYSIS

The systematic evaluation of the response of the optimal solution to changes in input data is referred to as *sensitivity analysis*. It is a highly valuable and important part of evaluating the optimal solution and should always be performed on all crucial input data. The three main uses of sensitivity analysis are:

1. to determine the accuracy required for input data for the model;
2. to establish control ranges for changes in input parameters and constants over which the present optimal solution remains near-optimal;
3. to evaluate for planning purposes the marginal value of scarce resources (i.e., the effect on the decision variables of changes in constraints).

Consider again the economic order quantity model with a relevant total annual cost given by expression (1-3) and its solution (1-6):

(1-3A) $$T_i(Q_i) = c_1 V_i Q_i/2 + c_{2i} R_i/Q_i$$

and

(1-6A) $$Q_i^* = \sqrt{\frac{2R_i c_{2i}}{c_1 V_i}}$$

Substituting Q_i^* into expression (1-3A) and simplifying we get:

(1-7) $$T_i(Q_i^*) = \sqrt{2R_i c_1 V_i c_{2i}}$$

If the demand for product i amounts to R_i during the coming year and inventory for product i is replenished by an amount Q_i^* whenever it has been reduced to zero, the total relevant cost is given by expression (1-7).

When this model is implemented the value of R_i used is based on the forecast of the expected demand for the coming year. Let $\hat{R}_i$ denote this forecast. Being a forecast, $\hat{R}_i$ might differ from the true but unknown demand R_i. By how much will actual incurred costs be off if the forecast were in error by a factor of k, i.e.,

(1-8) $$\hat{R}_i = kR_i$$

Using $\hat{R}_i = kR_i$ in (1-6A) we get an "optimal" order quantity of

(1-9) $$\hat{Q}_i = \sqrt{\frac{2\hat{R}_i c_{2i}}{c_1 V_i}} = \sqrt{\frac{2kR_i c_{2i}}{c_1 V_i}} = \sqrt{k}\, Q_i^*$$

and the true annual cost of using $\hat{Q}_i$, given the true demand is R_i, is

(1-10) $$T_i(\hat{Q}_i) = c_1 V_i \hat{Q}_i/2 + c_{2i} R_i/\hat{Q}_i$$
$$= c_1 V_i \sqrt{k}\, Q_i^*/2 + c_{2i} R_i/\sqrt{k}\, Q_i^*$$
$$= \sqrt{2R_i c_1 V_i c_{2i}}\left(\frac{k+1}{2\sqrt{k}}\right)$$

or

(1-11) $$T_i(\hat{Q}_i) = T_i(Q_i^*)\left(\frac{k+1}{2\sqrt{k}}\right)$$

The answer to our question is thus that the true cost will be off by a factor of $(k+1)/2\sqrt{k}$. $(k+1)/2\sqrt{k} = 1$ if $k = 1$ and will be larger than 1 for all values of $k \neq 1$, as is to be expected. Figure 1-7 shows $(k+1)/2\sqrt{k}$ as a function of k.

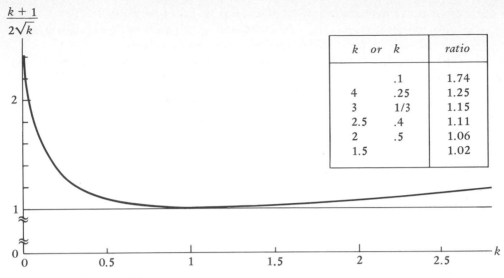

k	or	k	ratio
		.1	1.74
	4	.25	1.25
	3	1/3	1.15
	2.5	.4	1.11
	2	.5	1.06
	1.5		1.02

Figure 1-7. *Error factor of EOQ model.*

Say that the forecast overestimated the true demand by 44 percent, i.e., $k = 1.44$. Then

$$\hat{Q}_i = \sqrt{k}\, Q_i{}^* = 1.2 Q_i{}^*$$

and

$$(k+1)/2\sqrt{k} = (1.44+1)/2\sqrt{1.44} = 1.0167$$

The actual cost of using $\hat{Q}_i$ will be only 1.67 percent larger than the minimum cost if $Q_i{}^*$ had been used. On the other hand under-estimating the demand by 44 percent, i.e., $k = 0.56$, using $\hat{Q} = \sqrt{0.56}Q^* = 0.75Q^*$ results in an actual cost that is larger by 4.23 percent. Overestimation is thus less costly than underestimation. However, the EOQ model is not very sensitive to fairly large errors in the demand forecast, and therefore does not require a high forecasting accuracy.

To what degree of accuracy do the various parameters and constants used as inputs into a model have to be evaluated? This a matter of both the cost of data collection as a function of the degree of accuracy achieved and the sensitivity of the optimal solution and, in particular, the optimal value of the measure of effectiveness to changes in input parameters and constants. Increased accuracy can usually only be obtained at increased costs of data collection. However, increased costs are only justified if the improvement in the optimal value of the measure of effectiveness more than compensates for this increase—by now the familiar problem of balancing increased costs with increased benefits that constantly haunts the operations researcher.

1-16 TESTING THE SOLUTION FOR PERFORMANCE

Usually the purpose of an operations research project is to improve the performance of the system. Before deciding whether to implement the proposed solution or shelf it, usually the decision maker will want convincing proof that the proposed solution performs better than the present rules, say, reduces total costs or increases total profits. Demonstration of such superiority may help to have the solution accepted more than full understanding of how the model works in all its complexities.

When testing the solution, the operations researcher wants to ascertain (1) that the decision rules derived from the optimal solution perform as expected and (2) what the expected net benefits of implementing the solution will be. Unless the project deals with a one-shot problem, we are usually interested in the average long-run performance.

A solution may be tested retrospectively (against past observed behavior), or prospectively (against future behavior). In either case the test has to entail a detailed comparison of the "actual" performance of the optimal solution derived from the model, as if it were implemented, with the actual performance of present decision rules based on the same set of data.

For instance, the test could consist of running both sets of rules in parallel over a length of time, such as a year. The actual operations would be based on the present decision rules; the new decision rules would be simulated on paper alongside the old ones. Disregarding certain problems associated with such simulation, this clearly would permit a very realistic evaluation, but would also result in an unreasonably long delay before any conclusions could be drawn. For this reason, testing is usually done by simulation alone. The performance of the system is simulated, i.e., observed on paper, separately for each set of decision rules, over a sufficient length of operations on the same set of data.

There are a few traps that have to be avoided when testing a solution:

1. The evaluation of the proposed solution has to be done by observing its actual (simulated) performance and not on the basis of the optimal value of the measure of effectiveness associated with the data used, for instance, expression (1-7) for the EOQ-model. Such a test would be meaningless since it reflects an idealized and simplified reality as a result of the problem reduction process during the model construction.

2. The test should be independent of how the optimal solution was derived. For instance, a test against past data, demand figures, for example, that also served to estimate the various input parameters of the model used to derive the optimal solution, will not yield an independent test. Since the model supposedly optimizes the performance, it should perform better than the present decision rules on these data. Either part of the data has to be set aside specifically for the test and not used to derive the optimal solution, or data have to be generated artificially on the basis of projected behavior of the system, such as the projected demand distribution.

3. The data used should be "representative" of future behavior, i.e., they should cover the range of behavior likely to be observed in the future. Testing on the basis of particularly favorable or unfavorable time periods is not a valid test.

4. Tests should cover a sufficiently long time interval to allow for evaluation of not only a *point estimate* but also of the *variability* of the outcome. If the same model is applied to a number of operations, such as the same inventory model

applied to a large number of products, the test should cover a random sample of these products (usually on the basis of stratification so as to cover all important types of product characteristics).

The difference in average benefits for the present and proposed sets of rules derived from the tests is adjusted for any difference in the cost of applying and maintaining the two sets of rules to derive an average net benefit. The present value of this average net benefit over the projected lifetime of the project is finally compared with any further costs projected for the project, such as costs of initial data collection, further model refinements and implementation—similar to the evaluation of investment proposals in capital budgeting. Note that at this point only future costs are relevant. All costs incurred so far are *sunk costs* and no longer relevant to whether or not the project should be completed.

Many operations research projects have similar characteristics as *research and development projects*. Before a decision can be made as to whether a project is worthwhile, some expenditures have to be made, similar to the initial research into new product development—expenditures that will not be recovered if the project is never implemented. Therefore, the initial expenditures have to be financed from general funds specifically set aside for this purpose, as is done for research and development.

For these reasons it is important that the decision as to the economic feasibility of a project be made as early as possible. Thus, overall model testing should start on the earliest version of the model that seems to capture the most important features of the problem, before any bells and whistles, such as ancillary computer programs, have been added.

Operations research projects are usually high risk investments. Even if testing turns out to be favorable, unforeseen snags during implementation or further refinements of the model tend to cause cost overruns, whereas benefits may be highly variable. This calls for relatively high discount rates in the order of 20 to 100 percent. Furthermore, full benefits will not be realized from the very beginning, but only after a transition period that may easily extend over several months. It is essential that the decision maker is made aware of this fact or else he or she might decide to abandon the project well before it has reached its full potential.

1-17 PROBLEMS OF IMPLEMENTATION

Implementation of an operations research project is putting the tested solution to work. This means translating the mathematical solution into a set of easily understood operating procedures or decision rules for each of the persons involved in using and applying the solution; training these people in the proper use of these rules; planning and executing the transition from the present to the desired mode of operations; instituting controls to maintain and update the solution; and, finally, checking the initial performance periodically until the new mode of operation has become routine.

R. L. Ackoff in his talk given at the Symposium "Case Histories Five Years After" (*Operations Research*, March–April 1960) concludes with the statement:

"We must continually remind ourselves that the ultimate objective of O.R. is the improvement of operations. This improvement cannot come about without implementation of the solution obtained. Unless the researcher is involved in and concerned with implementation, we shall succeed only in amassing technical success and practical failures. We must avoid operations of which it can be said that the surgery was successful, but the patient died. The surgeon [the operations researcher] cannot survive many such deaths."

Implementation of all the recommendations of an operations research project is rare. It is more useful to talk about the degree of implementation achieved. The objective of the operations researcher is to achieve a sufficiently high degree of implementation to capture the major portion of the potential benefits that can be derived from the solution. Unfortunately, we do not yet have sufficient knowledge of how to approach the task of implementation to guarantee this objective. Although substantial research has been and is still being undertaken in this field, implementation remains largely an art. All we can do here is to point out some of the problems and suggest some approaches that may help overcome them.

Problems of implementation can be reduced to three basic factors—

1. those relating to the task of implementation, such as the complexity of the solution, the sensitivity of the solution to implementation, the degree of deviation of the solution from current practice (the greater any of these, the greater the problems created).
2. those relating to the individuals using the solution, such as the personality of of the users (Any change from current practices brings uncertainties about the future. For example, are they risk-averters?); their motivation and pride in the job (Does the proposed solution restrict their freedom of action, reduce their importance, transform a challenging job that requires years of experience to one of merely feeding data into a computer program?); their age (Routine becomes more entrenched with age and change therefore more difficult to accept); their intelligence, and the importance of the activities related to the solution in the framework of their total job (The less important they are, the less attention they receive).
3. those relating to the environment, such as the support given to the solution by higher echelons in the hierarchy, organizational implications of the solution (Does one department become more dependent on another?); or possible threat implications of the solution to other participants, such as employees (labor-replacement through automation) or customers.

Generally, the operations researcher pays full attention to the first factor which is a question of technology. The tendency is to neglect the human factors of 2 and 3, which are qualitative in nature and evade the formal treatment that can be given to the technological factors of implementation. One should, however, not be surprised that neglecting the human element in a system could well lead to a "solution" that in fact is a solution on paper only, but one that is not workable in practice. In other words, the human constraints that were neglected in the problem formulation may turn out to be binding in practice and, as a consequence, the proposed solution will not be implemented. From this point of view, the implementation problem can be viewed as a problem of relaxing the human constraint versus adjusting the technical solution.

The human constraints can be relaxed by replacing individuals that could become obstacles to proper implementation (for instance, by promoting them, or shifting them to other equally attractive jobs, and, in general, giving proper regard to the human side of such actions) or increasing their understanding and acceptance of the solution (for instance, by proper training or soliciting active participation in the project). The technical solution can be adjusted by simplifying the solution policy (for instance, by the use of close quick-and-dirty rules), by reducing the scope of the project, or by breaking the model into partially autonomous parts that maintain decentralized decision making, sacrificing part of the potential benefits.

1-18 PLANNING FOR IMPLEMENTATION

Reading through the literature, one comes to the conclusion that lack of implementation or improper implementation can usually be traced back to the operations research team, although there are instances of failures that are out of the team's control, such as reorganization of the sponsoring organization or economic pressures that lead to a general reduction of expenditures.

Lack of proper planning for implementation is probably the most common cause of failure. **Planning for implementation has to start with the formulation of the problem and the groundwork laid throughout all other phases.** It is not sufficient to start planning this phase once the model has been completed and tested. This includes technical aspects of implementation, such as preparing the proper data base and data collection procedures needed for implementation and continued maintenance of the solution, which may have to be initiated very early in the project analysis; deciding what to do with bad data; preparing detailed instruction manuals for all people involved with using and maintaining the solution; and preparing any special stationery and forms as well as tools needed for using the solution. Chances for successful implementation are substantially enhanced by creating and maintaining close links during all phases of the project, not only with the sponsor of the project (the person controlling the purse strings), but also with all people who will apply and maintain the solution. In fact, keeping them constantly informed and consulting them on major developments or, better still, obtaining their active participation in the project is almost a certain guarantee for successful implementation.

The actual process of changing from the present mode of operation to the new solution requires a detailed timetable of the various activities that have to be undertaken, their sequence and precedence relationships, and their assignment to the people or department best equipped to execute them. In fact, the operations research team may wish to apply one of its own techniques, namely critical path scheduling (discussed in Chapter 6) to this job. Prior to execution, the implementation plan should be pretested with all people involved and "debugged."

For large projects or projects that cover a large number of identical activities, such as an inventory control project, the solution may have to be implemented in stages rather than as a whole in order to avoid straining the resources and facilities available. For instance, although an inventory control project may promise reducing the average inventory investment by a substantial percentage, implementing the model for all products simultaneously will often result in an initial increase in the total inventory (Why?), followed by a gradual decline to the projected level over a number of months, straining limited warehouse capacity. Gradual introduction of the new rules may avoid such a situation.

1-19 CONTROLLING AND MAINTAINING THE SOLUTION

The environment in which most organizations operate is constantly undergoing change. Such change may be quantitative—environmental parameters or relationships change in magnitude only—or structural—the form or nature of environmental parameters or relationships changes. In the first case, the form of the operations research solution usually remains valid. Only the values of the decision variables may have to be adjusted to reflect quantitative changes in the environment. For example, the value of the products stored in inventory may change, calling for a corresponding adjustment in the economic order quantities. In the second case, the form of the solution may not be valid any longer, necessitating a reformulation of the model. For instance (in terms of the example in Section 1-9), introduction of new mixing and filling equipment may result in substantial savings in production set-up costs if all container sizes of the same oil are replenished jointly, whereas the present solution may be based on separate replenishments for each container size.

Procedures have to be set up to monitor such quantitative and qualitative changes in the environment, and corrective action undertaken when such changes become significant. A change is considered significant if the improvement in the benefits that can be gained by adjusting the solution exceeds the cost of making the adjustment. Establishing controls over the solution consists of

1. listing for each variable, parameter, constraint or relationship—for those that are explicitly included in the model as well as for those that have been excluded as insignificant—the range of values for which the present solution remains optimal or near-optimal and the type of qualitative change which invalidates the current form of the solution;
2. specifying in detail how each variable and parameter has to be measured, which relationships have to be checked, and the occasion and frequency of such controls and checks;
3. determining who is responsible for each item to be controlled and who has to be notified if significant changes are detected;
4. specifying in detail how the solution has to be adjusted for significant quantitative changes and what action has to be taken to deal with qualitative changes in the environment. For certain systems such as an inventory control system,

the solution may be updated periodically, say once a year for all products, regardless of whether significant quantitative changes have occurred or not. The rules of adjustments to reflect significant changes for individual products may then be relaxed accordingly.

Responsibilities should be part of a job specification rather than assigned to a specific individual.

Detailed documentation for control procedures have to be worked out by the operations researcher. Unless these responsibilities are properly assigned and documented, needed corrective measures may not be taken or may be taken incorrectly by someone not equipped to make the adjustment.

The job of the operations researcher is not finished once the solution has been implemented. In order to assure that the implementation does not deteriorate after a while, the actual performance of the solution (including control procedures) has to be carefully checked and the actual benefits achieved compared to those projected prior to implementation. Significant deviations have to be examined and adjustments made. Training of all people involved may have to be followed up. Only then can the success of the project be judged.

EXERCISES

1.1 The marketing department of a firm proposes to introduce a new item to its product line. The product would be produced by the firm's own production facilities. Analyze how such a decision might affect the performance of each of the other departments (parts) of the firm (system)? Do the same for a decision to adjust the price of a product in response to a general price increase by the competition.

1.2 Identify the components of the following decision problems:
a. assigning the course grade to each student in a class in quantitative methods;
b. buying a second-hand car;
c. designing a new advertising campaign.

1.3 Identify the major parts and subsystems associated with the following operations and draw an information and material flow diagram, indicating all decision points:
a. processing final course grades within a university or college;
b. operation of an airline;
c. operation of the postal services in a medium-sized city.

1.4 A small bakery produces only one type of whole meal bread, which it sells to a number of local supermarkets and delicatessen stores at a contractually fixed price of $0.40 per 2-pound loaf. Fixed costs associated with the operation amount to $2000.00 per month. Each baker hired has a salary including fringe benefits of $600.00 per month and can produce 8000 loaves of bread. The cost of the ingredients depends on the output, and is 20 cents a loaf for a monthly output of 12,000 loaves or less, 18 cents for a monthly output of more than 12,000, but at most 20,000, 16 cents for more than 20,000 and at most 40,000, and 15 cents for an output of more than 40,000.

   a. Construct a mathematical model for the difference between total monthly revenue and total monthly cost, as a function of output and number of bakers.
   b. Construct a mathematical model for the break-even point if the firm hires four bakers.
   c. Contrast your models with the real-life operation of such a small bakery. What approximations did you make in these models?

1.5   When testing a model, the following deficiencies may be discovered:
   a. the model may include irrelevant factors;
   b. it may exclude relevant factors;
   c. constants or parameters may be evaluated incorrectly;
   d. functional relationships may be misrepresented.
   Consider the case study discussed in Section 1-9 and the simplified model given in Section 1-11, and give examples for each of these deficiencies.

1.6   Discuss the apparent contradiction that if at the start of an operations research project all costs and the potential benefits were known accurately, the project would not be undertaken at all, whereas if the total costs and the potential benefits only can be ascertained at a later stage, e.g., once the model is tested for performance (but prior to implementation), the correct decision may be to implement the model. What implications does this have for the evaluation of operations research projects?

1.7   From the working definition of operations research given at the beginning of this chapter it follows that the operations researcher should take a systems approach and incorporate into the model all aspects that are affected by changes in the values of the decision variables or that limit or affect, in any other way, the optimal values of the decision variables. On the other hand, in real life the approach often used by operations researchers to model a complex problem is to build a series of separate models that may only be very loosely connected with each other (effects are only considered in one direction while reactions are ignored). Each subproblem is then solved separately or in a given sequence. Discuss this apparent contradiction.

REFERENCES—GENERAL

Ackoff, R. L., and P. Rivett, *A Manager's Guide to Operations Research* (New York: Wiley, 1963). A short introduction into "What is Operations Research?" and, "How should a manager approach operations research?" geared to provide a manager with some basic appreciation for operations research.

Churchman, C. West, *The Systems Approach* (New York: Dell Publ. Co., 1968). A must on the reading list of any student in operations research and systems analysis. Lucid, challenging, inspiring, and critical review in a climate of debate, of what the systems approach means, in less than 250 pages of easy reading.

Churchman, C. W., "Operations Research as a Profession," *Management Science*, Vol. 17 (Oct. 1970). The paper defines operations research and discusses each component of the definition in detail—in the light of the preparation for the operations research profession.

Miller, D. W., and M. K. Starr, *Executive Decisions and Operations Research* (Englewood Cliffs, N.J.: Prentice-Hall, 1969). Pragmatic and thorough treatment of the methodology of operations research (Chapters 1 to 9, 13 to 15) including an elementary discussion of the most basic operations research techniques for decisions in production, marketing, and finance. The text is intended for the executive and manager who wishes to obtain a good appreciation of the operations research approach rather than for the operations research student.

"Guidelines for the Practice of Operations Research," *Operations Research*, Vol. 19 (Sept. 1971, pp. 1123–48). Proposes professional standards for the practice of operations research.

METHODOLOGY

Ackoff, Russell L., "Optimization + Objectivity = Opt Out" *European Journal of Operational Research*, 1, 1977, pp. 1-7. It is argued that the preoccupation of operations researchers with optimization and objectivity leads to their withdrawal from reality. By clinging to optimality, reality is lost. Optimal solutions deteriorate because the system and environment change. Therefore, operations research should engage in designing models that adapt well rather than optimize.

Ackoff, Russell L., and Maurice W. Sasieni, *Fundamentals of Operations Research* (New York: Wiley, 1968). This text is in some sense an updated version of "*Introduction to Operations Research*" by Churchman, Ackoff, and Arnoff. Excellent treatment of methodology in chapters 1 to 4, 15 to 17. Recommended as alternative reading on this subject to Churchman. The methods part is organized by areas of applications rather than techniques and does not come up to the same standard as the methodology part.

Churchman, C. West, Russell L. Ackoff, and E. L. Arnoff, *Introduction to Operations Research* (New York: Wiley, 1957). The first complete text on operations research published. It contains one of the best treatments of the methodology of operations research, from problem formulation to implementation. (Chapters 1 to 7, 20 to 22.) Highly recommended as additional reading on this subject. Chapter 2 discusses the complete case history of an operations research project. The methods part is organized by areas of applications rather than by techniques and is somewhat outdated now. Chapter 15 discusses an actual simulation project of a waiting line problem.

Hitch, C., "Sub-optimization in Operations Problems," *Operations Research*, Vol. 1 (May–June 1953). Distinguishes between two levels of optimization and analyzes the problem of selecting appropriate optimization criteria in the light of economic history.

Little, John D. C., "Models and Managers: The Concept of a Decision Calculus," *Management Science*, Vol. 16 (April 1970). A model that is to be used by a manager should be simple, robust, easy to control, adaptive, complete, and easy to communicate with. This paper looks into these properties and gives a real example.

Rivett, Patrick, *Principles of Model Building* (New York: Wiley, 1972). "Model construction is an amalgam of theory and practice in which, unfortunately, either theory or practice appears from time to time as the dominant constituent. When theory is dominant, elegance of mathematical exposition may lead to consequences which are incapable of implementation. On the other hand, hurried problem solving which conceals within it a technical ineptitude may mean that insight into the structure is lost. . . . This book seeks to explore the middle ground." Quote from the preface of the book. Short, easy to read for an audience with some familiarity in operations research techniques, including aspects of data sources.

Wagner, Harvey M., "The Design of Production and Inventory Systems for Multifacility and Multiwarehouse Companies," *Operations Research*, Vol. 22 (March–April 1974). The paper presents the overall structure of the systems design for such problems, discussing in detail the steps that have to be followed, the management functions involved and the usefulness of operations research for such systems.

SENSITIVITY ANALYSIS

Blanning, Robert W., "The Sources and Uses of Sensitivity Information," *Interfaces*, Vol. 4 (Aug. 1974). Briefly reviews the various approaches of sensitivity analysis.

Feeney, G. J., "A Basis for Strategic Decisions on Inventory Control Operations," *Management Science*, Vol. 1 (September 1955). Shows how sensitivity analysis may be used to derive ranges for hard-to-evaluate cost factors based on past decisions.

IMPLEMENTATION

Churchman, C. W., and A. H. Schainblatt, "The Researcher and the Manager: A Dialectic of Implementation," *Management Science*, Vol. 11 (February 1965). Conceptual analysis of the activities and attitudes by the operations researcher and the manager which are most appropriate to bring about a climate conducive to proper implementation. Develops four levels of communication and understanding between the two. See also *Management Science*, October 1965, for a follow-up discussion on this very provocative paper, particularly the commentary by W. Alderson.

Stillson, P., "Implementation of Problems in Operations Research," *Operations Research*, Vol. 11 (Jan.–Feb., 1963). A searching analysis of the reasons why so few operations research projects are properly implemented.

Urban, Glen L., "Building Models for Decision Makers," *Interfaces*, Vol. 4 (May 1974). The paper draws on the literature along with practical experience to propose a process of building models that may have a high chance of being implemented. The steps are: (1) formulation of priors, (2) entry, (3) problem finding, (4) specification of model development criteria, (5) model building, (6) estimation and fitting, (7) tracking, and (8) continuing use. Contains a good list of more recent references.

2

Linear Programming— A Graphical Introduction

Linear programming, or LP as it is called for short, is one of the most important tools used in operations research. Linear programming is a mathematical structure, involving particular mathematical assumptions, that can be solved using a standard solution technique, called the *simplex method*. Any problem that satisfies the assumptions of this structure can be formulated as a linear program and solved by the simplex method. It is thus a general purpose model.

2-1 THE PROBLEM

Consider the following example, necessarily simplified for expository purposes. The management of a coal-fired electric power generating plant is studying the plant's operational setup in order to comply with the latest emission standards under the air pollution control laws. For the plant in question, maximum emission rates are—

- Maximum sulfur oxide emission: 3000 parts per million (PPM)
- Maximum particulate emission (smoke): 12 kg/hr

Coal is brought to the plant by railroad and dumped onto stockpiles near the plant. From there it is carried by a conveyor belt to the pulverizer unit, where it is pulverized and fed directly into the combustion chamber at the desired rate. The heat produced in the combustion chamber is used to make steam to drive the turbines.

Two types of coal are used at the plant: grade A which is a hard and clean-burning coal with a low sulfur content—fairly expensive though—and grade B which is a cheap, relatively soft and smoky coal with a high sulfur content.

Table 2-1. *Emission of Pollutants.*

Coal	Sulfur oxides in flue gases	Particulate emission/ton
A	1800 PPM	0.5 kg
B	3800 PPM	1.0 kg

The thermal value in terms of steam produced is higher for coal A than for coal B, namely 24,000 pounds per ton for A against 20,000 pounds per ton for B. Since coal A is a hard coal, the pulverizer unit can handle, at most, 16 tons of coal A per hour, whereas it can pulverize up to 24 tons of coal B per hour. The conveyor loading system has a capacity of 20 tons per hour regardless of which coal is loaded.

One of several questions management wants to have answered is: Given the constraints on emission of pollutants and given the grades of coal available, what is the maximum possible output of electricity of the plant? The answer will enable management to determine the margin of safety available to meet peak demands for power.

2-2 DECISION VARIABLES

In the short-run, the plant facilities are fixed. They form part of the environment of plant operating decisions. The only aspect of the problem which is controllable in the short-run and which can be used to affect the output of the plant is the amount of each type of coal to be burned. Thus the *decision variables* of the problem are:

- the amount of coal A used per hour denoted by x_1,
- the amount of coal B used per hour denoted by x_2.

In linear programming we often refer to the controllable aspects of a decision problem as *activities*. Hence x_1 and x_2 represent the *activity levels* of burning coal A and coal B, respectively.

LINEAR PROGRAMMING ASSUMPTION 1: DIVISIBILITY

All variables can assume any real value.

Some activities in the real world can be varied in an almost continuous manner, i.e., they are infinitely divisible. For instance, the amount of coal burned per hour can be adjusted to any value, integer, or fraction, within reasonable limits. However, many real activities can only occur in integer values such as the number of truck trips needed to haul a certain cargo from one location to another.

If the real activity is not infinitely divisible, but the normal activity level is a large number in terms of its units of measurement, then the assumption of divisibility may serve as a convenient approximation. This usually means that the solution value for the activity is in the tens or hundreds. Fractional values of the solution are simply rounded to the nearest integer. However, if the normal activity level is relatively small, say less than 10, a solution technique is needed that guarantees an integer solution. This is not the case for linear programming. The more advanced techniques called *integer programming* form the topic of Chapter 12.

This assumption seems to reflect well the nature of most activities in the real world, where it rarely makes sense within an economic or engineering context to talk about negative activity levels.   In our example, negative activity levels would represent a reversal of the process of generating electricity, i.e., converting electricity back into coal.

However, this assumption is not a loss of generality.   Remember that any number—positive, zero, or negative—can be expressed as the algebraic difference of two nonnegative numbers.   If an activity can occur at negative as well as positive levels, such as buying or selling marketable securities, we introduce two decision variables for this activity, one, say x^+, for nonnegative levels, the other, say x^-, for nonpositive levels.   Their difference $x = x^+ - x^-$ represents the actual level of the activity.   By this trick both x^+ and x^- are restricted to be nonnegative.

2-3 OBJECTIVE FUNCTION

Management's objective is to maximize the output of electricity of the plant.   Since electricity is produced through steam and since there is a direct relationship between the amount of steam produced and the output of electricity, maximizing electricity output is equivalent to maximizing steam output.   Therefore, management's objective can be reformulated as, "Find the combination of fuels that maximizes steam output."

What is the amount of steam produced for any arbitrary amounts of coal used? A simple and systematic way of determining this is shown in Table 2-2.

It is rather cumbersome to write numbers that are in the thousands.   Let us therefore *scale* this sum by a factor of 1000; i.e., rather than quoting the steam produced in pounds we express it in units of 1000 pounds.   Hence coal A produces

Table 2-2. *Construction of Objective Function.*

Coal	Steam in lbs/ton of fuel used	Fuel used/hour	Steam produced in lbs/hour
A	24,000	x_1	$24,000x_1$
B	20,000	x_2	$20,000x_2$

Total amount of steam/hour $= 24{,}000x_1 + 20{,}000x_2$

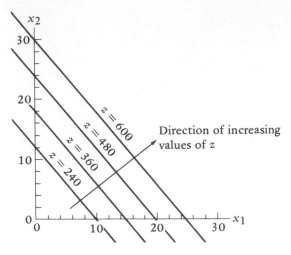

Figure 2-1. *Objective function.*

24 units and coal B 20 units of steam per ton of fuel. In terms of these new units, the total amount of steam produced per hour is

$$(2\text{-}1) \qquad\qquad 24x_1 + 20x_2 = z$$

The left-hand-side of expression (2-1) is called the *objective function* and z is the value of the objective function. The coefficients of the decision variables are referred to as *objective function coefficients*. The problem calls for finding values of x_1 and x_2 that maximize the value of z. Figure 2-1 depicts the objective function for arbitrary values of z in the form of *contour lines* of equal output.

Notice that in two-dimensional Euclidean space any given value of z yields a straight line for the objective function. As the value of z changes, this straight line moves parallel to itself. The objective function is thus seen to be *linear*.

LINEAR PROGRAMMING ASSUMPTION 3:
LINEARITY

All relationships between variables are linear. In linear programming this implies:

1. Proportionality of contributions. The individual contribution of each variable is strictly proportional to its value and the factor of proportionality is constant over the entire range of values that the variable can assume.
2. Additivity of contributions. The total contribution of all variables is equal to the sum of the individual contributions regardless of the values of the variables.

A relationship such as $z = (5x_1 + 3x_1^2 + 2x_2)$ or $z = (24x_1 + 20x_2$ for $x_1 \leqslant 5$ and $10 + 22x_1 + 20x_2$ for $x_1 > 5)$ would violate the condition of proportionality, whereas $z = (24x_1$ for $x_2 = 0$, $20x_2$ for $x_1 = 0$, and $22x_1 + 18x_2$ for $x_1 > 0$ and $x_2 > 0)$ would violate additivity.

Assumption 3 implies *constant returns to scale* and precludes *economies* or *diseconomies of scale*. In practice this assumption may not hold exactly, particularly for very small or very large values of the activity levels. However, if it holds approximately within the normal range of the solution values we may use the linear programming model as a convenient and powerful approximation. This assumption also excludes *fixed charges* which are incurred for positive activity levels but not for zero levels. Note that it is sometimes possible to approximate diseconomies of scale by the use of several variables, as will be discussed in Section 14-1.

2-4 CONSTRAINTS

In addition to the nonnegativity conditions, the activity levels are restricted by various constraints which may be of physical, technological, economic, or legal nature.

Constraint on Particulate Emission. The maximum amount of smoke that the plant is allowed to emit per hour is limited to 12 kg. According to Table 2-1, each ton of coal A produces 0.5 kg of smoke, and each ton of coal B produces 1 kg of smoke. If the plant burns x_1 tons of coal A and x_2 tons of coal B, the total amount of smoke emitted from both coals is equal to

$$0.5x_1 + x_2 \quad \text{(kg/hr)}$$

This sum cannot exceed 12 kg/hr. We thus have the following *inequality constraint*:

(2-2) $$0.5x_1 + x_2 \leqslant 12$$

The coefficients of the variables on the left-hand-side of the inequality sign are referred to as the *left-hand-side (LHS)* coefficients. The constant to the right of the inequality sign is the *right-hand-side (RHS) parameter*. Figure 2-2 depicts this constraint graphically.

Taken by itself, the smoke constraint restricts the values of the decision variables to those combinations of x_1 and x_2 that are on the line $0.5x_1 + x_2 = 12$ or to the left and below that line. Such an area is called a *closed half-space*—closed because it includes all of its boundaries.

We note again that the individual contribution of each variable is strictly proportional to its value and that the total contribution toward smoke emission is equal to the sum of the individual contributions. Hence the constraint satisfies the assumption of linearity as required by Assumption 3.

Constraint on Loading Facilities. The conveyor system transporting coal from the stockpiles to the pulverizer has an hourly capacity of 20 tons. The total number of tons loaded per hour is equal to the sum of the two decision variables.

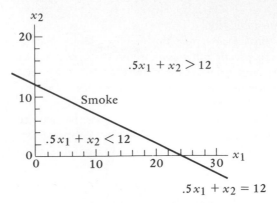

Figure 2-2. *Smoke constraint.*

Therefore, the loading constraint reads

(2-3) $$x_1 + x_2 \leqslant 20$$

You should show this constraint graphically.

Constraint on Pulverizer Unit.   The maximum pulverizer capacity is 16 tons per hour for coal A or 24 tons per hour for coal B.   In other words, it takes 1/16 of an hour to pulverize one ton of coal A and 1/24 of an hour to pulverize one ton of coal B.   If the solution calls for a combination of both coals, the amount of time taken to pulverize a mixture of x_1 tons of coal A and x_2 tons of coal B is $(1/16)\,x_1 + (1/24)\,x_2$. Only those combinations of x_1 and x_2 which require at most 1 hour of time are admissible.   Hence, the pulverizer constraint reads

(2-4) $$\tfrac{1}{16}x_1 + \tfrac{1}{24}x_2 \leqslant 1$$

Note how we overcame the difficulty introduced by different maximum rates for the two coals.   Since the effective maximum rate for a combination of coals is somewhere between the individual maximum rates, we translate these rates into length of time needed per ton and express the constraint in terms of time rather than capacity.

Constraint on Sulfur Oxide Emission.   The maximum sulfur oxide emission is not to exceed 3000 PPM at any time.   Given that the two coals are burned simultaneously, we assume that the combination of x_1 tons of coal A and x_2 tons of coal B is fed into the combustion chamber as a homogeneous mixture. $x_1/(x_1+x_2)$ of the mixture is coal A with a sulfur oxide emission rate of 1800 PPM and $x_2/(x_1+x_2)$ of it is coal B with an emission rate of 3800 PPM.   The emission rate of the mixture is equal to the weighted average of the individual emission rates, where the fractions of each coal used serve as weights.   This weighted average cannot exceed 3000 PPM:

$$\text{weighted average emission rate} \leqslant 3000 \text{ PPM}$$

or

$$1800\left(\frac{x_1}{x_1+x_2}\right) + 3800\left(\frac{x_2}{x_1+x_2}\right) \leqslant 3000$$

Multiplying both sides of the inequality through by (x_1+x_2) and rearranging terms, we get the sulfur constraint:

(2-5) $1200x_1 - 800x_2 \geqslant 0$

All four constraints are shown simultaneously in Figure 2-3.

2-5 THE FEASIBLE REGION

To be an admissible solution, a combination of activity levels must satisfy simultaneously all constraints, including the nonnegativity conditions.   Such a solution is called a *feasible solution* to the problem.   The set of all feasible solutions forms the *feasible region*.   A solution that does not fall in this region is an *infeasible solution*. Figure 2-3 shows all four constraints and the nonnegativity conditions on the same graph.   Inspection of the arrows shows that only those combinations of activity levels that are in the shaded area or its boundary satisfy all constraints simultaneously. This area therefore forms the feasible region.

Since each constraint and each nonnegativity condition represents a closed half-space, the feasible region is given by the *intersection* of these closed half-spaces. Note that the feasible region does not depend on the objective function.   This is an interesting property of most operations research models and has important effects on the solution method and the properties of the optimal solution.

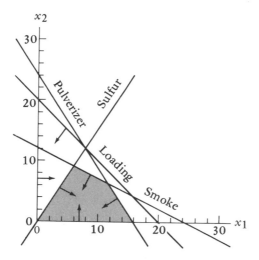

Figure 2-3. *The feasible region.*

If the boundary of a constraint has no point in common with the feasible region, then this constraint is *redundant*. It can be dropped from further consideration. It will never be limiting on the values of the decision variables. Is there a redundant constraint in our problem?

In practice where a problem may have hundreds of constraints and hundreds of variables, it is seldom possible to identify whether a constraint is redundant or not. Fortunately, the simplex method of solving linear programs works irrespective of whether the formulation contains redundant constraints.

2-6 GRAPHICAL SOLUTION

Let us now superimpose the objective function as shown in Figure 2-1 onto the graph of Figure 2-3. This gives us Figure 2-4. The contour lines for a steam output of $z = 240$, and $z = 360$ both have a segment that falls inside the feasible region,

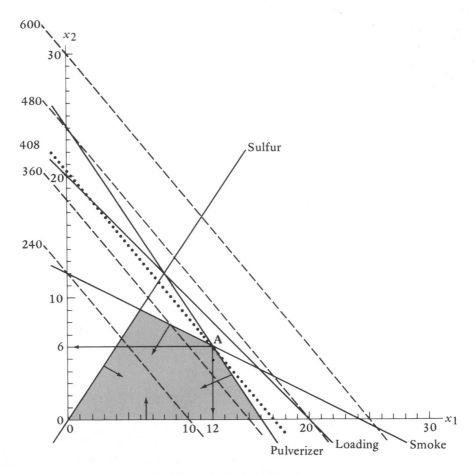

Figure 2-4. *Optimal solution.*

whereas the contour line for $z = 480$ has no point in common with the feasible region. Since our objective is to maximize the steam output of the plant, we want to find the highest contour line for z that contains at least one feasible solution. Consider the line given by $z = 408$ passing through point A. Note that if z is increased by an infinitesimal amount beyond 408, the resulting line has no point in common with the feasible region; whereas if z is decreased by an infinitesimal amount below 408 there is an infinite number of feasible solutions with a value higher than z. Hence $z = 408$ is the maximal value of the objective function that yields a feasible solution.

The optimal values of the decision variables can be read as $x_1 = 12$ and $x_2 = 6$. A combination of 12 tons of coal A and 6 tons of coal B per hour maximizes the steam output of the plant within the physical and legal restrictions imposed on the decision variables. Verify that this solution corresponds to a value of $z = 408$.

It seems intuitively obvious that the optimal solution will always occur at the boundary of the feasible region, either at a *corner point* (*extreme point*), or all along one of the edges, and thus again at an extreme point. As we shall see in Section 2-9 it is the *slope* of the objective function that determines where the optimal solution actually occurs on the boundary.

If the problem called for the minimization of the objective function, how would you change the graphical procedure to find the optimal solution? Say, we want to find the minimum cost solution to produce a steam output of at least 216 units per hour and the cost per ton of coal is $18 for coal A and $15 for coal B. Reformulate the problem to include an output constraint and the new objective function and find the least-cost solution graphically.

Finally, let us point out that not all linear programming problems have a happy ending. Two other types of solutions may occur occasionally. First, the constraints may be inconsistent in the sense that no feasible solution exists—the problem is *infeasible*. Second, the feasible region may be open in some direction such that the objective function can be increased indefinitely and no finite solution exists—the solution is *unbounded*. Note though that few real problems have infeasible or unbounded solutions. Often such solutions are the result of mistakes or misrepresentations in the mathematical formulation.

2-7 MATHEMATICAL SUMMARY

Let us now summarize the problem in mathematical form.

Objective function: Determine values for x_1 and x_2 that
maximize $z = 24x_1 + 20x_2$

Constraints: subject to

$$0.5x_1 + \quad x_2 \leqslant 12 \text{ (smoke)}$$

$$x_1 + \quad x_2 \leqslant 20 \text{ (loading)}$$

(2-6)

$$\tfrac{1}{16}x_1 + \tfrac{1}{24}x_2 \leqslant 1 \text{ (pulverizer)}$$

$$1200x_1 - 800x_2 \geqslant 0 \text{ (sulfur)}$$

and

Nonnegativity conditions: $\qquad\qquad\qquad\qquad x_1 \geqslant 0, \qquad x_2 \geqslant 0$

In general, if we denote x_j as the value of the jth activity or variable, a_{ij} as the LHS coefficient of variable j in constraint i, b_i as the RHS parameter of the ith constraint, and c_j as the objective function coefficient of the jth variable, then the structure of a linear program is as follows:

Determine values for $x_j, j = 1, 2, \dots, n$, that

$$\text{maximize} \qquad z = \sum_j c_j x_j$$

subject to

(2-7) $$\sum_j a_{ij} x_j \ [\leqslant \text{ or } = \text{ or } \geqslant] \ b_i, \qquad i = 1, 2, \dots, m$$

and

$$x_j \geqslant 0, \qquad j = 1, 2, \dots, n,$$

where n is the number of variables and m is the number of constraints, and the constraints may be inequalities of the type $\leqslant$ or $\geqslant$ or equalities.

2-8 SLACK VARIABLES

For any given feasible solution the difference between the LHS and the RHS of a constraint is called the amount of *slack* (for $\leqslant$ inequalities) or *surplus* (for $\geqslant$ inequalities). It is often convenient to show explicitly this difference by introducing an additional variable into each constraint. These variables are called *slack* or *surplus variables*. For convenience, we shall use the term *slack variables* for both. Slack variables are subject to the same assumptions as to divisibility (assumption 1) and nonnegativity (assumption 2) as the decision variables. Each constraint is then converted to an equality.

Let x_{i+2} be the slack variable for the ith constraint in our example. Introducing them into our constraints we get the following four equalities:

(2-2A) $\qquad 0.5x_1 + \quad x_2 + x_3 \qquad\qquad\qquad = 12$ (smoke)

(2-3A) $\qquad\quad x_1 + \quad x_2 \qquad + x_4 \qquad\qquad = 20$ (loading)

(2-4A) $\qquad \frac{1}{16}x_1 + \frac{1}{24}x_2 \qquad\qquad + x_5 \quad\ = 1$ (pulverizer)

(2-5A) $\qquad 1200x_1 - 800x_2 \qquad\qquad\quad - x_6 = 0$ (sulfur)

Why is the slack variable for the sulfur constraint (2-5A) subtracted from the LHS rather than added as for the other three constraints?

The slack variables can often be interpreted as the amount of *unused resources* or *unused capacity* for a given solution. For instance, x_3 is the amount of unused smoke emission capacity and x_4 the amount of unused loading capacity. What is the interpretation for x_5? Due to the way the sulfur constraint was obtained, there is no intuitively appealing interpretation for x_6. Each constraint converted in this manner to an equality says that the amount of resources or capacity used by the activities plus the unused amount of resources or capacity is equal to the total available amount of resources or capacity.

If a slack variable is equal to zero in a feasible solution, the corresponding constraint is *binding*. If a slack variable is positive, the corresponding constraint is *not binding* or *slack*. You should verify by substituting the values of the decision variables into each constraint that for the optimal solution we have:

Constraint	*Smoke*	*Loading*	*Pulverizer*	*Sulfur*
Amount of slack	0	2	0	9600
Status of constraint	binding	slack	binding	slack

2-9 SENSITIVITY ANALYSIS

Let us next consider some "what if" questions. We mentioned earlier that the slope of the objective function determines where the optimal solution occurs. The slope of the objective function is determined by the objective function coefficients. What happens if the value of one of the objective function coefficients changes?

Assume that the thermal value of coal A is equivalent to 32,000 pounds of steam rather than 24,000 with all other coefficients remaining unchanged at their present value, i.e., the objective function becomes

(2-8)
$$\text{maximize } 32x_1 + 20x_2$$

This new objective function is shown in Figure 2-5 as the broken line for various values of z. The optimal original objective function (2-1) is shown dotted. The maximal value of (2-8) occurs at point B.

A change in the value of an objective function coefficient—all other coefficients and parameters remaining unchanged—causes a change in the slope of the objective function. If the change in the slope is sufficiently large, the optimal solution shifts to another extreme point of the feasible region.

Let us study this effect a little more closely. What is the largest possible value of the original objective function coefficient of x_1, denoted by c_1, before the optimal solution shifts from point A to point B? From Figure 2-5 we see that as c_1 is increased the slope of the maximal value of the objective function gets closer and closer to the slope of the boundary of the pulverizer constraint and will ultimately coincide with the pulverizer constraint. At that value of c_1 any point along the line from A to B is optimal, i.e., we obtain *alternative optimal solutions* all with the same value of z. If c_1 is increased slightly more the optimal solution will occur only at point B. Thus, provided c_1 is no greater than the value needed to make the objective function parallel to the pulverizer constraint, the optimal solution will remain at A. The objective function and pulverizer constraint are parallel when their slopes are the same, i.e., when the ratio of the coefficients for the lines are the same. So we require that

$$\frac{c_1}{1/16} = \frac{20}{1/24} = 480$$

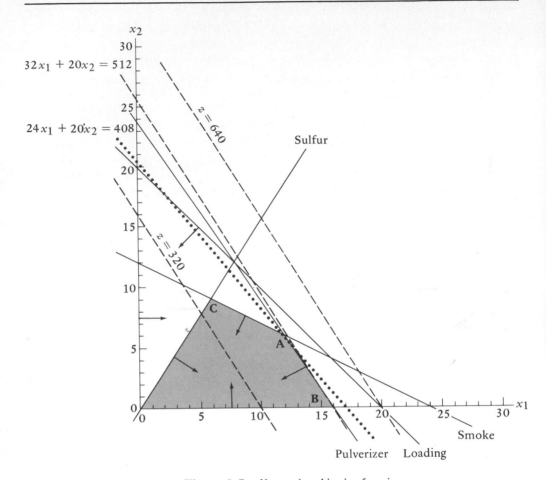

Figure 2-5. *Alternative objective function.*

This yields $c_1 = 30$. For an increase in c_1 beyond 30 the optimal solution will shift from point A to point B.

For $c_1 = 30$ the objective function $30x_1 + 20x_2$ assumes its maximal value of 480 for any point along the line from A to B, including both A and B.

By an analogous reasoning it follows that if c_1 is decreased to 10—all other coefficients and parameters remaining unchanged—the objective function will be parallel to the smoke constraint (2-2). A decrease of c_1 below 10 will cause a shift of the optimal solution from point A to point C. (See Figure 2-5).

The conclusion we can draw from this exercise is that, all other things remaining the same, the solution $x_1 = 12$ and $x_2 = 6$ remains optimal for any value of the objective function coefficient for x_1 in the range $10 \leqslant c_1 \leqslant 30$. Can you determine the range on c_2?

Let us next see how the optimal solution is affected by a change in the RHS parameter of a constraint. To motivate this analysis assume that management is contemplating the installation of emission control equipment that would reduce smoke by 20 percent.   This would allow the legal emission standards to be met by an uncontrolled emission of smoke from the combustion chamber of up to 15 kg/hr. How much would this be worth per hour in increased steam output?

Assume first that the maximum permissible smoke emission is increased from 12 kg to 13 kg/hr, all other coefficients and parameters remaining the same.   This will cause a parallel upward shift in the smoke constraint as shown in Figure 2-6. Since this constraint forms part of the boundary of the feasible region, the feasible region is enlarged by the dark shaded area.   In this enlarged feasible region, $z = 408$ is no longer the optimal value of the objective function—the best value is at point D. So the optimal solution shifts from point A to point D.   This change in the optimal solution occurs because originally the smoke emission constraint is binding at point A. The new optimal values of the decision variables are $x_1 = 11$ and $x_2 = 7.5$.   The decrease in x_1 causes a reduction in steam output of 24 units, whereas the increase in x_2 increases it by 30 units of steam.   The net increase is 6.   The new maximal value of z is thus $408 + 6 = 414$.

The change in the optimal value of the objective function for a unit change in the RHS parameter of a constraint is called the *shadow price* or *imputed value* of the constraint.   The shadow price of the smoke constraint (2-2) is 6.

What happens if the maximum smoke emission is further relaxed to 14, 15, 16, and 17 kg/hr?   The dotted lines in Figure 2-6 show how the smoke constraint shifts

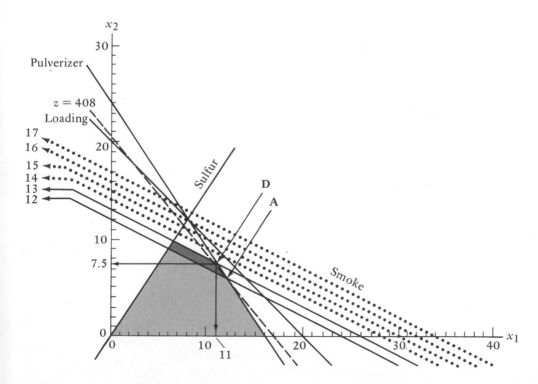

Figure 2-6. *Sensitivity analysis for RHS parameters.*

upward, adding an additional area to the feasible region for each such shift up to a maximum of 16. You should confirm that the resulting changes in the decision variables increase the maximal value of the objective function by 6 units for each unit increase in the RHS parameter.

For an increase of the RHS parameter beyond 16, the smoke constraint becomes redundant. The optimal solution is now constrained by the pulverizer and sulfur constraints (as well as by the loading constraint). Hence, for values of the RHS parameter of the smoke constraint larger than 16, the shadow price of the constraint is zero.

Our original question asked for the increase in steam output for a change in the permissible smoke level from 12 to 15 kg/hr. This will be 3×6 or 18 units of steam/hr.

What is the shadow price of a constraint that is not binding in the optimal solution? Clearly, if a portion of a resource remains unused—the corresponding slack variable is positive—additional amounts of that resource have no value. It would only increase the amount of slack. Hence, the shadow price of such a constraint is zero. Find the shadow prices for the remaining constraints.

Observe the interesting complementarity between the value of the shadow price of a constraint and the slack variable associated with the same constraint:

Status of constraint	Value of shadow price	Value of slack variable
binding	(usually) positive	zero
not binding	zero	(usually) positive

We hedge somewhat by saying "usually positive." We shall see in Chapter 4 that a more accurate statement is "nonnegative."

2-10 SOLUTION BY COMPUTER

The graphical solution is only possible if the number of decision variables does not exceed two (three?). Problems with more decision variables have to be solved mathematically by the simplex method. This method is developed in detail in Chapter 3. The computations of the simplex method are very time consuming. Even small problems of 5 to 10 variables and constraints take hours to be solved on a desk calculator. Real problems, however, have hundreds or thousands of constraints and variables. Access to computers is thus a necessity.

Due to its iterative nature, the simplex method can easily be programmed for a computer. Any problem that has the general structure of expressions (2-7) and satisfies the three assumptions of linear programming can be solved with the aid of such general purpose linear-programming computer codes.

Before we discuss the input into these computer codes let us represent the general form of a linear program, as it is shown by expressions (2-7), in the form of a table which has one row for each constraint plus an additional row for the objective function and one column for each variable plus an additional column for the RHS. At the intersection of each constraint row and variable column we insert the corresponding LHS coefficient. In the bottom row we insert the corresponding objective function coefficients and in the last column the RHS parameters, where we also show the type of constraint ($\leqslant$ or $=$ or $\geqslant$). This table is commonly referred to as the *linear program in detached coefficient form.* Instead of indicating the type of relationship in the column for the RHS, it is often convenient to add additional columns for the slack variables. Each constraint is then implied as an equality. This has been done in Table 2-3 for the original power plant capacity problem.

Table 2-3. *Linear Program in Detached Coefficient Form.*

constraint	variable						RHS
	x_1	x_2	x_3	x_4	x_5	x_6	
(2-2A)	0.5	1	1	0	0	0	12
(2-3A)	1	1	0	1	0	0	20
(2-4A)	1/16	1/24	0	0	1	0	1
(2-5A)	1200	-800	0	0	0	-1	0
Obj. function	24	20	0	0	0	0	maximize

This table essentially represents the input data for all computer codes. Therefore, the computer has to be told the size of the table, i.e., the number of variables (decision plus slack variables) and the number of constraints; the value of each entry in the table, usually identified by its row name and column name; and whether the objective function is to be minimized or maximized.

Rows and columns are usually identified by *mnemonic* names, i.e., words or suitable abbreviations that immediately hint at what activity or what constraint is being referred to. This avoids a lengthy translation process if the number of variables is large. For our example we could use the following names.

$$\begin{aligned}
\text{constraint (2-2A):} \quad &\text{SMOKE}\\
\text{(2-3A):} \quad &\text{LOAD}\\
\text{(2-4A):} \quad &\text{PULVER}\\
\text{(2-5A):} \quad &\text{SULFUR}\\
\text{variable} \quad x_1: \quad &\text{ACOAL}\\
x_2: \quad &\text{BCOAL}\\
x_3: \quad &\text{SMOKSL}\\
x_4: \quad &\text{LOADSL}\\
x_5: \quad &\text{PULVSL}\\
x_6: \quad &\text{SULFSL}
\end{aligned}$$

We have solved this problem using the simple linear programming computer code "LPGOGO" described in chapter 5 of Daellenbach and Bell, *User's Guide to Linear Programming*. This code, which is fairly typical of the input format of linear programming codes, requires that each nonzero entry of Table 2-3 is specified on a separate card. Figure 2-7 shows the printout of the optimal solution. The code first reproduces the input data. This is often a useful feature, since it allows us to check whether the problem actually solved was really the one we intended to solve!

Note that small rounding errors may occur when the data is read into the computer as well as during the computations of the simplex method. As a consequence the optimal solution printed may also contain small rounding errors, as is the case here.

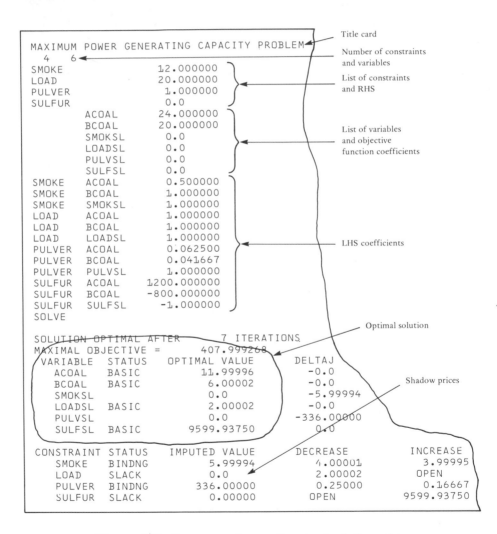

Figure 2-7. *Computer printout of optimal solution using LPGOGO.*

In addition to the optimal values of the variables and the objective function, LPGOGO also provides a considerable amount of information useful for sensitivity analysis. In particular, the shadow price of each constraint is shown under the heading "IMPUTED VALUE." The range of the RHS parameter over which each shadow price is valid, all other inputs remaining unchanged, is shown under the headings "DECREASE" and "INCREASE." For instance, the shadow price of 6.0 of the SMOKE constraint is valid for a decrease of up to 4 kg and an increase of up to 4 kg from the original value of 12 kg/hr, confirming our earlier results obtained graphically. On the other hand, the shadow price of the PULVER constraint is only valid for a decrease of up to 1/4 hour or an increase of up to 1/6 hour. The effect of changes in RHS parameters on the variables however is not shown.

The printout also provides sensitivity analysis with respect to the objective function coefficients of variables which have a zero value in the optimal solution. The numbers listed under the heading "DELTAJ" represent the change in the value of the objective function if the corresponding variable—which at present has a zero value—were forced to a value of one. Alternatively, the negative of the DELTAJ value is the amount by which the objective function coefficient of the corresponding variable would have to increase to make this variable a candidate to enter alternative optimal solutions.

In our example only the slack variables have nonzero DELTAJ values. Therefore, let us look at an expanded version of the power generating capacity problem.

2-11 AN EXPANDED VERSION OF THE POWER PLANT CAPACITY PROBLEM

The plant is offered a third type of fuel, namely grade C coal, which results in a sulfur oxide emission rate of 2000 PPM, a smoke emission rate of 0.8 kg/ton of fuel burnt, and requires 1/20 hour each of pulverizer and loader capacity per ton. Its thermal value is the equivalent of 21,000 lbs of steam per ton of fuel. Would it be advantageous for the plant to use this fuel?

Let us reformulate the problem with this third coal. Let x_3 be the number of tons per hour of coal C used. Then

$$\text{maximize} \quad 24x_1 + 20x_2 + 21x_3$$

$$\text{subject to} \quad 0.5x_1 + x_2 + 0.8x_3 \leqslant 12 \text{ (smoke)}$$

$$x_1 + x_2 + x_3 \leqslant 20 \text{ (loading)}$$

(2-9)

$$\tfrac{1}{16}x_1 + \tfrac{1}{24}x_2 + \tfrac{1}{20}x_3 \leqslant 1 \text{ (pulverizer)}$$

$$1200x_1 - 800x_2 + 1000x_3 \geqslant 0 \text{ (sulfur)}$$

$$x_1 \geqslant 0, \; x_2 \geqslant 0, \; x_3 \geqslant 0$$

Figure 2-8 illustrates the computer printout for this expanded version. The optimal solution is unchanged. Under the present conditions, it is not advantageous

```
MAXIMUM POWER PLANT CAPACITY PROBLEM - EXPANDED VERSION
   4    7
SMOKE                    12.000000
LOAD                     20.000000
PULVER                    1.000000
SULFUR                    0.0
          ACOAL          24.000000
          BCOAL          20.000000
          CCOAL          21.000000
          SMOKSL          0.0
          LOADSL          0.0
          PULVSL          0.0
          SULFSL          0.0
SMOKE     ACOAL           0.500000
SMOKE     BCOAL           1.000000
SMOKE     CCOAL           0.800000
SMOKE     SMOKSL          1.000000
LOAD      ACOAL           1.000000
LOAD      BCOAL           1.000000
LOAD      CCOAL           1.000000
LOAD      LOADSL          1.000000
PULVER    ACOAL           0.062500
PULVER    BCOAL           0.041667
PULVER    CCOAL           0.050000
PULVER    PULVSL          1.000000
SULFUR    ACOAL        1200.000000
SULFUR    BCOAL        -800.000000
SULFUR    CCOAL        1000.000000
SULFUR    SULFSL         -1.000000
SOLVE

SOLUTION OPTIMAL AFTER       7 ITERATIONS
MAXIMAL OBJECTIVE =      407.999512
 VARIABLE   STATUS   OPTIMAL VALUE      DELTAJ
   ACOAL    BASIC       12.00000        -0.0
   BCOAL    BASIC        6.00000        -0.0
   CCOAL                 0.0            -0.60001
   SMOKSL                0.0            -6.00000
   LOADSL   BASIC        2.00001        -0.0
   PULVSL                0.0          -335.99976
   SULFSL   BASIC     9599.99609         0.0

CONSTRAINT STATUS   IMPUTED VALUE    DECREASE      INCREASE
   SMOKE   BINDNG        6.00000       4.00000       4.00000
   LOAD    SLACK         0.0           2.00001       OPEN
   PULVER  BINDNG      335.99976       0.25000       0.16667
   SULFUR  SLACK         0.00000       OPEN       9599.99609
```

Figure 2-8. *Expanded version of power plant capacity problem.*

to use coal C. In fact, according to the DELTAJ value of variable CCOAL (x_3) the objective function would change by -0.6, i.e., it would decrease from 408 to 407.4 units of steam, if $x_3 = 1$. Alternatively, the thermal value of coal C would need to be 600 lbs/ton greater or the objective function coefficient of x_3 would need to be 21.6 rather than 21 (larger by the negative of -0.6) before variable x_3 becomes a candidate to assume positive values in alternative optimal solutions.

There was in fact no need to solve the expanded version of the problem to get this result. The shadow prices of the original problem give us all the information we need. Let us arbitrarily decide to use one ton of coal C and determine its effect on the maximal value of the objective function. Setting $x_3 = 1$ is equivalent to reducing the RHS parameters of the four constraints of the original problem as follows:

$$0.5x_1 + \quad x_2 \leqslant 12 - 0.8 \text{ or } 11.2 \text{ (smoke)}$$

$$x_1 + \quad x_2 \leqslant 20 - 1 \text{ or } 19 \text{ (loading)}$$

$$\tfrac{1}{16}x_1 + \tfrac{1}{24}x_2 \leqslant 1.0 - 1/20 \text{ or } 19/20 \text{ (pulverizer)}$$

$$1200x_1 - 800x_2 \geqslant 0 - 1000 \text{ or } -1000 \text{ (sulfur)}$$

The loading constraint and the sulfur constraint are both slack and their shadow prices are therefore zero. But 1/20 hour of pulverizer capacity reduction results in a decrease of the value of the objective function of $1/20 \times 336$ or 16.8 and a reduction of 0.8 kg of the maximum smoke emission decreases the value of the objective function by 0.8×6 or 4.8. The total decrease of the objective function value is equal to the sum of 16.8 plus 4.8 or 21.6 units of steam. On the other hand, the additional steam output gained per hour by burning one ton of coal C is only 21 units. The net loss in steam output is thus 0.6 units, confirming our earlier finding.

2-12 A PRODUCTION SCHEDULING PROBLEM

A metal processing plant receives an order to produce 10,000 casings. The contract specifies a sales price of $4.85 per casing. The products design engineer proposes four alternative designs for the casings resulting in different variable machine time usages and material costs. The latter differ due to different amounts of wastage.

Table 2-4. *Input Data for Casing Production.*

Production design	Machine time in minutes				Material cost	Predicted average fraction of rejects produced
	Cutting	Forming	Welding	Finishing		
1	0.40	0.70	1.00	0.50	$3.355	3%
2	0.80	1.00	0.40	0.30	$4.150	1%
3	0.35	0.60	1.25	0.75	$2.995	4%
4	0.70	0.80	0.60	0.55	$3.705	2%
Variable cost/minute	$0.20	$0.30	$0.15	$0.10		

The customer wants to receive delivery within one month of signing of the contract. On the basis of the present production commitments, the production engineer forecasts that the plant has excess capacities of 90 hours of cutting machine time, 140 hours of forming machine time, 154 hours of welding time, and 120 hours of finishing time. The production engineer's problem is to determine which designs to use so as to guarantee delivery within the contractual arrangement.

What should we use as the firm's objective? The usual objective in problems of this sort is the maximization of profits. In this particular instance the relevant measure of profit is given as the difference between gross revenues and all variable costs.

What aspects provide the decision variables? In this simplified problem the production engineer is given four alternative designs that each yield exactly the same end product from the customer's point of view. His decision problem thus boils down to a choice of which design or combination of designs to use—in particular, how many casings of each design to produce. Let x_j denote the number of casings of design j produced.

This choice cannot be arbitrary, but in order to guarantee delivery on due date it has to be within the predicted excess capacities for each operation. Furthermore, the total amount of good casings produced has to be equal to 10,000.

Total Output Constraint. From past experience, it is possible to predict the average fraction of defectives resulting from each product design. This is shown in the last column of Table 2-4. To satisfy the total output requirement, only good casings can be counted. So, if x_1 casings of design 1 are scheduled, and on the average 3 percent defectives are produced or 97 percent are expected to be good casings, then $0.97x_1$ is the number of good casings of design 1 obtained. Similarly for the other designs. Therefore for all four designs we require that:

[expected total number of good casings produced] = [number of good casings required]

(2-10) $$0.97x_1 + 0.99x_2 + 0.96x_3 + 0.98x_4 = 10{,}000$$

Protecting ourselves only against the average rate of defectives may in practice not be sufficient since it results in a large probability of not producing enough good casings.

Machine Time Constraints. The amount of machine time used for each operation cannot be more than the amount of excess time available within the delivery period. For instance, each unit of design 1 requires 0.4 minutes of cutting time, so x_1 units require $0.4x_1$ minutes of cutting time. For all four designs, the amount of cutting time needed is

$$0.4x_1 + 0.8x_2 + 0.35x_3 + 0.7x_4.$$

The amount of cutting time available is 90 hours or 5400 minutes. Thus, we get the following relation:

Cutting Time Constraint

(2-11) $$0.4x_1 + 0.8x_2 + 0.35x_3 + 0.7x_4 \leqslant 5400$$

Similarly, for the other three operations:

Forming Time Constraint

(2-12) $$0.7x_1 + 1.0x_2 + 0.6x_3 + 0.8x_4 \leqslant 8400$$

Welding Time Constraint

(2-13) $$1.0x_1 + 0.4x_2 + 1.25x_3 + 0.6x_4 \leqslant 9240$$

Finishing Time Constraint

(2-14) $$0.5x_1 + 0.3x_2 + 0.75x_3 + 0.55x_4 \leqslant 7200$$

To determine the profits we need the unit costs. These are made up of the variable machine cost for each operation and the material cost. Table 2-5 shows the detailed components for each design.

Table 2-5. *Unit Profit Computations Rounded to $\frac{1}{2}$ Cents.*

Design	1	2	3	4
	$	$	$	$
Material cost	3.355	4.150	2.995	3.705
Cutting time	0.08	0.16	0.07	0.14
Forming time	0.21	0.30	0.18	0.24
Welding time	0.15	0.06	0.19	0.09
Finishing time	0.05	0.03	0.075	0.055
Total variable unit cost	3.845	4.700	3.510	4.230

Total profits are given by total revenues minus total costs:

$$4.85(10,000) - 3.845x_1 - 4.7x_2 - 3.51x_3 - 4.23x_4.$$

Substituting the left-hand side of expression (2-10) for 10,000 we get

$$4.85(0.97x_1 + 0.99x_2 + 0.96x_3 + 0.98x_4) - 3.845x_1 - 4.7x_2 - 3.51x_3 - 4.23x_4$$

Collecting terms and rounding to the nearest $\frac{1}{2}$ cent, we finally obtain the

Objective Function

(2-15) $$\text{maximize } 0.86x_1 + 0.1x_2 + 1.145x_3 + 0.525x_4$$

Nonnegativity Conditions

$$x_j \geqslant 0, \quad j = 1,2,3,4$$

```
PRODUCTION SCHEDULING
   5    8
OUTPUT            10000.000000
CUT                5400.000000
FORM               8400.000000
WELD               9240.000000
FINISH             7200.000000
            DES1      0.860000
            DES2      0.100000
            DES3      1.145000
            DES4      0.525000
            CUTSL     0.000000
            FORMSL    0.000000
            WELDSL    0.000000
            FINSL     0.000000
OUTPUT      DES1      0.970000
OUTPUT      DES2      0.990000
OUTPUT      DES3      0.960000
OUTPUT      DES4      0.980000
CUT         DES1      0.400000
CUT         DES2      0.800000
CUT         DES3      0.350000
CUT         DES4      0.700000
CUT         CUTSL     1.000000
FORM        DES1      0.700000
FORM        DES2      1.000000
FORM        DES3      0.600000
FORM        DES4      0.800000
FORM        FORMSL    1.000000
WELD        DES1      1.000000
WELD        DES2      0.400000
WELD        DES3      1.200000
WELD        DES4      0.600000
WELD        WELDSL    1.000000
FINISH      DES1      0.500000
FINISH      DES2      0.300000
FINISH      DES3      0.750000
FINISH      DES4      0.550000
FINISH      FINSL     1.000000
SOLVE


SOLUTION OPTIMAL AFTER        7 ITERATIONS
MAXIMAL OBJECTIVE =     8531.603325
  VARIABLE   STATUS    OPTIMAL VALUE       DELTAJ
    DES1     BASIC        476.00950        0.00000
    DES2                    0.00000       -0.19559
    DES3     BASIC       4776.24703        0.00000
    DES4     BASIC       5054.15677        0.00000
    CUTSL                   0.00000       -1.11188
    FORMSL   BASIC       1157.71971        0.00000
    WELDSL                  0.00000       -1.63985
    FINSL    BASIC        600.02375        0.00000

CONSTRAINT STATUS    IMPUTED VALUE      DECREASE        INCREASE
    OUTPUT   BINDNG      -1.26247       31.80952       437.13043
    CUT      BINDNG       1.11188      505.22613        33.40000
    FORM     SLACK        0.00000     1157.71971           OPEN
    WELD     BINDNG       1.63985      700.62718        60.91185
    FINISH   SLACK        0.00000      600.02375           OPEN
```

Figure 2-9. *Computer printout of optimal solution to production scheduling problem.*

We have solved this problem by computer using the linear programming computer code LPGOGO. Figure 2-9 is a facsimile of the computer printout of the input and the optimal solution. Note that for the computer solution we introduce slack variables for the machine time constraints which are all $\leq$ inequalities. With this change the problem has 8 variables and 5 equality constraints. Constraints and variables are given mnemonic names which are self-explanatory.

The optimal solution provides that approximately 476 units of design 1, 4776 units of design 3, and 5054 units of design 4, but none of design 2 are produced at a total profit of $8531.60. All available capacity of cutting and welding machine time is used up, whereas there still remain about 1158 minutes of forming machine time and 600 minutes of finishing machine time.

From the imputed value (our shadow prices for the constraints) we can infer that, at the margin, additional cutting machine time has a value of $1.11 per minute and additional welding time is valued at $1.64 per minute. These shadow prices are valid for increases of respectively 33 and 61 minutes only. If for instance 60 more minutes of welding machine time were available, profits would increase by $60 \times \$1.64$ or $98.40. Such information may be highly useful for deciding whether or not to schedule overtime and on which machines it should be scheduled.

How are profits affected if the total output of good parts has to be increased by 100 units? The answer to this question is supplied by the shadow price of the total output constraint. For a unit increase in the RHS of constraint (2-10) profits change by $-1.26. In other words, total profit decreases by $1.26. For a 100-unit increase in output this amounts to a decrease in profits of 100($1.26), or $126. The reason for this rather unexpected result is that such an increase would force a proportionately larger shift from more profitable designs, such as design 3 to less profitable designs, such as 1 and 4.

Given the small number of units using design 1 required in the optimal solution, the production engineer may not wish to use design 1 at all. The unit costs may only be valid if sufficiently large quantities of a design are produced, say more than 1000 units. Under these circumstances, the production engineer would eliminate designs 1 and 2 and only produce designs 3 and 4. Solving the problem again, he will discover that with the present excess machine time constraints, no feasible solution exists. In fact, he needs at least 33.4 minutes of overtime on the cutting machine to produce an average of 10,000 units using designs 3 and 4 only. If this additional cutting time can be arranged, the optimal solution calls for 5092 units of design 3, 5216 of design 4 at a total profit of $8568.74 less the overtime cost of the additional cutting time. Ignoring the cost of overtime, this is $37.14 higher than the original maximum profit. Note that this number is equal to (33.4) (imputed value of CUT constraint) = (33.4) ($1.11188).

2-13 A CORPORATE PLANNING MODEL

Forest Industries Corporation has just signed contracts for the clear-felling of two large forest tracts of second-growth radiata pines. The harvested trees will supply

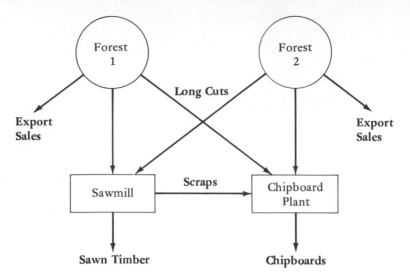

Figure 2-10. *Materials flow of Forest Industries.*

the firm's sawmill and chipboard plant.   Some of the logging output is also available for export.   Figure 2-10 depicts the materials flow schematically.

All trees harvested are cut on location into sections of 20 feet length, referred to as first cuts, second cuts, third cuts, etc.   On the basis of a detailed survey of each forest, the firm's chief forest engineer estimated the average composition of each forest's total output, as shown in Table 2-6.

Although each day's output may differ substantially from these proportions, the average daily output over one month is expected to be fairly close to these figures. The average daily output is 128 HC for forest 1 and 192 HC for forest 2 (1 HC = 100 cubic feet).

The log cuts are sorted and loaded onto logging trucks for transportation to either the sawmill or the chipboard plant, the two facilities being at different locations.   Transportation costs from forest 1 to the sawmill amount to $4 per HC and $7 per HC to the chipboard plant.   From forest 2 the costs are respectively $3 and $5.   Handling costs at the two plants depend on the type of log cuts, as shown in Table 2-7.

Table 2-6. *Composition of Logging Output.*

| | Composition | |
Log cuts	Forest 1	Forest 2
first and second	42%	46%
third and fourth	40%	41%
fifth and over	18%	13%

Table 2-7. *Handling Costs at Plants.*

Log cuts	Handling costs per HC at Sawmill	Handling costs per HC at Chipboard plant
first and second	$2.50	$1.20
third and fourth	$3.50	$1.50
fifth and over	$5.00	$2.00

At the sawmill, logs are sawn into three grades of finished products: clear grades, dressing grades, and construction grades. A substantial fraction of the incoming volume of wood ends up as scraps and sawdust. Table 2-8 shows the average

Table 2-8. *Log Conversion Factors at Sawmill.*

Log cuts	Sawn timber MBF/HC*	Scraps HC/HC	Sawdust HC/HC	Processing time per HC
first and second	0.72	0.26	0.14	1.8
third and fourth	0.66	0.30	0.15	2.6
fifth and over	0.54	0.39	0.16	3.9

* 1 MBF = 1000 board feet

log conversion factors at the sawmill, as well as the average processing rates. Excluding breakdowns, the productive capacity at the mill averages 360 minutes per day.

From sample logs processed at the sawmill, average yields for each grade of sawn timber were determined. They are summarized in Table 2-9.

The ex-mill wholesale price per MBF is $150 for clear grades, $110 for dressing grades, and $80 for construction grades. Scraps at the sawmill are transferred by truck to the chipboard plant for chipping. The transportation cost is $4 per HC. Sawdust is used as fuel in the mill's drying kiln and saves $12 in other fuel costs per HC.

Table 2-9. *Sawn Timber Yields by Grades.*

Log cuts	Clear grades Forest 1	Clear grades Forest 2	Dressing grades Forest 1	Dressing grades Forest 2	Construction grades Forest 1	Construction grades Forest 2
first and second	35%	28%	48%	42%	17%	30%
third and fourth	10%	3%	18%	9%	72%	88%
fifth and over	0	0	5%	0	95%	100%

At the chipboard plant, logs and scraps are chipped, the chips are then mixed with additives and glues, filled into 4' by 8' forms, and then compressed into boards of various thicknesses. The whole process is highly automated. Each HC of wood yields 0.76 $M_{\frac{3}{4}}$ of chipboard or equivalent (1 $M_{\frac{3}{4}}$ = 1000 square feet of $\frac{3}{4}$ inch thickness). The plant can produce up to 112 $M_{\frac{3}{4}}$ of chipboard per day. Chipboard prices ex-factory are $105 per $M_{\frac{3}{4}}$.

In the light of predicted demand and desired stock levels, certain minimum daily output rates of finished products are set by Forest Industries' management for a given planning period. These are 36 MBF of clear grades, 40 MBF of dressing grades, 48 MBF of construction grades and 96 $M_{\frac{3}{4}}$ of chipboards. Export prices valid during the same planning period are: $95 per HC for first and second cuts and $88 per HC of third and fourth cuts. Fifth or higher cuts are not exported.

What is the optimal daily operating policy during the planning period in question?

This problem deals with the operation of an entire firm. Admittedly, these operations are considered only in their most essential aspects, with most of the details ignored. For instance, the final products are lumped into a small number of sawn timber grades. Similarly, only the most important operation at the sawmill, namely the actual sawing of the logs, is represented. No doubt, for real applications considerably more detail would normally be included; but even then, some aggregation would still have to be made to keep the problem at a manageable size.

Our approach to formulate this problem as a linear program is to divide the operations into sequential phases where the outputs of one phase become inputs into subsequent phases. For each phase we construct a submodel and then tie these submodels together appropriately to form a single model. In this example, there are four logical phases: a log supply phase, the operation of the sawmill, the operations of the chipboard plant, and finally the finished product distribution phase which in our case boils down to a specification of minimum daily outputs.

Since we shall at the end solve this problem by computer, we will use mnemonic labels for the constraints and mnemonic names for the variables.

Supply Phase

The output for each type of log cuts at each forest can either be allocated to the sawmill, to the chipboard plant or export orders, or any combination of these uses. This is depicted schematically in Figure 2-11.

Each allocation of a cut to a given use requires a separate decision variable. The decision variables will thus have the interpretation of "cut i from forest j allocated to use k". Let LijSAW, LijCH, and LijEXP denote the number of HC per day of cut i from forest j allocated to the sawmill, the chipboard plant and to export respectively; $i = 1$ refers to first and second cuts, $i = 2$ refers to third and fourth cuts, and $i = 3$ refers to fifth and higher cuts.

Consider cuts $i = 1$ at forest 1. According to Table 2-6 the average daily output of first and second cuts is 42 percent of 128 HC or 53.76. If L11SAW, L11CH, and L11EXP are the amounts per day allocated to the three uses, then their total has to equal 53.76 HC, assuming that the firm does not wish to stockpile any

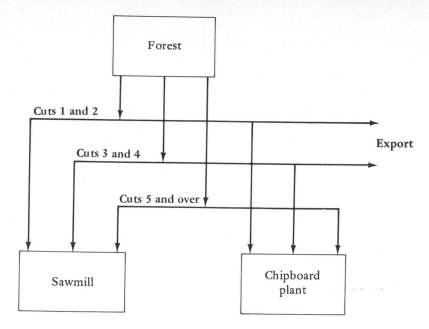

Figure 2-11. *Possible allocation of cuts.*

output at the forests.   This yields the following availability constraint, labelled (L1F1AV):

(L1F1AV)   L11SAW + L11CH + L11EXP = 53.76

If Forest Industries would consider stockpiling some of the cuts at the forests for use in later planning periods, then (L1F1AV) would be expressed in the form of a $\leqslant$ inequality.   We get a similar constraint for each of the other types of cuts at each forest:

(L2F1AV)   L21SAW + L21CH + L21EXP = 51.20

(L3F1AV)   L31SAW + L31CH   = 23.04

(L1F2AV)   L12SAW + L12CH + L12EXP = 88.32

(L2F2AV)   L22SAW + L22CH + L22EXP = 78.72

(L3F2AV)   L32SAW + L32CH   = 24.96

Note that log cuts $i = 3$ are not exported.

The LijSAW variables now become the input into the next phase.

Sawmill Phase

At the sawmill log cuts are converted to three grades of timber, scraps, and sawdust. Consider first the production of sawn timber.   According to Table 2-8, only a portion of each log cut ends up as sawn timber.   For instance, one HC of log cuts $i = 1$ from forest 1 yields 0.72 MBF of sawn timber, of which, according to Table 2-9, 35 percent becomes clear grades, 48 percent dressing grades, and 17 percent construction grades.   So one HC of log cuts $i = 1$ from forest 1 yields 0.72 times 0.35, or 0.252 MBF of clear grades.   Similarly,

1 HC of	cuts $i = 2$ from forest 1	cuts $i = 1$ from forest 2	cuts $i = 2$ from forest 2
yields	$0.66 (0.10) = 0.066$	$0.72 (0.28) = 0.2016$	$0.66 (0.3) = 0.0198$

MBF of clear grades.

Multiplying these coefficients by the daily number of HC of each type of cut brought to the sawmill gives the average daily output of clear grades.   Letting CLEAR denote the number of MBF of clear grades produced per day, we obtain

$$0.252 \text{ L11SAW} + 0.066 \text{ L21SAW} + 0.2016 \text{ L12SAW}$$
$$+ 0.0198 \text{ L22SAW} = \text{CLEAR}$$

Expressed in the usual linear programming form, we have the following constraint, labelled (CLPROD):

(CLPROD) $0.252 \text{ L11SAW} + 0.066 \text{ L21SAW} + 0.2016 \text{ L12SAW}$
$$+ 0.0198 \text{ L22SAW} - \text{CLEAR} = 0$$

Such a constraint is referred to as a *material balance equation* or an *input-output relation*.   Verify the following input-output relations for the production of dressing and construction grades:

(DRPROD)
$$0.3456 \text{ L11SAW} + 0.1188 \text{ L21SAW} + 0.027 \text{ L31SAW} + 0.3024 \text{ L12SAW}$$
$$+ 0.0594 \text{ L22SAW} - \text{DRESS} = 0$$

(COPROD)
$$0.1224 \text{ L11SAW} + 0.4752 \text{ L21SAW} + 0.513 \text{ L31SAW} + 0.216 \text{ L12SAW}$$
$$+ 0.5808 \text{ L22SAW} + 0.54 \text{ L32SAW} - \text{CONST} = 0$$

Similar input-output relations are obtained for the production of scraps and sawdust (using the data in Table 2-8):

(SCPROD)
$$0.26 \text{ L11SAW} + 0.3 \text{ L21SAW} + 0.39 \text{ L31SAW} + 0.26 \text{ L12SAW}$$
$$+ 0.3 \text{ L22SAW} + 0.39 \text{ L32SAW} - \text{SCRAP} = 0$$

(SDPROD)
$$0.14 \text{ L11SAW} + 0.15 \text{ L21SAW} + 0.16 \text{ L31SAW} + 0.14 \text{ L12SAW}$$
$$+ 0.15 \text{ L22SAW} + 0.16 \text{ L32SAW} - \text{SDUST} = 0$$

Finally, the sawmill time required to process the amounts of the various log cuts must not exceed the average productive capacity of 360 minutes per day.

Multiplying the processing times per HC for each type of cuts by the log input into the sawmill and summing, we obtain

(SAWCAP)
$$1.8 \text{ L11SAW} + 2.6 \text{ L21SAW} + 3.9 \text{ L31SAW} + 1.8 \text{ L12SAW}$$
$$+ 2.6 \text{ L22SAW} + 3.9 \text{ L32SAW} \leqslant 360$$

This completes the submodel for the sawmill operation. The variable for SCRAP becomes an input into the chipboard plant phase. The variables for CLEAR, DRESS, and CONST become inputs into the finished products distribution phase.

Chipboard Plant Phase

The inputs into this phase consist of the various amounts of log cuts allocated from each forest and the scraps transferred from the sawmill. Each HC of input yields 0.76 M_4^3 of chipboards. We therefore obtain the following input-output relation:

(CBPROD)
$$0.76 \text{ (L11CH} + \text{L21CH} + \text{L31CH} + \text{L12CH} + \text{L22CH} + \text{L32CH} + \text{SCRAP)}$$
$$- \text{ CBOARD} = 0$$

The output of chipboard is restricted to at most 112 M_4^3 per day. Thus

(CBCAP) $$\text{CBOARD} \leqslant 112$$

The variable CBOARD becomes another input into the last phase.

Finished Products Distribution Phase

For this example, the finished products distribution phase takes the simplified form of lower bounds to the decision variables:

(CLMIN) $$\text{CLEAR} \geqslant 32$$

(DRMIN) $$\text{DRESS} \geqslant 36$$

(COMIN) $$\text{CONST} \geqslant 48$$

(CBMIN) $$\text{CBOARD} \geqslant 96$$

All that is left is to formulate the objective function. The objective is to maximize the difference between revenues and variable costs which we shall loosely refer to as the gross profit. Revenues are generated from sales of sawn timber and chipboards. Costs are incurred from the transportation and handling of the log cuts and scraps; costs are reduced by burning sawdust. All other costs are assumed to be fixed and not affected by the allocation of logs to the various uses, nor the mix in the final products. Such an assumption is clearly true for the logging operation and, in

```
        SOLUTION OPTIMAL AFTER      26 ITERATIONS
        MAXIMAL OBJECTIVE =    27865.577036
        VARIABLE  STATUS    OPTIMAL VALUE        DELTAJ
          L11SAW  BASIC       53.76000         0.00000
          L21SAW  BASIC        8.96336         0.00000
          L31SAW                0.00000       -12.52445
          L12SAW  BASIC       88.32000         0.00000
          L22SAW  BASIC       31.13510         0.00000
          L32SAW                0.00000       -13.30764
          L11CH                 0.00000       -14.01491
          L21CH                 0.00000        -2.00000
          L31CH   BASIC       23.04000         0.00000
          L12CH                 0.00000       -11.75055
          L22CH   BASIC       29.34545         0.00000
          L32CH   BASIC       24.96000         0.00000
          L11EXP                0.00000        -5.31491
          L21EXP  BASIC       42.23664         0.00000
          L12EXP                0.00000        -5.05055
          L22EXP  BASIC       18.23944         0.00000
          CLEAR   BASIC       32.56089         0.00000
          DRESS   BASIC       48.20170         0.00000
          CONST   BASIC       48.00000         0.00000
          SCRAP   BASIC       48.97034         0.00000
          SDUST   BASIC       25.90597         0.00000
          CBOARD  BASIC       96.00000         0.00000
(SAWCAP)  SAWSL                0.00000        -4.81000
(CBCAP)   CBSL    BASIC       16.00000         0.00000
(CLMIN)   CLXS    BASIC        0.56089         0.00000
(DRMIN)   DRXS    BASIC       12.20170         0.00000
(COMIN)   COXS                 0.00000       -38.03030
(CBMIN)   CBXS                 0.00000       -19.34211

        CONSTRAINT STATUS  IMPUTED VALUE       DECREASE          INCREASE
          L1F1AV  BINDNG      100.31491        4.83829           3.38418
          L2F1AV  BINDNG       88.00000       42.23664           OPEN
          L3F1AV  BINDNG       85.50000       18.23944          29.34545
          L1F2AV  BINDNG      100.05055        5.26770           5.08635
          L2F2AV  BINDNG       88.00000       18.23944           OPEN
          L3F2AV  BINDNG       87.50000       18.23944          29.34545
          CLPROD  BINDNG     -150.00000        OPEN              0.56089
          DRPROD  BINDNG     -110.00000        OPEN             12.20170
          COPROD  BINDNG     -118.03030        3.28787           0.94653
          SCPROD  BINDNG      -90.50000       29.34545          18.23944
          SDPROD  BINDNG      -12.00000        OPEN             25.90597
          SAWCAP  BINDNG        4.81000        4.23722          17.98917
          CBPROD  BINDNG     -124.34211       22.30254          13.86198
          CBCAP   SLACK        -0.00000       16.00000           OPEN
          CLMIN   SLACK        -0.00000        OPEN              0.56089
          DRMIN   SLACK        -0.00000        OPEN             12.20170
          COMIN   BINDNG      -38.03030        3.28787           0.94653
          CBMIN   BINDNG      -19.34211       22.30254          13.86198
```

Figure 2-12. *Computer printout of optimal solution for Forest Industries Corporation.*

the short run, may be a good approximation for the costs of the sawmill and chipboard plants. The objective function is

maximize 150 CLEAR + 110 DRESS + 80 CONST + 105 CBOARD

$$+ 95 \text{ L11EXP} + 88 \text{ L21EXP} + 95 \text{ L12EXP} + 88 \text{ L22EXP}$$

$$+ 12 \text{ SDUST} - 4 \text{ SCRAP} - 6.5 \text{ L11SAW} - 7.5 \text{ L21SAW}$$

$$- 9 \text{ L31SAW} - 5.5 \text{ L12SAW} - 6.5 \text{ L22SAW} - 8 \text{ L32SAW}$$

$$- 8.2 \text{ L11CH} - 8.5 \text{ L21CH} - 9 \text{ L31CH} - 6.2 \text{ L12CH}$$

$$- 6.5 \text{ L22CH} - 7 \text{ L32CH}$$

The coefficients for LijSAW and LijCH are obtained by adding the handling costs shown in Table 2-7 to the transportation costs.

This completes the formulation of this problem. We have a total of 18 constraints and 22 decision variables. (A real corporate model may easily have several hundred constraints with several thousand variables.)

Figure 2-12 is a facsimile of the computer printout for the optimal solution (without a listing of the data input). Note that to solve this problem using LPGOGO, we converted all inequality constraints to equality constraints, by adding or subtracting slack variables. In the printout, we have flagged each slack variable with its corresponding constraint label. Figure 2-13 shows the optimal solution in the form of a materials flow chart.

The daily gross profit for the optimal solution amounts to $27,865.60. The optimal mode of operation provides for meeting the minimum requirements for construction grades and chipboards, with a small excess for clear grades and a substantial excess for dressing grades. The sawmill is used to full capacity. The chipboard plant has some unused capacity left. Export sales amount to slightly more than 60 HC per day, all of which come from third and fourth log cuts.

The output allows for some interesting sensitivity analysis. Under what conditions would it become profitable to have some of the first and second log cuts exported? From the DELTAJ values for the variables L11EXP and L12EXP we see that the export prices ex-forest for the first and second cuts would have to increase from $95 by at least $5.32 and $5.05 to reach $100.32 and $100.05. At that point, these variables would become candidates to enter alternative optimal solutions.

The shadow prices (imputed values) for the log cuts availability constraints LiFjAV provide management with information as to the increase in gross profit for additional output. For instance, each additional HC per day of first and second cuts from forest 1 increases gross profit by $100.32 (= imputed value for L1F1AV). Additional sawmill capacity has a value of $4.81 per minute (= imputed value for SAWCAP). On the other hand, increases in the minimum daily requirements for construction grades and chipboards would have a detrimental effect on gross profit. Each additional M$\frac{3}{4}$ of chipboard produces a loss of $19.34 (= imputed value for CBMIN). Hence, it would be a bad move to launch a sales promotion for chipboard now. In fact, by lowering the minimum daily requirement from the present

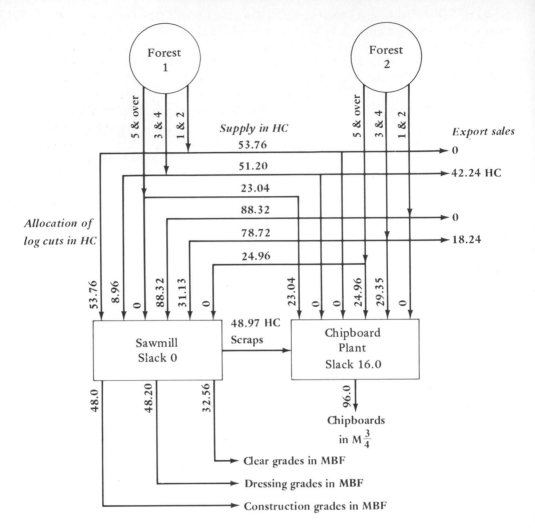

Figure 2-13. *Detailed materials flow for optimal solution to Forest Industries.*

96 $M\frac{3}{4}$ to 73.7 (= 96 less the entry of 22.3 shown under DECREASE for the CBMIN constraint), and optimally allocating to all other uses the log cuts thus freed, gross profits are increased by 22.3 × \$19.34 or \$431.28. (Note that the imputed values for input-output relations do not lend themselves to an easy interpretation.)

2-14 ADVERTISING MEDIA SELECTION—AN EXAMPLE OF GOAL PROGRAMMING

A firm is the distributor of a seasonal, packaged product for a given region that covers a large metropolitan area. The product is especially appealing to housewives with children.   The manufacturer of the product has offered to participate in a pre-season price discount promotion and the firm is planning to launch an advertising campaign.   Full-page color advertisements in the supplements to the Sunday editions of the two major daily newspapers are planned.   The advertising message and copy have been prepared.   The only point that remains to be settled is the media schedule, i.e., the number of consecutive insertions in each newspaper.

Ideally, one would like to relate this to the profit that can be generated by each insertion.   However, it is extremely difficult to measure the profits of a media schedule.   Therefore, in practice, one uses surrogate measures that from experience have shown to be positively correlated with profits.   Examples of such measures include the *reach* of the media schedule, defined as the fraction of people in the target population exposed at least once to the advertisement, or the *frequency* of the schedule, defined as the average number of exposures among target population members who have been reached at least once.   One may also wish to appeal to different segments of the target population to a different degree.   Let us assume that, for our problem, reach is the most appropriate criterion and that we want to differentiate between a *primary* target group of all women with at least one child of primary school age (goal 1) and a *secondary* target that covers all women from families with an annual income of over $8000 (goal 2).

Data about the reach of the Sunday supplements for various target populations can be obtained from the newspapers.   For instance, for newspaper X and the primary target group they indicate the following average fraction of the people in the group reached as a function of the number of insertions:

Number of insertions x	1	2	3	4	5	6
Cumulative fraction y	0.51	0.64	0.74	0.82	0.88	0.93

Unfortunately, this is a nonlinear relationship, but we may approximate it fairly closely by the following equation:

$$y = 0.49 + 0.08x$$

As the number of insertions will most likely lie between 2 and 5, the approximation error is small.   Applying this procedure to similar data (not shown) on reach for the other media/target group combinations, we obtain the following equations:

Newspaper	Target	Equation
X	primary	$0.49 + 0.08x$
Y	primary	$0.47 + 0.12x$
X	secondary	$0.44 + 0.12x$
Y	secondary	$0.37 + 0.09x$

Note that we also make the approximation that we allow all variables to assume any nonnegative real value and not just integer values.

Estimates indicate that the two newspapers share the primary target group evenly, but newspaper X has 60 percent of the secondary target group. Management would like to reach at least 80 percent of the primary target group and 70 percent of the secondary target group. Furthermore, they want to keep the past tradition of having at least twice as many insertions in newspaper X as in newspaper Y (goal 3). Newspaper X charges $2800 per insertion; newspaper Y, which uses a lower quality paper, charges $1600 per insertion. Management has allocated an advertising campaign budget of $14,400 (budget constraint).

The problem as it stands now is somewhat ill defined. We have several objectives or goals that management would like to achieve, some acquisitive such as goal 1 and 2, others retentive, such as goal 3 and to some extent the budget constraint. We have seen in Section 1-12 that one way to deal with multiple goals is to select the most important one as the basis for the objective function and express the others as constraints. Suppose management considers reach as the most important objective and wishes to maximize reach subject to achieving goal 3 and the budget allocation.

Our decision variables are the number of insertions in newspaper X and newspaper Y, denoted by x_1 and x_2, respectively. The reach achieved for each target population is calculated as the weighted average of the reach for each newspaper. Using the four equations listed earlier, the weighted average reach is

$$0.5(0.49+0.08x_1) + 0.5(0.47+0.12x_2)$$

for the primary target population and

$$0.6(0.44+0.12x_1) + 0.4(0.37+0.09x_2)$$

for the secondary target population. If management assigns to the reach for each target population equal importance, then we could define the objective as maximizing the average total reach given as the sum of the reach for both targets divided by 2:

$$\text{maximize } \tfrac{1}{2}[0.5(0.49+0.08x_1) + 0.5(0.47+0.12x_2)$$

$$+ 0.6(0.44+0.12x_1) + 0.4(0.37+0.09x_2)]$$

Collecting terms and dropping the constant (as it does not affect the optimal values of the decision variables), we obtain

(2-19) $$\text{maximize } 0.056x_1 + 0.048x_2$$

Note that this implies that goals 1 and 2 are commensurable in the sense that it is possible to quantify a trade-off function between them, which in this instance has a simple linear form. To ensure that at least twice as many insertions are made in newspaper X as in Y, we restrict the decision variables to

$$x_1 - 2x_2 \leqslant 0 \quad \text{(goal 3)}$$

while the budget allocation imposes that

(2-20) $$2800x_1 + 1600x_2 \leqslant 14{,}400 \quad \text{(budget constraint)}$$

with x_1 and x_2 restricted to assume nonnegative values only. Figure 2-14 shows the feasible region for this problem. The optimal solution occurs at point *A* and calls

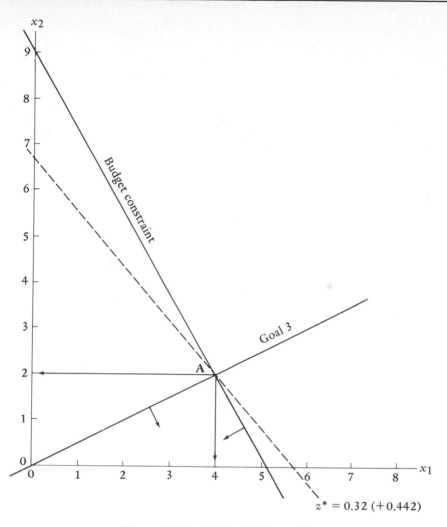

Figure 2-14. *Media selection problem.*

for 4 insertions in newspaper X and 2 in newspaper Y. All funds allocated are used up and the desired relationship between the number of insertions in each newspaper is maintained. Verify that the total average reach is 0.762 or 76.2 percent.

A more detailed analysis shows that the reach for the primary target population is 76 percent or 4 percentage points below the desired level of 80 percent, while the reach for the secondary target population is 76.4 percent or 6.4 percentage points above the desired level. This does not correspond to the desired goals management initially set out to achieve. The overachievement of the secondary target level may not really compensate for the underachievement in the primary target level. The acquisitive (and presumably more important) goals were not achieved completely, while the retentive (and presumably less important) goals were achieved completely, largely due to the fact that they were expresesd in the form of constraints. It would be useful to formulate the problem in such a manner that the character of objectives is explicitly retained for all goals. It is exactly this that a variation of linear programming, called *goal programming*, attempts to achieve.

In goal programming, each objective or goal is expressed in equality form by introducing slack variables that represent the deviations from the goal. Let s_i^- denote an underachievement of the goal i and let s_i^+ denote an overachievement. Retaining the budget constraint (2-20) in its present form, the three goals of our problem can then be expressed as follows:

(2-21) $0.04x_1 + 0.06x_2 + s_1^- - s_1^+ = 0.32$ (goal 1)

(2-22) $0.072x_1 + 0.036x_2 + s_2^- - s_2^+ = 0.288$ (goal 2)

(2-23) $x_1 - 2x_2 + s_3^- - s_3^+ = 0$ (goal 3)

where all s_i^+ and s_i^- are restricted to nonnegative values.

Management would like to achieve each of the three objectives as closely as possible, subject to the budget constraint. It is at this point where certain difficulties of interpretation arise. What is meant by "achieve each objective as closely as possible?" Does it mean "minimize the weighted sum of the deviations" and what should be the proper weights? Let a_i^- and a_i^+ be the weights for goal i. Then our objective function is

(2-24)   minimize $a_1^- s_1^- + a_1^+ s_1^+ + a_2^- s_2^- + a_2^+ s_2^+ + a_3^- s_3^- + a_3^+ s_3^+$

(Note that the simplex method will guarantee that of each pair s_i^- and s_i^+ only one variable may be positive, since if both were positive the total value of the objective function could be decreased by reducing both variables by an amount equal to the smaller of the two.) Say we decide that we only want to penalize underachievement. Setting $a_i^+ = 0$ and $a_i^- = 1$, for each i the objective function becomes

(2-25)   minimize $1(s_1^- + s_2^- + s_3^-) + 0(s_i^+ + s_2^+ + s_3^+)$

subject to the budget constraint. Figure 2-15 shows the new feasible region for the two original variables x_1 and x_2 as the shaded triangle BEH. We also show one goal line for each objective representing all solutions for which the corresponding objective is satisfied without any deviation. (Note that our problem has now more than two variables. In Figure 2-15 only the solution space for the original variables x_1 and x_2 is shown explicitly. The values of all other variables can be inferred implicitly from the deviation of solutions from the goal lines.) The optimal solution with a value of $z_2^* = 0.04$ occurs again at point A for which only goal 3 is satisfied without deviation. We thus see that the first formulation corresponds to a goal programming formulation with equal penalties for underachievements of all three objectives. Had we assigned different penalties to deviations from the three goals, different solutions might become optimal. For instance had we given a_1^- a value of $\frac{900}{13}a_3^-$ with $a_i^+ = 0$, all i, and any value for a_2^-, then any point along the line from F to A would be optimal.

No doubt, it is extremely difficult to derive an objective function like expression (2-24) where the penalties attached to underachievement and overachievement of

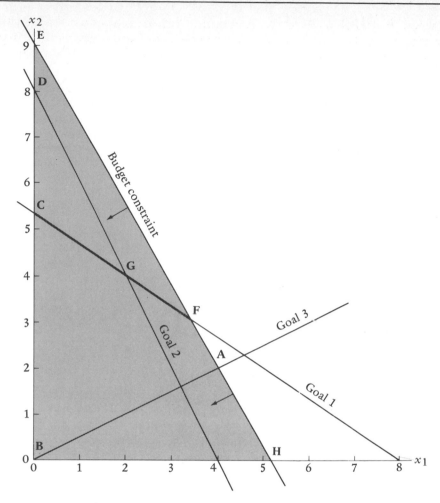

Figure 2-15. *Media selection by goal programming.*

goals properly represent the preferences of the decision maker. In fact, it is only possible if the objectives are commensurable. In most applications, some of the objectives may lack any common basis for comparison or trade-offs between them. Clearly this is the case here. Although the two goals as to reach may be commensurable, it would be rather hard to find a trade-off function between them and the third goal.

An alternative approach that avoids the necessity of constructing trade-off functions between objectives is to rank the objectives in a *preference ordering*. The solution procedure would then attempt to first satisfy the objective with the highest preference ranking as closely as possible, while completely ignoring all lower ranking objectives. If the highest ranking objective has been achieved, then the second highest ranking one is satisfied as closely as possible, without, however, impairing the achievement level of the highest ranking one. The same steps are followed for each of the lower ranking objectives in descending order of preference. The procedure usually terminates as soon as one of the objectives cannot be satisfied completely.

Say, that for our example management gives the highest priority to achieving the desired reach for the primary target population (goal 1), the second ranking to achieve the desired reach for the secondary target population (goal 2) and the lowest priority to the relationship between the number of insertions in X and Y (goal 3). Referring back to Figure 2-15, goal 1 is satisfied completely for any solution of x_1 and x_2 along the heavy line from point C to F, while remaining within the budget constraint. We can now proceed to satisfy the second ranking objective as closely as possible without impairing the achievement level for the first objective. Hence only solutions on the line from C to F may be considered. Goal 2 is completely satisfied at the intersection of the goal lines for goal 1 and goal 2, point G. Finally we can turn to the third ranking objective. No improvements can be made on goal 3 without impairing the achievement level of the two higher ranking goals. Hence the optimal solution for this preference ranking is given at point G which calls for 2 insertions in newspaper X and 4 in newspaper Y (with $s_3^- = 2$ and all other s_i^- and s_i^+ zero) at a cost of $12,000. This is $2400 below the budget allocation. (The simplex method can easily be adapted to perform these successive optimizations. See the texts by Charnes and Cooper, or Lee, listed in the references.)

2-15 SOME FURTHER APPLICATIONS

The list of possible applications for linear programming is enormous. It ranges from allocation of scarce resources for various end uses to the determination of the optimal phasing pattern for traffic lights along city streets.

1. *Allocation of scarce resources.* The decision variables are given by the various activities that consume the resources, such as products to manufacture. Each scarce resource gives rise to a constraint. The objective consists of maximizing total output or of minimizing total costs subject to achieving some specified output. A special case of this is the allocation of funds to potential investment projects. Each possible project is represented by a decision variable for each time period in which it can be undertaken. The amount of funds available in each time period gives rise to a constraint. Additional constraints may result from precedence relations between projects.

2. *Smoothing problems.* This term refers to scheduling overtime of production or manpower to satisfy seasonal demands for products or services. The level of and changes in manpower in each period, the number of idle employees or the amount of overtime, the size of the production during regular time and overtime in each period, and the size of the inventory carried forward to each succeeding period give rise to decision variables. The material balance or input-output relations between levels of manpower of consecutive periods and

similar relations between production, inventories, and demand form constraints. The objective is usually to minimize total production costs, including costs for training manpower and severance pay, and inventory carrying costs.

3. *Distribution problems.* A firm may operate a number of plants supplying a number of different regional marketing centers. The decision variables are given by the amount produced by each plant to be shipped to each marketing center. The production capacities at the plants and the demand requirements at the marketing centers, as well as any possible limitations on shared transportation facilities, give rise to constraints.

4. *Blending problems.* Various raw materials of different composition and chemical or physical properties have to be blended to final products. The amounts of each raw material used for each final product constitute the decision variables. The amounts of the raw materials available, or the amounts of the final products required, the limitations as to the composition of the final products and their required properties give rise to constraints. A possible objective is minimizing the cost of the raw materials used.

5. *Diet and feed-mix problems.* Such problems are special forms of blending problems where the output usually consists of a single blend or mix. If some of the inputs are only available in limited quantities and are shared by a number of different mixes, the formulation may cover several mixes at the same time.

6. *Trim problems.* Given quantities of goods of different shapes to be cut from a material that comes in various sizes, such as widths, a number of possible efficient patterns are considered. How much of each pattern should be cut? The numbers of each pattern cut represent the decision variables. The constraints are given by the required quantities and by the amount of material of each size available. The objective may be to minimize the cost of the material used or the amount of waste produced.

7. *Planning problems.* Planning the operation of a whole organization or firm. The Forest Industries example discussed in Section 2-13 belongs to this category.

In the business world, few problems occur in one of these pure forms; rather, they exhibit characteristics of several different types of basic linear programming models.

EXERCISES

2.1   A furniture manufacturer produces two types of desks: Standard and Executive. These desks are sold to an office furniture wholesaler, and for all practical purposes, there is an unlimited market for any mix of these desks, at least within the manufacturer's production capacity. Each desk has to go through four basic operations: cutting of the lumber, joining of the pieces, prefinishing, and final finish. Each unit of the Standard desk produced takes 48 minutes of cutting time, 2 hours of joining, 40 minutes of prefinishing, and 5 hours and 20 minutes of final finishing time.   Each unit of the Executive desk requires 72 minutes of cutting, 3 hours of joining, 2 hours of prefinishing, and 4 hours of final finishing time.   The daily capacity for each operation amounts to 16 hours of cutting, 30 hours of joining, 16 hours of prefinishing, and 64 hours of final finishing time. The profit per unit produced is $40 for the Standard desk and $50 for the Executive desk.   What product mix is optimal?   Required:

(a) Formulate this problem as a linear program with the objective of maximizing daily profit, and show each constraint graphically.   Show the objective function for $z = \$400$ and $z = \$600$.   Are there any redundant constraints?   Which ones?

(b) Find the optimal solution graphically.   What is the amount of slack for each constraint?

(c) Find the shadow price for each constraint graphically and interpret its meaning.

(d) Determine for each objective function coefficient individually the range of values for which the present solution remains optimal.

(e) The firm receives an inquiry to produce 1 unit per day of a third type of desk style called the Economy desk which requires 30 minutes of cutting, 90 minutes of joining, 30 minutes of prefinishing and 3 hours of finishing time.   The profit would amount to $20 per unit.   Should the firm offer to make one unit of Economy per day?   Why or why not?

2.2   A chicken feed manufacturer wants to find the lowest cost mix for a high-protein formula that contains 90 grams of nutrient A, 48 grams of nutrient B, 20 grams of nutrient C, and 1.5 grams of vitamin X for each kilogram of feed.   He can mix the formula from two ingredients and a filler.   Ingredient 1 contains 100 grams of nutrient A, 80 grams of nutrient B, 40 grams of nutrient C, and 10 grams of vitamin X.   It costs 40 cents per kilogram.   Ingredient 2 contains 200 grams of A, 150 grams of B, 20 grams of C, none of vitamin X.   It costs 60 cents a kilogram. Required:

(a) Formulate this problem as a linear program minimizing cost per kilogram of mix.   Note that you do not need a variable for the filler.   The amount of filler that has to be added can be determined once the optimal mix of ingredients 1 and 2 has been found.   Show each constraint graphically, and show the objective function for $z = 24$ cents and $z = 36$ cents.   Are there any redundant constraints?   Which ones?

(b) Find the optimal solution that minimizes the cost of the mix.   What is the amount of slack for each constraint?   How much filler has to be added?

(c) Find the shadow price for each constraint graphically and interpret its meaning.

(d) Determine for each objective function coefficient individually the range of values for which the present solution remains optimal.

(e) The firm receives a call from a supplier offering a third ingredient which contains 120 grams of A, 100 grams of B and 20 grams of C and no X per kilogram at a cost of 50 cents per kilogram.   Should they buy any of it for use in this formula?   Why or why not?

2.3   A firm produces 3 types of refined chemicals: A, B, and C.   At least 4 tons of A, 2 tons of B, and 1 ton of C have to be produced per day.   The inputs used are compounds X and Y.   Each ton of X yields 1/4 ton of A, 1/4 ton of B and 1/12 ton af C.   Each ton of Y yields 1/2 ton of A, 1/10 ton of B and 1/12 ton of C.   Compound

X costs $250 per ton, compound Y $400 per ton. The cost of processing is $250 per ton of X and $200 per ton of Y. Amounts produced in excess of the daily requirements have no value as the products undergo chemical changes if not used immediately. The problem is to find the minimum cost input mix. Required:

(a) Formulate this problem as a linear program with the objective of minimizing total daily costs. Show each constraint graphically and the objective function for $z = \$6000$ and $z = \$12,000$.

(b) Find the optimal solution graphically. What is the amount of excess produced for each chemical?

(c) The daily requirement for C is increased to 1.25 tons. By how much does the daily cost increase? The daily requirement for B is increased to 2.25 tons. By how much does the daily cost increase? The requirement for A is reduced by 1/2 ton. By how much does the daily cost change?

(d) Determine for each compound individually the range of prices for which the present solution remains optimal.

(e) The firm receives an offer for a third compound that yields 1/5 ton of A, 1/2 ton of B and 1/10 ton of C at a price of $300 per ton and a processing cost of $300 per ton. Should the firm accept this offer? Why or why not?

2.4 A farmer wishes to determine the best selection of stock for his farm, his objective being to maximize the profit after the sale of the animals at the end of the period. The alternatives available are Merino sheep, Romney sheep, Southdown sheep, Hereford cattle and Jersey cattle. The farmer has calculated that each Merino would require one acre of land, and would cost $1.50 in extra feed, treatment, etc. The purchase price is $6 and the farmer estimates that the selling price at the end of the period will be $10. For Romneys, the corresponding figures are 1 acre, $1.75, $4.25, $9.00; for Southdowns: 1 acre, $1, $3, $6; for Herefords: 4 acres, $15, $30, $60; for Jerseys: 6 acres, $12, $28, $58. The size of the farm is 400 acres, and the farmer has $3800 with which to purchase and maintain the stock. Formulate this problem as a linear program maximizing profits.

2.5 A paper company has received an order for the following stationery

Type	A	B	C	D
No. of reams ordered	4000	8000	3000	5000

In order to facilitate cutting it is customary that the actual amount supplied may exceed the order by up to 5 percent. Any excess beyond 5 percent becomes wastage. The stationery can be cut from paper rolls of 3 widths by a number of patterns that result in little waste (or trim) as shown in the following table.

Pattern	24″ Width Weight 1 ton		30″ Width Weight 1.25 tons		36″ Width Weight 1.5 tons			Weight per 1000
Type	1	2	1	2	1	2	3	reams
A	36	—	—	6	—	16	24	25.5
B	—	24	40	12	—	12	—	28.1
C	—	6	—	—	27	16	32	16.8
D	—	6	—	24	30	14	10	29.1
Waste per roll	8.2%	5%	10%	5.6%	8.8%	5.2%	6.6%	

Formulate this problem as a linear program:
(a) minimize total wastage.
(b) minimize the total cost of the rolls used, given that the 24″ width has a cost of $30, the 30″ width costs $34, and the 36″ width costs $37 per roll.

2.6   A firm would like to find the least cost production schedule for a seasonal product. The demand is 2000 units in May, 4000 in June, 6000 in July, 6000 in August and 2000 in September. The product cannot be kept in storage for more than 2 months, e.g., if produced in April, it has to be sold by the end of June. The workforce of seasonal workers has to be hired at the beginning of the season (early April) and kept until the close of the season (end of September). Initial training costs per worker amount to $200. Each worker can produce 400 units a month on regular time and, if desired, up to an additional 100 units on overtime. Each worker has a cost of $800 per month for regular time work. Overtime is paid at 1.5 times the regular rate in proportion to the amount of overtime actually worked in a given month. Units produced each month are available for sale that month. Each unit put into storage incurs a handling cost of $0.5. The cost of holding one unit in storage amounts to $0.4 per month carried forward. Formulate this problem as a linear program minimizing the sum of all costs.

2.7   A firm produces two products, S and T, which have to go through two manufacturing operations. The first operation is performed either at machine center 1 or 2, and the second either at machine center 3 or 4. Operation times for each machine center per unit produced, machine center capacities and machine center costs per minute are shown in the following table.

	Machine Centers			
	1 or 2		3 or 4	
Product S	10	6	16	12 minutes
Product T	20	8	12	10 minutes
Capacity	4800	3600	6000	6000 minutes
Cost/Minute	30	50	30	50 cents

Daily requirements are 600 units for product S and 300 units for product T. The objective is to find a production schedule that minimizes total machine center production costs. Formulate this problem as a linear program.

2.8   A sawmill can obtain three qualities of radiata pines that differ mainly in terms of diameter. Three products are made from these logs: grade A 1 × 4, grade A 2 × 4, grade B 2 × 4. Any scraps produced are sold to a wood chipping mill. The table

Log Type	Price per HC $	Sawmill hours in hours/MBF	Yield in MBF/HC			scraps in HC/HC	Maximum daily supply in HC
			grade A 1 × 4	grade A 2 × 4	grade B 2 × 4		
1	120	0.04	0.15	0.50	0.30	0.10	100
2	110	0.05	0.20	0.30	0.40	0.15	80
3	90	0.06	0.20	0.10	0.60	0.20	50
	Daily demand in MBF		60	50	75	0	

(MBF denotes units of 1000 board feet, HC denotes units of 100 cubic feet.)

on the previous page gives the yield conversion table, production rates, log supply, and lumber demand positions. Scraps are sold to the chipping mill at $40 per HC. The sawmill works 10 hours per day at most. The hourly cost is $20. Grade A 2 × 4 can be broken down to grade A 1 × 4 by an additional cutting operation, performed on a special saw at a rate of 5 MBF per hour and a cost of $5.00 per hour.

Under present market conditions any excess lumber produced has to be sold at a loss of $5 per MBF. Formulate this problem as a linear program minimizing total daily costs.

2.9   The administrative planner of a large city hospital wants to determine the number of orderlies he should hire for the coming two-month period based on the following tentative estimates for the requirements in terms of ward-hours:

Period	Jan/Feb	March/Apr	May/June	July/Aug	Sep/Oct	Nov/Dec
Hours	8000	7600	7200	7000	8000	9000

During the first two months an orderly hired will receive training requiring 90 hours of the time of an experienced orderly, who will have that much less time available to do normal duties. Each trainee is able to do 160 hours of productive work during the first two months of service. Each experienced orderly can put in an average of 320 hours of work during a two-month period. As of the beginning of January the hospital will have 28 experienced orderlies on the staff. This includes those who have just completed their two-month training period. At the end of each two-month period, approximately 10 percent of the experienced orderlies quit their job. Only 80 percent of the trainees complete their training, the others quit during training and on the average receive about 50 percent of the training and put in an equal fraction of productive work. No orderlies are laid off. It is desired to have at least 30 experienced orderlies by the beginning of January next year. An experienced orderly cost the hospital $2200 and a trainee $1800 for a two-month period. Formulate this problem as a linear programming problem, minimizing total costs. Note that only the optimal decision for the first period will be implemented and the problem solved again for a new interval of 6 periods prior to next period's decision. Can you explain why?

2.10   A firm has contracted to manufacture two types of industrial components. The contract calls for certain quantities each year for the next five years. There is no prospect of production after that. The contracted quantities are

	Demand	
Year	Type A	Type B
1	4,000	6,000
2	15,000	20,000
3	12,000	15,000
4	20,000	10,000
5	8,000	2,000

A special type of machine is required to handle both types of components at a certain stage in manufacture. One machine will handle 3000 Type A components or 2000 Type B components a year, or any proportional combination of them.

These machines can be either purchased or rented. To buy the machine costs $120,000 in year 1 and will increase $6000 each year. Each year of its life the machine loses $12,000 of its value, except in the first year where its loss is $20,000. Machines purchased can be sold at their salvage value at the end of each year. Machines can be rented for either a 1-year, 2-year, or 5-year term at rental charges starting at $28,000, $25,000, $24,000 per year, respectively. Each year the rental charges will increase by $2000 except that machines already on hire stay at their original charge until their rental period expires. All expenditures are assumed to occur at the beginning of each year. Machines can be hired or purchased at the beginning of each year. The firm wishes to minimize the present value of the net cost of acquiring or renting these machines. Assume the firm's discount rate is $\alpha = 0.9$ per annum. Formulate the problem as a linear program, and carefully note any assumptions you make. Can linear programming really solve this problem satisfactorily? (See Section 9-1 for a review of the principles of discounting.)

2.11 Consider the production scheduling example discussed in Section 2-12. Note that for an output of 10,000 casings the shadow price for the total output constraint (2-10) is negative. This indicates that it would be desirable to reduce the required total output somewhat.

(a) Indicate what will happen to the value of the shadow price as the total output requirement is gradually reduced.

(b) How would you reformulate the problem so as to find the optimal total output level?

REFERENCES

Charnes, A., and W. W. Cooper. *Management Models and Industrial Applications of Linear Programming*, vols. I and II. New York: Wiley, 1961. In addition to a thorough treatment of linear programming and extensions, this text contains a variety of formulations, including an introduction to goal programming.

———. "Goal Programming and Multiple Objective Optimizations", *European Journal of Operational Research*, I, 1977, pp. 39-54. A comprehensive survey of recent developments in goal programming and directions for future fruitful research.

Daellenbach, H. G., and E. J. Bell. *User's Guide to Linear Programming*. Englewood Cliffs, N.J.: Prentice-Hall, 1970. Introduction to linear programming at an elementary level, stressing graphical interpretation of concepts, including sensitivity analysis, with emphasis on problem formulations and solution by computer and detailed analysis of computer sensitivity analysis printout. Easy to read. Chapters 2, 3, and 5 give graphical representation, Chapter 4 develops step-by-step a number of different types of problem formulations, and Chapter 8 gives the formulation of company-wide operations of a firm from supplies of raw materials to the distribution of finished products. Contains a listing of a linear program computer code with input/output and sensitivity analysis (LPGOGO).

Dricbeek, Norman J. *Applied Linear Programming*. Reading, Mass.: Addison Wesley, 1969. This text has a flavor of real-life applications at a fairly elementary level.

Hadley, G. *Linear Programming*. Reading, Mass.: Addison Wesley, 1962. Chapter 12 contains a number of problem formulations in general form at a somewhat advanced level. No number examples are included.

Lee, Sang M. *Goal Programming for Decision Analysis*. Philadelphia: Auerbach, 1972. One of few texts devoted entirely to goal programming.

Levin, R. I., and R. P. Lamone. *Linear Programming for Management Decisions*. Homewood, Ill.: Irwin, 1969. Chapter 2 gives an Introduction to graphical solution. Chapter 9 shows a number of interesting and detailed applications of linear programming.

Smythe, William R., and Lynwood A. Johnson. *Introduction to Linear Programming with Applications*. Englewood Cliffs, N.J.: Prentice-Hall, 1966. Chapters 1 and 2 give the general linear programming model with graphical representation. Chapter 5 contains an excellent treatment of a number of formulations.

Most texts in operations research give a number of formulations, usually with few or no intermediate steps. See the list of general operations research texts in the Bibliography.

3

The
Simplex
Method

The algebraic technique for finding the optimal solution to a linear program is called the *simplex method*. It was developed in 1947 by the American mathematician, George B. Dantzig. The aim of this chapter is to provide an intuitive understanding of the mathematical theory behind the simplex method and spell out in detail the rules of its computations.

If you are not familiar with the concepts of *vectors* and *systems of linear equations* you should study first the short introduction to linear algebra in Appendix A.

3-1 EXTREME POINT IN SOLUTION SPACE

In the following sections we shall work with a simplified version of the power generating problem studied in Chapter 2. Only the two constraints that are binding at the optimal solution, namely the smoke and pulverizer constraints, will be retained. The optimal solution to both problems will thus be the same. The reduced problem in two decision variables x_1 and x_2 is then: Find values for x_1 and x_2 which

$$\text{maximize } 24x_1 + 20x_2$$

$$\text{subject to } 0.5x_1 + x_2 \leqslant 12 \text{ (smoke)}$$

(3-1)

$$\tfrac{1}{16}x_1 + \tfrac{1}{24}x_2 \leqslant 1 \text{ (pulverizer)}$$

$$x_1 \geqslant 0, \ x_2 \geqslant 0$$

Figure 3-1 represents the constraints and nonnegativity conditions for this problem in two-dimensional space, where each dimension corresponds to a decision variable. This is called a *representation in solution space*.

In Chapter 2 we pointed out that if a linear program has a finite optimal solution, at least one extreme point of the feasible region will be optimal. Consider now the two simultaneous equations (3-2) in four variables, namely, the constraints of (3-1) converted to equalities by the introduction of the two slack variables x_3 and x_5,

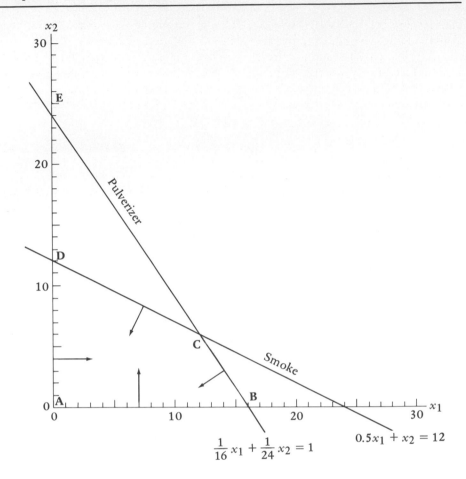

Figure 3-1. *Representation in solution space.*

retaining the subscripts used in Section 2-8:

$$0.5x_1 + x_2 + x_3 = 12$$

(3-2)

$$\tfrac{1}{16}x_1 + \tfrac{1}{24}x_2 + x_5 = 1$$

Each extreme point of the feasible region can be generated by setting two appropriately chosen variables equal to zero and solving (3-2) for the remaining two. For example, the optimal extreme point $(x_1 = 12, x_2 = 6)$ (labeled C in Figure 3-1) is obtained by setting $x_3 = 0$, $x_5 = 0$ and solving in (3-2) for x_1 and x_2. The extreme point B in Figure 3-1 is obtained by setting $x_2 = 0$ and $x_5 = 0$ and solving in (3-2) for x_1 and x_3. Verify that the solution is $x_1 = 16$, $x_3 = 4$.

The choice of which variables to set equal to zero is not arbitrary. Not every such choice yields a feasible solution. For example, setting $x_1 = 0$ and $x_5 = 0$, we get the solution $x_2 = 24$, $x_3 = -12$, which corresponds to point E in Figure 3-1. This solution is not feasible since one of the variables is negative; hence it is not an extreme point of the feasible region.   However, every solution obtained by this procedure which is a feasible solution is an extreme point and vice versa.

Extreme points are thus directly related to the algebraic structure of solving equations using only a subset of variables.   The importance of relating the geometric structure with an algebraic one is that any practicable solution technique must be algebraic, since a geometric representation is limited to two or three dimensions.

3-2 REPRESENTATION IN REQUIREMENT SPACE

The analysis using solution space is of limited value for developing a proper understanding of the mathematical concepts underlying the simplex method.   By changing our line of attack, we can go a long way further.   Instead of having a dimension for each variable, we have a dimension associated with each constraint.   This is referred to as *representation in requirement space*.   For instance, for the two-constraint problem (3-1) or (3-2) one dimension measures smoke emission and the other the pulverizer time.   In a general sense, smoke emission capacity and pulverizer capacity are our scarce resources.   So each dimension measures the use of a resource and each point in the nonnegative quadrant represents a combination of resources used.

These resources are used up by the activities of the problem—in our case the activities of burning coal A, burning coal B and the slack activities of leaving the resources unused.   Each of these activities can thus be represented in this space. For instance, the activity of burning one ton of coal A, which uses 0.5 kg of smoke emission capacity and $1/16$ of a hour of pulverizer capacity corresponds to the point

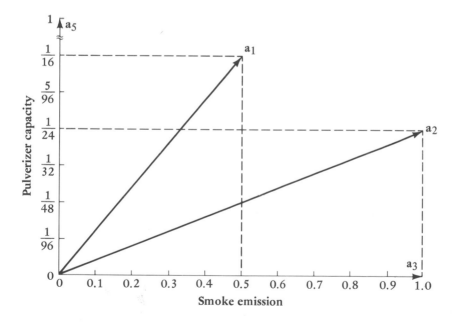

Figure 3-2. *Representation in requirement space.*

(0.5, 1/16) in Figure 3-2. From problem (3-2) you see that these two numbers correspond to the LHS coefficients of variable x_1. Viewing these coefficients as the vector of a unit activity, we see that each unit activity forms a vector in this space. Similarly, the vector corresponding to the right-hand-sides of the two constraints also forms a vector in this space.

Let a_1, a_2, a_3 and a_5 be the vectors of the four activities and b the vector for the right-hand-side, i.e.,

$$(3\text{-}3) \quad a_1 = \begin{bmatrix} 0.5 \\ 1/16 \end{bmatrix}, \quad a_2 = \begin{bmatrix} 1 \\ 1/24 \end{bmatrix}, \quad a_3 = \begin{bmatrix} 1 \\ 0 \end{bmatrix}, \quad a_5 = \begin{bmatrix} 0 \\ 1 \end{bmatrix}, \quad b = \begin{bmatrix} 12 \\ 1 \end{bmatrix}$$

Some of these vectors are shown graphically in Figure 3-2. The set of simultaneous equations (3-2) can be rewritten as

$$(3\text{-}4) \quad a_1 x_1 + a_2 x_2 + a_3 x_3 + a_5 x_5 = b$$

or

$$(3\text{-}5) \quad \begin{bmatrix} 0.5 \\ 1/16 \end{bmatrix} x_1 + \begin{bmatrix} 1 \\ 1/24 \end{bmatrix} x_2 + \begin{bmatrix} 1 \\ 0 \end{bmatrix} x_3 + \begin{bmatrix} 0 \\ 1 \end{bmatrix} x_5 = \begin{bmatrix} 12 \\ 1 \end{bmatrix}$$

3-3 BASIC FEASIBLE SOLUTIONS

Every possible vector in the plane in Figure 3-2 can be written as the sum of some multiple of any two of the vectors a_1, a_2, a_3 and a_5. Take the pair (a_1, a_2); a_5 can be expressed as

$$a_5 = \gamma_1 a_1 + \gamma_2 a_2$$

(When we express a vector in terms of a set of vectors the coefficient of the ith vector of the set is usually called γ_i. The γ_i's will have different values and maybe different meanings depending on which vector is being expressed and what set of vectors is being used.) Setting $\gamma_1 = 24$ and $\gamma_2 = -12$ produces the desired result, i.e.,

$$\begin{bmatrix} 0 \\ 1 \end{bmatrix} = 24 \begin{bmatrix} 0.5 \\ 1/16 \end{bmatrix} + (-12) \begin{bmatrix} 1 \\ 1/24 \end{bmatrix}$$

The vectors (a_1, a_2) are said to *span the space*. Not every arbitrary pair of vectors will span a two-dimensional space. The vectors used have to be *independent* in the sense that neither can be obtained from the other. In two-dimensional space this means that neither is a multiple of the other. In our example any pair from a_1, a_2, a_3, and a_5 forms an independent set of vectors that span the space.

If the requirement space has m dimensions, i.e., each vector contains m elements, then m independent vectors are needed to span the space. A set of m vectors that span the space is called a *basis* and the vectors that form the basis are referred to as *basic vectors*.

Let us choose the pair (a_1, a_3) as a basis. Since b is one of the vectors in the space, it can be represented in terms of this basis as follows:

$$(3\text{-}6) \quad \gamma_1 a_1 + \gamma_2 a_3 = b$$

or

(3-7)
$$\gamma_1 \begin{bmatrix} 0.5 \\ 1/16 \end{bmatrix} + \gamma_2 \begin{bmatrix} 1 \\ 0 \end{bmatrix} = \begin{bmatrix} 12 \\ 1 \end{bmatrix}$$

The solution to (3-7) is $\gamma_1 = 16$ and $\gamma_2 = 4$. Let us compare this with the equations in (3-2). By substituting x_1 for γ_1 and x_3 for γ_2 we see that (3-7) is equivalent to the equations obtained from (3-2) with $x_2 = 0$ and $x_5 = 0$. Expressing **b** in terms of a basis is thus equivalent to solving the constraint equations for the variables associated with the basic vectors. Such a solution is called a *basic solution*. If the solution is also feasible—all variables being nonnegative—it is a *basic feasible solution*. The basic solution implied in (3-7) is a basic feasible solution, since $x_1 = 16$, $x_2 = 0$, $x_3 = 4$ and $x_5 = 0$. Furthermore, we have also seen in Section 3-1 that this solution is an extreme point of the feasible region. Thus we see the important property: that the extreme points of the feasible region correspond to the basic feasible solutions of the constraint equations. Since at least one optimal solution occurs at an extreme point of the feasible region, we obtain a result that is fundamental for the simplex method: if a linear program has a finite optimal solution then at least one optimal solution is a basic feasible solution.

Let us generalize these results. Consider a linear program of the form (3-8) with m constraints—converted to equalities by the introduction of slack variables where needed—and a total of n (decision and slack) variables:

(3-8)
$$\text{maximize } c_1 x_1 + c_2 x_2 + c_3 x_3 + \cdots + c_n x_n$$
$$\text{subject to } \mathbf{a}_1 x_1 + \mathbf{a}_2 x_2 + \mathbf{a}_3 x_3 + \cdots + \mathbf{a}_n x_n = \mathbf{b}$$
$$x_1, x_2, \ldots, x_n \geqslant 0$$

(where the $\mathbf{a}_j$ and $\mathbf{b}$ vectors are m-dimensional).

A basis is formed by any set of m independent columns from the n columns of LHS coefficients. Solving the corresponding set of simultaneous equations for the m variables associated with the basic vectors yields a basic solution. All remaining variables are set equal to zero. Thus, at a basic solution, at least $(n-m)$ variables are equal to zero. These variables are referred to as *nonbasic variables* (the vectors of their LHS coefficients are called *nonbasic vectors*), whereas those variables whose LHS coefficients provide the basic vectors are called *basic variables*.

The fact that the optimal solution is a basic (feasible) solution, has some interesting practical consequences as to the form of the solution. Suppose, a problem consists of finding the optimal activity levels for k activities (other than slack activities), subject to m resource constraints, and $k > m$. The optimal solution will never have more than m of the k activities at positive levels and may have fewer, if any slack variables are positive.

3-4 GENERAL IDEAS OF THE SIMPLEX METHOD

The general idea of the simplex method is to move from one basic feasible solution to another basic feasible solution which has a better value of the objective function, until no further improvement can be obtained. At that point an optimal solution has been found. To achieve this change of basic feasible solutions we need to know—

- how to generate a new basic solution from the previous one,
- how to ensure that the new solution is feasible,
- how to make sure that the new solution is better than the previous one.

To move from one basic feasible solution to the next, the simplex method changes only one vector in the basis at a time, i.e., the new basis has one of the old basic vectors removed and one new vector introduced in its place. We select a *vector to enter the basis* which improves the value of the objective function at the new basic feasible solution. The *vector to leave the basis* is chosen to ensure that the new basic solution is feasible.

We will only discuss the simplex method for a maximization problem. This is not really a loss of generality since any minimization problem can be converted readily into a maximization problem by reversing the signs of the coefficients in the objective function.

For example,

$$\text{minimize } z = 2x_1 + 3x_2$$

gives the same solution as

$$\text{maximize } (-z) = -2x_1 - 3x_2$$

So we can transform a minimizing problem to a maximizing problem using:

$$\text{minimize } z = -\text{maximize } (-z)$$

Hence, the same method can handle both maximization and minimization problems. In graphical terms the reversing of signs leaves the slope of the objective function unchanged but reverses the direction of movement when the function increases in value. In a two-dimensional representation in solution space (such as Figure 3-1) the value of the objective function now increases for movements toward the origin rather than away from the origin.

3-5 THE VECTOR ENTERING THE BASIS

In (3-6) we expressed the vector $\mathbf{b}$ in terms of the basic vectors $\mathbf{a}_1$ and $\mathbf{a}_3$. The nonbasic vectors $\mathbf{a}_2$ and $\mathbf{a}_5$ can also be written in terms of this basis. Consider $\mathbf{a}_2$:

(3-9) $$\mathbf{a}_2 = \gamma_1 \mathbf{a}_1 + \gamma_2 \mathbf{a}_3$$

or

$$\begin{bmatrix} 1 \\ 1/24 \end{bmatrix} = \gamma_1 \begin{bmatrix} 0.5 \\ 1/16 \end{bmatrix} + \gamma_2 \begin{bmatrix} 1 \\ 0 \end{bmatrix}$$

The vector $\mathbf{a}_2$ represents the amount of the two resources smoke emission capacity and pulverizer capacity required to burn one ton of coal B; $\mathbf{a}_1$ represents the amount of the two resources required to burn one ton of coal A; $\mathbf{a}_3$ represents the amount of the two resources needed to have a slack of one kilogram of smoke emission capacity. Therefore, equation (3-9) says:

take a proportion γ_1 of the resources required to burn one ton of coal A, add to it γ_2 times the resources required for one kilogram of slack of smoke emission capacity; this sum equals the resources needed to burn one ton of coal B.

The solution to (3-9) is $\gamma_1 = 2/3$, $\gamma_2 = 2/3$. Burning one ton of coal B requires the same resources as burning 2/3 ton of coal A plus slack of 2/3 kilogram of smoke emission capacity. Algebraically, and in terms of resources required the right-hand-side of (3-9) is equivalent to burning one ton of coal B (although it is not so physically). We will call the right-hand-side of (3-9) the *equivalent vector* to $\mathbf{a}_2$.

Let us now compare the contribution to the objective function of $\mathbf{a}_2$ and that of the equivalent vector to $\mathbf{a}_2$. Since both vectors involve the use of identical amounts of the two resources, is it more advantageous to use these resources to produce steam by burning coal B directly or by the activities implied in the equivalent vector to $\mathbf{a}_2$? The steam produced by one ton of coal B (or the direct contribution to the objective function of one unit activity $\mathbf{a}_2$) is 20. It is equal to the objective function coefficient c_2. To find the contribution to the objective function implied by the activities of the equivalent vector to $\mathbf{a}_2$, we refer back to the solution to equation (3-9). The equivalent vector to $\mathbf{a}_2$ is made up of proportions γ_1 and γ_2 of $\mathbf{a}_1$ and $\mathbf{a}_3$. One unit of each of $\mathbf{a}_1$ and $\mathbf{a}_3$ contributes respectively c_1 and c_3 toward the objective function. Hence a proportion γ_1 of $\mathbf{a}_1$ contributes $\gamma_1 c_1$ and a proportion γ_2 of $\mathbf{a}_3$ contributes $\gamma_2 c_3$. Let z_2 denote the sum of the contributions implied by the equivalent vector to $\mathbf{a}_2$. Hence:

$$(3\text{-}10) \qquad z_2 = \gamma_1 c_1 + \gamma_2 c_3 = \tfrac{2}{3}(24) + \tfrac{2}{3}(0) = 16$$

It is intuitively appealing that if the direct contribution c_2 exceeds the implied contribution z_2, it is better to use $\mathbf{a}_2$ than the equivalent vector to $\mathbf{a}_2$, i.e., it is better to have the vector $\mathbf{a}_2$ in the basis. In our case $c_2 = 20 > z_2 = 16$, so $\mathbf{a}_2$ should enter the basis. In fact, each unit of activity $\mathbf{a}_2$ increases the value of the objective function by $c_2 - z_2 = (20 - 16) = 4$.

No matter what the meanings of the vectors in a linear program are, if a non-basic vector $\mathbf{a}_j$ makes a higher direct contribution (i.e., higher profit, higher output, or lower cost) as measured by its c_j value than the contribution implied by its equivalent vector as measured by its z_j value, then that vector should replace one of the basic vectors. Tradition has it that the test quantity for the nonbasic vector $\mathbf{a}_j$ is the difference $(z_j - c_j)$, i.e., the negative of $c_j - z_j$ used above. If this value is negative, then $\mathbf{a}_j$ is eligible to enter the basis. If more than one nonbasic vector has this property, then we choose the one which yields the greatest improvement in the objective function per unit of the vector.

SIMPLEX CRITERION 1: VECTOR ENTERING BASIS

The vector to enter the basis is the one that has the most negative $(z_j - c_j)$ value.

If no nonbasic vector has a negative $(z_j - c_j)$ value, nothing more can be gained by introducing one of these vectors into a new basis. The optimal basic feasible solution has been reached. We shall accept this optimality criterion here without proof.

OPTIMALITY CRITERION

The solution associated with a given basis is optimal if all $(z_j - c_j) \geqslant 0$.

3-6 THE VECTOR LEAVING THE BASIS

Assume that $\mathbf{a}_2$ enters the new basis. The solution for the old basis is $x_1 = 16$, $x_3 = 4$, and from (3-6) $\mathbf{b}$ is given as

$$(3\text{-}11) \qquad \mathbf{b} = 16\mathbf{a}_1 + 4\mathbf{a}_3$$

From (3-9) the equivalent vector to $\mathbf{a}_2$ in terms of the old basis is

$$(3\text{-}12) \qquad \mathbf{a}_2 = \gamma_1 \mathbf{a}_1 + \gamma_2 \mathbf{a}_3 = \tfrac{2}{3}\mathbf{a}_1 + \tfrac{2}{3}\mathbf{a}_3$$

With $\mathbf{a}_2$ entering the new basis, x_2 will normally become positive, since it is no longer a nonbasic variable. Similarly, either $\mathbf{a}_1$ or $\mathbf{a}_3$ will leave the basis, so either x_1 or x_3 must go to zero when it becomes nonbasic.

To help us trace the solution from one basis to the other let us increase x_2 to an amount θ. Now (3-11) is replaced by the expression $\mathbf{b} = x_1 \mathbf{a}_1 + x_3 \mathbf{a}_3 + \theta \mathbf{a}_2$. What will be the values of x_1 and x_3?

From (3-12) it follows that

$$(3\text{-}13) \qquad \theta \mathbf{a}_2 = \tfrac{2}{3}\theta \mathbf{a}_1 + \tfrac{2}{3}\theta \mathbf{a}_3$$

We now add the left-hand-side of (3-13) to the right-hand-side of (3-11) and then subtract the right-hand-side of (3-13). The net effect of this calculation is zero:

$$(3\text{-}14) \qquad \mathbf{b} = (16 - \tfrac{2}{3}\theta)\mathbf{a}_1 + (4 - \tfrac{2}{3}\theta)\mathbf{a}_3 + \theta \mathbf{a}_2$$

Since equation (3-14) is of the form $\mathbf{b} = x_1 \mathbf{a}_1 + x_3 \mathbf{a}_3 + x_2 \mathbf{a}_2$, if we put $x_2 = \theta$, x_1 is reduced by $\tfrac{2}{3}\theta$ to $(16 - \tfrac{2}{3}\theta)$ and x_3 by $\tfrac{2}{3}\theta$ to $(4 - \tfrac{2}{3}\theta)$. We should increase θ by as much as possible, since the greater x_2 is, the greater is the increase in the value of the objective function. But as θ is increased, first one, then the other variable will go to zero and then become negative.

The vector to leave the basis is the one whose variable first goes to zero.

This variable changes then to a nonbasic variable. We find the variable that first goes to zero by setting both x_1 and x_3 equal to zero and solving each for θ. The vector whose variable has the smallest θ leaves the basis. The smallest $\theta = \text{minimum}[16/(2/3), 4/(2/3)] = 6$ is obtained for x_3; so $\mathbf{a}_3$ is the vector to leave. The ratios in this minimization can be derived directly from (3-11) and (3-12). The numerator of the ratio is the x_i value from (3-11) and the denominator is the corresponding γ_i value in (3-12). Had any of the γ_i's in the equivalent vector to the vector entering the basis—expressions (3-9) and (3-12) in our example—been zero or negative, the corresponding basic variable would not have decreased as θ increased. Hence to find the vector leaving the basis we need consider only those with positive γ_i's.

SIMPLEX CRITERION 2: VECTOR LEAVING BASIS

Given the γ_i's in the equivalent vector to the vector entering the basis, the vector leaving the basis is the one that minimizes the ratio—

$$\frac{(\text{value of basis variable } x_i)}{(\text{corresponding } \gamma_i)} \quad \text{for all } \gamma_i > 0$$

Verify that if z is the objective function value for the basis $[\mathbf{a}_1, \mathbf{a}_3]$ and $\hat{z}$ is the value for the basis $[\mathbf{a}_1, \mathbf{a}_2]$ then $\hat{z} = z - \theta(z_2 - c_2)$.

If there are no positive γ_i's, θ can be increased without bound because none of the variables in the present basis will go to zero. As θ increases, so does the value of the objective function, and since θ can be increased without bound the objective function also goes to infinity. This is called an *unbounded solution*.

CRITERION FOR UNBOUNDED SOLUTION

If, for some $(z_j - c_j) < 0$, all γ_i are nonpositive, the linear programming problem has no finite optimal solution.

The calculations of this section and the preceding section are those required for the change of basis discussed in Section 3-9.

3-7 THE INITIAL BASIC FEASIBLE SOLUTION

How do we find a basic feasible solution to start with? Trial and error is not satisfactory, because in larger problems the number of infeasible bases far outweighs the number of feasible ones. We must have a foolproof, systematic technique. For reasons that will be apparent shortly, we would like to start with a basis that consists of independent *unit vectors*. In fact, unit vectors are the most fundamental basis of any space. The elements of any vector are the same as the γ_i values of the equivalent vector in terms of the unit basic vectors. Most actual problems do not have this basis, and finding an initial basis may in itself be a formidable task. In some cases, as in our example, the set of vectors corresponding to the slack variables with $+1$ LHS coefficients forms a basis of unit vectors. The corresponding basic solution is the origin in Figure 3-1.

For any basis of unit vectors, the basic solution is given by the elements of **b**. However, this basic solution is feasible only if **b** is nonnegative. Sections 3-10 to 3-12 deal with the problem of finding a feasible basis, when there is no complete basis of positive slack vectors corresponding to a nonnegative **b** vector.

The computations of the simplex method are most conveniently performed in a tableau structure, known as the *simplex tableau*. For the reduced version of the power generating problem (3-1) the simplex tableau for the initial basis of slack vectors $(\mathbf{a}_3, \mathbf{a}_5)$ is shown in Table 3-1.

The first two rows are header rows for reference purposes only. The first has the values of the objective function coefficients c_j for each vector $\mathbf{a}_j$ and the second indicates to which vector each column refers. The c_j column on the extreme left contains the objective function coefficients for the basic variables. They are required to find the z_j values. The vectors that form the basis are listed in the second column. The columns in the main body give the proportions of each basic vector needed to make up the equivalent vector to the vector shown in the second header row. For a basis of unit vectors, these proportions are simply the elements of each vector.

The column labeled **b** contains the values of the basic variables. By the principle developed in expressions (3-6) and (3-7) the values of the basic variables can be found by solving

$$(3\text{-}15) \qquad\qquad x_3\,\mathbf{a}_3 + x_5\,\mathbf{a}_5 = \mathbf{b}$$

Table 3-1. *Initial Simplex Tableau.*

c_j				24	20	0	0	ratio
c_j	Vectors / Basis		**b**	$\mathbf{a}_1$	$\mathbf{a}_2$	$\mathbf{a}_3$	$\mathbf{a}_5$	$\dfrac{\mathbf{b}}{\mathbf{a}_1}$
0	$\mathbf{a}_3$		12	0.5	1	1	0	$\dfrac{12}{0.5} = 24$
← 0	$\mathbf{a}_5$		1	$\boxed{\dfrac{1}{16}}$	$\dfrac{1}{24}$	0	1	$\dfrac{1}{1/16} = 16$
	$z_j - c_j$		0	-24	-20	0	0	

Vector out

↑ Vector in

whereas the nonbasic variables are equal to zero. Since $\mathbf{a}_3$ and $\mathbf{a}_5$ are unit vectors, the basic variables are equal to the elements of $\mathbf{b}$, i.e., $x_3 = 12$, and $x_5 = 1$.

The last row of the tableau shows the $(z_j - c_j)$ value for each vector. They are computed on the basis of expression (3-10). For instance

$$(z_1 - c_1) = 0.5c_3 + \tfrac{1}{16}c_5 - c_1 = 0.5(0) + \tfrac{1}{16}(0) - 24 = -24$$

The $(z_j - c_j)$ values for the basic vectors are zero since the equivalent vector to a basic vector is the basic vector itself and therefore $z_j = c_j$.

The first term in the $(z_j - c_j)$ row is the value of the objective function for this basic feasible solution, i.e.,

$$z = \sum_j c_j x_j = 24(0) + 20(0) + 0(12) + 0(1) = 0$$

Since the nonbasic variables are zero, this sum only needs to be taken over the basic variables.

(For our subsequent discussion, when we refer to the rows of the simplex tableau, the two header rows will be ignored. For example, row 1 is the $\mathbf{a}_3$ row in Table 3-1.)

We will say that a tableau is in *canonical form* when the columns of the tableau corresponding to the basic vectors are independent unit vectors.

3-8 FIRST ITERATION OF THE SIMPLEX METHOD

We are now ready for the first iteration of the simplex method. By simplex criterion 1 the nonbasic vector $\mathbf{a}_1$ enters the basis since it has the most negative $(z_j - c_j)$ value, as shown by the arrow below $(z_1 - c_1)$ in Table 3-1.

As we have seen, the values of the basic variables are the corresponding elements in column $\mathbf{b}$ and the proportions γ_i of the unit basic vectors to make up the equivalent vector to $\mathbf{a}_1$ are the corresponding elements in column $\mathbf{a}_1$. To find the vector leaving the basis we compute the ratio of these two numbers for all $\gamma_i > 0$, as shown in the last column of Table 3-1. By simplex criterion 2, $\mathbf{a}_5$ leaves the basis since it has the smallest value of this ratio. The new basis is $(\mathbf{a}_3, \mathbf{a}_1)$.

Our next task is to transform this tableau into the canonical form corresponding to the new basis. We will define the *pivot row* as the row of the vector leaving the basis which becomes the row of the new basic variable. This is row 2 in Table 3-1. We will define the *pivot column* as the column associated with the vector entering the basis—in our case column $\mathbf{a}_1$ in Table 3-1. The *pivot element* is defined as the element which is in both the pivot row and the pivot column. In our case it is the number 1/16 shown circled in Table 3-1.

To get the tableau to the new canonical form, the pivot column has to be transformed to a unit vector with the pivot element equal to 1. This is achieved by the following rules:

TRANSFORMATION RULES

1. The pivot row is transformed by dividing it through by the pivot element.
2. All other rows are transformed as follows: if $\bar{y}_i$ is the element in the pivot column and row i, then row i is transformed by subtracting $\bar{y}_i$ times the new pivot row from row i.

Table 3-2 shows the results of the transformation. The new row 2 was obtained by dividing the pivot row through by 1/16. The new row 1 was obtained by subtracting 0.5 times the new row 2 from the old row 1, and the new $(z_j - c_j)$ row was obtained by subtracting -24 times the new row 2 from the old $(z_j - c_j)$ row.

The columns in the main body of the tableau again give the proportions of the basic vectors $\mathbf{a}_3$ and $\mathbf{a}_1$ needed to obtain the equivalent vectors. The new basic feasible solution can be read off from the $\mathbf{b}$ column as $x_3 = 4$, $x_1 = 16$ with the nonbasic variables x_2 and x_5 equal to zero and a value of $z = 384$. This solution corresponds to extreme point B in Figure 3-1.

We can interpret Table 3-2 in a different way. The set of simultaneous equations implicit in Table 3-1 has been transformed into a new set of equations, namely,

$$0x_1 + \tfrac{2}{3}x_2 + x_3 - 8x_5 = 4$$

$$x_1 + \tfrac{2}{3}x_2 + 0x_3 + 16x_5 = 16$$

which have exactly the same solution as the first set. The transformation is such that the new basic solution (x_3, x_1) is obtained trivially, just as the basic solution (x_3, x_5) was obtained trivially from equations (3-2). The transformation rules transform the vectors of the columns of Table 3-1 in such a way that the relationship between them is preserved.

Table 3-2. *Second Simplex Tableau.*

		c_j		24	20	0	0	ratio
		Vectors	$\mathbf{b}$	$\mathbf{a}_1$	$\mathbf{a}_2$	$\mathbf{a}_3$	$\mathbf{a}_5$	$\dfrac{\mathbf{b}}{\mathbf{a}_2}$
	c_j	Basis						
$\leftarrow$	0	$\mathbf{a}_3$	4	0	$\left(\dfrac{2}{3}\right)$	1	-8	$\dfrac{4}{2/3} = 6$
Vector out	24	$\mathbf{a}_1$	16	1	$\dfrac{2}{3}$	0	16	$\dfrac{16}{2/3} = 24$
	$z_j - c_j$		384	0	-4	0	384	

$\uparrow$ Vector in

Let us use the following notation for the columns in Tables 3-2:

$$\bar{\mathbf{b}} = \begin{bmatrix} 4 \\ 16 \end{bmatrix}, \quad \bar{\mathbf{a}}_1 = \begin{bmatrix} 0 \\ 1 \end{bmatrix}, \quad \bar{\mathbf{a}}_2 = \begin{bmatrix} 2/3 \\ 2/3 \end{bmatrix}, \quad \bar{\mathbf{a}}_3 = \begin{bmatrix} 1 \\ 0 \end{bmatrix}, \quad \bar{\mathbf{a}}_5 = \begin{bmatrix} -8 \\ 16 \end{bmatrix}$$

In Table 3-1 we have

$$x_3 \ \mathbf{a}_3 \ + x_5 \ \mathbf{a}_5 \ = \mathbf{b}$$

or

$$12 \begin{bmatrix} 1 \\ 0 \end{bmatrix} + 1 \begin{bmatrix} 0 \\ 1 \end{bmatrix} = \begin{bmatrix} 12 \\ 1 \end{bmatrix}$$

This relationship also holds in Table 3-2 for the $\bar{\mathbf{a}}_j$ and $\bar{\mathbf{b}}$ vectors:

$$x_3 \ \bar{\mathbf{a}}_3 \ + x_5 \ \bar{\mathbf{a}}_5 \ = \bar{\mathbf{b}}$$

$$12 \begin{bmatrix} 1 \\ 0 \end{bmatrix} + 1 \begin{bmatrix} -8 \\ 16 \end{bmatrix} = \begin{bmatrix} 4 \\ 16 \end{bmatrix}$$

Similarly,

$$\mathbf{a}_1 = 0.5\mathbf{a}_3 + \frac{1}{16}\mathbf{a}_5 = 0.5 \begin{bmatrix} 1 \\ 0 \end{bmatrix} + \frac{1}{16} \begin{bmatrix} 0 \\ 1 \end{bmatrix} = \begin{bmatrix} 0.5 \\ 1/16 \end{bmatrix}$$

and

$$\bar{\mathbf{a}}_1 = 0.5\bar{\mathbf{a}}_3 + \frac{1}{16}\bar{\mathbf{a}}_5 = 0.5 \begin{bmatrix} 1 \\ 0 \end{bmatrix} + \frac{1}{16} \begin{bmatrix} -8 \\ 16 \end{bmatrix} = \begin{bmatrix} 0 \\ 1 \end{bmatrix}$$

3-9 SECOND ITERATION OF THE SIMPLEX METHOD

The basic feasible solution in the second simplex tableau (Table 3-2) is not optimal since not all $(z_j - c_j)$ values are nonnegative. We therefore start a second iteration. By simplex criterion 1, $\mathbf{a}_2$ enters the basis and, by simplex criterion 2, $\mathbf{a}_3$ leaves the basis as shown in Table 3-2. The new basis is $(\mathbf{a}_2, \mathbf{a}_1)$. These are results we developed in Sections 3-5 and 3-6. You may wish to refer back to those sections to

Table 3-3. *Third Simplex Tableau.*

c_j				24	20	0	0
		Vectors					
c_j	Basis		$\mathbf{b}$	$\mathbf{a}_1$	$\mathbf{a}_2$	$\mathbf{a}_3$	$\mathbf{a}_5$
20	$\mathbf{a}_2$		6	0	1	$\frac{3}{2}$	-12
24	$\mathbf{a}_1$		12	1	0	-1	24
	$z_j - c_j$		408	0	0	6	336

strengthen your understanding of the data of Table 3-2 and the reasons for the simplex criteria.

Applying the transformation rules we find the new canonical form as shown in the third simplex tableau in Table 3-3.

From the **b** column we can read off the basic feasible solution $x_2 = 6$, $x_1 = 12$ with the nonbasic variables x_3 and x_5 equal to zero and a value of $z = 408$.

By the optimality criterion we also have reached the optimal solution, since no $(z_j - c_j)$ values are negative.

3-10 ARTIFICIAL VARIABLES

Most linear programming problems do not have an initial basis of slack vectors, since some constraints may be equality constraints or "larger-than-or-equal" constraints.   One of the outstanding features of the simplex method is that the method itself can be used to generate its own initial feasible basis—provided one exists—or otherwise indicate that the problem has no feasible solution.

Since no basis of unit vectors exists to initiate the simplex method we use the trick of creating such a basis artificially.   We do this by introducing into each constraint which does not have a slack variable with a $+1$ LHS coefficient, a so-called *artificial variable* which does have that property.   The new problem thus created—called the *augmented problem*—has a basis of unit vectors made up of slack vectors and *artificial vectors*.   Geometrically, we are expanding the feasible region to include the origin of the space when we represent it in terms of all variables other than the slack and artificial variables.

Let us illustrate this idea with the original power generating problem as summarized below:

$$\text{maximize} \quad 24x_1 + 20x_2$$

$$\text{subject to} \quad 0.5x_1 + x_2 + x_3 \qquad\qquad = 12$$

$$x_1 + x_2 + x_4 \qquad\quad = 20$$

(3-16)
$$(1/16)\,x_1 + (1/24)\,x_2 \qquad\quad + x_5 \quad = 1$$

$$1200x_1 - 800x_2 \qquad\qquad - x_6 = 0$$

$$x_1, x_2, x_3, x_4, x_5, x_6 \geqslant 0$$

The unit vectors associated with the slack variables x_3, x_4, and x_5 can be used as unit basic vectors.   Since the sulfur constraint is a $\geqslant$ inequality, its slack variable has the wrong sign.   This prevents the existence of a full basis of unit vectors.   (Note that in this example we could obtain such a basis by multiplying this constraint by -1.   However, for demonstration purposes, we will not do that here.)

We now augment the original problem by adding the artificial variable x_7 to the fourth constraint:

$$0.5x_1 + \quad x_2 + x_3 \qquad\qquad\qquad\quad = 12$$

$$x_1 + \quad x_2 \qquad + x_4 \qquad\qquad\quad = 20$$

(3-17) $\qquad (1/16)x_1 + (1/24)x_2 \qquad\quad + x_5 \qquad\quad = 1$

$$1200x_1 - \quad 800x_2 \qquad\qquad\quad - x_6 + x_7 = 0$$

$$x_1, \ldots, x_7 \geqslant 0$$

The unit vectors $(\mathbf{a}_3, \mathbf{a}_4, \mathbf{a}_5, \mathbf{a}_7)$ form an initial basis to equations (3-17). The artificial variable x_7 has no meaning in terms of the original linear program (3-16). So, although we have an initial basic feasible solution to the augmented problem, the solution is not basic for the original problem since $\mathbf{a}_7$ is not a part of that problem. Our task is to construct, from the initial solution to the augmented problem, a basic feasible solution to the original problem by removing all artificial variables from the basis and then to find an optimal solution to the original problem. We will consider two methods of doing this—the *big* M *method* and the *two-phase method*. The big M method is attractive because it is a simple extension of the simplex method developed so far. However, most large-scale codes use the two-phase method.

3-11 THE BIG *M* METHOD

The basic idea of the big M method is very simple. We give the augmented problem the same objective function as the original problem, except that we penalize each artificial variable heavily with a large negative objective function coefficient, say an amount $-M$ (hence the name of the method). So any basic feasible solution that includes artificial variables is most unattractive. In the process of reaching the optimal solution to the augmented problem, the simplex method will get rid of the artificial vectors from the basis if at all possible. The big M method just uses the inherent logic of linear programming and the simplex method to provide an optimal solution to the augmented problem that is also optimal for the original problem.

What if the optimal solution to the augmented problem has artificial variables at nonzero level? We must argue that the simplex method would have excluded these variables if it could. Since it cannot exclude them there is no feasible solution to the augmented problem which is also feasible for the original problem. That simply means that there is no feasible solution to the original problem because its feasible region is completely contained in the feasible region of the augmented problem.

We have then the following two criteria.

BIG *M* METHOD CRITERION: OPTIMALITY

The optimal solution to the augmented problem is optimal to the original problem if there are no artificial variables, with nonzero value, in the optimal solution.

BIG *M* METHOD CRITERION: NO FEASIBLE SOLUTION

If any artificial vector is basic with nonzero value at the optimal solution of the augmented problem, the original problem has no feasible solution.

Table 3-4. *The Big* M *Method for Problem (3-18).*

c_j			24	20	0	0	0	0	$-M$	ratio
c_j	Vectors / Basis	$\mathbf{b}$	$\mathbf{a}_1$	$\mathbf{a}_2$	$\mathbf{a}_3$	$\mathbf{a}_4$	$\mathbf{a}_5$	$\mathbf{a}_6$	$\mathbf{a}_7$	$\dfrac{\mathbf{b}}{\mathbf{a}_j}$
0	$\mathbf{a}_3$	12	$\dfrac{1}{2}$	1	1	0	0	0	0	24
0	$\mathbf{a}_4$	20	1	1	0	1	0	0	0	20
0	$\mathbf{a}_5$	1	$\dfrac{1}{16}$	$\dfrac{1}{24}$	0	0	1	0	0	16
← $-M$	$\mathbf{a}_7$	0	⟨1200⟩	-800	0	0	0	-1	1	0
$z_j - c_j$		0	$(-1200M - 24)\uparrow$	$(800M - 20)$	0	0	0	M	0	
← 0	$\mathbf{a}_3$	12	0	⟨$\dfrac{4}{3}$⟩	1	0	0	$\dfrac{1}{2400}$	$-\dfrac{1}{2400}$	9
0	$\mathbf{a}_4$	20	0	$\dfrac{5}{3}$	0	1	0	$\dfrac{1}{1200}$	$-\dfrac{1}{1200}$	12
0	$\mathbf{a}_5$	1	0	$\dfrac{1}{12}$	0	0	1	$\dfrac{1}{19200}$	$-\dfrac{1}{19200}$	12
24	$\mathbf{a}_1$	0	1	$-\dfrac{2}{3}$	0	0	0	$-\dfrac{1}{1200}$	$\dfrac{1}{1200}$	
$z_j - c_j$		0	0	$-36\uparrow$	0	0	0	$-\dfrac{1}{50}$	$\dfrac{1}{50}+M$	
20	$\mathbf{a}_2$	9	0	1	$\dfrac{3}{4}$	0	0	$\dfrac{1}{3200}$	$-\dfrac{1}{3200}$	28800
0	$\mathbf{a}_4$	5	0	0	$-\dfrac{5}{4}$	1	0	$\dfrac{1}{3200}$	$-\dfrac{1}{3200}$	16000
← 0	$\mathbf{a}_5$	$\dfrac{1}{4}$	0	0	$-\dfrac{1}{16}$	0	1	⟨$\dfrac{1}{38400}$⟩	$-\dfrac{1}{38400}$	9600
24	$\mathbf{a}_1$	6	1	0	$\dfrac{1}{2}$	0	0	$-\dfrac{1}{1600}$	$\dfrac{1}{1600}$	
$z_j - c_j$		324	0	0	27	0	0	$-\dfrac{7}{800}$	$\dfrac{7}{800}+M$ $\uparrow$	
20	$\mathbf{a}_2$	6	0	1	$\dfrac{3}{2}$	0	-12	0	0	
0	$\mathbf{a}_4$	2	0	0	$-\dfrac{1}{2}$	1	-12	0	0	
0	$\mathbf{a}_6$	9600	0	0	-2400	0	38400	1	-1	
24	$\mathbf{a}_1$	12	1	0	-1	0	24	0	0	
$z_j - c_j$		408	0	0	6	0	336	0	M	

So to solve (3-17) we give an objective function coefficient of $-M$ to x_7, whereas all other variables have the original coefficients shown in (3-16). Thus we have the linear program:

(3-18)
$$\text{maximize } 24x_1 + 20x_2 - Mx_7$$

subject to the constraint set (3-17).

We see in Table 3-4 the sequence of tableaux for solving (3-18). In the first iteration the choice of $\mathbf{a}_1$ to enter the basis is determined by the $-1200M$ part of $(z_1 - c_1)$ since that completely dominates the term -24. By coincidence $\mathbf{a}_7$ is removed immediately—that need not have been the case since it is the ratio $(\mathbf{b}/\mathbf{a}_j)$ that determines the vector to leave the basis. The rest of the iterations are not affected by the penalty cost, except that it prevents $\mathbf{a}_7$ from entering the basis again. In fact, the $\mathbf{a}_7$ column could be removed from the tableau after the first iteration without altering the outcome.

The big M method may lead to difficulties when used on a computer. The first difficulty is that if M is very large the non-M part of each $(z_j - c_j)$ (i.e., the part which is not a multiple of M) may get lost because of the machine's finite precision. Naturally, $(z_j - c_j)$ could be computed from first principles at each iteration but this would be extravagant in computing time. On the other hand if M is too small, wrong answers may arise through the non-M part of $(z_j - c_j)$ negating the effect of the penalty cost. Unfortunately, the best value for M will vary from problem to problem.

3-12 THE TWO-PHASE METHOD

The two-phase method avoids the weakness of the big M method by distinguishing the two phases implicit in it. We saw that the big M method simultaneously seeks a feasible solution to the original problem and an optimal solution to the original problem. In the two-phase method we find the initial basic feasible solution to the original problem in phase 1. If no feasible solution exists phase 1 indicates that also. Phase 2 starts with this initial feasible basis and finds the optimal solution to the original problem. So we use the simplex method to find its own starting solution as well as to find an optimal solution. (We can also use phase 1 on its own to find a solution to a set of linear inequalities or equations that has no objective function.)

In the two-phase method we remove the artificial vectors from the basis in the following way. In phase 1 we introduce a separate objective function, often referred to as the *infeasibility form*, which gives each artificial vector an objective function coefficient of -1 and each true vector a coefficient of 0. By maximizing the infeasibility form we endeavor to force the artificial vectors to leave the basis. If a feasible solution exists for the original problem the maximum value of the infeasibility form is zero. If phase 1 terminates with basic artificial variables at a positive value, no feasible solution exists for the original problem. (It is, though, possible to have basic artificial variables with a value of zero at the end of phase 1. These will not be permitted to assume positive values in the phase 2 optimization.)

TWO-PHASE METHOD CRITERION: NO FEASIBLE SOLUTION

If phase 1 terminates with positive valued basic artificial variables, then there is no feasible solution to the original linear programming problem.

For our example, the phase 1 problem consists of:

$$(3\text{-}19) \qquad \text{maximize } 0x_1 + 0x_2 + 0x_3 + 0x_4 + 0x_5 + 0x_6 - x_7$$

subject to the constraint set (3-17).

Table 3-5. *Phase 1 of Two-Phase Method.*

				First Simplex Tableau							
		c_j		24	20	0	0	0	0	0	ratio
		$\bar{c}_j$		0	0	0	0	0	0	-1	
c_J	$\bar{c}_J$	Vectors / Basis	$\mathbf{b}$	$\mathbf{a}_1$	$\mathbf{a}_2$	$\mathbf{a}_3$	$\mathbf{a}_4$	$\mathbf{a}_5$	$\mathbf{a}_6$	$\mathbf{a}_7$	$\dfrac{\mathbf{b}}{\mathbf{a}_j}$
0	0	$\mathbf{a}_3$	12	$\frac{1}{2}$	1	1	0	0	0	0	24
0	0	$\mathbf{a}_4$	20	1	1	0	1	0	0	0	20
0	0	$\mathbf{a}_5$	1	$\frac{1}{16}$	$\frac{1}{24}$	0	0	1	0	0	16
← 0	-1	$\mathbf{a}_7$	0	(1200)	-800	0	0	0	-1	1	0
		$z_j - c_j$	0	-24	-20	0	0	0	0	0	
		$\bar{z}_j - \bar{c}_j$	0	-1200 ↑	800	0	0	0	1	0	
				Second Simplex Tableau							
0	0	$\mathbf{a}_3$	12	0	$\frac{4}{3}$	1	0	0	$\frac{1}{2400}$	$-\frac{1}{2400}$	
0	0	$\mathbf{a}_4$	20	0	$\frac{5}{3}$	0	1	0	$\frac{1}{1200}$	$-\frac{1}{1200}$	
0	0	$\mathbf{a}_5$	1	0	$\frac{1}{12}$	0	0	1	$\frac{1}{19200}$	$-\frac{1}{19200}$	
24	0	$\mathbf{a}_1$	0	1	$-\frac{2}{3}$	0	0	0	$-\frac{1}{1200}$	$\frac{1}{1200}$	
		$z_j - c_j$	0	0	-36	0	0	0	$-\frac{1}{50}$	$\frac{1}{50}$	
		$\bar{z}_j - \bar{c}_j$	0	0	0	0	0	0	0	1	

The simplex tableaux for phase 1 are shown in Table 3-5.   The $(z_j - c_j)$ values of the infeasibility form are denoted by $(\bar{z}_j - \bar{c}_j)$.   They are obtained in the usual way, using the infeasibility form as the objective function.   During the phase 1 computations it is also useful to carry the $(z_j - c_j)$ values of the original objective function along in the usual manner, except that they are not used to find the vectors entering the basis.

At the first iteration on the infeasibility form the vector $\mathbf{a}_1$ enters the basis and drives out $\mathbf{a}_7$.   The resulting canonical form for the new basis of $(\mathbf{a}_3, \mathbf{a}_4, \mathbf{a}_5, \mathbf{a}_1)$ is shown in the second tableau.   The infeasibility form has a value of zero and no negative $(\bar{z}_j - \bar{c}_j)$ values remain.   Phase 1 has terminated in a basic feasible solution to the original problem in one iteration.

Table 3-6. *Phase 2 of Two-Phase Method.*

c_j	Vectors / Basis	b	$\mathbf{a}_1$	$\mathbf{a}_2$	$\mathbf{a}_3$	$\mathbf{a}_4$	$\mathbf{a}_5$	$\mathbf{a}_6$	$\mathbf{a}_7$	$\dfrac{b}{a_j}$
c_j			24	20	0	0	0	0	—	ratio
0	$\mathbf{a}_3$	12	0	$\dfrac{4}{3}$	1	0	0	$\dfrac{1}{2400}$	$-\dfrac{1}{2400}$	9
0	$\mathbf{a}_4$	20	0	$\dfrac{5}{3}$	0	1	0	$\dfrac{1}{1200}$	$-\dfrac{1}{1200}$	12
0	$\mathbf{a}_5$	1	0	$\dfrac{1}{12}$	0	0	1	$\dfrac{1}{19200}$	$-\dfrac{1}{19200}$	12
24	$\mathbf{a}_1$	0	1	$-\dfrac{2}{3}$	0	0	0	$-\dfrac{1}{1200}$	$\dfrac{1}{1200}$	—
$z_j - c_j$		0	0	-36	0	0	0	$-\dfrac{1}{50}$	—	
20	$\mathbf{a}_2$	9	0	1	$\dfrac{3}{4}$	0	0	$\dfrac{1}{3200}$	$-\dfrac{1}{3200}$	28800
0	$\mathbf{a}_4$	5	0	0	$-\dfrac{5}{4}$	1	0	$\dfrac{1}{3200}$	$-\dfrac{1}{3200}$	16000
0	$\mathbf{a}_5$	$\dfrac{1}{4}$	0	0	$-\dfrac{1}{16}$	0	1	$\dfrac{1}{38400}$	$-\dfrac{1}{38400}$	9600
24	$\mathbf{a}_1$	6	1	0	$\dfrac{1}{2}$	0	0	$-\dfrac{1}{1600}$	$\dfrac{1}{1600}$	—
$z_j - c_j$		324	0	0	27	0	0	$-\dfrac{7}{800}$	—	
20	$\mathbf{a}_2$	6	0	1	$\dfrac{3}{2}$	0	-12	0	0	
0	$\mathbf{a}_4$	2	0	0	$-\dfrac{1}{2}$	1	-12	0	0	
0	$\mathbf{a}_6$	9600	0	0	-2400	0	38400	1	-1	
24	$\mathbf{a}_1$	12	1	0	-1	0	24	0	0	
$z_j - c_j$		408	0	0	6	0	336	0	—	

As an interesting footnote let us point out that x_1 is a basic variable at a zero value. Such a solution is called a *degenerate solution*. We shall discuss this further in Section 3-14.

Once phase 1 has yielded a basic feasible solution to the original linear program, we

- reinstate the original objective function, and
- ignore the artificial vectors for future consideration.

If we carry the original objective function along during the phase 1 computations, phase 2 can start immediately, because the original linear program is in canonical form. Otherwise the $(z_j - c_j)$ row has to be computed in the manner described in Section 3-5. For reasons that will become clear in Chapter 4 it is also advantageous to carry the columns for the artificial vectors along in the usual manner during the phase 2 computations, except that the artificial variables will never be allowed to become positive.

The phase 2 tableaux are shown in Table 3-6. The optimality condition is satisfied at the third tableau with the optimal solution of $x_1 = 12$, $x_2 = 6$, $x_3 = 0$, $x_4 = 2$, $x_5 = 0$, $x_6 = 9600$, $z = 408$. The reader may find it instructive to trace the sequence of solutions of phase 1 and phase 2 on Figure 2-3 in Chapter 2.

3-13 ALTERNATIVE OPTIMAL SOLUTIONS

When the objective function is parallel to the edge of a constraint, the optimal solution is not unique, as we illustrated in Section 2-9. This condition can be identified as follows:

ALTERNATIVE OPTIMAL SOLUTIONS

If at the optimal tableau one or more of the nonbasic vectors have $(z_j - c_j) = 0$ then each one of them is a candidate to enter alternative optimal bases.

This is intuitively reasonable, because a $(z_j - c_j)$ value of zero means that it is neither beneficial nor detrimental to have that vector in the basis—the value of the objective function will not change. The alternative optimal basic solutions can be found by evaluating each basis formed by all combinations of vectors with $(z_j - c_j)$ values of zero at the optimal solution. Furthermore, any convex combinations (linear combinations with proportions summing to 1) of the alternative optimal basic solutions will yield an optimal nonbasic solution. The set of all convex combinations is the edge of the feasible region along which the objective function lies. (Section A-4 of Appendix A discusses convex combinations.) Table 3-7 illustrates the example

Table 3-7. *Alternative Optimal Solutions.*

c_j			30	20	0	0	0	0	—
c_j	Vectors / Basis	b	a_1	a_2	a_3	a_4	a_5	a_6	a_7
← 20	a_2	6	0	1	$\boxed{\frac{3}{2}}$	0	-12	0	0
0	a_4	2	0	0	$-\frac{1}{2}$	1	-12	0	0
0	a_6	9600	0	0	-2400	0	38400	1	-1
30	a_1	12	1	0	-1	0	24	0	0
$z_j - c_j$		480	0	0	0	0	480	0	—
					↑				
0	a_3	4	0	$\frac{2}{3}$	1	0	-8	0	0
0	a_4	4	0	$\frac{1}{3}$	0	1	-16	0	0
0	a_6	19200	0	1600	0	0	19200	1	-1
30	a_1	16	1	$\frac{2}{3}$	0	0	16	0	0
$z_j - c_j$		480	0	0	0	0	480	0	—

of Section 2-9 with the objective function

$$\text{maximize } 30x_1 + 20x_2$$

The simplex method arrives at an optimal basis of (a_2, a_4, a_6, a_1) with $(z_3 - c_3) = 0$. Introducing a_3 into the basis, we get the alternative optimal basis of (a_3, a_4, a_6, a_1).

Not only are the two basic solutions optimal, i.e.,

$$x_1 = 12, \quad x_2 = 6, \quad x_3 = 0, \quad x_4 = 2, \quad x_5 = 0, \quad x_6 = 9600,$$

and

$$\bar{x}_1 = 16, \quad \bar{x}_2 = 0, \quad \bar{x}_3 = 4, \quad \bar{x}_4 = 4, \quad \bar{x}_5 = 0, \quad \bar{x}_6 = 19200,$$

but so are all the points on the line segment between these two solutions, i.e.,

(3-20) $$\hat{x}_j = (1 - \lambda) x_j + \lambda \bar{x}_j, \quad 0 < \lambda < 1$$

These are optimal solutions (though not basic), all with the same value of the objective function of $z = 408$.

3-14 DEGENERACY

When one or more basic variables have a value of zero (as x_1 did at the end of phase 1 in Table 3-5), the basic solution is called a *degenerate solution*. Theoretically, this may spell trouble for the simplex method. To prove the convergence of the simplex method in a finite number of iterations we must assume that the value of the objective function increases at each iteration. When this occurs, each basis in the sequence traced out by the simplex method has a unique value of z and so no basis can appear more than once. Since there is only a finite number of basic feasible solutions, the simplex method converges to the optimal solution in a finite number of iterations.

However, when a variable enters a basic solution at a zero value, the value of the objective function does not change at that iteration. If this occurs a number of times in sequence, it is conceivable that a previous basis will reappear. If we then follow exactly the same sequence of computations and selection rules as we did when this basis was encountered for the first time, we are caught in a circle without exit. This is known as *cycling*.

Although degeneracy is fairly common, the danger of cycling seems to be negligible, and is usually ignored. So for practical purposes we can assume finite convergence even though there is degeneracy in the problem. However, there are a number of ways of preventing cycling. The most satisfactory and sophisticated one is a special version of the simplex method called the *lexicographic form of the simplex method*. (See M. Simmonard, *Linear Programming*, pp. 63–66.) Another method of preventing cycling is to remove the degeneracy. This can be done by *perturbing* the degenerate variable (i.e., giving it a very small nonzero value). If the perturbation is very small, the effect on the optimal solution is also small, although it may rise substantially over many iterations. This is a danger. Computer codes by the very nature of their computational system, accumulate rounding errors during the arithmetic operations from iteration to iteration and thus automatically introduce minute perturbations. Thus, in practice, cycling can be safely ignored. Most of the examples of cycling reported in the literature are mathematical fabrications, designed to illustrate the problem.

3-15 COMPUTER CODES AND THE SIMPLEX METHOD

Most commercial linear programming computer codes do not use the *full tableau simplex method* as described in this chapter. Instead they work with the *revised simplex method* in which less data is updated at each iteration and which retains the original tableau of LHS coefficients, RHS parameters, and objective function coefficients. With this method it is possible to periodically (after a predetermined number of iterations) rid the current solution of many of the rounding errors accumulated during the updating operations. This is done by computing again, from scratch, the tableau data via a procedure referred to as *inversion*. It is also possible to determine the final errors contained in the optimal solution.

The accuracy of the final solution is not only a function of the frequency of recomputing the basis data but also of the various *tolerances* built into the computer code, or specified by the user at data input time. At various points in the computations of both phases of the simplex method, checks are made on certain entries in the tableau, such as the $(z_j - c_j)$ values and the pivot column, to determine whether they are equal to zero. Unfortunately, a computer seldom carries a number that is zero (theoretically) at exactly this value. Errors may be introduced by the manner in which the computer stores decimal numbers or through truncation (rounding down) during computations. Therefore, for all practical purposes entries with small deviations from zero, such as plus or minus 10^{-6}, are taken to be equal to zero. These limits are referred to as tolerances.

Choosing the tolerances is not always easy. The tighter these tolerances, the more computer errors are excluded by them and the more difficult they are to satisfy. Unfortunately, tight tolerances do not always result in better final answers, since important true data may be eliminated. For example, the authors have experienced cases where too tight a tolerance for the optimality condition of the infeasibility form resulted in problems being diagnosed wrongly as having no feasible solution. Loosening of this tolerance resolved the difficulty and produced a feasible solution.

The accuracy of the final answer can also be improved by proper *scaling* of the input data. Extremely large and extremely small numbers in the same problem should, whenever possible, be avoided since their simultaneous presence increases the danger of large error accumulation. By suitable elementary row-and-column operations on the input data, some of these variations can be eliminated. This is called scaling. An example of this was done on the objective function of the power generating problem. Rather than specify the objective function coefficients in pounds, we used units of 1000 pounds. This is equivalent to multiplying the objective function through by $1/1000$.

EXERCISES

3.1 Graph the constraint set in solution space:

$$2x_1 + 4x_2 \leqslant 8$$
$$x_1 - x_2 \leqslant 1$$
$$x_1, x_2 \geqslant 0$$

Find the bases that correspond to each of the extreme points of the feasible region. Remember to add slack variables.

3.2 For the constraint set

$$2x_1 + 4x_2 + x_3 + 2x_4 \leqslant 8$$
$$3x_1 + 2x_2 + 6x_3 + x_4 \leqslant 6$$
$$x_1, x_2, x_3, x_4 \geqslant 0$$

draw the vectors $\mathbf{a}_1, \mathbf{a}_2, \mathbf{a}_3, \mathbf{a}_4$ and $\mathbf{b}$ in requirements space.

(a) Which of the following sets of vectors span the two-dimensional space, and which ones are bases?

   (i) $(\mathbf{a}_1, \mathbf{a}_2)$
   (ii) $(\mathbf{a}_1, \mathbf{a}_3, \mathbf{a}_4)$
   (iii) $(\mathbf{a}_2, \mathbf{a}_4)$
   (iv) $(\mathbf{a}_2, \mathbf{a}_3, \mathbf{a}_4)$

(b) Express graphically, and algebraically:

   (i) $\mathbf{b}$ in terms of $(\mathbf{a}_1, \mathbf{a}_2)$
   (ii) $\mathbf{a}_3$ in terms of $(\mathbf{a}_1, \mathbf{a}_2)$
   (iii) $\mathbf{a}_4$ in terms of $(\mathbf{a}_1, \mathbf{a}_2)$

(c) Is (x_1, x_2) a basic feasible solution?

3.3 Using the constraint set of question 3.2, and the objective function

$$\text{maximize } z = 5x_1 + 6x_2 + 4x_3 + 2x_4$$

construct the simplex tableau for the basis $(\mathbf{a}_1, \mathbf{a}_2)$.

3.4 Solve the following problems by the simplex method:

(a)
$$\begin{aligned}
\text{maximize } z = {}& 4x_1 + 5x_2 \\
\text{subject to } {}& 2x_1 + 3x_2 \leqslant 6 \\
& 2x_1 + 2x_2 \leqslant 5 \\
& x_1, x_2 \geqslant 0
\end{aligned}$$

(b)
$$\begin{aligned}
\text{minimize } z = {}& x_1 - 2x_2 \\
\text{subject to } {}& 4x_1 + 2x_2 \leqslant 6 \\
& -x_1 + x_2 \leqslant 0 \\
& x_1, x_2 \geqslant 0
\end{aligned}$$

3.5 Solve the following problems using the big M or the 2-phase method.

(a)
$$\begin{aligned}
\text{maximize } z = {}& 4x_1 + 5x_2 \\
\text{subject to } {}& 2x_1 + 3x_2 \leqslant 6 \\
& 3x_1 + x_2 \geqslant 3 \\
& x_1, x_2 \geqslant 0
\end{aligned}$$

(b)
$$\begin{aligned}
\text{minimize } z = {}& x_1 - 2x_2 \\
\text{subject to } {}& 4x_1 + 2x_2 \leqslant 6 \\
& -2x_1 + 3x_2 \leqslant -1 \\
& x_1, x_2 \geqslant 0
\end{aligned}$$

3.6 Using the optimal tableau of question 3.5(a), replace the objective function with

$$\text{maximize } z = 6x_1 + 9x_2$$

Hint: You need only work out new $(z_j - c_j)$'s.
(a) Find the optimal solution.
(b) Find the alternative optimal basic feasible solution.
(c) Find two nonbasic optimal solutions.

3.7 Show by the 2-phase method that the following problem has no feasible solution.

$$\text{maximize } z = 4x_1 + 5x_2$$
$$\text{subject to } 2x_1 + 4x_2 \leqslant 8$$
$$x_1 + 3x_2 \geqslant 9$$
$$x_1, x_2 \geqslant 0$$

3.8 Show by the simplex method that the following problem has an unbounded solution.

$$\text{maximize } z = 2x_1 + x_2$$
$$\text{subject to } x_1 - x_2 \leqslant 1$$
$$-x_1 + x_2 \leqslant 1$$
$$x_1, x_2 \geqslant 0$$

3.9 Consider the following simplex tableau:

c_j			2	1	2	4	0	0
	Vectors							
c_j		$\mathbf{b}$	$\mathbf{a}_1$	$\mathbf{a}_2$	$\mathbf{a}_3$	$\mathbf{a}_4$	$\mathbf{a}_5$	$\mathbf{a}_6$
	Basis							
2	$\mathbf{a}_1$	4	1	-1	0	1.4	-0.6	0.4
2	$\mathbf{a}_3$	1.5	0	1	1	0.4	0.2	-0.1
	$z_j - c_j$	11.0	0	-1	0	-0.4	-0.4	0.6

(a) Write the following vectors in terms of the basis $(\mathbf{a}_1, \mathbf{a}_3)$. (i) $\mathbf{a}_1$, (ii) $\mathbf{a}_4$, (iii) $\mathbf{a}_5$, (iv) $\mathbf{a}_6$.

(b) Write the vector $(\mathbf{b} + 5\mathbf{a}_5)$ in terms of the basis.

(c) If the vectors $\mathbf{a}_5 = \mathbf{e}_1$, and $\mathbf{a}_6 = \mathbf{e}_2$ (the unit vectors) write the vector $\mathbf{a}_7 = \begin{bmatrix} 4 \\ 1 \end{bmatrix}$ in terms of the basis. Hint: $\mathbf{a}_7 = 4\mathbf{e}_1 + 1\mathbf{e}_2$ by definition of the unit vectors.

(d) If the vector $\mathbf{b}$ is changed to

$$\hat{\mathbf{b}} = \begin{bmatrix} b_1 + 10 \\ b_2 + 10 \end{bmatrix} = \mathbf{b} + \begin{bmatrix} 10 \\ 10 \end{bmatrix}$$

Write down $\hat{\mathbf{b}}$ in terms of the basis. Assume again that $\mathbf{a}_5 = \mathbf{e}_1$, and $\mathbf{a}_6 = \mathbf{e}_2$.

Hint: $\begin{bmatrix} 10 \\ 10 \end{bmatrix} = 10\mathbf{e}_1 + 10\mathbf{e}_2$.

3.10 Consider the following linear programming problem:

$$\text{maximize } z = c_1 x_1 + c_2 x_2 + c_3 x_3$$

subject to

$$\begin{bmatrix} a_{11} \\ a_{21} \end{bmatrix} x_1 + \begin{bmatrix} a_{12} \\ a_{22} \end{bmatrix} x_2 + \begin{bmatrix} a_{13} \\ a_{23} \end{bmatrix} x_3 + \begin{bmatrix} 1 \\ 0 \end{bmatrix} x_4 + \begin{bmatrix} 0 \\ 1 \end{bmatrix} x_5 = \begin{bmatrix} b_1 \\ b_2 \end{bmatrix}$$

$$x_1, \ldots, x_5 \geqslant 0$$

The optimal tableau follows:

c_j			c_1	c_2	c_3	c_4	c_5
c_j	Vectors Basis	$\mathbf{b}$	$\mathbf{a}_1$	$\mathbf{a}_2$	$\mathbf{a}_3$	$\mathbf{a}_4$	$\mathbf{a}_5$
c_3	$\mathbf{a}_3$	$\dfrac{3}{2}$	1	0	1	$\dfrac{1}{2}$	$-\dfrac{1}{2}$
c_2	$\mathbf{a}_2$	2	$\dfrac{1}{2}$	1	0	-1	2
	$z_j - c_j$	20	3	0	0	0	4

(a) Find the values of

$$\begin{bmatrix} a_{11} \\ a_{21} \end{bmatrix}, \begin{bmatrix} a_{12} \\ a_{22} \end{bmatrix}, \begin{bmatrix} a_{13} \\ a_{23} \end{bmatrix}, \quad \text{and} \quad \begin{bmatrix} b_1 \\ b_2 \end{bmatrix}.$$

(b) Find the values of c_1, c_2, c_3, c_4 and c_5.

REFERENCES

Daellenbach, H. G., and E. J. Bell. *User's Guide to Linear Programming.* Englewood Cliffs, N.J.: Prentice-Hall, 1970. Chapter 9 gives a cookbook treatment of the simplex method at an elementary level.

Fraser, J. Ronald. *Applied Linear Programming.* Englewood Cliffs, N.J.: Prentice-Hall, 1968. Chapter 4 of this text systematically traces the logic of a simple FORTRAN computer code for the simplex method. The treatment is easy to follow for the average reader.

Garvin, W. W. *Introduction to Linear Programming.* New York: McGraw-Hill, 1960. In general this book, though not a recent publication, provides a remarkably thorough treatment of all aspects of linear programming without requiring advanced mathematics. Chapters 2 and 3 develop the simplex method. Extensions to the simplex method are found in Chapter 11 (upperbounded variables), Chapter 13 (revised simplex method), and Chapter 14 (degeneracy). A good reference for the average reader.

Gass, Saul I, *Linear Programming*, 3rd Ed. New York: McGraw-Hill, 1969. A readable advanced text in linear programming, requiring expertise in matrix algebra.

Chapters 2 and 3 provide the development of the simplex method. Chapter 9 is a useful chapter dealing with additional computational techniques—the dual simplex method, decomposition of large-scale systems, and bounded variables in particular.

Hadley, G. *Linear Algebra*. Reading, Mass.: Addison Wesley, 1961. Sections 2-7 to 2-10 of this text give an excellent theoretical exposition of linear dependence and the concept of a basis.

Simmonard, M. *Linear Programming*. Englewood Cliffs, N.J.: Prentice-Hall, 1966. This is a high level book conceptually and mathematically. Only readers with expertise in mathematics should attempt it. Chapters 1–3 give the simplex method, and Chapter 4 introduces the revised simplex method. Specialized simplex algorithms like the dual simplex method and primal-dual algorithm are found in Chapter 6. Chapter 10 treats upper bounds and the decomposition of large-scale linear programs.

Wagner, Harvey M. *Principles of Operations Research*, 2nd Ed. Englewood Cliffs, N.J.: Prentice-Hall, 1975. The simplex method is introduced in Chapter 4 using the Gaussian elimination approach.

Many other specialized texts in operations research and linear programming exist. All of them (with the exception of only the most elementary) deal with the simplex method in one way or another. See the list of general operations research texts at end of Chapter 1 and the references to Chapter 2.

4

Duality
and
Postoptimal
Analysis

One of the features that greatly enhances linear programming as a decision-making tool is the ease and great scope of possible sensitivity analysis. This chapter studies the mathematical side of sensitivity analysis. We will first develop the theory, known as *duality*, upon which much of sensitivity analysis is based. For every linear programming problem there is another unique linear programming problem which has a special relationship to the first one. These two problems stand as a pair or *duals* of each other.

The second topic, *postoptimal analysis*, deals with the mechanical aspects of sensitivity analysis. We will study how the optimal solution reacts to changes in the input data. In particular, we will analyze how the optimal solution responds to changes in:

- the objective function coefficients,
- the RHS parameters, and
- the LHS coefficients.

Before proceeding to Section 4-5 you may wish to refer to Chapter 2, Section 2-9 where the concepts of sensitivity analysis were introduced graphically. This chapter assumes that you are familiar with the concepts of vectors and systems of linear equations, and that you have a thorough grasp of Chapter 3.

4-1 THE DUAL PROBLEM

The power generating problem was viewed in Chapter 2 as a problem of allocating scarce resources. Let us now look at this problem from an entirely different angle. The county council which is the largest customer of the power generating plant is considering making an offer to purchase the plant. In order to make such an offer they need to determine fair prices for the existing plant resources. For our purpose these resources can be viewed as the loading capacity available, the pulverizer capacity available, and the available capacity to emit smoke. (We shall for the moment neglect the "capacity" to emit sulfur and reintroduce it later on.)

Theoretically, the prices of resources are not necessarily related to their average or marginal costs, but rather to the revenues that they can produce. In our example these resources are used to produce steam. Therefore, the value of each resource depends on how much steam it will produce. Economics tells us that as long as the price offered for a resource is less than the *marginal revenue product* of the resource, i.e., the revenue produced by the last unit of the resource employed, the firm has no incentive to sell any of this resource. The marginal revenue products can also be viewed as the prices the firm should be willing to pay for additional amounts of scarce resources. In linear programming, these prices or marginal revenue products are called *imputed values* or *shadow prices*—imputed because they are not actual costs or prices, but the prices or values that can be inferred from the particular productive system in question.

The problem of finding these prices turns out to be another linear program. For our problem, rather than expressing these prices in monetary units, we shall express them in terms of steam equivalents. If we know the value of a unit of steam, then these steam equivalents can immediately be translated into monetary terms. Furthermore, since the original resource allocation problem is on a per hour basis, the prices of the resources will also be on the basis of a per hour use.

- Let w_1 be the steam that can be produced by using up 1 kg of smoke emission capacity.
- Let w_2 be the steam that can be produced by 1 ton of loading capacity.
- Let w_3 be the steam that can be produced by 1 hour of pulverizer capacity.

The objective of the problem is to find prices w_1, w_2, and w_3 that minimize the total cost to the council of acquiring the resources presently owned by the firm. The cost of acquiring the smoke capacity is $12w_1$ ($=$ quantity available $\times$ price), the cost of the loading capacity is $20w_2$ and the cost of the pulverizer capacity is $1w_3$. So the objective function is:

(4-1) $$\text{minimize } 12w_1 + 20w_2 + w_3$$

The prices that the firm is willing to accept depend on what the resources can do for it. The firm will insist on prices for the resources which give it a return that is at least equal to the return produced by each of the two activities, namely, burning coal A and burning coal B.

In burning 1 ton of coal A, 24 units of steam are produced. The resources required are 0.5 kg/hr of smoke emission capacity, 1 ton of loading capacity and 1/16 hr of pulverizer capacity. The council will pay $0.5w_1 + w_2 + (1/16)w_3$ per hour for these resources. However, since the firm can already make 24 units of steam from one ton of coal A, the amount the council has to be willing to pay (per hour) for these resources has to be at least equivalent to 24 units of steam, or

(4-2) $$0.5w_1 + w_2 + \tfrac{1}{16}w_3 \geqslant 24$$

Similarly, for coal B:

(4-3) $$w_1 + w_2 + \tfrac{1}{24}w_3 \geqslant 20$$

The prices must also be nonnegative:

(4-4) $$w_1, w_2, w_3 \geqslant 0$$

Let us write out this linear program again and compare it with problem (2-6) of Chapter 2 (without the sulfur constraint):

New problem: Pricing of resources	*Original problem: Allocation of resources*
minimize $Z = 12w_1 + 20w_2 + w_3$	maximize $z = 24x_1 + 20x_2$
subject to $\quad 0.5w_1 + w_2 + \tfrac{1}{16}w_3 \geqslant 24$	subject to $\quad 0.5x_1 + x_2 \leqslant 12$
(4-5) $\quad\quad w_1 + w_2 + \tfrac{1}{24}w_3 \geqslant 20$	(4-6) $\quad\quad x_1 + x_2 \leqslant 20$
$\quad\quad w_1, w_2, w_3 \geqslant 0$	$\quad\quad \tfrac{1}{16}x_1 + \tfrac{1}{24}x_2 \leqslant 1$
	$\quad\quad x_1, x_2 \geqslant 0$

How are problems (4-5) and (4-6) related?

DUALITY RELATION 1 (DR1)

a. Each constraint in one problem is associated with a variable in the other, and vice versa.

b. The LHS coefficients of each constraint of one problem are the same as the LHS coefficients of the corresponding variable of the other problem.

c. The RHS parameters of one problem are the objective function coefficients of the corresponding variables in the other problem, and vice versa.

d. One problem is a minimizing problem with $\geqslant$ constraints and nonnegative variables and the other is a maximizing problem with $\leqslant$ constraints and nonnegative variables.

Each problem is called the *dual* of the other problem. The relationship between them is two way: what applies from (4-5) to (4-6) also applies from (4-6) to (4-5). Some algebraic manipulations are needed to show this for part (d) of DR1. In the terminology of linear programming we call one problem the *primal* and the other problem the *dual*. It does not matter which problem is called the primal and which one is called the dual. Normally, we would only formulate from scratch one of the problems and the other would result from duality. The original problem is then referred to as the primal, the other is referred to as the dual. In this case, problem (4-6) is the primal, and problem (4-5) is the dual. (Note our convention to denote the value of the dual objective function by a capital Z in contrast to the value of the primal objective function which is denoted by lower case z.)

4-2 MORE ON DUALITY RELATIONS

Let us define *standard form problems* as follows:

1. A *standard form maximizing problem* is a linear program with all constraints as ⩽ inequalities and nonnegative variables.
2. A *standard form minimizing problem* is a linear program with all constraints as ⩾ inequalities and nonnegative variables.

The dual of a standard form maximizing problem is a standard form minimizing problem and vice versa. This is part (d) of DR1. If the primal is not in standard form, neither is the dual. Deviations from the standard form could mean that a problem has both ⩾ and ⩽ constraints or equality constraints and/or some non-positive or unrestricted variables. Fortunately, any nonstandard form problem can easily be converted to a standard form problem by some simple algebraic manipulations.

Let us demonstrate this with the original problem (2-6) from Chapter 2:

Original Primal

$$\text{maximize } z = 24x_1 + 20x_2$$

$$\text{subject to} \quad 0.5x_1 + x_2 \leqslant 12$$

$$x_1 + x_2 \leqslant 20$$

(4-7)

$$\tfrac{1}{16}x_1 + \tfrac{1}{24}x_2 \leqslant 1$$

$$1200x_1 - 800x_2 \geqslant 0$$

$$x_1, x_2 \geqslant 0$$

This problem is not in standard form. Since the objective function is maximized, all constraints should be ⩽ inequalities. The sulfur constraint is, however, a ⩾ inequality. The problem can easily be converted to a standard form by multiplying the sulfur constraint through by −1.

Standardized Primal

$$\text{maximize } z = 24x_1 + 20x_2$$

$$\text{subject to} \quad 0.5x_1 + x_2 \leqslant 12 \quad (w_1)$$

$$x_1 + x_2 \leqslant 20 \quad (w_2)$$

$$\tfrac{1}{16}x_1 + \tfrac{1}{24}x_2 \leqslant 1 \quad (w_3)$$

$$-1200x_1 + 800x_2 \leqslant -0 \quad (\hat{w}_4)$$

$$x_1, x_2 \geqslant 0$$

associated dual variable

The dual associated with this standardized primal is:

Standardized Dual

minimize $Z = 12w_1 + 20w_2 + w_3 - 0\hat{w}_4$

subject to $0.5w_1 + w_2 + \frac{1}{16}w_3 - 1200\hat{w}_4 \geqslant 24$

$w_1 + w_2 + \frac{1}{24}w_3 + 800\hat{w}_4 \geqslant 20$

$w_1, w_2, w_3, \hat{w}_4 \geqslant 0$

Compare now the original primal with the standardized dual. Properties (b) and (c) of DR1 are not satisfied for those coefficients associated with the sulfur constraint and $\hat{w}_4$. The standardized dual is thus not the proper dual of the original problem. The proper dual can, however, easily be obtained by reversing the standardization operation used to get the standardized primal. We multiply the coefficients of $\hat{w}_4$ through by -1 and define a new variable w_4 which is the negative of $\hat{w}_4$. This yields the

Dual of the Original Primal

minimize $Z = 12w_1 + 20w_2 + w_3 + 0w_4$

subject to $0.5w_1 + w_2 + \frac{1}{16}w_3 + 1200w_4 \geqslant 24$

(4-8) $\qquad w_1 + w_2 + \frac{1}{24}w_3 - 800w_4 \geqslant 20$

$w_1, w_2, w_3 \geqslant 0$

$w_4 \leqslant 0$

We now see that properties (b) and (c) of DR1 are satisfied. But we also note that the new dual variable w_4 is restricted to be nonpositive (since $\hat{w}_4$ was nonnegative):

DUALITY RELATION 2 (DR2)

If the direction of the inequality constraint in one problem deviates from the standard form, the corresponding variable in the other problem is restricted to be nonpositive and vice versa.

If the primal has equality constraints, we resort to the following trick for each such constraint. We replace the equality by two inequalities of opposite direction, i.e., one is a $\leqslant$ inequality, the other a $\geqslant$ inequality. The LHS coefficients and the RHS parameter are the same as in the original constraint. Since both have to be satisfied simultaneously, the feasible region will be identical to the original constraint. We have just seen how to handle this new problem, which has mixed inequality constraints. The dual will have two dual variables, say w_i^+ and w_i^-, one of which is restricted to be nonnegative and the other to be nonpositive. Both variables have, however, exactly the same coefficients in the dual. We now undo the trick of substituting two inequality constraints for the equality constraint. We define a new variable which can assume both nonnegative and nonpositive values, i.e., which is unrestricted in sign, and which replaces $w_i{}^+$ if nonnegative and $w_i{}^-$ if nonpositive.

DUALITY RELATION 3 (DR3)

If a constraint in the one problem is a strict equality, then the corresponding variable in the other problem has no sign restriction and vice versa.

You will be asked to test your understanding of DR2 and DR3 in problem 4.1 at the end of this chapter.

The duality relations include a number of theorems regarding the primal and dual problems. For the sake of stating these theorems, we will define the primal to be a standard form maximizing problem and the dual to be a standard form minimizing problem.

DUALITY RELATION 4 (DR4)

The objective function value of any feasible solution to the primal will be less than or equal to the objective function value of every feasible solution to the dual, i.e., $z \leqslant Z$.

DUALITY RELATION 5: DUALITY THEOREM (DR5)

If the primal and dual both have feasible solutions, then both have finite optimal solutions, and the optimal values of the objective functions of the two problems are equal, i.e., $z^* = Z^*$.

DUALITY RELATION 6: COMPLEMENTARY SLACKNESS THEOREM (DR6)

If a constraint of either problem is slack at any optimal solution to that problem, then in the other problem, the variable associated with that constraint is zero at every optimal solution. If a variable of either problem at an optimal solution is nonzero, then in the other problem the constraint associated with that variable is binding at every optimal solution.

We will use problems (4-7) and (4-8) to illustrate some of these ideas. From DR4 we get that for any feasible solutions $(x_1{}', x_2{}')$ to the primal and $(w_1{}', w_2{}', w_3{}', w_4{}')$

to the dual

$$z' = 24x_1' + 20x_2' \leqslant Z' = 12w_1' + 20w_2' + w_3' + 0w_4'$$

For example, let $(x_1', x_2') = (10, 4)$ and $(w_1', w_2', w_3', w_4') = (6, 1, 640, -0.01)$, which are feasible.   Then

$$z' = 240 + 80 = 320 < Z' = 72 + 20 + 640 = 732$$

From the way the dual was constructed it seems reasonable that no resource values that give a total resource valuation less than the total steam production would be feasible; otherwise the notion of marginal revenue product would be contradicted. In fact, we would expect that the optimal imputed values would equate total resource valuation and total steam production exactly.   This is true.   The optimal solution to the primal is $x_1 = 12$, $x_2 = 6$, and the optimal solution to the dual is $w_1 = 6$, $w_2 = 0$, $w_3 = 336$, $w_4 = 0$ (the reader who wishes to confirm this result can do so by the simplex method; we will establish it by other methods shortly), and

$$z^* = 24(12) + 20(6) = 408 = Z^* = 12(6) + 1(336)$$

This confirms the second part of the duality theorem (DR5).   If $w_1 = 6, w_3 = 336$ were not optimal, DR4 would be contradicted.

Next, let us apply the complementary slackness theorem (DR6):

Optimal Primal Solution		*Optimal Dual Solution*
$x_1 = 12 > 0$	implies	constraint 1 binding
$x_2 = 6 > 0$	implies	constraint 2 binding
constraint 2 is slack	implies	$w_2 = 0$
constraint 4 is slack	implies	$w_4 = 0$

With this information, problem (4-8) is now reduced to

$$\text{minimize } Z = 12w_1 + w_3$$
$$\text{subject to} \quad 0.5w_1 + \tfrac{1}{16}w_3 = 24$$
$$w_1 + \tfrac{1}{24}w_3 = 20$$
$$w_1, w_3 \geqslant 0$$

The two constraints define a unique solution: $w_1 = 6, w_3 = 336$; and $Z^* = 408$, as stated previously.

4-3   FURTHER INTERPRETATION OF THE DUAL PROBLEM

We have already noted in Section 4-2 that there is a close relationship between the primal constraints and the dual variables.   In fact, we interpreted the dual variables in problem (4-5) as imputed values (i.e., the marginal revenue product, where the constraint refers to a resource) of each of the primal constraints.   This concept can be generalized and applies to other primal problems.

INTERPRETATION OF THE OPTIMAL VALUES OF DUAL VARIABLES

The optimal value of a dual variable associated with a particular primal constraint gives the marginal change (increase, if positive, or decrease, if negative) in the optimal value of the primal objective function for a marginal increase in the RHS parameter of that constraint.

Note that this does not mean that we can always find an intuitively appealing interpretation of the dual variable. The dual variable, w_4, associated with the sulfur constraint is an example. The manner in which the constraint was constructed renders an appealing interpretation impossible.

4-4 THE DUAL VARIABLES, $(z_j - c_j)$, AND THE SIMPLEX MULTIPLIERS

In Section 3-5 we saw that each z_j gives the contribution to the objective function of the equivalent vector to $\mathbf{a}_j$—constructed in terms of the basis. The value this basis gives to the bundle of resources represented by $\mathbf{a}_j$ is z_j. At the optimal solution the values of z_j are the contributions imputed by the optimal basis—they are thus optimal valuations the system gives to the $\mathbf{a}_j$ vectors.

Let us consider in particular the vector $\mathbf{a}_3$, the slack vector of constraint 1. At the optimal tableau, z_3 is the optimal contribution, or valuation, of a unit level of $\mathbf{a}_3$. But a unit level of $\mathbf{a}_3$ is simply a unit of smoke emission capacity, and the valuation of $\mathbf{a}_3$ is the valuation on one unit of smoke emission capacity. However, coming from another direction, we have already defined the value of a unit of smoke emission capacity as w_1. So we can equate the optimal value of w_1 and the valuation z_3 in the optimal simplex tableau. The same reasoning applies to w_2 and z_4, w_3 and z_5, and w_4 and z_7. We choose z_7 rather than z_6 to give the value of w_4 because $\mathbf{a}_6$ represents the negative of a unit of the RHS of constraint 4 and so z_6 is the negative of w_4.

Hence, we can find the optimal values of the dual variables from the final simplex tableau as follows:

z_j VALUES AND OPTIMAL DUAL VARIABLES:

The z_j value of the slack or artificial vector of each constraint in the optimal simplex tableau of the primal gives the optimal value of the dual variable associated with that constraint.

Since the c_j values of the slack and artificial vectors in the primal objective function are all zero, the z_j values are equal to the $(z_j - c_j)$ values. For the dual

Table 4-1. *Initial and Final Simplex Tableaux.*

Tableau	Objective Function (c_j)			24	20	0	0	0	0	0
	c_j \ Basis		**b**	$\mathbf{a}_1$	$\mathbf{a}_2$	$\mathbf{a}_3$	$\mathbf{a}_4$	$\mathbf{a}_5$	$\mathbf{a}_6$	$\mathbf{a}_7$
Initial	0	$\mathbf{a}_3$	12	$\frac{1}{2}$	1	1	0	0	0	0
	0	$\mathbf{a}_4$	20	1	1	0	1	0	0	0
	0	$\mathbf{a}_5$	1	$\frac{1}{16}$	$\frac{1}{24}$	0	0	1	0	0
	0	$\mathbf{a}_7$	0	1200	-800	0	0	0	-1	1
	$z_j - c_j$		0	-24	-20	0	0	0	0	0
Final	20	$\mathbf{a}_2$	6	0	1	$\frac{3}{2}$	0	-12	0	0
	0	$\mathbf{a}_4$	2	0	0	$-\frac{1}{2}$	1	-12	0	0
	0	$\mathbf{a}_6$	9600	0	0	-2400	0	38400	1	-1
	24	$\mathbf{a}_1$	12	1	0	-1	0	24	0	0
	$z_j - c_j$		408	0	0	6	0	336	0	0

problem in (4-8) we can read off the optimal simplex tableau for the primal problem in Table 4-1 as

$$w_1 = z_3 = 6$$
$$w_2 = z_4 = 0$$
$$w_3 = z_5 = 336$$
$$w_4 = z_7 = 0$$

This analysis also indicates how the numbers shown under the heading, *IMPUTED VALUE*, of the computer printout (Figure 2-7 in Chapter 2) were derived.

If we consider a vector $\mathbf{a}_j$, other than the slack or artificial vectors, the corresponding z_j at the optimal solution gives the valuation of a more complex bundle of resources. For example, the optimal valuation of the vector $\mathbf{a}_1$ (=burning 1 ton of coal A) is the sum of the values of the individual resources involved in burning 1 ton of coal A (=0.5 kg smoke emission, 1 ton of loading capacity, 1/16 hr of pulverizer capacity, and 1200 units of sulfur emission). The optimal valuation of $\mathbf{a}_1$ is $z_1 = 24$.

The optimal valuation of the individual resources is

$$0.5w_1 + 1w_2 + \tfrac{1}{16}w_3 + 1200w_4 =$$
$$0.5(6) + 1(0) + \tfrac{1}{16}(336) + 1200(0) = 24$$

Thus we have the relationship:

$$z_1 = 0.5w_1 + 1w_2 + \tfrac{1}{16}w_3 + 1200w_4$$

Verify that $z_2 = 1w_1 + 1w_2 + (1/24)\,w_3 - 800w_4$.

Let us compare these results with the dual (4-8). The value of the left-hand-side of the first constraint of (4-8) at the optimal solution is z_1. In general, z_j is the value of the left-hand-side of the jth dual constraint. Since the RHS parameter of the jth dual constraint is c_j, the optimal values of the slack variables of the dual gives us the negative of the optimal $(z_j - c_j)$ values. Furthermore, for all basic variables at the primal optimum $(z_j - c_j) = 0$. Therefore, the slack variables of the dual constraints associated with the optimal basic primal variables are zero. Thus, these constraints are binding. But this is just one of the complementary slackness conditions.

Can the dual equations be used to provide the $(z_j - c_j)$ values for nonoptimal primal tableaux? Let us apply the complementary slackness conditions for the basis $(\mathbf{a}_3, \mathbf{a}_4, \mathbf{a}_5, \mathbf{a}_1)$ shown in the first tableau of Table 3-6. We can conclude that the first dual constraint is binding because $x_1 > 0$; similarly, $w_1 = w_2 = w_3 = 0$ because the first three primal constraints are slack. The dual (4-8) thus reduces to $1200w_4 = 24$ or $w_4 = 1/50$. Using $w_4 = 1/50$ in the second equation of (4-8), we obtain a value of the left-hand side of $-800\,(1/50)$ which is also the value of z_2 in Table 3-6, and the difference between the left-hand-side value and the RHS parameter of $(-16 - 20) = -36$ which is the $(z_2 - c_2)$ value in Table 3-6. We again see that the value of the left-hand side of the dual constraint is the z_j of the corresponding primal variable and the RHS parameter is c_j. Thus, the difference between the value of the left-hand-side and the RHS parameter is $(z_j - c_j)$. However, the w_i are not a feasible solution to the dual. Rather than call them dual variables in this context, we call them *simplex multipliers*. At the optimal solution, with all $z_j \geqslant c_j$, the simplex multipliers become feasible and, at the same time, the optimal values for the dual variables.

To summarize, for any basic feasible solution of the primal, the simplex multipliers can be found by applying the complementary slackness conditions to the dual, i.e., by setting $z_j = c_j$ for all basic variables. All the other $(z_j - c_j)$ values can then be computed by substituting the simplex multipliers into the dual constraints.

4-5 POSTOPTIMAL ANALYSIS OF OBJECTIVE FUNCTION COEFFICIENTS

Most queries of postoptimal analysis can be readily answered on the basis of the information contained in the optimal simplex tableau. For this analysis we shall again use the original power generating problem, whose initial and final simplex tableaux are summarized in Table 4-1.

A change in the coefficients of the objective function, viewed in terms of a representation in solution space, is equivalent to a change in the slope of the objective function line (or hyperplane in more than two dimensions). If the slope is tilted sufficiently in one or another direction, the optimal solution may shift to another extreme point of the feasible region. Changes in the objective function coefficients may thus affect the optimality of the current solution. However, they can never affect the feasibility of this solution. In terms of the optimal simplex tableau this means that none of the entries are affected except some or all of the $(z_j - c_j)$ values.

The most common test of sensitivity of the objective function involves finding the range of values within which each objective function coefficient can lie without affecting the optimality of the solution. Thus we allow only that coefficient to change; all other input coefficients and parameters must be unchanged. It is important to remember that assumption when using this analysis.

Let us look at c_3. A change in c_3 does not alter any of the c_j values associated with the basic vectors because $\mathbf{a}_3$ is nonbasic. So none of the z_j values are changed, nor are any of the $(z_j - c_j)$ values, except $(z_3 - c_3)$ through the change in c_3. Hence, provided the change in c_3 does not violate $(z_3 - c_3) \geqslant 0$, the present solution remains optimal. Since $z_3 = 6$, $(z_3 - c_3) \geqslant 0$ if $c_3 \leqslant 6$. The range for c_3 is thus $-\infty \leqslant c_3 \leqslant 6$.

Next consider c_1. This time the corresponding vector, $\mathbf{a}_1$, is basic. A change in c_1 will potentially affect all the z_j and the $(z_j - c_j)$ values except the $(z_j - c_j)$ values for basic vectors. (These are always zero.) Let us find the range of c_1 that keeps $(z_j - c_j) \geqslant 0$ for all nonbasic vectors (except $(z_7 - c_7)$ because $\mathbf{a}_7$ is an artificial vector):

(4-9)

(a) $(z_3 - c_3)$

From Table 4-1 we see that as c_1 changes, z_3 changes also:

$$z_3 = 20(\tfrac{3}{2}) + 0 - (\tfrac{1}{2}) + 0(-2400) + c_1(-1) = 30 - c_1$$

For $(z_3 - c_3) \geqslant 0$ we need

$$(30 - c_1) - 0 \geqslant 0$$

or
$$c_1 \leqslant 30$$

(b) $(z_5 - c_5)$

As c_1 changes, z_5 becomes:

$$z_5 = 20(-12) + 0(-12) + 0(38400) + c_1(24) = -240 + 24c_1$$

For $(z_5 - c_5) \geqslant 0$ we need

$$(24c_1 - 240) - 0 \geqslant 0$$

or
$$c_1 \geqslant 10$$

For the current solution to remain optimal, c_1 has to satisfy both of these conditions, i.e., $(z_j - c_j)$ has to be nonnegative for all nonbasic variables. This will be so if c_1 lies in the range

(4-10) $10 \leqslant c_1 \leqslant 30$

This case was studied graphically in Section 2-9.

The interpretation of expression (4-10) is: provided that the steam output of coal A falls within the range of 10,000 to 30,000 lbs/ton, with all other coefficients or parameters unchanged, the solution in Table 4-1 remains optimal. This range is very large. It is unlikely that the steam output would ever go outside it. Since there could have been measurement errors when this coefficient was determined (or slight variation from load to load), it is useful to know the range of acceptable variations.

You should verify that similar analysis yields the following ranges for the remaining objective function coefficients, each taken by itself

$$16 \leqslant c_2 \leqslant 48$$

$$-\infty \leqslant c_4 \leqslant 12$$

$$-\infty \leqslant c_5 \leqslant 336$$

$$-\tfrac{7}{800} \leqslant c_6 \leqslant \tfrac{1}{400}$$

Looking at these ranges we conclude that the optimal solution is very insensitive to realistic changes in any one of the c_j coefficients—a comforting thought!

Table 4-2. *Solution of Postoptimal Change to Objective Function.*

c_j	New c_j / Vectors / Basis	b	$\mathbf{a}_1$	$\mathbf{a}_2$	$\mathbf{a}_3$	$\mathbf{a}_4$	$\mathbf{a}_5$	$\mathbf{a}_6$	$\mathbf{a}_7$
			28	18	0	0	0	0	0
18	$\mathbf{a}_2$	6	0	1	$\frac{3}{2}$	0	-12	0	0
0	$\mathbf{a}_4$	2	0	0	$-\frac{1}{2}$	1	-12	0	0
0	$\mathbf{a}_6$	9600	0	0	-2400	0	38400	1	-1
28	$\mathbf{a}_1$	12	1	0	-1	0	24	0	0
Adjusted $z_j - c_j$		444	0	0	-1	0	456	0	0
0	$\mathbf{a}_3$	4	0	$\frac{2}{3}$	1	0	-8	0	0
0	$\mathbf{a}_4$	4	0	$\frac{1}{3}$	0	1	-16	0	0
0	$\mathbf{a}_6$	19200	0	1600	0	0	19200	1	-1
28	$\mathbf{a}_1$	16	1	$\frac{2}{3}$	0	0	16	0	0
$z_j - c_j$		448	0	$\frac{2}{3}$	0	0	448	0	0

Next, let us look at simultaneous changes in more than one objective function coefficient. The engineers discovered a substantial error in the measurement of the steam produced by both coal A and coal B. The true coefficients are $c_1 = 28$ and $c_2 = 18$. Is the current solution in Table 4-1 still optimal?

It is not possible to use the ranges of values found for each coefficient individually, since these ranges require that all other input data including other objective function coefficients remain unchanged. We can, however, use similar reasoning as before. Since $\mathbf{a}_1$ and $\mathbf{a}_2$ are both basic vectors, some of the $(z_j - c_j)$ values for nonbasic vectors may change.

For the new values of c_1 and c_2 we obtain

$$z_3 \quad = 18(\tfrac{3}{2}) + 0(-\tfrac{1}{2}) + 0(-2400) + 28(-1) = -1$$

and $\quad z_3 - c_3 = -1$

$$z_5 \quad = 18 - (12) + 0(-12) + 0(38400) + 28(24) = 456$$

and $\quad z_5 - c_5 = 456$

$$z_0 = 18(6) + 0(2) + 0(9600) + 28(12) = 444$$

Since one of the new $(z_j - c_j)$ values is negative, namely, $(z_3 - c_3) = -1$, the basis of Table 4-1 is no longer optimal. To find the new optimal solution we insert the new c_j and $(z_j - c_j)$ values and then apply the simplex method. This is shown in Table 4-2. One iteration is needed to find the new optimal solution: $x_1 = 16$, $x_2 = 0$, $x_3 = 4$, $x_4 = 4$, $x_5 = 0$, $x_6 = 19200$, and $z = 448$.

4-6 PARAMETRIC PROGRAMMING OF OBJECTIVE FUNCTIONS

In *parametric programming* of the objective function we let some or all objective function coefficients change continuously over some range and trace the sequence of optimal solutions so obtained.

For example, if we consider the problem of varying c_1 on its own from zero to ∞, we form the following objective function involving the parameter, θ.

(4-11) $\qquad$ maximize $z = 24\theta x_1 + 20x_2, \qquad 0 \leqslant \theta \leqslant \infty$

Had we varied c_1 and c_2 together, the objective function would have been

(4-12) $\qquad$ maximize $z = \theta(24x_1 + 20x_2), \qquad 0 \leqslant \theta \leqslant \infty$

Note that in (4-12) the relative proportions of c_1 and c_2 remain constant at 24 and 20. This case is of no interest since it will not vary the slope of the objective function.

We will perform an example of parametric programming using (4-11). Starting at the tableau in Table 4-1, we find the optimal basic solution for $\theta = 0$, then increase θ to infinity, noting the changes of basis and the values of θ at which they occur. The sequences of simplex tableaux are given in Table 4-3. (We omitted $\mathbf{a}_7$ from the table because, being an artificial vector, it adds nothing to the analysis.)

Table 4-3. *Parametric Programming of c_1.*

	c_j		24θ	20	0	0	0	0
c_j	Basis	b	a_1	a_2	a_3	a_4	a_5	a_6
20	a_2	9	0	1	$\frac{3}{4}$	0	0	$\frac{1}{3200}$
0	a_4	5	0	0	$-\frac{5}{4}$	1	0	$\frac{1}{3200}$
0	a_5	$\frac{1}{4}$	0	0	$\frac{1}{16}$	0	1	$\frac{1}{38400}$
24θ	a_1	6	1	0	$\frac{1}{2}$	0	0	$-\frac{1}{1600}$
	$z_j - c_j$	$(180+144\theta)$	0	0	$(15+12\theta)$	0	0	$\frac{1}{160}-\frac{3\theta}{200}$
20	a_2	6	0	1	$\frac{3}{2}$	0	-12	0
0	a_4	2	0	0	$-\frac{1}{2}$	1	-12	0
0	a_6	9600	0	0	-2400	0	38400	1
24θ	a_1	12	1	0	-1	0	24	0
	$z_j - c_j$	$(120+288\theta)$	0	0	$(30-24\theta)$	0	$(-240+576\theta)$	0
0	a_3	4	0	$\frac{2}{3}$	1	0	-8	0
0	a_4	4	0	$\frac{1}{3}$	0	1	-16	0
0	a_6	19200	0	1600	0	0	19200	1
24θ	a_1	16	1	$\frac{2}{3}$	0	0	16	0
	$z_j - c_j$	3840θ	0	160θ	0	0	3840	0

$0 \leqslant \theta \leqslant \dfrac{5}{12}$

$\dfrac{5}{12} \leqslant \theta \leqslant \dfrac{5}{4}$

$\theta \geqslant \dfrac{5}{4}$

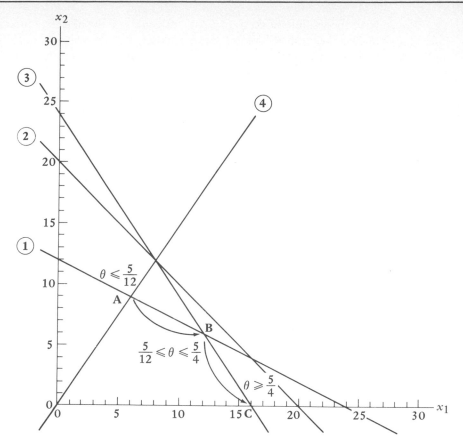

Figure 4-1. *Parametric programming on* c_1.

Table 4-4. *Results of the Parametric Programming on* c_1.

Variable	$0 \leqslant \theta \leqslant \dfrac{5}{12}$	$\dfrac{5}{12} \leqslant \theta \leqslant \dfrac{5}{4}$	$\dfrac{5}{4} \leqslant \theta \leqslant \infty$
	$0 \leqslant c_1 \leqslant 10$	$10 \leqslant c_1 \leqslant 30$	$30 \leqslant c_1 \leqslant \infty$
x_1	6	12	16
x_2	9	6	0
x_3	0	0	4
x_4	5	2	4
x_5	1/4	0	0
x_6	0	9600	19200

We can trace these solutions on Figure 4-1. When $\theta = 0$ the objective function line is horizontal, so the optimal solution occurs at point A and remains there as long as $\theta \leqslant \frac{5}{12}$. At $\theta = \frac{5}{12}$ which implies $c_1 = 10$ the basis changes. The optimal solution occurs at point B for $\frac{5}{12} \leqslant \theta \leqslant \frac{5}{4}$. Another change of basis occurs at $\theta = \frac{5}{4}$ or $c_1 = 30$ and the optimal solution remains at point C because at that basis, θ can then be increased indefinitely. Table 4-4 lists the set of optimal solutions. For example, if $c_1 = 45$, the optimal solution is $x_1 = 16$, $x_3 = 4$, $x_4 = 4$, $x_6 = 19200$.

4-7 POSTOPTIMAL ANALYSIS OF RHS PARAMETERS

In Section 3-3 we saw how a basic feasible solution is a representation of the vector **b** (the vector made up of the RHS parameters of the constraints) in terms of basic vectors. If any of the RHS parameters change, then this representation must also change.

To illustrate some of these ideas let us use the reduced version of the power generating problem so that we can have recourse to graphical reasoning. Only the smoke and pulverizer constraints are retained and the problem is

$$\text{maximize } 24x_1 + 20x_2 + 0x_3 + 0x_4$$

$$\text{subject to } 0.5x_1 + x_2 + x_3 \qquad = 12 \text{ (smoke)}$$

$$\tfrac{1}{16}x_1 + \tfrac{1}{24}x_2 \qquad + x_4 = 1 \text{ (pulverizer)}$$

$$x_1, x_2, x_3, x_4 \geqslant 0$$

Or in vector notation:

$$\text{maximize } 24x_1 + 20x_2 + 0x_3 + 0x_4$$

$$\text{subject to } \begin{bmatrix} 0.5 \\ 1/16 \end{bmatrix} x_1 + \begin{bmatrix} 1 \\ 1/24 \end{bmatrix} x_2 + \begin{bmatrix} 1 \\ 0 \end{bmatrix} x_3 + \begin{bmatrix} 0 \\ 1 \end{bmatrix} x_4 = \begin{bmatrix} 12 \\ 1 \end{bmatrix}$$

$$\quad\;\; \underset{\mathbf{a}_1}{\uparrow} \qquad\quad \underset{\mathbf{a}_2}{\uparrow} \qquad \underset{\mathbf{a}_3}{\uparrow} \qquad \underset{\mathbf{a}_4}{\uparrow} \qquad \underset{\mathbf{b}}{\uparrow}$$

$$x_1, \dots, x_4 \geqslant 0$$

When $\mathbf{b} = \begin{bmatrix} 12 \\ 1 \end{bmatrix}$, the optimal basic solution is $x_1 = 12$, $x_2 = 6$, and the representation of **b** in terms of the basic vectors $\mathbf{a}_1$ and $\mathbf{a}_2$ is $\mathbf{b} = 12\mathbf{a}_1 + 6\mathbf{a}_2$. This is shown graphically in requirement space in Figure 4-2.

Let the RHS parameter of the smoke constraint increase from 12 to $b_1 > 12$. The new vector $\mathbf{b} = \begin{bmatrix} b_1 \\ 1 \end{bmatrix}$ is tilted to the right. When $b_1 = 24$, it falls along the same line as the vector $\mathbf{a}_2$, i.e., **b** becomes *colinear* with $\mathbf{a}_2$, and its representation in terms of the current basis $(\mathbf{a}_1, \mathbf{a}_2)$ is $\mathbf{b} = 0\mathbf{a}_1 + 24\mathbf{a}_2$. As b_1 increases, x_1 decreases, and x_2 increases. If b_1 increases beyond 24, the vector **b** moves further to the right,

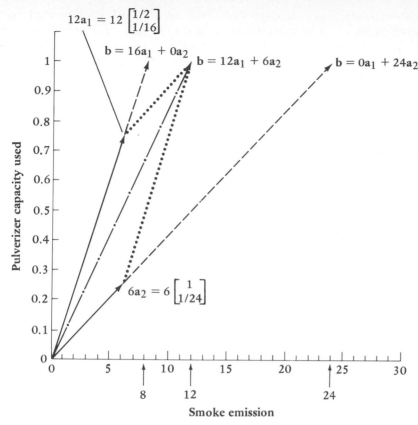

Figure 4-2. *Optimal solution of reduced problem in requirement space.*

and its representation in terms of the current basis requires x_1 to be negative. The solution ceases to be a feasible basic solution. A change of basis is required to obtain a feasible solution. Similarly, by decreasing the RHS parameter of the smoke constraint from 12 to 8, the new vector $\mathbf{b} = \begin{bmatrix} 8 \\ 1 \end{bmatrix}$ is colinear to $\mathbf{a}_1$, and its representation in terms of the current basis is $\mathbf{b} = 16\mathbf{a}_1 + 0\mathbf{a}_2$. Any further decrease causes the basis $(\mathbf{a}_1, \mathbf{a}_2)$ to be infeasible.

Hence, as long as the RHS parameter of the smoke constraint varies between 8 and 24, the basis $(\mathbf{a}_1, \mathbf{a}_2)$ remains feasible for the reduced problem. Furthermore, since a change in a RHS parameter does not affect the $(z_j - c_j)$ values, the present basis is also optimal as long as it remains feasible. However, a change in the RHS parameter always alters the representation of $\mathbf{b}$ in terms of the current basis and, therefore, alters the values of the optimal basic variables even if no change of basis occurs. This is in contrast to changes in an objective function coefficient where the values of the variables only change if optimality is affected and another basis becomes optimal.

After this short motivation, let us now look into the mathematics of finding, for each RHS parameter taken individually, the range of values for which the current basis remains optimal—all other input data remaining the same. The approach is similar to the one used in Section 4-4 to show the equivalence of the dual variables and the $(z_j - c_j)$ values of slack variables.

Consider the full version of the power generating problem. In particular, consider the pulverizer capacity constraint:

$$(4\text{-}15) \qquad \tfrac{1}{16}x_1 + \tfrac{1}{24}x_2 + x_5 = 1$$

At the optimal solution, $x_5 = 0$, so (4-15) reduces to

$$(4\text{-}16) \qquad \tfrac{1}{16}x_1 + \tfrac{1}{24}x_2 = 1$$

Let us increase the pulverizer capacity by Δ, and study its effect on the values of the optimal solution. (4-16) now becomes

$$(4\text{-}17) \qquad \tfrac{1}{16}x_1 + \tfrac{1}{24}x_2 = 1 + \Delta$$

If we let $\hat{b}_3 = b_3 + \Delta$, where $\hat{b}_3$ is the RHS parameter of the pulverizer constraint, then we obtain the new RHS

$$\hat{\mathbf{b}} = \mathbf{b} + \Delta \mathbf{e}_3 = \begin{bmatrix} 12 \\ 20 \\ 1 \\ 0 \end{bmatrix} + \Delta \begin{bmatrix} 0 \\ 0 \\ 1 \\ 0 \end{bmatrix}$$

(where $\mathbf{e}_3$ is a unit vector).

But the slack vector of the pulverizer constraint $\mathbf{a}_5$ is the vector $\mathbf{e}_3$. Hence, the new RHS can be rewritten as

$$(4\text{-}18) \qquad \hat{\mathbf{b}} = \mathbf{b} + \Delta \mathbf{a}_5$$

We want to know the new optimal solution for this new RHS vector $\hat{\mathbf{b}}$, i.e., we want the representation of $\hat{\mathbf{b}}$ in terms of the optimal basis. From the final tableau in Table 4-1 we have $x_2 = 6$, $x_4 = 2$, $x_6 = 9600$, and $x_1 = 12$, or

$$(4\text{-}19) \qquad \mathbf{b} = 6\mathbf{a}_2 + 2\mathbf{a}_4 + 9600\mathbf{a}_6 + 12\mathbf{a}_1$$

By definition of the elements in column $\mathbf{a}_5$ of the final tableau, we can represent $\mathbf{a}_5$ in terms of the optimal basis as

$$(4\text{-}20) \qquad \mathbf{a}_5 = -12\mathbf{a}_2 - 12\mathbf{a}_4 + 38400\mathbf{a}_6 + 24\mathbf{a}_1$$

Refer to Section 3-7 if you are uncertain about (4-19) and (4-20). Using (4-19) and (4-20), we can expand equation (4-18) to

$$(4\text{-}21) \quad \hat{\mathbf{b}} = \underbrace{(6 - 12\Delta)\mathbf{a}_2}_{x_2} + \underbrace{(2 - 12\Delta)\mathbf{a}_4}_{x_4} + \underbrace{(9600 + 38400\Delta)\mathbf{a}_6}_{x_6} + \underbrace{(12 + 24\Delta)\mathbf{a}_1}_{x_1}$$

If the solution in (4-21) is a feasible solution, it is also the optimal solution, since the only numbers changed in the final tableau of Table 4-1 are those in the

b column. What values of Δ will give a feasible solution to equation (4-21)? By definition, they must satisfy the nonnegativity conditions on all variables—

(4-22)

$$x_2 = 6 - 12\Delta \geqslant 0 \qquad \text{or} \qquad \Delta \leqslant \tfrac{6}{12} = \tfrac{1}{2}$$

$$x_4 = 2 - 12\Delta \geqslant 0 \qquad \text{or} \qquad \Delta \leqslant \tfrac{2}{12} = \tfrac{1}{6}$$

$$x_6 = 9600 + 38400\Delta \geqslant 0 \qquad \text{or} \qquad \Delta \geqslant -\tfrac{9600}{38400} = -\tfrac{1}{4}$$

$$x_1 = 12 + 24\Delta \geqslant 0 \qquad \text{or} \qquad \Delta \geqslant -\tfrac{12}{24} = -\tfrac{1}{2}$$

Let Δ^- be the maximum decrease in b_3 and Δ^+ be the maximum increase in b_3 for the solution to still be feasible. Then

(4-23)

$$\Delta^- = \text{minimum}(\tfrac{1}{4}, \tfrac{1}{2}) = \tfrac{1}{4}$$

$$\Delta^+ = \text{minimum}(\tfrac{1}{2}, \tfrac{1}{6}) = \tfrac{1}{6}$$

Since the existing value of the RHS parameter b_3 is 1, it can lie anywhere between 3/4 and 7/6 (all other parameters unchanged), and the corresponding solution will still be feasible and optimal.

Formalizing this procedure we get the following rules for determining the range within which each RHS parameter can be varied individually without violating the feasibility of the current optimal basis, all other input data remaining unchanged.

RANGES FOR RHS PARAMETERS

In the optimal simplex tableau let β_i denote the ith element in the **b** column, and let γ_i be the ith element of the column corresponding to the slack or artificial vector for constraint k. Then

(4-24) Maximum increase in RHS parameter of constraint k $= \begin{cases} \text{minimum}\,(-\beta_i/\gamma_i) & \text{for all } \gamma_i < 0 \\ +\infty \text{ if all } \gamma_i \geqslant 0 \end{cases}$

(4-25) Maximum decrease in RHS parameter of constraint k $= \begin{cases} \text{minimum}\,(\beta_i/\gamma_i) & \text{for all } \gamma_i > 0 \\ +\infty \text{ if all } \gamma_i \leqslant 0 \end{cases}$

You should verify that if $\gamma_i \geqslant 0$, then the range for the RHS parameter is open from above. Whereas, if $\gamma_i \leqslant 0$, then this range is open from below. Table 4-5 shows the ranges derived from the optimal simplex tableau in Table 4-1.

Expression (4-21) also allows us to determine the new values of the basic variables for a change in the RHS parameter b_3 within its permissible range. For example, assume that the pulverizer capacity can be increased by 10 percent, i.e., the pulverizer rate for coal A increases to 17.6 tons and the rate for coal B to 26.4 tons per hour. The pulverizer constraint changes to

$$\tfrac{1}{17.6}x_1 + \tfrac{1}{26.4}x_2 \leqslant 1$$

Table 4-5. *Ranges on RHS Parameters at Optimal Solution.*

Constraint	Original RHS	Maximum Decrease	Maximum Increase	Range
smoke	12	4	4	8 to 16
loading	20	2	$+\infty$	18 to $+\infty$
pulverizer	1	$\dfrac{1}{4}$	$\dfrac{1}{6}$	$\dfrac{3}{4}$ to $\dfrac{7}{6}$
sulfur	0	$+\infty$	9600	$-\infty$ to 9600

or, in terms of the previous rates (multiplying through by 1.1), this is equivalent to

$$\tfrac{1}{16}x_1 + \tfrac{1}{24}x_2 \leqslant 1.1$$

This change is within the permissible range. So letting $\Delta = 0.1$, expression (4-21) becomes

$$\hat{\mathbf{b}} = \underbrace{[6-(12)(0.1)]}_{x_2}\mathbf{a}_2 + \underbrace{[2-(12)(0.1)]}_{x_4}\mathbf{a}_4 + \underbrace{[9600+(38400)(0.1)]}_{x_6}\mathbf{a}_6$$

$$+ \underbrace{[12+24(0.1)]}_{x_1}\mathbf{a}_1$$

The new solution is $x_2 = 4.8$, $x_4 = 0.8$, $x_6 = 13440$, $x_1 = 14.4$, and x_3 and x_5 are zero.

An analysis of the RHS is not complete without considering the profitability of increasing the RHS. It is one thing to find the new solution for a change in the RHS, but it is another question to decide whether it is worth making the change. Yet, in the final analysis this is the fundamental question.

In Sections 4-3 and 4-4 we saw that the dual variable associated with a constraint gives us the change in the value of the objective function for a unit increase in the RHS of that constraint. These hold, of course, only within the ranges of values given in Table 4-5. From Table 4-1 we see that the dual variable associated with the pulverizer constraint ($= z_j$ of the corresponding slack variable) has a value of 336 units of steam per hour. An increase in the pulverizer capacity of 10 percent results, therefore, in an increase in the steam output of 33.6 units per hour. If we know the monetary value per unit of the steam, the change in the cost of the coal used, and the fraction of time when the incremental steam output would be used, then we can determine the average annual increase in net profits for the plant. Comparing this with the initial cost of installing the additional pulverizer capacity will allow us to determine whether this investment provides an acceptable rate of return.

The ranges of values developed in Table 4-5 do not apply to changes of more than one RHS parameter at a time. However, in theory the required analysis is a direct extension of the one-by-one analysis, although in practice without matrix algebra, it becomes cumbersome for more than two changes at the same time.

Let us consider decreases in the RHS parameters of both binding constraints 1 and 3, i.e., $\hat{b}_1 = b_1 + \Delta_1$, and $\hat{b}_3 = b_3 + \Delta_3$, or $\hat{\mathbf{b}} = \mathbf{b} + \Delta_1 \mathbf{e}_1 + \Delta_3 \mathbf{e}_3$. Using the slack vectors instead we obtain

$$\hat{\mathbf{b}} = \mathbf{b} + \Delta_1 \mathbf{a}_3 + \Delta_3 \mathbf{a}_5$$

From the representations for $\mathbf{b}$, $\mathbf{a}_3$, and $\mathbf{a}_5$ in terms of the optimal basis given in the final tableau of Table 4-1 we obtain

$$\hat{\mathbf{b}} = (6 + \tfrac{3}{2}\Delta_1 - 12\Delta_3)\,\mathbf{a}_2 + (2 - \tfrac{1}{2}\Delta_1 - 12\Delta_3)\,\mathbf{a}_4$$

$$+ (9600 - 2400\Delta_1 + 38400\Delta_3)\,\mathbf{a}_6 + (12 - \Delta_1 + 24\Delta_3)\,\mathbf{a}_1$$

Hence, the new solution is

$$x_2 = 6 + \tfrac{3}{2}\Delta_1 - 12\Delta_3$$

$$x_4 = 2 - \tfrac{1}{2}\Delta_1 - 12\Delta_3$$

(4-26)

$$x_6 = 9600 - 2400\Delta_1 + 38400\Delta_3$$

$$x_1 = 12 - \Delta_1 + 24\Delta_3$$

If we are interested in the range of values of Δ_1 and Δ_3, for which the current basis remains optional, we obtain the feasible set defined by the following inequalities:

$$6 + \tfrac{3}{2}\Delta_1 - 12\Delta_3 \geqslant 0$$

$$2 - \tfrac{1}{2}\Delta_1 - 12\Delta_3 \geqslant 0$$

$$9600 - 2400\Delta_1 + 38400\Delta_3 \geqslant 0$$

$$12 - \Delta_1 + 24\Delta_3 \geqslant 0$$

Note, that the one-by-one ranges are special cases of these; for example, setting $\Delta_3 = 0$, gives the range for Δ_1. Equations (4-26) can also be used to find the new solution values for a particular configuration of b_1 and b_3.

The previous analysis breaks down if we wish to consider changes in a RHS parameter beyond the permissible range over which the current basis remains feasible and, therefore, optimal. For instance, if the pulverizer capacity could be increased by 25 percent, the RHS parameter of this constraint would increase to 1.25. However, the current basis is only feasible for an increase to at most 7/6. For increases beyond this, a new feasible basis has to be found. Unless the problem is solved again from scratch, our present tools are not suitable for such an analysis. It is more easily and more elegantly handled with the *dual simplex method*. (This technique is explained in some of the more advanced texts listed in the bibliography to this chapter.)

4-8 PARAMETRIC PROGRAMMING OF THE RHS

In parametric programming of the RHS we let some or all of the RHS parameters change continuously over a range from 0 to $+\infty$. While the detailed computations of this technique go beyond the scope of this text, the principles of the process involved can easily be grasped conceptually from a graphical demonstration. If we let the RHS parameter of the pulverizer constraint, denoted by θ, vary continuously from 0 to $+\infty$, the problem to be solved, as a function of θ, is then

$$\text{maximize} \quad 24x_1 + 20x_2$$

$$\text{subject to} \quad 0.5x_1 + x_2 \leqslant 12$$

$$x_1 + x_2 \leqslant 20$$

(4-27)
$$\tfrac{1}{16}x_1 + \tfrac{1}{24}x_2 \leqslant \theta$$

$$1200x_1 - 800x_2 \geqslant 0$$

$$x_1, x_2 \geqslant 0$$

$$0 \leqslant \theta < +\infty$$

Figure 4-3 traces the optimal solution as θ increases. We note that the optimal basis changes at points A, B, C, and D. Unlike parametric programming of the objective function, the optimal solution changes continually along the path $ABCD$ until the constraint becomes redundant at point D. Between each change of basis the optimal solution changes linearly; but, at a change of basis the linear relationship (the slope of the line along the path of the optimal solution) itself changes.

Let us look at an example. What is the optimal solution for $\theta = 1$ (point E)? From the table in Figure 4-3 we see that the solution lies on a straight line between points B and C. If we denote by θ_B and θ_C the values of θ at B and C, then E is $(\theta - \theta_B)/(\theta_C - \theta_B)$ of the way from B to C. For $\theta = 1$, $\theta_B = 3/4$, $\theta_C = 7/6$, we obtain $(\theta - \theta_B)/(\theta_C - \theta_B) = 3/5$. We find the solution at $\theta = 1$ by adding to the solution at point B 3/5 of the difference between the solutions at B and C. This solution is

$$x_1 = 6 + \tfrac{3}{5}(16{-}6) = 12$$

$$x_2 = 9 + \tfrac{3}{5}(4{-}9) = 6$$

$$x_3 = 0 + \tfrac{3}{5}(0{-}0) = 0$$

$$x_4 = 5 + \tfrac{3}{5}(0{-}5) = 2$$

$$x_5 = 0 + \tfrac{3}{5}(0{-}0) = 0$$

$$x_6 = 0 + \tfrac{3}{5}(16000{-}0) = 9600$$

and

$$z = 324 + \tfrac{3}{5}(464{-}324) = 408$$

which is the optimal solution to the original problem.

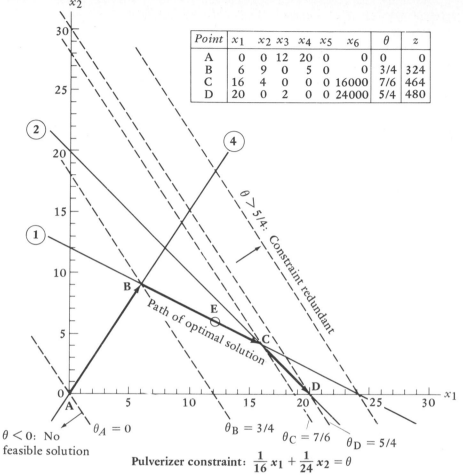

Point	x_1	x_2	x_3	x_4	x_5	x_6	θ	z
A	0	0	12	20	0	0	0	0
B	6	9	0	5	0	0	3/4	324
C	16	4	0	0	0	16000	7/6	464
D	20	0	2	0	0	24000	5/4	480

Pulverizer constraint: $\dfrac{1}{16} x_1 + \dfrac{1}{24} x_2 = \theta$

Figure 4-3. *Sequence of solutions for equations (4-27).*

It is possible, although not usual, to perform parametric programming of the RHS through the dual. Parametric programming of the RHS of the primal can be achieved by parametric programming of the objective function of the dual. Attempt to work out the details of this procedure for yourself.

4-9 POSTOPTIMAL ANALYSIS OF LHS COEFFICIENTS AND ADDITION OF NEW VARIABLES

When changing a LHS coefficient of a basic vector, we have in effect a different basis and all representations of vectors in terms of the basis must change. To find the new optimum by postoptimal analysis is usually a major undertaking. It may be quicker to solve the new problem from scratch.

When the changes in the LHS coefficients involve a nonbasic vector, the post-optimal analysis is more tractable. Let us view the changed LHS vector as a totally new activity, with the old one eliminated altogether. This is, of course, formally identical to the problem of adding a genuinely new activity (such as another type of coal in our example). Since both of these cases are of interest to us, we will deal with them together.

As we consider the addition of a new activity vector, we ask the question: Is the old optimal basis still optimal with the new vector present, or should the new vector enter the basis? In technical terms, we are asking whether the $(z_j - c_j)$ value of the new vector is negative.

We have seen in Section 4-4 that the z_j values at the optimal simplex tableau can be derived from the optimal values of the dual variables. Thus, the z_j value for the new vector (in terms of the current basis) can be computed in this manner. If the $(z_j - c_j)$ value so derived is nonnegative, the current basis remains optimal. If the $(z_j - c_j)$ value is negative, the new vector becomes a candidate to enter the basis.

To illustrate this idea consider the expanded version of the power generating problem in Section 2-11, where management is offered the possibility of an additional activity, namely, the burning of coal C. The vector for the activity of burning coal C is

$$\mathbf{a}_8 = \begin{bmatrix} 0.8 \\ 1 \\ 1/20 \\ 1000 \end{bmatrix}$$

and the objective function coefficient is $c_8 = 21$. Using the coefficients of $\mathbf{a}_8$ and the w_i values in the optimal simplex tableau in Table 4-1 we obtain

$$z_8 = 0.8w_1 + 1w_2 + \tfrac{1}{20}w_3 + 1000w_4$$
$$= 0.8\,(6) + 1\,(0) + \tfrac{1}{20}(336) + 1000\,(0) = 21.6$$

and $(z_8 - c_8) = 21.6 - 21 = 0.6 > 0$. Therefore, $\mathbf{a}_8$ is not eligible to enter the basis. The current basis is still optimal. There is no need to proceed any further with the analysis.

Let us next assume that 24 tons of coal C can be pulverized per hour. (Had $\mathbf{a}_8$ been an activity in the optimal tableau, this change would be a change in a LHS coefficient.) The new vector for the activity of burning coal C is

$$(4\text{-}28) \qquad\qquad \mathbf{a}_9 = \begin{bmatrix} 0.8 \\ 1 \\ 1/24 \\ 1000 \end{bmatrix}$$

Using the same analysis as previously we obtain

$$z_9 = 0.8\,(6) + 1\,(0) + \tfrac{1}{24}(336) + 1000\,(0) = 18.8$$

The $(z_j - c_j)$ value is $(z_9 - c_9) = 18.8 - 21 = -2.2 < 0$. The current basis is not optimal any longer. Vector $\mathbf{a}_9$ is a candidate to enter the basis. First, $\mathbf{a}_9$ is to be added to the old optimal simplex tableau. However, the tableau entries are not the coefficients shown in (4-28), but are the coefficients of $\mathbf{a}_9$ represented in terms of the current basis, namely, the γ_i values of

$$(4\text{-}29)\qquad\qquad \mathbf{a}_9 = \gamma_1\,\mathbf{a}_2 + \gamma_2\,\mathbf{a}_4 + \gamma_3\,\mathbf{a}_6 + \gamma_4\,\mathbf{a}_1$$

By the nature of the vectors $\mathbf{a}_3$, $\mathbf{a}_4$, $\mathbf{a}_5$ and $\mathbf{a}_7$ (they are the unit vectors $\mathbf{e}_1, \mathbf{e}_2, \mathbf{e}_3, \mathbf{e}_4$, respectively) (4-28) gives us

$$(4\text{-}30)\qquad\qquad \mathbf{a}_9 = 0.8\mathbf{a}_3 + 1\mathbf{a}_4 + \tfrac{1}{24}\mathbf{a}_5 + 1000\mathbf{a}_7$$

To express $\mathbf{a}_9$ in the form of (4-29), all we need do is express each of the vectors on the right-hand side of (4-30) in terms of the basis $(\mathbf{a}_2, \mathbf{a}_4, \mathbf{a}_6, \mathbf{a}_1)$. Table 4-1 gives us the necessary coefficients. So

$$\mathbf{a}_3 = \tfrac{3}{2}\mathbf{a}_2 - \tfrac{1}{2}\mathbf{a}_4 - 2400\mathbf{a}_6 - \mathbf{a}_1$$

$$\mathbf{a}_4 = 0\mathbf{a}_2 + 1\mathbf{a}_4 + 0\mathbf{a}_6 + 0\mathbf{a}_1$$

$$\mathbf{a}_5 = -12\mathbf{a}_2 - 12\mathbf{a}_4 + 38400\mathbf{a}_6 + 24\mathbf{a}_1$$

$$\mathbf{a}_7 = 0\mathbf{a}_2 + 0\mathbf{a}_4 - \mathbf{a}_6 + 0\mathbf{a}_1$$

Equation (4-30) then becomes

$$\begin{aligned}
\mathbf{a}_9 = \;& [(\tfrac{3}{2})\,(0.8) + (0)\,(1) + (-12)\,(\tfrac{1}{24}) + (0)\,(1000)]\,\mathbf{a}_2 \\
& + [(-\tfrac{1}{2})\,(0.8) + (1)\,(1) + (-12)\,(\tfrac{1}{24}) + (0)\,(1000)]\,\mathbf{a}_4 \\
& + [(-2400)\,(0.8) + (0)\,(1) + (38400)\,(\tfrac{1}{24}) + (-1)\,(1000)]\,\mathbf{a}_6 \\
& + [(-1)\,(0.8) + (0)\,(1) + (24)\,(\tfrac{1}{24}) + (0)\,(1000)]\,\mathbf{a}_1
\end{aligned}$$

or

$$(4\text{-}31)\qquad\qquad \mathbf{a}_9 = 0.7\mathbf{a}_2 + 0.1\mathbf{a}_4 - 1320\mathbf{a}_6 + 0.2\mathbf{a}_1$$

From (4-29) and (4-31) we find that $\gamma_1 = 0.7$, $\gamma_2 = 0.1$, $\gamma_3 = -1320$, $\gamma_4 = 0.2$. These γ_i values and $(z_9 - c_9) = -2.2$ are added to the simplex tableau, and a new iteration of the simplex method is initiated. Table 4-6 shows this analysis and the new optimal solution.

Let us consider now another issue: For what range of values of the pulverizer coefficient in vector $\mathbf{a}_9$ does the optimal basis of Table 4-1 remain optimal? The requirement is that $(z_9 - c_9) \geqslant 0$. Let α denote the pulverizer coefficient. Then, by the principle discussed earlier,

$$z_9 = 0.8\,(6) + 1\,(0) + \alpha\,(336) + 1000\,(0) = 4.8 + 336\alpha$$

and

$$(z_9 - c_9) = 4.8 + 336\alpha - 21 = 336\alpha - 16.2$$

Table 4-6. *Inserting the New Vector* a_9.

c_j			24	20	0	0	0	0	0	21
c_j	Vectors / Basis	b	a_1	a_2	a_3	a_4	a_5	a_6	a_7	a_9
← 20	a_2	6	0	1	$\frac{3}{2}$	0	-12	0	0	$\frac{7}{10}$
0	a_4	2	0	0	$-\frac{1}{2}$	1	-12	0	0	$\frac{1}{10}$
0	a_6	9600	0	0	-2400	0	38400	1	-1	-1320
24	a_1	12	1	0	-1	0	24	0	0	$\frac{2}{10}$
	$z_j - c_j$	408	0	0	6	0	336	0	0	$-\frac{22}{10}$
21	a_9	$\frac{60}{7}$	0	$\frac{10}{7}$	$\frac{15}{7}$	0	$\frac{-120}{7}$	0	0	1
0	a_4	$\frac{8}{7}$	0	$\frac{-1}{7}$	$\frac{-5}{7}$	1	$\frac{-72}{7}$	0	0	0
0	a_6	$\frac{146400}{7}$	0	$\frac{13200}{7}$	$\frac{3000}{7}$	0	$\frac{110400}{7}$	1	-1	0
24	a_1	$\frac{72}{7}$	1	$\frac{-2}{7}$	$\frac{-10}{7}$	0	$\frac{192}{7}$	0	0	0
	$z_j - c_j$	$426\frac{6}{7}$	0	$\frac{22}{7}$	$\frac{75}{7}$	0	$\frac{2088}{7}$	0	0	0

As long as $336\alpha \geqslant 16.2$, or as long as $\alpha \geqslant 16.2/336$ (or approximately 0.048), $(z_9 - c_9) \geqslant 0$. Interpreted another way, Table 4-1 gives the optimal solution as long as no more than $1/\alpha = 20.74$ tons of coal C can be pulverized per hour.

For some LHS coefficients, such as the loading coefficient or the sulfur co-efficient, sensitivity analysis is trivial. Since both w_2 and w_4 (the dual variable for these resources) are zero, no z_j value involves either of these two coefficients, and $(z_j - c_j)$ can never become negative as a function of them.

4-10 COMPUTER CODES AND POSTOPTIMAL ANALYSIS

Most commercially available linear programming computer codes provide, as a routine procedure, a large portion of the sensitivity analysis that can be determined from the optimal simplex tableau. They give

- optimal dual variables or shadow prices,
- individual ranges on RHS parameters for which the corresponding dual variables remain unchanged,

- variable to leave and variable to enter the basis for each RHS change beyond these ranges,
- $(z_j - c_j)$ values for nonbasic variables,
- individual ranges on c_j for basic variables,
- variable to enter for changes beyond these ranges on each c_j.

However, they will not provide any sensitivity analysis with respect to LHS coefficients, since this would require a tremendous amount of output that may not be justified or ever used for most real-life applications.

They may also allow the user to specify a series of different right-hand sides and/or objective functions which are solved in sequence, usually using the previous optimal solution as the new initial solution. As a rule, this reduces the additional computations required, provided the changes are relatively small. Some computer codes can perform parametric programming with respect to both the objective function and the RHS.

Most computer codes also allow the solution to be saved on disc or magnetic tape and provide *restart* procedures at which point new variables or constraints can be added, as well as old variables or constraints deleted.

EXERCISES

4.1 (a) Convert the following linear program into standard form:

$$\text{maximize } z = 3x_1 + 4x_2 + x_3$$
$$\text{subject to } \quad x_1 + 3x_2 + 2x_3 \geqslant 10$$
$$6x_1 + 2x_2 + \quad x_3 \leqslant 30$$
$$x_1 + \quad x_2 + \quad x_3 = \quad 5$$
$$x_1, x_2, x_3 \geqslant \quad 0$$

(b) Write (i) the dual of the linear program in (a), and (ii) the dual of the standard form of the linear program in (a). Show that these two dual problems are equivalent.

4.2 (a) Find the dual of the following problem:

$$\text{maximize } z = 4x_1 + 6x_2 + 10x_3 + 12x_4$$
$$\text{subject to } \quad x_1 + 3x_2 + \quad 2x_3 + \quad 4x_4 \leqslant \quad 5$$
$$x_1 + \quad x_2 + \quad 5x_3 + \quad 3x_4 \leqslant 15$$
$$x_1, \ldots, x_4 \geqslant \quad 0$$

(b) Graph the dual, and using DR6 (Complementary Slackness Theorem), find the solution of the primal. Check your answer using DR5 (Duality Theorem). Show that your solution to the primal is an extreme point to that problem.

4.3 Give the interpretations of the optimal values of w_2 and w_3 of the power generating problem, summarized in Table 4-1.

4.4 (a) Verify that c_2, in the power generating problem, must lie in the range $16 \leqslant c_2 \leqslant 48$, for the final tableau in Table 4-1 to give the optimal solution.

(b) Verify that b_1, the RHS parameter of the smoke constraint, must lie in the range $8 \leqslant b_1 \leqslant 16$, for the basis $(\mathbf{a}_2, \mathbf{a}_4, \mathbf{a}_6, \mathbf{a}_1)$ to give the optimal basic feasible solution.

(c) From Figure 4-3, find the optimal solution when $b_3 = \frac{1}{2}$.

(d) A device is marketed to reduce the sulfur oxide content of the gases by 10 percent. How much extra steam can be generated?

(e) A newly available coal (very hard and low in pollutants) is contemplated. It has a smoke emission rate of $\frac{1}{3}$ kg/ton. The pulverizer can handle 12 tons of it per hour. The coal has a sulfur content of 1500 PPM. Like all other coals, it uses loader capacity. It produces 30,000 lbs of steam/ton. Should it be used?

4.5 A cabinet maker has recently taken over an enterprise making luxury mahogany desks. The only constraints he has are on the capacity of the plant (in machine hours), and the availability of mahogany, which is delivered to him weekly by a regular supplier. The following table summarizes the data for each week for four possible types of desks.

Desk Type	1	2	3	4	Available
Machine hours	1	3	4	3	1000 hours
Mahogany (m²)	4	2	6	8	2500 m²
Profit/desk ($)	20	20	50	40	

He sets the problem up as a linear program to maximize profit. The number of desks (in hundreds) of type j desk to be produced is x_j.

$$\text{maximize } z = 2x_1 + 2x_2 + 5x_3 + 4x_4 \qquad \text{(profit in \$1000.)}$$
$$\text{subject to} \quad x_1 + 3x_2 + 4x_3 + 3x_4 \leqslant 10 \qquad \text{(plant capacity in 100 hours)}$$
$$4x_1 + 2x_2 + 6x_3 + 8x_4 \leqslant 25 \qquad \text{(mahogany in 100 m}^2\text{)}$$
$$x_j \geqslant 0, \qquad j = 1,\dots,4.$$

The optimal tableau is

c_j			2	2	5	4	0	0
c_j	Vectors	**b**	$\mathbf{a}_1$	$\mathbf{a}_2$	$\mathbf{a}_3$	$\mathbf{a}_4$	$\mathbf{a}_5$	$\mathbf{a}_6$
	Basis							
2	$\mathbf{a}_1$	4	1	-1	0	1.4	-0.6	0.4
5	$\mathbf{a}_3$	1.5	0	1	1	0.4	0.4	-0.1
	$z_j - c_j$	15.5	0	1	0	0.8	0.8	0.3

Starting at this optimal solution consider the following questions separately.

(a) Perform parametric programming of the profit values of desk 3, $0 \leqslant \theta \leqslant \infty$.

(b) A major customer insists that 100 desks of type 2 be delivered each week for 4 weeks. What is the optimal production for each of those weeks, and the weekly profit?

(c) A shipping delay forces the regular supplier to reduce weekly mahogany supplies to 2000 m². What is now the optimal production schedule and profit? However, another source is willing to supply him up to 1000 m² at \$6/m² instead of the normal price he pays of \$4/m². How much should he buy at this price? Why?

(d) He is considering another type of desk that uses 4 hours of machine time and only 2 m² of mahogany. It would yield a profit of \$36 per desk. Should he produce it?

4.6 A firm can produce four products in its factory. It takes only one day to produce a unit of each product, but production is limited by floor space in the factory and the amount of labor available. The relevant data are as follows:

	Product 1	Product 2	Product 3	Product 4	Availability
Floor area, (m²)/unit	10	30	80	40	900 m²
Labor/unit	2	1	1	3	80 men
Variable cost/unit	20	30	45	58	
Sales revenue/unit	30	50	85	90	

The following linear program is formulated where x_j is the daily production of product j:

$$\text{maximize } z = x_1 + 2x_2 + 4x_3 + 3.2x_4 \qquad \text{(profit in units of \$10)}$$
$$\text{subject to} \quad x_1 + 3x_2 + 8x_3 + \ 4x_4 \leqslant 90 \qquad \text{(factory space in units of 10 m}^2\text{)}$$
$$2x_1 + \ x_2 + \ x_3 + \ 3x_4 \leqslant 80 \qquad \text{(labor)}$$
$$x_j \geqslant 0 \qquad \text{all } j$$

The optimal tableau is:

	c_j		1	2	4	3.2	0	0
c_j	Vectors / Basis	**b**	$\mathbf{a_1}$	$\mathbf{a_2}$	$\mathbf{a_3}$	$\mathbf{a_4}$	$\mathbf{a_5}$	$\mathbf{a_6}$
1	$\mathbf{a_1}$	10	1	-1	-4	0	$-\dfrac{3}{5}$	$\dfrac{4}{5}$
3.2	$\mathbf{a_4}$	20	0	1	3	1	$\dfrac{2}{5}$	$-\dfrac{1}{5}$
	$z_j - c_j$	74	0	$\dfrac{1}{5}$	$\dfrac{8}{5}$	0	$\dfrac{17}{25}$	$\dfrac{4}{25}$

(a) A raw material used in products 1 and 3 is very unstable in price. At the moment it costs \$100 a ton. Product 1 uses 1/10 of a ton, and product 3 uses 1/5 of a ton. The cost of the raw material is included in the variable costs shown above. What is the price range of this raw material for which the present solution is still optimal?

(b) What are the optimal values of the dual variables of this problem? Interpret these variables. What is the range of RHS values in which these values hold?

(c) The firm can increase its effective floor space to 1000 m² by renting a new conveyor and stacking system. The machine costs $50 a day to rent and operate. Should they rent it? If so, what is the new production schedule?

4.7 A farmer has just bought an unstocked farm of 1040 acres, all in pasture. He has $10,400 available to spend on stocking the farm. He can buy breeding ewes, wethers, or beef breeding cattle. The current market price, his estimate of annual profit per animal, and the number of acres required per animal are as follows:

	Market Price per Animal in Dollars	Acres per Animal	Annual Profit per Animal in Dollars
Ewes	7.00	1.0	12.00
Wethers	10.00	0.5	7.00
Cattle	100.00	3.0	40.00

He uses a linear programming model to determine how he should stock his farm if he is to maximize profit in the first year. The initial tableau and a subsequent tableau in the computations are shown below.

Respectively, a_4 and a_5 are vectors representing unused land and capital.

Initial Tableau

c_j			12	7	40	0	0
c_j	Vectors / Basis	b	a_1	a_2	a_3	a_4	a_5
0	a_4	1040	1.0	0.5	3.0	1	0
0	a_5	10400	7.0	10.0	100.0	0	1
	$z_j - c_j$	0	-12	-7	-40	0	0

Final Tableau

12	a_1	800	1	0	-3.077	1.538	-0.077
7	a_2	480	0	1	12.154	-1.077	0.154
	$z_j - c_j$	12960	0	1	8.154	10.923	0.154

(a) If the portion of the profit from ewes and wethers due to the sale of wool is $4.00 in each case, by what percentage can the assumed wool price drop before cattle should be stocked?

(b) The farmer can borrow up to $7800 at 10 percent interest for use either as further working capital or to purchase more land. An additional 104 acres of farm land is for sale, and the cost of buying this land and getting it ready for use is $50 per acre. What action should the farmer take? What will his optimal stocking policy be now?

(c) Another possible way of increasing the productivity of the farm is the application of more fertilizer. Fertilizer costing $6 per acre will increase the carrying capacity of the land for ewes, wethers, and cattle to 0.6, 0.33, and 2.0 acres per animal respectively. Assuming that not all the farm needs to be fertilized, and that animals can be separated to these different portions of the farm, how many acres (if any) should be fertilized. What will the optimal stocking policy be now? The $6/acre fertilizer cost must be paid from working capital.

REFERENCES

Daellenbach, H. G., and E. J. Bell. *User's Guide to Linear Programming*. Englewood Cliffs, N.J.: Prentice-Hall, 1970. An elementary treatment of duality is given in Chapter 6. A feature of this chapter is the solution of problems via their duals using LPGOGO.

Gale, D. *The Theory of Linear Economic Models*. N.Y.: McGraw-Hill, 1960. Chapter 1 has an interesting set of linear programming applications and an interpretation of their duals.

Garvin, W. W. *Linear Programming*. N.Y.: McGraw-Hill, 1960. This text deals with sensitivity analysis in Chapter 4. Chapter 7 gives a treatment of duality from a definitional rather than conceptual point of view. The simplex multipliers are introduced in Chapter 4.

Gass, Saul I. *Linear Programming*, 3rd ed. N.Y.: McGraw-Hill, 1969. Duality is developed in Chapter 5. In Chapter 8, sensitivity analysis and parametric programming are considered. Both topics are handled in a theoretical manner.

Hadley, G. *Linear Programming*. Reading, Mass.: Addison-Wesley, 1962. Sections 11-2 to 11-6 give a terse but complete treatment of postoptimality changes using matrix algebra. An interesting application of linear programming and duality to the theory of the firm is given in Sections 13-2 to 13-4.

5

Networks
and
the
Transportation
Problem

A number of operations research problems can be represented diagrammatically as a series of points called *nodes*, *vertices*, or *points*, joined by *lines*, also referred to as *links*, *arcs*, *edges*, or *branches*. An example is the problem of a rural mail carrier who must deliver mail to a number of farms. The mail carrier would like to know how to schedule a route, so as to minimize the distance to be traveled. Figure 5-1 is a map of the area with each farm represented by a node, and the shortest route from one farm to another represented by a link. Each link has a distance associated with it.

A diagram like Figure 5-1 is called a *graph*. Although this graph was derived from a meaningful problem, in general, a graph is a totally abstract mathematical concept. Our concern with graphs lies only in finding how they can help us formulate and solve operations research problems. There are a number of classes of problems in operations research which can be viewed as graphs. Some can be solved by one of several solution techniques that make direct use of the graph structure of the

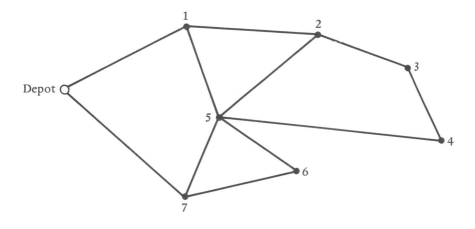

Figure 5-1. *Map of rural mail delivery.*

problems. Many can be solved by linear programming. For others, graph theory is helpful to understand the nature of the problem, but does not lead to a solution technique. The rural mail problem is an example of the so-called traveling salesman problem. Starting at a given node, the objective is to visit all other nodes and return to the starting point in minimum time or distance, or at minimum cost. This problem, though simple in concept, has proved resistant to a computationally efficient general solution technique, although a number of algorithms exist that find itineraries that are close to optimal.

This chapter looks at only two problems related to graph theory: the problem of *maximum flow in a network* and the *transportation problem*, both of which can also be formulated as linear programs. We shall see that in both cases there is a more satisfactory solution technique than the usual application of the simplex method. Chapter 6 takes up a third topic in graphs, namely, *critical path analysis*.

5-1 MAXIMUM FLOW IN A NETWORK

Consider a graph with a distance, cost, or capacity associated with each link and a *flow* of material or information through the links. Such a graph is called a *network*. The two most common network problems entail either finding the maximum capacity of the network, or the shortest (longest) path through the network.

Let us first introduce some definitions and notation:

- A *link* or line joining nodes i and j is written (i, j). With each link we associate a flow from i to j, or j to i, or both.
- A link is *directed* if the flow is limited to a given direction. A directed link from i to j is written $(i \rightarrow j)$. When a link (i, j) can have a flow in either direction, it can be thought of as the two directed links $(i \rightarrow j)$ and $(j \rightarrow i)$.
- A *source* is a node such that all links connected to it are directed away from it.
- A *sink* is a node such that all the links connected to it are directed toward it.
- A *path* between two nodes i and j is a set of connected links $(i, p), (p, q), ...,$ $(t, u), (u, j)$ such that any node is passed through only once.

In the network in Figure 5-2 an arrow on a link indicates the direction of possible flow and the number beside the arrow gives the capacity limit of that flow. The nodes are numbered with 1 as the source and 5 as the sink. A path through this network may be represented as: $(1 \rightarrow 2), (2 \rightarrow 4), (4 \rightarrow 5)$.

The network in Figure 5-2 could represent the following problem. An oil company has pipelines across a country from its unloading port (node 1) to its refinery (node 5). There are three pumping stations along the pipelines (nodes 2, 3, and 4). Between nodes 3 and 4 the flow can go in either direction at different capacities. The numbers attached to each link in Figure 5-2 are the capacities for each section of the pipelines in units of 1000 barrels per hour. The company wants to know the maximum hourly amount of oil it can pump through the links from the unloading port to the refinery.

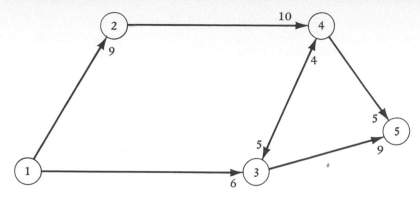

Figure 5-2. *Example of a network.*

We will first consider formulating the maximum flow problem in general terms. The decision variables are the amount of flow through each section of the pipeline network or each link. Let x_{ij} be the flow through link $(i \to j)$, with node $i = 1$ denoting the source and $j = N$ denoting the sink. If d_{ij} is the capacity limit in $(i \to j)$, then

$$(5\text{-}1) \qquad\qquad 0 \leqslant x_{ij} \leqslant d_{ij}$$

We will assume that no flow is lost within the network. This is called the assumption of a *conservation of flow*. So for all nodes other than the source and sink, the flow into node i $(= \sum_k x_{ki}$ for all k connected to i by a link $(k \to i))$ must equal the flow out of node i $(= \sum_r x_{ir}$ for all r connected to i by a link $(i \to r))$:

$$(5\text{-}2) \qquad\qquad \sum_k x_{ki} = \sum_r x_{ir}, \qquad i = 2, ..., N-1$$

The objective is to maximize the flow from source to sink. But this is the same as maximizing the total flow out of the source (or into the sink), i.e.,

$$(5\text{-}3) \qquad\qquad \text{maximize } z = \sum_s x_{1s} \quad \left(\text{or } \sum_q x_{qN} \right)$$

Expressions (5-1), (5-2), and (5-3) represent a linear program. The problem associated with Figure 5-2 in linear programming form has 7 decision variables, 3 artificial variables, 3 constraints, and 7 upper-bound restrictions. Although it can be solved by the simplex method, there is a much more efficient solution technique for this type of problem called the *labeling technique*. Also based on an iterative algorithm, its approach has no analogy with the simplex method.

The above example is a one-source-one-sink problem. There is no difficulty in handling multiple sources and multiple sinks. A more complex problem can be converted into a simple problem by linking all sources back to a *super-source*, and linking all sinks forward to a *super-sink*. The flow from the super-source to each source gives the total flow from that source, and the flow from each sink to the super-sink gives the total flow into that sink.

We will assume that all links can have a flow in either direction. If a flow exists in both directions the actual flow is the difference of the two opposing flows or the net flow $(x_{ij} - x_{ji})$. A flow direction that is not permitted is given a capacity limit of zero.

Let us now consider the network with a flow going through it, e.g., the zero flow with $x_{ij} = 0$ for all i and j. We define the *excess capacity* g_{ij} from i to j of link $(i{\to}j)$, as the difference between the capacity limit d_{ij} and the net flow $(x_{ij} - x_{ji})$ in that direction:

$$(5\text{-}4) \qquad\qquad g_{ij} = d_{ij} - x_{ij} + x_{ji} \qquad \text{for all } i \text{ and } j.$$

The excess capacity is the greatest feasible increase in x_{ij}. Thus we obtain the following result:

CRITERION 1: INCREASING THE FLOW IN A NETWORK

Given a flow through the network, the total flow can be increased if there exists a path from source to sink with a positive excess capacity in every link in the path.

Let us assume a flow of zero in the network of Figure 5-2. Consider the path $(1{\to}2)$, $(2{\to}4)$, $(4{\to}5)$, with excess capacities $g_{12} = 9$, $g_{24} = 10$, and $g_{45} = 5$, respectively. It is thus possible to increase the flow through the network. By what amount can the flow be increased? Clearly, the largest amount by which the flow can be increased using that path cannot exceed the smallest excess capacity of any link on that path. In our example, this is 5.

CRITERION 2: OPTIMALITY OF FLOW IN A NETWORK

If no path exists from source to sink with positive excess capacities in every link, then the solution is optimal.

5-2 THE LABELING TECHNIQUE

The purpose of the labeling technique is to find at each iteration a path from source to sink with a positive excess capacity in every link of the path. The iterations continue until no such path exists any longer.

Consider a path from the source to some node j. We will define the *excess capacity of the path* as the minimum of the excess capacities of the links in the path. Also, we will call a path from the source to node j a *feasible path*, if it has a positive excess capacity.

The operations of the labeling technique have two purposes. The first is to keep track of a feasible path (if one exists) from the source to each node of the network, until a feasible path is found from the source to the sink. The second is to record the excess capacity of each of those feasible paths. Not all feasible paths are considered at each iteration—it is sufficient to keep track of one such path to each node in the network.

If it is possible, each node j of the network, other than the source, is labeled with two numbers

(5-5) $$(\delta_j, \gamma_j)$$

where γ_j is the previous node on a feasible path from the source to node j, and δ_j is the excess capacity of that path.

If node i immediately precedes j on the feasible path, then $\gamma_j = i$, and δ_j will be given by

(5-6) $$\delta_j = \text{minimum}[\delta_i, g_{ij}]$$

The logic of the labeling technique is given in the flow chart of Figure 5-3. Some further explanation is needed concerning some of the eight steps involved.

Step 1. Any flow will suffice for initiating the algorithm. Often it will be most convenient to use a zero flow.
Step 2. Each iteration always starts at the source.
Step 4. Only unlabeled nodes can be labeled at this step. Previously labeled nodes are ignored.
Step 6. Once the sink has been labeled, one iteration is complete except for updating the data of the solution. The increase in flow is δ_N, the capacity of the feasible path generated. The feasible path is found by tracing back from $\gamma_N = k$ to $\gamma_k = r$, $\gamma_r = p$, etc., until the source is reached. The new values of the solution $\hat{x}_{ij}$ and the new excess capacities $\hat{g}_{ij}$ are given by:
(i) If link $(i{\rightarrow}j)$ is a member of the feasible path:

(5-7)
$$\hat{x}_{ij} = x_{ij} + \delta_N$$
$$\hat{x}_{ji} = x_{ji}$$
$$\hat{g}_{ij} = g_{ij} - \delta_N$$
$$\hat{g}_{ji} = g_{ji} + \delta_N$$

(ii) If link $(i{\rightarrow}j)$ is not a member of the feasible path:

(5-8)
$$\hat{x}_{ij} = x_{ij}$$
$$\hat{g}_{ij} = g_{ij}$$

(iii) The total flow in the network is,

(5-9) $$\hat{z} = z + \delta_N.$$

This new flow is used as the flow for the next iteration of the procedure. So, we return to Step 2.

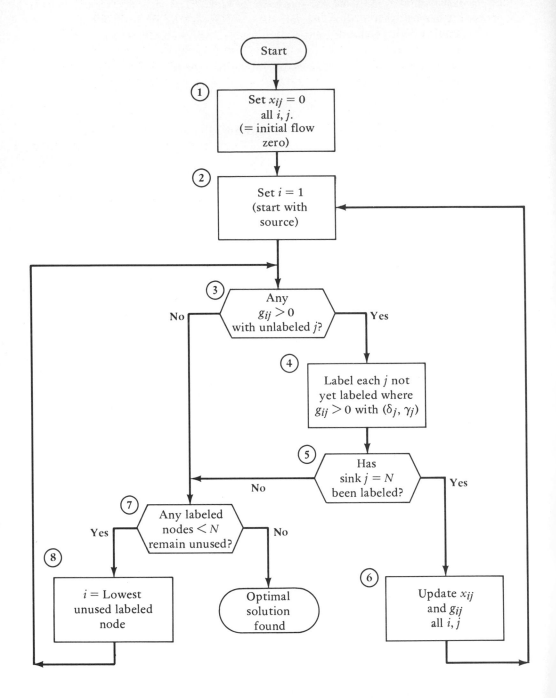

Figure 5-3. *Flow chart of labeling technique.*

Steps 7 When a node has been used to label other nodes it is eliminated from
and 8. further consideration. The next node chosen from which to label subsequent nodes must itself be labeled, and it is to be the lowest numbered
node not yet used. If all labeled nodes have been used up and the sink
has not been labeled, the optimality criterion has been fulfilled. The
total flow at the end of the previous iteration is the maximum flow for
the network.

5-3 DIAGRAMMATIC SOLUTION BY USE OF THE LABELING TECHNIQUE

Consider again the pipeline problem. In Figure 5-4 the excess capacities for an
initial flow of zero are shown on each line. Starting at node 1 we find that $g_{12} = 9 > 0$.
So in terms of (5-5), node 2 is labeled $(\delta_2 = 9, \ \gamma_2 = 1)$. Similarly, $g_{13} = 6 > 0$,
and node 3 is labeled $(6, 1)$. We now proceed to the next labeled node in ascending
numerical order. This is node 2. Since $g_{24} = 10 > 0$, we label node 4. The value
of δ_4 is found from expression (5-6), as $\delta_4 = \text{minimum}(9, 10) = 9$, and $\gamma_4 = 2$.
No other nodes can be labeled from node 2. Proceeding to node 3, we find $g_{34} =$
$4 > 0$, and $g_{35} = 9 > 0$. But since node 4 is already labeled, it cannot be labeled
again. Thus, only node 5 can be labeled from node 3, with $\delta_5 = \text{minimum}(6, 9) = 6$,
and $\gamma_5 = 3$. We have now labeled the sink and can find the feasible path by tracing
back from node 5. From $\gamma_5 = 3$, we find that the prior node in the path is node 3.
From $\gamma_3 = 1$, we find that the node prior to node 3 is node 1, the source. So the
feasible path is $(1 \rightarrow 3)$, $(3 \rightarrow 5)$. The increase in flow through the network is $\delta_5 = 6$.

To find a new flow through the network and the corresponding excess capacities,
we use expressions (5-7) and (5-8). From (5-7) we obtain $\hat{x}_{13} = 0 + 6 = 6$, and
$\hat{x}_{35} = 0 + 6 = 6$. From expression (5-8) we obtain $\hat{x}_{12} = 0$, $\hat{x}_{24} = 0$, $\hat{x}_{34} = 0$,

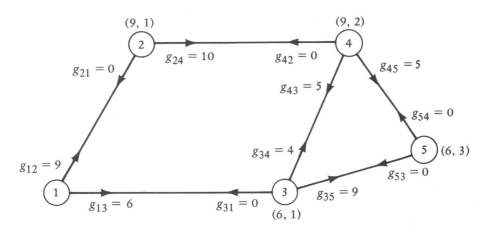

Figure 5-4. *First iteration of labeling technique.*

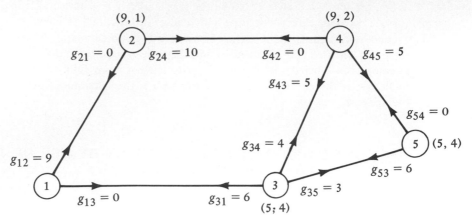

Figure 5-5. *Second iteration.*

$\hat{x}_{42} = 0$, $\hat{x}_{43} = 0$ and $\hat{x}_{45} = 0$. Since no flow can go into the source, or out of the sink, x_{21}, x_{31}, x_{53} and x_{54} are always zero (they can be ignored). So we obtain the new flows or updated solution:

$$x_{12} = 0 \qquad x_{24} = 0 \qquad x_{35} = 6 \qquad x_{43} = 0$$
$$x_{13} = 6 \qquad x_{34} = 0 \qquad x_{42} = 0 \qquad x_{45} = 0$$

From (5-9), $\hat{z} = 0 + 6 = 6$ is the total flow through the network. Expressions (5-7) and (5-8) also enable us to update the excess capacities. For instance, from (5-7), $\hat{g}_{13} = 6 - 6 = 0$, $\hat{g}_{31} = 0 + 6 = 6$, etc., and from (5-8), $\hat{g}_{12} = 9$, $\hat{g}_{21} = 0$, etc. The whole set of new excess capacities is shown in Figure 5-5.

At the second iteration, node 3 cannot be labeled from node 1, since $g_{13} = 0$. The labeling technique finds a path through node 2, allowing us to label the sink.

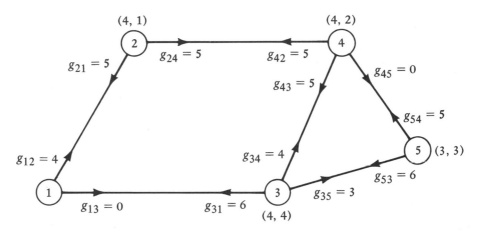

Figure 5-6. *Third iteration.*

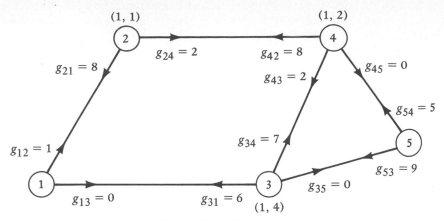

Figure 5-7. *Final iteration.*

The increase in the flow is $\delta_5 = 5$, and the feasible path is $(1 \to 2)$, $(2 \to 4)$, $(4 \to 5)$. From (5-7), (5-8), and (5-9) we obtain:

$$\hat{x}_{12} = 0 + \delta_5 = 5 \qquad \hat{x}_{24} = 0 + \delta_5 = 5 \qquad \hat{x}_{35} = 6$$
$$\hat{x}_{43} = 0 \qquad \hat{x}_{13} = 6 \qquad \hat{x}_{34} = 0 \qquad \hat{x}_{42} = 0$$
$$\hat{x}_{45} = 0 + \delta_5 = 5 \qquad \text{and} \qquad \hat{z} = 6 + \delta_5 = 11$$

The updated excess capacities are given in Figure 5-6.

The third iteration yields the feasible path $(1 \to 2)$, $(2 \to 4)$, $(4 \to 3)$, $(3 \to 5)$, with $\delta_5 = 3$. By (5-7), (5-8), and (5-9), the new flows are:

(5-10)

$$\hat{x}_{12} = 8 \qquad \hat{x}_{24} = 8 \qquad \hat{x}_{35} = 9 \qquad \hat{x}_{43} = 3$$
$$\hat{x}_{13} = 6 \qquad \hat{x}_{34} = 0 \qquad \hat{x}_{42} = 0 \qquad \hat{x}_{45} = 5 \qquad \hat{z} = 11 + \delta_5 = 14$$

At the fourth iteration we see from Figure 5-7 that we can label nodes 2, 3, and 4, but not the sink. So there does not exist another feasible path through this network. The solution given by (5-10) is thus the optimal flow.

We have calculated the flows at each iteration to help us see the progression towards the optimum. However, this is not necessary. It is possible to calculate the optimal net flows in each link directly from the original capacity limits (the d_{ij} values) and the final excess capacities (the g_{ij} values). Using equation (5-4), we can write the value of the net flows as

$$(x_{ij} - x_{ji}) = d_{ij} - g_{ij} \qquad \text{for all } i \text{ and } j.$$

5-4 THE MAX FLOW/MIN CUT THEOREM

We can establish that this solution is optimal by use of the *Max Flow/Min Cut theorem*. A *cut* in a network is defined as a collection of directed links such that every directed path from source to sink contains at least one link in the cut. The *capacity value* of a cut is the sum of the capacities of the links in the cut. The *minimum cut* is the cut with the smallest capacity value.

MAX FLOW/MIN CUT THEOREM

The maximum flow in a network equals the capacity value of the minimum cut.

This theorem is conceptually reasonable. Since each flow in every path from source to sink must go through the links in the minimum cut, the maximum flow can be no more than the capacity value of the minimum cut. Conversely, if the flow were less than the capacity value of the minimum cut, it could be increased until it reached that value.

In the pipeline problem the minimum cut is the pair of links $(3 \to 5)$ and $(4 \to 5)$. All paths from source to sink contain one or the other of these two links. The capacity value of the cut is $d_{35} + d_{45} = 9 + 5 = 14$ and hence the maximum flow is 14.

5-5 AN APPLICATION OF THE MAXIMUM FLOW PROBLEM

A number of uses have been found for the maximum flow idea other than the pipeline type problem we introduced in Section 5-1. It has been used in transport studies to maximize the traffic through a transport network such as a railroad or a highway system. These studies usually include a time dimension, so that a node is defined as a physical position (e.g., railway station, highway interchange) at a particular time. The links between the nodes then represent a traffic flow over space and time.

For example, a traffic engineer is studying the links between two cities at morning peak traffic, 7.00 A.M. to 9.00 A.M. During that period workers travel from the satellite city 1 to city 3. Two routes exist, one direct and one through an interchange at 2. Figure 5-8 gives the physical network. He wishes to find the maximum flow from city 1 to city 3 over this peak period.

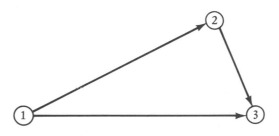

Figure 5-8. *Highway network from city 1 to city 3.*

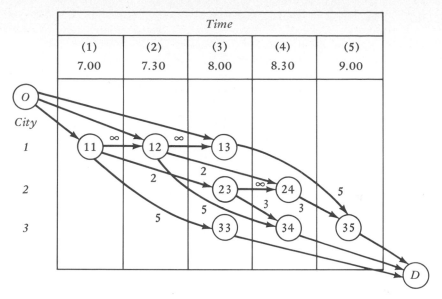

Figure 5-9. *Time/space network for highway flow.*

Data are available for maximum traffic capacity over a 30 minute interval for each link. These are: city 1 to city 2 has 2000 units capacity; city 1 to city 3 has 5000 units capacity; and city 2 to city 3 has 3000 units capacity. The average trip times are: city 1 to city 2 requires 60 minutes; city 1 to city 3 requires 60 minutes; and city 2 to city 3 requires 30 minutes. It is assumed that any number of vehicles can queue at city 1 or city 2.

Figure 5-9 gives a network, assuming traffic flow in 30-minute periods. Node O is a super-source, and node D is a super-sink. Each of the other nodes is designated ij, where i is the city and j is the time. Each link represents either a trip from one city to another or a 30-minute wait at a city. We define only those links that enable a worker to leave city 1 no earlier than 7.00 A.M. and arrive at city 3 no later than 9.00 A.M. The flow into D is the maximum possible flow into city 3 within the time restriction. The capacities on the links are given in thousands of units per 30 minutes.

Further applications of maximum flow in a network include routing calls in a telephone network, cargo flows in a particular transport node or a complex of nodes, and flows in electrical circuits.

5-6 FORMULATING THE TRANSPORTATION PROBLEM

Like the network flow problem, the *transportation problem* is a problem that bridges linear programming and graph theory. It also has a special solution technique—a variant of the simplex method—which is more efficient than the regular simplex method. Transportation problems should be viewed as problems with a specific

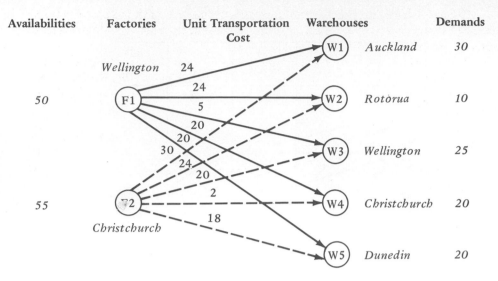

Figure 5-10. *Graph of transportation problem.*

linear programming or graph structure rather than problems with a particular inter-pretation as to the activities involved. A desirable feature of the transportation problem is that not only can it be solved by a special technique, but if the RHS of the linear programming formulation is integer, then the optimal solution will be integer—an enviable characteristic as we will see in Chapter 12.

A great variety of problems, seemingly unrelated, can be formulated as trans-portation problems. However, the most celebrated problem of this structure is the one that gave its name—the transportation problem.

Imagine a company in New Zealand producing a single commodity in two factories, one in Wellington (in the North Island), and one in Christchurch (in the South Island). The product is sold through five regional warehouses, Auckland, Rotorua, and Wellington in the North Island, and Christchurch and Dunedin in the South Island, as shown in the graph of Figure 5-10. Each node represents a factory or a warehouse, and each link represents a possible distribution path directed from a factory to a warehouse. The problem is to determine a transportation schedule from the two factories to the five warehouses so as to minimize total transportation costs.

Table 5-1. *Table of Unit Transportation Costs.*

Factories	Warehouses				
	W1	W2	W3	W4	W5
F1	24	24	5	20	20
F2	30	24	20	2	18

Table 5-1 reproduces the costs of transporting one unit of the commodity from factory Fi to warehouse Wj. Total shipping costs from a factory to a warehouse are directly proportional to the quantity shipped.

The decision variables of the problem are the quantities of the commodity shipped from each factory to each warehouse. Let x_{ij} be the quantity shipped from factory Fi to warehouse Wj. We shall first formulate this problem as a linear program.

Objective Function:

The objective is to minimize total transportation costs. From Table 5-1 we obtain the function

(5-11)
$$\text{minimize } z = 24x_{11} + 24x_{12} + 5x_{13} + 20x_{14} + 20x_{15} + 30x_{21}$$
$$+ 24x_{22} + 20x_{23} + 2x_{24} + 18x_{25}$$

Constraints:

The supply situation at factory F1 is shown in Figure 5-11.

The total amount shipped from factory F1 to all the warehouses must be no more than the amount available at the factory:

(5-12) $x_{11} + x_{12} + x_{13} + x_{14} + x_{15} \leqslant 50$ (*availability constraint*)

Similarly for factory F2:

(5-13) $x_{21} + x_{22} + x_{23} + x_{24} + x_{25} \leqslant 55$

The demand situation at warehouse W1 is depicted in Figure 5-12.

The total amount shipped to warehouse W1 from all the factories must be no

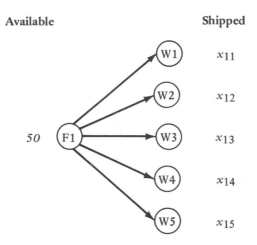

Figure 5-11. *Availability at factory F1.*

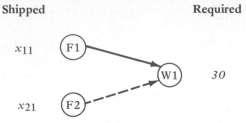

Figure 5-12. *Requirements at warehouse W1.*

less than the amount required at the warehouse:

(5-14) $x_{11} + x_{21} \geqslant 30$ *(demand constraint)*

Similarly for the other warehouses:

$$x_{12} + x_{22} \geqslant 10$$
$$x_{13} + x_{23} \geqslant 25$$
(5-15)
$$x_{14} + x_{24} \geqslant 20$$
$$x_{15} + x_{25} \geqslant 20.$$

Finally we have the usual nonnegativity conditions:

(5-16) $x_{ij} \geqslant 0$ for all i and j.

Equations (5-11) to (5-16) show the linear programming formulation of the transportation problem. Table 5-2 shows the linear program in detached coefficient form (without slack variables).

We notice from Table 5-2 that all the LHS coefficients are unity and that they have a special horizontal and diagonal structure. Each activity vector has only two nonzero elements, one in the row associated with its factory, and one in the row associated with its warehouse.

Table 5-2. *Transportation Problem in Detached Coefficient Form.*

x_{11}	x_{12}	x_{13}	x_{14}	x_{15}	x_{21}	x_{22}	x_{23}	x_{24}	x_{25}		RHS
1	1	1	1	1						$\leqslant$	50
					1	1	1	1	1	$\leqslant$	55
1					1					$\geqslant$	30
	1					1				$\geqslant$	10
		1					1			$\geqslant$	25
			1					1		$\geqslant$	20
				1					1	$\geqslant$	20

5-7 TRANSPORTATION PROBLEM IN GENERAL TERMS

Until now we have talked about factories and warehouses. Since the importance of the structure is mathematical, an identical analysis holds for *sources* and *destinations* of quite different sorts. If a particular problem can be thought of as the allocation of something from sources to destinations (in any sense of the words), then it is probably a transportation problem. For instance, the sources might be given by production capacity, the destinations by sales requirements, and the allocation be from sources to destination in various time periods. A sure way to identify a transportation problem is to look at the structure of the associated linear program in detached coefficient form.

There exists a feasible solution to the transportation problem only if the amount available at the factories (sources) is at least as much as the amount required by the warehouses (destinations). However, in order to use the special solution technique to be discussed, the amount available at the sources *must equal* the amount required by the destinations, and equality must hold for all the availability and demand constraints. Often in practice these equality assumptions do not hold, because availability is greater than requirements. In that case we add a dummy warehouse or destination whose demand for the commodity is equal to the difference between the quantity available from the sources and the quantity required by the real destinations. Transportation costs to the dummy destinations are zero from all sources. This restores the assumption that total availability equals total demand. Units shipped from a source to a dummy destination are interpreted as slack capacity at that source. Refer to exercise 5.5 at the end of this chapter for an example of the use of dummy warehouses.

Let us write out the transportation problem in general terms for m sources and n destinations. Let c_{ij} be the unit transportation cost from source i to destination j, a_i the quantity available at source i, and b_j the quantity required at destination j. Then the problem is:

$$\text{minimize} \quad z = \sum_{i=1}^{m} \sum_{j=1}^{n} c_{ij} x_{ij}$$

$$\text{subject to} \sum_{j=1}^{n} x_{ij} = a_i, \quad i = 1, \ldots, m \quad \text{(availability constraints)}$$

(5-17)

$$\sum_{i=1}^{m} x_{ij} = b_j, \quad j = 1, \ldots, n \quad \text{(demand constraints)}$$

$$x_{ij} \geqslant 0 \qquad \text{for all } i \text{ and } j$$

There are m times n variables and $m+n$ constraints. Since, by assumption $\sum_i a_i = \sum_j b_j$, one of the constraints of (5-17) is redundant. Therefore, a basis for this linear program contains only $(m+n-1)$ basic vectors.

Each vector in the linear program represents the shipping of the commodity from some source to some destination. Let us call the shipping of the commodity from source i to destination j the activity $\mathbf{P}_{ij}$. These vectors are given by the columns of Table 5-2.

5-8 REPRESENTING A VECTOR IN TERMS OF A BASIS

The key to the transportation technique is the special structure that results when we express a vector in terms of a basis for the transportation problem. The underlying logic is the same as that for the simplex method, but substantial simplifications, that enable a seemingly totally different method to be derived, are possible.

Let us look at what happens when we express a vector in terms of the basis. (For ease of identification, we give the basic vectors the superscript B.) We arbitrarily use the basis:

$$(5\text{-}18) \qquad (\mathbf{P}^B_{11}, \mathbf{P}^B_{12}, \mathbf{P}^B_{14}, \mathbf{P}^B_{23}, \mathbf{P}^B_{24}, \mathbf{P}^B_{25})$$

From Table 5-2 we see that, for instance, $\mathbf{P}_{13}$ can be written in terms of the three basic vectors $\mathbf{P}^B_{14}$, $\mathbf{P}^B_{24}$ and $\mathbf{P}^B_{23}$ as follows:

$$(5\text{-}19) \qquad \mathbf{P}_{13} \;=\; \mathbf{P}^B_{14} \;-\; \mathbf{P}^B_{24} \;+\; \mathbf{P}^B_{23}$$

$$
\begin{bmatrix} 1 \\ 0 \\ 0 \\ 0 \\ 1 \\ 0 \\ 0 \end{bmatrix}
=
\begin{bmatrix} 1 \\ 0 \\ 0 \\ 0 \\ 0 \\ 1 \\ 0 \end{bmatrix}
-
\begin{bmatrix} 0 \\ 1 \\ 0 \\ 0 \\ 0 \\ 1 \\ 0 \end{bmatrix}
+
\begin{bmatrix} 0 \\ 1 \\ 0 \\ 0 \\ 1 \\ 0 \\ 0 \end{bmatrix}
$$

Note how the signs of the basic vectors used alternate $(+, -, +)$. By the special structure of transportation problems, any nonbasic vector can always be represented by alternately adding and subtracting some of the basic vectors. Equation (5-19) can be interpreted as follows: $\mathbf{P}_{13}$ is the activity of shipping one unit from F1 to W3. Expressing $\mathbf{P}_{13}$ in terms of the basis is the same as shipping from F1 to W3 solely through the activities in the basis. This is achieved by shipping one unit from F1 to W4, then from W4 to F2, and finally from F2 to W3. The activity of shipping W4 to F2 is the reverse of $\mathbf{P}_{24}$, i.e., it is $(-\mathbf{P}_{24})$. This is shown diagrammatically in Figure 5-13, where all basic vectors are shown as solid lines and all nonbasic vectors as broken lines. The left-hand side of (5-19) is the heavy broken line from F1 to W3, while the right-hand side is the path of heavy solid lines from F1 to W3 via W4 and F2. (Ignore the direction of the arrows.)

In terms of the full basis, the coefficients resulting from expressing a vector in terms of the basis are either $+1$, or -1, or 0. The basic vectors are ordered in a string so that the coefficients alternate between $+1$ and -1, where a $+1$ refers to shipping from a factory to a warehouse, and a -1 represents the activity of shipping from a warehouse to a factory or, equivalently, refraining from shipping from a factory to a warehouse. Since the pattern always starts with a factory and finishes

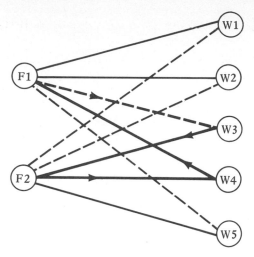

Figure 5-13. *Representation of nonbasic vectors.*

with a warehouse, there must be an odd number of basic vectors in the string, with the first and last coefficients equal to $+1$. All basic vectors not used in this representation have a coefficient of zero.

Rearranging equation (5-19) as

$$(5\text{-}20) \qquad\qquad \mathbf{P}_{13} - \mathbf{P}_{14}^{\mathrm{B}} + \mathbf{P}_{24}^{\mathrm{B}} - \mathbf{P}_{23}^{\mathrm{B}} = 0$$

it can be interpreted to mean that a unit sent from F1 to W3 requires a unit less from F1 to W4, a unit more from F2 to W4, and a unit less from F2 to W3. This process forms the "loop" in the graph of Figure 5-13.

No additional units are sent from any factory, and no fewer units are received by any warehouse. Equation (5-20) is merely a rearrangement of the schedule. This leads us to consider the effect of bringing $\mathbf{P}_{13}$ into the basis. As we send more units from F1 to W3 we are sending less from F2 to W3, more from F2 to W4, and less from F1 to W4. The most we can send from F1 to W3 is that amount which just drives the quantity from F2 to W3, or F1 to W4 to zero, i.e., we will send from F1 to W3, the minimum of the existing quantities being sent from F2 to W3 and F1 to W4.

5-9 STEPPING-STONE ALGORITHM

The *stepping-stone algorithm* is an adaptation of the simplex method. The special graph structure of the problem leads to considerable simplifications. The criterion for the vector to enter the basis carries over fairly simply from the simplex method. The only difference is that the transportation problem is usually a minimizing problem and this reverses the signs of all the $(z_{ij} - c_{ij})$ values, the subscripts here being ij rather than only j. Now we choose the most positive $(z_{ij} - c_{ij})$ value rather than the most negative.

CRITERION 1: VECTOR TO ENTER THE BASIS

The vector to enter the basis is the nonbasic vector with maximum $[(z_{ij} - c_{ij})$ for all $(z_{ij} - c_{ij}) > 0]$.

By analogy to the simplex method, if no $(z_{ij} - c_{ij}) > 0$ exist, the optimal solution has been found.

OPTIMALITY CRITERION

The solution associated with a given basis is optimal if all $(z_{ij} - c_{ij}) \leqslant 0$.

Assume that the vector to enter the basis $\mathbf{P}_{qr}$ has been decided and that the representation of that vector in terms of the basis has been made. The coefficient $+1$, -1, or 0 of the basic vector $\mathbf{P}_{ij}^{B}$ resulting from representing $\mathbf{P}_{qr}$ in terms of the basis, will be called the *coordinate of* $\mathbf{P}_{ij}^{B}$. The reasoning at the end of Section 5-8 gives:

CRITERION 2: VECTOR TO LEAVE THE BASIS

The vector to leave the basis $\mathbf{P}_{st}^{B}$ is the vector such that $x_{st} = $ minimum $[x_{ij}$ for all $\mathbf{P}_{ij}^{B}$ with $+1$ coordinates$]$.

NEW BASIC FEASIBLE SOLUTION

$$(1) \quad \hat{x}_{qr} = x_{st}$$

$$(2) \quad \hat{x}_{ij} = x_{ij} - x_{st} \quad \text{for } \mathbf{P}_{ij}^{B} \text{ with } +1 \text{ coordinates}$$

$(5\text{-}21)$

$$(3) \quad \hat{x}_{ij} = x_{ij} + x_{st} \quad \text{for } \mathbf{P}_{ij}^{B} \text{ with } -1 \text{ coordinates}$$

$$(4) \quad \hat{x}_{ij} = x_{ij} \quad \text{for } \mathbf{P}_{ij}^{B} \text{ with } 0 \text{ coordinates.}$$

Also, of course, $\hat{x}_{st} = 0$ since $\mathbf{P}_{st}$ is no longer a basic vector.

If there is a tie for the vector to satisfy criterion 2, any of the tied vectors may be chosen. However, at the next tableau the other vectors in the tie will be *degenerate*, i.e., they will be basic at zero value. Verify this with equations (5-21). We shall have more to say about this issue in Section 5-11.

While the graph theory representation of the transportation problem has been useful for exposition, for calculation purposes a tableau form is better. Table 5-3

Table 5-3. *Tableau Structure for Transportation Problem.*

	Warehouses					Availability a_i
	W1	W2	W3	W4	W5	
Factories F1	0 $\mathbf{P}^{\mathrm{B}}_{11}$	0 $\mathbf{P}^{\mathrm{B}}_{12}$	$\mathbf{P}_{13} \longrightarrow$	$+1$ $\mathbf{P}^{\mathrm{B}}_{14}$	$\mathbf{P}_{15}$	a_1
F2	$\mathbf{P}_{21}$	$\mathbf{P}_{22}$	$+1$ $\mathbf{P}^{\mathrm{B}}_{23} \longleftarrow$	-1 $\mathbf{P}^{\mathrm{B}}_{24}$	0 $\mathbf{P}^{\mathrm{B}}_{25}$	a_2
Require- ment b_j	b_1	b_2	b_3	b_4	b_5	

shows the tableau structure suitable for the transportation problem.   Each square (or *cell*) represents an activity $\mathbf{P}_{ij}$.   The cells are arranged with the sources vertical and the destinations horizontal.   In fact, each row corresponds to a source or availability constraint and each column to a destination or demand constraint.   The sum of the basic variables in row i equals a_i, and the sum for column j equals b_j.

Let us circle each basic vector in Table 5-3.   Note again that the representation of a nonbasic vector, such as $\mathbf{P}_{13}$, in terms of the basis has a "loop" structure.   Each corner of the loop is either a basic vector, or the nonbasic vector being expressed. The coordinates of the basic vectors start with a $+1$ for the basic vector in the loop which is adjacent to the nonbasic vector, and they alternate $(+1, -1)$ around the corners of the loop.   Basic vectors not on a corner of the loop have a coordinate of 0.

For actual computations each cell will contain the information shown in Figure 5-14.   In cells for nonbasic vectors, x_{ij} is left blank.   For basic vectors, $(z_{ij} - c_{ij})$ is left blank.   Degenerate basic variables are shown by a zero entry for x_{ij}.

Since we have not yet discussed how to choose an initial basis, we will again use the basis of equation (5-18) to illustrate the stepping-stone algorithm.

How do we find a better basic feasible solution?   The basis

$$(\mathbf{P}^{\mathrm{B}}_{11}, \mathbf{P}^{\mathrm{B}}_{12}, \mathbf{P}^{\mathrm{B}}_{14}, \mathbf{P}^{\mathrm{B}}_{23}, \mathbf{P}^{\mathrm{B}}_{24}, \mathbf{P}^{\mathrm{B}}_{25})$$

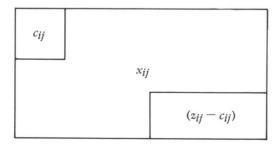

Figure 5-14. *The structure of cell* $\mathbf{P}_{ij}$.

Table 5-4. *First Transportation Tableau.*

	W1	W2	W3	W4	W5	a_i
F1	24 ㉚	24 ⑩	5 X⟶	20 +1 ⑩	20	50
			33		16	
F2	30	24	20 +1 ㉕◄	2 -1 ⑩	18 ⑳	55
	-24	-18				
b_j	30	10	25	20	20	Total Cost 2040

yields the solution $x_{11} = 30$, $x_{12} = 10$, $x_{14} = 10$, $x_{23} = 25$, $x_{24} = 10$, and $x_{25} = 20$. These values, the c_{ij} values, and the RHS parameters (availability and requirement), are all shown in Table 5-4. The total cost of this solution has been inserted in the bottom right-hand side cell as

$$24(30) + 24(10) + 20(10) + 20(25) + 2(10) + 18(20) = 2040.$$

To determine which vector, if any, should enter the basis, we need the $(z_{ij} - c_{ij})$ values for all nonbasic vectors. Consider $\mathbf{P}_{13} = \mathbf{P}_{14}^B - \mathbf{P}_{24}^B + \mathbf{P}_{23}^B$. The value z_{13} [the cost of sending one unit by the equivalent vector to $\mathbf{P}_{13}$, namely, $(\mathbf{P}_{14}^B - \mathbf{P}_{24}^B + \mathbf{P}_{23}^B)$], is $c_{14} - c_{24} + c_{23} = 20 - 2 + 20 = 38$. These are the costs in the left-hand corner of the corresponding cells in Table 5-4. The cost of sending directly from F1 to W3 (i.e., using $\mathbf{P}_{13}$) is $c_{13} = 5$. Hence $(z_{13} - c_{13})$ is $(38 - 5) = 33$. The unit cost of the equivalent vector to shipping from F1 to W3 is \$33 more than the unit cost of shipping directly. This number is inserted in the lower-right-hand corner of the cell for $\mathbf{P}_{13}$ in Table 5-4. You should verify what loops define the equivalent vectors to find the $(z_{ij} - c_{ij})$ values for $\mathbf{P}_{15}$, $\mathbf{P}_{21}$, and $\mathbf{P}_{22}$.

The $(z_{13} - c_{13})$ value is the greatest $(z_{ij} - c_{ij})$ value of all nonbasic vectors. So according to criterion 1, $\mathbf{P}_{qr} = \mathbf{P}_{13}$ enters the basis. From the loop of the equivalent vector to $\mathbf{P}_{13}$ we find the sequences of $+1$ and -1 associated with the basic vectors in the loop as shown in Table 5-4. By criterion 2 we take the vectors with $+1$ coordinates, $\mathbf{P}_{14}^B$ and $\mathbf{P}_{23}^B$, and obtain:

$$\text{minimum}(x_{14}, x_{23}) = \text{minimum}(10, 25) = 10 = x_{14}$$

Hence, $\mathbf{P}_{st}^B = \mathbf{P}_{14}^B$ leaves the basis, and by equations (5-21) the values of the variables at the new basis are:

$$\hat{x}_{13} = 10$$

$$\hat{x}_{23} = 25 - 10 = 15 \qquad \text{(the coordinate of } \mathbf{P}_{23} \text{ is } +1)$$

$$\hat{x}_{24} = 10 + 10 = 20 \qquad \text{(the coordinate of } \mathbf{P}_{24} \text{ is } -1).$$

x_{14} is now nonbasic.

Table 5-5. *Second Transportation Tableau.*

	W1	W2	W3	W4	W5	a_i
F1	24 ⟨30⟩	24 +1 ⟨10⟩	5 −1 ⟨10⟩	20 −33	20 −17	50
F2	30 / 9	24 X / 15	20 +1 ⟨15⟩	2 ⟨20⟩	18 ⟨20⟩	55
b_j	30	10	25	20	20	Total cost 1710

Table 5-6. *Third and Fourth Transportation Tableaux.*

	W1	W2	W3	W4	W5	a_i
F1	24 +1 ⟨30⟩	24 −15	5 −1 ⟨20⟩	20 −33	20 −17	50
F2	30 X / 9	24 ⟨10⟩	20 +1 ⟨5⟩	2 ⟨20⟩	18 ⟨20⟩	55
b_j	30	10	25	20	20	Total cost 1560
F1	24 ⟨25⟩	24 −6	5 ⟨25⟩	20 −24	20 −8	50
F2	30 ⟨5⟩	24 ⟨10⟩	20 −9	2 ⟨20⟩	18 ⟨20⟩	55
b_j	30	10	25	20	20	Minimum cost 1515

All other x_{ij} values are unaffected by the change of basis. This completes the first iteration. The new solution is given in Table 5-5. Its total cost is 1710, which is smaller than the previous solution by $(z_{qr} - c_{qr}) \hat{x}_{qr} = 33(10)$ or 330.

We are now ready for the second iteration. The first step is to find the updated $(z_{ij} - c_{ij})$ values for the nonbasic vectors, $\mathbf{P}_{14}$, $\mathbf{P}_{15}$, $\mathbf{P}_{21}$ and $\mathbf{P}_{22}$. Since $(z_{21} - c_{21})$ and $(z_{22} - c_{22})$ are positive, the solution reached at the end of iteration 1 is not optimal by the optimality criterion. Applying criterion 1, $\mathbf{P}_{22}$ enters the basis and, by criterion 2, $\mathbf{P}_{12}^B$ leaves the basis. The new basic solution is shown as the first tableau in Table 5-6. By the optimality criterion, this solution is not yet optimal. After a third iteration, all $(z_{ij} - c_{ij}) > 0$, and the optimal solution has been found with a minimum cost of 1515. The optimal shipping schedule is:

$$
\begin{array}{ll}
\text{F1 to W1} & \text{25 units,} \\
\text{F1 to W3} & \text{25 units,} \\
\text{F2 to W1} & \text{5 units,} \\
\text{F2 to W2} & \text{10 units,} \\
\text{F2 to W4} & \text{20 units,} \\
\text{F2 to W5} & \text{20 units.}
\end{array}
$$

5-10 INITIAL BASIC FEASIBLE SOLUTION

How do we find an initial basic feasible solution? One of the simplest ways is called the *northwest corner rule*. We start at the top left-hand cell, the northwest corner, and proceed down and to the right (in this order of preference), allocating to each cell as much as possible until the b_j requirement is satisfied but no a_i availability is violated. Starting at cell $\mathbf{P}_{11}$, the most it can take is minimum$(b_1, a_1) =$ minimum$(30, 50) = 30$. The first column is now satisfied, leaving $a_1 - b_1 = 50 - 30$ still to be allocated from F1, and x_{21} will be nonbasic. We now proceed to the second column. Here $x_{12} = $ minimum$(b_2, a_1 - b_1) = $ minimum$(10, 50 - 30) = 10$, leaving $a_1 - b_1 - b_2 = 50 - 40 = 10$ still to be allocated from F1. The third column gives $x_{13} = $ minimum$(25, 50 - 40) = 10$. The availability at F1 is now exhausted, so we proceed down column 3 to row 2: $x_{23} = $ minimum$(25 - 10, 55) = 15$; $x_{24} = $ minimum$(20, 55 - 15) = 20$; and $x_{25} = 25$. The resulting basis is shown in Table 5-7.

Table 5-7. *Initial Basis by Northwest Corner Rule.*

	W1	W2	W3	W4	W5	a_i
F1	30	10	10			50
F2			15	20	25	55
b_j	30	10	25	20	20	

The method used guarantees that the initial solution is feasible. The set of basic vectors is $(\mathbf{P}^B_{11}, \mathbf{P}^B_{12}, \mathbf{P}^B_{13}, \mathbf{P}^B_{23}, \mathbf{P}^B_{24}, \mathbf{P}^B_{25})$. As required, there are $(m+n-1)$ or 6 basic vectors. Having found an initial basic feasible solution, we can use the stepping-stone algorithm to proceed to the optimal solution.

There are other more sophisticated and efficient techniques for finding an initial basic feasible solution. Such methods take into account the values of the cost co-efficients, and tend to give a better initial solution than that of the northwest corner rule. One method called *column minimization* is introduced in Section 5-13. The advanced texts listed at the end of the chapter present more of these techniques.

At present, most computer codes for solving transportation problems do not use the stepping-stone algorithm. The codes are based on a minimal cost flow network algorithm, called the *out-of-kilter* algorithm, developed by D. Fulkerson. (See L. Ford and D. Fulkerson, *Flows in Networks*, Princeton University Press, 1962).

5-11 DEGENERACY

Degeneracy is a frequent occurrence in the transportation problem. While finding an initial basic feasible solution, degeneracy occurs when the allocation to a given cell satisfies both the unfilled requirement of the column and the remaining avail-ability of a row, except for the very last cell. Unless one appropriate cell is given a zero value, and made basic, the resulting set of vectors will not form a basis. Not many sets of $m+n-1$ vectors will form a basis. For a set of vectors to be basic there must be at least one basic vector in every row and one in every column, and it must not be possible to form loops consisting of basic vectors only. The simplest way of choosing the degenerate vector while finding an initial basic solution is to leave open either the row or the column with an amount zero still to be allocated from it. This ensures that some cell, in an appropriate position, is rendered basic with zero value. This case is illustrated in Table 5-8, where we have slightly altered the previous problem.

When the allocation is made to $\mathbf{P}_{12}$, both row 1 and column 2 are satisfied. We leave open row 1 with 0 to be assigned. Thus, $x_{13} = \mathrm{minimum}(0, 15) = 0$. (We could have left column 2 open, in which case x_{22} equals zero with $\mathbf{P}_{22}$ basic. The choice is arbitrary.)

As is true for the simplex method, degeneracy may cause the stepping-stone algorithm to go from iteration to iteration without any improvement of the objective

Table 5-8. *Initial Basis with Degeneracy.*

	W1	W2	W3	W4	W5	a_i
F1	30	20	0			50
F2			15	20	20	55
b_j	30	20	15	20	20	

function and occasionally may cause cycling among the same set of basic feasible
solutions. To prevent cycling, we could allocate to each degenerate cell (if there is
more than one) an infinitesimal amount, e_k, with magnitude $e_1 > e_2 > e_3, \ldots$. With
this convention, we can again apply the stepping-stone algorithm in the usual manner.
Once the optimal solution has been found, the values of all degenerate cells are set
equal to zero. In practice it is not usual to perturb the solution in this way.

*5-12 DUALITY AND THE *uv* METHOD

The dual of a transportation problem has a particularly interesting structure that is
useful for deriving a quick method of finding the $(z_{ij} - c_{ij})$ values of the primal transportation problems. The method is known as the *uv method*.

Let us derive the dual of our transportation problem using Table 5-2. First,
we define a dual variable for each constraint of the primal. In the primal there is an
availability constraint for each factory, Fi, and a demand constraint for each warehouse, Wj. We will find it useful to distinguish between these two types of constraint.
So, we define u_i to be the dual variable associated with the availability constraint of
Fi, and v_j to be the dual variable associated with the demand constraint of Wj.
Table 5-9 shows, in detached coefficient form, the result of applying the duality
relation 1 of Section 4-1. All u_i and v_j are unrestricted in sign.

We can see that each dual constraint contains exactly two variables—the ones
for the source and destination of the associated primal activity. For example, the
dual constraint associated with $\mathbf{P}_{23}$ is $u_2 + v_3 \leqslant 20$.

This structure permits us to effectively use the simplex multipliers (developed
in Section 4-4) for finding all of the $(z_{ij} - c_{ij})$ values. You will recall that we first

Table 5-9. *Dual Transportation Problem in Detached Coefficient Form.*

Dual Variable / Primal Variable	u_1	u_2	v_1	v_2	v_3	v_4	v_5		RHS
x_{11}	1		1					$\leqslant$	24
x_{12}	1			1				$\leqslant$	24
x_{13}	1				1			$\leqslant$	5
x_{14}	1					1		$\leqslant$	20
x_{15}	1						1	$\leqslant$	20
x_{21}		1	1					$\leqslant$	30
x_{22}		1		1				$\leqslant$	24
x_{23}		1			1			$\leqslant$	20
x_{24}		1				1		$\leqslant$	2
x_{25}		1					1	$\leqslant$	18
Objective Function	50	55	30	10	25	20	20		maximize

solve the dual for the simplex multipliers by applying the complementary slackness theorem. For example, for the basic solution of Table 5-4, the complementary slackness conditions give us the following set of equations:

$$
\begin{aligned}
u_1 &+ v_1 && && && = 24 \\
u_1 && + v_2 && && && = 24 \\
u_1 && && + v_4 && && = 20 \\
u_2 && && + v_3 && && = 20 \\
u_2 && && + v_4 && && = 2 \\
u_2 && && && + v_5 && = 18
\end{aligned}
$$

(5-22)

We see from equations (5-22) that all u_i and v_j are present in the set of equations, because a basis must have a vector in every row and column of the tableau. Also, there are seven variables $(m+n)$ but only six equations $(m+n-1)$, because of the redundancy noted in Section 5-7. We can solve equations (5-22) recursively as soon as one of the variables has been given an arbitrary value. Let us follow the usual tradition and set u_1 equal to zero. We immediately obtain $v_1 = 24$, $v_2 = 24$, and $v_4 = 20$. From $v_4 = 20$, we obtain $u_2 = -18$, and then $v_3 = 38$, and $v_5 = 36$.

It is now easy to write the $(z_{ij}-c_{ij})$ values for the nonbasic vectors. For example, z_{13} is the value of the left-hand-side of the dual constraint associated with x_{13}, i.e., $z_{13} = u_1 + v_3 = 0+38$, and c_{13} is the right-hand-side of that constraint, i.e., $c_{13} = 5$. So $(z_{13}-c_{13}) = u_1+v_3-c_{13} = 38-5 = 33$. In general we have

SIMPLEX MULTIPLIERS FOR THE TRANSPORTATION PROBLEM

(5-23) $$z_{ij} - c_{ij} = u_i + v_j - c_{ij}$$

These calculations can be performed much more compactly by incorporating the u_i and v_j values into the tableau format. Table 5-10 repeats Table 5-4, using the *uv* method. It is unnecessary to write out the dual constraints, since the relationships are so simple. We start by entering $u_1 = 0$ into the u_i column, and calculate the appropriate v_j values from basic vectors in the first row using $u_i+v_j = c_{ij}$ for these vectors. Starting from the left, the first basic vector in the first row is $\mathbf{P}^B_{11}$, so $v_1 = c_{11}-u_1 = 24-0 = 24$; the next is $\mathbf{P}^B_{12}$, so $v_2 = c_{12}-u_1 = 24-0 = 24$; and then $\mathbf{P}^B_{14}$—giving $v_4 = c_{14}-u_1 = 20$. We now use the columns of the v_j values which we have just determined to calculate further u_i values. There are no further basic vectors in either column 1 or column 2, so no additional u_i values can be found using them. In column 4, however, $\mathbf{P}^B_{24}$ is basic so we have $u_2 = c_{24}-v_4 = 2-20 = -18$. We do not know any more v_j values, so we now look at the rows for the u_i values we have just calculated—in our case row 2. The procedure we used for row 1 is repeated for row 2, and so on, until all u and v_j have been calculated.

Table 5-10. *First transportation tableau—uv method.*

	W1	W2	W3	W4	W5	a_i	u_i
F1	24 (30)	24 (10)	5	20 (10)	20	50	0
			33		16		
F2	30	24	20 (25)	2 (10)	18 (20)	55	−18
	−24	−18					
b_j	30	10	25	20	20	2040	
v_j	24	24	38	20	26		

To find the $(z_{ij} - c_{ij})$ values of the nonbasic vectors, we use equations (5-23), as we did previously. No matter how large the problem, only mental arithmetic is required.

Returning to the question of duality, the simplex multipliers become the optimal dual solution at the optimal primal tableau. The perceptive reader may be uneasy because the values are relative and not absolute. With a little more thought, we realize that not one of the a_i or b_j values can be changed on its own since $\sum a_i = \sum b_j$, but must always be accompanied by a change in at least one of the other RHS parameters. It is not hard to show that the net effect of the two (or more) changes is absolute. You are asked to consider this sort of postoptimal analysis in exercise 5.6.

5-13 ALLOCATION OVER TIME—A REGULAR TIME/OVERTIME PROBLEM

A manufacturer has orders for one of its products for the next four months as follows:

Month	1	2	3	4
Units Ordered	5000	8000	12000	7000

Each month the manufacturer can produce 6000 units in regular time and 3000 units in overtime. The unit cost of production is $10 in regular time and $15 in overtime. Inventory costs from one month to the next are $2 per unit. The manufacturer wishes to schedule production in regular time and overtime to meet the demand, minimizing total cost. No back ordering is permitted.

Let us formulate this problem as a linear program. We define

- r_{ij} to be regular time production in month i to meet demand in month j, and
- q_{ij} to be overtime production in month i to meet demand in month j.

In both cases the variables are defined only for $j \geqslant i$.
The cost of production is

$$\sum_{i=1}^{4} \sum_{j=i}^{4} (10r_{ij} + 15q_{ij})$$

The inventory cost is

$$\sum_{i=1}^{4} \sum_{j=i}^{4} [2(j-i)(r_{ij} + q_{ij})]$$

So, the objective function is

$$\text{minimize } z = \sum_{i=1}^{4} \sum_{j=i}^{4} [(10 + 2(j-i))r_{ij} + (15 + 2(j-i))q_{ij}]$$

There are three sets of constraints: production capacity regular time, production capacity overtime, and demand requirements—one constraint of each type for each month.
Production capacity regular time month i:

$$\sum_{j=i}^{4} r_{ij} \leqslant 6000$$

Production capacity overtime month i:

$$\sum_{j=i}^{4} q_{ij} \leqslant 3000$$

Demand requirements month j:

$$\sum_{i=1}^{j} (r_{ij} + q_{ij}) \geqslant D_j$$

where D_j is the number of units ordered for month j.

Table 5-11 gives this linear program in detached coefficient form. From Table 5-11 we see that the problem has almost the transportation structure, only the absence of variables r_{ij} and q_{ij} for $j < i$ precludes it. If we could introduce them, but at the same time also make sure that they would never appear in the optimal solution, then the transportation structure would be complete without violating the original problem. This can easily be achieved by arbitrarily assigning to these variables extremely large objective function coefficients, say $+\infty$.
Using this trick, we can now cast the problem into the format of the transportation tableau, as shown in Table 5-12. Our sources are regular-time capacity

Table 5-11. *A Linear Program in Detached Coefficient Form.*

	r_{11}	r_{12}	r_{13}	r_{14}	q_{11}	q_{12}	q_{13}	q_{14}	r_{22}	r_{23}	r_{24}	q_{22}	q_{23}	q_{24}	r_{33}	r_{34}	q_{33}	q_{34}	r_{44}	q_{44}	
Objective Function	10	12	14	16	15	17	19	21	10	12	14	15	17	19	10	12	15	17	10	15	minimize
Production Capacity																					
regular time month 1	1	1	1	1																	$\leqslant$ 6000
overtime month 1					1	1	1	1													$\leqslant$ 3000
regular time month 2									1	1	1										$\leqslant$ 6000
overtime month 2												1	1	1							$\leqslant$ 3000
regular time month 3															1	1					$\leqslant$ 6000
overtime month 3																	1	1			$\leqslant$ 3000
regular time month 4																			1		$\leqslant$ 6000
overtime month 4																				1	$\leqslant$ 3000
Demand																					
month 1	1				1																$\geqslant$ 5000
month 2		1				1			1			1									$\geqslant$ 8000
month 3			1				1			1			1		1		1				$\geqslant$ 12000
month 4				1				1			1			1		1		1	1	1	$\geqslant$ 7000

Table 5-12. *Regular Time/Overtime Transportation Tableau.*

	Demand					
Production	Month 1	Month 2	Month 3	Month 4	Slack	a_i
Regular time month 1	10 — 5000	12 — 1000	14 — (0)	16 — (−6)	0 — (−5)	6000
Overtime month 1	15 — (0)	17 — (0)	19 — 1000	21 — (−6)	0 — 2000	3000
Regular time month 2	✕	10 — 6000	12 — (0)	14 — (−6)	0 — (−7)	6000
Overtime month 2	✕	15 — 1000	17 — 2000	19 — (−6)	0 — (−2)	3000
Regular time month 3	✕	✕	10 — 6000	12 — (−6)	0 — (−9)	6000
Overtime month 3	✕	✕	15 — 3000	17 — (−6)	0 — (−4)	3000
Regular time month 4	✕	✕	✕	10 — 6000	0 — (−5)	6000
Overtime month 4	✕	✕	✕	15 — 1000	0 — 2000	3000
b_j	5000	8000	12000	7000	4000	

and overtime capacity in each of the months—the source of the production. Our destinations are orders to be filled in each of the months—the destination of the production. We also include a destination called "slack". This is a dummy destination of the form mentioned in Section 5-7. The demand of the slack destination is the amount of capacity available in excess of that required to meet the true demand of the four month period, i.e., $36000 - 32000 = 4000$. We assume that the slack capacity is costless. In this problem our allocation is not over space, as in the previous problem, but over time.

The inadmissible activities (those with $+\infty$) are represented by crossed out cells in Table 5-12. Also, the difference between production capacity and demand is assigned to the slack, or dummy, column. A feasible solution exists only if the accumulated production capacity is at least as great as the accumulated demand at each month.

For this problem we find the initial basic feasible solution by a rule called *column minimization*. Starting in column 1, the cells to be allocated are chosen not by the downward-and-to-the-right rule as in the northwest corner rule, but in ascending order of cost value. First, the cell with the lowest cost in column 1, i.e. P_{11} (since $c_{11} = 10$), is filled as much as possible: (minimum $(6000, 5000) = 5000$). If the column is not satisfied, the next lowest cost is chosen and the procedure repeated until the column is fully allocated. The same procedure is followed for column 2, i.e., minimum $(c_{i2}, \text{all } i) = c_{32} = 10$. So, $x_{32} = $ minimum $(6000, 8000) = 6000$. The column is not satisfied. The next lowest c_{i2} is $c_{12} = 12$, so

$$x_{12} = \text{minimum} (6000 - 5000, 8000 - 6000) = 1000.$$

Still column 2 is not satisfied. Next lowest c_{i2} is $c_{42} = 15$, so

$$x_{42} = \text{minimum} (3000, 1000) = 1000.$$

When column 2 is finished, we start column 3, and so on. In column 3 neither P_{13} nor P_{33} can be allocated anything because rows 1 and 3 are already fully used.

We have described the column minimization method because when it is used on a simple regular time/overtime problem like this, it always gives the optimal solution immediately—as we see from the $(z_{ij} - c_{ij})$ values in Table 5-12.

The minimum cost schedule is achieved by producing at full regular time capacity every month, and full overtime capacity in months 2 and 3, but only 1000 units in overtime in months 1 and 4.

The regular-time/overtime problem with back ordering involving a late delivery penalty is considered in exercise 5.12.

*5-14 A THREE-STAGE TRANSPORTATION PROBLEM

A company has two factories, two warehouses, and three stores. Each month it ships its production to the two warehouses where it is redistributed to the three stores. Figure 5-15 gives the configuration with factory capacities and store requirements. The unit cost for each line is also shown. At present, we assume that the warehouses have unlimited capacity. We wish to minimize distribution costs.

Available

Required

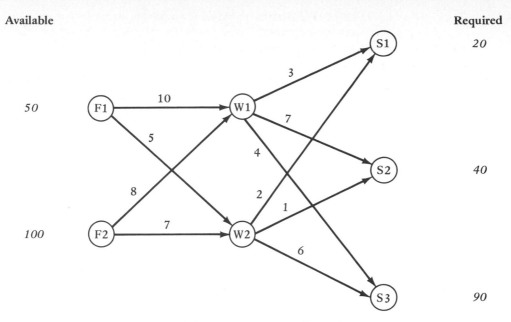

Figure 5-15. *Three-stage transportation problem.*

We can solve this as a simple 2×3 transportation problem by using the fundamental principle for deriving the c_{ij} values—they are the *least costs* from the sources to destinations. By inspection we can verify that the least cost from F1 to S1 is minimum $(10+3, 5+2) = 7$, i.e., from F1 to W2 to S1. Hence, we obtain Table 5-13, and the transportation tableau in Table 5-14.

Let us now alter this problem somewhat. First, we assume that W1 is rather small, with a maximum handling capacity of only 50 units. We see from Table 5-12 that the old optimum is not now feasible. Secondly, we assume that attached to W2 is a store which requires 30 units per month, and we increase the available supply at F1 to 60 and at F2 to 120 accordingly.

Let us consider the a_i and b_j values for warehouses W1 and W2. The most W1 can accept from all sources is its handling capacity of 50 units. If it receives less, some of its capacity remains unused. Since W1 is now both a source and a destination, we can, by stretching our imagination, view unused capacity as shipping from

Table 5-13. *Least Costs from Factories to Stores.*

	S1	S2	S3
F1	7 via W2	6 via W2	11 via W2
F2	9 via W2	8 via W2	12 via W1

Table 5-14. *Optimal Transportation Tableau Three-stage Problem.*

	S1	S2	S3	a_i
F1	7 \ 20	6 \ 30	11 \ (−1)	50
F2	9 \ (0)	8 \ 10	12 \ 90	100
b_j	20	40	90	

W1 to itself. With this consideration, the demand at W1 can thus be set equal to its handling capacity, i.e., $b_j = 50$ for W1. Similarly, no more than its handling capacity can be shipped from W1, including shipments to itself. Hence, its $a_i = 50$.

W2 has no upper handling capacity. However, we can arbitrarily introduce a handling capacity. All we have to ensure is that it is sufficiently large so as to never be restrictive on the optimal solution. Setting the handling capacity equal to the total supply of 180 units is one way of guaranteeing this. Hence its $b_j = 180$. However,

Table 5-15. *Revised Three-stage Transportation Problem.*

		Destinations					
		W1	W2	S1	S2	S3	a_i
Sources	F1	10 \ 50	5 \ 10	✕	✕	✕	60
	F2	8 \ (4)	7 \ 120	✕	✕	✕	120
	W1	0 \ (11)	✕	3 \ 20	7 \ 30	4 \ (8)	50
	W2	✕	0 \ 50	2 \ (−5)	1 \ 10	6 \ 90	150
	b_j	50	180	20	40	90	

at most, 150 units can leave W2, because W2 has a true destination demand of 30 units. Thus, its a_i value is only 150.

With these tricks we can now construct the transportation tableau shown in Table 5-15 for the revised problem. The cells representing slack capacity or shipments from a warehouse to itself—activities P_{31} and P_{42}—clearly have zero cost coefficients. All inadmissible cells involving shipments from factories directly to stores or from one warehouse to the other are shown as crossed cells.

The feasible solution shown in Table 5-15 sends 50 units from F1 through W1 to S1 and S2; 10 units from F1, and 120 units from F2 through W2 to W2 (itself), S2, and S3. The 50 units in the W2/W2 cell constitutes the amount of the 180 units of capacity at W2, which is unused. The solution is clearly not optimal, but you may wish to find the optimal solution.

This last example involves most of the concepts of the *transshipment problem*, which is a transportation problem that allows a shipment from source to destination through other sources and destinations. The nature of W2 is that it is both a destination in its own right, and a transshipment point.

*5-15 EXTENSIONS TO MAXIMUM FLOW AND TRANSPORTATION PROBLEMS

The network flow problem can be extended to include a cost per unit flow in each link. The *minimum cost flow* problem entails finding the system of flows that will send a certain flow from source to sink. A generalization of this problem places upper and lower bounds on the flows in each link, and finds the minimum cost feasible flow. The solution method that solves this general problem is known as the *out-of-kilter algorithm*, which is an extension of the labeling technique of this chapter.

We can formulate the transportation problem as a minimum cost flow problem with upper and lower bounds on the links. Figure 5-16 shows the transportation problem of Figure 5-10 as a minimum cost flow problem.

The sources are linked back to a supersource (SO), and the sinks are linked forward to a supersink (SI). The vector (U, L, c) associated with each link gives the upperbound, lowerbound, and unit cost respectively for that link. The links from Fi to Wj have as their upperbound the maximum amount available at Fi; their lowerbound is zero, and the costs are the unit transport costs on this route. All this information comes from Figure 5-10. The links from SO to Fi have as their upperbound the amount available at Fi; the lowerbound is zero to allow for the destinations taken together to require less than the sources have available. This link has no cost. The link from Wj to SI has upper and lower bounds equal to the amount required at Wi. The upper bound could be given a higher value if more than the minimum required was acceptable. The cost for the link again is zero. It is the upper and lower bounds on the links that force a feasible flow through the system when we minimize cost.

The particular advantage of this formulation is that it allows a genuine capacity bounds on the links. For example, there may be an upper limit on the number of

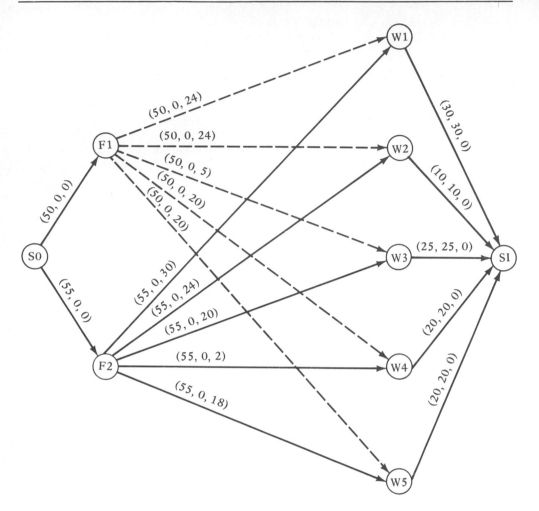

Figure 5-16. *Network-flow version of the transportation problem.*

units that can be sent from a particular source to a particular destination. The upper limit will then become the U value for that link. A transportation problem with such capacity limits is called a *capacitated transportation problem*.

Until recently it appeared that the out-of-kilter algorithm was the most efficient method to solve even an ordinary transportation problem. In their interesting study F. Glover, D. Karney, D. Klingman and A. Napier ("A Computation Study on Start Procedures, Basis Change Criteria and Solution Algorithms for Transportation Problems", *Management Science*, 20, Jan. 1974.) developed a computer program for the stepping-stone algorithm that is considerably better for the ordinary transportation problem than the most efficient out-of-kilter program they could obtain. It is even competitive for capacitated transportation problems.

EXERCISES

5.1   Using the labeling technique find the maximum flow in the following network.

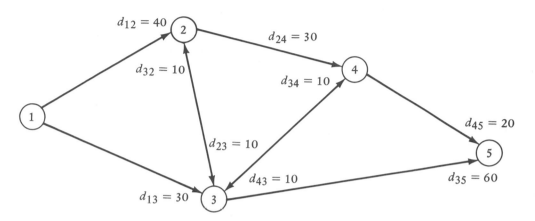

5.2   Find the maximum flow from 1 to 6 and 7 in the following network.

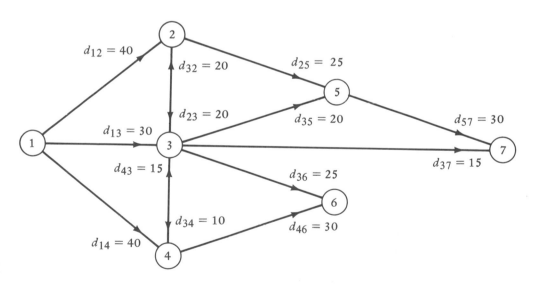

5.3   Beginning at Figure 5-7, find the maximum flow for each of the following changes, considered separately.

(i) d_{35} increases from 9 to 11.

(ii) d_{13} increases from 6 to 8, and d_{45} increases from 5 to 9.

(iii) A new link from 1 to 4 is opened with a capacity limit $d_{14} = 6$, and d_{45} increases from 5 to 9.

5.4 A manufacturer has three factories, one each at cities A, B, and C, and four warehouses located at cities 1, 2, 3, and 4. The following table gives the monthly production capacities of the factories, the monthly requirements at the warehouses, and the per unit transportation costs.

		Warehouses				Available
		1	2	3	4	at Factories
	A	2	3	6	2	5000
Factories	B	4	6	1	7	10000
	C	9	8	3	9	15000
Required by Warehouses		4000	10000	8000	8000	

Solve this transportation problem.

5.5 Solve problem 5.4 with the amount available at factory A changed to 10000.

5.6 Consider the following transportation tableau

		1	2	Warehouses 3	4	Dummy	a_i
Factories 1	4		1 100	4	2 150	0 50	300
2	1 200		4	5	1	0	200
3	2 0		2	6 175	1	0 25	200
b_j		200	100	175	150	75	

(i)   Find the optimal solution.
(ii)   Write schedules for the production manager and the distribution manager.
(iii)* Find the new optimum for $c_{34} = 3$. Do *not* start from scratch.
(iv)* Using the optimal dual variables, find the change in minimum cost if warehouse 4 requires 50 more units.

5.7 A nationwide retailing organization, Bargains Inc., is running a special line of shirts. Three suppliers have bid for the job, the first offering to supply up to 200,000 shirts at $3 each, the second up to 150,000 at $3.50 each, and the third 150,000 at $3.20 each. The company has five warehouses which service the retailing stores. These warehouses estimate requirements of 40,000; 70,000; 60,000; 100,000; and 50,000 shirts respectively. Bargains Inc. will pay freight from the suppliers to their warehouses. Freight costs per 1000 shirts are given in the following table.

Freight Costs per 1000 Shirts, in $100.

	To Warehouse				
From	1	2	3	4	5
Supplier					
1	4	2	7	2	1.5
2	3	6	1	2.5	3
3	3.5	3	4	1.5	1

The company wants to know how many shirts to buy from each supplier, and the shipping schedule from suppliers to warehouses. The objective is to minimize total cost.

5.8 An engineering company has the problem of assigning the day's jobs to various machines. Most machines can do most of the jobs, but with differing efficiency. Also to be considered is the setting up cost of each machine for each job; this varies according to what the machine was previously set up to do, and the job which is now assigned to it. With the data detailed below, the company wishes to minimize the total cost of today's work. (The tasks that the machines were previously set up to do are implicit in the table of set-up costs.) Formulate this problem as a transportation problem and find the first three tableaux. (This problem is an example of the so-called *assignment problem*—a variant of the transportation problem where all variables are restricted to assume values of 0 or 1 only. There exists a special solution technique that takes advantage of its mathematical structure.) See C. McMillan, *Mathematical Programming*, 2nd ed. (New York: John Wiley, 1975), pp. 120–122.)

Cost of Each Job on Each Machine in Multiples of $100.

		Jobs					
		1	2	3	4	5	6
	1	8	4	10	2	1	6
	2	6	6	12	4	3	5
Machines	3	2	4	8	1	1	4
	4	10	8	15	6	2	3
	5	5	7	20	4	4	1
	6	8	2	10	4	2	4

Set-up Cost of Each Machine for Each Job in Multiples of $100.

		Job					
		1	2	3	4	5	6
	1	1.0	0.5	1.5	0.8	0	0.1
	2	1.0	0.8	1.0	0.5	0.1	0.2
Machines	3	0	1.0	2.5	1.5	1.0	0.5
	4	1.5	1.5	0	2.0	1.0	1.0
	5	2.0	1.0	1.0	1.0	0.5	0.5
	6	0.5	0.8	0	0.4	0.5	1.0

5.9   Set up the following network as a transportation problem showing transshipment through all nodes. The amount available at each node is indicated. A negative value indicates a requirement at that node. The following table indicates the cost per unit of shipping between the nodes.

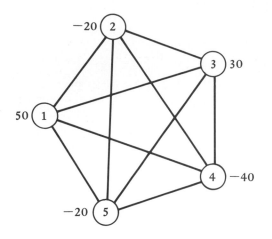

Shipping Costs in $100

	1	2	3	4	5	Nodes
	–	2	3	5	1	1
		–	2	4	3	2
			–	1	2	3
				–	6	4
					–	5

5.10   A manufacturer can normally produce 450 units of product X in a month. But, with special arrangements, at a cost of $1.50 for each additional unit, the capacity can be increased to 600 units a month. Demand for the next four months is as follows:

Month	Demand
1	200
2	800
3	600
4	400

The company stores and distributes its product from its warehouse some distance away. Transport from the factory to the warehouse presents a problem because the manufacturer has only one suitable truck that can deliver up to 300 units a month at a cost of $2 per unit. However, an identical vehicle is available for hire for any portion of the month, but costs, using this truck, are $2.50 per unit. Inventory cost is $1.00 per unit per month, and inventory on hand at the beginning of month 1 is 100 units. Formulate this problem as a transportation problem to minimize cost. Set out the initial tableau.

5.11   A medical research center is planning to conduct an important 5-day experiment. The experiment uses a large number of a special type of container which must be thoroughly cleaned after each day used. Since the cleaning process is intricate and costly, an industrial cleaner has contracted to do it. To have a container ready for the next day the cleaning charge is $3 per container. A slower process, taking a day longer, costs $2 per container. The price of a new container is $10, and these containers are available on demand. They do not need cleaning. The research center estimates that it needs the following number of containers for each of the five days:

Day 1	3000
Day 2	2500
Day 3	4000
Day 4	2000
Day 5	2500

Each day approximately 10 percent of these containers will be broken. The medical research center wishes to minimize the cost of purchasing and cleaning the containers. Set up the problem as a transportation problem. Perform the first iteration.

5.12 Solve the regular time/overtime problem of Section 5-13 with the following extension:

Back ordering (i.e., postponement of delivery) is permitted for two months. The cost of back ordering (administration and loss of goodwill) for one month is $1 per unit, and for two months is a total of $5 per unit.

Does the column minimization method produce the optimal solution at the initial basic feasible solution?

REFERENCES

Bennington, G. E. "An Efficient Minimal Cost Flow Algorithm," *Management Science*, 19, May 1973. A superior technique to the out-of-kilter algorithm for the minimum cost flow probelm.

Daellenbach, H. D., and E. Bell. *A User's Guide to Linear Programming*. Englewood Cliffs, N.J.: Prentice-Hall, 1970. Section 7-1 introduces the transportation problem at an elementary level. A good treatment of the production scheduling problem (regular time/overtime problem) is presented in Sections 4-4 and 7-4.

Elmaghraby, Salah E. "The Theory of Networks and Management Science: Part I," *Management Science*, 17, Sept. 1970. An expository treatment of two network models (shortest path and flow networks) with examples.

Glover, F., D. Karney, D. Klingman, and A. Napier. "A Computation Study on Short Procedures, Basis Change Criteria, and Solution Algorithms for Transportation Problems," *Management Science*, 20, Jan. 1974. This is a comparative study of different techniques for solving the transportation problem. It assumes a thorough knowledge of the subject and a good idea of computer programming. The conclusion is that the stepping-stone algorithm, suitably streamlined, is superior to the out-of-kilter algorithm.

Hadley, G. *Linear Programming*. Reading, Mass.: Addison Wesley, 1962. Chapter 9 develops the stepping-stone algorithm by rigorous mathematics. Sections 10-1 to 10-8 present the labeling technique. In particular, Sections 10-6 and 10-7 give a matrix method for the labeling technique.

Hu, T. C. *Integer Programming and Network Flows*. Reading, Mass.: Addison Wesley, 1969. A thorough and advanced text. Part II gives a complete treatment of network flows commencing with the maximal flow problem.

Kaufmann, A. *Graphs, Dynamic Programming and Finite Games*. New York: Academic Press, 1967. Section 6B of Chapter I describes the maximal flow problem applied to a traffic system, and 6E outlines an actual study made on the railroad between Paris and Lyons.

Noble, K. J., and R. B. Potts.   "Network Flow Model of the Australia–Europe Container Service," in G. F. Newell, ed., *Traffic Flow and Transportation*.   New York: American Elsevier Publishing Co., 1972.   This study builds on a time/space traffic flow network of container movements between Australia and Europe.

Plane, D. R., and C. McMillan, Jr.   *Discrete Optimization*.   Englewood Cliffs, N.J.: Prentice-Hall, 1971.   Chapter 6 develops, at a level suitable for the average reader, network optimization techniques.   Of very special interest is a description of the out-of-kilter algorithm, since this important algorithm is rarely developed at this level.

Sprinivasan, V.   "A Transshipment Model for Cash Management Decision," *Management Science*, 20, June 1974.   This article presents an interesting and efficient use of the transportation problem to cash management.

6

Project Planning and Scheduling Techniques

Research and development projects usually consist of a number of interrelated tasks or activities. Certain tasks can be executed simultaneously. Some tasks can only be started after other tasks have been completed, i.e., precedence relationships exist between the various tasks. Each task takes a given time to complete, and tasks may require scarce resources, such as manpower or funds. We may be interested in finding the earliest time that the project can be completed with the resources available. A number of other planning and scheduling problems, such as construction projects, periodic overhaul or maintenance of large installations, most capital expenditure projects, or the introduction of new products or procedures all require a coordinated plan that involves sequencing of interrelated ordered tasks and deployment of limited resources.

In the late 1950s a number of closely related approaches based on network analysis were developed to deal with such problems. Chapter 6 gives a brief survey of the two best known techniques, the *critical path method* or *CPM* and the *program evaluation and review technique* or *PERT*. Both have proved themselves not only as tools of planning but also as tools of controlling the execution of the plans.

Section 6-5 requires some elementary knowledge of random variables and their probability distributions, as reviewed in Appendix B, Sections B-2 and B-4.

6-1 NETWORK EVENT REPRESENTATION

Let us digress to the abbreviated case study discussed in Section 1-9 of Chapter 1. The problem there deals with an inventory control project. After a two-week orientation period, the operations researcher begins working out a detailed project proposal for an integrated inventory control and demand forecasting system. He produces the flow chart, Figure 6-1, which lists the various tasks (somewhat simplified) that have to be undertaken to complete the project. It shows the order in which the tasks have to be undertaken. For instance, task C (formulate a mathematical model for the proposed inventory control system, or ICS) can only start when task A (detailed

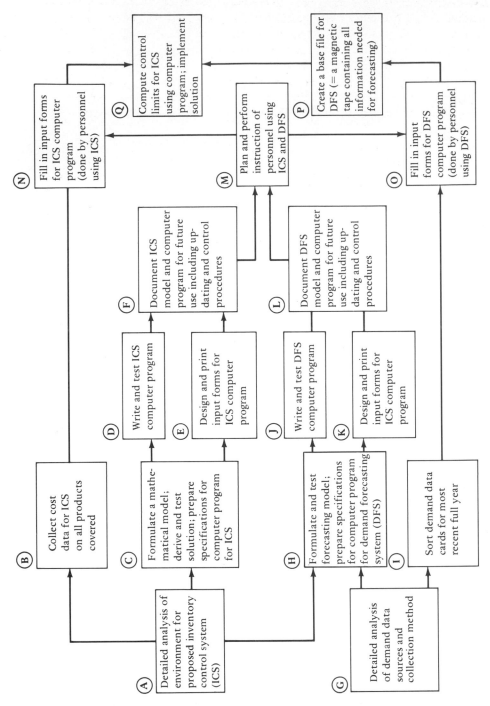

Figure 6-1. *Flow of tasks for an inventory control project.*

192

analysis of environment for proposed ICS) has been completed.   Task H (formulate forecasting model) can only start after the detailed analysis of the environment for the proposed inventory control system and of the demand data sources, i.e., after tasks A and G have been completed.   Similarly, the computation of the control limits for the products stored in inventory (task Q) can only start if both the input forms for the ICS program have been filled in (task N) and the demand forecasting base file, from where the ICS program obtains demand forecasts, has been created (task P).   Table 6-1 lists the precedence relations and estimates for the durations of the seventeen tasks.

Assume that we can draw on a sufficient number of people to have any number of tasks executed simultaneously.   If the project is given the go-ahead, what is the earliest project completion date?   This is one of the questions we would like to have answered.

For small problems, such as ours, the answer can easily be found by enumerating all possible sequences of tasks.   In our example, there are 14 different sequences. The project is only completed when the sequence with the longest time has been completed.

The critical path method or CPM provides an efficient technique to find the longest time sequence.   In Figure 6-1, we use blocks (or nodes) to represent each activity.   The arrows between the nodes simply indicate the precedence relations. Although this flow chart could be used directly to perform the computations of the critical path method, there are certain advantages in reversing this convention and

Table 6-1. *List of Tasks for Inventory Control Project.*

Tasks	Precedence	Duration in Weeks
A	—	3
B	A	12
C	A	4
D	C	10
E	C	2
F	D, E	3
G	—	2
H	A, G	4
I	G	3
J	H	16
K	H	2
L	J, K	2
M	F, L	2
N	B, M	2
O	I, M	1
P	O	2
Q	N, P	3

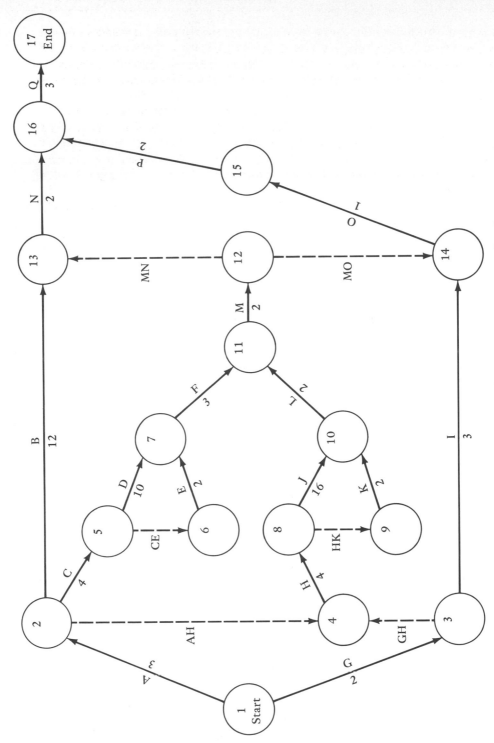

Figure 6-2. *Network diagram for an inventory control project.*

drawing a network where directed lines or links represent tasks, and nodes indicate the precedence relationships. With each link we associate a number that represents the duration of the task. Since each link starts at a node and ends at a node, nodes also represent the event of starting or completing a task. Often nodes are therefore referred to as *events*.

Figure 6-2 depicts the network associated with the tasks listed in Table 6-1 using this principle. The nodes are numbered consecutively in such a manner that each link always leads from a lower order node to a higher order node. Node 1 represents the start of the project. The length of the link is usually not drawn proportionally to the duration of the tasks. The number under each link is the duration of the corresponding task.

In this representation each task is uniquely defined by the two nodes where the corresponding link starts and ends. For instance, task A can be denoted by $(1, 2)$. The duration of task A is denoted by t_{12}. In general a task is identified by nodes (i, j) and its duration by t_{ij}. If the problem is solved on a computer, this is a convenient way to specify tasks and task durations.

Our network shows several links as broken lines. They are introduced to avoid ambiguities in the network logic or to allow proper representation of precedence relations. Consider, for instance, the sequence of tasks C, D, E, and F as shown in Figure 6-1. Tasks D and E both follow C, and F requires both D and E to be completed. This ordering could be represented as shown in Figure 6-3.

Tasks D and E both start and end at the same nodes. If tasks are referred to by the starting and ending nodes, then both would be denoted by $(5, 7)$. To avoid this we would introduce a *dummy task* which has a zero duration, and which leads to a new node. In Figure 6-2 the dummy task gives rise to link CE (connecting tasks C and E) which leads from node 5 to node 6. Task E is then started from this new node 6. Each task is now again uniquely defined by two node numbers. Exactly the same reasoning leads to the introduction of dummy task HK. Note that the dummy task could precede task D rather than task E, or it could follow either task D or E rather than precede it. (However, whenever possible the dummy task should precede a task that gives rise to it, otherwise the computations of free float, described in Section 6-3, are less straightforward.)

A somewhat different situation gives rise to the remaining four dummy tasks. For instance, the dummy tasks AH and GH are required because task H has both

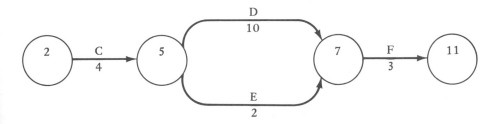

Figure 6-3. *An ambiguous representation of tasks.*

A and G as predecessors, whereas tasks B and C only depend on task A, but not on task G, and task I only requires task G, but not task A. The dependence of task H on tasks A and G is indicated by the dummy tasks AH and GH. Explain why dummy tasks MN and MO are needed.

In terms of this network, the earliest project completion date is equivalent to finding the longest path through the network.

6-2 EARLIEST PROJECT COMPLETION TIME

Assume that we were able to determine that the *earliest finish times* for tasks N and P are the end of week 29 and the end of week 30, respectively. Thus, the *earliest time* at which all tasks prior to node 16 are finished is the end of week 30—the latest of the two earliest finish times. Only at that time can task Q be started. The *earliest start time* of a task is therefore defined to be equal to the earliest time of the node where the task starts, i.e., the latest of the earliest finish times of all preceding tasks. In our case, this is the end of week 30. The duration of task Q is 3; hence we find that the earliest finish time of task Q is the end of week 33. Task Q being the last task to be performed, the end of week 33 is also the earliest completion time of the entire project.

In fact, we do not yet know the earliest finish times of tasks N and P. They could be determined if we knew the earliest times of nodes 13 and 15. These in turn could be found if we had the earliest finish times of the preceding tasks, etc. This gives us the idea to begin at the starting node and systematically evaluate the earliest times for each node until we reach the final node.

For this evaluation it is convenient to divide each node circle into three parts, as shown in Figure 6-4.

Initially we are only interested in the ET_j portion. Here we insert the earliest time (ET) that node j can be reached. At least that many periods (weeks in our case) must have elapsed since the beginning of the project before any task following node j can be started. The earliest time refers thus to the end of period ET_j.

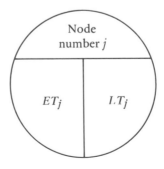

Figure 6-4. *Use of node circles in computations.*

EARLIEST TIME ET_j OF NODE j

ET_j is equal to the latest of the earliest finish times for all tasks preceding node j, i.e.,

(6-1) $$ET_j = \text{maximum}(EF_{i_k j}, \text{all } i_k)$$

where (i_k, j) is a task ending at node j, and
$EF_{i_k j}$ is the earliest finish time of task (i_k, j).

EARLIEST FINISH TIME OF TASK (i, j)

Let t_{ij} be the duration of task (i, j), then the earliest finish time of task (i, j) is

(6-2) $$EF_{ij} = ET_i + t_{ij}$$

The complete evaluation for our project is shown in Figure 6-5.   If the nodes have been properly numbered, i.e., no higher numbered node leads to a lower numbered node, then the nodes can be evaluated in numerical order.   The evaluation uses the following simple algorithm:

ALGORITHM FOR EVALUATING EARLIEST PROJECT COMPLETION TIME

1. Set $ET_1 = 0$
2. Go to next higher numbered node.   Evaluate earliest finish times of all tasks that end at that node.   Find the earliest time for that node, using equation (6-1).
3. If there remain any nodes that have not been evaluated, return to step 2, otherwise terminate iterations.

You should now test your understanding of this algorithm.   Work out the earliest times of all nodes using Figure 6-2, and verify the result with the solution shown in Figure 6-5.

It is usually convenient to have only one terminal node.   If the original problem has more than one terminal node, simply introduce dummy tasks as needed.   In this case, the earliest time of the last node evaluated gives the earliest project completion time.

6-3 THE CRITICAL PATH

We now have a method for finding the earliest project completion time.   Our next problem is to find which path of tasks has the longest completion time.   Any delay in these tasks will delay the earliest project completion time.   Thus, the tasks on this

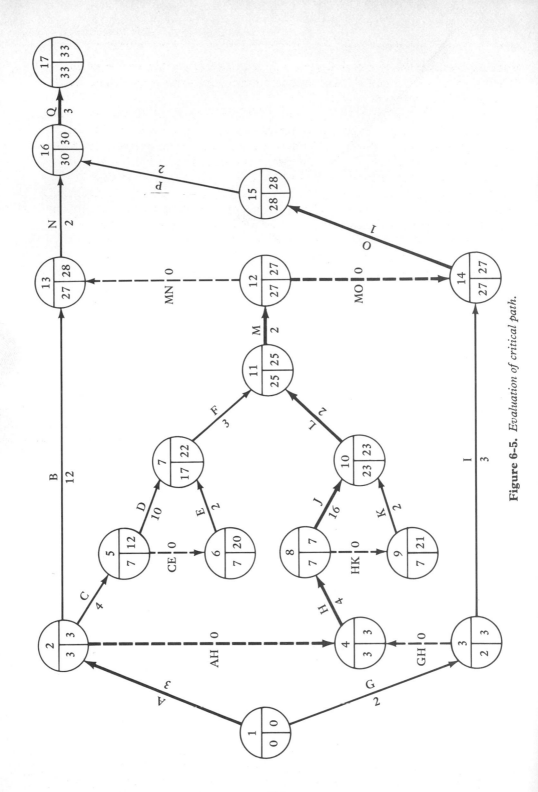

Figure 6-5. *Evaluation of critical path.*

path are the critical ones, and this path is referred to as a *critical path* of the network. There may be several paths that all have the same longest completion time. Each such path is a critical path.

How can we identify a critical path? Consider node 13 in Figure 6-5. The earliest time all tasks preceding it can be finished is $ET_{13} = 27$. (Remember that it denotes the end of a period.) This is also the earliest start time for task N. However, since task N only takes 2 weeks and the earliest time of node 16 is $ET_{16} = 30$, task N can be delayed by at least one week without delaying the completion time of the entire project. The *latest start time* for task N is the end of week 28. If any tasks preceding task N are delayed such that the start time for tasks from node 13 is later than the end of week 28, the project completion time is also delayed. In other words, the *latest time, LT,* all tasks preceding node 13 have to be finished without delaying the whole project is the end of week 28.

On the other hand, task P can be started, at the earliest, by the end of week 28, the earliest time of node 15. Given that task P takes 2 weeks to complete, and the earliest time of node 16 is 30, the latest start time of task P is also the end of week 28. There is no leeway. Unless all tasks preceding node 15 are finished by this time, the project completion will be delayed. In other words, the latest start time of task P is the same as the earliest time of node 15. This property holds for all tasks on a critical path.

CRITICAL TASKS AND CRITICAL PATHS

A task for which the latest start time is equal to the earliest time of its starting node is a critical task. Each path from the start node to the end node of the network that consists of critical tasks only is a critical path.

Thus, we found a simple way to identify the critical tasks of a network and all critical paths.

To determine the latest times of all nodes, we use an algorithm similar to the one we used to find the earliest times.

LATEST TIME LT_i OF NODE i

LT_i is equal to the earliest of the latest start times for all tasks following node i, i.e.,

(6-3) $$LT_i = \text{minimum}(LS_{ij_k}, \text{all } j_k)$$

where (i, j_k) is a task starting at node i, and LS_{ij_k} is the latest start time of task (i, j_k).

LATEST START TIME OF TASK (i, j)

The latest start time of task (i, j) is

(6-4) $$LS_{ij} = LT_j - t_{ij}$$

ALGORITHM FOR FINDING LATEST TIMES

1. Set $LT_I = ET_I$, where I is the terminal node.
2. Go to the first lower numbered node. Evaluate latest start times of all tasks that begin at that node. Find the latest time for that node, using equation (6-3).
3. If the starting node has been evaluated, terminate iterations; otherwise, return to step 2.

These computations are also shown in Figure 6-5 in the right-hand-side portion of the node circles which was labeled by LT_j in Figure 6-4.   Verify the results!

We can now identify the critical path by the nodes with $ET_i = LT_j - t_{ij}$;

nodes	1 → 2	→	4 → 8 → 10 → 11 → 12	→	14 → 15 → 16 → 17
tasks	A	dummy	H J L M	dummy	O P Q

This path is identified by the heavy line in Figure 6-5.

Any task not on the critical path can be delayed, within limits.   If we consider each task by itself (neglecting any interactions with preceding or subsequent tasks), then the difference between the earliest time of the node from which the task starts and its latest start time is the largest amount by which the task can be delayed without affecting the earliest completion time of the project.   This difference is called the *total slack* or *total float* (*TF*) of the task.   Thus, critical tasks have zero total float.

TOTAL FLOAT OF TASK (i, j)

(6-5)
$$TF_{ij} = LS_{ij} - ET_i = LT_j - ET_i - t_{ij}.$$

For example, the noncritical task B $= (2, 13)$ has a

$$TF_{2,13} = LS_{2,13} - ET_2 = (28-12) - 3 = 13$$

If task B is delayed by more than 13 weeks, then the earliest completion time of the entire project will be delayed.

However, delaying one task may affect the amount by which subsequent tasks can be delayed, since the float along a segment of the network is shared by all the tasks along that segment.   For example, tasks C, D, and F all share the same float of 5. The largest amount by which a task may be delayed without affecting the earliest start time of any subsequent tasks is called *free slack* or *free float* (*FF*).   Free float is the amount of float available when all other tasks take place at their earliest times. For instance, the noncritical task B may be delayed by up to 12 weeks without affecting task N.   Its free float is thus 12.   On the other hand, the noncritical task G cannot be delayed at all without delaying any of the subsequent tasks.   Free float can never exceed total float.   Along any segment of the network where all tasks have the same total float, only the last task has a positive free float.   For example, of tasks C, D, and F, which have the same total float of 5, only F has a free float and its free float is 5.

FREE FLOAT OF TASK (i, j)

(6-6) $$FF_{ij} = ET_j - EF_{ij} = ET_j - ET_i - t_{ij}.$$

Again, for task B = $(2, 13)$

$$FF_{2, 13} = ET_{13} - EF_{2, 13} = 27 - (3+12) = 12.$$

Both free float and total float are useful for planning decisions.   The planner has some choice as to when to start tasks with float.   This may allow him to schedule such tasks in a manner that reduces the amount of manpower needed.   For instance, tasks E and K are similar in nature and, thus, require the same professional training. Both could be started after week 7.   Since both have float, they can be scheduled in such a manner that the same person can do both tasks consecutively.

6-4 ACTUAL PROJECT PLANNING AND CONTROL THROUGH CPM

The computations for determining the critical path and the amount of total and free float are so simple that projects with up to a few hundred tasks can still be performed by hand.   Any self-contained segments of the network that have only a beginning and an ending node in common with other parts can be analyzed separately.   By inserting only the final results of this analysis into the total project structure, the whole segment can be regarded as a single task.   Using this trick, a complex network can be broken down into a number of smaller networks, each of which is analyzed for its critical paths.

Larger projects are best analyzed by computer, and most computer manu-facturers provide computer programs to analyze critical path networks.   These can handle projects with several thousand tasks and automatically keep track of the amount of various resources required during the project.   Some programs allow the input to be in the form of Figure 6-1, i.e., tasks are attached to nodes rather than to links, eliminating the translation process.   The program may contain a calendar covering up to 25 years, which includes all official holidays.   All start and finish dates are assigned by the program to their projected calendar date.   The program may also allow special work and shift patterns to be specified.

The practical use of CPM is twofold.   It is a tool for detailed planning and scheduling of projects made up of a large number of interconnected tasks.   However, it is also a highly useful aid in continuously measuring the actual progress of the project according to the plan.   Such continuous control allows management to predict delays or pinpoint situations that could lead to delays—often well ahead of the actual occurrence of the delays.   Corrective and remedial action can thus be taken early enough to counteract some of the consequences of late project completion. Furthermore, by using the current progress status as the starting point, management

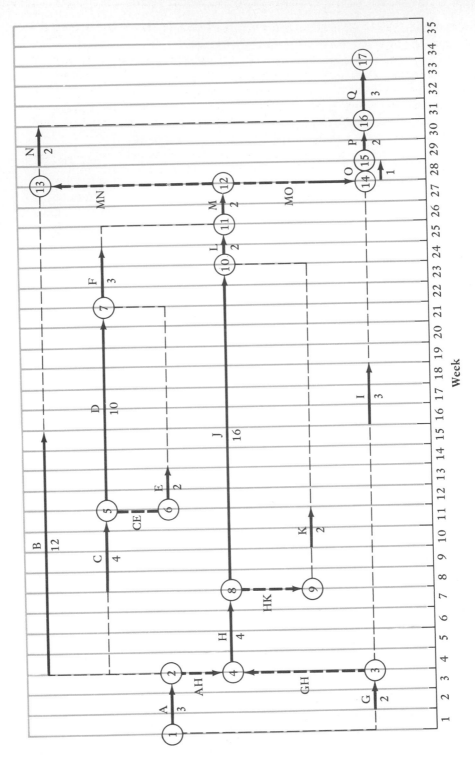

Figure 6-6. *Schedule graph of a CPM network.*

202

can work out the new projected critical path and earliest completion time in the light of the latest information.

Continuous control is more effectively achieved if we redraw the CPM network as a *schedule graph*. On this graph the horizontal projection of all links is drawn to a time scale representing their task duration. Usually, we also have to plan the starting dates for noncritical tasks. Figure 6-6 shows a possible schedule graph for the inventory control project studied earlier. Actual task times are drawn as solid lines, and float times as dotted lines.

In this project, tasks that require the same professional training are scheduled, as far as possible, in such a manner that the same person can perform them. For example, task H (formulate forecasting model) is followed by task C (formulate inventory control model). The former is on the critical path, the latter has considerable float.

As the project progresses, we continuously monitor the actual execution by marking the progress of each task on the schedule graph. When we observe or predict any irregularities, such as late starts or excessive task durations, we can immediately determine whether they will cause a delay in project completion. Self-contained segments of a project can be controlled individually.

For large projects, this control is best done directly by computer. Some CPM computer programs are specifically designed for control purposes by keeping the current status of a project on a random access memory file, such as a disk. Progress on task completions, as well as any new estimates of task durations for tasks not yet started or completed or any other changes in the project can be fed into the computer at any time. The program can also be instructed to provide a new status report, flag present and predicted delays in task completions, and update the critical path and float times.

6-5 PROGRAM EVALUATION AND REVIEW TECHNIQUE—PERT

Although PERT was developed concurrently and independently of CPM, it can be approached as an extension of CPM to deal with uncertainties in the task durations. All our computations to find the critical path were based on estimated or expected duration times. PERT is an attempt to determine not only the expected length of the critical path, but also to obtain some measure of the variability of the earliest project completion time. We say *attempt* because PERT does not fully succeed in this objective.

In PERT, task durations are assumed to be independent random variables, each with expected value t_{ij} and variance σ_{ij}^2. Thus, any path through the network represents a sum of independent random variables. In particular, the length of the critical path as determined by CPM is such a random variable with

(6-7)
$$\text{expected value } \mu = \sum_{\substack{\text{all } (i,j) \text{ on} \\ \text{critical path}}} t_{ij}$$

and

(6-8)
$$\text{variance } \sigma^2 = \sum_{\substack{\text{all } (i,\,j) \text{ on} \\ \text{critical path}}} \sigma_{ij}^2$$

(Expression (6-8) follows from the fact that the variance of the sum of independent random variables is equal to the sum of the variances of the random variables. See Section B-2 of Appendix B.)

Traditionally, PERT assumes that the individual tasks follow a particular form of the *Beta distribution,* which lends itself to an intuitively appealing interpretation for the task duration, as shown in Figure 6-7.

The operations researcher may be hard pressed to determine the actual distribution of task durations. On the other hand, management may be less reluctant to summarize the distributions by the minimum, maximum, and most likely duration times. Using the transformation shown in Section B-4 of Appendix B for the Beta distribution, the three estimates yield the following values for the expected task duration and its variance:

(6-9)
$$t_{ij} = \tfrac{1}{3}(2m + \tfrac{1}{2}(a+b))$$
$$\sigma_{ij}^2 = (\tfrac{1}{6}(b-a))^2$$

Consider a simple example. The heavy-duty diesel motor of the emergency power generating plant of a factory needs an extensive overhaul job. At the same time, the concrete base which is cracked also has to be remade. Management plans to have this job performed during the annual vacation closing of the factory. The factory remains closed for only 3 weeks or 15 working days. Management would like to know whether the overhaul job can be finished during the closing. Table 6-2 summarizes the various tasks of the job.

The t_{ij} and σ_{ij}^2 values are found using expressions (6-9). Note that if the minimum and the maximum times are equal, there is no variability in the task duration, and hence, the variance is zero. This is the case for tasks A and E. For task B we obtain:

$$t_{ij} = \tfrac{1}{3}(2m + \tfrac{1}{2}(a+b)) = \tfrac{1}{3}(2(7) + \tfrac{1}{2}(6+14)) = \tfrac{24}{3} = 8$$
$$\sigma_{ij}^2 = (\tfrac{1}{6}(b-a))^2 = (\tfrac{1}{6}(14-6))^2 = (\tfrac{4}{3})^2 = \tfrac{16}{9}$$

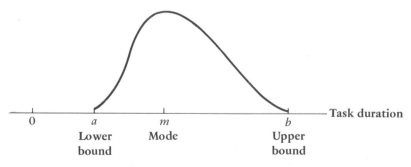

Figure 6-7. *Beta distribution and task duration.*

Table 6-2. *Diesel Motor Overhaul.*

		In Days				
Task	Precedence	Mode m	Minimum a	Maximum b	t_{ij}	σ_{ij}^2
A. Dismantle motor	—	2	2	2	2	0
B. Overhaul motor	A	7	6	14	8	$\frac{16}{9}$
C. Rebuild motor base and cure	A	9	8	10	9	$\frac{1}{9}$
D. Test and adjust motor	B	2.5	2	6	3	$\frac{4}{9}$
E. Mount motor on base	C, D	2	2	2	2	0

The t_{ij} values so computed are now used as input in finding the critical path in the same manner as for CPM. Since the t_{ij} values are estimates of expected values, the duration of the critical path is also an estimate of an expected value. For our simple problem, the critical path can be found by inspection. It consists of tasks A, B, D, E. By expressions (6-7) and (6-8) we find the following statistics for the expected length of the critical path and its variance or standard deviation:

$$\text{Expected length of critical path} = 2 + 8 + 3 + 2 = 15 \text{ days}$$

$$\text{Variance of duration} = 0 + \tfrac{16}{9} + \tfrac{4}{9} + 0 = \tfrac{20}{9}$$

$$\text{Standard deviation} = \sqrt{\tfrac{20}{9}} = 1.49 \text{ days}$$

Thus, the expected length of the critical path is just equal to the closing period.

What is the probability distribution of the length of the critical path? From probability theory we know that, no matter what the form of the individual probability distributions, the probability distribution of a sum of independent random variables is approximately normal for a sufficiently large number of variables. We also assume that the contribution of each random variable is small in comparison to the total. If the individual distributions are not highly skewed and none of the tasks dominate all others as to length, this property holds approximately for as few as $n = 10$ tasks. (Obviously, if the individual distributions are close to normal, it holds for even smaller numbers.) Therefore, we can use the normal distribution to make probability statements about the duration of any path through the network and, in particular, about the length of the critical path.

For the sake of demonstrating the principle, let us assume that for our problem the normal distribution is a sufficiently good approximation. We can then state that with probability 0.9099 the duration of the critical path does not exceed 17 days, and with probability 0.9778 the duration does not exceed 18 days, as shown in Figure 6-8.

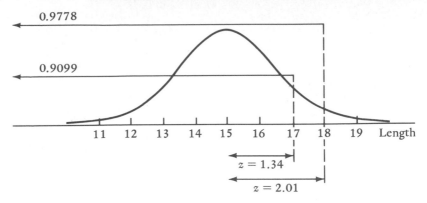

Figure 6-8. *Probability of length of critical path.*

Since the expected earliest project completion time is equal to the length of the critical path, it is easy to fall into the trap of concluding that the probability of an earliest project completion time of no more than 17 days is 0.9099. This would be a fallacy! Let us see why.

Although noncritical tasks will not affect the *expected* earliest project completion time, they may affect its variability. Tasks with a small amount of slack, but large variability, may have a significant probability that the length of the paths on which they lie may turn out to be longer than the critical path. PERT simply ignores these effects and, therefore, tends to underestimate the variability of the earliest project completion time. Unfortunately there exist no analytic methods to deal with this problem. *Stochastic simulation* is the only way to derive the empirical distribution of the earliest project completion time. (Refer to Chapter 15 on simulation.)

In our particular example, a probabilistic statement about the length of the critical path is practically equivalent to a statement about the earliest project completion time. The reason for this is the very small variance of the only noncritical task—task C.

Since the variability of the earliest project completion time depends on the variability of all tasks on the critical path, as well as on tasks of "near" or "close-to-critical" paths, any action that can reduce the variance of these tasks reduces the variability of the earliest project completion time, and therefore increases the probability of meeting project target dates.

6-6 THE CRITICAL PATH METHOD COST MODEL

The cost of completing a project usually can be divided into the costs directly related to the individual tasks, such as manpower and equipment applied to the task; and the costs related to the duration of the project as a whole, such as managerial services and other overhead items. Most tasks can be expedited if more resources are applied to them. Figure 6-9 illustrates such relationships. In simplest form, they are linear.

Direct costs are lowest at a normal level, b_{ij}. Any slow-down beyond this level

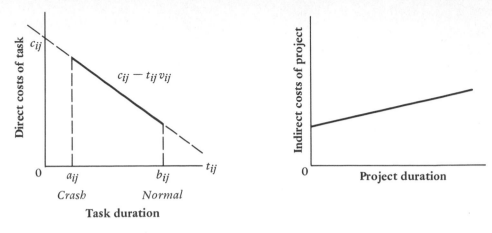

Figure 6-9. *Costs associated with a project.*

does not produce further cost savings. The duration cannot be cut below the *crash* level, a_{ij}. Our objective is to find a schedule of task durations that minimizes total direct and indirect costs.

For small problems the following heuristic reasoning will usually find the optimal schedule. We start out with an initial schedule using normal duration times for all tasks, yielding, in some sense, the maximum length critical path. We now attempt to stepwise reduce the total project duration by expediting one or more of the critical tasks. As critical tasks are shortened, the float of parallel noncritical tasks decreases and ultimately vanishes. Therefore, further decreases in the earliest project completion time may entail reducing several critical tasks on parallel critical paths simultaneously. Any critical task or combination of parallel critical tasks are candidates for being expedited when the combined rate of increase of direct costs as measured by their v_{ij} components is less than the rate of savings of indirect costs. At each stepwise reduction or iteration, the critical task or combination of critical tasks with the smallest total rate of increase of direct costs is chosen as the candidate for expediting. At least one candidate task is shortened to its crash level, a_{ij}, in each iteration unless a noncritical task becomes critical on a parallel path prior to reaching this level. For small projects these computations are best done on a schedule graph.

Consider the data shown in Table 6-3. Indirect project costs amount to $500

Table 6-3. *CPM Cost Project.*

Task	Precedence	Normal Time b_{ij}	Crash Time a_{ij}	Direct Costs c_{ij}	v_{ij}
A	—	8 weeks	4 weeks	3200	300
B	—	4	3	1000	100
C	B	2	1	1800	400
D	A, C	3	2	700	200

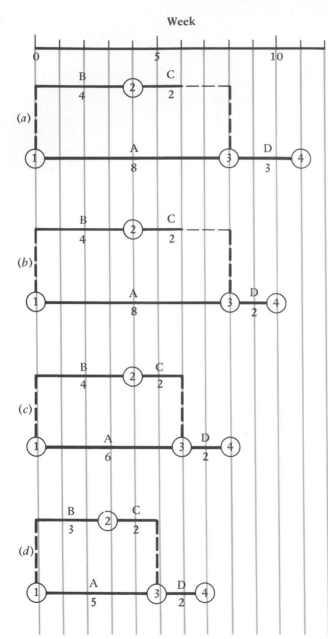

Week

Critical path for normal times:
Total cost $8000
Task D has lowest $v_{ij} = 200 \leqslant 500$ and is a candidate for expediting.

First iteration:
Task D reduced to $a_{ij} = 2$; new total cost $7700
Task A now has lowest $v_{ij} = 300 \leqslant 500$ and is a candidate for expediting.

Second iteration:
Task A reduced to $t_{ij} = 6$; B and C now become critical. New total cost $7300
Tasks A and B together have sum of v_{ij} of $300 + 100 \leqslant 500$ and are candidates for expediting.

Third iteration:
Task B reduced to $a_{ij} = 3$, task A reduced to $t_{ij} = 5$. New total cost $7200
No combinations of tasks on critical paths have rates of direct costs totalling less than 500. Minimum cost schedule reached.

Figure 6-10. *Iterations of CPM cost model.*

per week.   Part (a) of Figure 6-10 shows the schedule graph of the critical path for normal task durations, $t_{ij} = b_{ij}$.   Its length is 11 weeks.   The total cost is found by summing over all tasks the direct costs, $c_{ij} - t_{ij} v_{ij}$, and adding the indirect project costs.   The latter amount to $500 multiplied by the length of the critical path, or $5500.   The direct cost for task A is $3200 - 8(300) = \$800$.   Verify that direct costs for the remaining tasks are $600, $1000, and $100.   The total for normal task duration is thus $8000.

We now find the task on the critical path with the lowest rate of increase of direct costs, v_{ij}.   This is task D with $v_{ij} = \$200$.   Since this is less than the weekly rate of indirect project costs, task D is expedited, in this case to its crash time of $a_{ij} = 2$.   Costs go up by $200 in direct costs and down by $500 in indirect costs. The next critical path has a length of 10 weeks and a total cost of $7700.   This is shown in part (b) of Figure 6-10.   At the second iteration, task A is expedited by 2 weeks.   At that point the total float for tasks B and C has been reduced to zero, and they become critical tasks.   The new critical path of length 8 is shown in part (c). We now search for combinations of tasks on parallel critical paths for simultaneous time reductions.   Tasks A and B have a rate of increase of direct costs of $300 + $100 or $400, which is less than the rate of indirect project costs.   The maximum reduction possible is one week, at which point task B reaches its crash time.   The new critical path of 8 weeks is shown in part (d).   No further time reduction can be made now without increasing total costs.   Why?   The optimal project duration is thus 8 weeks at a cost of $7200.

Although this method is fairly effective for small problems, it becomes cumbersome for even moderate size problems of several dozen tasks, and at that point an optimal solution can no longer be guaranteed.   More powerful approaches are then needed to tackle the problem.   This is the topic of the next section.

*6-7 THE LINEAR PROGRAMMING FORMULATION OF A SCHEDULING PROBLEM

As we have seen in Chapter 5, some network problems can be formulated as linear programs.   Let x_i denote the time (earliest or latest) of completing all tasks preceding node i.   Then the time of node j has to satisfy

(6-10) $$x_j - x_i \geqslant t_{ij}, \qquad \text{all tasks } (i, j)$$

Let I denote the terminal node.   Then x_I is the total project completion time. The objective is to minimize this number:

(6-11) $$\text{minimize } x_I$$

By expression (6-10), $x_1 \leqslant x_i$ for all i, and from expressions (6-10) and (6-11) it follows that the optimal value of $x_1 = 0$.

If we wish to find the earliest time at all nodes, then we wish to make all x_i as small as possible.   This can be achieved with the alternative objective function of

(6-12) $$\text{minimize } \sum_i x_i$$

Both formulations have as many variables as nodes and as many constraints as tasks. Let us point out that CPM is a much more efficient technique for finding the critical path than the simplex method. It is possible, however, to reformulate the problem as a transportation problem which can be solved by inspection in a single pass through the table. (See text by G. Thornley listed in the bibliography.)

Next, we introduce cost considerations. Let the direct costs associated with task (i, j) be a linear function of the task duration t_{ij} (a variable now) as follows:

$$c_{ij} - v_{ij} t_{ij}, \qquad a_{ij} \leqslant t_{ij} \leqslant b_{ij}$$

where c_{ij} is the (theoretical) intercept of the cost curve with the ordinate for $t_{ij} = 0$,

and v_{ij} is the cost reduction gained by increasing the task duration by one period.

(See Figure (6-9).) The value of t_{ij} is restricted to values between the crash level, a_{ij}, and the normal level, b_{ij}. The objective is to find activity levels, t_{ij}, that

(6-13)   minimize $\sum_{ij} (c_{ij} - v_{ij} t_{ij}) + C x_I$

where C is the indirect project cost per period, and, if x_1 is set to zero, x_I represents the earliest project completion time. Since $\sum_{ij} c_{ij}$ is a constant, this equivalent to

(6-14)   maximize $\sum_{ij} v_{ij} t_{ij} - C x_I$

The linear programming variables, $x_i, i = 1, 2, ..., I$; and t_{ij}, all (i, j), are subject to the following constraints lower and upper bounds on task duration:

(6-15) $a_{ij} \leqslant t_{ij} \leqslant b_{ij}$ all (i, j)

and

(6-16) $x_j - x_i - t_{ij} \geqslant 0$ all (i, j)

For a cost formulation, the number of variables increases to the number of nodes plus the number of tasks, and the number of constraints becomes three times the number of tasks. However, with advanced linear programming computer codes, constraints (6-15) can be handled by upper and lower bounding and do not give rise to actual constraints.

If the project completion time should not exceed T periods, then this can easily be added to the formulation by setting an upper bound of T to x_I.

J. E. Kelley in the article listed in the bibliography shows how the special structure of the critical path cost linear programming model gives rise to a computational approach that is more efficient than the simplex method.

The linear programming formulation also makes it possible to include, in the model, restrictions on manpower and other resources shared by several tasks, and to find the optimal schedule under these conditions. Conventional critical path analysis cannot properly cope with such restrictions.

EXERCISES

6.1 The following maintenance job has to be performed periodically on the heat exchangers in a refinery.

	Task	Precedence	Duration in hours
A	Dismantle pipe connections	—	14
B	Dismantle header, closure, and floating head front	A	22
C	Remove tube bundle	B	10
D	Clean bolts	B	16
E	Clean header and floating head front	B	12
F	Clean tube bundle	C	10
G	Clean shell	C	6
H	Replace tube bundle	F, G	8
I	Prepare shell pressure test	D, E, H	24
J	Prepare tube pressure test and make the final reassembly	I	16

(a) Draw a CPM network. Introduce dummy tasks as needed.
(b) Find the earliest and latest times for each node. Identify the critical path. What is its length?
(c) Find the total float and free float for each task.
(d) Draw a schedule graph.

6.2 The brain trust of Creative Toys has just come up with the idea for a new plastic toy. Can it be ready for Christmas sales? It is July now. Working from past experience the assistant manager breaks the project into the following tasks.

	Task	Precedence	Duration in weeks
A	Initial market survey	—	1
B	Detailed design of toys and dies	A	3
C	Cost and demand analysis	B	2
D	Manufacture of dies	B	2
E	Procurement of materials for toy	B	4
F	Trial manufacture	D	1
G	Planning of sales promotion	C, F	4
H	Retooling of injection molding machines	F	2
I	Training of labor	F	1
J	Production run	C, E, H, I	8
K	Distribution to wholesalers	G, J	2
L	Distribution to retailers	K	2
M	Advertising campaign "watch for"	G	4
N	Advertising campaign "hard sell"	L, M	2

(a) Draw a CPM network. Introduce dummy tasks as needed.

(b) Find the earliest and latest times for each node. Identify the critical path. What is its length? If it is now July 10, when is the project completion date?

(c) Find the total float and free float for each task.

(d) Draw a schedule graph.

6.3 A firm has developed a new product and wishes to plan its prerelease marketing campaign to be started on August 20. The individual tasks are:

	Task	Precedence	Duration in weeks
A	Project plan, budget prepared and approved	—	1
B	Training of servicemen	A	8
C	Training of salesmen	A	4
D	Sales promotion to distributors	C	4
E	TV and radio advertising brief	A	4
F	TV and radio contract negotiation with agent	E	1
G	TV film making	F	8
H	Radio script taping and approval	F	4
I	Approval of TV film from management	G	3
J	Press and household advertising brief	A	2
K	Press and household advertising contract negotiations	J	1
L	Illustrations, text and block making for press and household advertising	K	4
M	Printing of above	L	4
N	Distribution of product to distributors	D	2
O	Distribution of product to retailers	N	4
P	Press conference	B,O,I,H,M	0

(a) Draw a CPM network, and determine the critical path. When will the press conference be held at the earliest?

(b) Determine the amount of total float and free float for each task.

6.4 Consider the following construction project for a boiler house.

	Task	Precedence	Duration in days
A	Construct floor slabs	—	8
B	Erect boiler house frame	A	21
C	Construct chimney base	A	3
D	Erect precast chimney	C	6
E	Construct boiler bases	A	6
F	Position boilers	E	2
G	Construct pump bases	A	4
H	Construct oil tank piers	A	3
I	Position oil tanks	H	1
J	Construct oil line trenches	A	5

	Task	Precedence	Duration in days
K	Position pumps	G	1
L	Install roof decking	B, D, F	8
M	Erect structures for chimney flue and vent	D	3
N	Erect flue headers	D, F	3
O	Brick out and fit burners	D, F	6
P	Fit boiler mountings and controls	F	2
Q	Install oil lines	F, I, J	10
R	Install water pipe system	F, K, L	25
S	Test pipe system	R	2
T	Install plant wiring	M, O, P, Q, S	20
U	Commissioning of boiler house	N, T	1

(a) Draw a CPM network. Find the critical path. What is its length?

(b) The suppliers require the following delivery lead times:

Boilers   90 days
Burners   105 days
Oil tank   60 days
Pumps   72 days

If construction is planned to begin (task A) on July 12, at what date do these various units have to be ordered at the latest so as not to cause any delay in the completion of the project?

(c) Find the amount of total float and free float for each activity.

(d) The following jobs require the same skills:
1. Concreting skills: A, C, D, E, G, H, J
2. Carpentry skills: B, L
3. Technical installations: F, I, K, Q, R, S
4. Masonry skills: D, M, N, O
5. Electrical wiring: P, T

Plan a schedule graph such that tasks requiring similar skills have minimum overlap without causing any delay in project completion time.

6.5   A sociologist plans a questionnaire survey consisting of the following tasks.

			Duration in Days		
			Mode	Minimum	Maximum
	Task	Precedence	m	a	b
A	Design of questionnaire	—	5	4	6
B	Sampling design	—	12	8	16
C	Testing of questionnaire and refinements	A	5	4	12
D	Recruiting for interviewers	B	3	1	5
E	Training of interviewers	D, A	2	2	2
F	Allocation of areas to interviewers	B	5	4	6
G	Conducting interviews	C, E, F	14	10	18
H	Evaluation of results	G	20	18	34

(a) For this PERT network find the expected task durations, t_{ij}, and the variances of task durations, σ_{ij}^2.

(b) Draw a network for this project and find the critical path. What is the expected length of the critical path? What is the variance of the length of the critical path?

(c) What is the probability that the length of the critical path does not exceed 60 days?

6.6   A publisher has just signed a contract for the publication of a book. What is the earliest date that the book can be ready for distribution? The following tasks with time estimates are involved.

			Duration in Weeks		
			Mode	Minimum	Maximum
	Task	Precedence	m	a	b
A	Appraisal of book by reviewers	—	8	4	10
B	Initial pricing of book	—	2	2	2
C	Assessment of marketability	A, B	2	1	3
D	Revisions by author	A	6	4	12
E	Editing of final draft	C, D	4	3	5
F	Type setting of text	E	3	3	3
G	Preparation of plates for art work	E	4	3	5
H	Design and printing of jacket	C, D	6	4	9
I	Printing and binding of book	F, G	8	6	16
J	Inspection and final assembly	I, H	1	1	1

(a) For this PERT network find the expected task durations, t_{ij}, and the variances of task duration, σ_{ij}^2.

(b) Draw a network and find the critical path. What is the expected length of the critical path and what is its variance?

(c) What is the probability that the length of the critical path does not exceed 32 weeks? 36 weeks?

6.7   Holiday Prefabs Inc. assembles prefabricated vacation houses in its factory, and transports them to the site where they are attached to the foundations. Each transaction covers the following tasks.

					Direct Labor Costs	
			Time in Days		at Normal	at Crash
	Task	Precedence	Normal	Crash	Time	Time
A	Inspection of site, preparation of detail plans	—	3	2	$180	$230
B	Levelling of foundation site, building foundations	A	4	2	$240	$360

Task		Precedence	Time in Days Normal	Crash	Direct Labor Costs at Normal Time	at Crash Time
C	Construction of wall panels, floors, and roof, and assembly	A	5	2	$800	$950
D	Transportation to site and positioning on foundations	C	1	1	$200	$200
E	Attaching prefab to foundations, and final installations	B, D	4	2	$220	$350

Indirect project labor costs amount to $100 per day.

(a) From the cost figures for normal and crash durations, determine the coefficients of the equations of $c_{ij} - t_{ij}v_{ij}$ for each task.

(b) Find the critical path for normal task duration and the total labor cost associated with the project.

(c) Using the method described in Section 6-6, determine the least cost schedule and the associated project duration.

(d) What is the total project cost for a minimum project completion time?

6.8 Consider the following pipeline laying project, where the tasks for the various sections are overlapping:

Task		Precedence	Duration in Weeks Normal	Crash	Direct Costs in $1000 c_{ij}	v_{ij}
A	Install pump 1	—	12	10	48	2
B	Dig trench section 1	—	4	3	15	3
C	Lay pipe section 1	A, B	6	3	48	4
D	Fill trench section 1	C	2	1	4	1
E	Dig trench section 2	B	6	4	21	3
F	Lay pipe section 2	C, E	8	5	64	4
G	Fill trench section 2	D, F	3	2	6	1
H	Install transmission pump	—	14	10	48	2
I	Dig trench section 3	E, H	4	3	15	3
J	Lay pipe section 3	F, H, I	6	3	48	4
K	Fill trench section 3	G, J	2	1	4	1
L	Dig trench section 4	I	4	3	15	3
M	Lay pipe section 4	J, L	6	3	48	4
N	Fill trench section 4	K, M	2	1	4	1
O	Connect pipe to terminal	M	3	2	12	2

(a) Determine the critical path for normal task duration and draw a schedule graph, allowing all tasks to start at their earliest start time.

(b) The indirect costs amount to $6000 per week. Use the scheme explained in Section 6-6 to find the least cost schedule. What is the total cost reduction achieved and what is the decrease in project completion time? (Hint: The costs for sections 1, 3, and 4 are exactly the same; therefore, any time reductions can be made on all three sections in one iteration.)

6.9 Consider the CPM cost example discussed in Section 6-6.
(a) Formulate a linear program to find the critical path.
(b) Formulate a linear program to find the least cost schedule.

6.10 Consider exercise 6.7.
(a) Formulate a linear program to find the critical path.
(b) Formulate a linear program to find the least cost schedule.

REFERENCES

Burman, P. J. *Precedence Networks for Project Planning and Control.* London: McGraw-Hill, 1972. A voluminous 350-page text that covers most aspects of CPM from bar charting, project budgeting, use of computers, project control, to implementation with real-life type examples.

Elmaghraby, Salah E. "The Theory of Networks and Management Science: Part II," *Management Science*, 17, Oct. 1970. An expository treatment of activity networks, reviewing CPM, PERT, and some generalizations, where activities may not necessarily be executed, i.e., may be probabilistic: generalized activity networks or GAN and graphical evaluation and review technique or GERT.

Fulkerson, D. R. "A Network Flow Computation for Project Cost Curves", *Management Science*, 7, January 1961. Shows that the dual to the least cost linear programming model corresponds to a maximum flow model that can be solved via the maximum flow network algorithm. An excellent review is contained in A. Kaufmann and G. Desbazeille. (See the following entry.)

————. "Expected Critical Path Length in PERT Networks", *Operations Research*, 10, Nov.–Dec., 1962. Gives an approximate method for determining the bias in the variability of the critical path length of the PERT model.

Horowitz, J. *Critical Path Scheduling.* New York: Ronald Press, 1967. A detailed and complete development of CPM and PERT and extensions at an elementary level. Easy-to-read with a strong bias towards practical use of the tools.

Kaufmann, A., and G. Desbazeille. *The Critical Path Method.* New York: Gordon and Breach, 1969. As is the case for all of Kaufmann's books, this short text is concise, to the point, and well organized. More than a third is devoted to advanced approaches for cost minimization. Although it is at a higher level mathematically than most CPM texts, it is very practical with excellent realistic examples.

Kelley, J. "Critical-Path Planning and Scheduling: Mathematical Basis", *Operations Research*, 9, May–June 1961. Critical path least cost linear programming model that takes advantage of the problem's special structure to derive a solution algorithm more efficient than the simplex method.

Siemens, Nicolai. "A Simple CPM Time-Cost Tradeoff Algorithm", *Management Science*, 17, Feb. 1971. A simple algorithm ideally suited for hand computations is explained with an example. The method gives either optimal or near-optimal solutions.

Thornley, Gail. *Critical Path Analysis in Practice*. London: Tavistock Publications, 1968 (paperback). This short text contains a collection of excellent papers on various aspects of project control including aspects of implementation, communication and training. No print is wasted. It also gives a summary of all major CPM computer programs available in Britain in 1967. Shows how the problem can be formulated as a transportation problem solved by inspection in one pass through the table.

Van Slyke, R. M. "Monte Carlo Methods and the PERT Problem", *Operations Research*, 11, Sept.–Oct., 1963. Uses simulation to determine a critical index (equal to probability) that a task is on the critical path.

Weist, Jerome D., and Ferdinand K. Levy. *A Management Guide to PERT/CPM*. Englewood Cliffs, N.J.: Prentice-Hall, 1969 (paperback). A thorough discussion at an elementary level of PERT, CPM, and various extensions. Also shows how to construct schedule graphs and their use for manpower and resource scheduling. Contains a short CPM FORTRAN computer program. Extensive bibliography up to 1968.

7

Dynamic
Programming

In contrast to linear programming, *dynamic programming* is not a mathematical model with which we can associate an algorithm and which can be programmed once and for all to solve all problems that satisfy the assumptions of the model. Rather, dynamic programming is a *computational method* that allows us to break up a complex problem into a sequence of easier subproblems by means of a *recursive relation*, which can be evaluated by stages. If you have never encountered this type of reasoning, then you may find the mathematical notation somewhat strange, even confusing, and many of the basic concepts difficult to grasp. For this reason, learning about dynamic programming can be slow. It is only by studying a number of typical examples of different types that you will become accustomed to viewing a problem in terms of a recursive solution technique rather than as a mathematical model. This is what we propose to do in this chapter.

Some parts of this chapter assume that you are familiar with the concepts of random variables, probability distributions, and expected values of random variables. Section B-2 in Appendix B, on Probability, provides a short review.

7-1 A SOMEWHAT DISGUISED ROUTING PROBLEM

An electric power supply company considers upgrading one of its power transmission lines which serves a number of communities. A preliminary analysis indicates that four transformer stations will be able to economically supply all communities involved. However, each transformer station could be placed at a number of alternative sites. A detailed survey of the area also suggests alternative possible routes over which the transmission line could be taken. Figure 7-1 shows the network of possible transformer sites, represented by circles, and the alternative routes of the transmission line, depicted by lines. The number attached to each line gives the construction cost of each section of the transmission line, and the number in each circle is the cost of the transformer station and the additions to the feeder lines required for that site. Which route and set of transformer sites has the lowest total cost?

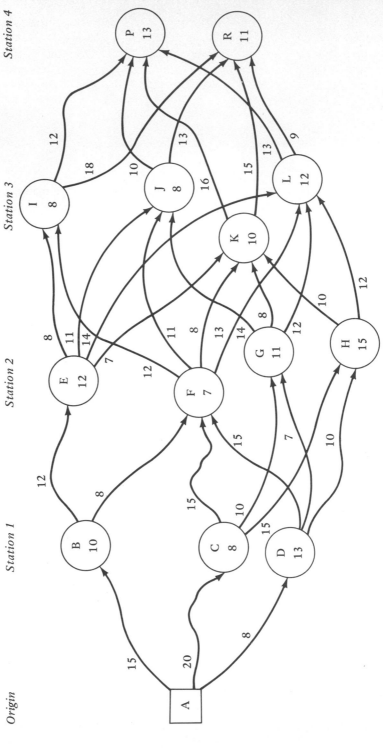

Figure 7-1. *A routing problem.*

For this simple example, it would be an easy matter to find the cheapest route by evaluating all possible routes—a procedure called *enumeration*.   Check that there are fifty-two different routes that have to be evaluated.   For larger problems, enumeration can become prohibitively expensive in terms of the number of computations that have to be performed.   Dynamic programming provides a computationally more efficient approach to solving such problems.

7-2 SOLUTION OF ROUTING PROBLEM BY STAGES

The construction of the transmission line can be viewed as a multi-stage process where each of the four stages involves the choice of a transformer site and the transmission line section connecting it with the preceding transformer (or the origin in the case of the first section).   Similarly, if we are to restrict our attention to only a subproblem, for example, the continuation of the transmission line from site B, the problem again can be viewed as a multi-stage process with a structure analogous to that of the original problem, i.e., each stage involves the choice of a transformation site and the associated transmission line section.   In this instance, only three stages remain to be completed.   The same observation can be made not only for all other sites of the first transformer station, but also for the second and third, except that fewer stages are left to be completed.

This suggests an efficient line of attack for finding the optimal route.   Let us say that by some means or another we are able to find that the minimum cost of completing the line to station 4 from each of the three alternative sites for station 1 is 67 for site B, 72 for site C, and 75 for site D.   (The transformer cost for station 1 is already included.)   It is now a simple matter to find the minimum cost from the origin A.   From A we have the following choices:

Route	Cost of Line Section	Minimum Cost of Completing Line	Total Cost
from A to B	15	67	82
from A to C	20	72	92
from A to D	8	75	83

The lowest cost is achieved by the section from A to B and then continuing on the best route from there.   Thus, we could find the optimal route from the origin A to station 4, if we knew the optimal route to station 4 from each of the sites for station 1. But, we really do not know this.   However, we observed earlier that the problem of completing the line from each site for station 1 is also a multi-stage process.   Hence, we could use the same trick as before, if we knew the minimum cost of completing the line from each of the sites for station 2, and so on.

These "ifs" provide us with the basic idea underlying dynamic programming. Starting with only one stage to be completed, we find the minimum cost of completing

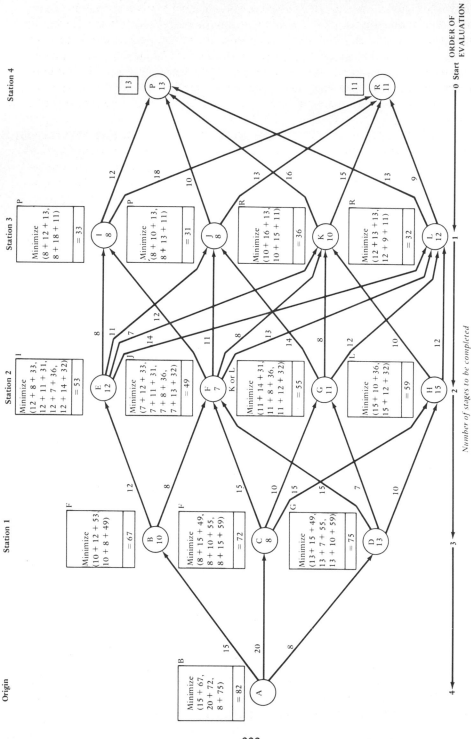

Figure 7-2. *Evaluation of a routing problem.*

the line for each site of station 3.   Then, working backwards stage by stage, we evaluate the minimum cost of completing the line from each site of the preceding station, until we have reached the origin A and found the overall minimum cost solution.   For each site we ask the hypothetical question: "If we were to complete the line from this site with n stages left to go, what is the best site to go to?"   We have to answer this question separately from each site at each stage, as we do not know at this moment in our evaluation which sites will be on the optimal route for the whole problem.

Figure 7-2 shows the evaluation for the entire network.   Note that we number the stages backward, starting at the end (i.e., in reverse order of the stations), so that the stage number gives the number of stages left to be completed.   We start out by recording the cost of each of the two possible sites for station 4, i.e., at the end of the line.   These costs are inserted in the square boxes above the circles depicting sites P and R.   We now evaluate the best decision for each site of station 3 (i.e., at stage 1 or with one stage left to be completed).   What is the best decision for site I?

Choice	Cost of Station at Site I	Cost of Line Section	Cost at Last Site	Total
Route I to P	8	12	13	33
Route I to R	8	18	11	37

The best decision at site I is a line to site P, at a cost of 33.   These computations are shown in the box attached to circle I.   The best site to go to next is indicated by the letter P above this box.

We now proceed to evaluate each of the other three sites at that stage.   Verify the computations in Figure 7-2 for station 3 or stage 1.

But now, knowing the optimal route from each site at stage 1, we can go back another step and find the best decision for each site at stage 2, or with two stages left to be completed, as shown in Figure 7-2.   Proceeding in this manner, stage by stage, we finally evaluate the minimum cost for the origin A.

The optimal route from the origin A can easily be found by unrolling the sequence of best decisions, given the best decision at site A.   The optimal route leads us from site A to site B (as indicated by the letter B shown above the box attached to circle A), from site B to site F, from site F to site J and on to site P at a total cost of 82.   There is no solution that has a lower cost.   Although this is not the case here, a problem may have two or more alternative optimal routes, all having the same minimum cost.

This problem, and the approach used to solve it, contains most basic aspects of dynamic programming and the structurally related theory of optimal control, which will not be studied in this text.   All problems solved by these two techniques consist of taking a particular process in stages from a given initial position to a desired ending position, passing through a sequence of alternative intermediate positions.

These positions—the alternative transformer sites in our example—are referred to as *states*. In general, the state description has to contain all information relevant for future decisions about the process from that state on. It can be viewed as reflecting the cumulative effect of all decisions that can be made prior to reaching that state. In our example, the only piece of information relevant for deciding how to continue the route is the current site position. Many problems may require several distinct elements about the process for a complete state description.

For every state at each stage, a decision has to be made. Any sequence of decisions that leads the process from the initial state to the desired state is called a *policy* in dynamic programming and a *trajectory* in optimal control theory. The objective is to find the *optimal policy*.

Note that in this example we started at the states where we wanted to end, i.e., sites P and R, rather than at the beginning, the origin A, and then we worked backward, stage by stage, until we reached the beginning. This particular formulation is called the *backward solution*. At each state we found the optimal immediate decision for leaving that stage given n stages left to go. We could also have solved the problem working forward, resulting in the *forward solution*. We then reword the crucial question to be answered at each state as, "If we were to reach state i after completing n stages, which is the best state from which to come?" Note: this implies that the state description now reflects all relevant aspects of the position in which the process ends after completing n stages, rather than those in which it starts with n stages remaining. It is then convenient to number the stages in a chronological order starting from the beginning position rather than the ending position. It is clear that the optimal route (or routes if alternative optima exist) will be the same for the forward and backward solutions.

7-3 REVIEW AND IMPLICATIONS OF COMPUTATIONAL PROCESS

We shall now look at this problem in more general terms, using the backward solution. Let i_n be the state of the process with n stages remaining. A route from the initial state to the final state consists of a sequence of decisions. Each decision involves defining a link between two states at consecutive stages. A policy can thus be described by a sequence of pairs of states (i_n, i_{n-1}), (i_{n-1}, i_{n-2}), ..., (i_1, i_0). With each link (k, j) we associate a cost t_{kj}, the cost of the one-step transition from state k to state j. In our example, this included the cost of the transformer station at state (site) k plus the cost of the transmission line from state k to state j. For an N-stage process the cost of each feasible policy is the sum of N variables,

$$(7-1) \qquad \sum_{n=1}^{N} t_{i_n, i_{n-1}}$$

where consecutive pairs of states are properly linked together. We wish to find the optimal policy. In our example this is the least-cost policy. In terms of expression (7-1), this is a minimization problem involving N variables—one variable for each stage of the process.

PROPERTY 1

Dynamic programming solves an N-variable problem sequentially in N stages where each stage involves optimization over one variable only.

Consider now the truncated problem of being in state s with $n < N$ stages left to go. We have seen that this new problem has the same structure as the original problem. With this new problem we can associate an optimal subpolicy. Let $f_n(s)$ be the cost of this optimal subpolicy. We wish to stress that $f_n(s)$ is already the result of a minimization operation, not merely the cost of any arbitrary subpolicy. This optimal subpolicy depends on both the number of stages left to go (as indicated by the subscript n) and the state which the process is in at that point (as indicated by the arguments). We refer to s as the *state variable*. In our example, for $s = P$ and $s = R$ and $n = 0$ stages left to go, $f_0(P) = 13$ and $f_0(R) = 11$. From this we can determine $f_1(s)$. For instance, for $s = I$:

$$f_1(I) = \underset{i_0 = P, R}{\text{minimum}}\, [t_{I, i_0} + f_0(i_0)] = \text{minimum}\,[20 + 13, 26 + 11] = 33$$

In general

(7-2) $$f_1(s) = \underset{i_0}{\text{minimum}}\, [t_{s, i_0} + f_0(i_0)], \quad \text{all } s$$

Using the $f_1(s)$ evaluated in this fashion, we then proceed to find $f_2(s)$, etc., by the same principle. In general, the expression for n stages remaining is

---

PROPERTY 2

(7-3) $$f_n(s) = \underset{i_{n-1}}{\text{minimum}}\, [t_{s, i_{n-1}} + f_{n-1}(i_{n-1})], \quad \text{all } s, \quad \text{all } n \geqslant 1,$$

where $\quad f_0(i_0) = c_{i_0} \;(= \text{given constants}).$

This is known as the *recursive relation of dynamic programming*. At each state it is evaluated for all values of the state variable. Property 2 can also be expressed in another form known as the *principle of optimality of dynamic programming*, which exists in different versions.

PROPERTY 3

An optimal policy has the property that whatever state the process is in at a given stage and whatever the decision taken from that state, the remaining decisions must constitute an optimal subpolicy for the state resulting from this decision.

Or, an optimal policy must have the property that regardless of how the process entered into a given state, the remaining decisions must constitute an optimal subpolicy.

Or, the optimal policy can be formed only from optimal subpolicies.

The principle of optimality contains the necessary condition which a problem has to satisfy for it to be formulated by dynamic programming.

PROPERTY 4

The measure of effectiveness of a given subpolicy from any state depends only on the state which the process is in and the number of stages remaining, but not on how the process entered that state.

This is known as the *Markovian property* due to its similarity with one of the assumptions inherent in Markov chains or Markov processes. (See Chapter 8.) The current state at any stage has to be a sufficient summary of all aspects about the current condition of the process that are relevant for future decisions or for the future performance of the process. The optimal subpolicy is then independent of the decisions made prior to reaching this state. In terms of the backward solution, this property implies that to find the optimal subpolicy from the current state, we only have to worry about decisions to be taken at the current and subsequent stages and can ignore decisions taken at all stages prior to reaching the current state. This allows us to effectively separate "past" and "future" decisions at each stage. However, this is not the same as asserting that the decisions taken at each stage are independent of all other stages. Clearly, the best decision in the current state depends on the best decisions at subsequent stages. On the other hand, if the best current decision also depended on decisions of preceding stages, the N-variable problem could not be separated into N one-variable problems.

Note that Properties 2 and 4 imply only that the overall measure of effectiveness to be optimized can be separated into n stages that satisfy the Markovian property. Beyond this, there are no assumptions or restrictions on the particular mathematical form taken by the measure of effectiveness or the state and decision variables. The functional relationships may be linear or nonlinear, and the variable may assume any real value or be restricted to discrete values only. Dynamic programming always finds the overall optimum. Hand in hand with this, however, goes the fact that dynamic programming is not a mathematical model like linear programming, with which we can associate a computational algorithm and which can be programmed once and for all to solve all problems satisfying the assumptions of the model. Rather, dynamic programming is a computational method for solving certain problems that have a particular structure. So each problem usually requires its own tailor-made computer program that solves it using this computational method. Although dynamic programming solves the problem in a sequential manner, not every multi-stage decision problem can be formulated by dynamic programming, nor is it restricted to *a priori* multi-stage decision problem. In fact, many decision problems that are not multi-stage problems can, by some trick, or another, be converted to a multi-stage decision problem. Hence, dynamic programming seldom reduces to rote, but leaves ample room for ingenuity and imagination, making it, as a tool, rather deceptive.   Usually, a problem may look simple once it has been formulated. Yet, prior to formulation many problems look rather forbidding.

7-4 A RENTAL DECISION PROBLEM

Problems that involve decisions to be made at specific points in time are natural multi-stage processes, and hence, they are usually ideal for dynamic-programming formulations.   Consider the following rental equipment problem.

   A highway construction firm rents certain of its specialized earth-moving equipment from a leasing company, as needed during the various phases of a construction job.   However, the number of units required during any time period of one week cannot be predicted exactly, since the requirement depends on a variety of factors, such as the weather and soil conditions.   It is possible, however, to specify a probability distribution for weekly requirements.   Equipment has to be rented for full weeks, and it can only be obtained at the beginning of a week and released at the end of a week.   Assume that the beginning of a week coincides with the end of the preceding week.   The rental cost per week is $200.   Each time a unit is rented, there is a preparation and delivery charge of $120 by the leasing company.   Each time a unit is returned to the leasing company, there is a servicing, cleaning, and delivery charge of $150.   If, during any week, the construction firm has fewer units on hand than the number required, i.e., the company is short, it has to farm out the excess work to a local contractor at a cost of $400 per unit short per week or any part of a week.   Over a 6-week period, the requirements are distributed as shown in Table 7-1.   No units will be required after 6 weeks.   Therefore, all units are released at the beginning of week 7.   Given that the firm has 3 units on hand initially, what is the minimum cost policy?

   What comprises a rental policy?   It can be defined either in terms of the number of rental units on hand during each week or in terms of the change in the number of rental units on hand from week to week.   Let us assume that the decision as to whether to increase or decrease the number of rental units on hand during a particular week is made at the beginning of that week.   Thus, we define the decision variable

- $x_n > 0$ as the number of additional units hired at the beginning of week n,

   and

- $x_n < 0$ as the number of units released at the beginning of week n

At the beginning of week n, prior to any change, we start out with y_n rental units. Hence the number of units on hand during week n and consequently at the end of the week is

(7-4) $$z_n = y_n + x_n$$

with

$$y_1 = 3.$$

Table 7-1. *Distribution of Weekly Requirements.*

Requirements in Week n: d_n	Probability of a Requirement of Size d_n in Week n: $p_n(d_n)$					
	$n=1$	$n=2$	$n=3$	$n=4$	$n=5$	$n=6$
0	0.2	0	0.8	0.5	0	0
1	0.4	0.3	0.2	0.5	0.2	0.2
2	0.4	0.4			0.5	0.6
3		0.3			0.2	0.2
4					0.1	

Note that z_n is the number of units carried forward to period $n+1$. Similarly, y_n is the number of units carried forward from period $n-1$, and, therefore, $y_n = z_{n-1}$. Eliminating y_n in (7-4) we have

(7-5)
$$z_n = z_{n-1} + x_n$$

The cost of a rental decision during period n consists of

(7-6)

$$\begin{bmatrix} \text{Cost in} \\ \text{period} \end{bmatrix} = \begin{bmatrix} \text{Cost of hiring} \\ \text{or releasing units} \end{bmatrix} + \begin{bmatrix} \text{Rental} \\ \text{cost} \end{bmatrix} + \begin{bmatrix} \text{Cost of} \\ \text{being short} \end{bmatrix}$$

$$C_n(x_n, z_n) = \begin{bmatrix} 120x_n & \text{for } x_n \geq 0 \\ -150x_n & \text{for } x_n < 0 \end{bmatrix} + 200z_n + 400 \sum_{d_n > z_n} (d_n - z_n)p_n(d_n)$$

(Do you understand why the coefficient of x_n in the bottom part of the first term of expression (7-6) has to be negative?)

The cost of being short is an expected cost, and it is derived as follows: For any required d_n, the number of units short is

$$\begin{cases} 0 & \text{for } d_n \leq z_n, \quad \text{and} \\ (d_n - z_n) & \text{for } d_n > z_n \end{cases}$$

Since d_n is a random variable and the number of units short is a function of d_n, it is also a random variable. It assumes the value 0 with probability $\sum_{d_n \leq z_n} p_n(d_n)$ (=probability that demand is at most z_n) and the values $(d_n - z_n)$ with probabilities $p_n(d_n)$. Therefore (by the usual method of computing expected values as given by expression B-6 in Appendix B), the expected number of units short is

$$0 \cdot \left(\sum_{d_n \leq z_n} p_n(d_n) \right) + \sum_{d_n > z_n} (d_n - z_n)p_n(d_n)$$

The first part is zero, and only the second part remains. The expected shortage cost is then equal to the product of the expected number of units short and the shortage cost of $400 per unit.

Expressions (7-5) and (7-6) hold for each of the first six periods. At the beginning of period 7, all units are returned, hence, $x_7 = -z_6$, and (7-6) simplifies to

(7-7)
$$C_7(x_7 = -z_6, z_7 = 0) = 150z_6$$

The total cost over all 7 periods is given as the sum

(7-8)
$$\sum_{n=1}^{7} C_n(x_n, z_n)$$

We wish to determine values for x_n, $n = 1, 2, \ldots, 7$, so as to minimize expression (7-8).

7-5 DYNAMIC PROGRAMMING FORMULATION OF THE RENTAL PROBLEM

Let us solve this problem using a forward solution, i.e., the numbering of the stages coincides with the chronological sequence of decisions. In our case the decision involves the choice of a value for x_n for each of the first six weeks and at the beginning of week 7. Given three units on hand at the beginning of the six weeks, all possible sequences of decisions can be represented by the network shown in Figure 7-3. The maximum requirement never exceeds 4, so if we wish to be ready for the highest possible demand, we will never rent more than four units.

The first job in our formulation is to identify what aspect of the problem represents a stage and what aspect will serve as the state variable. The network representation immediately suggests that each week corresponds to a stage and that the number of units on hand at the end of each week serves as the state variable.

These two conclusions can also be reached without having recourse to a network diagram. From Property 1 it follows that with each decision variable we associate a stage. Thus, the stage description can be inferred from the decision process. In this example the decision process involves making a decision at the beginning of each week. Therefore, each week forms a stage. We have to make a decision at the beginning of each of the first six weeks as to the total number of units we should have on hand and a further decision at the beginning of week 7 of how many units to return. Thus, the problem has 7 stages. For the forward solution, the numbering of the stages coincides with the chronological ordering of the weeks.

For the forward solution, we ask for each state at stage n, "What is the best state s_{n-1} to come from, given that we want to end up in state s_n after one transition?" The state description refers to the ending position of the process after a decision has been made. Furthermore, the state description has to satisfy Property 4, implying that, given the value of the state variable and given the value of the decision variable, the value of the state variable at the preceding stage is uniquely defined. The variable z_n satisfies both of these requirements. It refers to the ending position each week, and by expression (7-5) the value of the state variable at the preceding stage is uniquely defined by z_n and x_n, namely,

(7-9)
$$z_{n-1} = z_n - x_n$$

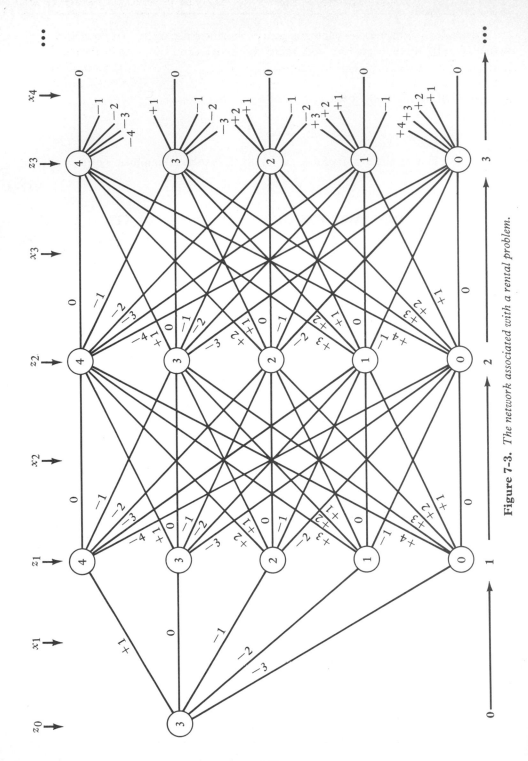

Figure 7-3. The network associated with a rental problem.

Now we are ready to formulate the recursive relation of dynamic programming. It states that the optimum cost to reach state z_n after n transitions is given by the minimum, over all feasible values of the decision variable x_n, of the sum of the immediate cost in period n and the cost of the optimal policy for state z_{n-1} resulting from z_n and the choice of x_n. If we let

(7-10) $$f_0(z_0) = 0, \qquad \text{all } z_0 \text{ (we only need } z_0 = 3)$$

then,

(7-11) $$f_n(z_n) = \underset{x_n \leqslant z_n}{\text{minimum}}[C_n(x_n, z_n) + f_{n-1}\underbrace{(z_n - x_n)}_{z_{n-1}}], \qquad \text{all } z_n, \quad \text{all } n \geqslant 1$$

7-6 EVALUATION OF RECURSIVE RELATION FOR RENTAL PROBLEM

To evaluate the recursive relation we need two tables at each stage n. The first one, referred to here as table 1, contains the $f_{n-1}(z_{n-1})$ values determined at the preceding stage. The second, referred to here as table 2, is used to find $f_n(z_n)$ using the recursive relation (7-11). For $n = 1$, table 1 consists of the single number $f_0(z_0 = 3) = 0$. Determining table 2 for $f_1(z_1)$ is also trivial. Since $z_0 = 3$, it follows by expression (7-9) that x_1 can assume only one value for each value of z_1, namely $x_1 = z_1 - 3$, and (7-11) simplifies to $f_1(z_1) = C_1(x_1, z_1)$. The value of $f_1(z_1)$ must be determined for all viable values of z_1.

Often, the range of values of the state variable for which the recursive relation has to be evaluated cannot be inferred exactly from the problem. This is the case for most inventory control problems. We then make a first choice based on an educated guess and subsequently alter it as needed during the computations. For our example, however, the exact range can be inferred from the requirement data in Table 7-1.

As we have seen, the maximum requirement never exceeds 4, so it will never be optimal to have more than 4 rental units on hand. Furthermore, since the number of units rented cannot be negative, expression (7-11) will only have to be evaluated for $z_n = 0, 1, 2, 3,$ and 4.

Table 7-2. *Table 2 for n = 1.*

(1) z_1	(2) x_1	(3) $C_1(z_1, x_1)$	(4) $f_1(z_1)$
0	-3	930	930
1	-2	660	660
2	-1	550	550
3	0	600	600
4	$+1$	920	920

Table 7-2 shows the evaluation of $f_1(z_1)$ (table 2 for $n = 1$). For instance, $z_1 = 0$ implies that $x_1 = -3$ and expression (7-6) yields

$$C_1(-3,0) = -150(-3) + 200(0) + 400[(1-0)(0.4)+(2-0)(0.4)] = 930$$

For $n = 2$, table 1 is formed of columns (1) and (4) of Table 7-2. It is convenient to include additional columns in table 2 for this and later stages, as shown in Table 7-3.

To illustrate some of the calculations in Table 7-3, let us outline how the value for $f_2(z_2 = 1)$ was determined. By expression (7-9), x_2 can assume values of -3, -2, -1, 0, and 1, implying values for z_1 of 4, 3, 2, 1, and 0, respectively, as shown in columns 2 and 4 of Table 7-3. For each x_2, we find $C_2(x_2, z_2)$, using expression (7-6). Next, we find in Table 7-2, which is now table 1 for $n = 2$, the value of $f_1(z_1)$ associated with each choice of x_2 (repeated in column 5 of Table 7-3) and find the sum of corresponding pairs of $C_2(x_2, z_2)$ and $f_1(z_1)$ (columns 3 and 5), shown in

Table 7-3. *Table 2 for $n = 2$.*

(1) z_2	(2) x_2	(3) $C_2(z_2, x_2)$	(4) $z_1 = z_2 - x_2$	(5) $f_1(z_1)$	(6) Total	(7) $f_2(z_2)$
0	-4	1400	4	920	2320	
	-3	1250	3	600	1850	
	-2	1100	2	550	1650	
	-1	950	1	660	1610	1610
	0	800	0	930	1730	
1	-3	1050	4	920	1970	
	-2	900	3	600	1500	
	-1	750	2	550	1300	
	0	600	1	660	1260	1260
	1	720	0	930	1650	
2	-2	820	4	920	1740	
	-1	670	3	600	1270	
	0	520	2	550	1070	1070
	1	640	1	660	1300	
	2	760	0	930	1690	
3	-1	750	4	920	1670	
	0	600	3	600	1200	1200
	1	720	2	550	1270	
	2	840	1	660	1500	
	3	960	0	930	1890	
4	0	800	4	920	1720	
	1	920	3	600	1520	1520
	2	1040	2	550	1590	
	3	1160	1	660	1820	
	4	1280	0	930	2210	

column 6.   By the recursive relation (7-11), $f_2(z_2 = 1)$ is the minimum of the values in column 6, i.e., 1260, the value for $x_2 = 0$.

This process repeats itself now for each state at all remaining 5 stages.   At each stage n we obtain table 1 from columns 1 and 7 of table 2 for the preceding stage $n-1$.   Note that table 1 never has to be written out explicitly since it is contained as part of table 2 of the preceding stage.

Table 7-4. $f_n(z_n)$ *Evaluated for All Seven Stages.*

Stage	z_n	$f_n(z_n)$	Optimal x_n	z_{n-1} Implied
1	0	930	−3	3
	1	660	−2	3
	2	550	−1	3
	3	600	0	3
	4	920	1	3
2	0	1610	−1	1
	1	1260	0	1
	2	1070	0	2
	3	1200	0	3
	4	1520	1	3
3	0	1450	−2	2
	1	1420	−1	2
	2	1470	0	2
	3	1790	1	2
	4	2110	2	2
4	0	1650	0	0
	1	1620	0	1
	2	1870	0	2
	3	2190	1	2
	4	2510	2	2
5	0	2530	0	0
	1	2300	0	1
	2	2300	1	1
	3	2500	2	1
	4	2780	3	1
6	0	3250	−1	1
	1	2900	0	1
	2	2780	0	2
	3	3020	1	2
	4	3340	2	2
7	0	3050	−1	1

Start

Since all units are to be returned at the beginning of week 7, $z_7 = 0$ is the only value of the state variable that has to be evaluated at the last stage.

Table 7-4 shows the $f_n(z_n)$ values and the corresponding optimal x_n values for all 7 stages. The minimum cost of the optimal rental policy is seen to be $f_7(z_7=0) = 3050$. We can now backtrack through this table to find the optimal policy. The last line in Table 7-4 indicates that the optimal $x_7 = -1$. Expression (7-9) implies that $z_6 = 1$. We now go to the panel for $n = 6$, and find the optimal decision associated with $z_6 = 1$. This is $x_6 = 0$. Again, expression (7-9) implies that $z_5 = 1$, and from the panel for $n = 5$ and $z_5 = 1$, we find the optimal $x_5 = 0$. Continuing in this fashion, as shown by the arrows in Table 7-4, we find that the optimal policy is:

Week	1	2	3	4	5	6	7
Number of Units Rented	2	2	1	1	1	1	0
Change from Previous Week	-1	0	-1	0	0	0	-1

This example could also have been solved using the backward solution. It goes without saying that the optimal solution would be the same.

7-7 COMPUTATIONAL ASPECTS

As was true for linear programming, few real-life dynamic programming problems are ever solved by hand. Although dynamic programming tremendously reduces and simplifies the number of computations that have to be made to find the optimal solution, the computational effort is still very large. Therefore, the analyst usually writes a computer program to actually evaluate the recursive relation.

Figure 7-4 shows a flowchart of the exact sequence of computations for the rental problem, which could serve as a basis for such a computer program. The evaluation of the recursive relation for all types of problems has basically the same structure, but the exact details in the various boxes may differ.

7-8 A RESOURCE ALLOCATION PROBLEM

Three factories are located along a river. All three discharge their industrial waste water into the river, with little or no processing. As a result, the water quality of the river has suffered severely. Under the pressure of government and various citizens groups, the managements of the three factories decide to implement a joint plan for waste water treatment, so as to upgrade the water quality of the river to a standard that would permit the river to purify itself prior to reaching a main recreational area. A water pollution expert is called in. His analysis indicates that the total biological oxygen demand on the river water by all three factories combined should not exceed 1.6 parts per million (PPM).

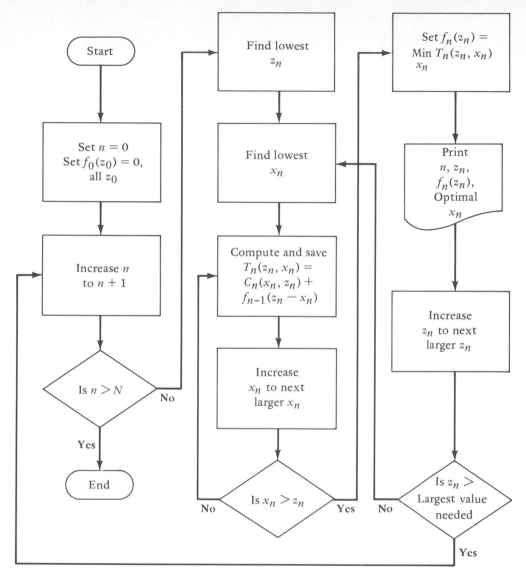

Figure 7-4. *Flowchart of computations.*

Each factory can process waste water either by primary treatment only, primary and secondary, or primary, secondary, and tertiary treatment, each reducing the oxygen demand of the treated effluent to progressively lower levels. Table 7-5 lists the oxygen demand by each factory for the various degrees of waste water treatment and the cost of the installations.

The three managements agree to cooperate by allocating the combined cost of waste water treatment to each factory proportional to the oxygen demand of its

Table 7-5. *Oxygen Demand and Installation Costs.*

Highest Degree of Treatment	Oxygen Demand PPM x_{nj} Factory			Installation Costs in $1000 Factory		
	$n=1$	$n=2$	$n=3$	$n=1$	$n=2$	$n=3$
$j=0$: none	1.2	0.8	1.6	0	0	0
$j=1$: primary	0.6	0.6	1.0	80	40	100
$j=2$: secondary	0.2	0.4	0.6	140	80	150
$j=3$: tertiary	0	0	0	170	140	220

untreated waste water, regardless of the extent of effluent treatment installed at each factory. The objective is to determine the degree of treatment at each factory such that the sum of the oxygen demand by all three factories does not exceed 1.6 PPM, minimizing the combined cost for all installations.

This problem is a version of the resource allocation problem, known under such descriptive names as the *knap-sack problem* or the *fly-away-kit problem*. The scarce resource to be allocated is the river's capacity to support a certain amount of oxygen demand. It is to be allocated in an optimal fashion to one or several uses or activities (in our case, to the final purification of partially treated effluent from each factory).

Our first task in solving this problem by dynamic programming is, again, to identify which aspects of the problem represent the decision variables, which aspects will serve as the stage, and what should be used as the state variable. The highest degree of treatment to be used in each factory is the natural choice for the decision variable. Recall that with each stage we associate a decision variable. Hence, each factory represents a stage. The amount of the scarce resource left to be allocated at each stage serves as the state variable.

By the principle of optimality, the formulation implies the following type of reasoning: If there is an amount s of the resource left to be allocated to the nth, $(n-1)$th, ..., second, and first use (or factory in our case), and we allocate an amount x_{nj} to the nth use, then the balance of the resource $s - x_{nj}$ is to be allocated optimally to the remaining $n-1$ uses. This will allow us to find the optimal allocation to the nth use. Starting with $n = 1$ (or only one factory left), we go through this exercise for each possible value of s, then move on to the next value of n until n equals the total number of factories, or $n = 3$ in our case.

We now translate this reasoning into mathematics. Let $f_n(s)$ be the cost of allocating an amount s of the resource optimally to the first n factories. The value $f_n(s)$ is a minimum. If c_{nj} is the cost, and x_{nj} is the oxygen demand of alternative j for factory n, then

(7-12)
$$f_1(s) = \operatorname*{minimum}_{\substack{j \\ x_{1j} \leqslant s}} c_{1j}$$

and

(7-13)
$$f_n(s) = \operatorname*{minimum}_{\substack{j \\ x_{nj} \leqslant s}} [c_{nj} + f_{n-1}(s - x_{nj})], \qquad n > 1$$

Note, that by defining $f_0(s) = 0$, for all s, expression (7-13) can also be used for $n = 1$. The condition $x_{nj} \leqslant s$ guarantees that the minimum is only taken over those alternatives which have an oxygen demand not exceeding the amount left to be allocated. The state variable ranges over the values 0 to 1.6. Since all oxygen demands are multiples of 0.2, $f_n(s)$ only has to be evaluated for $s = 0, 0.2, 0.4, ..., 1.4$, and 1.6. Table 7-6 shows the computations. The evaluation for $n = 1$ is trivial. The minimum is always obtained for the highest degree of treatment feasible for the given value of s. At stage 3, we only need to evaluate $f_3(s)$ for $s = 1.6$. However, it is interesting to perform some sensitivity analysis with respect to the maximum s.

Table 7-6. *Evaluation of the Water Pollution Project.*

(1) n	(2) s	(3) j	(4) x_{nj}	(5) c_{nj}	(6) $s - x_{nj}$	(7) $f_{n-1}(s - x_{nj})$	(8) Total	(9) $f_n(s)$
1	0	3	0	170	0	0	170	170
	0.2	2	0.2	140	0	0	140	140
	0.4	2	0.2	140	0.2	0	140	140
	0.6	1	0.6	80	0	0	80	80
	0.8	1	0.6	80	0.2	0	80	80
	1.0	1	0.6	80	0.4	0	80	80
	1.2	0	1.2	0	0	0	0	0
	1.4	0	1.2	0	0.2	0	0	0
	1.6	0	1.2	0	0.4	0	0	0
2	0	3	0	140	0	170	310	310
	0.2	3	0	140	0.2	140	280	280
	0.4	3	0	140	0.4	140	280	
		2	0.4	80	0	170	250	250
	0.6	3	0	140	0.6	80	220	
		2	0.4	80	0.2	140	220	
		1	0.6	40	0	170	210	210
	0.8	3	0	140	0.8	80	220	
		2	0.4	80	0.4	140	220	
		1	0.6	40	0.2	140	180	
		0	0.8	0	0	170	170	170
	1.0	3	0	140	1.0	80	220	
		2	0.4	80	0.6	80	160	
		1	0.6	40	0.4	140	180	
		0	0.8	0	0.2	140	140	140
	1.2	3	0	140	1.2	0	140	
		2	0.4	80	0.8	80	160	
		1	0.6	40	0.6	80	120	120
		0	0.8	0	0.4	140	140	
	1.4	3	0	140	1.4	0	140	
		2	0.4	80	1.0	80	160	
		1	0.6	40	0.8	80	120	
		0	0.8	0	0.6	80	80	80
	1.6	3	0	140	1.6	0	140	
		2	0.4	80	1.2	0	80	
		1	0.6	40	1.0	80	120	80
		0	0.8	0	0.8	80	80	

Table 7-6 (continued)

(1) n	(2) s	(3) j	(4) x_{nj}	(5) c_{nj}	(6) $s - x_{nj}$	(7) $f_{n-1}(s - x_{nj})$	(8) Total	(9) $f_n(s)$
3	0	3	0	220	0	310	530	530
	0.2	3	0	220	0.2	280	500	500
	0.4	3	0	220	0.4	250	470	470
	0.6	3	0	220	0.6	210	430	430
		2	0.6	150	0	310	460	
	0.8	3	0	220	0.8	170	390	390
		2	0.6	150	0.2	280	430	
	1.0	3	0	220	1.0	140	360	360
		2	0.6	150	0.4	250	400	
		1	1.0	100	0	310	410	
	1.2	3	0	220	1.2	120	340	340
		2	0.6	150	0.6	210	360	
		1	1.0	100	0.2	280	380	
	1.4	3	0	220	1.4	80	300	300
		2	0.6	150	0.8	170	320	
		1	1.0	100	0.4	250	350	
		0	1.6	0	0	310	310	
	1.6	3	0	220	1.6	80	300	
		2	0.6	150	1.0	140	290	290
		1	1.0	100	0.6	210	310	
		0	1.6	0	0	310	310	

The optimal solution is shown by the arrows in Table 7-6. For a maximum permissible oxygen demand level of $s = 1.6$, the optimal solution calls for factory 3 to install $j = 2$, or first and secondary waste water treatment; factory 2 to install $j = 0$, or no treatment whatsoever; and factory 1 to install $j = 2$, or first and secondary treatment.

Figure 7-5 depicts the increase in cost as the maximum permissible oxygen demand is decreased from 1.6 to 0.

Note that an initial tightening of 0.2 PPM down to 1.4 PPM is relatively cheap and, thereafter, increases to about $30,000 per 0.2 PPM.

7-9 AN EQUIPMENT REPLACEMENT MODEL

As a piece of equipment, such as a machine, a truck or an airplane, ages its efficiency decreases, whereas operating and maintenance costs increase. Therefore, there comes a time when it becomes more economical to replace it by a new similar piece of equipment. What is the optimal time of replacement? This section deals with this question.

Dump trucks are subjected to a lot of beating. They age fast. Past records of a

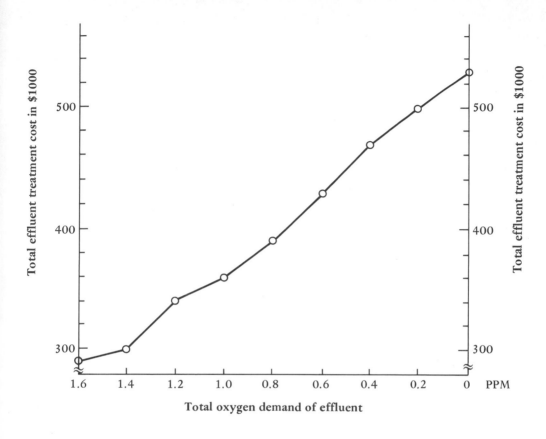

Figure 7-5. *Sensitivity of optimal solution to tightening of the effluent standards.*

cartage contractor show the following pattern of operating and maintenance costs, opportunity costs of down-time (=lost revenue), and resale or salvage value for a given model:

Year of operation	1	2	3	4	5	6
	$	$	$	$	$	$
Operating and maintenance costs	8000	8200	9000	8400	9400	8800
Opportunity cost for down time	1000	1100	1600	1200	2000	1600
End-of-year salvage value	14000	12000	11000	8000	7000	5000

No truck was ever used for more than six years.   The maintenance costs reflect major overhauls at the beginning of the third and fifth years.   A new truck has a cost of $18,000.   When should this model be replaced?

Let us initially look at this problem over an arbitrarily chosen planning horizon of nine years.   We start out with a new truck, and we will sell whatever truck we have on hand at the end of the ninth year.   Starting with the second year a decision has to be made at the beginning of each year.   The alternatives are: (1) keep the truck for at least another year, or (2) replace the truck with a new one of the same model.   (Although models and prices change slightly over the years, such changes are assumed not to affect the relative operating characteristics to any major degree. The same operating data are thus assumed to be valid over the entire nine years.)

This decision process is depicted graphically in Figure 7-6.   The numbers in the circles denote the age of the truck prior to making a decision.   We start out with a truck of age 0 (new) at the beginning of the 9-year period.   After one year that truck is age 1 (1 year old).   At that point we can either keep it (top branch) and end up with a truck of age 2 at the end of year 2, or trade it in for a new truck (bottom branch) and have a truck of age 1 at the end of year 2, and so on.   No truck is kept for more than 6 years.   The numbers attached to the branches are the total net annual cost associated with the corresponding action.   All branches leading to a one-year old truck in years 2 through 9 are obtained as

(purchase price of new truck) − (salvage value of truck replaced)

+ (sum of operating, maintenance, and down-time costs for new truck)

For instance, branches leading from a 3-year-old truck to a 1-year-old truck have a cost of $(\$18,000 - \$11,000) + (\$8000 + \$1000) = \$16,000$.   The negative numbers shown at the end of the planning horizon are the cash inflow from salvage values of the truck.

The diagram immediately suggests that each year represents a stage, and the age of the truck on hand at the end of a year serves as the state variable.   Stage 10 represents the action of selling the truck on hand at the end of year 9.   The objective is to determine a policy that minimizes total costs over the planning horizon.

We shall use a forward formulation.   Let $f_n(s)$ be the total minimum cost through period n if the truck on hand at the end of period n is of age s.   Let c_s be the sum of all operating, maintenance, and down-time costs during a truck's sth year of operation. Let p be the purchase price of a new truck, and let b_s be the salvage value of a truck of age s.   Then

$$f_1(1) = c_1$$

(7-14) $$f_n(s) = c_s + f_{n-1}(s-1), \qquad \text{for} \quad s > 1, \quad n > 1,$$

and

$$f_n(1) = \text{minimum}_s [(p - b_s) + c_1 + f_{n-1}(s)], \qquad 1 < n \leqslant 9.$$

Finally, let f_{10} be the minimum cost, given that the truck is sold at the end of year 9:

(7-15) $$f_{10} = \text{minimum}_s [f_9(s) - b_s]$$

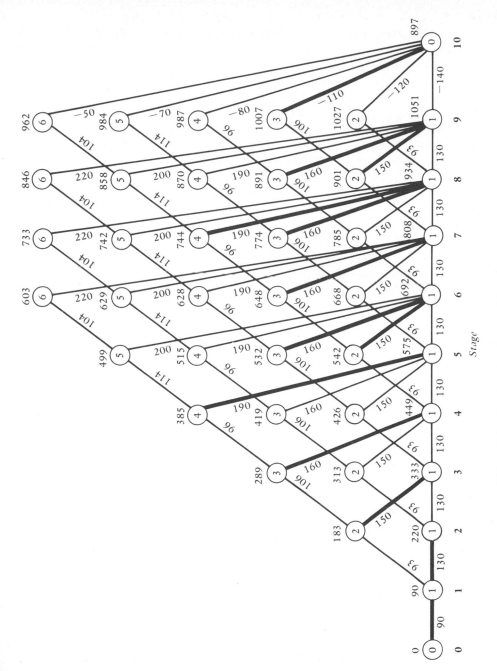

Figure 7-6. *Truck replacement problem—decision diagram.*

Note that only for $f_n(1)$, $n > 1$, does the evaluation of expression (7-14) involve any minimization. All other terms of $f_n(s)$, $s > 1$, are obtained by a simple addition of two numbers.

For a small problem like this, the diagram might as well be directly used for the evaluation of the forward solution. The number shown immediately above each circle in Figure 7-6 is $f_n(s)$ for $n \leqslant 9$ and f_{10} for $n = 10$. You should check these computations to test your understanding.

The heavy lines leading to the bottom row of circles (age 1) indicate the optimal action. The optimal action for stage 10 is to sell a truck of age 3. A heavy line leads from state 3 of stage 9 (end of year 9) to the end point. This implies that this truck was age 1 at stage 7 (end of year 7). The heavy line leading from state 3 of stage 6 to state 1 at stage 7 indicates that a truck replacement occurred at the end of year 6. Tracing the optimal policy back to the initial point in this manner, we see that the first truck was replaced at the end of year 3. So the optimal policy is to replace the truck every three years.

Let us push the analysis a bit further. Replacement problems essentially have to be viewed as part of a continuous sequence of replacement decisions. The operation for which the equipment is used may change in nature, but rarely will it disappear. Only the reliability of the information about the type of equipment available a few years from now may be in doubt. Thus, it becomes important to analyze how our initial replacement decision changes as we lengthen the planning horizon. It is only the first replacement decision that is of immediate concern to us. For our problem, this information can readily be obtained from the diagram. You should ascertain that the optimal subpolicy implied by each $f_n(1)$ gives the answer for our cost structure, since $f_n(1)$, the minimum cost of ending up with a truck of age 1 at the end of year n, differs from f_n, the minimum cost when the truck on hand is sold at the end of year $n-1$, only by a constant. Tracing these optimal subpolicies, as n increases, we note that for $n > 5$ it is always optimal to have the first replacement after three years.

7-10 TWO OR MORE STATE VARIABLES

Sometimes more than one state variable is needed to provide a complete description of the state of a process. For instance, in the preceding problem, the firm may require equipment at more than one location. Equipment rented may be transferred from one location to another at a certain cost. Rather than have only one state variable for the total number of pieces rented, we introduce a separate state variable for each location. Similarly, the firm may rent more than one type of equipment, and costs may depend on the combination of equipment rented. Again, a separate state variable would be introduced for each type of equipment. In fact, probably most dynamic programming problems need more than one state variable.

There is no conceptual difficulty in having more than one state variable. However, there are severe computational limitations on the viable number of state variables. Let us look at the number of computations required to evaluate the recursive relation for more than one state variable. Assume that each state variable can take on 100 different values. Then, for two state variables it is neccessary to evaluate 100^2 combinations. This may not pose any problems other than increasing the computational time by 100-fold. For three state variables, the number of combinations at each stage is 100^3 or 1 million, resulting in a 10,000-fold increase in computational time. For example, if a one-state variable problem takes 1 second of computation time on a computer, an equivalent three-state variable problem would take close to three hours. Furthermore, the amount of computer memory needed at each stage is now also at least 2 times 100^3 (if f_n and f_{n-1} are stored only). Therefore, to handle more than two state variables by internal memory alone, the number of states for each variable has to be drastically reduced. It is hardly ever feasible to go beyond three state variables. (However, see R. E. Larson's text listed in the bibliography.)

7-11 CONTINUOUS STATE VARIABLES

So far we have discussed the case where the state and decision variables assume only a finite set of discrete values. In fact, dynamic programming is admirably suited for discrete problems. If the state and decision variables may assume any real value a number of difficulties appear and the temptation is great to make an arbitrary discrete approximation. For many applications this is adequate. If the state variable is left real-valued, the usual approach to the problem is to evaluate the state variable for a discrete set of values only—a so-called *finite grid*. If f_{n-1} is needed for values other than the ones evaluated, linear interpolation is usually applied to find the required values. Note that no global optimum can now be guaranteed if the problem has several local optima, some of which may be missed by a finite grid. This is, however, not a shortcoming of dynamic programming, but a failure caused by an inadequate approximation.

7-12 DYNAMIC PROGRAMMING WITH STOCHASTIC STATE SPACE

Consider the network in Figure 7-7. The problem consists of getting from state 1 to state 8 or 9 at the lowest cost. As for the routing problem in Section 7-1, the states can be partitioned into four sets. Each route from state 1 to state 8 or 9 has to go through one state at each of the four sets. In each state of sets 1, 2, and 3, one of two possible actions can be taken: action A or action B, each leading to a new state with a certain probability. We can thus look at this problem again as a sequential decision process with three stages. In contrast to our earlier analysis of deterministic sequential decision problems (where the new state resulting from a decision is known with certainty), in this problem the new state resulting from a decision is only known in terms of probability. The new state variable is therefore a *random variable*. For instance, if we take decision A at state 5 (at a cost of 5), then with probability 0.3

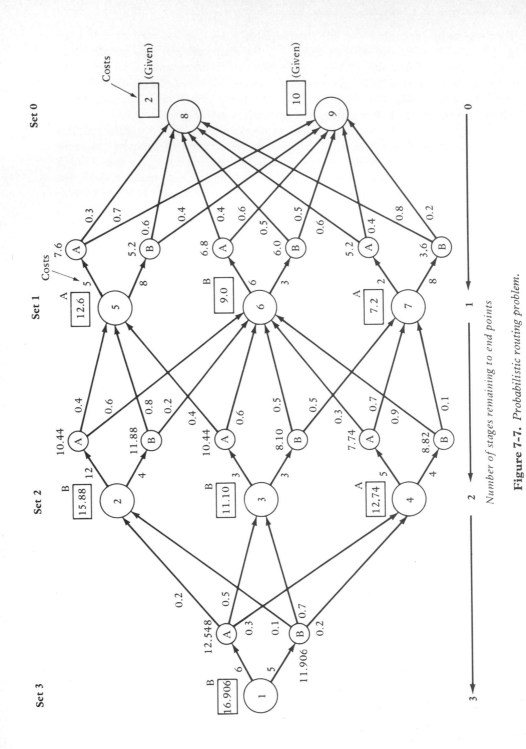

Figure 7-7. *Probabilistic routing problem.*

will we go to state 8, and with probability 0.7 to state 9. In other words, the random variable for the new state assumes either the value 8 or 9. If we reach state 8, a cost of 2 is incurred, whereas if we reach state 9, a cost of 10 is incurred. The cost associated with the new state is therefore also a random variable. For this reason the criterion for optimization usually applied is *minimization of the expected cost* (or *maximization of the expected return*).

To solve this problem, we start again at the end and, working backwards, evaluate each state at each stage until we reach the known starting position. For each state and each action we compute the expected cost over all states that can be reached for this action. These are the numbers shown above the small circles denoting the action in Figure 7-7. Adding the immediate cost for a given action to the corresponding expected cost over all future states, we obtain the total cost associated with each action. The action with the minimum total cost is the optimal action at each state. The minimum expected cost and the corresponding action are shown in the rectangles above each of the large circles denoting the states. For instance, given that the costs in states 8 and 9 are 2 and 10, respectively, the expected cost from state 5 to the end is $5 + (0.3)2 + (0.7)10 = 12.6$, if action A is taken, or

$$8 + (0.6)2 + (0.4)10 = 13.2,$$

if action B is taken. Action A has the lower expected cost, so it is the optimal action at state 5. Verify the other computations.

The recursive relation now is:

(7-16)

$$f_n(i_n) = \operatorname*{minimum}_{\text{all } u \in I_n} \left[t_{u, i_n} + \sum_{i_{n-1}} p_{i_n, i_{n-1}}(u) f_{n-1}(i_{n-1}) \right], \qquad \text{all } i_n, \qquad \text{all } n \geqslant 1$$

where: $f_0(i_0) = c_{i_0}$, all i_0, and c_{i_0} is given and
  t_{u, i_n} denotes the cost of taking action u in state i_n,
  $p_{i_n, i_{n-1}}(u)$ is the probability of going from state i_n to state i_{n-1} if action u is taken in state i_n and
  I_n is the set of all possible actions in state i_n.

What is the meaning and form of an optimal solution to a dynamic programming problem with a stochastic state space? Once the supposedly known (chronological) starting point has been evaluated, we know the minimum expected cost. Furthermore, we also know the optimal initial decision or action. However, in contrast to a deterministic dynamic programming problem, we now do not know what the subsequent decisions will be, since these depend on the outcome of random events. The optimal decision rules are of the form "if the state is . . ., then take . . .", i.e., a *strategy of conditional actions*—one for each state at each stage. Only the initial decision can be implemented. For instance, in the present example the optimal action at state 1 is action B. This decision is the only one that can be implemented. Only when we have observed the outcome of a random event (i.e., when we know which state at stage 2 has resulted from this decision) can we implement the next decision at stage 2.

One further point has to be stressed. **Dynamic programming problems for which the state is a random variable can only be solved by the backward solution.** Why? This is immediately clear if we consider the chronological sequence of events. At the beginning of a period (or transition) the process is in a given known state. At this point an action is taken that leads to one of several future states—each one reached with a known probability. We cannot decide which particular state we want to reach. The backward solution maintains this chronological sequence of a decision followed by a random event. In a forward solution we would ask ourselves what is the best path to reach a given state, i.e., the state reached by a random event is arbitrarily fixed—which is a contradiction. Furthermore, even if it were possible, it would be of little use to know what action should have been taken in the preceding period, i.e., after the fact. This difficulty is not present in deterministic problems. Note that for the problem in Section 7-4 the randomness is contained within each period and not carried forward to subsequent periods. The state variable remains deterministic. Therefore, the forward solution can be used.

7-13 INVENTORY PRODUCTION PROBLEM WITH PROBABILISTIC DEMANDS

The inventory of a given product is reviewed once a week, and a decision is made whether to replenish inventory or not, i.e., whether to schedule a production run or not. Goods from a production run scheduled for the coming period will be available for sale during the same period. In addition to costs of holding goods in inventory and fixed and variable production costs, any shortages incurred due to insufficient inventories cause a shortage cost which is linear with respect to the amount short. No sales are lost. Shortages are made up during the following week. The demand during each period is a random variable with known probability distribution. The problem is to find an optimal inventory and production policy so as to minimize total expected costs over a finite planning horizon of N periods.

We first introduce some symbols. The periods are numbered consecutively from end to beginning. The last period in the planning horizon is period 1, and the first period is period N. Let—

- z_n denote the beginning inventory with n periods left to go to the end of the planning horizon;
- x_n denote the amount produced in the nth to last period, $x_n \in X_n$, where X_n is the set of all feasible production levels;
- d_n denote the demand in the nth to last period, subject to a discrete probability distribution with terms $p_n(d_n)$;
- c_h denote the holding cost per period per unit carried forward from the preceding period;
- c_s denote the shortage cost per unit short;
- $k_n(x_n)$ denote the fixed and variable production cost to produce x_n units in period n, $k_n(0) = 0$, $k_n(x_n) \geqslant a$ for $x_n > 0$, where a represents the fixed cost.

The cost in the nth to last period is equal to the sum of the fixed and variable production cost, the inventory holding cost and the shortage cost:

(7-17)
$$C_n(z_n, x_n) = k_n(x_n) + \begin{bmatrix} z_n c_h & \text{for} & z_n > 0 \\ 0 & \text{for} & z_n \leqslant 0 \end{bmatrix} + c_s \sum_{d_n > z_n + x_n} (d_n - z_n - x_n) \, p_n(d_n)$$

where $d_n - z_n - x_n$ is the amount short with probability $p_n(d_n)$, and inventories of two successive periods are related as follows:

(7-18)
$$z_{n-1} = z_n + x_n - d_n$$

The expected total cost is given by the $C_n(z_n, x_n)$ terms summed over all N periods. For the dynamic programming formulation, let the periods denote the stages. The state of the process is given by the beginning inventory level z_n. Then by the principle of optimality, the minimum expected total cost $f_n(z_n)$ of starting with an inventory level of size z_n and n periods left to go to the end of the planning horizon is given by the following recursive relations:

(7-19)
$$f_n(z_n) = \underset{x_n \in X_n}{\text{minimum}} \left[C_n(z_n, x_n) + \sum_{d_n} f_{n-1}(z_n + x_n - d_n) \, p_n(d_n) \right], \qquad \text{all } z_n, \quad n \geqslant 1,$$

where $f_0(z_0) = C_0(z_0)$, all z_0, is given.

For instance, $C_0(z_0)$ could reflect the cost of ending up with an inventory of z_0 at the end of the planning horizon. This cost might include a penalty for deviating from a given target ending inventory of z.

Expression (7-19) is evaluated stage by stage, starting with $n = 1$. The range of values for which the state variable z_n is to be evaluated at each stage is determined from economic considerations about the maximum plausible inventory level. Also, since shortages may occur, z_n may become negative. This in turn will restrict the range of the production levels x_n. No definite guidelines can be given. It is largely a matter of experience with the particular situation and, unfortunately, trial and error. An example using this model is given in the exercise set at the end of this chapter.

7-14 SOME FURTHER POTENTIAL APPLICATIONS

The following is a short list of some additional applications.

1. Allocation of scarce resources to several projects that can be undertaken at varying levels. Examples:
   - Funds allocated to promotion of a product in several marketing areas (stage: areas; state: unused funds; decision: amount of funds allocated to area).
   - Water in reservoir to be allocated to several uses (try to define stage, state, and decision).

2. Scheduling over time. Examples:
   - Production scheduling over time (stage: time period; state: inventory level; decision: production level).
   - Water releases from a reservoir over time (try to define stage, state, and decision). This problem may be combined with an allocation to various uses over time, resulting in a nested problem.
3. Control of chemical processes (stage: reactor; state: composition of entering material; decision: temperature, catalyst), or (stage: time period; state: temperature level; decision: change in temperature).
4. Location of highways (stage: distance from either end; state: elevation, geographical coordinates; decision: link to next state, subject to curvature and grade).

*7-15 NEXT BEST POLICIES

So far we have always been looking for optimal policies. In the real world there may be many reasons why a decision maker may not be willing to implement the optimal policy. In particular, the model used may ignore certain aspects of the real world which are hard to quantify, but which are nevertheless important to the decision maker and which may render the optimal policy undesirable. For this and other reasons it may be desirable to explore the neighborhood of the optimal policy by finding next best policies that may not be in conflict with the aspects ignored.

In this section we shall briefly explore how to adapt the recursive relation so as to obtain the optimal policy and the second best policy for a problem where the state variable is deterministic. Consider the following general form of the recursive relation of a deterministic dynamic programming problem:

(7-20)

$$f_n(z_n) = \operatorname*{minimum}_{x_n \in P_n} \left[C_n(x_n, z_n) + f_{n-1}\left(t(z_n, x_n) \right) \right] \qquad \text{all } z_n, \qquad \text{all } n \geqslant 1$$

where z_n denotes the state variable at stage n;

x_n denotes the decision variable at stage n, and P_n is the set of feasible decisions at stage n;

$C_n(x_n, z_n)$ denotes the one-stage cost for stage n; and

$t(z_n, x_n)$ denotes the new state resulting from decision x_n and state z_n.

As usual, $f_n(z_n)$ is the cost of the optimal policy with n stages remaining, given that we start out in state z_n, and $f_0(z_0) = 0$, for all z_0.

Next, let us introduce the new notation:

(7-21)

$$\text{minimum }_2(y_1, y_2, \ldots, y_k) = \text{the second lowest value of the quantities } y_i,$$

and

$$f_n^{(2)}(z_n) = \text{the cost of the second best policy with } n \text{ stages remaining.}$$

To determine $f_n^{(2)}(z_n)$, we adapt the principle of optimality as follows: **No matter what our initial decision x_n at stage n, the subpolicy over the remaining $n-1$ stages either has to be an optimal one or a second best one.** In the first case the total cost is

(7-22) $$C_n(x_n, z_n) + f_{n-1}(t(z_n, x_n))$$

and in the second case the total cost is

(7-23) $$C_n(x_n, z_n) + f_{n-1}^{(2)}(t(z_n, x_n))$$

Therefore, $f_n^{(2)}(z_n)$ must be equal to either

(7-24) $$\operatorname*{minimum}_{x_n \in P_n}{}_2 \left[C_n(x_n, z_n) + f_{n-1}(t(z_n, x_n)) \right]$$

or

(7-25) $$\operatorname*{minimum}_{x_n \in P_n} \left[C_n(x_n, z_n) + f_{n-1}^{(2)}(t(z_n, x_n)) \right]$$

In fact, to be the cost of the second best policy with n stages remaining, it has to be equal to the smaller of (7-24) and (7-25), or

(7-26) $$f_n^{(2)}(z_n) = \operatorname{minimum} \begin{bmatrix} \operatorname*{minimum}_{x_n \in P_n}{}_2 [C_n(x_n, z_n) + f_{n-1}(t(z_n, x_n))], \\ \operatorname*{minimum}_{x_n \in P_n} [C_n(x_n, z_n) + f_{n-1}^{(2)}(t(z_n, x_n))] \end{bmatrix} \quad \text{all } z_n,$$

$$\text{all} \quad n \geqslant 1,$$

where $f_0(z_0) = 0$, and $f_0^{(2)}(z_0) = 0$

To evaluate the recursive relation (7-26), we need both $f_n(z_n)$ and $f_n^{(2)}(z_n)$ for all but the last stage, N. Therefore, to obtain the second best policy, the recursive relation (7-20) has also to be evaluated for all but one stage.

In practice, one would usually wish to evaluate both the optimal and the second best policies simultaneously. The computational effort would be slightly more than double.

In Figure 7-8, the optimal and the next best policies for the routing problem Figure 7-1 have been evaluated. To ease the task of tracing the second best policy once state 1 has been evaluated, we record for each state evaluated not only the cost of the second best subpolicy, and the second best decision at that state, but also whether the second best decision involves f_{n-1} (i.e., the optimal subpolicy from stage $n-1$ on) or $f_{n-1}^{(2)}$ (i.e., the second best subpolicy from stage $n-1$ on). Thus, the box shown above each state contains two lines. The first line has the entries: (1), (optimal subpolicy from that state on), (next state at stage $n-1$); and the second line shows: (2), (cost of the second best subpolicy from that state on), (next state at stage $n-1$), (policy to be followed from stage $n-1$: 1 for optimal subpolicy, 2 for second best subpolicy).

Tracing back the second best policy, we see that there are two second best policies with equal costs of 83. We can follow the optimal policy initially and go from A to B to F to J, and then take the second best decision from there on, leading to R. Or we can take the second best decision at A, which leads to D, and then follow the optimal subpolicy from D on, which passes through G, K, or L, to R.

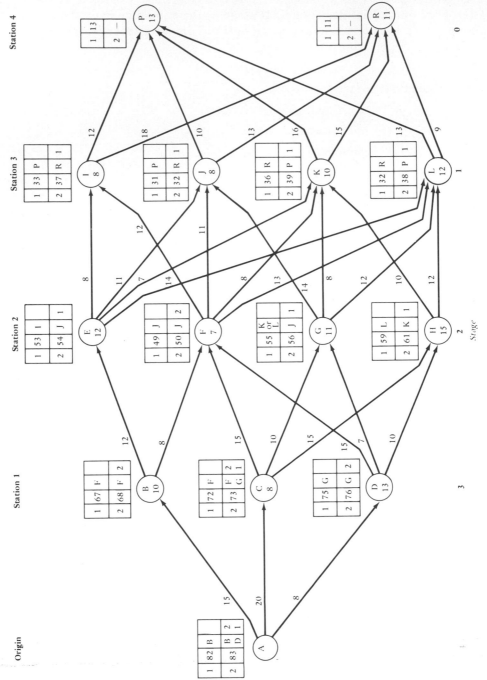

Figure 7-8. *Optimal and next best policy for routing problem.*

250

EXERCISES

7.1 Consider the following network where the numbers attached to the links are the distance between two points.

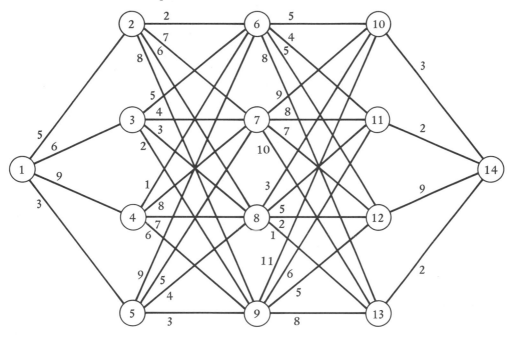

(a) Using the backward solution of dynamic programming, find the shortest path from point 1 to point 14.

(b) Using the forward solution of dynamic programming, find the shortest path from point 1 to point 14.

7.2 A firm has just developed a new product. Management figures that it has about three months before its main competitor will have a similar product on the market, and, therefore, wishes to contact as many potential customers as possible. The territory to be covered is divided into five sales areas. For each sales area the incremental number of customers that can be contacted by the 1st, 2nd, 3rd, etc., salesmen within the three-month period is as follows:

Number of Salesmen Assigned to the Area	Sales Area 1	2	3	4	5
1	31	36	40	28	32
2	31	33	36	25	30
3	30	31	32	24	29
4	28	24	29	22	27
5	25	20	25	12	18
6	20	14	18	8	12
7	12	9	10	0	6
8	8	0	0	0	0

(a) The firm has ten salesmen trained for this promotion. Formulate the recursive relation of dynamic programming. Find the optimal assignment of salesmen to each sales area so as to maximize the number of potential customers contacted.

(b) How many additional customers could be contacted if the firm trained one additional salesman? two additional salesmen?

(c) Is there any conceptual difference in the dynamic programming formulation between a forward and a backward solution for this problem?

7.3 A weather monitoring station is supplied once a month by air drop. The plane making the air drop has an excess weight capacity for nonessential items of W kg. Each month the weather station radios its needs for various nonessential items, by assigning utility values for the first, second, ..., kth item included in the shipment. On a particular occasion the list is as follows:

Item	1st	2nd	3rd	4th	5th	Weight per Unit in kg
	Incremental Utility for Units					
1	12	8	4	0	0	2
2	15	5	1	0	0	3
3	6	6	5	4	2	1
4	8	5	2	1	0	1
5	20	10	0	0	0	4

The total excess weight capacity is $W = 10$kg. Formulate the recursive relation of dynamic programming maximizing total utility, and use it to evaluate the optimal solution.

7.4 A product is produced by a batch process. The setup cost per batch amounts to $10. The variable production cost is $8 for the first unit produced, $6 for the second, $4 for the third, and $3 for each additional unit. The maximum production capacity per week is 6 units. The product can be stored in inventory at a cost of $2 per week. The beginning inventory is zero, and no inventory is wanted at the end of the planning horizon.

(a) If the demand over the next 8 weeks is 2, 1, 2, 3, 0, 1, 3, and 3, formulate the recursive relation of dynamic programming, and find the optimal solution using a backward formulation, i.e., starting at the end of the planning horizon.

(b) If the demand is 1 unit per week over the next 8 weeks, formulate the recursive relation of dynamic programming using a forward formulation, and find the optimal solution.

(c) If there is also a handling cost of $1 for each unit put into inventory, how does this change the form of the recursive relation for (a)? You do not have to solve the problem again, but merely reformulate it.

7.5 The price of one of the raw materials needed in the manufacturing process of a firm is subject to fairly regular seasonal fluctuations. The prices predicted and the amounts required for the coming 6 months are:

Month	1	2	3	4	5	6
Price/Unit	$11000	$13000	$18000	$19000	$19000	$21000
Requirement	2	4	4	4	4	2

Material purchased in a given month can be used in the production process of the same month or stored for later use. The maximum storage capacity is 8 units. Material carried forward in inventory for one period incurs a holding cost of $2000 per unit. Each purchase requires a trip by a specialized vehicle at a cost of $3000 per purchase, regardless of the amount procured. Beginning inventory and ending inventory is zero. Formulate the recursive relations of dynamic programming minimizing total cost and find the optimal purchasing and storage policy.

7.6 An electronic monitoring device consists of N components that work in series. Each must function for the device to function as a whole. Each component is subject to random failure, thus causing the device to fail as a whole. The reliability of the device can be improved by installing more than one unit of a component. If this component fails, one of the spare units is automatically switched into the circuit to take its place. The number of units installed for each component is restricted by the total cost of the device. Consider the following simple example for $N = 4$.

Component	1	2	3	4
Probability of No Failure for				
0 spare units	0.7	0.9	0.8	0.6
1 spare unit	0.85	0.96	0.9	0.8
2 spare units	0.97	0.99	0.98	0.95
Cost of One Unit	$100	$300	$100	$200

Assume that one unit of each component has been included. If $600 of additional funds are available for spare units, how many spare units of each component should be included in the device so as to maximize the probability that the device will not fail. Formulate the recursive relations of dynamic programming and find the optimal solution. *Hint:* The probability that the device will not fail is equal to the product of the probabilities of each component not failing. For example, if no spare units are included for components 1, 2, and 3, and 1 spare unit for component 4, the probability of no failure is $(0.7)(0.9)(0.8)(0.8)$. Let $f_n(s)$ denote the maximum probability of no failure if s dollars are allocated for spares for the first n components.

7.7 Consider the following costs associated with operating and maintaining a machine.

Operating Year	1	2	3	4	5	6	7	8	9
	$	$	$	$	$	$	$	$	$
Operating and Maintenance costs/year	200	200	210	240	280	350	450	600	800
Salvage Value of Machine (end of year)	900	750	600	450	300	200	100	50	0

The cost of a new machine is $1200. The present machine is 3 years old. Using a 12-year planning horizon, formulate the recursive relations of dynamic programming and find the least-cost replacement policy. How is the initial decision affected by the age of the machine in year 12.

7.8   The replacement costs and net revenue of a machine depend on the year in which the machine is purchased.

Purchased in years 1 through 3: purchase price $1000

Operating year	1	2	3	4	5	6	7
Net revenue	$500	$500	$450	$400	$300	$250	$200
Salvage value	800	700	550	350	200	100	0

Purchased in years 4 through 8: purchase price $1200

Operating year	1	2	3	4	5	6	7
Net revenue	$600	$600	$550	$500	$400	$300	$250
Salvage value	900	800	650	450	250	100	0

Purchased in years 9 through 12: purchase price $1300

Operating year	1	2	3	4	5	6	7
Net revenue	$650	$650	$600	$550	$450	$300	$250
Salvage value	1000	800	650	450	250	100	0

The present machine is 3 years old. Using a 12-year planning horizon, determine the optimal replacement policy that maximizes net revenues minus net replacement costs. Machines are replaced at the beginning of the year. The present machine has the same operating characteristics as the machines bought in years 1 to 3.

7.9   Consider problem 7.3. Assume that there is not only a maximum excess weight limit, but also a limit on the excess space, S. The amount of space required per unit for the five items is:

Item	1	2	3	4	5
Space in cubic feet	1	2	1	2	3

Assume that for a given flight, the excess space is $S = 5$, and the excess weight is $W = 6$. Formulate the recursive relations of dynamic programming, maximizing total utility, and use it to evaluate the optimal solution. *Hint:* two state variables are needed.

7.10 A product is produced by a continuous production process. Each month the production engineer has to set the rate of production. Changes in the rate of production result in a so-called smoothing cost. If x_{t-1} is the rate of production in period $t-1$, and x_t is the rate of production in period t, then the smoothing cost is equal to $c_s(x_t - x_{t-1})^2$. Other costs involved are: a cost of c_h per unit carried in inventory from one period to the next, and a variable unit production cost which depends on the rate of production as follows:

Rate of production	$x_t \leqslant 6$	$7 \leqslant x_t \leqslant 8$	$x_t \geqslant 9$
Cost per unit	c_1	c_2	c_3

The demand in period t is d_t. All demand has to be met. The beginning inventory and ending inventory are both zero. The present production rate is $\hat{x}$. The final rate can be arbitrary.

(a) Formulate this problem as a dynamic programming problem using a backward formulation. Show the recursive relations for $t = 1$, $1 < t < N$, and $t = N$.

(b) If $c_s = 4$, $c_h = 2$, and $c_1 = 5$, $c_2 = 4$, $c_3 = 6$, the demand over a 6-month planning horizon is $d_6 = 6$, $d_5 = 8$, $d_4 = 10$, $d_3 = 7$, $d_2 = 8$, $d_1 = 6$, and $\hat{x} = 7$, what is the optimal production plan?

7.11 Using the stochastic inventory control model formulated in Section 7-13, find the optimal production policy over a 6-month planning horizon for the following data: $c_h = \$1.00$, $c_s = \$4.00$, $k_n(x_n) = \$4$, $x_n > 0$, all n (i.e., the production cost consists only of a setup cost that is constant), and $p_n(d_n)$ as follows:

n	6	5	4	3	2	1
$d_n = 0$	0.5	0.2	0.4	0.5	0.2	0.2
$d_n = 1$	0.3	0.3	0.2	0.5	0.3	0.3
$d_n = 2$	0.2	0.4	0.2	0	0.3	0.3
$d_n = 3$	0	0.1	0.2	0	0.2	0.2

Due to storage restrictions, no more than 6 units can be kept in inventory from one period to the next. The beginning inventory is 2.

7.12 A stockbroker has speculated on the forward market and signed an agreement to deliver a certain stock at a price of $49 per share on Friday. He does not hold any of this stock on Monday, but will have to buy it prior to the due date. The present price is $48. The price per share changes randomly from day to day. His subjective estimates of the probability distribution of price changes from day n to day $n+1$ are

Change of price	-1	0	$+1$
Probability if price decreased from day $n-1$ to n	0.4	0.4	0.2
Otherwise	0.3	0.35	0.35

He would like to buy the shares at the lowest possible price.   Once he has made his purchase, he will hold the shares until the evening of Friday when he makes the delivery.   He would like to find the optimal purchasing strategy, given that the last price change observed was a decrease.   Formulate the recursive relations of dynamic programming so as to maximize his expected gain or minimize his expected loss.   *Hint:* Let the current price be the state variable.   Use a second state variable to denote the price change on the preceding day.

7.13   A machine is subject to random failure.   If a failure occurs, it has to be replaced with a new one by the beginning of the following year.   The operating efficiency of the machine also decreases with time.   Consider the following data.

Year of operation	1	2	3	4	5	6
Probability of failure	0	0.1	0.2	0.3	0.4	0.5
Operating costs	$100	$110	$140	$170	$210	$260
Salvage value if machine is sold prior to failure	$600	$500	$350	$200	$100	$50

If a failure occurs, an additional cost of $200 is incurred.   A new machine costs $800.   Solve this problem by dynamic programming for an 8-year planning horizon.   Formulate the recursive relations in general terms first.   The current machine on hand has had one year of use.   Whatever machine is on hand at the end of the planning horizon is sold provided it has not failed.

7.14   Find the second best policy for the river pollution control problem discussed in Section 7-8.   What is the cost difference with the optimal policy, and how does each factory's treatment differ.

REFERENCES

Bellman, Richard E.   *Dynamic Programming*.   Princeton Univ. Press, 1957.   The first text in dynamic programming by the father of this most versatile tool.   The treatment is highly abstract.   This is not an easy text to study.

———, and Stuart E. Dreyfus.   *Applied Dynamic Programming*.   Princeton Univ. Press, 1962.   A thorough discussion of numerous completely worked examples, including a number of computer program flowcharts.   More easily readable than Bellman's first book.   It is somewhat dated now due to the vast progress made in dynamic programming since its publication.   Gives full details of a number of refinements, such as the method of Lagrange multipliers and the method of successive approximation to overcome problems of multi-dimensionality of the state variables (Chapter 2), and various search methods to reduce computational effort (Chapter 4).

———, and Robert Kalaba.   "On *k*th Best Policies," *SIAM J. on Applied Mathematics*, 8 (1960), pp. 582–88.   A generalization of the material in Section 7-15.

Bertele, Umberto, and Francesco Brioschi.   *Nonserial Dynamic Programming*.   New York: Academic Press, 1972.   In serial problems, the interactions are restricted to occur only between consecutive state variables, e.g., x_{n-1} and x_n. This permits the problem to be decomposed serially into subproblems, where interactions occur only between consecutive subproblems. Nonserial problems allow interactions between other variables also. Provided these interactions are sparse or occur in groupings, generalizations of the concepts of dynamic programming may be possible to solve such problems. This text addresses itself to such problems. In addition to the standard procedure of eliminating variables one by one, it considers elimination of variables in blocks and multilevel elimination of variables. This is definitely an advanced text.

Hadley, George. *Nonlinear and Dynamic Programming*. Reading, Mass.: Addison Wesley, 1964. Chapters 10 and 11 have a thorough treatment of dynamic programming and computational refinements. Mathematically somewhat demanding. But clarity of development is outstanding. Highly recommended as additional reading to this chapter.

Jewell, William S. "Markov-Renewal Programming, I: Formulation, Finite Return Models," *Operations Research*, 11, 1963, pp. 938–48; "Markov-Renewal Programming, II: Infinite Return Models, Example," 11, 1963, pp. 949–71.

Kaufmann, A. *Graphs, Dynamic Programming and Finite Games*. New York: Academic Press, 1967. The nature of dynamic programming is taken up in Chapter 2 with a number of fully worked examples. The graph of the decision process is shown for most examples. The presentation is somewhat cumbersome as the author never uses the compact and efficient table method to evaluate the recursive relations. Chapter 5 deals with the mathematical properties of dynamic programming. The treatment is, however, almost exclusively devoted to Markov Chains and dynamic programming, discussed in Chapter 9 of this text.

Larson, Robert E. *State Increment Dynamic Programming*. New York: Elsevier, 1968. A variant of dynamic programming that attempts to overcome the computational problems of a multi-dimensional state space by limiting the search to adjacent points only. Highly successful for problems where the state changes in small steps.

Luenberger, David G. "Cyclic Dynamic Programming: A Procedure for Problems with Fixed Delay," *Operations Research*, 19, July–August 1971. A dynamic decision problem in which the effect of an action is delayed for a number of periods or has an effect that lasts for a fixed interval normally requires a multi-dimensional state space. This note shows how this structure may be exploited to reduce the dimensionality.

Nemhauser, George L. *Introduction to Dynamic Programming*. New York: Wiley, 1966. Not an easy text to read, its main detraction is the somewhat difficult and unconventional notation. The book has a whole chapter on computational refinements.

Wagner, H. M. *Principles of Operations Research*, 2nd Ed. Englewood Cliffs: Prentice-Hall, 1975. Chapters 8, 9, and 10 discuss deterministic models, with Chapter 9 entirely devoted to inventory control. Considerable emphasis is put on the effect of the length of the planning horizon on the optimal policy. General level of treatment is fairly easy. Chapter 17 deals with stochastic problems. Chapters 11 and 12 extend dynamic programming to infinite period models for the deterministic case. These aspects are taken up in Chapter 9 of this text.

———, and T. M. Whitin. "Dynamic Versions of Economic Lot Size Model," *Management Science*, 5, Sept. 1958. One of the most basic deterministic dynamic inventory control models with a linear holding cost and a constant setup cost per batch. The authors show that this cost structure implies a specific form of the optimal policy. The reasoning used has many applications in completely different type problems. For a more easily readable version of the same paper, see G. Hadley and T. M. Whitin, *Analysis of Inventory Systems*, Englewood Cliffs: Prentice-Hall, 1963, pp. 326–45, or H. Wagner. *Principles of Operations Research*, 2nd Ed. Englewood Cliffs: Prentice-Hall, 1975, pp. 303–8.

Whisler, W. D. "A Stochastic Inventory Model for Rented Equipment," *Management Science*, 13, May 1967. Derives the form of the optimal policy for the example developed in Sections 7-4 to 7-6. This policy has two control limits, L_n and U_n, for each period. If $z_n < L_n$, additional equipment is rented, if $z_n > U_n$, some equipment may be returned, and if $L_n < z_n < U_n$, no action is taken. This same structure of the optimal policy holds for a number of different problems. See the following papers: Eppen, Gary D., and Eugene F. Fama. "Cash Balance and Simple Dynamic Portfolio Problems with Proportional Costs," *International Economic Review*, 10, June 1969; Daellenbach, H. G. "A Stochastic Cash Balance Model with Two Sources of Short-term Funds," *International Economic Review*, 12, June 1971; Daellenbach, H. G. "Note on a Stochastic Manpower Smoothing and Production Model," *Operational Research Quarterly*, 27, 3, 1976; and Mann, Stuart H. "On the Optimal Size for Exploited Natural Animal Populations," *Operations Research*, 21, May–June 1973.

White, D. J. "An Example of Loosely Coupled Stages in Dynamic Programming," *Management Science*, 19, March 1973. Considers a scheduling problem where the dependence between successive stages is weak, resulting in a reduction in the computational effort.

————. *Dynamic Programming*. Edinburgh: Oliver & Boyd and San Francisco: Holden-Day, 1969. An advanced text that tends to indulge in the mathematical aspects of the method, including the connections with optimal control theory and adaptive processes. Recommended for mathematics majors only.

Williams, Jack F. "Multi-Echelon Production Scheduling when Demand is Stochastic," *Management Science*, 20, May 1974. A multi-stage inventory system with set-up costs at each stage.

Wong, Peter J., and David G. Luenberger. "Reducing the Memory Requirements of Dynamic Programming," *Operations Research*, 16, Nov.–Dec. 1968. This paper presents a decomposition procedure for extending the size of problems that can be solved with limited high-speed computer memory.

8

Markov
Chains

A *Markov process* is a mathematical model that describes, in probabilistic terms, the dynamic behavior of certain types of systems over time. In this chapter we shall study a type of Markov process known as a *Markov chain*. In particular, we will study aspects and properties of Markov chains needed to analyze their long-run behavior. Chapter 9 will look at so-called *Markovian decision processes* that can be formulated as dynamic-programming problems.

This chapter assumes that the reader is familar with the concepts of matrices and vectors and the operations of vector and matrix multiplication. If you have any doubts about these operations, we suggest that you review Appendix A and, in particular, Section A-5. Sections B-1 and B-2 of Appendix B review the basic probability concepts needed for this chapter.

8-1 TRANSITION MATRIX

A regional water board plans to build a reservoir for flood control and irrigation purposes on one of the rivers under its jurisdiction. The proposed maximum capacity of the reservoir is 4 million cubic meters or, for short, 4 units of water. Before proceeding with the construction, the board wishes to have some idea about the reservoir's long-run effectiveness.

The weekly flow of the river can be approximated by the following discrete probability distribution:

Weekly water flow in units of one million cubic meters	2	3	4	5
Probability	0.3	0.4	0.2	0.1

The board considers acceptance of water contracts for irrigation of 2 units of water per week. Furthermore, to maintain minimum water quality standards downstream of the reservoir, at least one unit of water per week would have to be released over the spillway. So, the total weekly target release is 3 units. If the reservoir level plus the water inflow is less than that, any shortages would always be at the expense of irrigation. If the reservoir is full, any further inflow would immediately be released over the spillway. The reservoir level cannot be reduced below one unit of water.

The two most basic concepts of the behavior of such a system are the *state* of the system and the *state transitions* that the system may undergo. The state of a system represents all those aspects that completely describe the "position" of the system at any instant of time and which are relevant for the future behavior of the system. In physical systems, the *state space* can often be specified in terms of the values of one or several variables, referred to as *state variables*. Note the analogy to dynamic programming. For the reservoir problem, the variable that completely defines the state of the system is the reservoir level at the beginning (or end) of a week. If s denotes this variable, then the state space covers all real numbers between 1 and 4 units of water, inclusive. Thus, the state space is continuous. For many real life problems, the state variable may be restricted to assume discrete values only. For instance, the process studied may deal with customers arriving at a counter to receive a service. For such problems the state variable often represents the number of customers being serviced or waiting for service and, hence, assumes only non-negative integer values. In other instances, a continuous state space is arbitrarily approximated by a discrete state space, usually to simplify the analysis. This is what we will do for the reservoir problem. In view of the fairly crude form of the weekly water inflow data, we shall approximate the state space by the discrete values $s = 1, 2, 3,$ and 4. In fact, in this chapter we will only discuss processes with a finite discrete state space.

As time passes the system may move from a given state to another state, i.e., it may undergo a *transition* from one state to another. Say, we observe our reservoir at the beginning of each week. Then, from one week to the next, depending on the water inflow (a random variable) and the water releases (a controllable variable), the reservoir level may rise, fall, or remain the same. Figure 8-1 depicts states and possible transitions in the form of a *transition diagram* for this example. Each circle denotes a state and the arrows represent possible transitions. Note that for completeness, no change in the water level is depicted as a transition back to the same state. For instance, if the reservoir is in state 1 (i.e., contains 1 unit of water) at the beginning

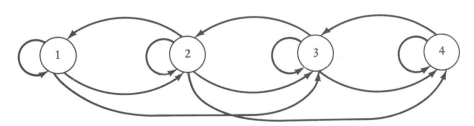

Figure 8-1. *Transition diagram for reservoir system.*

of a week, the water inflow during the week is 5 units of water, and the total outflow to satisfy the target release is 3, then the reservoir will move to state 3 (i.e., it will contain 3 units of water) by the end of the week (=beginning of next week). If the water inflow is 4, the system will move to state 2. If the water inflow is 3, the reservoir will remain in state 1. However, the reservoir will also remain in state 1 if the water inflow is only 2 and, consequently, the target release cannot be satisfied completely. You should verify the meaning of all other arrows. Again, we shall restrict our discussion in this chapter to processes where a transition occurs at discrete points in time. In our example this means that, strictly speaking, the inflow and outflow occur simultaneously at an instant of time either at the beginning or at the end of each week. However, this results in the same end-of-week reservoir levels as if inflows and outflows occur at constant rates throughout the week. Chapter 10 looks at processes where a transition can occur at any instant of time.

With each possible transition from state $s = i$ to state $s = j$ we associate a probability, p_{ij}, called a *one-step transition probability*. If no transition can occur from state i to state j, $p_{ij} = 0$. On the other hand, if the system, when it is in state i, can only move to state j at the next transition, $p_{ij} = 1$. With this convention, transition probabilities can be defined from each state i to each state j. For a system with r states, the p_{ij} values can be arranged as an $(r \times r)$ matrix, called a *transition matrix*:

(8-1)
$$\mathbf{P} = \begin{bmatrix} p_{11} & p_{12} & \cdots & p_{1r} \\ \cdot & \cdot & & \cdot \\ \cdot & \cdot & & \cdot \\ \cdot & \cdot & & \cdot \\ p_{r1} & p_{r2} & \cdots & p_{rr} \end{bmatrix}$$

Each row represents the *one-step transition probability distribution* over all states. From this it follows immediately that the row sums of $\mathbf{P}$ are equal to 1:

(8-2)
$$\sum_j p_{ij} = 1, \quad \text{all } i$$

Any matrix with elements $0 \leqslant p_{ij} \leqslant 1$, whose row sums are 1, is called a *stochastic matrix*.

For our reservoir system, the one-step transition probabilities can be determined from the probability distribution of the weekly water inflows and the target release. For instance, the one-step transition probabilities for state 1 (=row 1) are obtained as follows: (Referring back to Figure 8-1 will be helpful at this point.)

Water Inflow	Probability	Water Outflow	New State j	p_{ij}
5	0.1	3	3	$p_{13} = 0.1$
4	0.2	3	2	$p_{12} = 0.2$
3	0.4	3	1⎱	
2	0.3	2	1⎰	$p_{11} = 0.7$

From state 1, no transition is possible to state 4, and the sum $p_{11}+p_{12}+p_{13}+p_{14} = 1$ as required.   By the same reasoning we obtain the other elements in **P**.

$$(8\text{-}3) \qquad \mathbf{P} = \begin{bmatrix} 0.7 & 0.2 & 0.1 & 0 \\ 0.3 & 0.4 & 0.2 & 0.1 \\ 0 & 0.3 & 0.4 & 0.3 \\ 0 & 0 & 0.3 & 0.7 \end{bmatrix} \begin{matrix} (\text{row } 1) \\ (\text{row } 2) \\ (\text{row } 3) \\ (\text{row } 4) \end{matrix}$$

(col. 1) (col. 2) (col. 3) (col. 4)

If we observe the system in state i at the beginning of any week, then the ith row of the transition matrix **P** represents the probability distribution over the states at the beginning of the next week.   The same transition matrix completely describes the probabilistic behavior of the system for all future one-step transitions.   The probabilistic behavior of such a system over time is called a *Markov chain with stationary transition probabilities*—stationary because **P** remains constant over time.

Note that the future (probabilistic) behavior of this system only depends on the current state of the system and not on how it entered this state.   Knowledge of the past history of the process does not alter the probability of any future transition. This lack of memory is known as the *Markovian assumption*.

MARKOVIAN ASSUMPTION

Given the transition matrix **P**, knowledge of the current state occupied by the process is sufficient to completely describe the future probabilistic behavior of the process.

Again, note the analogy to dynamic programming.

8-2 n-STEP TRANSITION PROBABILITIES

Suppose the system is in state 2 (i.e., the reservoir has 2 units of water) at the beginning of a week, and we would like to know the probability of finding the system in each of the 4 states after 16 weeks or 16 transitions.   We call these the *state probabilities* after 16 transitions.

Let $p_{ij}^{(n)}$ denote the probability of finding the system in state j after n transitions given that the initial state is i.   (Note that n is not a power.)   The term, $p_{ij}^{(n)}$, is called an *n-step transition probability*.   Clearly, by definition, $p_{ij}^{(1)} = p_{ij}$, the one-step transition probability.   In 2 transitions, the process can move from state i to state k in the first transition, and then on to state j in the second transition.   The probability of this is $p_{ik}^{(1)}p_{kj}$.   Since state k can be any one of r states, there are r mutually exclusive ways of doing this.   Hence, $p_{ij}^{(2)}$ is equal to the sum of their probabilities:

$$(8\text{-}4) \qquad p_{ij}^{(2)} = \sum_k p_{ik}^{(1)} p_{kj}, \qquad \text{all } i, \quad \text{all } j.$$

Repeated use of the same reasoning allows us to build up the n-step transition probabilities, $p_{ij}^{(n)}$ for $n = 3, 4, \ldots$, as follows:

$$(8\text{-}5) \qquad\qquad p_{ij}^{(n)} = \sum_k p_{ik}^{(n-1)} p_{kj}, \qquad \text{all } i, \quad \text{all } j$$

Let us look at expression (8-4) more carefully. The values of the $p_{ik}^{(1)}$ $(= p_{ik})$, for all k, are the elements of row i in the transition matrix **P**. Similarly, the p_{kj} values are the elements of column j in **P**. Thus, each $p_{ij}^{(2)}$ is the result of multiplying the vector of transition probabilities given by row i in **P** with the vector of transition probabilities given by column j in **P**. Hence, the $p_{ij}^{(2)}$ values are the elements of a stochastic matrix which is obtained by multiplying the transition matrix by itself. In other words, the matrix of the two-step transition probabilities is simply equal to $\mathbf{PP} = \mathbf{P}^2$. By analogy to expression (8-5), we find that the matrix of the three-step transition probabilities with elements $p_{ij}^{(3)}$ is given by $\mathbf{P}^2 \mathbf{P} = \mathbf{P}^3$. In general, the matrix of the n-step transition probabilities $p_{ij}^{(n)}$ is equal to

$$(8\text{-}6) \qquad\qquad \mathbf{P}^{n-1} \mathbf{P} = \mathbf{P}^n$$

Each row i of $\mathbf{P}^n$ represents the *state probability distribution* after n transitions, given that the process starts out in state i.

Applied to the reservoir problem, we get:

$$\mathbf{P}^2 = \mathbf{PP} = \begin{bmatrix} 0.7 & 0.2 & 0.1 & 0 \\ 0.3 & 0.4 & 0.2 & 0.1 \\ 0 & 0.3 & 0.4 & 0.3 \\ 0 & 0 & 0.3 & 0.7 \end{bmatrix} \begin{bmatrix} 0.7 & 0.2 & 0.1 & 0 \\ 0.3 & 0.4 & 0.2 & 0.1 \\ 0 & 0.3 & 0.4 & 0.3 \\ 0 & 0 & 0.3 & 0.7 \end{bmatrix}$$

$$= \begin{bmatrix} 0.55 & 0.25 & 0.15 & 0.05 \\ 0.33 & 0.28 & 0.22 & 0.17 \\ 0.09 & 0.24 & 0.31 & 0.36 \\ 0 & 0.09 & 0.33 & 0.58 \end{bmatrix}$$

$$\mathbf{P}^4 = \mathbf{P}^3 \mathbf{P} = \mathbf{P}^2 \mathbf{P}^2 = \begin{bmatrix} 0.399 & 0.248 & 0.200 & 0.153 \\ 0.294 & 0.229 & 0.235 & 0.242 \\ 0.157 & 0.196 & 0.281 & 0.366 \\ 0.059 & 0.157 & 0.314 & 0.470 \end{bmatrix}$$

$$\mathbf{P}^8 = \mathbf{P}^7 \mathbf{P} = \mathbf{P}^4 \mathbf{P}^4 = \begin{bmatrix} 0.272 & 0.219 & 0.243 & 0.266 \\ 0.236 & 0.209 & 0.255 & 0.300 \\ 0.186 & 0.196 & 0.271 & 0.347 \\ 0.147 & 0.186 & 0.284 & 0.383 \end{bmatrix}$$

$$\mathbf{P}^{16} = \mathbf{P}^8\,\mathbf{P}^8 = \begin{bmatrix} 0.210 & 0.203 & 0.263 & 0.324 \\ 0.205 & 0.201 & 0.265 & 0.329 \\ 0.198 & 0.200 & 0.265 & 0.335 \\ 0.193 & 0.198 & 0.269 & 0.340 \end{bmatrix}$$

Note how we obtained higher powers of $\mathbf{P}$.

If the process starts out in state 2 as assumed, then the state probability distribution after 16 weeks is given by row 2 of $\mathbf{P}^{16}$. So the probability is 0.205 of finding the process in state $s = 1$ after 16 weeks, 0.201 for $s = 2$, 0.265 for $s = 3$, and 0.329 for $s = 4$, given that we begin in state 2.

8-3 CLASSIFICATION OF FINITE MARKOV CHAINS

Before we study the long-run behavior of finite Markov chains, it is helpful to classify them according to the general structure of the transition matrix.

State j is said to be *accessible* from state i, if it is possible to go from state i to state j in a sufficiently large number of transitions. Mathematically, this means that $p_{ij}^{(n)} > 0$ for some n. Two states i and j are said to *communicate* if j is accessible from i and i is accessible from j, i.e., it is possible to go from state i to j and back to i after a sufficiently large number of transitions. Communication is a class property. If state i communicates with j and with k, then j also communicates with k. Thus, all states that communicate with i also communicate among each other. Let us clarify these concepts with a few examples.

$$\mathbf{P}_1 = \begin{array}{c} \\ 1 \\ 2 \\ 3 \\ 4 \end{array} \begin{array}{cccc} 1 & 2 & 3 & 4 \\ \left[\begin{array}{cccc} \frac{1}{2} & \frac{1}{2} & 0 & 0 \\ \frac{1}{3} & \frac{2}{3} & 0 & 0 \\ \frac{1}{4} & \frac{1}{4} & \frac{1}{6} & \frac{1}{3} \\ 0 & 0 & \frac{1}{4} & \frac{3}{4} \end{array}\right] \end{array} \qquad \mathbf{P}_2 = \begin{array}{c} \\ 1 \\ 2 \\ 3 \\ 4 \end{array} \begin{array}{cccc} 1 & 2 & 3 & 4 \\ \left[\begin{array}{cccc} 1 & 0 & 0 & 0 \\ 0 & 1 & 0 & 0 \\ \frac{1}{2} & 0 & \frac{1}{6} & \frac{1}{3} \\ 0 & \frac{1}{3} & \frac{1}{2} & \frac{1}{6} \end{array}\right] \end{array}$$

$$\mathbf{P}_3 = \begin{array}{c} \\ 1 \\ 2 \\ 3 \end{array} \begin{array}{ccc} 1 & 2 & 3 \\ \left[\begin{array}{ccc} 0.2 & 0.5 & 0.3 \\ 0.1 & 0.2 & 0.7 \\ 0.6 & 0.3 & 0.1 \end{array}\right] \end{array} \qquad \mathbf{P}_4 = \begin{array}{c} \\ 1 \\ 2 \\ 3 \\ 4 \end{array} \begin{array}{cccc} 1 & 2 & 3 & 4 \\ \left[\begin{array}{cccc} 0 & 0 & 0.7 & 0.3 \\ 0 & 0 & 0.4 & 0.6 \\ 0.2 & 0.8 & 0 & 0 \\ 0.6 & 0.4 & 0 & 0 \end{array}\right] \end{array}$$

In the process of matrix $\mathbf{P}_1$, states 1 and 2 are both accessible from states 3 and 4, but not vice versa. States 1 and 2 can be reached from state 3 in one transition, whereas from state 4 they can only be reached in $n = 2$ transitions. States 1 and 2 communicate with each other and so do states 3 and 4. Each set forms a class of communicating states. Note, however, that once the process has made a transition to either state 1 or 2, it cannot return to states 3 or 4. The process has been absorbed in the set of states 1 and 2. Such a set of states is called an *ergodic set*, and the states that belong to it are called *ergodic states*, whereas states 3 and 4 are called *transient states*. No matter where the process starts out, it will sooner or later end up in the ergodic set. If we are only interested in the long-run behavior of the chain, we can forget about the transient states. In fact, higher powers of $\mathbf{P}_1$ will still have zeros in the upper right-hand portion, whereas the probabilities in the lower right-hand portion will get smaller and smaller.

It is possible for a process to have more than one ergodic set of states. For a chain of this sort it may be interesting to know the probability with which the process is absorbed in each of the ergodic sets, given that it starts out in a transient state.

In $\mathbf{P}_2$ the process will be absorbed, sooner or later, in either state 1 or state 2, and then never leave that state again. This can be seen from the one-step transition probabilities, p_{11} and p_{22}, which are both equal to 1, with all other p_{1j} and p_{2j} zero. A state that has this property is called an *absorbing state*.

In $\mathbf{P}_3$, all states communicate and form a single ergodic set. Such a chain is called *irreducible*. The states in $\mathbf{P}_4$ also communicate with each other, and thus also form a single ergodic set. However, note that if the process is in state 1 or 2, it will always move to either state 3 or 4, and similarly if it is in state 3 or 4, it will move back to state 1 or 2. Thus, if the process starts out in state 1 or 2, after every odd number of transitions it will be in states 3 or 4, and after every even number of transitions it will be back in states 1 or 2. Such a chain is called *cyclic*. The states in $\mathbf{P}_4$ can be divided into two cyclic sets, namely $(1, 2)$ and $(3, 4)$. The process can only return to either set after $d = 2$ transitions. The number, d, of transitions needed for returning is known as the *period*. Note that the period is equal to the number of cyclic sets. The long-run behavior of such a chain will remain cyclic.

A chain that is not cyclic is called *aperiodic*. A Markov chain that is irreducible and aperiodic is called *regular*. Which of the four transition matrices belongs to a regular chain?

8-4 LIMITING STATE PROBABILITIES

Consider again in the four matrices, $\mathbf{P}^2$, $\mathbf{P}^4$, $\mathbf{P}^8$, and $\mathbf{P}^{16}$ in Section 8-2 and, in particular, compare the columns. The differences in the elements of a given column become smaller as n increases. In other words, all elements of a given column tend towards a common limit as n increases. Since this is true for each column, it follows that all rows tend to the same limiting row vector. Does this imply that the state probability distribution approaches a common limiting distribution as n increases irrespective of the initial state in which the process started? The answer is yes for all *regular* Markov chains. This is not the case for cyclic chains nor for chains with transient states or several ergodic sets (although each of these may be analyzed individually as a regular chain).

THEOREM: LIMITING BEHAVIOR OF REGULAR MARKOV CHAINS

If **P** is the transition matrix of a regular Markov chain, then $\mathbf{P}^n$ approaches a unique limiting matrix **A** with all rows equal to $\mathbf{a} = (a_1, a_2, ..., a_r)$ as n tends to infinity.

The common row vector **a** represents the *limiting state probability distribution* or the *steady state probability distribution* that the process approaches regardless of the initial state.

How do we find these limiting state probabilities? From the preceding theorem it follows that for n arbitrarily large

$$p_{ij}^{(n)} = p_{ij}^{(n+1)} = a_j, \qquad \text{all } j.$$

Using this result in expression (8-5) we obtain

(8-7) $$a_j = \sum_k a_k\, p_{kj}, \qquad \text{all } j$$

or expressed in matrix notation, (8-7) is equivalent to

(8-8) $$\mathbf{a} = \mathbf{a}\mathbf{P}$$

The limiting state probabilities are thus the solution of the system of linear equations, such that the row sum of **a** is 1, i.e.,

(8-9) $$\sum_j a_j = 1$$

With condition (8-9), we have $r + 1$ linear equations in r unknowns. To solve for the unknowns we may discard any one of the r linear equations obtained from (8-8), but never (8-9).

Let us now find the limiting state probabilities for the reservoir problem. The 5 equations are:

(8-10)
$$a_1 = 0.7a_1 + 0.3a_2$$
$$a_2 = 0.2a_1 + 0.4a_2 + 0.3a_3$$
$$a_3 = 0.1a_1 + 0.2a_2 + 0.4a_3 + 0.3a_4$$
$$a_4 = \qquad\quad\; 0.1a_2 + 0.3a_3 + 0.7a_4$$

and

$$1 = \quad a_1 + \quad a_2 + \quad a_3 + \quad a_4$$

Discarding any one of the first four equations and solving the remaining ones we obtain

$$a_1 = \tfrac{1}{5}, \qquad a_2 = \tfrac{1}{5}, \qquad a_3 = \tfrac{4}{15}, \qquad a_4 = \tfrac{1}{3}$$

In many applications of finite Markov chains the limiting state probabilities are the only quantities of interest.

From the theorem and from expression (8-8) it follows that if the transition matrix **P** has the special feature that all rows are equal, then the limiting matrix **A** is equal to **P**.   For such a process the one-step transition probabilities are independent of the state.

There is another special case that warrants mentioning.   If the transition matrix of a finite Markov chain is *doubly stochastic*, i.e., row and column totals are equal to 1, and the chain is regular, then and only then does the limiting matrix **A** have all elements equal to $1/r$, where r is the number of states.   The limiting state distribution is thus a uniform distribution.

8-5 INTERPRETATION OF LIMITING STATE PROBABILITIES

What do these limiting state probabilities mean?

INTERPRETATION OF LIMITING STATE PROBABILITIES

They represent the approximate probabilities of finding the system in each state at the beginning (or end) of a transition after a sufficiently large number of transitions has occurred for the memory of the initial state to be more or less lost.

There is a second even more useful interpretation.   Instead of predicting the state of the process at a random point in time in the more distant future, we look at the process over a large number of transitions in the future.   Define a dichotomous random variable that assumes the value 1 if the process occupies state i (or makes a transition to state i) and 0 otherwise.   In the steady state these two values are assumed with probabilities a_i and $1 - a_i$, respectively.   We would like to know the expected value of this random variable over k transitions once the process is approximately in steady state.   For one transition this is $1a_i + 0(1 - a_i) = a_i$, and summing over k transitions we obtain

$$(8\text{-}11) \qquad \sum_{n=1}^{k} a_i = ka_i$$

The fraction of transitions that the process occupies state i is

$$(8\text{-}12) \qquad \frac{ka_i}{k} = a_i$$

FREQUENCY INTERPRETATION OF LIMITING STATE PROBABILITIES

The limiting state probabilities represent the fraction of transitions that the process occupies each state in the long run or makes a transition to each state in the long run.

In the reservoir problem we therefore expect that in the long run the reservoir will start, or end, with a level of

1	2	3	4	units of water
20%	20%	$26\frac{2}{3}$%	$33\frac{1}{3}$%	of all weeks.

Often, in practice, the number of transitions needed for these approximations to be useful does not have to be very large, particularly if the transition matrix is relatively well balanced, i.e., it does not contain large concentrations of zeros in the lower left-hand and upper right-hand corners. Also, the larger the number of states and/or the smaller the tendency of the process to move significantly away from the current state, the larger the number of transitions needed to approach a steady state situation.

8-6 A SHARE-OF-THE-MARKET MODEL

Suppose that for the last few months a firm has experienced a decreasing share of the market, attributed largely to the entry of a newcomer into the field. Last year the firm managed to capture about 40 percent of the total market. Before deciding on the best counterstrategy, management would like to have some indication of how this trend is likely to affect its share of the market over time. Maybe the decline is only temporary, and the firm's sales might recover without active intervention.

This situation can be studied by a *brand-share* or *brand-switching model*. The purchasing pattern of a typical customer for this product can be viewed as a Markov chain. Suppose interviewers are stationed at a number of randomly selected supermarkets which carry all the competitive brands of this product. Each customer who buys one of the brands is asked for the name of the brand previously purchased. Let us say that 400 such observations are made. They can be grouped into the following pattern for two consecutive purchases where brand A is our firm's brand, and brand X represents the products of all competitors combined:

Previous Purchase	Present Purchase		
	brand A	brand X	total
brand A	117	98	225
brand X	35	140	175

From these results we can conclude that of 225 customers who bought brand A previously, 117 or 52 percent bought the same brand, whereas 98 customers or

48 percent deserted to one of the competitive brands. Similarly, of those who bought a competitive brand last time, 20 percent switched to brand A, and 80 percent stayed with the competitive brands. The astute reader will immediately discern that these proportions can be viewed as the transition probabilities of a two-state Markov process, where state 1 denotes "customer buys brand A" and state 2 "customer buys brand X", and a transition represents the time between two purchases. The transition matrix associated with this process is

$$\mathbf{P} = \begin{bmatrix} 0.52 & 0.48 \\ 0.20 & 0.80 \end{bmatrix}$$

The state probabilities after n transitions can be used to predict the firm's share of the market. We use last year's split in the market share between brand A and its competitors as the initial position or the initial state distribution. Denoting the initial state distribution by the vector $\pi^{(0)} = [\pi_1^{(0)}, \pi_2^{(0)}]$, then for a share of the market for brand A of 40 percent,

$$\pi^{(0)} = [0.4, 0.6]$$

You recall that each row i of $\mathbf{P}^n$ represents the state probability distribution, if the process starts out in state i. With $\pi^{(0)}$ as the initial state distribution, the state probabilities after n transitions are given by

(8-13) $$\pi^{(n)} = \pi^{(0)}\mathbf{P}^n$$

For our problem, $\pi^{(n)}$ behaves as follows:

n	0	1	2	3	4	6	12	$n \to \infty$
$\pi_1^{(n)}$	0.4	0.328	0.305	0.2076	0.2052	0.2942	0.2941	0.2941
$\pi_2^{(n)}$	0.6	0.672	0.695	0.7024	0.7048	0.7058	0.7059	0.7059

Thus, the firm's share of the market will ultimately decline to 29.41 percent if no counter action is undertaken to reverse the trend.

This model can be made more sophisticated by observing the purchasing pattern between sets of two overlapping consecutive purchases. The market share predictions are then likely to be more reliable. Consider the following sequence of purchases: AAXAXXXAAXAAAA. The first two purchases are a set of two consecutive purchases of brand A denoted by AA. The next set is formed by dropping the first purchase and adding the third—the customer switches to the sequence AX. The third set consists of the third and fourth purchase, the sequence XA. This is followed by AX, XX, etc. Viewing each possible sequence of two consecutive purchases as a state, we get the four states AA, AX, XA, and XX. Figure 8-2 shows the transition diagram associated with this process. The numbers attached to the branches are the transition probabilities.

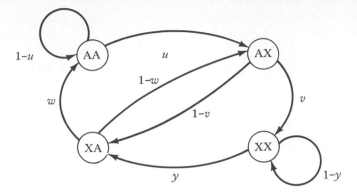

Figure 8-2. *Brand-switching transition diagram.*

The transition matrix for this model is

$$
\begin{array}{c c c c c}
 & \text{AA} & \text{AX} & \text{XA} & \text{XX} \\
\text{AA} & \left[\begin{array}{cccc} 1-u & u & 0 & 0 \\
\text{AX} & 0 & 0 & 1-v & v \\
\text{XA} & w & 1-w & 0 & 0 \\
\text{XX} & 0 & 0 & y & 1-y \end{array}\right]
\end{array}
$$

The limiting share of the market for brand A is obtained by adding the steady-state probabilities for states AA and XA. Both have A as the second purchase. It turns out that the steady-state probabilities for states AX and XA are equal. That this has to be so, seems to be intuitively obvious. The state probabilities for AX and XA represent the rate of switching from one brand to the other. Unless these rates cancel each other, the process cannot be in equilibrium or in steady state.

8-7 MARKOV CHAINS WITH REWARDS

Let us continue with our analysis of the reservoir problem. We are interested in finding the net benefit that could be gained by operating the reservoir as outlined, namely, having a target release of 3 units, 1 of which is used to maintain minimum downstream water quality and the remainder used for irrigation. The weekly return from 2 units of water for irrigation in terms of additional agricultural output is $5000 and a loss of $3000 if the irrigation target of 2 units is missed, i.e., if only 1 unit is available. The reservoir would also be available for recreational purposes for the residents of the area. Assuming that the transportation cost of getting to the reservoir is a measure of its recreational value, the regional water board figures that, given the attendance rates projected, the reservoir would be able to generate the following dollar equivalents for recreational value.

Reservoir level in units at the beginning of a week	1	2	3	4
Weekly recreational benefits in dollars	0	1000	6000	2000

Finally, if the downstream water flow exceeds 2 units per week, flood risks are incurred with expected damages of $5000.

With each state and each possible water flow we can associate the weekly benefits and costs shown in Table 8-1 in units of $1000. These costs are used to find the expected value of the weekly net benefits for each state, as the sum of the total net benefits for a given water inflow times the probability of that water inflow. For instance, for state 1, it is equal to $(-3)(0.3)+(5)(0.7) = 2.6$ thousand dollars.

Let us denote the expected weekly net benefits associated with state i by c_i. Given the long-run average fraction of transitions that the process is in each state (starts out in each state)—the limiting state probabilities a_i—the long-run average benefits or returns, g, are given by

$$(8\text{-}14) \qquad\qquad g = \sum_i c_i a_i$$

The a_i serve as weights.

For the proposed reservoir operating policy the long-run average net benefits per week are

$$g = \tfrac{1}{5}(2.6) + \tfrac{1}{5}(6.0) + \tfrac{4}{15}(11.0) + \tfrac{1}{3}(6.5)$$

$$= 6.82 \text{ thousand dollars}$$

In downstream areas this policy has a risk of flooding that is equal to the product of the probability of being in state 4 and experiencing a water inflow of 5, or $(1/3)(0.1) = 1/30$. In view of this danger, the water board wishes to consider the

Table 8-1. *Weekly Benefits and Costs of Reservoir Operating Policy in $1000.*

State	Water Flow Amount	Prob- ability	Irrigation Benefits	Recreational Benefits	Flood Damages	Total Net Benefits	Expected Net Benefits
1	2	0.3	-3	0	0	-3	2.6
	3 or more	0.7	5	0	0	5	
2	all levels		5	1	0	6	6.0
3	all levels		5	6	0	11	11.0
4	4 or less	0.9	5	2	0	7	6.5
	5	0.1	5	2	-5	2	

alternative policy of increasing the minimum water release over the spillway to 2 units whenever the reservoir level at the beginning of a week is at its maximum of 4. No change in policy would occur for the other 3 states. This would tend to keep the reservoir level away from its maximum and, hence, reduce the risk of flooding. Check that under this alternative policy the transition matrix becomes

$$\mathbf{P} = \begin{bmatrix} 0.7 & 0.2 & 0.1 & 0 \\ 0.3 & 0.4 & 0.2 & 0.1 \\ 0 & 0.3 & 0.4 & 0.3 \\ 0 & 0.3 & 0.4 & 0.3 \end{bmatrix}$$

Only the last row changes. The limiting state probabilities for this alternative policy are

$$a_1 = 0.3, \qquad a_2 = 0.3, \qquad a_3 = 0.25, \qquad a_4 = 0.15$$

The risk of flooding is reduced to $(0.15)(0.1) = 0.015$, less than half of the first policy. The net benefits and costs associated with each state are exactly the same as shown in Table 8-1. Therefore the long-run average benefits per week become

$$g = 0.3(2.6) + 0.3(6.0) + 0.25(11.0) + 0.15(6.5)$$

$$= 6.305 \text{ thousand dollars}$$

or about 0.5 less than the first policy. Apparently the gain obtained by reducing the risk of flooding is more than offset by smaller benefits from irrigation and recreation.

If the maximum reservoir level is allowed to become a decision variable, the same analysis could be made for different maximum reservoir levels, such as 3, 5, and 6, and the one with the highest expected total benefits would be recommended as the best choice.

8-8 A FAILURE MODEL

A control device contains N parallel circuits, all of which have to function for the device as a whole to operate properly. Each circuit is subject to random failure. The failure rate increases with the age of the circuit units. Past records of 122 units give the following *survival function:*

Number of weeks used	0	1	2	3	4	5	6	7
Number of units surviving	122	122	116	109	98	78	39	0
Fraction of surviving units failing during following week	0	0.05	0.06	0.10	0.20	0.50	1.0	

Any circuit unit that fails is replaced by the beginning of the following week. No unit survives to age 7 weeks. For this reason, all six-week-old units are replaced automatically. The failure and replacement pattern of each circuit, considered individually, over time can be modeled as a Markov chain. Each week represents a transition. The age (in weeks) of the circuit unit is the state of the process. The states are thus 0, 1, 2, 3, 4, and 5. A unit of age 6 is replaced and becomes a unit of age 0. The transition probabilities can be determined from the survival function. For instance, all new units survive to age 1, so $p_{01} = 1$ and $p_{0j} = 0$, all $j \neq 1$. A fraction of 0.05 of one-week-old units will fail during their second week of use. Failure means that the unit is replaced at the beginning of the next period and the process moves to state 0. Hence $p_{10} = 0.05$. Any one-week-old unit that does not fail survives to age 2. Hence $p_{12} = 1 - p_{10} = 0.95$, and the transition probabilities to all other states are 0, i.e., $p_{1j} = 0$, $j \neq 0,2$. Continuing in this manner, we obtain the following transition matrix:

$$(8\text{-}15) \qquad \mathbf{P} = \begin{array}{c} \text{Age} \\ 0 \\ 1 \\ 2 \\ 3 \\ 4 \\ 5 \end{array} \begin{array}{cccccc} 0 & 1 & 2 & 3 & 4 & 5 \\ \left[\begin{array}{cccccc} 0 & 1 & 0 & 0 & 0 & 0 \\ 0.05 & 0 & 0.95 & 0 & 0 & 0 \\ 0.06 & 0 & 0 & 0.94 & 0 & 0 \\ 0.10 & 0 & 0 & 0 & 0.9 & 0 \\ 0.20 & 0 & 0 & 0 & 0 & 0.8 \\ 1 & 0 & 0 & 0 & 0 & 0 \end{array}\right] \end{array}$$

Since no unit is used for more than 6 weeks, even those that survive to age 6, $p_{50} = 1$.

We may wish to find the answer to a number of questions about the operating characteristics of this process. How often, on the average, does the device fail? What is the average rate of replacements of units? If each failure costs $8, and each circuit unit replaced costs $6 if replaced individually, would a policy of forced individual replacement at an earlier age, say after 4 or even 3 weeks, lower the average weekly cost? Let us now answer these questions.

What is the percentage of weeks, in the long-run, that the device fails? This is the same as the probability that the device fails each week. This probability is equal to (1 − probability that the device works). The device works only if all circuits work. Since each circuit is independent, the probability that the device works is the product of the probabilities that each circuit works. For instance, if there are $N = 3$ circuits, one of age 0, one of age 1, and one of age 3, then P (device works) = (1)(0.95)(0.9). However, what we want is not the probability for a certain age combination of the circuit units, but the long-run probability, once the process has approached sufficiently close to the steady state. At that point, the age of each circuit unit is only known in terms of probability. Thus, before we can find the long-run probability that the device works we need to know the long-run age distribution of the circuits.

Let us first consider one circuit unit only. The long-run age distribution of an individual unit is given by the steady state probabilities of the Markov process associated with its failure and replacement pattern. For the transition matrix (8-15), we find the following steady-state probabilities.

$$a_0 = 0.189, \quad a_1 = 0.189, \quad a_2 = 0.180, \quad a_3 = 0.169, \quad a_4 = 0.152, \quad a_5 = 0.121$$

Each a_i represents the probability that at the beginning of a week the circuit unit is of age i. For each age we know the probability of failure during the following week of use. Let us denote these by b_i. Then the probability that an individual unit fails is

(8-16) $$P(\text{unit fails}) = \sum_i a_i b_i$$

Using the data of our example, we obtain

$$P(\text{unit fails}) = (0.189)(0) + (0.189)(0.05) + (0.180)(0.06)$$
$$+ (0.169)(0.1) + (0.152)(0.2) + (0.121)(0.5)$$
$$= 0.128.$$

The probability that the circuit works is $1 - P(\text{unit fails})$ or $1 - 0.128 = 0.872$.

In the steady state, each circuit unit has the same probability of failure. Hence, for three circuit units the probability that the device fails is

(8-17)
$$P(\text{device fails}) = 1 - P(\text{device works})$$
$$= 1 - (1 - P(\text{unit fails}))^3$$
$$= 1 - (0.872)^3 = 0.337$$

Thus we conclude that, on the average, the device fails in 33.7 percent of all weeks.

Let us next find the long-run average rate of replacements of units, remembering that the average long-run behavior of each circuit unit is the same. Each time the process moves to state 0, the circuit unit is replaced, regardless of whether it failed or not. Using a version of the long-run frequency interpretation of the steady-state probabilities, a_0 can be taken as the fraction of units replaced, on the average, each week. If there are N units, then $a_0 N$ units are replaced, on the average, each week. For $N = 3$, this is $(0.189)(3) = 0.567$ units.

What is the average cost per week of the present policy? This cost is the sum of the expected cost of failure of the device plus the expected cost of the number of units replaced per week:

Total average cost per week

= expected cost of failure + expected cost of units replaced

= (cost of failure) P(device fails)
+ (cost of units replaced)(expected number of units replaced)

= $8(0.337) + $6(0.567) = $6.10.

To answer the last question, we perform this analysis for each alternative policy of forced replacement of individual units. For a forced replacement after 4 weeks of use, we drop state 5 and adjust the transition probabilities for state 4 accordingly:

$$
\mathbf{P} = \begin{array}{c} \\ 0 \\ 1 \\ 2 \\ 3 \\ 4 \end{array}
\begin{array}{c} \text{Age} \\ \begin{bmatrix} \end{bmatrix} \end{array}
$$

Age	0	1	2	3	4
0	0	1	0	0	0
1	0.05	0	0.95	0	0
2	0.06	0	0	0.94	0
3	0.10	0	0	0	0.9
4	1	0	0	0	0

The steady state probabilities are $\mathbf{a} = [0.215, 0.215, 0.205, 0.192, 0.173]$. By expression (8-16), the probability that a circuit unit fails is 0.077, and by expression (8-17), the probability that the device fails is 0.214. The average number of units replaced is 0.645. The long-run average cost can then be found:

$$\$8(0.214) + \$6(0.645) = \$5.58.$$

The analogous computations for forced replacements of individual units after 3 weeks yield a long-run average cost per week of \$5.85. Therefore, forced replacement of individual units after 4 weeks is the optimal policy.

A forced replacement policy of individual units requires keeping track of the age of each individual unit. If the number of units is large or their individual value is small, in relative terms, the clerical work involved may prove expensive. A different sort of replacement policy, where all units are replaced periodically as a group regardless of their age, may become more attractive, particularly if the cost of each unit is lower for group replacements. This is the topic of the next section.

*8-9 A GROUP REPLACEMENT MODEL—ANALYSIS OF THE TRANSIENT BEHAVIOR

In group replacement all units are replaced at specific regular time intervals, regardless of their age, and between group replacements, individual units are replaced as they fail. Such a scheme becomes attractive if it costs less to replace units in groups than individually. Assume that for the problem we discussed in Section 8-8, it costs $c_1 = \$3$ per unit for group replacements, and $c_2 = \$6$ for individual replacements.

Each time a group replacement occurs, all units start out in state 0 (new). Then, we allow the process to go over n transitions, at which point all units are again replaced and the process starts back in state 0 for each unit. Thus, the process for each unit is periodically interrupted and brought back to square one. It never reaches a steady state. So we are only interested in the *transient behavior* of the process.

For this analysis, we do not provide for individual forced replacements of units, but we let each unit potentially go to the end of its productive life, which in this case is age 6, thus adding state 6 to the transition matrix (8-15). **P** is now

$$
\text{(8-18)} \qquad \mathbf{P} = \begin{array}{c}
\text{Age} \\
0 \\
1 \\
2 \\
3 \\
4 \\
5 \\
6
\end{array}
\begin{array}{ccccccc}
0 & 1 & 2 & 3 & 4 & 5 & 6 \\
\left[\begin{array}{ccccccc}
0 & 1 & 0 & 0 & 0 & 0 & 0 \\
0.05 & 0 & 0.95 & 0 & 0 & 0 & 0 \\
0.06 & 0 & 0 & 0.94 & 0 & 0 & 0 \\
0.1 & 0 & 0 & 0 & 0.9 & 0 & 0 \\
0.2 & 0 & 0 & 0 & 0 & 0.8 & 0 \\
0.5 & 0 & 0 & 0 & 0 & 0 & 0.5 \\
1 & 0 & 0 & 0 & 0 & 0 & 0
\end{array}\right]
\end{array}
$$

Let us start out by finding the total expected cost over n transitions (n weeks), if a group replacement occurs every n transitions. This cost is made up of the initial cost of starting with a complement of N new units, the cost of replacing the units that fail prior to the next group replacement, and the cost of the device failing.

The cost of the initial group replacement is $c_1 N$. For the second term, we need the average number of individual replacements at failure between group replacements. Units just failing prior to a scheduled group replacement will not be replaced individually. In the previous section, we interpreted the steady-state probability for state 0 as the fraction of units that are replaced each week. Here, we use the state probability for state 0 for the same purpose. We interpret this probability as the average fraction of units that failed in the preceding transition. To find the average fraction of units that fail over the $n-1$ weeks between group replacements, we need to sum the state probability for state 0 over all $n-1$ transitions starting with new units in week 1. Table 8-2 lists the state probabilities for $n = 1, 2, 3, 4$, and 5 transitions for the transition matrix (8-18) and for an initial state vector $\pi^{(0)} = [1, 0, 0, 0, 0, 0]$, i.e., $\pi^{(n)} = \pi^{(0)} \mathbf{P}^n$. Note that since no unit survives past age 6, we do not need to consider a group replacement policy for an interval of $n > 6$. The $\pi_0^{(n)}$ column of

Table 8-2. *State Probabilities for Individual Replacement at Failure.*

n	$\pi_0^{(n)}$	$\pi_1^{(n)}$	$\pi_2^{(n)}$	$\pi_3^{(n)}$	$\pi_4^{(n)}$	$\pi_5^{(n)}$	$\sum_{k=1}^{n} \pi_0^{(k)}$
1	0	1	0	0	0	0	0
2	0.05	0	0.95	0	0	0	0.05
3	0.057	0.05	0	0.893	0	0	0.107
4	0.0918	0.057	0.0475	0	0.8037	0	0.1988
5	0.1664	0.0918	0.0542	0.0446	0	0.6430	0.3652

Table 8-2 gives the average fraction of units that fail in the nth week after group replacement, and the final column of the table gives the accumulated average fraction through week n.   The average number of units that fail where there are N units in total, for an interval of n weeks between group replacements is

$$N \sum_{k=1}^{n-1} \pi_0^{(k)}.$$

For $N = 3$, we get the following average number of individual replacements at failure and associated cost for group replacements every $n = 2, 3, 4,$ and 5 weeks:

Group replacement interval, n	2	3	4	5
Fraction replaced at failure through week $n-1$	0	0.05	0.107	0.1988
Total expected number replaced individually	0	0.15	0.321	0.5964
Expected cost of individual replacements at $6.00/unit	$0	$0.90	$1.93	$3.58

The failure probability for the device is now different from week to week.   Let us consider first the probability of failure of an individual unit in the kth week.   The state probabilities $\pi_i^{(k-1)}$ give us the age distribution at the start of the kth week. Multiplying these by the conditional probabilities of failure, b_i, and summing over all ages yields the probability of failure in the kth week.   You should verify that if no individual forced replacements occur, this sum is equal to the state probability for state 0 after k transitions, $\pi_0^{(k)}$.   We can thus use the results computed in Table 8-2 directly.   Then, by (8-17)

Week n	1	2	3	4	5
$P(\text{unit fails}) = \pi_0^{(n)}$	0	0.05	0.057	0.0918	0.1664
$P(\text{device fails}) = 1 - (1 - \pi_0^{(n)})^n$	0	0.1426	0.1614	0.2509	0.4207
Expected cost of failure at $8/failure	$0	$1.14	$1.29	$2.01	$3.37

We now have all the ingredients needed to find the optimal length of the group replacement interval n.   Table 8-3 contains the computations.

Thus, the lowest average cost per week is obtained for group replacements every 4 weeks.   This is lower than the best forced individual replacement policy and thus, is the optimal replacement policy.

Table 8-3. *Cost Computations for Group Replacements.*

Replacement Interval, n	2	3	4	5
Cost of initial group replacement	$9.00	$9.00	$9.00	$9.00
Cost of individual replacements at failure	0	0.90	1.93	3.58
Cost of failure $k=2$	1.14	1.14	1.14	1.14
$k=3$		1.29	1.29	1.29
$k=4$			2.01	2.01
$k=5$				3.37
Total costs for n weeks	. $10.14	$12.33	$15.37	$20.39
Average cost per week	$5.07	$4.11	$3.84	$4.08

EXERCISES

8.1   A delicate precision instrument has a component that is subject to random failure. In fact, if the instrument is operating properly at a given moment in time, then with probability 0.1 it will fail within the next 10-minute period. If the component fails, it can be replaced by a new one, an operation that also takes 10 minutes. The present supplier of replacement components does not guarantee that all replacement components are in proper working condition. The present quality standards are such that about 1 percent of the components supplied are defective. However, this can be discovered only after the defective component has been installed. If defective, the instrument has to go through a new replacement operation. Assume that when a failure occurs, it always occurs at the end of a 10-minute period.

(a) Find the transition matrix associated with this process.

(b) Given that it was properly working initially, what is the probability of finding the instrument not in proper working condition after 30 minutes? after 60 minutes?

(c) Find the steady state probabilities. What fraction of time is the instrument being repaired?

(d) Assume that each replacement component has a cost of 30 cents, and the opportunity cost in terms of lost profit during the time that the instrument is not working is $10.80 per hour. What is the average cost per 10-minute period?

8.2   The market for a product is shared by 4 brands. The table below gives the present share-of-the-market distribution and the percentage of people that switch from each brand to the other brands for consecutive purchases.

from	to Brand				Market
Brand	1	2	3	4	Share
1	60	8	20	12	40%
2	15	40	25	20	20%
3	25	16	50	9	30%
4	28	12	20	40	10%

(a) If, on the average, 1 purchase is made every 2 months, predict the distribution of the share of the market after 6 months.

(b) What is the long-run average share of the market for each brand if present purchasing patterns are not altered?

8.3   A machine shop operates two identical machines supervised by one operator. Each machine requires the operator's attention at random points in time. The probability that the machine requires a service in a period of 5-minutes is $p = 0.4$. The operator is able to service a machine in 5 minutes. Let us approximate this situation by assuming that a machine requires service always at the beginning of a 5-minute period.

(a) Construct a transition diagram for this problem and find the transition matrix associated with it.

(b) If both machines are operating properly at 8 A.M., find the state probabilities after 5 minutes, 10 minutes, and 40 minutes.

(c) Find the steady state probabilities for this process. What is the long-run probability that the operator is idle for a 5-minute period? What fraction of 5-minute periods is the operator busy? What is the long-run average number of machines that require service within any 5-minute period?

(d) Assume that the opportunity cost in terms of lost production, if a machine is down or being serviced for a 5-minute period, is $5. What is the long-run average opportunity cost for an 8-hour shift (96 5-minute periods)?

8.4   An independent taxi operator works in the area of San Francisco and Oakland. In San Francisco chances are 3 out of 5 that the next rider wants to make a trip within San Francisco, and 2 out of 5 that the rider wants to go to Oakland. In Oakland, 1 out of 4 riders want to go to San Francisco, and 3 out of 4 want a trip within Oakland.

(a) Find the transition matrix associated with this process. What aspect of the problem represents the states, and what aspect is a transition?

(b) If the driver starts out in San Francisco, what is the probability of finding him in San Francisco after 4 trips? in Oakland after 4 trips?

(c) What is the long-run average fraction of calls that have the taxi go from
   • San Francisco to San Francisco,
   • San Francisco to Oakland,
   • Oakland to Oakland,
   • Oakland to San Francisco.

(d) If a trip within San Francisco produces, on the average, an intake of $7.00, a trip from San Francisco to Oakland $8.00, and trip within Oakland $3.00, and a trip from Oakland to San Francisco $6.00, what is the long-run average intake per call.

(e) The present method of attracting customers is to cruise until the taxi is hailed. The driver experiments with a different approach, namely, to always return to the main bus terminal in each city after a call. He finds that for this approach, 50 percent of all calls involve trips in San Francisco to Oakland, and 40 percent of all calls in Oakland involve trips to San Francisco. What is his optimal policy, given that he is willing to allow any combination of the two approaches in each city?

8.5   The operational efficiency of a machine producing parts tends to deteriorate randomly from a condition of (1), properly adjusted, to (2), slightly out of adjustment, and from that condition to (3), completely out of adjustment. The condition of the machine can only be ascertained at the end of each one-hour period on the basis of the number of defective parts produced during the preceding hour. If the machine was properly adjusted in the preceding hour, the rate of defective parts is 1 percent; if slightly out of adjustment, the rate is 5 percent and if completely out of adjustment the rate is 20 percent. Past experience indicates that if the machine is found properly adjusted at the end of a one-hour period, the probability that at the end of the next one-hour period it is found slightly out of adjustment is 0.1. If slightly out of adjustment, the probability that it is found completely out of adjustment by the end of the next hour is 0.25. Once completely out of adjustment, it will remain in that condition. Each hour, 100 parts are produced by the machine. At the beginning of any hour, the machine can be properly adjusted by an operation that takes 12 minutes and, thus, reduces the output of the machine during the coming hour by 20 percent. Defective parts have to be reworked on a different machine at a cost of $2.50 per part. Each part produced brings in a net revenue (gross revenue less cost of material) of $2.00.

(a) Find the transition matrix for this process if the machine is adjusted whenever it is found that the rate of defective parts produced during the preceding hour is 20 percent.

(b) Find the steady state probabilities for this mode of operation, and determine the long-run average total number of parts and the long-run average number of defective parts produced per hour. What is the long-run average gross profit per hour (net revenue less cost of reworking defective parts).

(c) Find the optimal policy for adjusting the machine.

8.6 A car testing station has one attendant. He takes exactly 1 hour to check a car. He works 8 hours per day. Cars arrive for testing in a random fashion. The probability, $p(d)$, that d cars arrive in one hour is $p(0)=0.3$, $p(1)=0.4$, $p(2)=0.3$. Any cars arriving, when there are already 2 cars waiting to be tested (plus the one being tested) departs without waiting (and goes to a competitor). Assume for sake of simplicity that all cars arrive exactly at the beginning of each hour.

(a) Construct the transition matrix for this process. What constitutes the states and the transition of the process? (Only 3 states are needed.)

(b) Determine the state probabilities after 1, 2, 4, and 8 hours, assuming that the attendant started in the morning with no cars in the shop. How many cars are in the station, on the average, at the end of 4 hours? 8 hours?

(c) Assuming that any cars waiting at the end of the day will be processed first the next morning, find the steady-state probabilities for this process. What is the long-run probability that the shop attendant is idle? What is the long-run probability that he is busy? What is the long-run average number of cars in the station at the end of an hour?

(d) What is the long-run average fraction of customers lost per hour? What is the long-run average number of customers served per hour?

8.7 As a by-product of crude oil processing, an oil refinery produces light petroleum gas (LPG) which is sold to LPG dealers in tank truck loads. LPG is produced at a constant rate and stored in a tank from which the tank trucks are filled for delivery to the customers. The daily production rate is the equivalent of 4 tank truck loads. Deliveries are made throughout the day and night, and demand is randomly distributed as follows:

Daily demand in truck loads, d	0	1	2	3	4	5	6	7	8
Probability, $p(d)$	0.03	0.07	0.12	0.18	0.20	0.20	0.10	0.05	0.05

The present tank has a capacity of 10 tank truck equivalents. If the tank is empty and a customer demand occurs, the customer does not wait for the tank to fill. The sale is lost and the customer goes to the nearby competitor. If the tank is full to capacity, any LPG produced is diverted for fuel to the refinery's distilling units. The profit lost from not being able to deliver immediately is $120 per tank truck equivalent. The opportunity cost of diverting LPG to the distilling unit is $200 per tank truck equivalent.

(a) Assume that all transactions occur at an instant of time—at the end of each day. Consider this situation as a Markov process, and find its transition matrix.

(b) Find expressions for the long-run expected amount of lost sales per day, the long-run expected amount of LPG diverted to the distilling unit per day and the long-run average daily cost associated with lost sales and diverting LPG to the distilling unit? (No numerical answer is needed.)

(c) (This part of the exercise requires access to computers.) The tank has to be replaced. Standard tank sizes available are 10, 16, 24, and 36 tank truck equivalents. Maintenance and capital depreciation costs amount to $20, $30, $40, and $50 per day, respectively. What is the optimal tank size that minimizes average daily costs?

8.8 Past records indicate that the survival function for light bulbs of traffic lights has the following pattern:

Age, n, of bulbs in months	0	1	2	3	4	5
Number surviving to age n	1000	950	874	769	615	0

(a) If each light bulb is replaced after failure, find the transition matrix associated with this process. Assume that a replacement during the month is equivalent to a replacement at the end of the month.

(b) Determine the steady state probabilities. What is the long-run average length of time that a bulb is used prior to being replaced? If an intersection has 40 bulbs, how many bulbs fail on the average per month? If individual replacements have a cost of $2, what is the long-run average cost per month?

8.9 Consider the survival function of problem 8.8.

(a) Assume now that all bulbs, regardless of age, are replaced every 3 months and individual bulbs are replaced at failure, including those that fail during the month prior to a scheduled group replacement. On the basis of the transition matrix for the failure pattern of an individual bulb, determine the number of bulbs that are replaced at failure between group replacements. Note that failures in the month just prior to a group replacement are replaced also at failure. If group replacements cost $0.20 per bulb plus a $5.00 fixed cost per intersection, find the average cost per month for this policy.

(b) Find the least cost group replacement policy. Is its average monthly cost lower than a policy of individual replacements at failure only?

8.10   Past records of a department store indicate that 20 percent of all new charge account customers become delinquent in the following month.   Of all charge accounts delinquent for one month, 50 percent become fully paid during the next month, 30 percent remain delinquent by one month, and 20 percent become delinquent for 2 months purchases.   Of the 2-month delinquent group, 10 percent become fully paid, 20 percent pay partially and become delinquent by one month, 30 percent remain delinquent by 2 months, and 40 percent become delinquent by 3 months. Any charge account that is delinquent for 3 months is cancelled.

(a) Find the transition matrix for this process.   What type of Markov process is it?

(b) During a given month, 100 new charge accounts were opened.   What percentage of those have their charge account cancelled after 4 months? after 8 months?

8.11   An investor bought shares of a certain speculative stock at \$38, and has given orders to his broker to sell the stock as soon as its price rises to \$40 or above or falls to \$37 or below.   From observations about this stock over the last few weeks, he estimates that the probability of a price rise of one dollar is 0.5, and the probability of a price decline of one dollar is 0.2 for each day.

(a) Find the transition matrix for this process.   Which states are transient states and which are absorbing?

(b) What is the probability that the broker sells the stock within four days?   What is the expected net gain, or loss, per share if he sells within these four days if the selling conditions are met or at the current price at the end of the fourth day?

REFERENCES

Howard, Ronald A. *Dynamic Programming and Markov Processes*. Cambridge, Mass.: M.I.T. Press, 1960.   A doctoral dissertation turned best seller.   Chapters 1 and 2 discuss Markov processes.   Later chapters are relevant to Chapter 9 of this text. Easy reading.   All future operations researchers should look at this book.

———. *Dynamic Probabilistic Systems—Vol. 1: Markov Models, Vol. 2: Semimarkov and Decision Processes*, New York: John Wiley, 1971.   The most complete treatment on Markov processes published recently.   Uses transform analysis.   Contains numerous examples.   An ambitious but not necessarily difficult text.   Should be part of any reference library.

Karlin, S. *A First Course in Stochastic Processes*.   New York: Academic Press, 1969. See comments for Parzen.

Kemeny, John G., Arthur Schleifer, J. Laurie Snell, and Gerald L. Thompson. *Finite Mathematics with Business Applications*.   Englewood Cliffs, N.J.: Prentice-Hall, 1962.   Markov processes are discussed on pages 193–197, and 274–294, at a level similar to this chapter.   The discussion of absorbing Markov processes is more extensive.   Recommended as first reading on this subject.

Kemeny, John G. and J. Laurie Snell, *Finite Markov Chains*.   Princeton: Van Nostrand, 1960 (out of print).   Thorough development of Markov processes, both regular and absorbing, using matrix algebra only.   Contains a number of interesting examples. This is a highly readable text.

Parzen, E. *Stochastic Processes*. San Francisco: Holden-Day, 1962. Markov processes are part of the much wider field of stochastic processes. This and Karlin's text give a complete development of the theory of stochastic processes. Both require a high degree of mathematical sophistication. Their development is based on the theory of Eigenvectors.

The following articles give some interesting applications.

Cyert, R. M., H. J. Davidson, and G. L. Thompson. "Estimation of the Allowance for Doubtful Accounts by Markov Chains", *Management Science*, 8, April 1962.

Kemeny, John G., and J. Laurie Snell. *Mathematical Models in the Social Sciences*. Waltham, Mass.: Blaisdell, 1962. Chapter 5 discusses an application in Sociology. Appendix C gives a short summary of the essentials of Markov Processes.

Meliha, Dileep. "Markov Processes and Credit Collection Policy", *Decision Sciences*, 3, April 1972.

9

Markovian
Decision
Processes

With the exception of Chapter 8, the decision models discussed so far all covered either a single period or a finite planning horizon. The future beyond the finite planning horizon was ignored. This approach implicitly assumes that current decisions are independent of future events and decisions. Undoubtedly, this assumption applies to many one-shot or limited-time decision problems. However, much more decision making has to be viewed as being an integral part of a never-ending sequence of actions, where current decisions leave their imprint on the future, and future decisions influence the present. In this chapter we shall look at a class of sequential decision models where the unboundedness of the planning horizon is explicitly incorporated into the analysis. In particular, we shall study how optimization problems whose probabilistic behavior can be described by Markov chains are solved by dynamic programming.

The material discussed in this chapter is more demanding than that of earlier chapters. Some of the mathematical basis cannot be developed fully, as this would require a mathematical sophistication well beyond the level of this text. Therefore, we often have recourse to subtle reasoning that is a distinct departure from previous chapters and may call for more than one thorough reading before it will be understood properly.

9-1 OPTIMIZATION OVER AN UNBOUNDED PLANNING HORIZON

When dealing with decision problems that have no well defined terminal point but will go on indefinitely over the foreseeable future, the model builder has several options.

1. He may consider a finite planning horizon and select terminal conditions that the system has to satisfy (for deterministic problems) or deviations from which are penalized (for stochastic problems). For instance, in an inventory control

model the terminal condition consists of the inventory level desired at the end of the planning horizon. This approach is particularly suitable for problems subject to seasonal cycles where the carry-over from one cycle to the next is small.

2. He may choose a planning horizon long enough so that the optimal current decisions are invariant to reasonable changes in events and decisions towards the end of the planning horizon. The exact length required is best determined by sensitivity analysis. It may only cover a few months if we are dealing with decisions of a routine type, but may cover ten to twenty years for strategic decisions such as those dealing with investments. Since information about the future behavior of the system becomes less and less reliable as we project into the more distant future, this approach has considerable appeal. Only the current optimal decision would ever be implemented. The problem would be reoptimized for each later decision, at which time better information about the more distant future would probably be available. For each optimization, the planning horizon is maintained at a predetermined constant length as shown in Figure 9-1.

3. He may build a model for an *unbounded planning horizon*.

Once we let the planning horizon become unbounded, we have to introduce restrictive assumptions about the behavior of the system studied.

ASSUMPTION OF STATIONARITY

We assume that the environment in which the decisions have to be made and the actions available to the decision maker remain stationary over time.

For instance, for an inventory control problem this implies that the demand levels (in the deterministic case) or the demand probability distributions (in the stochastic case) are identical in each period, and that all costs associated with a given decision and the set of possible decisions available in each period remain the same. This is analogous to the assumption of stationarity already encountered for Markov chains in Chapter 8. Note that in a narrow sense this assumption excludes seasonal variations even if they are identical from year to year. (Although it is possible, by suitable redefinition of the states and transitions of the process and greatly increased size and complexity of the model, to handle seasonal variations which remain stationary.)

Admittedly, few real-life processes remain stationary for any extended length of time. Nevertheless, this assumption may be a suitable approximation to reality for many problems, such as routine day-to-day decisions in a slowly changing environment, or long-term recurrent strategic decisions. In the first instance, the potential increase in benefits of a nonstationary analysis is not usually justified by the higher cost of data collection for such an analysis. This is the case for most inventory control

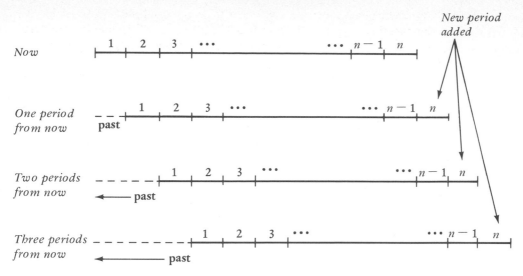

Figure 9-1. *Rolling planning horizon of constant length.*

problems covering hundreds or thousands of products, each generating only small savings.   In the second instance, uncertainty about events and alternative courses of action in the more distant future and the fact that they have a small impact on the present, due to discounting of future benefits and costs (as shown below), may justify the assumption of stationarity and result in better current decisions than those obtained by ignoring the distant and uncertain future altogether.   We shall see this shortly.

As our focus shifts from a finite to an infinite planning horizon, the optimization criteria of the finite case have to be altered or adapted appropriately.   Since the sum of a stream of finite returns or costs per period may become infinitely large as the number of periods considered goes to infinity, we may look at either

1. the *present value* of a discounted stream of returns or costs, discussed in Sections 9-2 to 9-5, or
2. the *average return* or *average cost* per period, discussed in Sections 9-6 to 9-8.

Let us briefly review some of the principles of discounting.   If \$1 invested now has a value of \$$(1+r)$ one period from now, where r is the *rate of return* (e.g., interest), then \$1 received in one period's time has a *present value* now of:

(9-1)
$$\alpha = \frac{1}{1+r}$$

α is called the discount rate.   From expression (9-1) and the fact that $r > 0$, it follows that $0 < \alpha < 1$.   If $r = 0$, then $\alpha = 1$, i.e., future funds are not discounted.

R dollars received one period from now have a present value of αR. R dollars received two periods from now have to be discounted for two periods.   Discounting

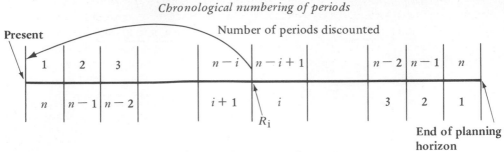

Chronological numbering of periods

Figure 9-2. *Present value of R_i dollars received at the beginning of the ith from last period.*

for one period reduces their value to αR, and discounting this amount for a second period gives a present value of $\alpha^2 R$. In general, R dollars received k periods from now have a present value of $\alpha^k R$.

Let R_i be the funds received at the beginning of the ith from last period in the planning horizon. As you can see from Figure 9-2, if the planning horizon is n periods long, then this corresponds to funds received $(n-i)$ periods from now. The present value of these funds is thus $\alpha^{n-i} R_i$.

Consider now the stream of funds $R_n, R_{n-1}, R_{n-2}, ..., R_i, ..., R_2, R_1$, where the subscript refers to the number of periods to the end of the planning horizon. The present value of this stream of funds, discounted at a rate α is

(9-2) $\qquad S_n = R_n + \alpha R_{n-1} + \alpha^2 R_{n-2} + \alpha^3 R_{n-3} + \cdots + \alpha^{n-1} R_1$

Similarly,

$$S_{n+1} = R_{n+1} + \alpha R_n + \alpha^2 R_{n-1} + \alpha^3 R_{n-2} + \cdots + \alpha^n R_1$$
$$= R_{n+1} + \alpha(R_n + \alpha R_{n-1} + \alpha^2 R_{n-2} + \cdots + \alpha^{n-1} R_1)$$

But the term in parentheses is equal to expression (9-2), and is the present value one period from now of a stream of funds. We thus get the following recursive formula:

(9-3) $\qquad S_{n+1} = R_{n+1} + \alpha S_n$

or

$$S_n = R_n + \alpha S_{n-1}.$$

We will find this result useful for later analysis.

If $R_n = R$, for all n, and we consider an unbounded planning horizon, the present value of a stream of funds R over all future periods becomes

(9-4) $\qquad S = \sum_{n=1}^{\infty} \alpha^{n-1} R = \frac{R}{1-\alpha}$

for $0 < \alpha < 1$.

In the finite period case, the optimal policy or strategy depends on the state occupied by the system and the number of periods (or stages) remaining. For an unbounded planning horizon the number of periods remaining stays the same from period to period. Therefore, the optimal policy is no longer dependent on the number of periods remaining, but becomes uniquely a function of the state of the system.

STATIONARY POLICIES

A stationary policy has the property that whenever the process returns to a given state, the same decision is taken, i.e., the decision taken in each period only depends on the current state of the system.

It can be shown that for a large class of problems with an unbounded planning horizon and, in particular, all those discussed in this chapter, stationary policies are optimal among all possible policies.

9-2   FUNCTIONAL EQUATIONS

Consider again the N-period inventory model discussed in Section 7-13. Expression (7-19) represents the minimum (undiscounted) cost with n periods remaining, repeated here for your convenience.

$$f_n(z_n) = \operatorname*{minimum}_{x_n \in X_n}\left[C_n(z_n, x_n) + \sum_{d_n} f_{n-1}(z_n + x_n - d_n)\, p_n(d_n) \right]$$

where z_n is the state variable denoting the beginning inventory level;
x_n is the decision variable denoting the amount produced in period n;
X_n is the set of possible production levels;
$C_n(z_n, x_n)$ is the sum of production, inventory holding, and shortage costs;
d_n is the random variable of demand with probability distribution $p_n(d_n)$, all with respect to period n (numbered backwards from the end of the planning horizon).

Let us now discount future costs at a rate α. To apply formula (9-3) we let $S_n = f_n(z_n)$, $R_n = C_n(z_n, x_n)$ and $S_{n-1} = \sum_{d_n} f_{n-1}(z_n + x_n - d_n)\, p_n(d_n)$. Then the recursive relation (7-15) becomes

(9-5)

$$f_n(z_n) = \operatorname*{minimum}_{x_n \in X_n}\left[C_n(z_n, x_n) + \alpha \sum_{d_n} f_{n-1}(z_n + x_n - d_n)\, p_n(d_n) \right], \qquad \text{all} \quad n \geqslant 1$$

The term, $f_n(z_n)$, now represents the present value of the minimum cost with n periods remaining, and the term corresponding to S_{n-1} is the present value one period from now of the expected value of the minimum cost with $n-1$ periods remaining to the end of the planning horizon, with the expectation taken over all possible values of the state variable.

Suppose that the planning horizon becomes unbounded. Then by the assumption of stationarity,

$$(9\text{-}6) \qquad\qquad C_n(z_n, x_n) = C(z, x),$$

$$p_n(d_n) = p(d),$$

and

$$X_n = X, \qquad \text{all } n$$

After each period the decision maker again faces an unbounded planning horizon. The number of stages left to go remains therefore infinitely large and the subscript n on f may be dropped. Substituting the terms (9-6) into (9-5), the recursive relation for the minimum discounted expected cost over all future periods becomes

$$(9\text{-}7) \quad f(z) = \underset{x \in X}{\text{minimum}} \left[C(z, x) + \alpha \sum_d f(z + x - d)\, p(d) \right], \qquad \text{all } z$$

where z is the state variable.

Expression (9-7) is the present value of the minimum cost over all future periods starting in state z. It is equal to the minimum, over all possible decisions, of two cost terms. The first is the cost in the current period. The second is the present value, one period from now, of the expected value of the minimum cost over all future periods, discounted to the present.

Note that the same value of the state variable z may appear in f on both sides of the equal sign. A relation of the form (9-7) is called a *functional* or *extremal equation*. The set of functional equations (9-7) states what optimization condition f has to satisfy for all values of the state variable z.

It is also immediately clear that the conventional approach of dynamic programming for finding the optimal policy, namely to evaluate the recursive relation stage by stage starting with the last stage in the planning horizon, cannot be used any longer. There is no last period in the planning horizon.

Before looking into how to find the optimal policy, let us study first the probabilistic structure of expression (9-7).

9-3 MARKOVIAN DECISION PROCESSES

Suppose the demand distribution for a given product is as follows:

Weekly demand, d	0	1	2	3	4 or more
Probability, $p(d)$	0.4	0.3	0.2	0.1	0

The inventory level is reviewed at the beginning of each week. Any demand not met in a period is lost. Let us arbitrarily decide that the maximum inventory level cannot exceed 5. Therefore, the state variable in (9-7) which stands for the beginning inventory (carried forward from the preceding week) can assume values 0, 1, 2, 3, 4, or 5. An inventory policy or strategy consists of a replenishment decision—a value of x—for each value of the state variable. Given that the maximum inventory cannot exceed 5, we have the following choice of decisions in each state:

State z	Choices for x
0	0, 1, 2, 3, 4, 5
1	0, 1, 2, 3, 4,
2	0, 1, 2, 3
3	0, 1, 2
4	0, 1
5	0

For instance, $(4, 3, 0, 0, 0, 0)$ would be a possible policy. It says that whenever the state of the system (beginning inventory) is 0 or 1, the state is instantaneously increased to 4, whereas no change (no replenishment) is made if the state of the system is 2 or more.

During the week, a random demand d occurs with probability $p(d)$. It affects the inventory level carried forward to the next period. In the terminology for Markov chains we say that, given the decision x, the state of the system undergoes a transition from state i to state $j = i + x - d$ with probability $p_{ij}(x) = p(d)$. The transition probabilities, $p_{ij}(x)$, are seen to be a function of both the probability distribution of the demand and the particular decision chosen in state i. For any given strategy, i.e., a decision for each state, the probabilistic behavior of the system is that of a Markov chain.

With each state i and each decision x we also associate a one-period cost $c_i(x)$. Table 9-1 lists the transition probabilities and the associated cost for each state and each decision. The former are based on $p(d)$ and the latter on the assumption that (a) the cost of carrying one unit in inventory from the preceding period to the current period is \$1, (b) the cost of replenishing inventory is fixed and amounts to \$3 and (c) the cost of a lost sale is \$20 per unit. For instance, the first row in Table 9-1 refers to a beginning inventory of $i = 0$ and a production of $x = 0$. In this case, no goods are available to meet the demand and the entire demand is lost. The inventory level at the beginning of the next period is $j = 0$, with probability $p_{00}(0) = 1$ and all other transition probabilities equal to 0. No costs are incurred for carrying goods in inventory (column a is 0) and for replenishing inventory (column b is 0). Shortage costs are found as the expected value of the amount short times the shortage cost per unit:

$$E(\text{shortage cost}) = \$20 \left[\sum_{d > i + x} (d - i - x)\, p(d) \right]$$

$$= \$20 \left[(1 - 0)\, 0.3 + (2 - 0)\, 0.2 + (3 - 0)\, 0.1 \right] = \$20$$

Table 9-1. *Transition Probabilities and Costs for Inventory Control Problem.*

Row	State i	Decision x	$j=0$	$j=1$	$j=2$	$j=3$	$j=4$	$j=5$	(a)	(b)	(c)	Total $c_i(x)$
1	0	0	1	0	0	0	0	0	0	0	20	20
2		1	0.6	0.4	0	0	0	0	0	3	8	11
3		2	0.3	0.3	0.4	0	0	0	0	3	2	5
4		3	0.1	0.2	0.3	0.4	0	0	0	3	0	3
5		4	0	0.1	0.2	0.3	0.4	0	0	3	0	3
6		5	0	0	0.1	0.2	0.3	0.4	0	3	0	3
7	1	0	0.6	0.4	0	0	0	0	1	0	8	9
8		1	0.3	0.3	0.4	0	0	0	1	3	2	6
9		2	0.1	0.2	0.3	0.4	0	0	1	3	0	4
10		3	0	0.1	0.2	0.3	0.4	0	1	3	0	4
11		4	0	0	0.1	0.2	0.3	0.4	1	3	0	4
12	2	0	0.3	0.3	0.4	0	0	0	2	0	2	4
13		1	0.1	0.2	0.3	0.4	0	0	2	3	0	5
14		2	0	0.1	0.2	0.3	0.4	0	2	3	0	5
15		3	0	0	0.1	0.2	0.3	0.4	2	3	0	5
16	3	0	0.1	0.2	0.3	0.4	0	0	3	0	0	3
17		1	0	0.1	0.2	0.3	0.4	0	3	3	0	6
18		2	0	0	0.1	0.2	0.3	0.4	3	3	0	6
19	4	0	0	0.1	0.2	0.3	0.4	0	4	0	0	4
20		1	0	0	0.1	0.2	0.3	0.4	4	3	0	7
21	5	0	0	0	0.1	0.2	0.3	0.4	5	0	0	5

In the computations of the expected shortage cost, we only have to consider values of d larger than $i+x$, since for $d \leqslant i+x$ no shortages are incurred. The total cost $c_0(0) = \$20$.

Let us consider another row, e.g., row 8 for a beginning inventory of $i = 1$ and a production of $x = 1$. If demand is $d = 0$, then the new inventory is $j = i+x-0$ or $j = 2$. This demand occurs with probability 0.4, so $p_{12}(1) = 0.4$. If demand is $d = 1$, then $j = i+x-1$ or $j = 1$ with probability 0.3, so $p_{11}(1) = 0.3$. If demand is $d = 2$ or $d = 3$, then the new inventory is $j = 0$. These demands occur with probability 0.2 and 0.1, so $p_{10}(1) = 0.2+0.1 = 0.3$. All other transition probabilities are again 0. One unit is carried forward to the current period at a cost of \$1 (column a). Inventory is replenished at a cost of \$3 (column b). Finally, shortage costs are incurred when demand exceeds $i+x = 2$. Hence column c is $\$20(3-2)(0.1) = \$2$. The total cost $c_1(1)$ amounts to $\$(1+3+2) = \$6$. To test your understanding, you should verify some of the other rows!

For the policy $(4, 3, 0, 0, 0, 0)$, the corresponding transition matrix **P** and the vector of one-period costs (c_i) is constructed from Table 9-1 by taking, for each i, the row of transition probabilities associated with the decision x taken in state i. So we take rows 5, 10, 12, 16, 19, and 21.

$$(9\text{-}8) \quad \mathbf{P} = \begin{bmatrix} 0 & 0.1 & 0.2 & 0.3 & 0.4 & 0 \\ 0 & 0.1 & 0.2 & 0.3 & 0.4 & 0 \\ 0.3 & 0.3 & 0.4 & 0 & 0 & 0 \\ 0.1 & 0.2 & 0.3 & 0.4 & 0 & 0 \\ 0 & 0.1 & 0.2 & 0.3 & 0.4 & 0 \\ 0 & 0 & 0.1 & 0.2 & 0.3 & 0.4 \end{bmatrix} \quad \text{and} \quad \begin{bmatrix} c_0(4) \\ c_1(3) \\ c_2(0) \\ c_3(0) \\ c_4(0) \\ c_5(0) \end{bmatrix} = \begin{bmatrix} 3 \\ 4 \\ 4 \\ 3 \\ 4 \\ 5 \end{bmatrix}$$

State 5 is a transient state, whereas the remaining states form an ergodic subset. Since each policy generates a transition matrix and a vector of costs, selecting the optimal policy is equivalent to finding the optimal combination of transition probability rows and their related costs. This can be seen by rewriting expression (9-7) in terms of our new notation as

$$(9\text{-}9) \qquad f_i = \underset{x \in X}{\text{minimum}} \left[c_i(x) + \alpha \sum_j p_{ij}(x) f_j \right], \qquad \text{all } i$$

where f_i stands for the cost of following an optimal policy over all future periods starting the process in state i. Such a problem is known as a *Markovian decision process*.

In this example, x is a numerical variable. There are many applications where the set of actions cannot be expressed numerically. For instance, in a maintenance problem the decisions may be "do nothing," "inspect and replace if needed only," and "replace without inspection." If each possible action is numbered from 1 to M_i, where M_i is the number of possible actions in state i, then x stands for this number. However, the numerical value x has no significance in itself.

9-4 APPROXIMATION IN POLICY SPACE WITH DISCOUNTING

How can the optimal values of x and the minimum f_i be determined for all i? The boot strap operation, which follows, turns out to be a powerful approach to tackle this problem.

STEP 1: INITIAL POLICY

Guess an initial policy labeled by the superscript $k = 0$ by choosing for each state i a decision $x = x_i^{(0)}$.

For instance, we could decide to use in each state that decision x which minimizes the one-period cost $c_i(x)$.

Having decided on a policy k, we associate with each decision $x_i^{(k)}$ the transition probabilities $p_{ij}(x_i^{(k)})$ and the one-period cost $c_i(x_i^{(k)})$. With these we can find $f_i^{(k)}$, the discounted cost using policy k over all future periods, starting in state i, all i. This is our next step. (For the first time through $k = 0$.)

STEP 2: POLICY EVALUATION ROUTINE

Determine the values $f_i^{(k)}$ which are the solution of the system of linear equations:

$$(9\text{-}10) \qquad f_i^{(k)} = c_i(x_i^{(k)}) + \alpha \sum_j p_{ij}(x_i^{(k)}) f_j^{(k)}, \qquad \text{all } i$$

Equations (9-10) arise from the following reasoning: If the process starts out in state i using policy k, it first incurs the cost associated with this policy in state i $(= c_i(x_i^{(k)}))$ and then moves to state j by the beginning of the next period. The present value of the cost from state j over all future periods, one period from now, is $f_j^{(k)}$. This cost is weighted by the probability of going from state i to state j using policy k. The sum of all these terms is then discounted by one period.

The term, $f_j^{(k)}$, should not be confused with f_j of expression (9-9). Except for the last iteration, $f_j^{(k)}$ is not the minimum cost, but simply the present value of the cost associated with the (arbitrary) policy k which may not be the optimal policy.

Step 2 implies that we commit ourselves to use policy k for all future periods and want to know the cost of starting it in each state.

We now have some second thoughts. We decide to postpone the use of this policy by one period and at the same time try to find a better policy for the current period.

STEP 3: POLICY IMPROVEMENT ROUTINE

Determine a new policy $k+1$ by finding for each i the decision $x_i^{(k+1)}$ that will

$$(9\text{-}11) \qquad \text{minimize}_x \left[c_i(x) + \alpha \sum_j p_{ij}(x) f_j^{(k)} \right]$$

Expression (9-11) arises from a reasoning similar to that behind (9-10).

If the minimum is obtained for several decisions, the choice for $x_i^{(k+1)}$ is arbitrary, except if $x_i^{(k)}$ is one of them in which case $x_i^{(k+1)} = x_i^{(k)}$. This avoids cycling of the iterative scheme.

Now we examine the new policy $k+1$. If $x_i^{(k+1)} = x_i^{(k)}$ for all states, then we have a policy that satisfies expression (9-9) with $f_i = f_i^{(k)} = f_i^{(k+1)}$, which is what we were looking for. On the other hand, if policy $k+1$ differs from policy k in at least one state, we reason that if policy $k+1$ is better for the first period, surely it is also better for all subsequent periods! Fortunately, it can be shown that this is so. Since the trick worked this time, we go back to step 2 for a new iteration of this algorithm.

STEP 4: STOPPING RULE

If $x_i^{(k+1)} = x_i^{(k)}$, all i, the optimal policy has been found and the $f_i^{(k+1)}$ are the minimum expected discounted costs of starting in state i. If the new policy $k+1$ differs from the previous one in at least one state, increase the count k by one and go back to step 2.

The better the initial choice in step 1, the faster the algorithm finds the optimal solution. Often, the analyst may have a fairly good feel of what is a good initial policy.

For a maximization problem the only change needed is to substitute maximize for minimize in expression (9-11).

If the number of possible decisions in each state i is finite, then the number of possible combination of decisions or the number of possible different policies is also finite. In step 2, expression (9-10) results in a unique solution for the $f_i^{(k)}$ values for each policy. By step 3, each new policy is at least as good as the preceding one, and by step 4, no policy can repeat itself without terminating the algorithm. Therefore, this method will converge to the optimal solution in a finite number of iterations.

This advantage has to be paid for, however, by a large amount of computation. If there are r different states, then step 2 involves solving a system of r linear equations in r unknowns. For practically all real-life problems, this job has to be done on high-speed electronic computers. However, in contrast to n stage dynamic programming problems, this algorithm can be programmed for computers as a *general purpose code* for a standard input format that can solve all Markovian decisions processes.

9-5 SOLUTION OF INVENTORY CONTROL PROBLEM FOR DISCOUNTING

To apply this algorithm it is always helpful to first set up a table listing the transition probabilities and expected costs for each action in each state, as we did in Table 9-1. Let us use a discount rate of $\alpha = 0.99$ per week (this corresponds to an annual interest rate of about 60 percent).

First iteration

Step 1: Initial policy $= (x_0^{(0)} = 4,\ x_1^{(0)} = 3,\ x_2^{(0)} = 0,\ x_3^{(0)} = 0,\ x_4^{(0)} = 0,\ x_5^{(0)} = 0)$
with transition probabilities and costs as shown in expression (9-8).

Step 2: Solve the following set of linear equations:

$$f_0^{(0)} = 3 + 0.99(0.1f_1^{(0)} + 0.2f_2^{(0)} + 0.3f_3^{(0)} + 0.4f_4^{(0)})$$
$$f_1^{(0)} = 4 + 0.99(0.1f_1^{(0)} + 0.2f_2^{(0)} + 0.3f_3^{(0)} + 0.4f_4^{(0)})$$
$$f_2^{(0)} = 4 + 0.99(0.3f_0^{(0)} + 0.3f_1^{(0)} + 0.4f_2^{(0)})$$
$$f_3^{(0)} = 3 + 0.99(0.1f_0^{(0)} + 0.2f_1^{(0)} + 0.3f_2^{(0)} + 0.4f_3^{(0)})$$
$$f_4^{(0)} = 4 + 0.99(0.1f_1^{(0)} + 0.2f_2^{(0)} + 0.3f_3^{(0)} + 0.4f_4^{(0)})$$
$$f_5^{(0)} = 5 + 0.99(0.1f_2^{(0)} + 0.2f_3^{(0)} + 0.3f_4^{(0)} + 0.4f_5^{(0)})$$

The solution is

$$f_0^{(0)} = 364.6, \ f_1^{(0)} = 365.6, \ f_2^{(0)} = 365.7, \ f_3^{(0)} = 364.3, \ f_4^{(0)} = 365.6, \ f_5^{(0)} = 367.4$$

Step 3: Find a new action for each state using expression (9-11).

State i	Action x	$c_i(x) + \alpha \sum_j p_{ij}(x) f_j^{(0)}$		Minimum for x
0	0	$20 + 0.99 \ [(1 \ ) 364.6]$	$= 380.9$	
	1	$11 + 0.99 \ [(0.6) 364.6 + (0.4) 365.6]$	$= 372.3$	
	2	$5 + 0.99 \ [(0.3) 364.6 + (0.3) 365.6 + (0.4) 365.7]$	$= 366.6$	
	3	$3 + 0.99 \ [(0.1) 364.6 + (0.2) 365.6 + (0.3) 365.7 + (0.4) 364.3] = 364.3$		$x = 3$
	4	$3 + 0.99 \ [(0.1) 365.6 + (0.2) 365.7 + (0.3) 364.3 + (0.4) 365.6] = 364.6$		
	5	$3 + 0.99 \ [(0.1) 365.7 + (0.2) 364.3 + (0.3) 365.6 + (0.4) 367.4] = 365.4$		
1	0	$9 + 0.99 \ [(0.6) 364.6 + (0.4) 365.6]$	$= 370.3$	
	1	$6 + 0.99 \ [(0.3) 364.6 + (0.3) 365.6 + (0.4) 365.7]$	$= 367.6$	
	2	$4 + 0.99 \ [(0.1) 364.6 + (0.2) 365.6 + (0.3) 365.7 + (0.4) 364.3] = 365.3$		$x = 2$
	3	$4 + 0.99 \ [(0.1) 365.6 + (0.2) 365.7 + (0.3) 364.3 + (0.4) 365.6] = 365.6$		
	4	$4 + 0.99 \ [(0.1) 365.7 + (0.2) 364.3 + (0.3) 365.6 + (0.4) 367.4] = 366.4$		
2	0	$4 + 0.99 \ [(0.3) 364.6 + (0.3) 365.6 + (0.4) 365.7]$	$= 365.7$	$x = 0$
	1	$5 + 0.99 \ [(0.1) 364.6 + (0.2) 365.6 + (0.3) 365.7 + (0.4) 364.3] = 366.3$		
	2	$5 + 0.99 \ [(0.1) 365.6 + (0.2) 365.7 + (0.3) 364.3 + (0.4) 365.6] = 366.6$		
	3	$5 + 0.99 \ [(0.1) 365.7 + (0.2) 364.3 + (0.3) 365.6 + (0.4) 367.4] = 367.4$		
3	0	$3 + 0.99 \ [(0.1) 364.6 + (0.2) 365.6 + (0.3) 365.7 + (0.4) 364.3] = 364.3$		$x = 0$
	1	$6 + 0.99 \ [(0.1) 365.6 + (0.2) 365.7 + (0.3) 364.3 + (0.4) 365.6] = 367.6$		
	2	$6 + 0.99 \ [(0.1) 365.7 + (0.2) 364.3 + (0.3) 365.6 + (0.4) 367.4] = 368.4$		
4	0	$4 + 0.99 \ [(0.1) 365.6 + (0.2) 365.7 + (0.3) 364.3 + (0.4) 365.6] = 365.6$		$x = 0$
	1	$7 + 0.99 \ [(0.1) 365.7 + (0.2) 364.3 + (0.3) 365.6 + (0.4) 367.4] = 369.4$		
5	0	$5 + 0.99 \ [(0.1) 365.7 + (0.2) 364.3 + (0.3) 365.6 + (0.4) 367.4] = 367.4$		$x = 0$

Step 4: From the last column of the previous table we find the new policy

$$(x_0^{(1)} = 3, \ x_1^{(1)} = 2, \ x_2^{(1)} = 0, \ x_3^{(1)} = 0, \ x_4^{(1)} = 0, \ x_5^{(1)} = 0)$$

Going back to Table 9-1, we find the following transition probabilities and costs associated with this policy:

$$(9\text{-}12) \qquad
\begin{bmatrix}
0.1 & 0.2 & 0.3 & 0.4 & 0 & 0 \\
0.1 & 0.2 & 0.3 & 0.4 & 0 & 0 \\
0.3 & 0.3 & 0.4 & 0 & 0 & 0 \\
0.1 & 0.2 & 0.3 & 0.4 & 0 & 0 \\
0 & 0.1 & 0.2 & 0.3 & 0.4 & 0 \\
0 & 0 & 0.1 & 0.2 & 0.3 & 0.4
\end{bmatrix}
\quad \text{and} \quad
\begin{bmatrix}
3 \\ 4 \\ 4 \\ 3 \\ 4 \\ 5
\end{bmatrix}$$

This policy is different from the previous one; so we go through another iteration. Note that now both states 4 and 5 are transient states.

Second iteration

Step 2: Solve the following set of linear equations:

$$f_0^{(1)} = 3 + 0.99(0.1f_0^{(1)} + 0.2f_1^{(1)} + 0.3f_2^{(1)} + 0.4f_3^{(1)})$$

$$f_1^{(1)} = 4 + 0.99(0.1f_0^{(1)} + 0.2f_1^{(1)} + 0.3f_2^{(1)} + 0.4f_3^{(1)})$$

$$f_2^{(1)} = 4 + 0.99(0.3f_0^{(1)} + 0.3f_1^{(1)} + 0.4f_2^{(1)})$$

$$f_3^{(1)} = 3 + 0.99(0.1f_0^{(1)} + 0.2f_1^{(1)} + 0.3f_2^{(1)} + 0.4f_3^{(1)})$$

$$f_4^{(1)} = 4 + 0.99(0.1f_1^{(1)} + 0.2f_2^{(1)} + 0.3f_3^{(1)} + 0.4f_4^{(1)})$$

$$f_5^{(1)} = 5 + 0.99(0.1f_2^{(1)} + 0.2f_3^{(1)} + 0.3f_4^{(1)} + 0.4f_5^{(1)})$$

The solution is

$$f_0^{(1)} = 356.0, \ f_1^{(1)} = 357.0, \ f_2^{(1)} = 357.2, \ f_3^{(1)} = 356.0, \ f_4^{(1)} = 357.3, \ f_5^{(1)} = 359.2$$

Step 3: Find a new action for each state using expression (9-11).

State i	Action x	$c_i(x) + \alpha \sum_j p_{ij}(x) f_j^{(1)}$		Minimum for x
0	0	$20 + 0.99 \ [(1 \ \ )356.0]$	$= 372.5$	
	1	$11 + 0.99 \ [(0.6)356.0 + (0.4)357.0]$	$= 363.8$	
	2	$5 + 0.99 \ [(0.3)356.0 + (0.3)357.0 + (0.4)357.2]$	$= 358.2$	
	3	$3 + 0.99 \ [(0.1)356.0 + (0.2)357.0 + (0.3)357.2 + (0.4)356.0] = 356.0$		$x = 3$
	4	$3 + 0.99 \ [(0.1)357.0 + (0.2)357.2 + (0.3)356.0 + (0.4)357.3] = 356.3$		
	5	$3 + 0.99 \ [(0.1)357.2 + (0.2)356.0 + (0.3)357.3 + (0.4)359.2] = 357.2$		
1	0	$9 + 0.99 \ [(0.6)356.0 + (0.4)357.0]$	$= 361.8$	
	1	$6 + 0.99 \ [(0.3)356.0 + (0.3)357.0 + (0.4)357.2]$	$= 359.2$	
	2	$4 + 0.99 \ [(0.1)356.0 + (0.2)357.0 + (0.3)357.2 + (0.4)356.0] = 357.0$		$x = 2$
	3	$4 + 0.99 \ [(0.1)357.0 + (0.2)357.2 + (0.3)356.0 + (0.4)357.3] = 357.3$		
	4	$4 + 0.99 \ [(0.1)357.2 + (0.2)356.0 + (0.3)357.3 + (0.4)359.2] = 358.2$		
2	0	$4 + 0.99 \ [(0.3)356.0 + (0.3)357.0 + (0.4)357.2]$	$= 357.2$	$x = 0$
	1	$5 + 0.99 \ [(0.1)356.0 + (0.2)357.0 + (0.3)357.2 + (0.4)356.0] = 358.0$		
	2	$5 + 0.99 \ [(0.1)357.0 + (0.2)357.2 + (0.3)356.0 + (0.4)357.3] = 358.3$		
	3	$5 + 0.99 \ [(0.1)357.2 + (0.2)356.0 + (0.3)357.3 + (0.4)359.2] = 359.2$		
3	0	$3 + 0.99 \ [(0.1)356.0 + (0.2)357.0 + (0.3)357.2 + (0.4)356.0] = 356.0$		$x = 0$
	1	$6 + 0.99 \ [(0.1)357.0 + (0.2)357.2 + (0.3)356.0 + (0.4)357.3] = 357.3$		
	2	$6 + 0.99 \ [(0.1)357.2 + (0.2)356.0 + (0.3)357.3 + (0.4)359.2] = 360.2$		
4	0	$4 + 0.99 \ [(0.1)357.0 + (0.2)357.2 + (0.3)356.0 + (0.4)357.3] = 357.3$		$x = 0$
	1	$7 + 0.99 \ [(0.1)357.2 + (0.2)356.0 + (0.3)357.3 + (0.4)359.2] = 361.2$		
5	0	$5 + 0.99 \ [(0.1)357.2 + (0.2)356.0 + (0.3)357.3 + (0.4)359.2] = 359.2$		$x = 0$

Step 4: The new policy

$$(x_0^{(2)} = 3, \ x_1^{(2)} = 2, \ x_2^{(2)} = 0, \ x_3^{(2)} = 0, \ x_4^{(2)} = 0, \ x_5^{(2)} = 0)$$

is the same as at the end of the preceding iteration and is the optimal policy. The minimum discounted costs are those found in step 3 of this iteration, i.e., $f_0 = 356.0, \ f_1 = 357.0, \ f_2 = 357.2, \ f_3 = 356.0, \ f_4 = 357.3$, and $f_5 = 359.2$.

The algorithm converged on the optimal solution in two iterations. The policy found says: replenish inventory to a level of 3 whenever it has been reduced to 1 or less, and do nothing otherwise. Such an optimal policy is known as an (S, s) *policy* with the replenishment level, $S = 3$, and the reorder point, $s = 1$. It can be shown that for inventory control problems with fixed inventory replenishment costs, linear holding costs, and constant per unit shortage cost, as is the case here, the optimal policy always has the form of an (S, s) policy. Note that the initial policy also had this form with $S = 4$ and $s = 1$.

How does the optimal policy change as a function of the discount rate α? Sensitivity analysis, with respect to the discount rate, often provides useful insight to the decision maker. In this particular case, the present policy remains optimal for all α, $0 \leqslant \alpha \leqslant 1$.

9-6 AVERAGE GAIN PER PERIOD

When dealing with routine day-to-day or month-to-month decisions, the appropriate discount factor per period may be close to 1. Then, the discounted gain over all future periods tends to become extremely large. Furthermore, the discounting procedure implies a long-term behavioral pattern, whereas the stationary assumptions may have been introduced as a convenient approximation of the short-term or intermediate-term behavior of the system. Thus, we may not be interested in the discounted gain over all future periods, but only in the average gain per (short) period or the total gain for a limited interval of perhaps one year, where the effect of discounting may be negligible. Maximizing average gain (or minimizing average cost) then becomes the more appropriate criterion to use.

As we have seen in Section 8-7, with each Markov chain containing only one ergodic subset of states we can associate the unique long-run average benefit (or cost) per period given by expression (8-14), i.e.,

$$g = \sum_i c_i a_i$$

Here, c_i is the one-period benefit (or cost) of starting the process in state i and the a_i are the steady state probabilities associated with the transition matrix **P**. In this chapter we study systems that can be governed by any one of a number of alternative policies, each defining its own Markov chain, and resulting in a unique long-run average benefit (or cost) per period.

Suppose we operate the inventory system discussed in Section 9-3 under a given (arbitrary) policy for n periods. Let $v_i(n)$ be the undiscounted expected cost of this policy over n periods given that the process starts out in state i (i.e., with an initial inventory of i). These costs satisfy the following recursive relation:

$$(9\text{-}13) \qquad v_i(n) = c_i(x) + \sum_j p_{ij}(x) v_j(n-1), \qquad \text{all } i, \quad n = 1, 2, \ldots$$

The reasoning used to obtain expression (9-13) is analogous to that used for expression (9-10). If the process starts out in state i, it first incurs the cost $c_i(x)$

associated with using a given policy, and then moves to state j with probability $p_{ij}(x)$. The cost over the remaining $n-1$ periods onward from state j is $v_j(n-1)$. Again, we take the expected value over all possible states j.

As we have seen, in the steady state the long-run average cost per period is g, and is independent of the initial state i. Thus, in the steady state, the average long-run cost over n periods is ng. On the other hand, for n finite the cost over n periods, $v_i(n)$, depends on the initial state i. Let n now be sufficiently large, and consider the difference between these two terms, denoted by v_i:

$$(9\text{-}14) \qquad\qquad v_i = v_i(n) - ng.$$

For n sufficiently large, v_i represents the *transient effect* of the initial state on the cost of the process. The difference of the transient effects for two different initial states, $(v_i - v_j)$, can be given the following economic interpretation: By (9-14), we have

$$v_i(n) = ng + v_i$$

$$(9\text{-}15) \qquad \text{and}$$

$$v_j(n) = ng + v_j, \qquad n \text{ sufficiently large}$$

The difference, $v_i(n) - v_j(n)$, is thus, $v_i - v_j$. It represents the difference in the total cost of starting the process in state i rather than state j. This is the amount that a rational person should be willing to pay (if $v_i < v_j$) or receive (if $v_i > v_j$) for being able to start the process in state i rather than in state j.

The v_i turn out to be useful quantities in our search for the optimal policy. But first, let us see how we can determine their values. Substituting equations (9-15) into (9-13), we obtain

$$(9\text{-}16) \qquad ng + v_i = c_i(x) + \sum_j p_{ij}(x)\,((n-1)g + v_j)$$

$$= c_i(x) + (n-1)g\sum_j p_{ij}(x) + \sum_j p_{ij}(x)\,v_j$$

But $\sum_j p_{ij}(x) = 1$, and (9-16) becomes

$$ng + v_i = c_i(x) + (n-1)g + \sum_j p_{ij}(x)\,v_j$$

Cancelling equal terms on both sides, we finally derive

$$(9\text{-}17) \qquad g + v_i = c_i(x) + \sum_j p_{ij}(x)\,v_j, \qquad \text{all } i$$

The term n conveniently drops from (9-16). For n sufficiently large the v_i are independent of n. Thus, g and the v_i are the solution to a system of r linear equations in $r+1$ variables, where r is the number of states. These equations will not have a unique solution. In general, we need to set the value of one variable in order to solve for the other r variables uniquely. Of special interest is the fact that if $(v_1, v_2, ..., v_r, g)$ is a solution to (9-17), so is $[(v_1+b), (v_2+b), ..., (v_r+b), g]$ for any scalar b. Clearly, the differences $(v_i - v_j)$ will then remain undisturbed for any b. So we might set b equal to any one of the v_i values, say v_0, and solve for the remaining v_i in terms of

v_0, i.e., the solution values are $\hat{v}_i = v_i - v_0$, all i. Therefore, we shall refer to them as *relative values*. Note that this approach implies that we simply set $\hat{v}_0 = 0$ to get a solution to the relative values. We shall now drop the separate notation, $\hat{v}_i$, and simply use v_i for the relative values.

Let us find the long-run average cost and the relative values for the policy $(4, 3, 0, 0, 0, 0)$ used earlier with the transition matrix $\mathbf{P}$ and the one-period costs $c_i(x)$ given by expression (9-8). By expression (9-17) they are the solution to the following system of 6 equations in 7 unknowns:

$$g + v_0 = 3 + 0v_0 \ + 0.1v_1 + 0.2v_2 + 0.3v_3 + 0.4v_4 + 0v_5$$

$$g + v_1 = 4 + 0v_0 \ + 0.1v_1 + 0.2v_2 + 0.3v_3 + 0.4v_4 + 0v_5$$

$$g + v_2 = 4 + 0.3v_0 + 0.3v_1 + 0.4v_2 + 0v_3 \ + 0v_4 \ + 0v_5$$

(9-18)

$$g + v_3 = 3 + 0.1v_0 + 0.2v_1 + 0.3v_2 + 0.4v_3 + 0v_4 \ + 0v_5$$

$$g + v_4 = 4 + 0v_0 \ + 0.1v_1 + 0.2v_2 + 0.3v_3 + 0.4v_4 + 0v_5$$

$$g + v_5 = 5 + 0v_0 \ + 0v_1 \ + 0.1v_2 + 0.2v_3 + 0.3v_4 + 0.4v_5$$

Setting $v_0 = 0$, we obtain

$$g = 3.652, \quad v_0 = 0.0, \quad v_1 = 1.0, \quad v_2 = 1.08,$$

$$v_3 = -0.213, \quad v_4 = 1.0, \quad v_5 = 2.856$$

9-7 APPROXIMATION IN POLICY SPACE FOR AVERAGE COST PER PERIOD

To determine the optimal policy that minimizes the average cost per period we shall again use a bootstrap operation analogous to the one developed for discounting.

STEP 1: INITIAL POLICY

Guess an initial policy labeled by the superscripts $k = 0$ by choosing for each state i a decision $x = x_i^{(0)}$.

STEP 2: POLICY EVALUATION ROUTINE

Determine, for policy k, the expected cost g and the relative values v_i, all i, which are the solution to the system of linear equations:

(9-19)
$$g^{(k)} + v_i^{(k)} = c_i(x_i^{(k)}) + \sum_j p_{ij}(x_i^{(k)}) v_j^{(k)}, \quad \text{all } i$$

by setting one of the relative values, v_i, equal to zero.

At this time we again decide to determine a new policy, $k+1$, for the first period, followed by policy k in all periods thereafter. To derive the appropriate expressions for this optimization, we will again revert to an n period case first. If we were to determine the optimal policy in the first period, given that we would use policy k in the remaining $n-1$ periods, we would find for each state i that action x which

$$(9\text{-}20) \qquad \text{minimizes}_x \left[c_i(x) + \sum_j p_{ij}(x) v_j(n-1) \right]$$

where $v_j(n-1)$ is the cost for policy k over the remaining $n-1$ periods.

For n sufficiently large, we may now again approximate (9-20) by substituting $(n-1)g^{(k)}+v_j^{(k)}$ for $v_j(n-1)$:

$$(9\text{-}21) \qquad \text{minimize } c_i(x) + \sum_j p_{ij}(x)[(n-1)g^{(k)}+v_j^{(k)}]$$

But, $\sum_j p_{ij}(x)(n-1)g^{(k)}$ is a constant and does not affect the minimization. We are left with $c_i(x)+\sum_j p_{ij}(x)v_j^{(k)}$. As for the policy evaluation routine, the resulting expression is independent of n. The relative values v_i hold the key to the policy improvement routine.

STEP 3: POLICY IMPROVEMENT ROUTINE

Determine a new policy $k+1$ by finding for each i the decision $x_i^{(k+1)} = x$ that will

$$(9\text{-}22) \qquad \text{minimize } c_i(x) + \sum_j p_{ij}(x)v_j^{(k)}$$

If $x_i^{(k)}$ is one of several for which the minimum in (9-22) is obtained, $x_i^{(k+1)} = x_i^{(k)}$ is retained as the best decision in state i to avoid cycling.

STEP 4: STOPPING RULE

If $x_i^{(k+1)} = x_i^{(k)}$, all i, the optimal policy has been found, and $g^{(k)}$ is the minimum average cost per period. If the new policy $k+1$ differs from the previous one in at least one state, increase the count k by one and go back to step 2.

It can again be shown that each new policy produced by the policy improvement routine has an average cost per period which is at most as high as for the previous policy. As for $\alpha < 1$, this algorithm converges to the optimal policy in a finite number of iterations.

For a maximization problem we simply substitute *maximize* for *minimize* in (9-22).

9-8 SOLUTION FOR AVERAGE GAIN PER PERIOD

Table 9-1 contains all information needed for the algorithm in Section 9-7.

Step 1: Initial policy $= (x_0^{(0)} = 4,\ x_1^{(0)} = 3,\ x_2^{(0)} = 0,\ x_3^{(0)} = 0,\ x_4^{(0)} = 0,\ x_5^{(0)} = 0)$ with transition probabilities and costs as shown by expressions (9-8) in Section 9-3.

Step 2: Solve the set of linear equations (9-18) whose solution is $g^{(0)} = 3.652$, $v_0^{(0)} = 0,\ v_1^{(0)} = 1.0,\ v_2^{(0)} = 1.08,\ v_3^{(0)} = -0.213,\ v_4^{(0)} = 1.0,\ v_5^{(0)} = 2.856$.

Step 3: Find a new action for each state using (9-22).

State i	Action x	$c_i(x) + \sum_j p_{ij}(x) v_j^{(0)}$								Minimum for x
0	0	$20 + (1\ )0$						$= 20$		
	1	$11 + (0.6)0$	$+(0.4)$	1				$= 11.4$		
	2	$5 + (0.3)0$	$+(0.3)$	1	$+(0.4)$	1.08		$= 5.732$		
	3	$3 + (0.1)0$	$+(0.2)$	1	$+(0.3)$	1.08	$+(0.4)(-0.213)$	$= 3.439$		$x = 3$
	4	$3 + (0.1)1$	$+(0.2)$	1.08	$+(0.3)(-0.213)$	$+(0.4)$	1	$= 3.652$		
	5	$3 + (0.1)1.08$	$+(0.2)(-0.213)$	$+(0.3)$	1	$+(0.4)$	2.856	$= 4.508$		
1	0	$9 + (0.6)0$	$+(0.4)$	1				$= 9.4$		
	1	$6 + (0.3)0$	$+(0.3)$	1	$+(0.4)$	1.08		$= 6.732$		
	2	$4 + (0.1)0$	$+(0.2)$	1	$+(0.3)$	1.08	$+(0.4)(-0.213)$	$= 4.439$		$x = 2$
	3	$4 + (0.1)1$	$+(0.2)$	1.08	$+(0.3)(-0.213)$	$+(0.4)$	1	$= 4.652$		
	4	$4 + (0.1)1.08$	$+(0.2)(-0.213)$	$+(0.3)$	1	$+(0.4)$	2.856	$= 5.508$		
2	0	$4 + (0.3)0$	$+(0.3)$	1	$+(0.4)$	1.08		$= 4.732$		$x = 0$
	1	$5 + (0.1)0$	$+(0.2)$	1	$+(0.3)$	1.08	$+(0.4)(-0.213)$	$= 5.439$		
	2	$5 + (0.1)1$	$+(0.2)$	1.08	$+(0.3)(-0.213)$	$+(0.4)$	1	$= 5.652$		
	3	$5 + (0.1)1.08$	$+(0.2)(-0.213)$	$+(0.3)$	1	$+(0.4)$	2.856	$= 6.508$		
3	0	$3 + (0.1)0$	$+(0.2)$	1	$+(0.3)$	1.08	$+(0.4)(-0.213)$	$= 3.439$		$x = 0$
	1	$6 + (0.1)1$	$+(0.2)$	1.08	$+(0.3)(-0.213)$	$+(0.4)$	1	$= 6.652$		
	2	$6 + (0.1)1.08$	$+(0.2)(-0.213)$	$+(0.3)$	1	$+(0.4)$	2.856	$= 7.508$		
4	0	$4 + (0.1)1$	$+(0.2)$	1.08	$+(0.3)(-0.213)$	$+(0.4)$	1	$= 4.652$		$x = 0$
	1	$7 + (0.1)1.08$	$+(0.2)(-0.213)$	$+(0.3)$	1	$+(0.4)$	2.856	$= 8.508$		
5	0	$5 + (0.1)1.08$	$+(0.2)(-0.213)$	$+(0.3)$	1	$+(0.4)$	2.856	$= 6.508$		$x = 0$

Step 4: The new policy is $(x_0^{(1)} = 3,\ x_1^{(1)} = 2,\ x_2^{(1)} = 0,\ x_3^{(1)} = 0,\ x_4^{(1)} = 0,\ x_5^{(1)} = 0)$. This policy is different from the initial policy, and hence we go through another iteration. The transition matrix and costs for the new policy are given by expressions (9-12) in Section 9-5.

Second iteration

Step 2: Solve the set of simultaneous equations obtained from (9-19): (for convenience, superscripts are deleted)

$$g + v_0 = 3 + 0.1v_0 + 0.2v_1 + 0.3v_2 + 0.4v_3$$

$$g + v_1 = 4 + 0.1v_0 + 0.2v_1 + 0.3v_2 + 0.4v_3$$

$$g + v_2 = 4 + 0.3v_0 + 0.3v_1 + 0.4v_2$$

$$g + v_3 = 3 + 0.1v_0 + 0.2v_1 + 0.3v_2 + 0.4v_3$$

$$g + v_4 = 4 + 0.1v_1 + 0.2v_2 + 0.3v_3 + 0.4v_4$$

$$g + v_5 = 5 + 0.1v_2 + 0.2v_3 + 0.3v_4 + 0.4v_5$$

Setting $v_0 = 0$, the solution is

$$g^{(1)} = 3.567, \qquad v_0^{(1)} = 0, \qquad v_1^{(1)} = 1, \qquad v_2^{(1)} = 1.222, \qquad v_3^{(1)} = 0,$$

$$v_4^{(1)} = 1.296, \qquad v_5^{(1)} = 3.241.$$

Step 3: Find a new action for each state using (9-22).

State i	Action x	$c_i(x) + \sum_j p_{ij}(x) v_j^{(1)}$				Minimum for x
0	0	$20 + (1\ )0$			$= 20$	
	1	$11 + (0.6)0$	$+(0.4)1$		$= 11.4$	
	2	$5 + (0.3)0$	$+(0.3)1$	$+(0.4)1.222$	$= 5.789$	
	3	$3 + (0.1)0$	$+(0.2)1$	$+(0.3)1.222 + (0.4)0$	$= 3.567$	$x = 3$
	4	$3 + (0.1)1$	$+(0.2)1.222 + (0.3)0$	$+(0.4)1.296 =$	3.863	
	5	$3 + (0.1)1.222 + (0.2)0$		$+(0.3)1.296 + (0.4)3.241 =$	4.807	
1	0	$9 + (0.6)0$	$+(0.4)1$		$= 9.4$	
	1	$6 + (0.3)0$	$+(0.3)1$	$+(0.4)1.222$	$= 6.789$	
	2	$4 + (0.1)0$	$+(0.2)1$	$+(0.3)1.222 + (0.4)0$	$= 4.567$	$x = 2$
	3	$4 + (0.1)1$	$+(0.2)1.222 + (0.3)0$	$+(0.4)1.296 =$	4.863	
	4	$4 + (0.1)1.222 + (0.2)0$		$+(0.3)1.296 + (0.4)3.241 =$	5.807	
2	0	$4 + (0.3)0$	$+(0.3)1$	$+(0.4)1.222$	$= 4.789$	$x = 0$
	1	$5 + (0.1)0$	$+(0.2)1$	$+(0.3)1.222 + (0.4)0$	$= 5.567$	
	2	$5 + (0.1)1$	$+(0.2)1.222 + (0.3)0$	$+(0.4)1.296 =$	5.863	
	3	$5 + (0.1)1.222 + (0.2)0$		$+(0.3)1.296 + (0.4)3.241 =$	6.807	
3	0	$3 + (0.1)0$	$+(0.2)1$	$+(0.3)1.222 + (0.4)0$	$= 3.567$	$x = 0$
	1	$6 + (0.1)1$	$+(0.2)1.222 + (0.3)0$	$+(0.4)1.296 =$	6.863	
	2	$6 + (0.1)1.222 + (0.2)0$		$+(0.3)1.296 + (0.4)3.241 =$	7.807	
4	0	$4 + (0.1)1$	$+(0.2)1.222 + (0.3)0$	$+(0.4)1.296 =$	4.863	$x = 0$
	1	$7 + (0.1)1.222 + (0.2)0$		$+(0.3)1.296 + (0.4)3.241 =$	8.807	
5	0	$5 + (0.1)1.222 + (0.2)0$		$+(0.3)1.296 + (0.4)3.241 =$	6.807	$x = 0$

Step 4: The new policy is the same as after the previous iteration. The optimal solution has been reached. The minimum average cost per period is $g = 3.567$.

The optimal policy turns out to have the same (S, s) form as for $\alpha < 1$.

*9-9 LINEAR PROGRAMMING FORMULATION OF MARKOVIAN DECISION PROCESSES

Numerical solutions to expression (9-9) can be obtained by linear programming. Consider expression (9-9) again.

$$f_i = \underset{x \in X}{\text{minimum}} \left[c_i(x) + \alpha \sum_j p_{ij}(x) f_j \right]$$

The term f_i being the minimum discounted expected cost, it must be true that

$$(9\text{-}23) \qquad f_i \leqslant c_i(x) + \alpha \sum_j p_{ij}(x) f_j, \qquad \text{all} \quad x \in X, \quad i = 1, 2, \ldots, r$$

For each i there is at least one x for which strict equality holds in (9-23). Re-arranging (9-23), we obtain

$$(9\text{-}24) \qquad f_i - \alpha \sum_i p_{ij}(x) f_j \leqslant c_i(x), \qquad \text{all} \quad x \in X, \quad i = 1, 2, \ldots, r$$

In the dynamic programming formulation, the f_i are constants. We now allow them to become variables. Let y_i be the variable denoting the expected discounted cost over all future periods starting in state i. Then (9-24) becomes

$$(9\text{-}25) \qquad y_i - \alpha \sum_j p_{ij}(x) y_j \leqslant c_i(x), \qquad \text{all} \quad x \in X, \quad i = 1, 2, \ldots, r$$

where for each i equality holds for at least one value of x. There are $\sum_i M_i$ constraints in r variables, where M_i is the number of possible actions in state i. Note that in this formulation, nothing is known about the sign of the y_i values. Hence, they are unrestricted in sign.

For linear programming we need an objective function. It can be shown that the f_i values of (9-9) are equal to the optimal y_i values obtained by using the following objective function:

$$(9\text{-}26) \qquad \qquad \text{maximize} \sum_i q_i y_i$$

where $q_i > 0$, all i. For instance, we could set all $q_i = 1$. Alternatively, by selecting the values of q_i such that $\sum_i q_i = 1$, each q_i can be interpreted as the probability of starting the process in state i.

To identify the optimal policy, all we have to do is to observe those constraints that are satisfied as an equality for each state i. The x associated with this constraint is the optimal action for that state i.

In this formulation, the number of constraints, $\sum_i M_i$, is usually very much larger than the number of variables. Since the computational effort to solve a linear program is much more sensitive to the number of constraints than the number of variables, it seems natural to solve the dual of (9-25) and (9-26). If w_{ix} is the dual variable associated with the primal constraint for action x in state i, then the dual is

$$\text{minimize} \sum_i \sum_x c_i(x)\, w_{ix}$$

(9-27) subject to

$$\sum_x w_{jx} - \alpha \sum_i \sum_x p_{ij}(x)\, w_{ix} = q_j, \qquad j = 1, 2, \ldots, r$$

and all $w_{jx} \geqslant 0$. Since the primal variables are unrestricted in sign, the dual constraints are all equalities.

The dual has r constraints in $\sum_i M_i$ variables. By complementary slackness, the optimal policy is given by the x in each i for which $w_{ix} > 0$.

Table 9-2 shows the structure of the primal problem in detached coefficient form and its optimal solution for $\alpha = 0.99$. Obviously, the optimal values of the variables y_i, $i = 0, 1, 2, 3, 4, 5$, coincide with the optimal f_i values obtained in Section 9-5.

Table 9-2. *Primal Problem of Linear Program Markovian Decision Process.*

State	x	y_0	y_1	y_2	y_3	y_4	y_5		$c_i(x)$	Binding Constraints	Optimal Decision
0	0	$1-\alpha$						$\leqslant$	20	Slack	
	1	$1-0.6\alpha$	-0.4α					$\leqslant$	11	Slack	
	2	$1-0.3\alpha$	-0.3α	-0.4α				$\leqslant$	5	Slack	
	3	$1-0.1\alpha$	-0.2α	-0.3α	-0.4α			$\leqslant$	3	Binding	$x = 3$
	4		-0.1α	-0.2α	-0.3α	-0.4α		$\leqslant$	3	Slack	
	5			-0.1α	-0.2α	-0.3α	-0.4α	$\leqslant$	3	Slack	
1	0	-0.6α	$1-0.4\alpha$					$\leqslant$	9	Slack	
	1	-0.3α	$1-0.3\alpha$	-0.4α				$\leqslant$	6	Slack	
	2	-0.1α	$1-0.2\alpha$	-0.3α	-0.4α			$\leqslant$	4	Binding	$x = 2$
	3		$1-0.1\alpha$	-0.2α	-0.3α	-0.4α		$\leqslant$	4	Slack	
	4			-0.1α	-0.2α	-0.3α	-0.4α	$\leqslant$	4	Slack	
2	0	-0.3α	-0.3α	$1-0.4\alpha$				$\leqslant$	4	Binding	$x = 0$
	1	-0.1α	-0.2α	$1-0.3\alpha$	-0.4α			$\leqslant$	5	Slack	
	2		-0.1α	$1-0.2\alpha$	-0.3α	-0.4α		$\leqslant$	5	Slack	
	3			$1-0.1\alpha$	-0.2α	-0.3α	-0.4α	$\leqslant$	5	Slack	
3	0	-0.1α	-0.2α	-0.3α	$1-0.4\alpha$			$\leqslant$	3	Binding	$x = 0$
	1		-0.1α	-0.2α	$1-0.3\alpha$	-0.4α		$\leqslant$	6	Slack	
	2			-0.1α	$1-0.2\alpha$	-0.3α	-0.4α	$\leqslant$	6	Slack	
4	0		-0.1α	-0.2α	-0.3α	$1-0.4\alpha$		$\leqslant$	4	Binding	$x = 0$
	1			-0.1α	-0.2α	$1-0.3\alpha$	-0.4α	$\leqslant$	7	Slack	
5	0			-0.1α	-0.2α	-0.3α	$1-0.4\alpha$	$\leqslant$	5	Binding	$x = 0$
Maximize		1	1	1	1	1	1				
Optimal solution for $\alpha = 0.99$		356.0	357.0	357.2	356.0	357.3	359.2				

EXERCISES

9.1   (a) If funds earn interest of 10 percent per period, find the present value for the following stream of funds received at the beginning of each period.

Period	1	2	3	4	5
Funds, R_i, in dollars	10	8	6	4	2

(b) Assume now that the stream of funds only starts occurring one period from now and requires a cash expenditure of $24. Using the result obtained for (a), find the present value of this new stream of expenditures and receipts of funds.

9.2   Each month the management of a small chain of service stations has to make a decision as to the promotion campaign for the coming month. If sales in the current month are high, three possible actions are available: (1) Management can decide to continue the current promotion for next month; then, with probability 0.4, sales in the next month will be high and generate a net revenue of $8000, and with probability 0.6, sales will be low and generate a net revenue of $4000. The costs incurred for continuing the present promotion amount to $1000. (2) They can offer a new free gift; then, with probability 0.8 sales in the month will be high and generate a net revenue of $7000, and with probability 0.2, sales will be low and generate a net revenue of $3000. The cost of this action is $2500. (3) No promotion is undertaken; then, with probability 0.25, sales will be high with a revenue of $10000, and with probability 0.75, sales will be low with a revenue of $5000. No costs are incurred then. If sales in the current month are low, two possible actions are available: (1) Management can decide to offer a new gift; then, with probability 0.5, sales will be high with a revenue of $6000, and with probability 0.5, sales will be low with a revenue of $2000. The cost of this action is $2500. (2) They can decide to copy the main competitor's promotional campaign; then, with probability 0.4, sales will be high with a revenue of $7000, and with probability 0.6, sales will be low with a revenue of $3000. The cost of this action is $1000.

(a) Construct a table similar to Table 9-1, showing columns for the current state, the decision, the transition probabilities, and the expected gross profit of the action (difference between expected net revenue and costs).

(b) For an initial policy of continuing the current promotion if sales are high and offering a new free gift if sales are low, find the present value of gross profits for each state for a discount factor of $\alpha = 0.9$.

(c) Use the four-step algorithm for approximation in policy space to find the optimal policy for a discount factor of 0.9. Note that this is a maximization problem!

(d) Determine the sensitivity of the optimal policy to $0 \leqslant \alpha < 1$.

9.3   A machine goes through several stages of deterioration that can be classified as 0 (properly adjusted), 1, 2, and 3 (inoperative). The state of the machine can be inferred with certainty from the number of defectives produced during the preceding day. At the beginning of each day a decision has to be made as to whether the machine should be adjusted or not. If the machine is not adjusted, then the probability that its state of deterioration will progress to the next higher one is as follows:

State i as of end of day	0	1	2
Probability of state $i+1$ as of end of next day	0.1	0.2	0.3

Once in state 3 it will remain there. If the machine is adjusted at the beginning of the day, its pattern of deterioration is the same as if it were in state 0. Total operating cost, including losses on defective parts are as follows:

State as of end of next day	0	1	2	3
Operating cost next day in dollars	10	12	15	30

The cost of an adjustment (including loss of production) is $8.
(a) Construct a table similar to Table 9-1, containing all information needed for the algorithm for approximation in policy space.
(b) Use the algorithm for approximation in policy space to find the optimal policy for a discount factor 0.99.

9.4 Consider the water reservoir example in Chapter 8, Sections 8-1 and 8-7. This can be viewed as a Markovian decision process, where for each state the size of the target release represents the decision variable. Indicate why the algorithm for approximation in policy space may result in an optimal policy that is nonoptimal for practical or technical reasons.

9.5 A reservoir is used to generate electric power for a small factory with a constant power demand equivalent to 4 units of water. The decision variables are the target releases to be scheduled for each reservoir level. If the target release cannot be met or is less than 4 units of water, power has to be purchased from a public utility at a cost of $5000 for the first unit and $6000 for the second unit of water. If more water is available than needed, excess power can be sold at a price of $3000 per unit of water. Use the water inflow pattern of the example in Section 8-1. The reservoir has a maximum capacity of 4, and can be emptied completely. Construct a table similar to Table 9-1 that contains all information needed to apply the algorithm. You do not have to solve the problem.

9.6 The emergency treatment station at a hospital has the policy of having two surgeons on duty at all times. Studying the records of the station, the chief medical officer notices that, at times, one surgeon would be able to handle all emergency calls, whereas at other times the number of emergencies is more than the two surgeons can cope with. Therefore, he wants to investigate this problem to determine an optimal staffing policy for the station. Some practical experimentation with the number of surgeons on duty yields the following information as to the probabilistic behavior of the system: $p(i,j|s) =$ the probability of finding j cases to be treated at the end of a one-hour period if i cases were waiting for treatment at the beginning of the period and s surgeons were on duty for $i, j = 0, 1, ..., K$, and $s = 1, 2, ..., S < K$. Calling a surgeon on duty has a fixed cost of a dollars and an hourly cost of c dollars. The intangible cost of having a patient waiting for treatment at the end of each one-hour period is assessed to amount to b. Construct, in general terms, a table similar to Table 9-1 which, given numbers for $K, S, p(i, j | s)$, a, c and b, could be completed to contain all information needed to use the algorithm for approximation in policy space. Indicate why such a model may not sufficiently represent the true situation.

9.7 Consider problem 9.2.

(a) For the policy listed under (b) of problem 9.2, find the average return per period and the relative values. Assume that sales in the current period are low. How much would it be worth to management to start out from a position of high current sales?

(b) Using the algorithm for approximation in policy space for the average return per period, find the optimal policy.

9.8 Consider the taxi problem 8.4 of Chapter 8. Find the optimal policy using the algorithm for approximation in policy space maximizing average return per trip. Initial policy: cruise in both cities.

9.9 Find the optimal policy that minimizes average cost per day for the machine adjustment problem 9.3.

9.10 Formulate the linear program associated with problem 9.3. If you have access to a computer, solve the linear program and interpret the optimal solution.

9.11 Formulate the linear program associated with problem 9.2. Note that this is a maximization problem. Therefore, expressions (9-23) through (9-26) have to be adjusted accordingly.

REFERENCES

Most texts on dynamic programming deal with Markovian decision processes. Also see the references to Chapter 7.

Blackwell, D. "Discrete Dynamic Programming", *Annals of Mathematical Statistics*, 33 (1962), pp. 719–26. Advanced development of the theory of successive approximation in policy space for average return per period. A classic paper in this field, only for the mathematically sophisticated.

de Ghellinck, Guy T., and Gary D. Eppen. "Linear Programming Solutions for Separable Markovian Decision Problems", *Management Science*, 15, Jan. 1967. This important paper shows that if the transition probabilities only depend on the decision taken in state i and not state i itself, and $c_i(x)$ can be separated into two parts, one depending on the state only and one depending on the decision only, the problem can be solved by a streamlined linear program that is considerably smaller than the normal linear programming formulation of the problem. Most inventory control problems and replacement problems are separable in this sense. The theoretical part of the paper is extremely difficult, but the examples shown at the end are simple enough to follow. See also Denardo, Eric V. "Separable Markovian Decision Problems", *Management Science*, 14, March 1968.

Hadley, George. *Nonlinear and Dynamic Programming*. Reading, Mass.: Addison Wesley, 1964. Chapter 11 has several excellent sections at an advanced level developing the theoretical basis of Markovian decision processes, including proofs.

Howard, Ronald A. *Dynamic Probabilistic Systems—Volume II: Semimarkov and Decision Processes*, New York: Wiley, 1971. Advanced treatment of Markovian Decision Processes, discrete and continuous. Cannot be properly studied without Volume I. (See References to Chapter 8).

————. *Dynamic Programming and Markov Processes*. Cambridge, Mass.: M.I.T. Press, 1960. This 130-page book is delightful reading on this subject at a very leisurely pace. It is a must on the reading list for any would-be operations researcher. It includes an extension to continuous-time processes where a transition can occur at any point in time.

Jewell, William S. "Markov-Renewal Programming I: Formulation, Finite Return Models", and "Markov-Renewal Programming II: Infinite Return Models, Example", *Operations Research*, 11, 1963, pp. 938–71.

Newman, J. M., and D. J. White. "A Method for Approximate Solutions to Stochastic Dynamic Problems Using Expectations", *Operations Research*, 16, March–April 1968. Describes and illustrates a technique for obtaining approximate solutions to Markovian decision processes. Useful as a choice of the initial policy.

Satia, J. K., and R. E. Lave. "Markovian Decision Processes with Probabilistic Observation of States", *Management Science*, 20, Sept. 1973. Develops an implicit enumeration algorithm for solving problems where the true state of the system can only be observed probabilitistically. Gives several numerical examples.

Wagner, Harvey M. "On the Optimality of Pure Strategies", *Management Science*, 6, April 1960. Proof that the optimal strategy of a Markovian decision problem will always involve taking a single decision in each state, rather than using a mixed strategy (as in game theory) where randomization over several strategies may be optimal.

————. *Principles of Operations Research*, 2nd ed., Englewood Cliffs, N.J.: Prentice-Hall, 1975. Chapters 11 and 12 deal with the principles of decision making over an unbounded planning horizon for deterministic problems, using discounting, and discusses the two solution methods "Approximation in function space" and Approximation in policy space." The first method approximates the optimal solution via the f_i values directly, rather than via the decision variables. Chapter 12 extends the results to the optimal policy for the average return and shows the linear programming formulation for the discounting case. Chapter 16 reviews optimizing criteria for stochastic models. Chapter 18 deals with Markovian decision processes. The treatment is in parts somewhat more advanced than given here.

The following articles discuss some applications of Markovian decision processes.

Derman, Cyrus. "Optimal Replacement and Maintenance under Markovian Deterioration with Probability Bounds on Failure", *Management Science*, 9, Jan. 1963.

Eppen, Gary D., and Eugene F. Fama. "Solutions for Cash Balance and Simple Dynamic Portfolio Problems", *Journal of Business*, 41, Jan. 1968.

Liebman, Leon H. "A Markov Decision Model for Selecting Optimal Credit Control Policies", *Management Science*, 18, June 1972.

10

Introduction to Waiting Line Models

Waiting lines or *queues* are everyday occurrences familiar to all of us. We experience them in our daily lives in one form or another—waiting at a bus stop or elevator, queuing at the cafeteria or ticket office, waiting in shops or at a gasoline station. Queues also occur extensively within an economic, industrial, or social context, sharing the common features of people or objects arriving at a service facility requiring some service and the ensuing delays when the service facility is occupied.

Although the number of potential uses of waiting-line or queuing theory is very large, two major types of situations give rise to successful economic applications. The first deals with the case where an organization controls a sufficiently large number of similar or identical service facilities, such as gasoline pumps, bank tellers, machine operators or repair crews (for looms and knitting machines in a textile factory, machine tools in a machine shop, copying machines in a geographical area), or telephone exchanges. In fact, the first applications of queuing theory dealt with the operation of telephone exchanges. Although queuing theory may offer only small economic incentives for each facility by itself, it is the pooling of large numbers of individually small gains that make such applications economically worthwhile. The second type of application deals with the planning and design of single facilities involving large capital investments, such as the purchase and operation of port facilities, or a computer installation.

In contrast to most other operations research tools, no general pattern of optimization exists for waiting line models. Waiting line theory is mainly concerned with determining, for a given service facility, certain crucial characteristics of a proposed mode of operation, such as average waiting times, average queue length, and average idle time of the facility. These operating characteristics serve as input into the decision-making process about the facility studied—a process that often reduces to the economic evaluation of a small number of possible facilities and operating modes, with the "best" solution found by enumeration.

Most real-life applications of waiting line theory are highly complex. Many defy any formal analytic treatment—simulation being the only approach with any hope of capturing their essential features. In other cases, the tools of waiting line

313

theory only serve as a first approximation to provide some quantitative information about the behavior of the more complex situation. Even so, the level of mathematics required to analyze such problems goes well beyond the scope of this text. The models discussed here are, therefore, a far cry from the complexities encountered in reality and are only intended to give some qualitative insights into waiting line phenomena.

Since this chapter deals with stochastic phenomena, it is essential that you are familiar with the basic operations of probability and expected values. Also, we will use two theoretical probability distributions extensively, namely, the *Poisson distribution* and the *negative exponential distribution*. Sections B-3 and B-4 of Appendix B summarize their most important characteristics. With the exception of a small proportion of Section 10-2 which involves integration of some simple exponential functions, the mathematical operations do not go beyond algebra. For this reason, certain results have to be stated without proof, whereas others are derived by heuristic reasoning. When results are derived formally and intermediate steps are shown, they are only intended to provide you with sufficient insight. You are not necessarily supposed to be able to reproduce them. It is only the proper application of the final results that is important.

10-1 GENERAL STRUCTURE OF WAITING LINES

The physical structure of waiting lines consists of three components:

- one or several *sources of arrivals*,
- *queues*, and
- a *service facility* consisting of one or several parts.

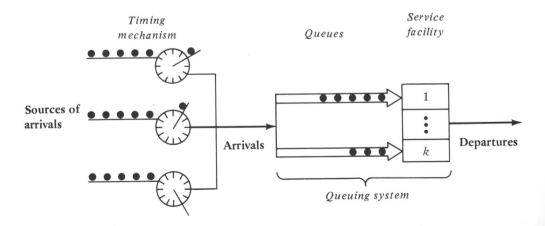

Figure 10-1. *Waiting line structure.*

Table 10-1. *Examples of Waiting Line Phenomena.*

Source of arrivals	Nature of service requested	Service facility
population of customers	sales transaction	shop attendant(s)
aircraft	landing or take off	runway(s)
ships at sea	unloading or loading	port dock(s)
telephones	telephone connection	telephone exchange
cars	crossing	ferry
machines on shop floor	repairs	operators or mechanics
mechanics on shop floor	tools or parts	attendants at tool crib
inventory withdrawals	inventory replenishment	supplier

The queues and service facility together are referred to as the *system*. Table 10-1 lists a few typical examples.

Arrivals may originate from one or several sources or pools of potential customers, referred to as the *calling populations*. We assume that each source has a well defined arrival pattern over time. It may be helpful to visualize that each source is equipped (figuratively speaking) with an *arrival timing mechanism* that releases units with a known pattern of *interarrival times*—the times between two consecutive arrivals. Arrivals may be uniformly spaced over time, i.e., the interarrival times are constant, or randomly spaced over time with a known *interarrival time probability distribution*.

A calling population may be inexhaustible in the sense that the number of potential customers in the source is assumed to be always very much larger than the number of units in the system, or a calling population may be sufficiently limited in size that the arrival pattern varies as a function of that size. The number of telephones serviced by a telephone exchange is an example of an inexhaustible source (under most conditions), whereas the number of machines on a factory floor is an example of a limited source. In the first instance, the call rate will hardly be affected by the number of telephones busy at any given moment in time, whereas in the second case, every machine that requires the attention of an operator, i.e., enters the queuing system, may significantly reduce the rate of arrivals, and every machine that has been serviced, i.e., departs from the system, may again significantly increase the rate of arrivals. If the number of units being served or waiting for service tends to be a relatively small fraction of the total calling population, an unlimited source model may be a satisfactory approximation.

The service facility may consist of one or several *stations* or *channels*. They may operate either *in parallel*, in which case an arrival has to go through one channel only before being discharged from the system, or they may operate *in series*, in which case an arrival has to go through several channels in sequence before being discharged. The service times at each channel may be constant or random with a known *service time distribution*.

There may be none, one, or several queues. Queues do not have to be physical in nature, as the queue in front of a bank teller, but may consist of geographically separated units awaiting service, such as equipment operated at different locations that requires some service. The manner in which units are taken from the queue is called the *queue discipline*. It may, for example, be on a first-come-first-served basis, random, or subject to *service priorities*, as for instance in an emergency clinic. We shall only look at the first scheme. It may also be possible to switch queues, and the choice of which queue to join may be open to an arrival. Furthermore, the maximum queue length may be unlimited or finite. In the latter case, units arriving when the queue is full immediately depart, i.e., are lost to the system. Finally, potential arrivals may *balk* if the queue length becomes excessive and decide not to join, or arrivals may join the queue and subsequently *renege*, i.e., become impatient and leave before being served. In either case they are lost to the system. The variety of possible waiting line configurations seems almost unlimited.

The waiting line problems of interest to us are those that have either random interarrival times or random service times, or both. In this case, queues of random lengths will occur. If no units are waiting most of the time, then the service facility will tend to be idle for a large portion of the time. If there are costs associated with idle service channels, then this is undesirable. On the other hand, if the service facility is busy and queues exist most of the time, arrivals will frequently have to wait prior to service. If the waiting times are long, this may again result in tangible or intangible costs, such as lost production time (mechanics waiting for parts or tools, machines down), deterioration of certain attributes of arrivals (cement trucks or banana boats waiting to be unloaded, patients waiting for surgery), or loss of goodwill (customers becoming impatient). The problem in waiting line models is to determine a system such that the sum of all costs associated with operating the system is minimized.

The controllable aspects of queuing systems are—

- arrival rate (e.g., by choosing quality of parts that may fail or require service);
- number of service facilities;
- service times, both in terms of average length as well as service time variations;
- maximum queue length (e.g., by providing a certain number of spaces, say, in a parking lot); and
- priority rules and queue discipline.

10-2 ARRIVAL TIME DISTRIBUTION

We shall consider only models where arrivals and services occur in single or individual units, rather than in groups of several units (called *bulk arrivals* or *bulk service*).

The simplest waiting line models assume that the number of arrivals occurring within a given interval of time, t, follows a *Poisson distribution* with parameter λt, where λt is the average number of arrivals in the interval of time t. (For the Poisson distribution, λt is also equal to the variance). If n denotes the number of arrivals in the interval t, then the probability function $p(n)$ is given by

(10-1)
$$p(n) = \frac{(\lambda t)^n}{n!} e^{-\lambda t}, \qquad n = 0, 1, 2, \ldots$$

This arrival process is called the *Poisson input*. λ represents the *arrival rate*.

What interarrival time distribution is implied by (10-1)? Assume that we start observing the process immediately after an arrival at time 0. What is the probability of no arrivals in the interval from 0 to t, denoted by $[0, t]$. This probability is given by the first term of (10-1):

(10-2) $$P(\text{no arrival in } [0, t]) = A_0(t) = e^{-\lambda t} = p(0)$$

But

$$P(\text{no arrival in } [0, t]) = P(\text{next arrival occurs after } t)$$

$$= P(\text{time between two successive arrivals exceeds } t)$$

since by assumption we had an arrival at time 0. Let t become a random variable. From (10-2) it follows that the shape of $A_0(t)$ is as shown in Figure 10-2. Now consider the process at time t, and again at time $t+h$. Clearly, $A_0(t) > A_0(t+h)$ for $h > 0$. The difference between the probability of no arrivals up to time t and the probability of no arrivals up to time $t+h$ is the probability that the next arrival occurs in the interval from t to $t+h$, i.e.,

(10-3) $$P(\text{next arrival occurs in } [t, t+h]) = A_0(t) - A_0(t+h)$$

We now introduce the probability density function of the time between successive arrivals or of the interarrival time, denoted by $a(t)$. Figure 10-3 depicts the shape of the density function associated with the Poisson input.

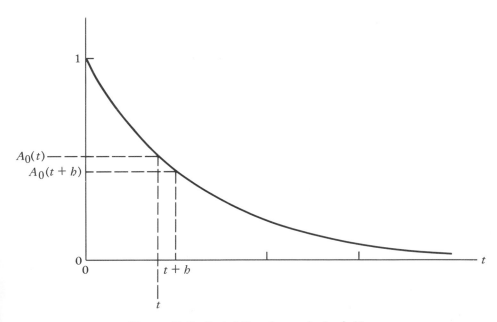

Figure 10-2. *Probability of no arrivals, $A_0(t)$.*

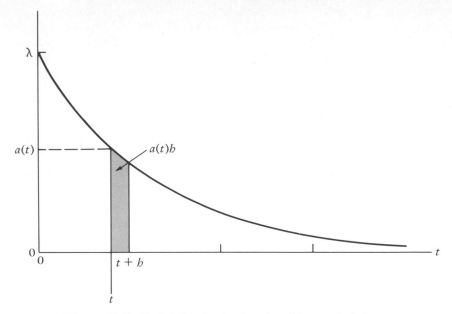

Figure 10-3. *Probability density function of interarrival time,*
a(t), for Poisson input.

For h sufficiently small, P(next arrival occurs in $[t, t+h]$) is approximately
equal to $a(t)h$, as shown in Figure 10-3. Hence

$$A_0(t) - A_0(t+h) \doteq a(t)h,$$

where $\doteq$ denotes approximately equal.

Dividing both sides through by h and letting h go to zero, we obtain

$$\frac{A_0(t) - A_0(t+h)}{h} \underset{h \to 0}{=} -\frac{d}{dt} A_0(t) = a(t)$$

Using this result for the Poisson input case, it follows from expression (10-2) that the
probability density function of interarrival times is given by

(10-4) $$a(t) = -\frac{d}{dt}(e^{-\lambda t}) = \lambda e^{-\lambda t}, \qquad t \geqslant 0$$

known as the *negative exponential distribution* with parameter λ. The mean interarrival time and the standard deviation of interarrival times both are $1/\lambda$.

A Poisson input implies certain behavioristic assumptions about the arrival
process that at first glance may look somewhat unrealistic but in practice turn out to
be surprisingly robust. Let us find the conditional probability that the first arrival

occurs in the interval $[t, t+h]$ given that no arrivals occurred up to time t:

$$\frac{\int_t^{t+h} a(t)\,dt}{A_0(t)} = \frac{\int_t^{t+h} \lambda e^{-\lambda t}\,dt}{e^{-\lambda t}} = \frac{1 - e^{-\lambda(t+h)} - (1 - e^{-\lambda t})}{e^{-\lambda t}}$$

$$= 1 - e^{-\lambda h}$$

But the probability of an arrival in the interval $[0, h]$ is also:

$$\int_0^h a(t)\,dt = \int_0^h \lambda e^{-\lambda t}\,dt = 1 - e^{-\lambda h}$$

i.e., the conditional probability for an arrival in an interval of length h, given no arrival in the preceding interval of length t, is the same as the unconditional probability of an arrival in an interval of length h. In other words:

PROPERTY OF STATIONARITY AND LACK OF MEMORY

A Poisson input implies that arrivals are completely independent of one another or of the state of the system, and the probability of an arrival in any interval of time h does not depend on the starting point of the interval or on the specific history of arrivals preceding it, but depends only on the length h of the interval.

Consider again a very short time interval of length h. What is the probability of exactly one arrival in $[0, h]$? By the second term of expression (10-1) we obtain

$$P(\text{exactly one arrival in } h) = \lambda h e^{-\lambda h}$$

For h very small, $e^{-\lambda h}$ is very close to 1 $(= e^0)$. Hence for h very small we get the approximation

(10-5) $$P(\text{exactly one arrival in } h) \doteq \lambda h$$

From expression (10-1) it also follows that for h very small the probability of observing more than 1 arrival in h is almost zero, since these terms contain higher order powers of h which are negligible for h very small. We can safely assume that for h sufficiently small, no more than one arrival can occur. Only the terms for no arrival and one arrival are thus significant, and

(10-6) $$P(\text{no arrival in } h) \doteq 1 - P(\text{exactly one arrival in } h)$$
$$A_0(h) \doteq 1 - \lambda h, \quad \text{for } h \text{ very small}$$

To verify that the Poisson input is a satisfactory representation of a particular real-life arrival process, we would gather data on the number of arrivals for a sufficiently large number of equal time intervals and compare the empirical distribution

Table 10-2. *Chi-square Test for Arrival Process.*

Arrivals 8-hour day	Observed F_i	Theoretical f_i	$(F_i-f_i)^2/f_i$
$i = 0$	28	24.7	0.44
1	35	34.5	0.01
2	20	24.1	0.70
3	8	11.3	0.96
4	6 ⎫	4.0 ⎫	
5	2 ⎬ 9	1.1 ⎬ 5.4	2.40
6	0 ⎪	0.2 ⎪	
7	1 ⎭	0.1 ⎭	
	100	100	4.51

The "Frequencies" header spans the Observed and Theoretical columns.

Number of classes = 5

Number of degrees of freedom = number of classes − number of estimated parameters − 1 = 5 − 1 − 1 = 3

$P(\text{Chi-square} > 4.51) > 0.2$

(Note that small classes with a frequency of less than 5 should be lumped together to give frequencies for all classes of at least 5. This reduces the effective number of classes available to 5.)

observed with the corresponding theoretical distribution, usually by performing a *goodness of fit test*.

Let us demonstrate this approach with the following example. A firm operates a 10-ton crane truck on a job contracting basis. Arrivals into the system are given by job requests. Data is gathered over a 100-day period and compiled to a frequency table as shown in the first two columns of Table 10-2. Does the daily number of job requests or arrivals have a Poisson distribution?

Thus, we want to test the null hypothesis that the distribution is Poisson with a mean of λ. To test this, we first determine an estimate of the daily arrival rate which turns out to be 1.4 job requests per day. This is used as the value of λ in the Poisson probability function (10-1) and the theoretical frequencies of this distribution—usually obtained from tables—are compared with the observed frequencies using a *Chi-square goodness-of-fit test*. The computations leading up to this test are shown in the last three columns of Table 10-2.

The observed Chi-square value corresponds to a level of significance of about 0.2. This means that the hypothesis of a Poisson distribution is not rejected for all smaller levels of significance. Hence, we can safely approximate the arrival process by a Poisson input.

Analysis of waiting line problems becomes immediately more difficult for arrival processes other than Poisson input. We shall postpone further discussion on this topic to Section 10-12.

10-3 SERVICE TIME DISTRIBUTIONS

Most simple waiting line models also assume that service times have a *negative exponential distribution* with parameter μ.

(10-7) $$s(t) = \mu e^{-\mu t}, \qquad t \geqslant 0$$

The mean service rate for a unit of time is represented by μ, and $1/\mu$ is the mean service time, as well as the standard deviation of service times. This implies again that the service times are independently and identically distributed, no matter when they are undertaken, no matter how many arrivals are waiting in the queue, and no matter what the previous service history has been.

By analogy to (10-5) and (10-6) we have for h very small

(10-8) $$P(\text{one service completion in } h) \doteq \mu h$$

(10-9) $$P(\text{no service completion in } h) \doteq 1 - \mu h$$

The property of lack of memory has some revealing consequences. If a unit arrives at the service facility (when the queue is empty) and finds the service facility busy, the probability that this unit has to wait a length of time of at least h is independent of how long the current service has been in progress. In fact, by the analogous reasoning used for the conditional arrival distribution, the conditional service time distribution is also negative exponential with parameter μ.

What is the expected waiting time for a unit that joins the queue and finds n units ahead of it ($n-1$ in the queue and one unit in the service facility)? Since each unit takes, on the average, a length of time $1/\mu$, the total expected time needed to process n units is n/μ, and by independence of the service times, the standard deviation is $\sqrt{n}/\mu$. Since the total waiting time is equal to the sum of n random variables, all with identical negative exponential distributions, its probability distribution is given by the *convolution* of n negative exponential distributions (see Section B-5 of Appendix B). It turns out that this produces a *gamma distribution* with parameters (n, μ), i.e.,

(10-10) $$f(t) = \frac{\mu^n t^{n-1} e^{-\mu t}}{(n-1)!}, \qquad t \geqslant 0$$

We shall again postpone further discussion of service time distributions other than the negative exponential to Section 10-12.

10-4 QUEUING MODEL NOMENCLATURE

The literature of queuing theory tends to use a standardized terminology, consisting of three symbols separated by vertical bars to describe the most basic types of models:

$$I \mid F \mid S$$

where I designates the input process,

          F the service time distribution, and

          S the number of service channels in parallel.

The standard symbols are:

     M = negative exponential time distribution (M stands for *Markovian*),

     D = deterministic or constant times,

     E_n = Erlang distribution of order n (see Section 10-13),

    GI = general independent interarrival time distribution,

     G = general service time distribution.

For instance, a waiting line model which has Poisson input, constant service times, and 1 service channel is denoted by $M|D|1$.

10-5 THE MOST BASIC WAITING LINE MODEL, $M|M|1$

Mathematically speaking, the simplest waiting line model assumes that arrivals join a queue that is unlimited in size, wait in line until their turn for service comes on a first-come-first-served basis, and then, enter a service facility consisting of a single channel, as depicted in Figure 10-4.

The input process is assumed to be Poisson, i.e., interarrival times have a negative exponential distribution with parameter λ, and the service channel has service times that also follow a negative exponential distribution with parameter μ.

As was the case with Markov processes in Chapter 8, in waiting line models we are often interested only in the long-run operating characteristics of such systems, i.e., when the system is in *statistical equilibrium* or in *steady state*. The time intervals needed to approach the steady state sufficiently closely—the so-called *transient* behavior of the process—is ignored. However, it should be realized that many systems never reach a steady state. This is the case for processes that are periodically interrupted, e.g., daily, before they approach a steady state and then are restarted, usually with empty queues, such as a bank teller service, or systems whose input distribution does not remain stationary but changes over time, such as the traffic flow at a toll bridge during various times of the day. In such cases we study the transient behavior of the system. However, this requires a level of mathematics far beyond the scope of this text.

At any moment in time, the state of a waiting line process is usually completely described by the number of units in the system. For an $M|M|1$ process, this is the number of units in the queue plus the number in the service channel—the latter is either 0 or 1. Thus, the state of the process can assume values 0 (service facility idle, no units in queue), 1 (service facility busy, no units in the queue), 2, 3, ..., n units (service facility busy, $n-1$ units in the queue).

In contrast to the type of Markov processes discussed in Chapter 8, in queuing systems a transition from one state to another can occur at any moment in time and not only at specified evenly spaced points in time. However, the process will nevertheless approach a steady state which is independent of its starting position or state.

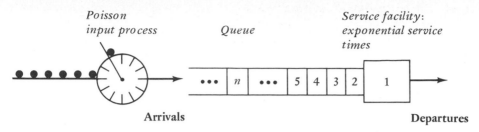

Figure 10-4. *Single channel system.*

Let these steady state probabilities be denoted by P_n, $n = 0, 1, 2, \ldots$, where the subscript refers to the number of units in the system. To derive these steady state probabilities we shall use the following heuristic reasoning. As we have seen, for a Poisson input and a negative exponential service time distribution, the probabilities that an arrival occurs or a service is completed in an interval of length h do not depend on any previous history, but are only a function of the length of time h. Hence the probability of a transition from a given state to another state in the interval h does not depend on how long the system already occupied that state. This allows us to look at the system at any random point in time without having to worry about the system's past history. The state occupied at that time contains all the information needed to describe the system's future behavior. If we look at the process in the steady state at two randomly chosen moments in time, separated by a short interval of time h, then it must be true that the probabilities of finding the process in the various states remains unchanged—by the very definition of the steady state. But this requires that, for each state, the probability of being in that state and leaving it during h exactly balances the probability of being in other states and entering that state during h.

As we have seen in Section 10-2, for h sufficiently small no more than one arrival can occur in the interval of length h. By analogous reasoning, no more than one service completion can occur. Similarly, the probability of observing an arrival and a service completion in the same interval, given by $\mu \lambda h^2$, is approximately zero for h very small, since it also involves a higher order term of h. This leaves only the following four compound events associated with each state for $n > 1$:

Events	Probability
(1) There are n units in the system	P_n
and one arrival occurs in h	λh
(2) There are n units in the system	P_n
and one service is completed in h	μh
(3) There are $n-1$ units in the system	P_{n-1}
and one arrival occurs in h	λh
(4) There are $n+1$ units in the system	P_{n+1}
and one service is completed in h	μh

For $n = 0$, only events 1 and 4 are possible. Figure 10-5 shows a transition diagram for these events:

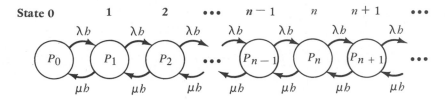

Figure 10-5. *Transition diagram for* M|M|1.

Now for $n > 1$

$$P\left(\begin{matrix} \text{being in state } n \text{ and} \\ \text{leaving it} \end{matrix}\right) = P\left(\begin{matrix} \text{being in state } n-1 \text{ or } n+1 \\ \text{and entering state } n \end{matrix}\right)$$

$$P(\text{event 1}) + P(\text{event 2}) = P(\text{event 3}) + P(\text{event 4})$$

This yields the following equation known as a *steady state balance equation*:

(10-11) $$P_n \lambda h + P_n \mu h = P_{n-1} \lambda h + P_{n+1} \mu h$$

In terms of Figure 10-3, the left-hand side of (10-11) is obtained by adding the products of the probabilities shown in circle n and on the arrows leaving circle n, whereas the right-hand side is obtained as the sum of the products of the probabilities shown in circles where arrows entering circle n originate and on these arrows. Dividing expression (10-11) through by h and rearranging we obtain

(10-12) $$P_{n+1} = \frac{1}{\mu}(P_n(\lambda+\mu) - P_{n-1}\lambda), \qquad n \geqslant 1$$

For $n = 0$, we equate the probabilities for event 1 and event 4. The steady state balance equation then simplifies to

$$P_0 \lambda h = P_1 \mu h$$

or

(10-13) $$P_1 = \frac{\lambda}{\mu}P_0$$

Using expression (10-13) in expression (10-12), P_n can be obtained recursively in terms of P_0 as follows:

$$P_2 = \frac{1}{\mu}(P_1(\lambda+\mu) - P_0\lambda) = \frac{1}{\mu}\left(\frac{\lambda}{\mu}P_0(\lambda+\mu) - P_0\lambda\right) = \left(\frac{\lambda}{\mu}\right)^2 P_0,$$

$$P_3 = \frac{1}{\mu}(P_2(\lambda+\mu) - P_1\lambda) = \frac{1}{\mu}\left[\left(\frac{\lambda}{\mu}\right)^2 P_0(\lambda+\mu) - \frac{\lambda}{\mu}P_0\lambda\right] = \left(\frac{\lambda}{\mu}\right)^3 P_0, \qquad \text{etc.}$$

In general:

(10-14)
$$P_n = \left(\frac{\lambda}{\mu}\right)^n P_0, \qquad n \geq 1$$

Using the fact that $\sum_n P_n = 1$ or $\sum_{n=0}^{\infty} (\lambda/\mu)^n P_0 = 1$, and $\sum_{n=0}^{\infty} (\lambda/\mu)^n = 1/(1 - \lambda/\mu)$ for $0 < \lambda/\mu < 1$, we find

$$P_0 = \frac{1}{\sum_{n=0}^{\infty} (\lambda/\mu)^n} = 1 \bigg/ \left(\frac{1}{1 - \lambda/\mu}\right)$$

or

(10-15)
$$P_0 = 1 - \frac{\lambda}{\mu}$$

and (10-14) simplifies to

(10-16)
$$P_n = \left(\frac{\lambda}{\mu}\right)^n \left(1 - \frac{\lambda}{\mu}\right), \qquad \text{all } n \geq 0 \qquad (geometric\ distribution)$$

The term, λ/μ, is known as the utilization factor or _traffic intensity_. It is also equal to the probability that the service channel is busy, referred to as P(busy period), or the probability that an arrival will have to wait. (Why?)

From the derivation of expression (10-15), we see that the arrival rate λ has to be smaller than the service rate μ. This is intuitively obvious. If the arrival rate is equal to or larger than the service rate, the queue tends to become longer and longer. The process never reaches a statistical equilibrium, and the above analysis does not apply.

Given the steady state distribution, we can derive a number of important system operating characteristics that may be needed as inputs into the measures of effectiveness of the system.

 (a) The average number of units in the system, denoted by L:

(10-17)
$$L = \sum_{n=1}^{\infty} nP_n = \sum_{n=1}^{\infty} n\left(\frac{\lambda}{\mu}\right)^n \left(1 - \frac{\lambda}{\mu}\right) = \left(1 - \frac{\lambda}{\mu}\right)\frac{\lambda}{\mu} \sum_{n=1}^{\infty} n\left(\frac{\lambda}{\mu}\right)^{n-1} = \frac{\lambda/\mu}{1 - \lambda/\mu}$$

(since $\sum_{n=1}^{\infty} n(\lambda/\mu)^{n-1}$ is the derivative of $\sum_{n=1}^{\infty} (\lambda/\mu)^n = (\lambda/\mu)/[1 - \lambda/\mu]$.)

 (b) The average number of units waiting in the queue, denoted by L_q:

(10-18)
$$L_q = \sum_{n=1}^{\infty} (n-1)P_n = \underbrace{\sum_{n=1}^{\infty} nP_n} - \underbrace{\sum_{n=1}^{\infty} P_n}$$

$$= \quad L \quad - (1 - P_0) = \frac{(\lambda/\mu)^2}{1 - \lambda/\mu}$$

 (c) The _average idle time_ and _average busy time_ of the service facility: An alternative interpretation for the steady state probabilities is that they represent the average fraction of time that the system is in each state. Hence, $P_0 =$

$1 - \lambda/\mu$ is the average fraction of time that no unit is in the system or the average idle time, and $P(\text{busy period}) = 1 - P_0 = \lambda/\mu$ is the average fraction of time that there is at least one unit in the system or the average busy time of the facility.

(d) The average time spent in the system by an arrival, denoted by W: This is the sum of the expected waiting time and the expected service time. In the steady state there cannot be, on the average, more units leaving than entering the system. Thus, the average rate of departure is equal to the average rate of arrivals, or the average rate of units passing through the system per unit time is λ. If on the average a unit spends a time W in the system and the average rate of units passing through the system per unit time is λ, then the product of the two is equal to the average number of units arriving during W. But this must also be equal to the average number of units in the system, i.e.,

(10-19)
$$L = \lambda W$$

This relationship holds for a wide class of arrival and service patterns, other than the Poisson input and exponential service times, as well as for multiserver queues. Solving expression (10-19) for W we obtain

(10-20)
$$W = \frac{L}{\lambda} = \frac{1}{\mu - \lambda}$$

(e) The average waiting time each arrival spends in the queue, denoted by W_q: Of the total time spent in the system, on the average, $1/\mu$ is spent in the service channel. Hence

(10-21)
$$W_q = W - \frac{1}{\mu} = \frac{\lambda}{\mu}\left(\frac{1}{\mu - \lambda}\right)$$

If the average rate of arrivals is λ per time unit, then the average time spent in the system by all units is λW per time unit and the average total waiting time is λW_q.

The operating characteristics of queuing systems tend to be highly sensitive to changes in the utilization factor and rise steeply as this factor approaches 1, as can be seen from Table 10-3. It is important that both λ and μ are estimated with a sufficiently high degree of accuracy.

Table 10-3. *Sensitivity of Operating Characteristics to Utilization Factor for $M|M|1$ Models.*

λ/μ*	0.2	0.4	0.5	0.6	0.7	0.8	0.9	0.95	0.98	0.99
L	0.25	0.667	1.0	1.5	2.333	4.0	9.0	19.0	49.0	99.0
W	1.25	1.667	2.0	2.5	3.333	5.0	10.0	20.0	50.0	100.0

*Assuming $\mu = 1$, λ is the rate of arrival per average service time, and W is in units of average service time.

10-6 EXAMPLES OF M|M|1

Let us return to the firm operating a 10-ton crane truck on a job contracting basis. We shall use one day as our basic time unit. From the data of Table 10-2 we conclude that the input process is Poisson with a mean arrival rate of $\lambda = 1.4$ per day. The average service time amounts to 4 hours or $\frac{1}{2}$ of an 8-hour day, and we assume that the service time distribution is approximately negative exponential with a mean service rate of $\mu = 2$ per day. The $M|M|1$ model applies, and we obtain the following operating characteristics:

$$\text{Utilization factor} = P(\text{crane busy}) = \frac{\lambda}{\mu} = 1.4/2 = 0.7$$

$$\text{Average idle time} = P_0 = 1 - \frac{\lambda}{\mu} = 0.3 \text{ or } 30\% \text{ of the time}$$

$$L = \frac{\lambda/\mu}{1-\lambda/\mu} = \frac{0.7}{1-0.7} = 2.33 \text{ jobs in the system}$$

$$L_q = \frac{(\lambda/\mu)^2}{1-\lambda/\mu} = \frac{0.7^2}{1-0.7} = 1.63 \text{ jobs waiting}$$

$$W = \frac{1}{\mu-\lambda} = \frac{1}{2-1.4} = 1.67 \text{ days in the system}$$

$$W_q = \frac{\lambda}{\mu}\left(\frac{1}{\mu-\lambda}\right) = 0.7(1.67) = 1.17 \text{ days waiting time}$$

$P(\text{more than 1 job waiting for service})$

$= P(\text{more than 2 jobs in the system})$

$= P(n \geq 3) = 1 - P_0 - P_1 - P_2 = 1 - 0.3 - (0.7)0.3 - (0.7)^2 0.3 = 0.343$

Therefore, about one-third of the time, the crane is more than one job behind.

Assume now that customers with job requests do not wait if there is already another job request ahead of them waiting for service. Hence, the maximum number of units in the system will never be more than 2. This particular type of balking is equivalent to the case where the maximum queue length is limited to a finite number. In the *finite queue* case, expressions (10-15) and (10-16) have to be adjusted accordingly. Now, $\sum_n P_n = 1$ only covers the terms for $n = 0, 1,$ and 2, i.e.,

$$\sum_{n=0}^{2}\left(\frac{\lambda}{\mu}\right)^n P_0 = 1$$

Since $\sum_{n=0}^{k}(\lambda/\mu)^n = 1-(\lambda/\mu)^{k+1}/1-(\lambda/\mu)$, this yields   ✳ *very important.*

(10-22) $$P_0 = \frac{1}{\sum_{n=0}^{2}(\lambda/\mu)^n} = \frac{1-(\lambda/\mu)}{1-(\lambda/\mu)^3} = 0.457$$

Note that here we do not need $\lambda < \mu$ any longer. ✳✳

From the result of expression (10-22) we note that if customers balk when there is already another job waiting, the average idle time of the crane increases from 30 percent to almost 46 percent. Furthermore, a certain fraction of jobs will be lost. Customers balk if the system is in state 2. The fraction of time the system is in state 2 is

$$P_2 = \left(\frac{\lambda}{\mu}\right)^2 P_0 = 0.7^2(0.457) = 0.224$$

This is also the fraction of jobs lost. On the average, almost one out of four job requests will be lost.

In general, if the length of the queue is limited to $N-1$ places, then

$$(10\text{-}23) \qquad P_n = \begin{cases} \dfrac{1-(\lambda/\mu)}{1-(\lambda/\mu)^{N+1}}\left(\dfrac{\lambda}{\mu}\right)^n & \text{for} \quad \lambda \neq \mu \\[2ex] \dfrac{1}{N+1} & \text{for} \quad \lambda = \mu \end{cases} \qquad 0 \leqslant n \leqslant N$$

The average number of jobs in the system, as well as the average number of jobs waiting can be computed from the definition of expected values:

$$L = \sum_{n=1}^{N} nP_n \qquad \text{and} \qquad L_q = \sum_{n=1}^{N} (n-1)P_n$$

To find W, we use the same reasoning as for expression (10-19), except that the average arrival rate is no longer λ, but $\lambda(1-P_N)$. Hence, $L = W\lambda(1-P_N)$ and

$$W = \frac{L}{\lambda(1-P_N)}$$

Verify that for our example $L = 0.76$, $L_q = 0.22$, and $W = 0.65$. All are substantially lower than the corresponding result for the unlimited queue case.

Limiting the queue length or arrivals that balk or renege has the following consequences: average idle time increases, average queue length and average waiting time decrease, and a portion of the customers will be lost. It is usually possible to assign costs and benefits to each of these effects. If the queue length is a controllable variable, then the optimal queue length can be determined.

10-7 MULTIPLE CHANNEL MODELS, $M|M|S$

Assume now that the service facility consists of S channels operating in parallel, each having an exponentially distributed service time with mean $1/\mu$. The arrival process is Poisson with rate λ. Arrivals join a single queue and enter the first available service channel on a first-come-first-served basis, as shown in Figure 10-6.

As long as the number of units in the system, n, is less than S, an arrival immediately enters an idle service channel. Since each channel services units at a rate μ, the average service rate is $n\mu$. A queue starts building up only when the number of

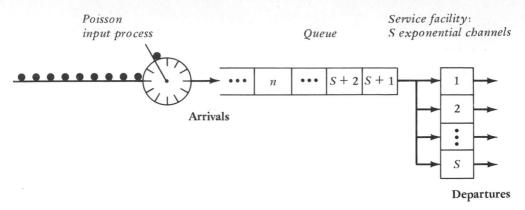

Figure 10-6. *Multiple channel system* M|M|S.

units in the system exceeds S.   At that point all service channels are busy and the average service rate attains its maximum $S\mu$.   If the queue length is unlimited, such a system can only reach a steady state if the arrival rate is less than the maximum service rate, i.e., $\lambda < S\mu$.   For a finite queue length where customers bypass the system once the queue is full, this restriction is not needed.

By the same reasoning as for $M|M|1$ systems (see the explanations after expression (10-11) in Section 10-5), Figure 10-7 allows us to derive the following steady state balance equations, where we have already divided both sides through by h:

$$\lambda P_0 = \mu P_1 \qquad\qquad \text{for}\quad n = 0$$

(10-24) $\quad (\lambda + n\mu) P_n = \lambda P_{n-1} + (n+1)\mu P_{n+1} \qquad \text{for}\quad 0 < n < S$

$$(\lambda + S\mu) P_n = \lambda P_{n-1} + S\mu P_{n+1} \qquad \text{for}\quad n \geqslant S$$

If the maximum queue length is $N - S$, and arrivals bypass the system once the queue is full, then the equation for $n = N$ is

$$S\mu P_N = \lambda P_{N-1}$$

From expression (10-24) we obtain

(10-25)
$$P_n = \begin{cases} \dfrac{(\lambda/\mu)^n}{n!}\, P_0 & \text{for}\quad n < S \\[2ex] \dfrac{(\lambda/\mu)^n}{S!\,S^{n-S}}\, P_0 & \text{for}\quad n \geqslant S \end{cases}$$

Using the property that $\sum_{n=0}^{\infty} P_n = 1$ and

(10-26)
$$\sum_{n=S}^{\infty} \frac{(\lambda/\mu)^n}{S!\,S^{n-S}} = \frac{(\lambda/\mu)^S}{S!} \sum_{n=0}^{\infty} \left(\frac{\lambda}{S\mu}\right)^n = \frac{(\lambda/\mu)^S}{S!(1 - \lambda/S\mu)}$$

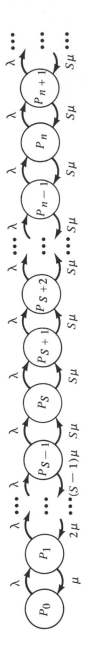

Figure 10-7. *Transition diagram for* M|M|S *system.*

we derive for the unlimited queue case of expression (10-24)

$$(10\text{-}27) \qquad P_0 = \frac{1}{\left(\sum_{n=0}^{S-1} (\lambda/\mu)^n/n!\right) + \left((\lambda/\mu)^S/S!(1-\lambda/S\mu)\right)}$$

All service channels are busy when $n \geqslant S$. Using the results of (10-26), the average fraction of time all service channels are busy or the probability that an arrival will have to wait, $P(\text{busy period})$, is

$$(10\text{-}28) \qquad P(n \geqslant S) = \sum_{n=S}^{\infty} P_n = \frac{(\lambda/\mu)^S}{S!(1-\lambda/S\mu)} P_0$$

and the average number of service channels busy is

$$(10\text{-}29) \qquad E(\text{channels busy}) = \sum_{n=1}^{S-1} nP_n + S \sum_{n=S}^{\infty} P_n = \frac{\lambda}{\mu}$$

It is independent of S. Dividing expression (10-29) by S gives the utilization factor per channel, $\lambda/\mu S$, or the average fraction of time that each channel is busy. Note that expression (10-29) also gives the average number of units in service.

The average number of units waiting in the queue is

$$(10\text{-}30) \quad L_q = \sum_{n=S+1}^{\infty} (n-S)P_n = P(n \geqslant S)\left(\frac{\lambda/\mu}{S-\lambda/\mu}\right) = \frac{(\lambda/\mu)^{S+1}}{SS![1-(\lambda/S\mu)]^2} P_0$$

Note that (10-30) can be expressed in terms of (10-28).

The average number of units in the system is equal to the average number waiting in the queue plus the average number in service:

$$(10\text{-}31) \qquad L = L_q + \frac{\lambda}{\mu}$$

To find the average time in the system, W, and the average waiting time in the queue, W_q, we use the same reasoning as for the single channel model, i.e., $\lambda W = L$. From expression (10-31) we obtain

$$(10\text{-}32) \qquad W = \frac{L}{\lambda} = \frac{L_q}{\lambda} + \frac{1}{\mu} = W_q + \frac{1}{\mu}$$

The last part of expression (10-32) follows from the fact that the average service time per unit is $1/\mu$.

For the case where the queue length is finite, P_0 is obtained from $\sum_{n=0}^{N} P_n = 1$, and all other operating statistics are adjusted appropriately.

Verify that for the same value of the utilization factor λ/μ, $M|M|S$ systems have smaller values for L, L_q, W, and W_q than $M|M|1$ systems.

10-8 A CASE STUDY OF AN $M|M|S$ SYSTEM

In large factories most tools for use by mechanics on the factory floor are stored in one or several tool cribs. How many clerks should man the counter of such a tool crib? This is a classical application of a multiple channel queuing system. The service facility consists of the counter of the tool crib where one or several clerks attend to mechanics requesting tools. Each clerk represents a service channel, working independently and in parallel. The mechanics on the factory floor form the source of arrivals. Although their number is finite, it is sufficiently large that the fraction of mechanics waiting for service or being served represents a negligible portion of the total population. If their number were relatively small such that the arrival rate would vary as a function of the number of mechanics at the tool crib, the model of the preceding section would not be suitable.

In the particular study on which this example is based (G. Brigham, "On a Congestion Problem in an Aircraft Factory", *Operations Research,* Nov. 1955), a sample of service times was measured with a stop watch by an observer stationed at the counter. An electrical device was used to record arrival times of mechanics at the counter. The average time between arrivals was found to be 35 seconds, corresponding to an arrival rate of $\lambda = 60/35 = 1.71$ per minute. The average service time amounted to 50 seconds, yielding a service rate of $\mu = 1.2$ per minute. The interarrival time and service time distributions found on this basis were compared to the corresponding negative exponential distributions by means of a Chi-square goodness of fit test and the associated null hypotheses were accepted.

Assuming an unlimited queue length, we need at least two clerks for the steady state analysis of the preceding Section to apply. (Why?) For $S = 2$, we find the following operating statistics:

$$P_0 = \frac{1}{\sum_{n=0}^{1}(1.71/1.2)^n/n! + \left((1.71/1.2)^2/2!(1-1.71/2(1.2))\right)} = 0.167$$

$$1 + 1.425 + 3.532$$

(by expression (10-27)),

i.e., the fraction of time both clerks are idle is 1/6.

$$P(\text{busy period}) = P(n \geqslant 2) = \frac{(1.71/1.2)^2}{2!\,(1-1.71/2(1.2))}0.167 = 0.595$$

(by expression (10-28)),

i.e., the fraction of time both clerks are busy is 59.5 percent. The average number of clerks busy or the average number of mechanics being serviced is

$$E(\text{channels busy}) = 1.71/1.2 = 1.43 \qquad \text{(by expression (10-29)).}$$

The average number of mechanics being serviced or waiting for service is

$$L = 0.595\left(\frac{1.71/1.2}{2-1.71/1.2}\right) + \left(\frac{1.71}{1.2}\right) = 2.92$$

(by expressions (10-30) and (10-31)),

from which we find the average time in the system as

$$W = \frac{L}{\lambda} = \frac{2.92}{1.71} = 1.70 \text{ minutes} \qquad \text{(by expression (10-32)) or 102 seconds.}$$

On the average, a mechanic requesting a tool will wait in the queue

$$W_q = W - \frac{1}{\mu} = 102 - 50 = 52 \text{ seconds}$$

For a working day of $7\frac{1}{2}$ hours or 450 minutes, on the average, 450λ mechanics request tools at the counter. Hence the average total waiting time in the queue by all arrivals is

(number of arrivals)(52) = ((1.71)(450))52 = 770(52) seconds = 11.12 hours/day

whereas the total service time amounts to (number of arrivals) $(1/\mu)$ seconds or $770(50)/3600 = 10.69$ hours/day. If two clerks are at the counter, working a total of 15 hours per day, the total idle time is $15 - 10.69 = 4.31$ hours.

Verify some of the operating characteristics for $S = 3$ and $S = 4$ clerks, summarized in Table 10-4.

For each additional server, the idle time increases by 7.5 hours. On the other hand, the number of mechanics in the system and their waiting time both decrease. Idle time of the servers and waiting time for the mechanics are both costly to the firm. The cost of the servers is monotonically increasing and the cost of waiting time is monotonically decreasing as the number of servers increases. Their total will therefore have a unique minimum for some number (or adjacent numbers) of servers.

Assume that the hourly rate including fringe benefits is $4.00 for clerks and $8.00 for mechanics. Then the total expected cost is lowest for $S = 3$ clerks.

Table 10-4. *Operating Characteristics for* $S = 2$, 3, *and* 4 *Servers.*

Operating characteristic	$S = 2$	$S = 3$	$S = 4$
P_0	0.167	0.229	0.239
P(busy period)	0.595	0.210	0.064
L	2.92 units	1.615 units	1.460 units
W_q	52 sec	6.67 sec	1.23 sec
daily waiting time	11.12 hrs	1.43 hrs	0.26 hrs
daily clerk time	15.0 hrs	22.5 hrs	30.0 hrs
daily service time	10.69 hrs	10.69 hrs	10.69 hrs
daily idle time	4.31 hrs	11.81 hrs	19.31 hrs
daily cost of clerk time at $4.00/hour	$60.00	$90.00	$120.00
daily cost of waiting time at $8.00/hour	$88.96	$11.44	$2.08
Total daily cost	$148.96	$101.44	$122.08

10-9 FINITE CALLING POPULATION

So far the pool of potential customers or the *calling population* was assumed to be infinitely large, such that the input process did not depend on the number of units in the system. For many industrial applications the calling population is finite.

For instance, it may consist of a limited number of machines on a factory floor that may break down. A breakdown represents an arrival, a repair service completion represents a departure. The system is formed, as for other models, by the queue of machines waiting for service and the service facility. Properly working machines are not part of the system. Once a machine has been repaired it re-enters the pool of potential arrivals. Therefore, each arrival decreases the rate of arrivals, and each departure increases the rate of arrivals.

Assume that there are M identical machines, such as looms on a production floor or copying machines in a geographical area. Each machine has a failure rate of λ (e.g., per day). If there are n units in the system (i.e., n units requiring service or being serviced), the calling population consists of the remaining $M-n$ machines, and the total arrival rate is $(M-n)\lambda$. We retain the assumption that for each level of the arrival rate the arrival process is Poisson. Figure 10-8 shows the transition diagram for a single-channel service facility with negative exponential service times.

This yields the following steady state balance equations:

$$((M-n)\lambda + \mu)P_n = (M-n+1)\lambda P_{n-1} + \mu P_{n+1} \quad \text{for} \quad 1 \leqslant n < M$$

$$(10\text{-}33) \qquad\qquad M\lambda P_0 = \mu P_1 \qquad\qquad\qquad \text{for} \quad n = 0$$

$$\text{and} \qquad\qquad \mu P_M = \lambda P_{M-1} \qquad\qquad\qquad \text{for} \quad n = M$$

From these we can find the following steady state results:

$$(10\text{-}34) \qquad\qquad P_0 = \frac{1}{1 + \sum_{n=1}^{M} (M!/(M-n)!)(\lambda/\mu)^n}$$

and

$$(10\text{-}35) \qquad\qquad P_n = \frac{M!}{(M-n)!}\left(\frac{\lambda}{\mu}\right)^n P_0, \qquad \text{for} \quad 1 \leqslant n \leqslant M$$

The average number of units in the system (i.e., waiting for service or being serviced) is

$$(10\text{-}36) \qquad\qquad L = \sum_{n=1}^{M} nP_n = M - \frac{\mu}{\lambda}(1-P_0)$$

The average number of units waiting in the queue is

$$(10\text{-}37) \qquad L_q = \sum_{n=1}^{M} (n-1)P_n = L - (1-P_0) = M - \frac{\lambda+\mu}{\lambda}(1-P_0)$$

For the average waiting time and the average time in the system per service request, we note that the average arrival rate is not λ, but

$$(10\text{-}38) \qquad\qquad \lambda \sum_{n=0}^{M} (M-n)P_n = \lambda\left(M - \sum_{n=1}^{M} nP_n\right) = \lambda(M-L)$$

By analogy to the infinite calling population case, the identity, $L = \lambda W$, now becomes $L = \lambda(M-L)W$. Hence

$$(10\text{-}39) \qquad W = \frac{L}{\lambda(M-L)} = \frac{1}{\mu}\left(\frac{M}{1-P_0} - \frac{\mu}{\lambda}\right) \qquad \text{per service request,}$$

State

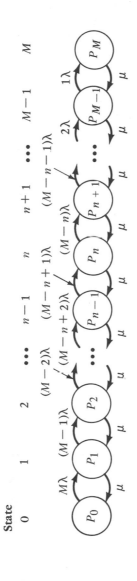

Figure 10-8. *Finite calling population M|M|1 system.*

335

and the waiting time in the queue per service request is as usual $W_q = W - (1/\mu)$. The average total time spent in the system by all arrivals is again obtained as the product of the average arrival rate and the average time in the system, namely, $\lambda(M-L)W$; similarly, the total average waiting time of all arrivals is $\lambda(M-L)W_q$. These results can easily be extended to the $M|M|S$ case with a finite population.

10-10 AN EXAMPLE OF A FINITE CALLING POPULATION

An operator is in charge of four identical machines. On the basis of the first few hours of operation for a new production run (after the operator has become thoroughly familiar with the process), the production engineer estimates that, on the average, each machine requires the operator's attention about 6 times per hour; and the operator takes, on the average, 2 minutes to service a machine. Both the interarrival and service time patterns seem to follow approximately negative exponential distributions. Can one operator properly handle four machines, or is the total machine down time excessively large? Expressing the arrival and service rates on an hourly basis, we obtain $\lambda = 6$, $\mu = 60/2 = 30$, and $\lambda/\mu = 0.2$. The term P_0 is the average idle time of the operator. In this case it is

$$P_0 = \frac{1}{1 + (4!/3!)\,0.2 + (4!/2!)\,0.2^2 + (4!/1!)\,0.2^3 + (4!/0!)\,0.2^4} = 0.398$$

(by expression (10-34))

The operator is idle about 40 percent of the time, waiting for machines to require service. From this result we can find P_n, the fraction of time that n machines require service.

$$P_1 = \frac{4!}{3!}0.2(0.398) = 0.319, \qquad P_2 = 0.191, \qquad P_3 = 0.077, \qquad P_4 = 0.015$$

(by expression (10-35))

These fractions drop off fairly quickly. The average number of machines being serviced or waiting for service is

$$L = 4 - \frac{30}{6}(1 - 0.398) = 0.990 \qquad \text{(by expression (10-36))}$$

On the average, only one machine is down and three are working. The average time per service request in the system, W, also represents the average down time per machine per service request:

$$W = \frac{0.99}{6(4 - 0.99)} = 0.0548 \text{ hours} \qquad \text{(by expression (10-39))}$$

or about 3.3 minutes per service request. During one hour of operation, the average number of arrivals is $6(4 - 0.99) = 18.06$ (by expression (10-38)). Hence the total down time per hour for all four machines taken together is 18.06(0.0548) = 0.99 hours or 59.4 minutes. Of this time, $18.06W_q = 18.06[0.0548 - (1/30)] = 0.388$ hours, or 23.3 minutes are spent waiting for service. So, on the average, a fraction of (0.388/4) = 0.097, or 9.7 percent of the productive capacity of all machines is lost as down time waiting for the operator.

10-11 QUEUING TABLES AND GRAPHS

The computations of operating characteristics are often extremely time consuming. Since they all depend on a small number of parameters, λ, μ, S, N, and M, a number of extensive tables and graphs have been published for the most commonly used operating characteristics. Some important ones are:

Peck, L. G. and R. N. Hazelwood. *Finite Queuing Tables*. N.Y.: Wiley, 1958.
Lists P_n for $M \mid M \mid S$ queues with finite calling population.

Bowman, E. H. and R. B. Fetter, ed. *Analysis of Industrial Operations*, Homewood, Ill.: Irwin, 1959.
(1) Graphs of μW_q versus λ/μ for $M \mid M \mid S$ queues (reprinted from T. M. Manglesdorf, "Waiting Line Theory applied to Manufacturing Problems);
(2) Graphs of optimum number of machines assigned to a service crew as a function of machine down cost and labor cost.

Bhat, U.N. "Two Measures of Describing Queue Behavior", *Operations Research*, March/April 1972.
Most queuing systems are periodically interrupted and then started anew, usually with empty queues. In order to determine whether a steady state analysis can adequately describe the behavior of the system during the major portion of its operation, one should know how fast the system approaches the steady state. Bhat gives extensive tables that show the transient behavior of the system as a function of the number of arrivals.

10-12 NONEXPONENTIAL ARRIVAL AND SERVICE DISTRIBUTIONS

We have seen that Poisson arrivals and negative exponential service time distributions give rise to relatively simple balance equations for the steady state probabilities. For other distributions where the probability of a transition depends on the length of time that the system occupies a given state, the expressions become much more complicated. Yet there are many real-life situations where both the interarrival time and the service time distributions are appreciably different from the exponential.

Although considerable progress has been made to describe the probabilistic behavior of waiting line systems with arbitrary distributions, relatively simple expressions for the operating characteristics have only been derived for $M \mid G \mid 1$ and $M \mid D \mid 1$ systems.

For Poisson input and arbitrary service time distribution with a mean $1/\mu$ and a variance σ^2, we find for infinite calling populations:

$$P_0 = 1 - \frac{\lambda}{\mu}$$

$$L_q = \frac{\lambda^2 \sigma^2 + (\lambda/\mu)^2}{2(1 - \lambda/\mu)}$$

(10-40)
$$L = L_q + \frac{\lambda}{\mu}$$

$$L = \lambda W$$

and

$$W_q = W - \frac{1}{\mu}$$

For a fixed average service rate μ, queue length and waiting times increase as the variance of the service time increases. Thus, the performance of the system can be improved by reducing the variance of the service time. If the variance of the service time can be reduced to zero, then service times become a constant and the operating characteristics are minimized and

(10-41)
$$L_q = \frac{(\lambda/\mu)^2}{2(1 - \lambda/\mu)}$$

Note that this is half as large as for $M|M|1$ systems.

*10-13 ERLANG AND HYPEREXPONENTIAL DISTRIBUTIONS

It is possible to "simulate" a number of arbitrary distributions by a compound system of negative exponential distributions. Suppose that the service consists of k independent tasks that have to be executed in sequence, all with identical negative exponential service time distributions with a mean of $1/k\mu$, and that a service channel can only perform one of these tasks at a time, i.e., only one unit can be held by any service channel at a time. A new unit is only admitted to the service channel after the preceding unit has gone through all k phases, as depicted in Figure 10-9.

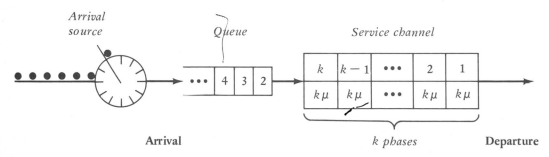

Figure 10-9. *Service channel with Erlang distribution.*

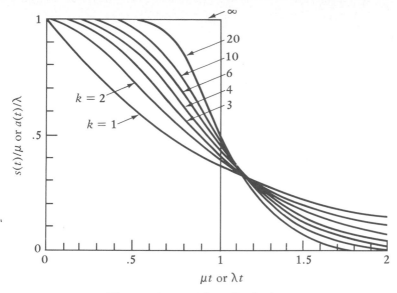

Figure 10-10. *Erlang distributions.*

Since each phase has a mean service time of $1/k\mu$, and there are k phases, the total mean service time over all k phases is $k(1/k\mu) = 1/\mu$, as for an exponential channel, but the total variance over all k phases, given that each phase has a variance of $(1/k\mu)^2$, and the phases are independent, is

$$k\left(\frac{1}{k\mu}\right)^2 = \frac{1}{k\mu^2} < \frac{1}{\mu^2}$$

i.e., the variance is smaller than for an exponential channel.

The resulting service time distribution is known as an *Erlang distribution*, after its Danish inventor. (If we set $k\mu = \mu'$, it can be seen that the Erlang distributions are in fact Gamma distributions with parameters μ' and k.)

Erlang distributions have been used to approximate arbitrary distributions, even though the separate phases have no physical counterpart in reality. By experimenting with the number k, it is often possible to closely match the distribution actually observed. Figure 10-10 depicts a number of Erlang distributions for various values of k.

The state of the system now has to be described not only in terms of the number of units in the system, but also in terms of the number of phases that a unit still has to complete before being discharged from the service channel, i.e., two state variables are needed. Each time a unit enters the service facility, the state variable representing the phase jumps to k and, then, gradually decreases one by one to zero as the unit works itself through the k phases, as shown in Figure 10-11, where P_{nj} denotes the probability of n units in the system with j phases remaining for the unit being served.

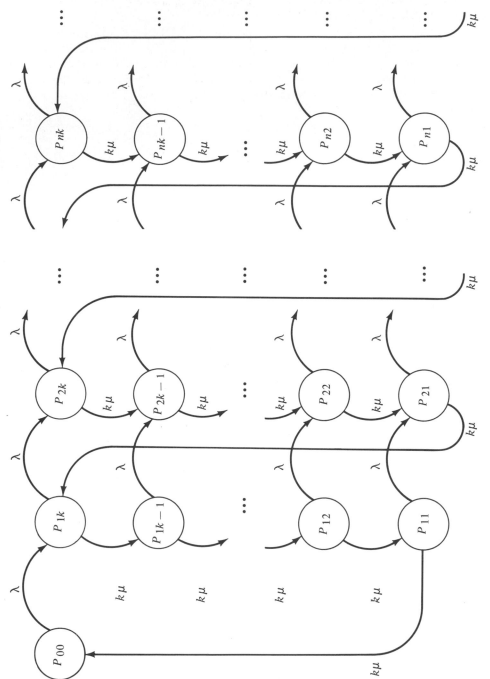

Figure 10-11. *Transition diagram for Erlang distributions.*

Transitions from one state to another are again independent of the length of time a given state has been occupied, and detailed steady state balance equations can be obtained in the usual manner, with expressions (10-40) holding for $\sigma^2 = 1/k\mu^2$.

The same trick can also be applied to simulate interarrival time distributions that have a smaller variance than implied by the Poisson input case. In this instance, we assume that the arrival timing mechanism consists of k exponential phases, each with parameter $k\lambda$. After each arrival, a new unit enters the arrival timing mechanism and works itself through the k phases, at which point it is released and becomes an arrival to the system. Since each phase has an average holding time of $1/k\lambda$, the average interarrival time is again $k(1/k\lambda) = 1/\lambda$, but the variance of interarrival times is $1/k\lambda^2 < 1/\lambda^2$.

Variances larger than for the negative exponential distributions can also be "simulated" by having the service channel or the arrival timing mechanism consist of two branches, which have different discharge rates of $2v\mu$ and $2(1-v)\mu$ and which are entered with probability v and $1-v$, respectively, where $0 < v \leqslant \frac{1}{2}$. The mean holding time remains $1/\mu$, but the variance of holding times increases to

$$\sigma^2 = \frac{1}{\mu^2}\left(1 + \frac{(1-2v)^2}{2v(1-v)}\right) > \frac{1}{\mu^2}$$

Such distributions are known as *hyperexponential distributions*. For more detailed treatment of such distributions, the reader is referred to the text by Philip M. Morse, Chapter 5.

EXERCISES

10.1 A coal mine operates its own barge loading port consisting of one berth with automatic railroad unloading facilities.
(a) Past records of barge arrivals over a 200-day interval show the following:

Number of arrivals per day	0	1	2	3	4	5	6
Number of days	18	61	60	37	16	4	4

For what levels of significance would you accept the hypothesis that the input pattern is Poisson? Do you conclude that the Poisson approximation is good enough? What is the average arrival rate per day?
(b) Past records of berth occupancy times for barges show the following cumulative frequencies.

Fraction of working day	0.1	0.2	0.3	0.4	0.5	0.6	0.7	0.8	0.9	1.0
Number of shorter occupancy times	24	42	53	63	75	85	90	94	98	100

The average berth occupancy time is about one-third of a working day. For what levels of significance would you accept the hypothesis that the occupancy times are approximately exponentially distributed with mean 1/3? What is your conclusion?

Hint: To determine the theoretical frequencies for the negative exponential distribution with parameter $\mu = 1/3$, use the property that $P(a \leqslant t < b) = e^{-\mu a} - e^{-\mu b}$. The value of e^{-t} can be obtained from tables of the exponential function.

10.2 Consider exercise 10.1 again. Assuming that the average daily arrival rate is 2, and occupancy times can be taken as the service times for loading barges with a mean time of one-third day:

(a) Determine the steady state probabilities for this queuing system.

(b) What fraction of time is the berth empty? busy?

(c) What is the average number of barges waiting to be loaded?

(d) What is the average waiting time per barge arrival?

10.3 The mine management of exercise 10.1 considers installing new rail unloading facilities that would accelerate the barge loading process. Two types of facilities are considered: one with an average barge loading time of 0.25 working day and a daily operating cost of $800.00, and the other with an average loading time of 0.2 working day and a daily operating cost of $1000.00. The present system has a daily operating cost of $700.00, and the cost of barge waiting and servicing time is $500.00 per day. Determine the operating characteristics required to compute operating costs for each of the three systems (the present one and the two new alternatives). Which installation has the lowest total daily cost?

10.4 The telephone switchboard of a firm is usually manned by one operator who handles incoming as well as outgoing calls. Incoming calls and outgoing calls both follow Poisson distributions with mean rates of 20 and 16 per hour respectively. The operator can handle, on the average, 60 calls per hour. The distribution of the time to service calls is approximately exponential.

(a) Find the average idle time, and average busy period of the operator, the average number of units in the queue, the average waiting time of calls, and the average total waiting time of outgoing calls per hour.

(b) The firm considers installing new equipment that would allow outgoing calls inside the local area to be made directly. This would reduce the arrival rate of outgoing calls to 8 per hour. The rental cost of this equipment is $240.00 per month (= 200 working hours). The average cost per hour for people requesting outgoing calls is estimated at $9. Should the firm install this equipment.

10.5 A downtown car service station has facilities for a maximum of 4 cars to be serviced or waiting for service on its premises. Past experience indicates that no potential customers join the queue once these four places are filled. The arrival rate of customers is 24 per hour during off-peak hours, and the input process is approximately Poisson. The service times are exponential with a mean of 3 minutes.

(a) Find the steady state probabilities for this system.

(b) What is the average idle time of the attendant?

(c) What is the fraction of customers lost? If the average profit per customer is $0.80, what is the lost profit per hour? What is the average waiting time of an arrival?

10.6   Consider exercise 10.4. An alternative to installing the equipment is to add a second telephone operator. Each operator would have the same average service rate of 60 per hour.

(a) Find the steady state probabilities for $n = 0, 1, 2,$ and 3.

(b) What fraction of time are both operators idle? only one operator idle? both operators busy?

(c) What is the average number of units waiting in the queue, and what is the average waiting time of calls? What is the average total waiting time of outgoing calls per hour?

(d) If each operator costs the firm $30.00 per day and the average cost per hour for people requesting outgoing calls is estimated at $9.00, what is the average total daily cost for 1 and 2 operators?

10.7   Consider exercise 10.5. The service station has two sets of pumps and considers using a second attendant at a cost of $5.00 per hour. His service time distribution would be the same as for the first attendant.

(a) Find the steady state probabilities for this system.

(b) What is the average fraction of time both attendants are idle? only one is idle? both are busy?

(c) What is the average fraction of customers lost now?

(d) If the average profit per customer is $0.80, is it more profitable to have one or two attendants?

10.8   A computer manufacturer has one maintenance and repair crew stationed in a locality to service the 5 computers and ancillary equipment installed in the area. Each computer installation has a Poisson breakdown pattern with mean breakdown rate of 0.125 per day. The time to service breakdowns including travel times is approximately exponential with a mean of $1\frac{1}{3}$ day.

(a) Find the steady state probabilities? What is the average arrival rate?

(b) What is the idle time of the service crew?

(c) What is the average down time per service call? What is the total average daily down time for all five installations?

10.9   Consider the example in Section 10-10. Determine the average number of machines down, the average down time per service call, the total average down time per hour for all machines for 3, 4 and 5 machines supervised by one operator. If the firm operates 60 machines of this type, each operator has a cost per hour of $6.00, and the lost profit per hour of down time per machine is $20.00, what is the optimal number of machines supervised by each operator?

10.10   Barges arrive at a river dam lock system at an average rate of 4 per hour. Each lock deals with traffic in only one direction to reduce the danger of collisions. The arrival pattern is approximately Poisson. The time to enter a barge into the lock, raise the barge, vacate the lock, and lower the water level in the lock is approximately normally distributed with a mean of 10 minutes and a standard deviation of 3 minutes. Using expressions (10-40)—

(a) Find the average busy time of the lock.

(b) Find the average number of barges waiting to be raised and the average waiting time per service request.

(c) If by redesigning the water valve system the standard deviation of service times can be reduced to 1 minute, by how much would this reduce average waiting time per service request?

10.11   Consider the service station problem in exercise 10.5. Assume now that customers balk (i.e. refuse to join the queue) in the following manner: All customers join if fewer than 2 cars are in the service station. If 2 cars are in the service station, only 75 percent of potential customers decide to join. If 3 cars are in the service station only 50 percent join, and if 4 cars are in the station, no additional customers join. Arrival and service distributions are otherwise unchanged.

(a) Construct a transition diagram for this system and attach transition rates to each arrow.

(b) Derive the state balance equations on the basis of this diagram. Find the steady state probabilities.

(c) What is the average idle time of the attendant? What is the average number of customers lost?

(d) What is the average number of customers waiting for service? What is the average waiting time per customer?

10.12   An operator supervises two identical machines. Each has an arrival rate of λ per hour, with negative exponential interarrival times. Service times follow an Erlang distribution with $k = 2$ phases and a mean service time of $1/\mu$.

(a) Construct a transition diagram for this system and attach transition rates to each arrow.

(b) Derive the state balance equations on the basis of this diagram for $\lambda = 1$ and $\mu = 2$. Find the steady state probabilities.

(c) What is the average idle time of the operator? What is the busy time?

(d) What is the average number of machines down (= being serviced or waiting for service)? What is the average arrival rate? What is the average down time per service request? What is the average total down time per hour for both machines?

REFERENCES

The literature on queuing theory is extermely large. The journal *Operations Research* has fromt he start devoted a substantial portion of its space to queuing problems. The reader is also referred to Chapter 15 on Simulation.

Bhat, U. N. "Sixty Years of Queuing Theory", *Management Science*, 15, Feb. 1969. Reviews the major strides taken by queuing theory. Refutes the accusation that the systems solvable mathematically are of little practical use, includes an extensive bibliography.

Cooper, Robert B. *Introduction to Queuing Theory*. New York: Macmillan, 1972. A text of intermediate difficulty for students with an engineering background, with the majority of the examples taken from traffic engineering and telephone operations.

Edie, Leslie C., "Traffic Delays at Toll Booths", *Operations Research*, Vol. 2, May 1954 (reprinted in C. W. Churchman *et. al.*, *Introduction to O.R.*, Wiley, 1957, Chapter 15). A complete case study of the Port of New York Authority toll booth operations.

Howard, Ronald A. *Dynamic Programming and Markov Processes*. Cambridge, Mass.: MIT Press, 1960. Chapter 8 deals with continuous-time Markovian decision processes and shows how the techniques discussed in Chapter 9 of this text can be adapted to such problems which cover some queuing systems.

Jaiswal, N. K. *Priority Queues.* New York: Academic Press, 1968. A text addressed to the reader interested in research into queues. It assumes familiarity with queuing theory in general and deals with a special class of queuing problems where arrivals belong to priority groups. Only for the reader well versed in mathematics.

Koenigsberg, E. "On Jockeying in Queues", *Management Science*, 12, Jan. 1966. Jockeying is the switching of waiting customers from one queue to another in anticipation of shorter delays. The paper considers several types of jockeying and shows that some are equivalent to simpler systems with no jockeying.

Lee, A. M. *Applied Queueing Theory.* New York: Macmillan, 1966. Contains some interesting case histories to apply queuing theory to practical problems.

Maaloe, Erik. "Approximation Formulae for Estimation of Waiting-Time in Multiple Channel Queueing System", *Management Science*, 19, Feb. 1973. Shows how the waiting time in a multiple channel system with Erlang service time distribution can be approximated as a fraction of the corresponding single channel system.

Morse, Philip M. *Queues, Inventories, and Maintenance.* New York: Wiley, 1958. An excellent text although somewhat outdated now, at an intermediate level. Chapters 1–5, 10, and 11 are introductory.

Newell, G. F. *Applications of Queueing Theory.* London: Chapman and Hall, 1971. The author takes a novel approach to queueing based on graphical methods of representation, deterministic fluid approximations, and diffusion approximations. His aim is to suggest approximate solutions to real problems which typically can neither be formulated nor solved accurately, rather than giving a survey of known solutions to hypothetical situations. Particular attention is given to systems that have the time dependent characteristics of rush-hour behavior. The book is written for students in engineering, particularly transportation engineering.

Panico, Joseph A. *Queuing Theory.* Englewood Cliffs, N.J.: Prentice-Hall, 1969. Although a somewhat poorly written text, it contains some interesting real-life case studies, including some using simulation.

Prabhu, N. U. *Queues and Inventories.* Wiley, New York, 1965. Classical treatment of queues using transforms. A very complete text, but intended for the advanced student, fairly demanding mathematically.

11

Classical Optimization Methods with Applications to Inventory Control

Many problems in operations research, particularly in inventory control, involve nonlinear functions in only a few decision variables, where the classical methods of continuous and discrete calculus may be powerful enough for finding the optimal solution. In this chapter, we start by briefly reviewing the classical approach, using differential calculus, for finding unconstrained extreme values of differentiable functions in one or several variables. Life will then become progressively more difficult as we introduce constraints and derive the famous Kuhn-Tucker conditions for a constrained optimum. Chapters 12, 13, and 14 will explore more recent and more powerful methods for solving classes of nonlinear optimization problems subject to constraints.

In parts this chapter will be somewhat uneven and seemingly arbitrary in its coverage, as we shall discuss mainly those aspects of classical optimization that may not be fully covered in an elementary text on differential calculus. All examples used deal with inventory control models of various degrees of sophistication.

We assume that you are familiar with the basic concepts and operations of differential calculus, in particular, differentiation and partial derivatives of simple polynomials. Some of the models presented are stochastic in the sense that the demand for the products stocked are assumed to be random variables. Thus you should be able to deal with probability distributions of continuous random variables, such as the normal distribution, the negative exponential and uniform distributions, and their expected values, as well as the distribution of functions of random variables. The essential concepts of probability used are reviewed in Sections B-2, B-4, and B-5 of Appendix B. We also urge you again to study briefly several parts of Chapter 1, in particular the abbreviated case study in Section 1-9, the formulation of the most basic inventory model—the EOQ model—in Section 1-11, the derivation of the solution to this model in Section 1-14, and the sensitivity analysis on this model in Section 1-15. This review will put you into the appropriate frame of mind needed to benefit fully from the discussion presented in this chapter.

11-1 OPTIMIZATION OF DIFFERENTIABLE FUNCTIONS OF ONE VARIABLE

Let f be a function in the variable x defined over the interval $a \leqslant x \leqslant b$, with first and second order derivatives, and let $f(x)$ be the value of the function evaluated at the point x. Suppose f assumes an *extreme value*—a *maximum* or a *minimum*—at the point x_0 in the interval from a to b (denoted as $[a,b]$). Let x be any other points in the interval $[a,b]$.

LOCAL MAXIMUM

The function f has a local or relative maximum at x_0, if and only if

(11-1) $f(x) \leqslant f(x_0)$

for all x in some neighborhood of x_0 in the interval $[a,b]$ (i.e., there exists a $\varepsilon > 0$ so that the inequality holds for all x in $[a,b]$ and for $0 < |x - x_0| < \varepsilon$).

GLOBAL MAXIMUM

The function f has a global or absolute maximum at x_0 if (11-1) holds for all x in the interval $[a,b]$.

If expression (11-1) holds with strict inequality, i.e., $f(x) < f(x_0)$, then x_0 is a *strict maximum*.

For a minimum of f, the inequality in expression (11-1) is reversed, i.e.,

(11-1A) $f(x) \geqslant f(x_0)$

The function f in Figure 11-1 has local maxima at x_2, x_4, and a, with x_4 being the global maximum; x_1, x_3, and b are local minima, with x_3 being the global minimum. Maxima correspond to the hilltops. The global maximum is the highest hilltop in the range considered. All other hilltops are local maxima. Minima correspond to the valley floors. The global minimum is the lowest of all the valley floors, whereas all other valley floors represent local minima in the range considered.

Consider again the definition of a maximum in expression (11-1) in conjunction with Figure 11-1. As we move from left to right toward the hilltop at x_2, we are going uphill. In geometric terms the slope of the hillside looking toward x_2 is positive for points to the left of x_2. If we proceed to the right past the hilltop at x_2, we are going downhill, i.e., the slope is now negative for points to the right of x_2. As we go past x_2, the slope has to change from positive to negative. At the hilltop itself the slope was horizontal or zero.

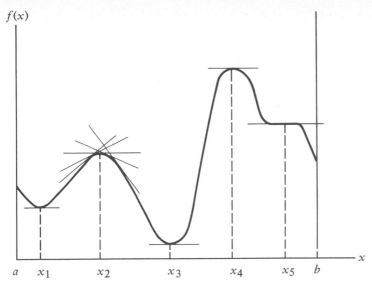

Figure 11-1. *Stationary points.*

In mathematical terms, the slope of a function f is given by its first derivative, denoted by $df\,(x)/dx = f'(x)$. Again, let us denote the hilltop by $f(x_0)$ as in (11-1). To the left of x_0, as we have just seen, the slope is positive (or at least zero), so $f'(x) \geqslant 0$, whereas to the right of x_0 the slope is negative (or at most zero), so $f'(x) \leqslant 0$. Unless x_0 coincides with one of the endpoints, a or b, the derivative thus changes from negative to positive as x increases through x_0. Therefore, at x_0 the derivative must be zero. Any point at which $f'(x) = 0$ is called a *stationary point*.

Analogous reasoning shows that if the function f assumes a local or a global minimum at a point x_0 its derivative is also equal to zero at x_0, except if x_0 coincides with one of the endpoints, a or b.

**NECESSARY CONDITION FOR AN EXTREME
VALUE OF f**

A necessary condition for the function f to assume an extreme value (a maximum or a minimum) at an interior point x_0 of the interval $[a, b]$ is that x_0 be a stationary point, i.e.,

(11-2) $f'(x) = 0$ at x_0

Unfortunately, the function also has a stationary point at x_5 which is an inflection point of f. A stationary point is therefore not a *sufficient condition* for an extreme value of f. The sufficient condition for a stationary point to yield an extreme value of f can be obtained by examining the Taylor expansion of f around x_0 for h small:

$$(11\text{-}3) \qquad f(x_0+h) = f(x_0) + hf'(x_0) + \frac{h^2}{2}f''(x_0) + R_2$$

where $f'(x_0)$ is the first derivative evaluated by x_0,

$f''(x_0)$ is the second derivative evaluated at x_0,

and, for h small, the remainder term R_2 is less, in absolute value, than the term containing $f''(x_0)$.

At the stationary point x_0 the term containing $f'(x)$ is zero, and h^2 is positive for all values of h, negative or positive. Hence, $f(x_0+h)$ will be less than $f(x_0)$ if $f''(x_0) < 0$, and larger than $f(x_0)$ if $f''(x_0) > 0$.

Let us view this in terms of our previous picture of approaching the hilltop from the left and going past it—assuming the hilltop is, mathematically speaking, "well behaved" (which in layman's language means round and smooth). As we approach from the left, the slope which is positive on that side becomes less and less steep until it reaches zero at x_0. To the right of x_0, the slope becomes negative and becomes steeper and steeper. Mathematically speaking, the slope is decreasing as we go through x_0 from left to right.

This situation is just reversed at the valley floor—the slope is increasing as we go from left to right through x_0. The rate of change of the slope corresponds to the second derivative of the function f. If the slope is decreasing, $f''(x) < 0$, and if the slope is increasing, $f''(x) > 0$.

SUFFICIENT CONDITION FOR AN EXTREME VALUE OF f

If x_0 is a stationary point, the function f has a maximum at x_0 if $f''(x_0) < 0$ and it has a minimum at x_0 if $f''(x_0) > 0$.

If $f''(x_0) = 0$, we find the first of the higher order derivatives of f which is non-zero at x_0. If the order of this derivative is odd, f has an inflection point at x_0. If the order of this derivative is even, this derivative is substituted for $f''(x_0)$ in the sufficient condition above.

You will have noticed that neither the necessary nor the sufficient conditions allow us to determine whether a stationary point yields a local or a global extreme value of the function f. This has to be determined by evaluating the function at all relevant stationary points as well as at the end points a and b of the interval on x.

Consider again the economic order quantity model (EOQ), discussed in Section 1-11 of Chapter 1. Demand is assumed to occur at a constant rate over time. Periodically, the inventory is replenished by an amount Q. This occurs whenever sales deplete the inventory to zero. The replenishment is assumed to be available instantaneously. Alternatively, the time to execute customer orders is longer than the time needed to replenish inventory (the *inventory lead time*). Given a constant demand rate, the time between successive replenishments is constant. (See Figure 1-5 of Chapter 1.) Under these conditions, the average inventory is equal to $\frac{1}{2}$ of the replenishment size Q. The objective is to determine a value for Q that minimizes the total costs associated with this replenishment policy.

The total annual cost is equal to the sum of inventory holding costs, inventory replenishment costs, and product costs (purchase price or production cost, including any variable transportation or handling charges). The inventory holding cost amounts to c_1 dollars for each dollar invested per year, the ordering cost is c_2 per replenishment, regardless of the size of Q, and the product cost of the goods stored in the warehouse is V dollars per unit. We saw in Section 1-11 that the total annual cost amounts to

(11-4)
$$T(Q) = c_1 V \frac{Q}{2} + c_2 \frac{R}{Q} + VR$$

where R is the annual demand,
$V(Q/2)$ is the average inventory investment, and
R/Q is the number of replenishments per year.

We want to determine for what value(s) of Q this function takes on its minimum value.

By the necessary condition (11-2) we first find the stationary point where $T'(Q) = 0$:

$$T'(Q) = \frac{c_1 V}{2} - \frac{c_2 R}{Q^2} = 0$$

Multiplying through by Q^2 and then solving for Q, we get the well known EOQ formula

(11-5)
$$Q^* = \sqrt{2Rc_2/c_1 V}.$$

Note that the term VR for the annual product cost does not influence the optimal Q^*. This term could be dropped without affecting the result.

If $R = 1200, V = \$8, c_1 = \$0.18/\text{per dollar}$, and $c_2 = \$24$, then expression (11-5) yields

$$Q^* = \sqrt{\frac{2(1200)24}{0.18(8)}} = 200$$

To determine whether this solution represents a minimum, a maximum, or neither, we use the sufficient condition for an extreme value. Taking the second derivative of T, we obtain

(11-6)
$$T''(Q) = \frac{2c_2 R}{Q^3}$$

Substituting $Q = 200$ into this expression, we obtain $T''(Q = 200) = 0.0072$. Since this is positive, T has a minimum at $Q = 200$. In fact, (11-6) will be positive for all $Q > 0$, $c_2 > 0$, and $R > 0$. Hence, T always assumes a minimum at Q^*. There is no need to actually substitute the solution for Q^* into expression (11-6) to determine its sign.

The total annual cost of replenishing inventory in lots of $Q = 200$ (which occurs every $Q/R = 200/1200 = 1/6$ year or 2 months) amounts to

$$T(200) = 0.18(8)\,200/2 + 24(1200)/200 + 8(1200) = \$9888,$$

of which \$9600 represents the annual cost for product value alone.

11-2 A CONSTANT-CYCLE INVENTORY REPLENISHMENT MODEL WITH RANDOM DEMAND

A meat processing firm prepares a batch of spicy sausages every Wednesday for sale by butchers and supermarkets prior to the weekend. The sausages are sold by weight. Any sausages not sold by the weekend, are sold to a petfood manufacturer on Monday. The petfood manufacturer accepts any amount of old sausages. The gross profit (i.e., wholesale price less manufacturing costs) is c_1 dollars per kilogram of fresh sausages sold. The gross loss per kg on sales to the petfood manufacturer (i.e., cost of manufacturing less proceeds) amounts to c_2 dollars. The weekly demand for spicy sausages is a random variable with a probability density function $h(r)$, $r \geqslant 0$, as depicted in Figure 11-2. The objective is to determine the size of the weekly batch, denoted by S, which maximizes the expected total net profit (i.e., gross profit less losses).

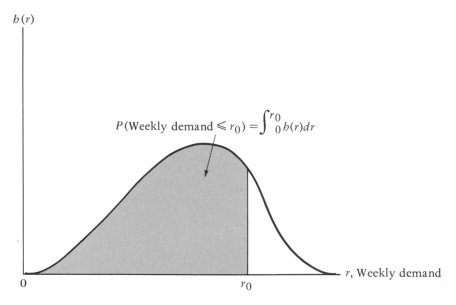

Figure 11-2. *Probability density function of weekly demand for fresh sausages.*

The net profit depends on the demand—a continuous random variable. Hence, the net profit π is a function of a continuous random variable and is, therefore, a random variable itself. If the weekly demand r exceeds S, the entire batch is sold fresh at a net profit of $c_1 S$, or

$$\pi(r) = c_1 S \qquad \text{for all} \quad r \geqslant S$$

If the weekly demand is less than S, an amount r is sold fresh at a gross profit of $c_1 r$, and an amount $S - r$ is sold old at a loss of $c_2(S - r)$. The net profit is

$$\pi(r) = c_1 r - c_2(S - r) \qquad \text{for all} \quad r < S$$

The expected value of the function π of the continuous random variable r is equal to $\int_0^{+\infty} \pi(r) h(r) \, dr$. Hence, for any given value of S, the expected net profit is

(11-7) $$T(S) = \int_0^S [c_1 r - c_2(S - r)] h(r) \, dr + \int_S^\infty c_1 S h(r) \, dr$$

To find the value of S for which expression (11-7) attains a maximum, we need $T'(S) = 0$. For this operation we have recourse to the following formula for differentiating an integral whose limits of integration are functions. Let

$$F(y) = \int_{g(y)}^{k(y)} f(x, y) \, dx$$

Then,

(11-8) $$\frac{d}{dy} F(y) = \int_{g(y)}^{k(y)} \frac{\partial f(x, y)}{\partial y} \, dx + f(k(y), y) \frac{dk(y)}{dy} - f(g(y), y) \frac{dg(y)}{dy}$$

We let $y = S$, $x = r$, and use expression (11-8) separately for each of the two parts in expression (11-7). The result is

(11-9) $$T'(S) = -c_2 \int_0^S h(r) \, dr + c_1 \int_S^\infty h(r) \, dr$$

All other parts are either zero or they cancel. Setting expression (11-9) equal to zero, we see that the optimal batch size S^* has to satisfy

(11-10) $$c_1 \int_{S^*}^\infty h(r) \, dr = c_2 \int_0^{S^*} h(r) \, dr$$

$\int_{S^*}^\infty h(r) \, dr$ is the probability that demand exceeds S^*, or that the marginal unit produced is sold. Hence, the left-hand side of (11-10) is the expected profit from selling the marginal unit produced by regular sales, and the right-hand side represents the expected loss from selling the marginal unit produced to the pet food manufacturer. At the optimum, these two must be equal. This is precisely the basic principle in economics that the optimal output equates marginal revenue and marginal cost.

Using the property that

$$\int_0^S h(r) \, dr + \int_S^\infty h(r) \, dr = 1$$

and rearranging (11-10) we obtain

(11-11) $$\int_0^{S^*} h(r) \, dr = \frac{c_1}{c_1 + c_2}$$

At the optimum, the probability that the weekly demand is at most S^* is equal to the ratio of gross profit over gross profit plus loss per unit.

Let $c_1 = \$0.50$, $c_2 = \$0.10$, and let the weekly demand be normally distributed with a mean of 800 and a standard deviation of 100.   Then

$$\frac{c_1}{c_1+c_2} = \frac{0.50}{0.50+0.10} = .833$$

and from the tables of the normal distribution we find that

$$P(\text{weekly demand} \leqslant S^*) = 0.833$$

implies that $S^* \cong 897$.   The optimum weekly batch is almost 900 kg.

The sufficient condition for a maximum is that $T''(S^*) < 0$.   From (11-9) we obtain

$$T''(S) = -(c_1+c_2)\,h(S)$$

Since $h(S) > 0$ for all values of S for a normal distribution, $c_1 > 0$, and $c_2 > 0$, $T''(S)$ is negative for all values of S.   Hence, expression (11-10) is the optimum S^* maximizing (11-7).

11-3 CONVEX AND CONCAVE FUNCTIONS IN ONE VARIABLE

The function f of the variable x is *convex* if the straight line between any two arbitrary points on its graphs falls on or above the graph of the function, as depicted in Figure 11-3a.   The function is *strictly convex* if the straight line between any two points is always above the graph of the function.

Consider the line segment between the values of the function f on its graph for any two points, x_1 and x_2.   The value of this line segment at the point x, $x_1 \leqslant x \leqslant x_2$, is given by a linear combination of $f(x_1)$ and $f(x_2)$.   Let the proportion of the interval $[x_1, x_2]$ from x_1 to x be λ.   Then

$$\lambda = \frac{x - x_1}{x_2 - x_1}$$

or

$$x = (1-\lambda)x_1 + \lambda x_2$$

with $0 \leqslant \lambda \leqslant 1$, by definition.   The value of the line segment at x is

$$f(x_1) + \lambda(f(x_2)-f(x_1)) = (1-\lambda)f(x_1) + \lambda f(x_2)$$

For a convex function, the value at the point x of the line segment joining any two points x_1 and x_2 on the graph of f will never be less than $f(x)$.   We will use this property as our mathematical definition of convexity.

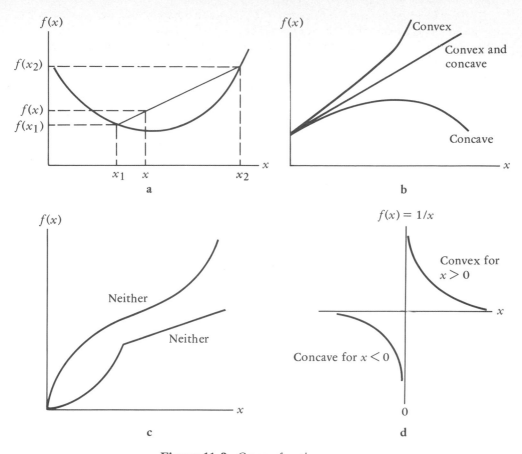

Figure 11-3. *Convex functions.*

CONVEX FUNCTIONS

A function f is convex if and only if for all pairs (x_1, x_2) of x, and for all λ, $0 \leqslant \lambda \leqslant 1$,

(11-12) $\qquad f((1-\lambda)x_1 + \lambda x_2) \leqslant (1-\lambda)f(x_1) + \lambda f(x_2)$

For instance, $f(x) = x^2$ is convex, but $f(x) = R/x$ is not convex for all values of x. However, if $f(x) = R/x$ is only defined for nonnegative values of x for a particular problem, then it is also convex. Suppose $f(x)$ represents the number of production batches, as a function of the size x of the production batches, needed to meet an annual demand of size R. Clearly, x cannot be negative. Therefore, it may be often useful to say that a function is convex between two points, x_1 and x_2, disregarding its shape outside this range.

A function f is said to be *concave* if the line segment joining any two points x_1 and x_2 on the graph of f is never above $f(x)$.

CONCAVE FUNCTIONS

A function f is concave if and only if for all pairs (x_1, x_2) of x and for all λ, $0 \leqslant \lambda \leqslant 1$,

(11-13) $$f((1-\lambda)x_1 + \lambda x_2) \geqslant (1-\lambda)f(x_1) + \lambda f(x_2)$$

You will observe that if f is convex, then $-f$ is concave. Note that a linear function is both convex and concave.

Consider the shape of the convex function in Figure 11-4. It is first decreasing at a decreasing rate (or at most at a constant rate), and then increasing at an increasing rate (or at least at a constant rate). The rate of change of the slope of the function is therefore everywhere positive (or at least nonnegative). However, the rate of change of the slope of the function is equal to its second derivative. Therefore, for differentiable functions

(11-14) $\qquad$ if $\quad f''(x) \geqslant 0$, $\quad$ all x, f is convex.

By analogous reasoning we find that

(11-15) $\qquad$ if $\quad f''(x) \leqslant 0$, $\quad$ all x, f is concave.

Note the strong analogy between these two properties and the sufficient conditions for an extremum of f.

In economic terms, if f is a cost function, then expression (11-14) corresponds to the case of *increasing marginal cost*, and if f is a profit function, then expression (11-15) implies *decreasing marginal return*.

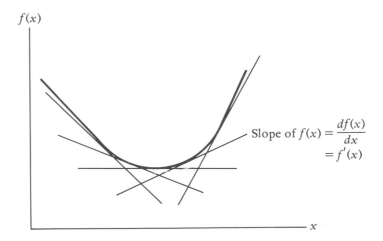

Figure 11-4. *Convex differentiable functions.*

The graphical representation of convex and concave functions reveals that these functions can have one stationary point at most, if one exists. The implications of this property in terms of finding the global optimum of a function are evident.

GLOBAL OPTIMA

CONVEX FUNCTIONS   **CONCAVE FUNCTIONS**

(i) GLOBAL MINIMUM

(i) At a stationary point if one exists;   (i) At one of the end points.
otherwise at one of the end points.

(ii) GLOBAL MAXIMUM

(ii) At one of the end points.   (ii) At a stationary point if one exists;
otherwise at one of the end points.

The sum of convex (concave) functions is also convex (concave), i.e., if $f_1, f_2, \ldots, f_n$ are convex (concave) functions in x, then the function defined by

$$(11\text{-}16) \qquad f(x) = \sum_i a_i f_i(x), \qquad \text{all} \quad a_i \geqslant 0$$

is also convex (concave). This is a very useful property since it allows us to determine whether a function consisting of the sum of several parts is convex or concave by considering each part separately.

Let us now apply these concepts to the sausage example in Section 11-2. The total expected net profit to be maximized is

$$(11\text{-}17) \qquad T(S) = \int_0^S \left[c_1 r - c_2 (S-r) \right] h(r)\, dr + \int_S^\infty c_1 S h(r)\, dr$$

with a stationary point defined by (11-10). Does this stationary point yield a global maximum? To answer this question we determine whether the function T is concave in S. Since we are dealing with a differentiable function we use expression (11-15). To demonstrate the use of the property summarized by expression (11-16), let us separate T into the two parts, multiplied by nonnegative constants c_1 and c_2.

$$(11\text{-}18) \qquad T_1(S) = \int_0^S r h(r)\, dr + \int_S^\infty S h(r)\, dr$$

and

$$T_2(S) = \int_0^S - (S-r) h(r)\, dr$$

Then, since $h(r) \geqslant 0$ for all probability distributions,

$$(11\text{-}19) \qquad T_1''(S) = -h(S) \leqslant 0, \qquad \text{for all} \quad S \geqslant 0$$

and

$$(11\text{-}20) \qquad T_2''(S) = -h(S) \leqslant 0, \qquad \text{for all} \quad S \geqslant 0$$

Therefore, each part of T is concave, and for $c_1, c_2 \geqslant 0$, their sum is also concave. S^* obtained from expression (11-10) is the global maximum.

To test your understanding, determine whether T in expression (11-4) is concave or convex in Q. What does your answer imply in terms of finding a global optimum?

11-4 PRICE-BREAKS—AN EXAMPLE OF A DISCONTINUOUS FUNCTION

Consider again the economic order quantity model discussed in Section 11-1. The total annual cost amounts to

(11-21)
$$T(Q) = c_1 V \frac{Q}{2} + c_2 \frac{R}{Q} + VR$$

The minimum of T occurs at

(11-22)
$$Q^* = \sqrt{2Rc_2/c_1 V}$$

Recall again that the annual product cost, VR, has no influence on the optimal value of Q.

Assume now that the unit product cost is a discontinuous function of the replenishment size Q, as shown in Figure 11-5.

The unit price for the product depends on the size of the replenishment order. For any order quantity Q less than B_1, the unit price is V_0 and the total annual product cost amounts to $V_0 R$. If the order quantity is increased to a value of B_1 or more, but less than B_2, the unit price decreases to V_1 for all units purchased, and the total annual product cost decreases to $V_1 R$, etc. Under these conditions, the total annual cost in expression (11-21) has to be modified as follows:

(11-23) $$T(Q) = c_2 \frac{R}{Q} + \begin{cases} c_1 V_0 (Q/2) + V_0 R & \text{for} \quad Q < B_1 \\ c_1 V_1 (Q/2) + V_1 R & \text{for} \quad B_1 \leqslant Q < B_2 \\ c_1 V_2 (Q/2) + V_2 R & \text{for} \quad Q \geqslant B_2 \end{cases}$$

Figure 11-6 depicts expression (11-23) graphically.

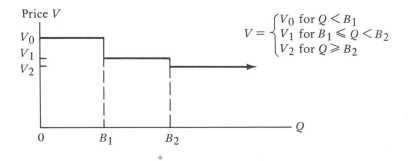

$$V = \begin{cases} V_0 \text{ for } Q < B_1 \\ V_1 \text{ for } B_1 \leqslant Q < B_2 \\ V_2 \text{ for } Q \geqslant B_2 \end{cases}$$

Figure 11-5. *Price-breaks.*

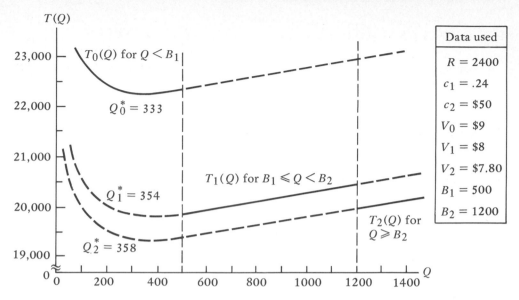

Figure 11-6. *Total annual costs for price-break model.*

Applying the necessary conditions for a minimum to expression (11-23), we derive again expression (11-22) for each segment of (11-23). However, the stationary point Q^* so derived for a given segment may not fall into the corresponding range of Q for which this segment is defined. If this occurs, it has to be discarded as not defined. Furthermore, since the annual product cost is a constant for each segment, it has no influence on where the stationary point is located. Finally, the global minimum may occur at one of the points of discontinuity in (11-23). The way out of this confusion is to evaluate (11-23) for all stationary points which fall into their proper segments, and also evaluate (11-23) at all points of discontinuity. The optimal Q^* is that value of Q which has the lowest $T(Q)$ from among all the $T(Q)$ values so evaluated. In many instances this approach can be refined to reduce the number of points evaluated by exploiting the shape of the function.

For the data shown in Figure 11-6 we obtain the following results:

Range	Q^* from (11–23)	Status	$T(Q)$
$Q < 500$	$Q_0^* = 333$		\$22,320
$500 \leqslant Q \leqslant 1200$	$Q_1^* = 354$	outside range	—
$Q \geqslant 1200$	$Q_2^* = 358$	outside range	—
$Q = 500$			\$19,920
$Q = 1200$			\$19,943

$Q = 500$ has the lowest annual cost and is, thus, the optimal order quantity.

11-5 DIFFERENTIABLE FUNCTIONS OF TWO VARIABLES

Optimization of functions of two decision variables warrants separate discussion not only because there are many practical applications, but also because the principles of classical optimization for several decision variables can best be demonstrated in terms of the two-variable case. Let f be a function in the variables x and y defined over some region R. Following the one-variable case, the function has a maximum at (x_0, y_0) if

$$(11\text{-}24) \qquad f(x_0, y_0) \geqslant f(x, y), \qquad \text{all } x, y \text{ in some neighborhood of } (x_0, y_0)$$

This maximum will be a global maximum if expression (11-24) holds for all values of (x, y) in R. It is a local maximum if (11-24) holds for all values around a neighborhood of (x_0, y_0). Geometrically, a maximum corresponds to a hilltop—this time viewed in three dimensions. For a minimum, the inequality in (11-24) is reversed.

As in the one-variable case, the necessary condition for f to have an extreme value at (x_0, y_0) is that (x_0, y_0) be a stationary point, unless the maximum occurs on the boundary of R.

NECESSARY CONDITION FOR AN EXTREME VALUE OF f

A necessary condition for the function f in x and y to assume an extreme value at (x_0, y_0) in the interior of R is that

$$(11\text{-}25) \qquad\qquad f_x = 0 \quad \text{and} \quad f_y = 0 \quad \text{at } (x_0, y_0)$$

where $\quad f_x = \dfrac{\partial f}{\partial x} \quad$ and $\quad f_y = \dfrac{\partial f}{\partial y}$

From the Taylor expansion of f around (x_0, y_0), we obtain the sufficient conditions for a maximum or a minimum.

SUFFICIENT CONDITIONS FOR AN EXTREME VALUE OF f

The stationary point (x_0, y_0) of the function f evaluated at (x_0, y_0) is a maximum if

$$(11\text{-}26) \qquad\qquad f_{xx} < 0 \quad \text{and} \quad f_{xx} f_{yy} - f_{xy}^2 > 0$$

It is a minimum if

$$(11\text{-}27) \qquad\qquad f_{xx} > 0 \quad \text{and} \quad f_{xx} f_{yy} - f_{xy}^2 > 0$$

It is neither if

$$(11\text{-}28) \qquad\qquad f_{xx} f_{yy} - f_{xy}^2 < 0$$

where $\quad f_{xx}, f_{yy},$ and f_{xy} are the second order partial derivatives of f.

For functions in $n > 2$ variables, the necessary conditions require that the partials of f with respect to each variable are equated to zero, and the sufficient conditions generalize to the evaluation of the $(n \times n)$ Hessian matrix at the stationary point considered. For further details see the text by Teichroew, pp. 547–548, listed among the references to this chapter.

11-6 AN INVENTORY CONTROL MODEL WITH SPECIAL PRODUCTION RUNS TO MEET LARGE DEMANDS

SLO, Inc. produces some of its superior lubricating oils by a batch process. The firm has the policy of shipping all customer orders on the third day after receipt of the order. This is also the time needed to schedule and complete a production batch for these products. Therefore, no safety stock is needed, since it is always possible to meet the demand of any customer by scheduling a production batch if the inventory level is less than the amount of customer orders received but not yet delivered. Figure 11-7 shows a typical probability distribution for the daily demand of most of the fast-selling lubricating oils. There are many days when demand is small or zero and few days when it is very large.

SLO's policy is to ship customer orders for a product from inventory during those days where the demand for that product is small. However, on days when the demand is large, a special production batch is scheduled for the exact amount of that day's demand. This batch is ready in time for delivery three days later. The second

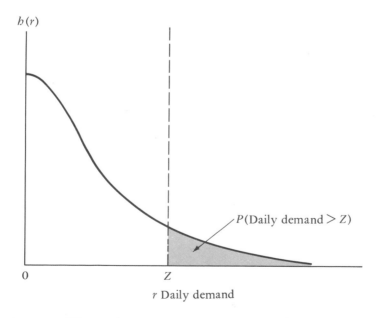

Figure 11-7. *Typical daily demand distribution.*

mode of operation provides substantial savings in handling costs, since the product has to be handled only once, namely, from the production plant to the shipping docks. If demand is met from inventory, the product is handled twice, first from the production plant to the inventory location and then from there to the shipping docks. Figure 11-8 is a flow diagram of the decision process.

For technical reasons it is not possible to produce jointly for inventory and for direct shipment to the customers. The problem consists of finding values for the cutoff point Z and the inventory replenishment quantity Q that minimize the total expected annual cost. Products stored in inventory incur a holding cost of c_1 dollar

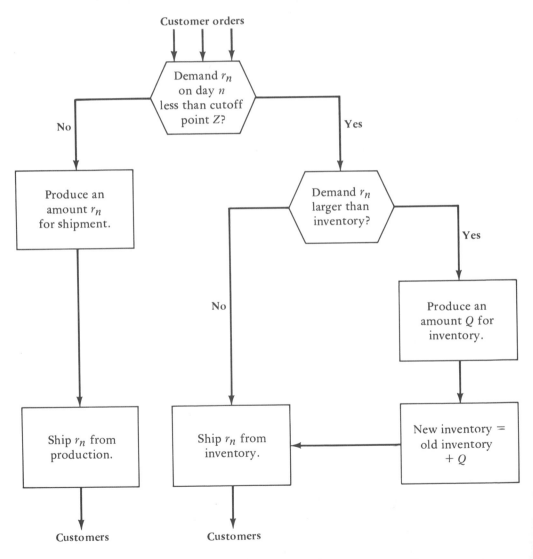

Figure 11-8. *Decision process of two-parameter policy.*

per dollar invested per year. Each production batch results in a set-up cost of c_2 dollars per batch regardless of the amount produced. Each time drums are handled a handling cost of c_3 dollars per unit (drum) is incurred.

Note that for any given product, the inventory is always equal to zero just prior to a replenishment, and Q just after receipt of a batch. If the entire demand were met from inventory, the average daily rate of depleting inventory would be constant and equal to the average daily demand $\int_0^\infty rh(r)\,dr$, where $h(r)$ stands for the probability density function of the daily demand. However, now the demand on any given day is only met from inventory if it is less than Z. So only a portion of the total demand is met from inventory. On the average, given a cutoff point of Z, this portion is

$$(11\text{-}29) \qquad\qquad \int_0^Z rh(r)\,dr$$

This is the average daily rate at which inventory is depleted. Again, it is a constant for any given value of Z. Thus, the inventory behavior over time can also be approximated by the saw-tooth pattern of Figure 1-5 in Chapter 1. By the same reasoning as for the EOQ formula, the average inventory is therefore $Q/2$, and the average annual inventory holding cost is

$$(11\text{-}30) \qquad\qquad c_1 V \frac{Q}{2}$$

where V is the value of the product per unit in inventory.

The total annual expected demand shipped from inventory, given a cut off point of Z, is equal to the number of days per year, N, times expression (11-29). The ratio of this product over Q is the expected number of set-ups for inventory replenishments. Therefore, the expected annual set-up cost for inventory replenishments is

$$(11\text{-}31) \qquad\qquad \frac{c_2\,N \int_0^Z rh(r)\,dr}{Q}$$

Whenever the daily demand is at least Z, a special production batch is scheduled for direct shipment to customers. This occurs with a probability of $P(\text{demand} \geqslant Z) = \int_Z^\infty h(r)\,dr$. In the long-run, this probability is also equal to the average fraction of days where a special production batch is scheduled. The average number of days per year with a special production batch is equal to $N\int_Z^\infty h(r)\,dr$. The expected annual set-up cost for special production batches is therefore

$$(11\text{-}32) \qquad\qquad c_2\,N \int_Z^\infty h(r)\,dr.$$

Every unit of the product has to be handled at least once. This portion of the annual handling cost is a constant which only depends on the total annual demand, and can thus be ignored. We only have to include the incremental handling cost incurred for that portion of the annual demand satisfied from inventory. By expression (11-29) this cost is

$$(11\text{-}33) \qquad\qquad c_3\,N \int_0^Z rh(r)\,dr$$

The total expected annual cost as a function of the two variables Q and Z is equal to the sum of expressions (11-30) to (11-33):

(11-34)

$$T(Q,Z) = c_1 V \frac{Q}{2} + \frac{c_2 N}{Q} \int_0^Z rh(r)\, dr + c_2 N \int_Z^\infty h(r)\, dr + c_3 N \int_0^Z rh(r)\, dr$$

From the necessary conditions (11-25), the minimum of expression (11-34) can be found by solving the partials of (11-34) for Q and Z:

(11-35)
$$\frac{\partial}{\partial Q} T(Q,Z) = \frac{c_1 V}{2} - \frac{c_2 N}{Q^2} \int_0^Z rh(r)\, dr = 0$$

(11-36)
$$\frac{\partial}{\partial Z} T(Q,Z) = \left(\frac{c_2 N}{Q}\right) Zh(Z) - c_2 Nh(Z) + c_3 NZh(Z) = 0$$

where we used formula (11-8) to obtain (11-36). Solving (11-35) for the optimal value of Q, and (11-36) for the optimal value of Z, we obtain

(11-37)
$$Q^* = \sqrt{\frac{2c_2 N \int_0^{Z^*} rh(r)\, dr}{c_1 V}}$$

and

(11-38)
$$Z^* = \frac{c_2 Q^*}{c_2 + c_3 Q^*}$$

No further simplification is possible. Unfortunately, each expression involves the optimal value of the other variable.

How can we find the optimal values of Z and Q from expressions (11-37) and (11-38)? Consider (11-37) as a function of Z, say $Q = G(Z)$, and (11-38) as a function of Q, say $Z = H(Q)$. Figure 11-9 depicts the shape of these functions for a negative exponential demand distribution $h(r) = \lambda e^{-\lambda r}$, where λ is the daily average rate of demand. Note that if Z is so large that the entire demand is met from inventory, expression (11-37) reduces to the EOQ formula, i.e.,

(11-39)
$$Q_0 = \left[2c_2 N \int_0^\infty rh(r)\, dr / c_1 V\right]^{1/2}$$

On the other hand, the optimal Z^* is always less than c_2/c_3. (Explain why.) Thus, both $G(Z)$ and $H(Q)$ are asymptotic.

Provided these functions are well behaved, they can be solved for the optimal values Q^* and Z^* by successive approximations. We guess an initial value for Q, say Q_0 of (11-39). Insert this value Q_0 into expression (11-38), and find a first approximation for Z of Z_1. Next, we substitute Z_1 into expression (11-37) and find a new approximation for Q of Q_1, which in turn is substituted into (11-38) to obtain a second approximation for Z of Z_2. Continuing in this fashion we can approximate

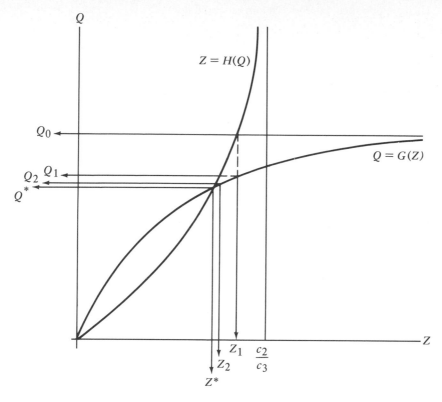

Figure 11-9. *Successive approximations for two-parameter inventory model.*

the optimal values of Z and Q as closely as we wish.   Usually, we would stop this iterative procedure as soon as the differences between two successive values of the two variables become smaller than some arbitrary chosen value.   These successive approximations are shown graphically by the broken line in Figure 11-9 using the following data:

$h(r) = \lambda e^{-\lambda r}$,   for $\lambda = 0.1$ (negative exponential distribution with mean $1/\lambda = 10$)

$N = 250$

$c_1 = 0.2$

$c_2 = \$10.00$

$c_3 = \$0.20$

$V = \$20.00$

Using expression (11-39) to obtain an initial guess for Q, we obtain the following progression of numerical approximations:

Iteration i	Q_i	Z_i
0	111.8	$+\infty$
1	103.6	34.55
2	103.08	33.73
3	103.04	33.67

We arbitrarily stopped the iterations as soon as consecutive approximations differed by less than 0.1 for both Q and Z.

This simple example demonstrates how the necessary conditions for stationary points of functions in more than one variable may easily result in expressions too complex to be solved by analytic methods. It is for such reasons that methods of classical optimization are often impractical from a computational point of view. Unfortunately, the tremendous advances in more powerful methods have so far not produced any general method for finding the global optimum of any arbitrary function in several variables. Some methods work better for some type of mathematical structures, some better for others.

11-7 CONVEX AND CONCAVE FUNCTIONS OF SEVERAL VARIABLES

A cereal bowl represents a typical example of a convex function in two variables. The definition of convexity for functions in two or more variables is a generalization of expression (11-12).

CONVEX FUNCTIONS IN SEVERAL VARIABLES

A function f of the variables $x, y, \ldots,$ and z is convex if and only if for any two points $(x_1, y_1, \ldots, z_1)$ and $(x_2, y_2, \ldots, z_2)$ and all $\lambda, 0 \leqslant \lambda \leqslant 1$,

(11-40)
$$f((1-\lambda)x_1 + \lambda x_2, (1-\lambda)y_1 + \lambda y_2, \ldots, (1-\lambda)z_1 + \lambda z_2)$$
$$\leqslant (1-\lambda)f(x_1, y_1, \ldots, z_1) + \lambda f(x_2, y_2, \ldots, z_2).$$

For differentiable functions of two variables, expression (11-40) is equivalent to

(11-41) $$f_{xx} \geqslant 0, \qquad f_{yy} \geqslant 0,$$

and

$$f_{xx}f_{yy} - (f_{xy})^2 \geqslant 0$$

For concave functions the inequality in (11-40) is reversed and (11-41) becomes

(11-42) $$f_{xx} \leqslant 0, \qquad f_{yy} \leqslant 0,$$

and

$$f_{xx} f_{yy} - (f_{xy})^2 \geqslant 0$$

(For differentiable functions of more than two variables, (11-41) and (11-42) generalize to the $(n \times n)$ Hessian matrix being positive semidefinite for convexity and negative semidefinite for concavity. See the text by Teichroew, p. 547, listed in the references to this chapter.)

Let us now apply this to the problem in the preceding section. If T is convex in Q and Z, then any stationary point found will yield a global minimum. From expressions (11-35) and (11-36) we obtain

$$T_{QQ} = \frac{2c_2 N}{Q^3} \int_0^z rh(r) \, dr$$

$$T_{ZZ} = \left[\frac{c_2 N}{Q} + c_3 N \right] (h(Z) + Zh'(Z)) - c_2 Nh'(Z)$$

and

$$T_{QZ} = \frac{-c_2 N}{Q^2} Zh(Z)$$

T_{QQ} is nonnegative for all $Q, Z \geqslant 0$. T_{ZZ} involves the derivative of the probability density function which for most distributions will be negative for some values of the random variable. Hence, T_{ZZ} may be negative depending on the shape of the distribution, and we cannot conclude that T is convex in Q and Z for all types of probability distributions. However, it can be shown that for a uniform distribution, $h(r) = 1/b, 0 \leqslant r \leqslant b$, T is convex. This is left as an exercise to the reader. (Note however, that T is convex in Q for any given value of Z.)

11-8 CONSTRAINED OPTIMIZATION AND LAGRANGE MULTIPLIERS

So far items stocked in inventory were always optimized individually. This approach is only permissible as long as there are no interactions among the items, such as limited production facilities, limited warehouse space, or necessity for joint ordering of groups of items. If such restrictions are present, then interdependent items will have to be considered jointly.

Consider the case where items compete for a limited amount of funds for inventory investments. The average inventory investment for all n items stocked is not to exceed an amount F. F could be a function of the firm's short-term funds available in the form of bank overdrafts, a line of credit, and/or a fraction of total yearly purchases. The latter would have the effect of forcing the overall inventory turnover to be at least equal to a certain size. If Q_i is the inventory replenishment quantity, and V_i the cost in the warehouse per unit of item i, then it must be true that the average inventory investment, $V_i Q_i/2$, summed over all n items, cannot exceed F, i.e.,

$$(11\text{-}43) \qquad \frac{1}{2} \sum_{i=1}^{n} V_i Q_i \leq F$$

Let R_i denote the annual demand for item i. Let c_1 denote the annual holding cost per dollar invested in inventory, and c_{2i} the fixed ordering incurred whenever item i is ordered. By analogy with the EOQ model of expression (11-4), the total annual cost for all n items is

$$(11\text{-}44) \qquad T(Q_1, Q_2, ..., Q_n) = \sum_{i=1}^{n} \left[\frac{R_i}{Q_i} c_{2i} + \frac{Q_i}{2} c_1 V_i \right]$$

The objective is to find optimal order quantities, $Q_1^*, Q_2^*, ..., Q_n^*$, that minimize expression (11-44) subject to the investment constraint (11-43).

Generalizing the principles of Section 11-5 to the n-variable case, the unconstrained optimum is obtained by setting all first order partial derivatives of (11-44) equal to zero and solving the equations obtained for the n variables:

$$(11\text{-}45) \qquad \frac{\partial T}{\partial Q_i} = -\frac{R_i}{Q_i^2} c_{2i} + \frac{c_1 V_i}{2} = 0, \qquad i = 1, 2, ..., n$$

The unconstrained optimal Q_i^* have the familiar EOQ form:

$$(11\text{-}46) \qquad Q_i^* = \sqrt{\frac{2 R_i c_{2i}}{c_1 V_i}}, \qquad i = 1, 2, ..., n$$

We now require that the solutions to expression (11-46) also satisfy expression (11-43). How should we approach this constrained optimization problem? We do not know *a priori* whether the constraint is binding at the optimal solution. The first step is therefore to find out whether or not this is the case.

CONSTRAINED OPTIMIZATION: STEP 1

Find the optimal values for the decision variables ignoring the constraint and check whether these unconstrained optimal values satisfy the constraint. If they do, the constraint is not active and the optimal solution to the constrained problem is the same as the optimal solution to the unconstrained problem. If the constraint is violated, go to step 2.

If the original constraint is in the form of an equation from the outset, rather than an inequality, step 1 can be skipped.

CONSTRAINED OPTIMIZATION: STEP 2

The constraint is binding and will hold as an equality at the optimal solution. Hence, solve the problem with the constraint in the form of an equality.

To motivate the solution method for minimizing a function subject to an equality constraint, we revert to a two-variable case. We want to minimize the function f in x and y, subject to the equality constraint $g(x, y) = b$. In Figure 11-10 we show *contour lines* for the objective function. Each line traces all combinations of x and y that yield the same value of f. The curve for $g(x, y) = b$ shows all combinations of x and y that satisfy the constraint as an equality. The optimal solution to the constrained problem occurs at the point (x_0, y_0), where a contour line just touches $g(x, y) = b$. This is the lowest value f can assume while still satisfying the constraint. At (x_0, y_0), the slopes of f and g coincide.

The change in f for marginal changes in x and y is given by the total differential

$$df = f_x\,dx + f_y\,dy$$

Along a contour line, $df = 0$. So we find that

$$\frac{dy}{dx} = -\frac{f_x}{f_y}$$

By the same reasoning we also find that

$$\frac{dy}{dx} = -\frac{g_x}{g_y}$$

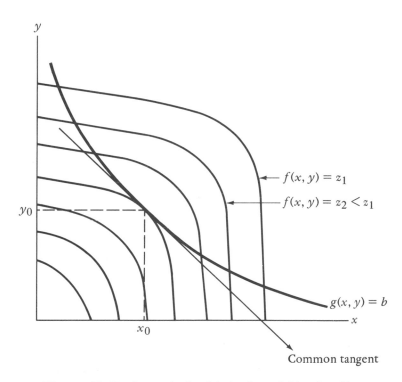

Figure **11-10.** *Constrained minimization of $f(x, y)$ subject to $g(x, y) = b$.*

At the point (x_0, y_0) these two slopes are equal, i.e.,

$$\frac{f_x}{f_y} = \frac{g_x}{g_y}$$

or, by rearranging terms,

(11-47) $$\frac{f_x}{g_x} = \frac{f_y}{g_y}$$

Let the common ratio of expression (11-47) be equal to λ. Hence the optimal values of x and y satisfy the following two equations:

(11-48) $$f_x - \lambda g_x = 0$$

and

$$f_y - \lambda g_y = 0$$

as well as the constraint $g(x, y) = b$. Letting λ become a variable, we can now take advantage of this property and use it to find the optimal constrained values for x and y and the new variable λ by solving the three simultaneous equations:

(11-49)
$$f_x - \lambda g_x = 0$$
$$f_y - \lambda g_y = 0$$
$$g(x, y) = b$$

It turns out that exactly the same set of equations can be generated by considering the unconstrained minimization of the following augmented objective function:

(11-50) $$L(x, y, \lambda) = \underbrace{f(x, y)}_{\substack{\text{original} \\ \text{function}}} + \lambda \underbrace{(b - g(x, y))}_{\text{constraint}}$$

known as the *Lagrangian function*. λ is called a *Lagrange multiplier*. The Lagrangian function for one constraint has one variable more than the original function—the price we must pay for being able to apply methods of classical optimization to such problems.

The stationary points of expression (11-50) are defined by

$$\frac{\partial L}{\partial x} = f_x - \lambda g_x = 0$$

(11-51) $$\frac{\partial L}{\partial y} = f_y - \lambda g_y = 0$$

$$\frac{\partial L}{\partial \lambda} = b - g(x, y) = 0$$

which is exactly the same as the set of equations derived in expression (11-49). (The reader is referred to more advanced texts for the sufficient conditions.)

We are now equipped to perform step 2 of constrained optimization. Combining (11-44) and (11-43) we obtain the Lagrangian function:

$$(11\text{-}52) \quad L(Q_1, Q_2, \ldots, Q_n, \lambda) = \sum_{i=1}^{n} \left[\frac{R_i}{Q_i} c_{2i} + \frac{Q_i}{2} c_1 V_i \right] + \lambda \left[F - \tfrac{1}{2} \sum_{i=1}^{n} V_i Q_i \right]$$

and the following necessary conditions for an optimum:

$$(11\text{-}53) \qquad \frac{\partial L}{\partial Q_i} = -\frac{R_i}{Q_i^2} c_{2i} + \frac{c_1 V_i}{2} - \frac{\lambda V_i}{2} = 0, \qquad i = 1, 2, \ldots, n$$

$$(11\text{-}54) \qquad \frac{\partial L}{\partial \lambda} = F - \tfrac{1}{2} \sum_{i=1}^{n} V_i Q_i = 0$$

Solving each equation (11-53) for Q_i, we obtain

$$(11\text{-}55) \qquad Q_i^* = \sqrt{\frac{2 R_i c_{2i}}{V_i (c_1 - \lambda^*)}}, \qquad i = 1, 2, \ldots, n$$

where λ^* is the value of λ, such that the Q_i^* of (11-55) satisfy (11-54). Viewing (11-55) as functions of λ, and substituting them into (11-43), we see that

$$(11\text{-}56) \qquad F - \tfrac{1}{2} \sum_{i=1}^{n} V_i [2 R_i c_{2i} / V_i (c_1 - \lambda)]^{1/2}$$

is a monotonic decreasing function of λ. Hence there is a unique value $\lambda < 0$, such that (11-53) is satisfied.

Table 11-1 gives the data for an example involving $n = 3$ items.

Table 11-1. *Data for Constrained Optimization Example.*

Item	1	2	3
R_i	2000	8000	4000
V_i	$200	$100	$40
c_{2i}	$150	$200	$100

The inventory holding cost per dollar invested per year is $c_1 = 0.2$, and the average inventory investment should not exceed $28,000.

Step 1. The unconstrained optimal order quantities are:

$$Q_1^* = \sqrt{\frac{2(2000)(150)}{(0.2)\,200}} = 122.5, \text{ or about } 122$$

$$Q_2^* = \sqrt{\frac{2(8000)(200)}{(0.2)\,100}} = 400.0$$

$$Q_3^* = \sqrt{\frac{2(4000)(100)}{(0.2)\,40}} = 316.2, \text{ or about } 316.$$

The average investment required amounts to

$$\tfrac{1}{2}[122(200)+400(100)+316(40)] = \$38{,}520$$

Since this violates the upper limit of $28,000, we go to

Step 2.   The constrained optimal Q_i^* values are found by solving the four equations generated from (11-53) and (11-54).   From (11-56) we find that the optimal λ^* is the solution to

$$\frac{1}{2}\left[200\left(\frac{2(2000)(150)}{200(0.2-\lambda^*)}\right)^{1/2} + 100\left(\frac{2(8000)(200)}{100(0.2-\lambda^*)}\right)^{1/2} + 40\left(\frac{2(4000)(100)}{40(0.2-\lambda^*)}\right)^{1/2}\right]$$

$$= 28{,}000$$

which yields $\lambda^* = -0.1795$.   Inserting this result in (11-53) we find the constrained optimal order quantities as

$$Q_1^* = \sqrt{\frac{2(2000)(150)}{200(0.2+0.1795)}} = 88.91, \text{ or about } 89$$

$$Q_2^* = \sqrt{\frac{2(8000)(200)}{100(0.2+0.1795)}} = 290.38, \text{ or about } 290$$

and

$$Q_3^* = \sqrt{\frac{2(4000)(100)}{40(0.2+0.1795)}} = 229.57, \text{ or about } 230$$

Verify that these values exactly use up the entire $28,000 available.   The total cost of the constrained optimal values is $24,491 versus $15,430 for the unconstrained optimum.   Therefore, the limit imposed on the average inventory investment costs the firm $9,061 per year in the form of higher inventory operating costs.

In this example, the Lagrange multiplier could be determined analytically. There are many problems where this is not so.   In such instances the approach used is to determine the optimal value of λ by a search method.   A systematic approach that is easily programmed for electronic computers is to select two initial values for λ (say λ_0 and λ_1), such that for λ_0 the constraint holds as a $<$ inequality, and for λ_1 as a $>$ inequality.   The next guess for λ is $\lambda_2 = \tfrac{1}{2}(\lambda_0+\lambda_1)$.   If λ_2 forces the constraint to hold as $>$, $\lambda_3 = \tfrac{1}{2}(\lambda_0+\lambda_2)$, otherwise $\lambda_3 = \tfrac{1}{2}(\lambda_2+\lambda_1)$.   Proceeding in this fashion the optimal λ can be approximated as closely as desired.

In theory the method of Lagrange multipliers can be extended to more than one constraint.   The Lagrangian function would include one Lagrange multiplier for each constraint.   Since it is not known *a priori* which constraints are binding at the optimal solution, all possible combinations of binding and slack constraints have to be evaluated.   For two constraints that means solving up to 4 problems: the unconstrained problem, 2 problems with one constraint only, and finally a fourth problem with both constraints included.   For 3 constraints up to 8 problems and for k constraints up to 2^k problems have to be evaluated.   Adding to this the disadvantage of the increased number of variables, the method of Lagrange multipliers is hardly a practical solution method for problems with more than 2 constraints.

11-9 INTERPRETATION OF LAGRANGE MULTIPLIERS

Assume now that the amount of funds is not limited, but that there is an inventory investment cost of α dollars for every dollar invested per year, assessed on the average inventory investment. Added to the total annual cost in (11-44) this gives

(11-57)
$$T(Q_1, Q_2, \ldots, Q_n) = \sum_{i=1}^{n} \left[\frac{R_i}{Q_i} c_{2i} + \frac{Q_i}{2} (c_1 V_i + V_i \alpha) \right]$$

The optimal order quantities are now

(11-58)
$$Q_i^* = \sqrt{\frac{2 R_i c_{2i}}{V_i (c_1 + \alpha)}}, \qquad \text{all } i$$

Comparing (11-58) with expression (11-55) obtained from the Lagrangian function, we see that if we set $\alpha = -\lambda^*$, the two formulas result in exactly the same optimal order quantities. Thus, the optimal value of the Lagrange multiplier can be interpreted as a cost assessed on a scarce resource.

In fact, if we let the scarce resource in the constraint $g(x, y) = b$ increase by a very small amount Δb, then the new optimal value of the Lagrangian function, say L_1, can be approximated in terms of the previous solution L by

(11-59)
$$L_1(x^*, y^*, \lambda^*) \doteq f(x^*, y^*) + \lambda^* [b + \Delta b - g(x^*, y^*)]$$

$$= f(x^*, y^*) + \lambda^* [b - g(x^*, y^*)] + \lambda^* \Delta b$$

$$= L(x^*, y^*, \lambda^*) + \lambda^* \Delta b, \qquad \text{for } \Delta b \text{ small}$$

The marginal change in the optimal value of L for a marginal change in b is proportional to the optimal value of the Lagrange multiplier. Recall that at the optimum solution, $L(x^*, y^*, \lambda^*) = f(x^*, y^*)$. Hence, λ^* can be interpreted in terms of f rather than L. Since b represents a scarce resource, the economic interpretation of this result is:

INTERPRETATION OF OPTIMAL LAGRANGE MULTIPLIERS

The optimal value of the Lagrange multiplier gives the marginal value of the scarce resource.

λ is a function of b. It will change as b changes. Figure 11-11 depicts how $-\lambda$ behaves as a function of the amount of funds available for inventory investment. When funds reach a value of \$38,520, the constraint just ceases to be binding, and the optimal $\lambda = 0$ from there on. (Why?)

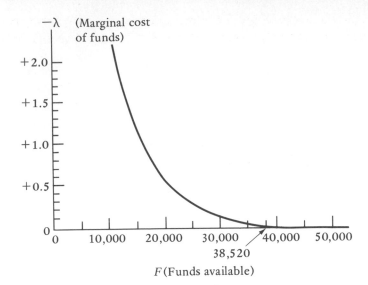

Figure 11-11. *Marginal cost of funds for inventory investment.*

*11-10 KUHN-TUCKER CONDITIONS

In this section we shall formalize the necessary conditions for constrained optimization, known as the *Kuhn-Tucker conditions*, after their founders H. W. Kuhn and A. W. Tucker ("Nonlinear Programming", *Proceedings Second Berkley Symposium on Mathematical Statistics and Probability*, University of California Press, 1951). Consider the following maximization problem, subject to an inequality constraint:

$$(11\text{-}60) \qquad \text{maximize } f(x, y)$$

$$\text{subject to } g(x, y) \leqslant b$$

The Lagrangian function for this problem is

$$(11\text{-}61) \qquad L(x, y, \lambda) = f(x, y) + \lambda\,(b - g(x, y))$$

As we have seen, if the constraint is slack at a maximum, the necessary conditions for a stationary point to expression (11-60) are those of the unconstrained case, which can be stated as

$$(11\text{-}62) \qquad f_x = 0,$$

$$f_y = 0,$$

$$g(x, y) < b$$

If the constraint is binding at a maximum, the necessary conditions are those for the Lagrangian problem with an equality constraint:

(11-63)
$$f_x - \lambda g_x = 0,$$
$$f_y - \lambda g_y = 0,$$
$$b - g(x, y) = 0$$

Since, *a priori* we do not know which case applies, we need necessary conditions that cover both cases. In the preceding section, we defined λ as the marginal change of f with respect to b. For a maximization problem subject to an inequality constraint of the form $g(x, y) \leqslant b$, a marginal increase in b enlarges the feasible region. If the constraint is binding, the maximal value of f increases or, at worst, is unchanged, and, if the constraint is slack, f remains unchanged. In the first instance $g(x, y) = b$ and $\lambda > 0$, in the second instance $g(x, y) < b$ and $\lambda = 0$. These conditions can be combined to

(11-64)
$$\lambda(b - g(x, y)) = 0,$$
$$\lambda \geqslant 0$$

At a maximum, the Lagrangian function L must have a stationary point with respect to x and y, i.e.,

(11-66)
$$\frac{\partial L}{\partial x} = f_x - \lambda g_x = 0,$$
$$\frac{\partial L}{\partial y} = f_y - \lambda g_y = 0$$

and, furthermore, this stationary point must be feasible, i.e.,

(11-67)
$$b - g(x, y) \geqslant 0$$

Expressions (11-64) through (11-67) are the Kuhn-Tucker conditions for a two-variable maximization problem, and are formally derived from the Lagrangian function as

(11-68)
$$\partial L / \partial x = f_x - \lambda g_x = 0,$$
$$\partial L / \partial y = f_y - \lambda g_y = 0,$$
$$\partial L / \partial \lambda = b - g(x, y) \geqslant 0,$$
$$\lambda \, \partial L / \partial \lambda = \lambda(b - g(x, y)) = 0,$$
$$\lambda \geqslant 0$$

An important extension deals with problems in which the variables have to be nonnegative, i.e., the constraints

(11-69) $$x \geqslant 0, \qquad y \geqslant 0$$

are added to problem (11-60).

Initially, we shall consider these conditions just like regular constraints, re-written in the form of $-x \leqslant 0$, $-y \leqslant 0$. The Lagrangian function for this en-larged problem is

(11-70) $\quad L(x, y, \lambda_1, \lambda_2, \lambda_3) = f(x, y) + \lambda_1(b - g(x, y)) + \lambda_2(0 + x) + \lambda_3(0 + y)$

Applying the Kuhn-Tucker conditions for this problem, we obtain

(11-71) $$\partial L/\partial x = f_x - \lambda_1 g_x + \lambda_2 = 0,$$

$$\partial L/\partial y = f_y - \lambda_1 g_y + \lambda_3 = 0,$$

$$\partial L/\partial \lambda_1 = b - g(x, y) \geqslant 0,$$

$$\partial L/\partial \lambda_2 = x \geqslant 0,$$

$$\partial L/\partial \lambda_3 = y \geqslant 0,$$

$$\lambda_1 \, \partial L/\partial \lambda_1 = \lambda_1(b - g(x, y)) = 0,$$

$$\lambda_2 \, \partial L/\partial \lambda_2 = \lambda_2 x = 0,$$

$$\lambda_3 \, \partial L/\partial \lambda_3 = \lambda_3 y = 0,$$

$$\lambda_1 \geqslant 0, \qquad \lambda_2 \geqslant 0, \qquad \lambda_3 \geqslant 0$$

We now eliminate λ_2 and λ_3. Since both are nonnegative, $\partial L/\partial x$ and $\partial L/\partial y$ become

(11-72) $$\frac{\partial L}{\partial x} = f_x - \lambda_1 g_x \leqslant 0, \qquad \frac{\partial L}{\partial y} = f_y - \lambda_1 g_y \leqslant 0$$

Furthermore, from the definition of the Lagrange multipliers λ_2 and λ_3, we know that $\lambda_2 > 0$ implies $x = 0$ and similarly $\lambda_3 > 0$ implies $y = 0$. In this instance, (11-72) hold as strict inequalities. On the other hand, $x > 0$ implies $\lambda_2 = 0$ and $y > 0$ implies $\lambda_3 = 0$ and (11-72) hold as a strict equalities. Taking advantage of this property, we combine these conditions to:

(11-73) $\quad x \, \partial L/\partial x = x(f_x - \lambda_1 g_x) = 0, \qquad y \, \partial L/\partial y = y(f_y - \lambda_1 g_y) = 0$

and eliminate λ_2 and λ_3 in the process. We can see also that expression (11-73) is equivalent to the conditions $\lambda_2 x = 0$ and $\lambda_3 y = 0$ in expression (11-71). So those two conditions can be eliminated also. The Kuhn-Tucker conditions for non-negative variables can be simplified to the following:

KUHN-TUCKER NECESSARY CONDITIONS FOR OPTIMUM TO CONSTRAINED MAXIMIZATION PROBLEM

The necessary conditions for an optimum to the constrained maximization problem:

$$\text{maximize } f(x, y)$$

$$\text{subject to } g(x, y) \leqslant b$$

$$x, y \geqslant 0$$

are:

(11-74)

$$\partial L/\partial x = f_x - \lambda_1 g_x \leqslant 0$$

$$\partial L/\partial y = f_y - \lambda_1 g_y \leqslant 0$$

$$\partial L/\partial \lambda_1 = b - g(x, y) \geqslant 0$$

$$x\, \partial L/\partial x = x(f_x - \lambda_1 g_x) = 0$$

$$y\, \partial L/\partial y = y(f_y - \lambda_1 g_y) = 0$$

$$\lambda_1\, \partial L/\partial \lambda_1 = \lambda_1(b - g(x, y)) = 0$$

$$x \geqslant 0, \qquad y \geqslant 0, \qquad \lambda_1 \geqslant 0.$$

(There is a further condition known as the *constraint qualifications* which must be satisfied before the Kuhn-Tucker conditions hold. For a discussion of this see W. I. Zangwill, *Non-linear Programming*, Prentice-Hall, 1969, pages 39–40.)

The astute reader may have noticed not only the similarity between the definition of λ and the dual variables of linear programming in Chapter 4, but also the similarity between the third and fourth set of equations in (11-74) and complementary slackness in Chapter 4.

Generalization of the Kuhn-Tucker conditions to the n variable case, subject to m constraints, with some or all variables restricted to be nonnegative is straightforward and left as an exercise to the reader.

In the derivation of the Kuhn-Tucker conditions above, we dealt with a standard maximization problem subject to a $(\leqslant)$ constraint, namely, $g(x, y) \leqslant b$. For the standard minimization problem subject to a $(\geqslant)$ constraint, the direction of the first three inequalities in (11-74) is reversed. If we deviate from either of these two standard forms, there will be other changes. For example, for a maximization problem subject to a $(\geqslant)$ constraint, namely, $g(x, y) \geqslant b$, in addition to the reversal of the direction of the third inequality in (11-74), the sign of the corresponding Lagrangian multiplier is also reversed. What are the changes to (11-74) when $g(x, y) = b$?

*11-11 SUFFICIENT CONDITIONS FOR MAXIMUM TO CONSTRAINED PROBLEM

The Kuhn-Tucker conditions are necessary conditions for an optimum. To guarantee that these conditions give the global optimum, we need to develop some sufficient conditions which ensure that the problem has a unique point at which the Kuhn-Tucker conditions hold, and that this point is a maximum.

First, we need an objective function that has a single stationary point that is a maximum. From Figure 11-3b we see that this will occur if the function is concave. So, the first part of our sufficient conditions is to require that f be a concave function.

This is not enough. We must also place conditions on the feasible region. For instance, Figure 11-12, parts a and b, illustrate cases where a concave objective function does not yield a unique optimum. In these examples, the point $\mathbf{x}^{(A)}$ is the

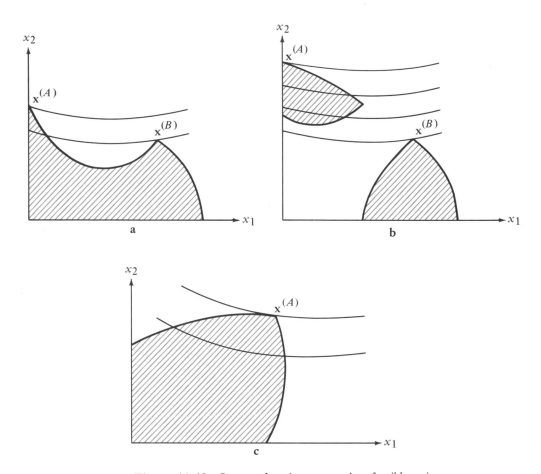

Figure 11-12. *Concave function over various feasible regions.*

global maximum and $\mathbf{x}^{(B)}$ is a local maximum. The local maximum exists because not all the points on the line segment between $\mathbf{x}^{(A)}$ and $\mathbf{x}^{(B)}$ are feasible solutions. We can establish fairly easily from the definition of a concave function that if all the points on this line segment are feasible, then $\mathbf{x}^{(B)}$ cannot be a local optimum. If we let $\hat{\mathbf{x}}$ be any point on the line segment between $\mathbf{x}^{(A)}$ and $\mathbf{x}^{(B)}$, then, by definition, $\hat{\mathbf{x}} = (1 - \lambda)\mathbf{x}^{(A)} + \lambda\mathbf{x}^{(B)}$, $0 \leqslant \lambda \leqslant 1$. Also, from expression (11-40) we can show that if the objective function is concave, $f(\hat{\mathbf{x}}) \geqslant (1 - \lambda)f(\mathbf{x}^{(A)}) + \lambda f(\mathbf{x}^{(B)})$. But we know that $f(\mathbf{x}^{(A)}) \geqslant f(\mathbf{x}^{(B)})$, because $\mathbf{x}^{(A)}$ is the global maximum. So,

$$(1 - \lambda)f(\mathbf{x}^{(A)}) + \lambda f(\mathbf{x}^{(B)}) \geqslant f(\mathbf{x}^B);$$

hence, $f(\hat{\mathbf{x}}) \geqslant f(\mathbf{x}^{(B)})$. The importance of this result is that if, for all λ, $\hat{\mathbf{x}}$ is a feasible solution to the constraints, there is no neighborhood around $\mathbf{x}^{(B)}$ where $f(\mathbf{x}) \leqslant f(\mathbf{x}^{(B)})$ for all feasible $\mathbf{x}$, i.e., $\mathbf{x}^{(B)}$ is not a local maximum. So if we extend the feasible region to include the line segment between $\mathbf{x}^{(A)}$ and $\mathbf{x}^{(B)}$ the local optimum disappears. To ensure that the constraint set does not create local optima, we require that any point on the line segment between any pair of feasible points is also feasible. This is the case in Figure 11-12c. A set with this property is called a *convex set* (not to be confused with a convex function).

CONVEX SET

A set is a convex set if, for any two members of the set, $\mathbf{x}^{(1)}$ and $\mathbf{x}^{(2)}$, any point on the line segment between them (i.e., $\mathbf{x} = (1 - \lambda)\mathbf{x}^{(1)} + \lambda\mathbf{x}^{(2)}$, for any λ, $0 \leqslant \lambda \leqslant 1$) is also a member of the set.

What can we say about the constraint functions that will ensure that the feasible region is a convex set? Figure 11-13 shows that if the constraint function g is a convex function, then $g(x, y) \leqslant b$ describes a convex set. Similarly, if g is a concave function, then $g(x, y) \geqslant b$ describes a convex set. If $g(x, y) = b$, the feasible region is a convex set if and only if g is a linear function. Verify this for yourself. Where there is more than one constraint, the feasible region is a convex set if each constraint describes a convex set. (The intersection of convex sets is a convex set.) So the feasible region of

$$g(x, y) \leqslant b$$

$$x \geqslant 0$$

$$y \geqslant 0$$

is a convex set if g is a convex function. (Since a linear function is both a concave function and a convex function, the nonnegativity conditions on the variables yield convex sets.)

We can now state sufficient conditions for the Kuhn-Tucker conditions to give a global optimum.

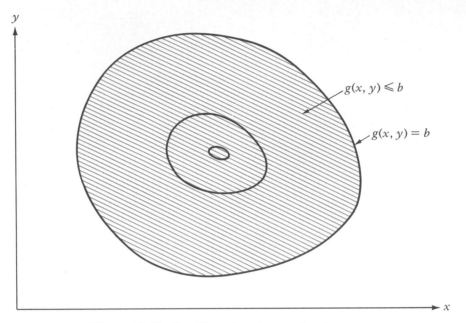

Figure 11-13. *Feasible region of convex function.*

SUFFICIENT CONDITIONS FOR GLOBAL OPTIMUM TO CONSTRAINED MAXIMIZATION PROBLEM

The Kuhn-Tucker conditions to the constrained maximization problem:

$$\text{maximize } f(x, y)$$

$$\text{subject to } g(x, y) \leqslant b$$

$$x, y \geqslant 0$$

are also sufficient conditions for a global optimum if f is a concave function and g is a convex function.

It is reasonably straightforward to develop sufficiency conditions for a general constrained maximization problem.

EXERCISES

11.1   For the EOQ model discussed in Section 11-1, find the optimal value of Q and the minimum annual cost for the following data: $c_1 = 0.24$, $c_2 = 200$, $V = 20$, $R = 3600$. Verify that the sufficient conditions are satisfied at the optimum.

11.2 Consider the following variation of the EOQ model. The replenishment is no longer assumed to be instantaneous, but once a replenishment has been ordered, it is filled at a rate b per day. This is the typical situation when goods are produced in the firm's own production facilities and become available for sale as soon as they come off the production floor, and the rate of production is b per day. All other aspects, in particular, all cost factors, remain the same.

(a) Show graphically the behavior of the inventory over time.

(b) Find a general expression for the total annual cost, and find an expression for the optimal order quantity minimizing total annual costs.

(c) For $c_1 = 0.2$, $c_2 = 24$, $V = 10$, $R = 1800$, and $b = 20$ per day, find the optimal order quantity Q^*, and check whether the sufficient conditions for a minimum are satisfied. Take the year at 360 days. How many replenishments are placed per year? How many days does each replenishment take to produce? What is the minimum annual cost?

(d) Determine whether the cost function is convex or concave.

11.3 A manufacturer procures n different products from the same supplier. His policy is to periodically place orders Q_i for all n products at the same time, and when stocks are depleted, he sends a truck to the supplier to take delivery for all products. The cost of trucking the goods amounts to c_2 dollars per trip. Other ordering costs are negligible. The capacity of the truck used is such that no more than one trip has to be made for the entire order. The value of product i is V_i, and the holding cost per dollar invested per year is c_1. The annual demand for product i is R_i, and it occurs at a constant rate.

(a) Find a general expression for the total annual cost consisting of inventory holding cost and ordering cost, and show that this cost can be expressed as a function of one decision variable only. (Hint: The proportion of the total annual requirement ordered for each replenishment is the same for all products.)

(b) Find the value of the decision variable that minimizes total annual costs and express each Q_i in terms of the optimal value of the decision variable. Show that the sufficient conditions are satisfied for all positive values of the cost factors.

(c) For $n = 3$ products, and $c_1 = 0.2$, $c_2 = 120$, $V_1 = 10$, $V_2 = 6$, $V_3 = 20$, $R_1 = 600$, $R_2 = 240$, $R_3 = 1500$, find the optimal order quantities and the total annual cost. How many times is inventory replenished per year?

(d) Determine whether the function is convex or concave.

11.4 A manufacturer of seasonal fashion clothing would like to determine the size of the production run for a given item which is subject to a random demand. Only one run will be made for the entire season. Each unit produced has a cost of k_1 dollars. Any goods not sold by the end of the season are essentially worthless. If the demand exceeds the production run, then the manufacturer suffers an opportunity cost for lost sales of k_2 dollars per unit short. The probability density function of the demand is $h(r)$, where r denotes demand.

(a) Find a general expression for the sum of production and opportunity costs if a run of size Q is made at the beginning of the season.

(b) Find an expression to determine the optimal value of Q that minimizes total costs. Verify that the sufficient conditions are satisfied for all positive cost factors. Find the optimal value of Q for $k_1 = \$9.50$, $k_2 = \$30$, and $h(r)$ normal with mean 400 and standard deviation 80.

11.5 For the model discussed in Section 11-2, find the optimal value of S for the following data: $c_1 = \$3$, $c_2 = \$7$, $h(r) = 0.02 - 0.0002r$ for $r \leqslant 100$ and 0 for $r > 100$ (i.e., a triangular distribution). Verify that the sufficient conditions are satisfied at the optimum.

11.6 Cost analysis had shown that the most advantageous procurement policy for a given product is to replenish inventory in whole truck loads, covering demand, on the average, for about 3 months. The replenishment lead time is one month. Demand is random with a probability density function $h(r)$, where r is the demand for one month. If stocks during the replenishment lead time are insufficient to cover demand, shortage costs are incurred which are proportional to the length of time short. Shortage costs per unit short for one month are c_2. Holding costs are equal to c_1 per unit carried forward to the following replenishment cycle. Holding costs are only assessed on the average ending inventory on hand when the new replenishment arrives. The problem is to find a reorder point, i.e., a critical inventory level which triggers off a replenishment order to be sent out to the supplier, that minimizes the sum of expected holding and shortage costs.
   (a) Let s be the reorder point. Find an expression for the expected cost per replenishment. It may help to draw a picture of the inventory behavior over time.
   (b) Find the necessary conditions for a minimum for this expression.
   (c) Determine whether the cost function is convex or concave.

11.7 Consider the following waiting line problem: Ships arrive at a port at a rate of λ ships per day. Unloading and loading of ships can be done at a rate of μ ships per day. Then (as shown in Chapter 10), the average time a ship is in port waiting and being unloaded is $1/(\mu - \lambda)$. Assume that the cost for unloading a ship is proportional to the rate μ, with factor of proportionality c_1, and assume that the cost of a ship in port is proportional to the average time it is in port, with factor of proportionality c_2.
   (a) Find an expression for the total cost per ship unloaded as a function of μ and λ.
   (b) Find an expression for the optimal rate μ^* of unloading ships so as to minimize total cost per ship.
   (c) Let $\lambda = 8$, $c_1 = \$2000$, $c_2 = 8000$. Find the optimal μ and verify if the sufficient conditions are satisfied.
   (d) Is the total cost function convex or concave?

11.8 A machine produces parts at a constant rate of 360 units per hour. The rate of defectives produced depends on the length of time t between adjustments of the machine as follows: $144t$, where $t = 1$ is one hour. Defective parts have to be reworked on a different machine at a cost of $\$2$ per unit. Whenever an adjustment is made, the output of the machine is temporarily stopped. The opportunity cost of the lost production amounts to $\$32$. The objective is to determine the length of time between successive adjustments so as to minimize the total cost.
   (a) Find an expression for the total cost as a function of the length of time between successive adjustments.
   (b) Find the optimal length of time between successive adjustments, and check whether the sufficient conditions are satisfied.
   (c) Determine whether the cost function is convex or concave.

11.9 For the model discussed in Section 11-4, find the optimal value of Q and the annual cost for the following data: $c_1 = 0.16$, $c_2 = 40$, $R = 800$, and the price-breaks of $V_0 = 10$ for $Q < 160$, $V_1 = 9.80$ for $160 \leqslant 240$, and $V_2 = 9.75$ for $Q \geqslant 240$.

11.10 A product is mixed in batches. There are 3 mixers available, each with different capacities and different costs.

Mixer	1	2	3
Minimum batch	200 gal	800 gal	2400 gal
Maximum batch	1000 gal	3000 gal	6000 gal
Set-up costs	$36	$48	$64 per batch
Variable cost of product	$1.20	$1.19	$1.18

The annual demand amounts to 12,000 gallons, and the inventory holding cost per dollar invested per year is $0.20.

(a) Find the total annual cost as a function of the batch size Q.

(b) Find the optimal batch size and the minimum annual cost. Which mixer is used.

11.11 For the model discussed in Section 11-6 find the optimal values of Q and Z for the following data: $N = 250$, $c_1 = 0.24$, $c_2 = \$5$, $c_3 = \$0.50$, $V = \$20$, and $h(r) = 0.05 - 0.00125r$ for $r < 40$ and 0 for $r > 40$.

11.12 Consider exercise 11.11. Replace the continuous probability density function $h(r)$ by the following discrete distribution.

r	0	1	2	3	4	5	6	7	8	9	10
$p(r)$	0.22	0.12	0.08	0.07	0.06	0.06	0.05	0.05	0.04	0.04	0.03

r	11	12	13	14	15	16	17	18	19	20
$p(r)$	0.03	0.03	0.02	0.02	0.02	0.02	0.01	0.01	0.01	0.01

Although the demand distribution is now discrete, you may still use expressions (11-37) and (11-38) to approximate the optimal solution rounded always to the nearest integer values. What are the approximate optimal values of Q and Z.

11.13 A subcontractor has to supply a given part at a rate of 20 units per day. One day's supply is brought to the customer every morning. The subcontractor produces these parts in batches of Q units at a rate of 50 units per day. It costs him $7.50 to hold one unit in stock for one month. The contract provides for a late delivery penalty of $2 per part per day late. Each time a production batch is started, there is a production set-up cost of $4000. The objective is to find the optimal batch size Q^* and the optimal amount Z^* of late deliveries each replenishment cycle. Assume a month has 20 working days.

(a) Find an expression for the sum of annual production set-up costs, inventory holding costs, and late delivery penalties as a function of Q and Z.

(b) Determine the optimal values of Q and Z, and check whether the sufficient conditions for a minimum are satisfied.

(c) Determine whether the total cost function is convex or concave.

11.14 Consider the following inventory replenishment policy: Whenever the inventory level has been reduced (through sales) to a level of s, a replenishment is placed for an amount Q. This replenishment is received in stock after 1 week. Sales are a random variable. The density function of demand for one week is $h(r)$. Holding costs are incurred on the average inventory and are proportional to the average stocks. If stocks during the lead time are insufficient to meet demand, customers wait until the replenishment arrives. The shortage cost is proportional to the amount short. Let c_1 be the holding cost per unit stored in inventory for one year, c_2 the fixed replenishment cost per order, c_3 the shortage cost per unit, and R be the annual demand, $R = N \int_0^\infty rh(r)\,dr$, where N is the number of weeks per year. The objective is to minimize average annual costs.

(a) Determine the expected annual cost associated with this policy. Assume that Q is sufficiently larger than s. (Hint: The average inventory level can be approximated as the sum of the average order quantity Q and the expected protection against shortages. The latter is equal to the reorder level s minus the expected demand during the replenishment lead time. To find the annual expected shortage cost, first find the expected shortage cost per replenishment cycle and then multiply this by the number of replenishment cycles.)

(b) Use the necessary conditions to determine expressions that, given data, allow you to find the optimal values of Q and s. What approach would you use to find these values?

11.15   For the problem discussed in Section 11-8, find the optimal order quantities Q_i and the unconstrained and constrained minimum cost for the following data: $c_1 = 0.24$, average inventory investment limit \$30,000, and

i	1	2
R_i	8000	6000
V_i	\$120	\$200
c_{2i}	\$ 80	\$ 50

11.16   A firm stocks different items in the same warehouse. Item i requires a_i square feet of warehouse space per unit. The total warehouse space available is A square feet. All N items are replenished independently in batches of size Q_i. Holding costs assessed on the average inventory level amount to c_1 dollars per dollar invested per year. The value of item i is V_i dollars per unit. The fixed ordering cost is c_{2i} per batch ordered for item i, and the annual demand for item i is R_i.

(a) Find an expression for the annual total inventory holding and ordering costs for all N items. If each item is allotted a space in the warehouse required to store Q_i, what is the total amount of warehouse space needed?

(b) Given that the warehouse space available is A, form the Lagrangian function and determine expressions to find the optimal order quantities Q_i^*.

(c) Use the following data to find the optimal Q^* and the minimum constrained cost:

i	1	2	3
R_i	12,000	5,000	2,000
V_i	\$20	\$40	\$50
c_{2i}	\$160	\$200	\$100
a_i in sq. ft.	1	2	4

and $A = 2000$ sq. ft., $c_1 = 0.2$. What is the cost of the warehouse restriction?

11.17 A firm produces N products on the same machine. Total productive capacity of the machine is 250 days per year. Each product is produced in batches of size Q_i. For every batch of product i produced, the set-up time amounts to a_i days. The product is produced at a rate b_i per day. Let R_i be the annual demand, V_i the product value per unit, c_1 the holding cost per dollar invested per year, and c_{2i} the fixed set-up cost per batch for product i.

(a) Find a general expression for the total annual cost and express the constraints on the production capacity mathematically.

(b) Find expressions that, given data, would allow you to determine the optimal constrained batch sizes Q_i.

(c) Using common sense, discuss why this model is only a suitable approximation if the number of products N is relatively large, and why it could not be implemented if N is small, say 2, 3, or 4.

11.18 For the example discussed in Section 11-8, define the Kuhn-Tucker conditions.

REFERENCES

Hadley, G. and T. M. Whitin. *Analysis for Inventory Systems*. Englewood Cliffs, N.J.: Prentice-Hall, 1963. Although over ten years old, this text remains one of the most important works in the field. The treatment is at a slightly more advanced level than in Chapter 11. Very clear exposition with many fully discussed examples. Contains two appendices listing properties of both the normal and the Poisson distribution useful for solving expressions involving these distributions. Highly recommended.

Holt, C. C., F. Modigliani, J. F. Muth, and H. A. Simon. *Planning Production, Inventories and Work Force*. Englewood Cliffs, N.J.: Prentice-Hall, 1960. Most of the text is devoted to an important multi-variable model with a quadratic cost structure whose solution leads to so-called *linear decision rules*.

Sasieni, M. W., A. Yaspan, and L. Friedman. *Operations Research: Methods and Problems*. New York: Wiley, 1959. Chapter 2 shows a number of inventory examples solved by classical methods of continuous and discrete calculus, showing all intermediate steps of the solution method.

Scarf, Herbert E. "The Optimality of (s, S) Policies in the Dynamic Inventory Problem", *Studies in Applied Probability and Management Science*, K. J. Arrow, S. Karlin, and H. E. Scarf, eds., Stanford University Press, 1962. An (s, S) policy works as follows: Whenever the inventory i falls to or below s, a replenishment of size $S-i$ is placed. This is the original work showing the conditions under which such a policy is optimal.

Teichroew, Daniel. *An Introduction to Management Science: Deterministic Models*. New York: Wiley, 1964. One of the few texts of operations research that contains an adequate treatment of the methods of classical optimization at an introductory level. Numerous fully worked examples involving differentiable functions of various forms. Good treatment of Lagrange multiplier approach.

Veinott, Arthur F., Jr. and Harvey M. Wagner. "Computing Optimal (s, S) Inventory Policies", *Management Science*, 11, Feb. 1965. Computational approaches for finding the optimal (s, S) policy under various cost structures. Advanced reading. (See also Chapter 9, Sections 9-5 and 9-8).

Wagner, Harvey M.   "A Manager's Survey of Inventory and Production Control Systems", *Interfaces*, 2, August 1972.   Reviews for managers the important components of an inventory control project, the steps to be taken, and the pitfalls to be avoided.   No specific models are discussed.

Inventory control problems covering several periods are usually solved by other methods, such as mathematical programming techniques (see Chapters 2, 13, and 14) or dynamic programming (see Chapters 7 and 9).

See G. Hadley.   *Elementary Calculus*.   San Francisco: Holden-Day, 1968, for an elementary treatment of Calculus.

12

Integer Programming

The assumptions of linear programming often do not hold in reality. Although sometimes a linear program can be used as an effective first approximation, there are times when we must depart from the linear programming structure for the sake of accuracy. In this chapter we deal with the situation where it is unreasonable to assume that all variables are continuous.

In many instances continuity is a good assumption and a fraction of a unit is meaningful, for example, where the commodity is in terms of time, or is a fluid or a powder, or the like. On other occasions, however, we are dealing with discrete commodities—airplanes, warehouses, cars, etc., and depending on the number of these involved, continuity may not be a reasonable assumption. If the solution to a linear program gives a variable a large value, it is usually safe to round it to the nearest integer and thereby obtain a solution that may be very close to optimal. However, when the optimal value of a variable is small, rounding it to the nearest integer may be far from optimal.

Techniques for solving linear programs with integer restrictions on some or all variables are called *integer programming techniques*. Before we deal with these, let us go through a few examples of how integer programming arises.

12-1 A SIMPLE INTEGER PROBLEM

A university has received a grant of $2.5 million for purchasing new computer equipment. It is impossible for it to supplement this sum from any other source. Feasibility studies indicate that only two machines are suitable. The set-up of the university is such that any number of either type of machine or any combination of them would be quite acceptable. Bench mark tests have enabled the university to evaluate the load capacity in units of "average jobs" per hour of the two types of machines.

Computer	Cost ($ million)	Capacity (average jobs/hour)
1	1.4	28
2	0.6	11

The university wishes to maximize its potential job capacity. Clearly, the machines can only be purchased in whole units.

Let x_1 be the number of computers type 1

Let x_2 be the number of computers type 2

The job capacity per hour (in average jobs) is $28x_1 + 11x_2$. This is to be maximized. Hence the objective is

$$\text{maximize } z = 28x_1 + 11x_2$$

subject to the finance constraint, nonnegativity conditions, and integrality constraints:

$$14x_1 + 6x_2 \leqslant 25 \quad \text{(units \$100,000)} \qquad \text{(Finance constraint)}$$

(12-1) $\qquad x_1, x_2 \geqslant 0 \qquad\qquad\qquad\qquad\qquad \text{(Nonnegativity conditions)}$

$\qquad\qquad x_1, x_2 \quad \text{integers} \qquad\qquad\qquad \text{(Integrality)}$

Although problem (12-1) has the structure of an ordinary linear programming problem, it must be solved by integer programming because of the small solution values of the variables. We will discuss the actual solution to this problem later.

The structure of integer programming allows some interesting twists in the formulations, such as the introduction of *zero-one variables*, i.e., integer variables restricted to the values 0 and 1. These can be ordinary decision variables as in the *assembly line balancing* problem or "dummy" variables introduced especially to permit logical statements to be formulated as linear constraints—as in the *fixed charge* problem.

12-2 ASSEMBLY LINE BALANCING PROBLEM

An assembly line consisting of a collection of work stations has to perform a series of jobs in order to assemble a product. At each work station one or more of the jobs may be performed. Normally there are some restrictions on the order in which jobs may be done. These are called *precedence relations*, and there is a limit on the time a product can stay at any particular work station. Consider an example of a product with 5 jobs. The decision involves allocating each job to a work station so that the number of work stations is minimized. Table 12-1 gives the jobs, any precedence relations that exist, and the time needed to complete each job.

Job i is either done at station j, or it is not done at station j. This is an either/or type situation which fits in well with zero-one variables.

$$\text{Let } x_{ij} = \begin{cases} 1 & \text{if } i \text{ is done at station } j \\ 0 & \text{if } i \text{ is not done at station } j. \end{cases}$$

Table 12-1. *Data for assembly line balancing.*

Job i	Time (p_i) in minutes	Predecessors
1	6	—
2	5	—
3	7	—
4	6	3
5	5	2, 4

Let us assume that there are 4 stations (this is certainly an upper limit). Suppose, the maximum time at each work station is 12 minutes. So we obtain the following time constraint on each solution:

$$(12\text{-}2) \qquad \sum_{i=1}^{5} p_i x_{ij} \leqslant 12, \qquad j = 1, \ldots, 4$$

(i.e., the time taken for jobs assigned to station j must be less than 12 minutes.) Equations (12-2) expand to

$$(12\text{-}3) \quad \begin{aligned} 6x_{11} + 5x_{21} + 7x_{31} + 6x_{41} + 5x_{51} &\leqslant 12 \\ 6x_{12} + 5x_{22} + 7x_{32} + 6x_{42} + 5x_{52} &\leqslant 12 \\ 6x_{13} + 5x_{23} + 7x_{33} + 6x_{43} + 5x_{53} &\leqslant 12 \\ 6x_{14} + 5x_{24} + 7x_{34} + 6x_{44} + 5x_{54} &\leqslant 12 \end{aligned}$$

Next, we must handle precedence relations between jobs. By saying that job 3 must be done before job 4, we mean that job 3 must be performed either at the same station as job 4 or at a prior station. Job i has been done at or before station k, if $\sum_{j=1}^{k} x_{ij} = 1$, and has not been done if $\sum_{j=1}^{k} x_{ij} = 0$. At station k, if $\sum_{j=1}^{k} x_{4j} \leqslant \sum_{j=1}^{k} x_{3j}$, then job 4 cannot be done unless job 3 has been done because $\sum_{j=1}^{k} x_{4j} = 1$ only if $\sum_{j=1}^{k} x_{3j} = 1$. For the precedence relations to be satisfied this must hold at all stations. So we obtain

$$(12\text{-}4) \qquad \sum_{j=1}^{k} x_{4j} \leqslant \sum_{j=1}^{k} x_{3j}, \qquad k = 1, \ldots, 4$$

If neither job is done by station k, expression (12-4) holds trivially (i.e., $0 \leqslant 0$), and it also holds if both jobs have been done (i.e., $1 \leqslant 1$).

The precedence relations for job 5 are

$$(12\text{-}5) \qquad \left. \begin{aligned} \sum_{j=1}^{k} x_{5j} &\leqslant \sum_{j=1}^{k} x_{2j} \\ \sum_{j=1}^{k} x_{5j} &\leqslant \sum_{j=1}^{k} x_{4j} \end{aligned} \right\} k = 1, \ldots, 4$$

It is also necessary to ensure that each job is done once and only once:

$$(12\text{-}6) \qquad \sum_{j=1}^{4} x_{ij} = 1, \qquad i = 1, \ldots, 5$$

The objective is to find the minimum number of stations to set up. This is achieved by allocating a lower "cost" to job i if it is done at station 1 than if it is done at station 2, etc. By minimizing these costs, we force the jobs to the earliest possible work stations. The costs are arbitrary. We will give a cost of j to x_{ij} ($=$job i done at station j). Thus we obtain

$$(12\text{-}7) \qquad \text{minimize } z = \sum_{i=1}^{5} x_{i1} + 2 \sum_{i=1}^{5} x_{i2} + 3 \sum_{i=1}^{5} x_{i3} + 4 \sum_{i=1}^{5} x_{i4}$$

The collection of equations (12-3) to (12-7), together with the nonnegativity and integrality conditions on the variables

$$(12\text{-}8) \qquad\qquad\qquad x_{ij} \geq 0 \text{ and integer}$$

make up the integer program for this problem. We do not need to put an upper limit of 1 on each x_{ij}; equation (12-6) does that implicitly.

12-3 THE FIXED-CHARGE PROBLEM

A firm can produce five products on its production line which goes through 3 different departments. Product j requires a_{ij} man hours in department i. Department i has M_i man hours per month available. A unit of product j makes a gross profit of $\$c_j$ (i.e., selling price less variable cost $= \$c_j$). However, it costs $\$F_j$ to set up the production line for producing a run of product j. The firm wants to schedule monthly production so as to maximize profits.

Where a fixed cost is incurred if, and only if, some variable is positive, an ordinary linear programming formulation does not work. In linear programming we assume that all costs are variable costs (i.e., proportional to the magnitude of the variable), whereas here there is both a fixed cost and a variable cost.

Let x_j be the size of the production run of product j. The profit from producing x_j is

$$(12\text{-}9) \qquad P_j = \begin{cases} c_j x_j - F_j & \text{for } x_j > 0 \\ 0 & \text{for } x_j = 0 \end{cases}, \qquad j = 1, \dots, 5$$

We define variables

$$(12\text{-}10) \qquad \delta_j = \begin{cases} 1 & \text{for } x_j > 0 \\ 0 & \text{for } x_j = 0 \end{cases}, \qquad j = 1, \dots, 5$$

Using (12-10), expressions (12-9) can be written

$$(12\text{-}11) \qquad\qquad P_j = (c_j x_j - F_j \delta_j) \qquad j = 1, \dots, 5$$

Since the objective is to maximize profits, it follows directly from (12-11) that the objective function is

$$(12\text{-}12) \qquad\qquad \text{maximize } z = \sum_{j=1}^{5} (c_j x_j - F_j \delta_j)$$

The man-hour production constraints are

(12-13)
$$\sum_{j=1}^{5} a_{ij} x_j \leqslant M_i, \qquad i = 1, 2, 3$$

Equations (12-10) must be written in linear constraint form in order to fit them into the integer programming structure. We do this by finding an upper limit on x_j—say U_j—which we know to be above any possible value of x_j. Then using (12-10) we form the constraints

(12-14)
$$x_j \leqslant U_j \delta_j, \qquad j = 1, \ldots, 5$$

(12-15)
$$\left. \begin{array}{l} x_j \geqslant 0 \\[4pt] 0 \leqslant \delta_j \leqslant 1 \quad \text{and integer} \end{array} \right\}, \qquad j = 1, \ldots, 5$$

Equations (12-12) to (12-15) are the integer programming formulation. Together they ensure that $\delta_j = 0$ only when $x_j \leqslant 0$ and $x_j \geqslant 0$ simultaneously (i.e., $x_j = 0$). The δ_j variables are referred to as *dummy variables* or *logical variables*. They are merely an aid to formulating the problem and are not decision variables.

12-4 A BUS SCHEDULING PROBLEM

An airline wishes to schedule a bus service between an airport and a downtown terminal. The buses are rented from another company at $25 for a round trip from downtown to the airport and back, plus $9 per hour waiting time at the airport. The service must give a passenger leaving on a flight at least 20 minutes but no more than 45 minutes to check in at the airport before the flight departure. Similarly, a bus must leave the airport between 15 minutes and 30 minutes of each flight arriving. It takes a bus at least 10 minutes to turn around at the airport. A simplified daily flight schedule is given in Table 12-2. The airline wants to minimize the cost of the bus service.

Since costs are related to the number of round trips made, we define variables for each round trip. Let x_j be the arrival time of trip j at the airport, and y_j the departure time of trip j from the airport, both expressed in minutes from midnight.

Table 12-2. *Daily Flight Schedule.*

	Departures			Arrivals	
Flight Number (i)	Time Hours Mins.	Minutes (a_i)	Flight Number (k)	Time Hours Mins.	Minutes (b_k)
1	7.40	460	1	9.50	590
2	10.55	655	2	11.00	660
3	11.15	675	3	13.00	780
4	14.50	890	4	15.30	930
5	16.35	995	5	18.30	1110

The objective function has a form similar to the fixed charge problem.   The cost of trip j is

$$(12\text{-}16) \qquad C_j = \begin{cases} 25 + (9/60)(y_j - x_j) & \text{if trip } j \text{ is made,} \\ 0 & \text{otherwise} \end{cases}$$

Trip j is made when $x_j > 0$, so we define variables

$$\delta_j = \begin{cases} 1 & \text{if } x_j > 0, \\ 0 & \text{otherwise} \end{cases}$$

and appropriate constraints

$$x_j \leqslant P\delta_j$$

where P is a large constant.

Let us give P the value 2000.   This is large enough not to constrain the value of x_j. So we obtain

$$(12\text{-}17) \qquad\qquad\qquad x_j \leqslant 2000\delta_j$$

or

$$x_j - 2000\delta_j \leqslant 0 \qquad\qquad\qquad (\text{TRIP}j)$$

The objective function is

$$(12\text{-}18) \qquad\qquad \text{minimize} \sum_j \left[25\delta_j + 0.15y_j - 0.15x_j\right] \qquad (\text{COST})$$

Waiting time for trip j at the airport is $(y_j - x_j)$, but only if trip j is run.   Since the waiting time is at least 10 minutes this yields the restriction

$$y_j - x_j \geqslant 10\delta_j$$

or

$$(12\text{-}19) \qquad\qquad\qquad -y_j + x_j + 10\delta_j \leqslant 0 \qquad\qquad (\text{WAIT}j)$$

If trip j is to service flight i scheduled to leave at time a_i, then the bus must arrive at the airport at least 20 minutes before time a_i, i.e.,

$$(12\text{-}20) \qquad\qquad\qquad a_i - x_j \geqslant 20$$

Similarly it must arrive no more than 45 minutes before a_i, i.e.,

$$(12\text{-}21) \qquad\qquad\qquad a_i - x_j \leqslant 45$$

Equations (12-20) and (12-21) are to hold only if bus trip j services departure flight i.   If trip j is not scheduled to service flight i, then

$$(12\text{-}22) \qquad\qquad\qquad -P \leqslant (a_i - x_j) \leqslant P$$

Expressions (12-20), (12-21), and (12-22) have to be combined.   For this purpose we define a zero-one logical variable

$$\gamma_{ij} = \begin{cases} 1 & \text{if trip } j \text{ services departure flight } i, \\ 0 & \text{otherwise} \end{cases}$$

We can combine $(a_i - x_j) \geqslant 20$ for $\gamma_{ij} = 1$, and $(a_i - x_j) \geqslant -2000$ for $\gamma_{ij} = 0$ as

$$(12\text{-}23) \qquad\qquad a_i - x_j \geqslant 20\gamma_{ij} - 2000(1 - \gamma_{ij})$$

or $\qquad\qquad x_j + 2020\gamma_{ij} \leqslant 2000 + a_i \qquad\qquad$ (MNDPij)

An examination of (12-23) shows that the right hand side of the equation has a value 20 for $\gamma_{ij} = 1$, and -2000 for $\gamma_{ij} = 0$. Similarly, $(a_i - x_j) \leqslant 45$ for $\gamma_{ij} = 1$, and $(a_i - x_j) \leqslant 2000$ for $\gamma_{ij} = 0$, i.e.,

$$(12\text{-}24) \qquad\qquad a_i - x_j \leqslant 45\gamma_{ij} + 2000(1 - \gamma_{ij})$$

or $\qquad\qquad -x_j + 1955\gamma_{ij} \leqslant 2000 - a_i \qquad\qquad$ (MXDPij)

Equations (12-23) and (12-24) must hold for all viable combinations of i and j.

One further condition is imposed on the γ_{ij}. Since every flight must be serviced and need only be serviced once, we obtain

$$(12\text{-}25) \qquad\qquad \sum_j \gamma_{ij} = 1 \qquad \text{for each } i \qquad\qquad \text{(FLTDPi)}$$

An analysis analogous to that for outgoing flights applies to incoming flights. If trip j is to service flight k scheduled to arrive at time b_k, then the bus must leave the airport at least 15 minutes later, i.e.,

$$(12\text{-}26) \qquad\qquad y_j - b_k \geqslant 15$$

Also, it must leave no more than 30 minutes later, i.e.,

$$(12\text{-}27) \qquad\qquad y_j - b_k \leqslant 30$$

For any flights k not serviced by trip j, we have again by analogy to (12-22)

$$(12\text{-}28) \qquad\qquad -2000 \leqslant (y_j - b_k) \leqslant 2000$$

To combine these equations we define logical variables for bus trips and incoming flights:

$$\beta_{kj} = \begin{cases} 1 & \text{if trip } j \text{ services arrival flight } k, \\ 0 & \text{otherwise} \end{cases}$$

You should verify that equations (12-26), (12-27), and (12-28) yield

$$(12\text{-}29) \qquad\qquad y_j - b_k \geqslant 15\beta_{kj} - 2000(1 - \beta_{kj})$$

or $\qquad\qquad -y_j + 2015\beta_{kj} \leqslant 2000 - b_k \qquad\qquad$ (MNARkj)

and

$$(12\text{-}30) \qquad\qquad y_j - b_k \leqslant 30\beta_{kj} + 2000(1 - \beta_{kj})$$

or $\qquad\qquad y_j + 1970\beta_{kj} \leqslant 2000 + b_k \qquad\qquad$ (MXARkj)

and

$$(12\text{-}31) \qquad\qquad \sum_j \beta_{kj} = 1 \qquad \text{for each } k \qquad\qquad \text{(FLTARk)}$$

Table 12-3. *Viable Trip/Flight Combinations.*

		Bus trip						
		1	2	3	4	5	6	7
Departure flight	1	x						
	2		x	x				
	3		x	x	x			
	4				x	x		
	5					x	x	
Arrival flight	1	x	x					
	2		x	x				
	3			x	x			
	4				x	x	x	
	5					x	x	x

There are also the following variable restrictions:

$$x_j, y_j \geqslant 0, \qquad \text{for all } j,$$

$$\gamma_{ij}, \beta_{kj}, \delta_j = 0 \text{ or } 1, \qquad \text{for all } i, j, \text{ and } k$$

For solution purposes we can eliminate, by inspection, many unrealistic combinations of flights and trips to reduce the number of variables and constraints. Table 12-3 marks with an x the viable combinations resulting from an inspection of the problem.   It appears that 7 trips are enough to satisfy the constraints optimally.

Table 12-4 shows, in detached coefficient form, the variables and constraints of this problem.   Only those variables indicated in Table 12-3 have been defined.

We will present the solution of this problem in Section 12-12.

12-5 FURTHER APPLICATIONS

Integer programming has been suggested and used to solve problems of a variety of sorts.   The following is a list of some further applications.

1. *Capital budgeting problem*: choosing between ways of using limited funds to maximize the discounted net return.
2. *Covering problem*: For example, a minimum cost selection of loads and routes for delivery trucks of limited capacity so that all consignments are covered.
3. *Location problems*: choosing between various alternative sites for the location of a factory, warehouse, store, etc., to minimize transport cost, maximize revenue, etc.
4. *Knapsack problem*: choosing between items to pack into a limited space, to get as much "value" in the space as possible.   There are a host of problems that fit this structure; some seemingly quite different.
5. *Matching problem*: selecting items to match from different groups so that as many matching sets as possible are formed, e.g., selecting gears, bearings and

shafts from batches of each of them, to form matching sets that conform to certain precision tolerances.

6. *Sequencing problems*: sequencing a number of jobs on a machine to minimize set-up cost, or time taken. (Enumeration of all possibilities, heuristic approaches, or dynamic programming, where applicable, are often better than integer programming.)

7. *Traveling salesman problem*: the problem of choosing an optimal route (e.g., minimum cost or distance) for a traveling salesman.

12-6 INTRODUCTION TO SOLVING INTEGER PROGRAMMING PROBLEMS

Consider again problem (12-1):

$$\text{maximize } z = 28x_1 + 11x_2$$
$$\text{subject to} \quad 14x_1 + 6x_2 \leqslant 25$$
$$x_1, x_2 \geqslant 0$$

The integer programming solution is $x_1 = 0,$ $x_2 = 4,$ $z = 44.$

The linear programming solution is $x_1 = 25/14,$ $x_2 = 0,$ $z = 50.$

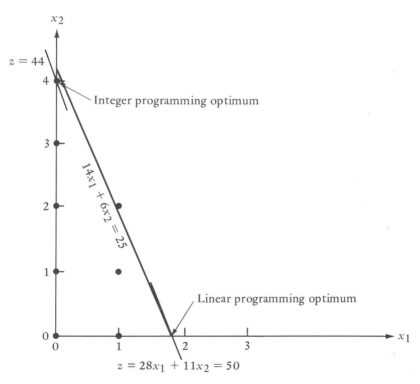

Figure 12-1. *Graphical solution to problem (12-1).*

Table 12-4. Bus Scheduling Problem in Detached Coefficient Form. (Inequalities are continued on page 400.)

Row Name	x_1	x_2	x_3	x_4	x_5	x_6	x_7	y_1	y_2	y_3	y_4	y_5	y_6	y_7	δ_1	δ_2	δ_3	δ_4	δ_5	δ_6	δ_7
WAIT1	1							−1							10						
WAIT2		1							−1							10					
WAIT3			1							−1							10				
WAIT4				1							−1							10			
WAIT5					1							−1							10		
WAIT6						1							−1							10	
WAIT7							1							−1							10
MNDP11	1																				
MNDP22		1																			
MNDP23			1																		
MNDP32		1																			
MNDP33			1																		
MNDP34				1																	
MNDP44				1																	
MNDP45					1																
MNDP55					1																
MNDP56						1															
MXDP11	−1																				
MXDP22		−1																			
MXDP23			−1																		
MXDP32		−1																			
MXDP33			−1																		
MXDP34				−1																	
MXDP44				−1																	
MXDP45					−1																
MXDP55					−1																
MXDP56						−1															
FLTDP1																					
FLTDP2																					
FLTDP3																					
FLTDP4																					
FLTDP5																					
MNAR11								−1													

Table 12-4. *Continued.* (*Inequalities are continued on page 401.*)

	1	2	3	4	5	6	7	8	9	10	11	12	13	14	15	16	17	18	19	20	21
MNAR12									−1												
MNAR22									−1												
MNAR23										−1											
MNAR33										−1											
MNAR34											−1										
MNAR44											−1										
MNAR45												−1									
MNAR46													−1								
MNAR55													−1								
MNAR56													−1								
MNAR57														−1							
MXAR11								1													
MXAR12									1												
MXAR22									1												
MXAR23										1											
MXAR33										1											
MXAR34											1										
MXAR44											1										
MXAR45												1									
MXAR46												1									
MXAR55													1								
MXAR56													1								
MXAR57														1							
FLTAR1																					
FLTAR2																					
FLTAR3																					
FLTAR4																					
FLTAR5																					
TRIP1	1														−2000						
TRIP2		1														−2000					
TRIP3			1														−2000				
TRIP4				1														−2000			
TRIP5					1														−2000		
TRIP6						1														−2000	
TRIP7							1														−2000
Cost	−0.15	−0.15	−0.15	−0.15	−0.15	−0.15	−0.15	0.15	0.15	0.15	0.15	0.15	0.15	0.15	25	25	25	25	25	25	25

Table 12-4. *Continued from page 398*

NAME	γ_{11}	γ_{22}	γ_{23}	γ_{32}	γ_{33}	γ_{34}	γ_{44}	γ_{45}	γ_{55}	γ_{56}	β_{11}	β_{12}	β_{22}	β_{23}	β_{33}	β_{34}	β_{44}	β_{45}	β_{46}	β_{55}	β_{56}	β_{57}	RHS
WAIT1																							≤ 0
WAIT2																							≤ 0
WAIT3																							≤ 0
WAIT4																							≤ 0
WAIT5																							≤ 0
WAIT6																							≤ 0
WAIT7																							≤ 0
MNDP11	2020																						≤ 2460
MNDP22		2020																					≤ 2655
MNDP23			2020																				≤ 2655
MNDP32				2020																			≤ 2675
MNDP33					2020																		≤ 2675
MNDP34						2020																	≤ 2890
MNDP44							2020																≤ 2890
MNDP45								2020															≤ 2995
MNDP55									2020														≤ 2995
MNDP56										2020													≤ 1540
MXDP11	1955																						≤ 1345
MXDP22		1955																					≤ 1345
MXDP23			1955																				≤ 1325
MXDP32				1955																			≤ 1325
MXDP33					1955																		≤ 1325
MXDP34						1955																	≤ 1110
MXDP44							1955																≤ 1110
MXDP45								1955															≤ 1005
MXDP55									1955														≤ 1005
MXDP56										1955													≤ 1005
FLTDP1	1																						= 1
FLTDP2		1	1																				= 1
FLTDP3				1	1	1																	= 1
FLTDP4							1	1															= 1
FLTDP5									1	1													= 1
MNAR11											2015												≤ 1410

400

Table 12-4. *Continued from page 399.*

MNAR12	2015	≤ 1410
MNAR22	2015	≤ 1340
MNAR23	2015	≤ 1340
MNAR33	2015	≤ 1220
MNAR34	2015	≤ 1220
MNAR44	2015	≤ 1070
MNAR45	2015	≤ 1070
MNAR46	2015	≤ 1070
MNAR55	2015	≤ 890
MNAR56	2015	≤ 890
MNAR57	2015	≤ 890
MXAR11	1970	≤ 2590
MXAR12	1970	≤ 2590
MXAR22	1970	≤ 2660
MXAR23	1970	≤ 2660
MXAR33	1970	≤ 2780
MXAR34	1970	≤ 2780
MXAR44	1970	≤ 2930
MXAR45	1970	≤ 2930
MXAR46	1970	≤ 2930
MXAR55	1970	≤ 3110
MXAR56	1970	≤ 3110
MXAR57	1970	≤ 3110
FLTAR1	1 1	= 1
FLTAR2	1 1	= 1
FLTAR3	1 1	= 1
FLTAR4	1 1	= 1
FLTAR5	1 1	= 1
TRIP1		≤ 0
TRIP2		≤ 0
TRIP3		≤ 0
TRIP4		≤ 0
TRIP5		≤ 0
TRIP6		≤ 0
TRIP7		≤ 0
Cost		minimize

401

Let us try rounding the linear programming solution to the nearest integer solution: i.e., $x_1 = 2$, $x_2 = 0$, $z = 56$. This yields a solution that is not feasible.

Trying the next nearest integer solution we obtain the solution: $x_1 = 1$, $x_2 = 0$, $z = 28$. This time, however, the solution is well below the optimal integer solution.

This case demonstrates that seeking the integer programming optimum by rounding the linear programming optimum even in simple examples may be unreliable. As the integer programming problem gets larger, such a naive technique is quite useless. We need techniques which systematically work to the optimal integer solution.

12-7 GENERAL STRUCTURE OF INTEGER PROGRAMMING TECHNIQUES

Several techniques exist to solve integer programming problems and they vary considerably in concept and detail. It is possible to summarize their basic approaches and their variations under three principles: *separation*, *relaxation*, and *fathoming*.

Consider the problem

$$\text{maximize } z = \sum_j c_j x_j$$

$$\text{subject to} \quad \sum_j a_{ij} x_j \leqslant b_i, \qquad i = 1, \ldots, m$$

(12-32)

$$x_j \geqslant 0, \qquad \text{all } j$$

$$x_j \qquad \text{integer for some of the } j$$

We have not assumed that all the variables take integer values. We call a problem a *mixed-integer problem* when it has both integer and continuous variables. A problem where variables all have integer restrictions is called an *all-integer problem*.

Let P be a maximization problem involving integer restriction, either a mixed-integer problem or an all-integer problem. Let $F(P)$ be the set of feasible solutions to the problem P, i.e., the set of solutions which satisfies the inequalities and integer restrictions.

It is sometimes more convenient to solve a problem through a series of smaller subproblems of the original. A valid separation of the problem into subproblems should satisfy the following principle

PRINCIPLE OF SEPARATION

P is separated into the subproblems or descendants $P_1, P_2, \ldots, P_q$, if:

S1. Every feasible solution to P is a feasible solution of one and only one of the descendants.

S2. Every feasible solution of every descendant is a feasible solution to P.

Separation can occur in a number of ways. The following example illustrates the most useful form of separation for our purposes.

Consider problem (12-1) again as problem P:

(P) maximize $z = 28x_1 + 11x_2$

subject to $14x_1 + 6x_2 \leqslant 25$

$$x_1, x_2 \geqslant 0 \quad \text{and integers}$$

This can be separated into the two descendants:

(P_1) maximize $z_1 = 28x_1 + 11x_2$

subject to $14x_1 + 6x_2 \leqslant 25$

$$x_2 \leqslant 2$$

$$x_1, x_2 \geqslant 0 \quad \text{and integers}$$

and

(P_2) maximize $z_2 = 28x_1 + 11x_2$

subject to $14x_1 + 6x_2 \leqslant 25$

$$x_2 \geqslant 3$$

$$x_1, x_2 \geqslant 0 \quad \text{and integers}$$

We have separated P around the interval: $2 < x_2 < 3$.

P_1 is the feasible region of P for $x_2 \leqslant 2$ and P_2 is the feasible region of P for $x_2 \geqslant 3$. Since the region $2 < x_2 < 3$ contains no integer values it can be excluded from consideration.

We can show that P, P_1 and P_2 satisfy $S1$ and $S2$. $S1$ is satisfied because every integer solution of P belongs to exactly one of P_1 and P_2. $S2$ is satisfied because there are no integer solutions to P_1 and P_2 which are not solutions of P.

Of course, there is nothing special about the interval, $2 < x_2 < 3$. Any other interval which excludes no integer solutions such as $0 < x_1 < 1$, or $4 < x_2 < 5$, will do just as well.

The problem P is relaxed by removing or weakening some of its constraints or restrictions. We call a relaxation of P the problem P_R. The most common use of relaxation in integer programming is to drop the integrality requirement, although other forms of relaxation are also used.

Relaxation requires that the following conditions be satisfied.

PRINCIPLE OF RELAXATION

When a problem P is relaxed to a problem P_R, every feasible solution to the problem P must be a feasible solution to the problem P_R. This leads to three results:

$R1$. If there is no feasible solution to P_R, there is no feasible solution to P.

$R2$. The maximum value of P_R is no less than the maximum value of P.

$R3$. If an optimal solution of P_R is a feasible solution of P, it is an optimal solution of P.

Finally, we have fathomed a problem when the problem needs no further analysis in the quest for the integer programming solution. The principle of fathoming gives three different ways in which a problem is fathomed. The importance of the second case will become clear in the next section.

PRINCIPLE OF FATHOMING

We say a problem P is fathomed when either

$F1.$ P has no feasible solution, or

$F2.$ P has no solution that has an objective function value better than some predetermined value z^*, or

$F3.$ An analysis of P reveals the optimal solution.

The integer programming techniques for solving expression (12-32) vary— nearly all relax the original problem by removing the integer restriction, some fathom it without separating it into descendants, and others fathom totally through the descendants. We will study how integer programming uses these principles by looking at two entirely different solution techniques, the first, a simple version of *branch and bound algorithms*, and the second, *Gomory's cutting plane algorithm*. For ease of exposition we will always deal with a maximizing problem.

12-8 A BRANCH AND BOUND ALGORITHM

A branch and bound algorithm solves the integer programming problem by a combination of relaxation and separation. Fathoming is done through the descendants of the original integer programming problem. The original integer program and its descendants that are generated by the branch and bound procedure are relaxed to linear programs for solution. If a particular descendant is not fathomed when its linear programming solution is found, it is separated or *branched* into two new descendants. If it is fathomed at the linear programming solution, then that branch is terminated. We have not fathomed the original problem until we have fathomed all of the descendants. The optimal solution to the original integer programming problem is the greatest of the optimal solutions of the descendant problems.

The collection of unfathomed problems is called the *reserve* or *candidate list*. Each time a problem is chosen for fathoming from the reserve, we start a new iteration of the branch and bound algorithm, and the problem chosen is referred to as the *candidate problem*, or CP. At the first iteration, the reserve only contains the original integer programming problem, which is thus the initial candidate problem.

Let us assume that at each iteration of the algorithm we know that the objective function value of the optimal solution to the integer programming problem is at least as great as some specified value. This value is a lower bound on the optimal integer programming solution. If, while solving a candidate problem we find a

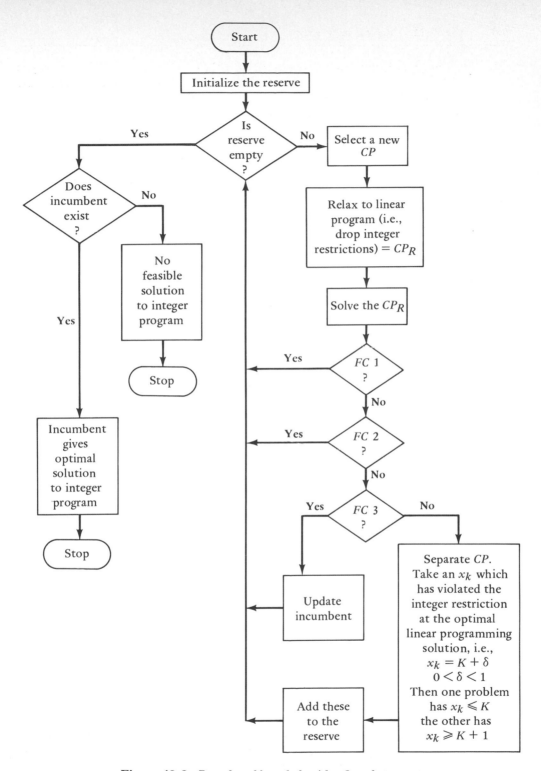

Figure 12-2. *Branch and bound algorithm flow chart.*

405

feasible integer solution with an objective function value higher than the previously greatest known lower bound, then we can update the greatest known lower bound to this new value. The integer programming solution that supplies this new greatest known lower bound is called the *incumbent*. Conversely, if the optimal objective function value of the candidate problem solved at an iteration is less than that of the incumbent, this candidate problem can be discarded from further consideration—it has been fathomed. Let CP_R be the problem created by relaxing the integer restrictions on CP.

BRANCH AND BOUND FATHOMING

If CP_R is a relaxation of CP, then CP is fathomed if:

FC1. The analysis of CP_R reveals that CP has no feasible solution. (See $R1$.)

FC2. The analysis of CP_R reveals that CP has no feasible solution better than the incumbent. (See $R2$.)

FC3. The analysis of CP_R reveals the optimal solution to CP. (See $R3$.)

The branch and bound algorithm is summarized in the flow chart of Figure 12-2.

12-9 EXAMPLE OF BRANCH AND BOUND ALGORITHM

Let us solve problem (12-1) by the branch and bound algorithm. Figure 12-3 shows the progression of candidate problems as they are created and solved. Each rectangle represents the solution to a problem. A branch is created where separation generates new descendent problems, and a branch is terminated when the fathoming criteria are satisfied by a problem. The order in which the problems have been extracted and solved from the reserve is given by the problem numbers in Figure 12-3.

Implicit in Figure 12-3 is a rule for the order of entering descendant problems into the reserve, and also a rule for choosing the candidate problem from the reserve. When two new descendants are created, the problem with $x_k \leqslant K$ is first entered at the top of the candidate list. Then the problem with $x_k \geqslant K + 1$ is entered ahead of it. Candidates are chosen from the top downward. This means that the latter problem is always solved prior to the former. In terms of Figure 12-3, the right-hand branch just created is always chosen first (this means that there are never any right-hand branches in the reserve), then the left-hand branches are chosen starting from the last one created.

For our problem, when the reserve is empty, all the branches have been terminated and the incumbent has the solution: $z = 44$, $x_1 = 0$, $x_2 = 4$. This is the optimal solution.

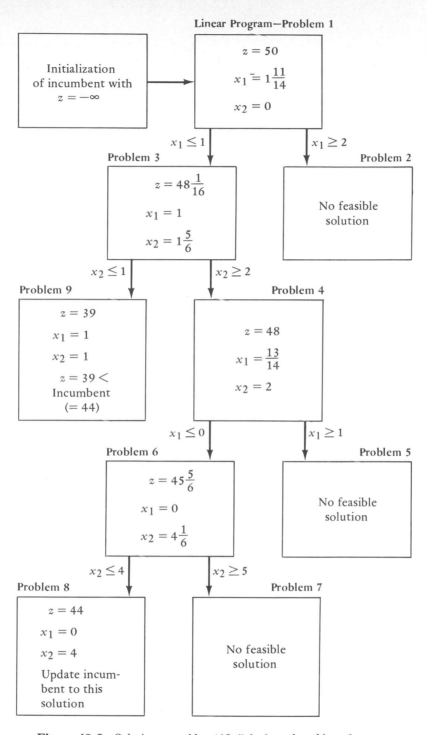

Figure 12-3. *Solution to problem (12-1) by branch and bound.*

Figure 12-4 depicts graphically the sequence of problems created by the branch and bound algorithm. The solution of problem i is shown as $SOLN(i)$.

More sophisticated branch and bound algorithms carefully choose the variable around which to separate and the candidate problem to be solved at each iteration. These choices can have a significant influence on the number of descendants created

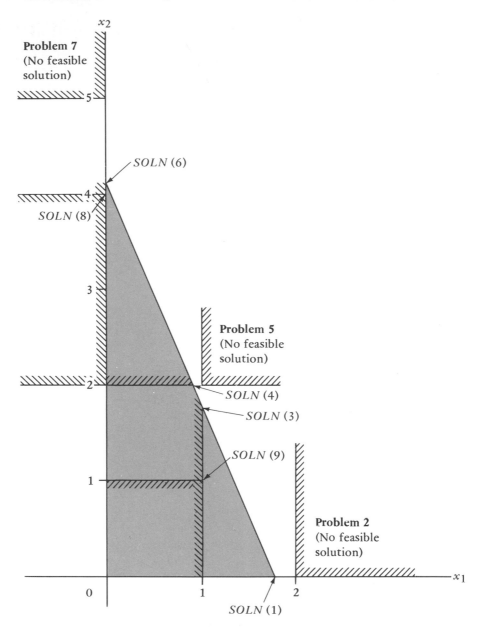

Figure 12-4. *Branch and bound for problem (12-1).*

and the order in which they are solved, which in turn influence the way each branch is terminated and, thus, the time the algorithm takes to reach the optimal solution.

Some algorithms take special account of zero-one variables. An all-zero-one problem can usually be solved more quickly by specialized branch and bound algorithms that specifically take advantage of the zero-one property.

12-10 CUTTING PLANE TECHNIQUE

The branch and bound technique does not persist in the fathoming of a particular problem. If it cannot fathom the problem, it separates it into descendants.

The technique we come to now is at the opposite extreme. It never separates but always persists in fathoming a problem until the solution is found. As with branch and bound, the initial step is to relax the integer programming problem by removing the integer restrictions, i.e., the integer programming problem is converted to an ordinary linear programming problem. The relaxed problem is then solved. If this does not fathom the integer programming problem, then the relaxation is modified—it is in fact tightened by adding a new constraint. The integer restrictions are never formally reimposed, but they are embodied in new constraints added to the continuous problem.

The principle behind this technique is illustrated in Figure 12-5.

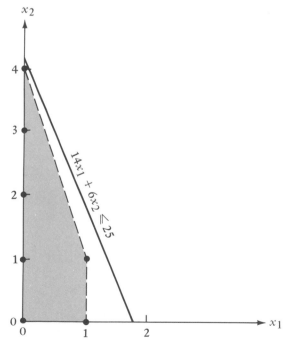

Figure 12-5. *Convex hull of the feasible solution to problem* *(12-1).*

If we solve the problem with dashed constraint lines instead of the one with the black constraint line, we obtain the optimal integer solution as the optimal solution of an ordinary linear programming problem (with continuous variables).

We can see some interesting things about this new problem:

(i) Every integer solution of the old problem is a solution of the new one.
(ii) Every corner point of this problem (and hence every basic feasible solution) is an integer solution.

The feasible region of the new problem is the *convex hull of the integer solutions* of problem (12-1). It is the smallest linear programming feasible region to contain all the integer solutions. For solution purposes it is not necessary to obtain the linear program which has property (ii), it is sufficient to obtain a linear program which has the optimal integer solution as its optimal continuous solution.

The solution techniques which are called *cutting plane techniques* add constraints which cut away some of the feasible region, but never cut away a feasible integer solution. The objective is to start at the optimal linear programming solution and create a new linear program with a smaller feasible region. If the new linear program does not have an integer solution as its optimum, the process is continued until a linear program is reached whose optimal solution is an integer solution. This process is a series of relaxations of the integer programming problems, each relaxation being more restrictive than the previous one. By principle $R3$ the integer solution obtained by this technique is optimal to the integer program.

One form of *cut*, for the all-integer problem, suggested by George B. Dantzig, ("Note on Solving Linear Programs in Integers," *Naval Research Logistics Quarterly*, 6, 1959, pp. 75–76) is as follows:

Consider the optimal linear programming basic solution. If this solution is not integer, some of the variables (including the slack variables) must change their values in order to reach the optimal integer programming solution. In particular, some of the nonbasic variables at the optimal linear programming solution must become positive, and they must be integer at the optimal integer programming solution. Since they must be positive and integer, they must be at least equal to 1.

Let R be the set of subscripts of the x_j for the nonbasic variables at the optimal linear programming basic solution. The following constraint must therefore hold at the optimal integer solution:

$$\sum_{j \in R} x_j \geqslant 1$$

If the new linear program (i.e., the old linear program with this constraint added) does not have an integer solution as its optimum, then a similar constraint is added for the new nonbasic variables.

This particular cut is simple in concept but, unfortunately, it has practical problems. As it stands, we cannot guarantee that the optimal integer programming solution will be reached.

R. E. Gomory ("An Algorithm for Integer Solutions to Linear Programming," *Princeton-IBM Mathematics Research Project, Technical Report* No. 1, Nov. 1958) is responsible for a type of cut that guarantees that the process will terminate, in theory, at the optimal solution in a finite number of stages.   To illustrate Gomory's reasoning for the all-integer problem, we will derive the cut equations for the relaxation of problem (12-1), i.e., for

$$\text{maximize } z = 28x_1 + 11x_2 + 0x_3$$

(12-33) $$\text{subject to} \quad 14x_1 + 6x_2 + x_3 = 25$$

$$x_1, x_2, x_3 \geqslant 0$$

In terms of the linear programming analysis of Chapter 3, let us define the following column vectors in problem (12-33). $\mathbf{a}_1 = [14]$, $\mathbf{a}_2 = [6]$, $\mathbf{a}_3 = [1]$, $\mathbf{b} = [25]$.   The optimal linear programming solution is $x_1 = 25/14$, corresponding to the basis $(\mathbf{a}_1)$ in E^1 (one-dimensional Euclidean space), i.e., it is the basic solution to the equation system.

(12-34) $$\mathbf{b} = x_1 \mathbf{a}_1$$

We can also express $\mathbf{a}_2$ and $\mathbf{a}_3$ in terms of the optimal basis:

(12-35)
$$\mathbf{a}_2 = \tfrac{6}{14}\mathbf{a}_1$$

$$\mathbf{a}_3 = \tfrac{1}{14}\mathbf{a}_1$$

Again, we reason that if the optimal linear programming solution is not integer, then at least one of the nonbasic variables at the optimal linear programming solution must become a positive integer at the optimal integer programming solution.   Let us consider the change in the basic solution if the nonbasic variables are allowed to assume positive values, i.e., what is the new value of x_1, if at least one of x_2 and x_3 is allowed to assume a positive integer value?   We must solve the following equation for x_1:

(12-36) $$\mathbf{b} = x_1 \mathbf{a}_1 + x_2 \mathbf{a}_2 + x_3 \mathbf{a}_3$$

Using (12-35) this gives

$$\mathbf{b} = (x_1 + \tfrac{6}{14}x_2 + \tfrac{1}{14}x_3)\mathbf{a}_1$$

From (12-34) we know that

$$(x_1 + \tfrac{6}{14}x_2 + \tfrac{1}{14}x_3) = \tfrac{25}{14}$$

or

(12-37) $$x_1 = \tfrac{25}{14} + \tfrac{6}{14}(-x_2) + \tfrac{1}{14}(-x_3)$$

Note carefully that the coefficients on the left-hand side of (12-37) are the coefficients of $(-x_j)$ for each nonbasic variable x_j.   Had there been more than one basic variable in (12-34), there would be an expression like (12-37) for each variable. Gomory's procedure takes only one of the noninteger basic variables at the optimal linear programming solution and its expression of the form of (12-37), and derives a cut constraint.   The choice is arbitrary.   In this case, x_1 is the only eligible variable.

Let us separate each coefficient and parameter on the right-hand side of (12-37) into its integer and its positive fractional parts.   For instance, a coefficient of 2.7 is separated into $+2$ and $+0.7$, whereas -2.7 is separated into -3 and $+0.3$. Thus (12-37) becomes

$$x_1 = (1 + \tfrac{11}{14}) + (0 + \tfrac{6}{14})(-x_2) + (0 + \tfrac{1}{14})(-x_3)$$

or

(12-38) $$x_1 = (1 - 0x_2 - 0x_3) + (\tfrac{11}{14} - \tfrac{6}{14}x_2 - \tfrac{1}{14}x_3)$$

Now, we want to derive from (12-38) a condition that must be met by all solutions (x_1, x_2, x_3) that are integer. Whenever x_2 and x_3 are integer, the first bracket on the right-hand side of (12-38) is an integer, since by construction, the parameters and coefficients in it are integer. We are left with the term

(12-39) $$(\tfrac{11}{14} - \tfrac{6}{14}x_2 - \tfrac{1}{14}x_3)$$

which must also be integer for x_1 to be integer. It is the integrality of (12-39) that determines the *Gomory cut*. For (12-39) to be integer, it cannot be positive since the only positive term, $\tfrac{11}{14}$, is by definition fractional, i.e., less than one.

So (x_1, x_2, x_3) can be integer only if

$$\tfrac{11}{14} - \tfrac{6}{14}x_2 - \tfrac{1}{14}x_3 \leqslant 0$$

or

(12-40) $$-\tfrac{6}{14}x_2 - \tfrac{1}{14}x_3 \leqslant -\tfrac{11}{14}$$

This is the first Gomory cut. Using the constraint of (12-33) to substitute for x_3 in (12-40), we see that it is equivalent to

(12-41) $$x_1 \leqslant 1$$

The whole reasoning holds for **any** feasible integer solution. Thus, no integer solutions are excluded by the cut. On the other hand, the old linear programming optimum is **not** satisfied by the cut. From (12-40) we see that the left-hand side is always zero at the old linear programming optimum (since the nonbasic variables are zero), while the right-hand side is by definition always a negative fraction. In fact, the cut always excludes the fractional part of the variable around which it was constructed, in this case, x_1.

When the new constraint (12-41) is added to (12-33), we obtain a new linear program with the optimal solution: $x_1 = 1$, $x_2 = \tfrac{11}{6}$. This is point A in Figure 12-6. This solution is not all integer, hence we introduce another Gomory cut using the linear programming problem which includes (12-41). The new Gomory cut is generated in a similar manner to (12-40).

$$\text{Let } \mathbf{b} = \begin{bmatrix} 25 \\ 1 \end{bmatrix}, \ \mathbf{a}_1 = \begin{bmatrix} 14 \\ 1 \end{bmatrix}, \ \mathbf{a}_2 = \begin{bmatrix} 6 \\ 0 \end{bmatrix}, \ \mathbf{a}_3 = \begin{bmatrix} 1 \\ 0 \end{bmatrix}, \ \mathbf{a}_4 = \begin{bmatrix} 0 \\ 1 \end{bmatrix},$$

with optimal basis $(\mathbf{a}_1, \mathbf{a}_2)$ and

(12-42)
$$\begin{aligned} \mathbf{b} &= 1\mathbf{a}_1 + \tfrac{11}{6}\mathbf{a}_2 \\ \mathbf{a}_3 &= 0\mathbf{a}_1 + \tfrac{1}{6}\mathbf{a}_2 \\ \mathbf{a}_4 &= 1\mathbf{a}_1 - \tfrac{14}{6}\mathbf{a}_2 \end{aligned}$$

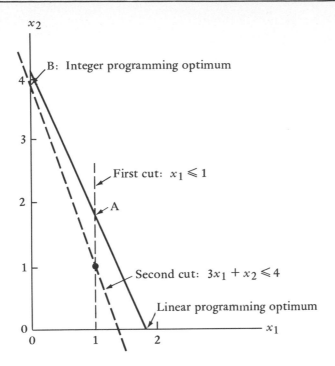

Figure 12-6. *The Gomory cuts for problem (12-1).*

Expressing $\mathbf{b} = x_1\mathbf{a}_1 + x_2\mathbf{a}_2 + x_3\mathbf{a}_3 + x_4\mathbf{a}_4$ in terms of (12-42), we obtain

(12-43) $\qquad \mathbf{b} = (x_1 + 0x_3 + x_4)\mathbf{a}_1 + (x_2 + \frac{1}{6}x_3 - \frac{14}{6}x_4)\mathbf{a}_2$

Take a noninteger valued basic variable—in this case $x_2 = \frac{11}{6}$—then we obtain from (12-43) and (12-42)

$$\frac{11}{6} = x_2 + \frac{1}{6}x_3 - \frac{14}{6}x_4$$

or $\qquad x_2 = \frac{11}{6} + \frac{1}{6}(-x_3) - \frac{14}{6}(-x_4)$

$$= (1 + \frac{5}{6}) + (0 + \frac{1}{6})(-x_3) + (-3 + \frac{4}{6})(-x_4)$$

$$= (1 - 0x_3 + 3x_4) + (\frac{5}{6} - \frac{1}{6}x_3 - \frac{4}{6}x_4).$$

The new Gomory cut can now be identified as

(12-44) $\qquad \frac{5}{6} - \frac{1}{6}x_3 - \frac{4}{6}x_4 \leqslant 0$

Using the definitions, $x_3 = 25 - 14x_1 - 6x_2$ and $x_4 = 1 - x_1$, (12-44) becomes

(12-45) $\qquad 3x_1 + x_2 \leqslant 4$

The linear program with both cuts (12-41) and (12-45) added is, in fact, the convex hull of the integer solutions and the optimal solution to this problem—point B in Figure 12-6 ($x_1 = 0$, $x_2 = 4$)—is an integer solution and hence the optimal integer solution.

12-11 GENERAL COMMENTS

The branch and bound algorithm and the cutting-plane technique represent extremes of the separation-relaxation-fathoming principles.   Many techniques fall somewhere in between.

Figure 12-7 is the flow chart for the general procedure.   Particular techniques omit certain stages, or treat certain stages in different ways.

For example, the branch and bound algorithm described earlier never persists in fathoming the same candidate problem (i.e., never pursues the Yes branch at the question "Persist?"), while the cutting plane procedure always persists.

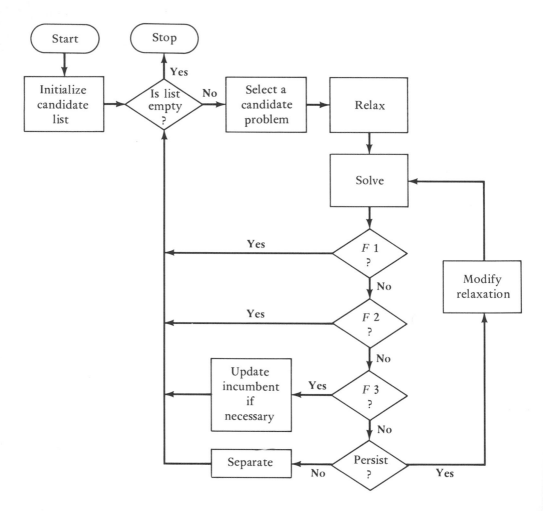

Figure 12-7. *Flow chart for general integer programming techniques.*

12-12 SOLUTION TO THE BUS SCHEDULING PROBLEM

The bus scheduling problem of Section 12-4, as given in Table 12-4, was solved using Burrough's TEMPO mathematical programming system.   The problem has 69 rows, including the objective function, and 43 nonslack variables, of which 29 are

NAME	STATUS	ACTIVITY	INPUT COST
X1	BS	440.0	−0.15
X2	BS	635.0	−0.15
X3	BS	785.0	−0.15
X4	LL	0.0	−0.15
X5	BS	845.0	−0.15
X6	BS	950.0	−0.15
X7	BS	1115.0	−0.15
Y1	BS	605.0	0.15
Y2	BS	675.0	0.15
Y3	BS	795.0	0.15
Y4	BS	0.0	0.15
Y5	BS	855.0	0.15
Y6	BS	960.0	0.15
Y7	BS	1125.0	0.15
DELTA1	IV	1.0	25.00
DELTA2	IV	1.0	25.00
DELTA3	IV	1.0	25.00
DELTA4	IV	0.0	25.00
DELTA5	IV	1.0	25.00
DELTA6	IV	1.0	25.00
DELTA7	IV	1.0	25.00
GAMMA11	IV	1.0	0.0
GAMMA22	IV	1.0	0.0
GAMMA23	IV	0.0	0.0
GAMMA32	IV	1.0	0.0
GAMMA33	IV	0.0	0.0
GAMMA34	IV	0.0	0.0
GAMMA44	IV	0.0	0.0
GAMMA45	IV	1.0	0.0
GAMMA55	IV	0.0	0.0
GAMMA56	IV	1.0	0.0
BETA11	IV	1.0	0.0
BETA12	IV	0.0	0.0
BETA22	IV	1.0	0.0
BETA23	IV	0.0	0.0
BETA33	IV	1.0	0.0
BETA34	IV	0.0	0.0
BETA44	IV	0.0	0.0
BETA45	IV	0.0	0.0
BETA46	IV	1.0	0.0
BETA55	IV	0.0	0.0
BETA56	IV	0.0	0.0
BETA57	IV	1.0	0.0

Note: BS Denotes *basic variable*
LL Denotes *variable at lower limit*
IV Denotes *integer variable*

Figure 12-8. *Optimal solution to bus scheduling problem.*

0—1 integers. TEMPO's branch and bound algorithm looked at approximately 300 nodes before it terminated. The incumbent was set initially to zero and was changed 4 times during computation. The total CPU time was 75 seconds on a Burrough's B6718.

Figure 12-8 gives the listing of the optimal solution. It has a cost of $186.75 per day. This solution is shown diagrammatically in Figure 12-9. It is an interesting solution in that it drops one bus—bus 4 (obviously the numbering is irrelevant).

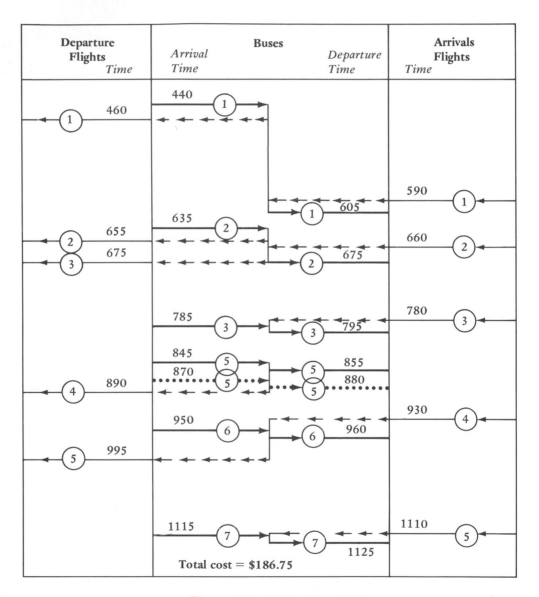

Figure 12-9. *Optimal bus schedule.*

Bus 1 is kept waiting at the airport 165 minutes, so that it can connect with the first arrival flight. Both buses 3 and 7 service only one arrival flight each, they do not connect with any departure flight, and bus 5 services only a departure flight. We have not assumed any capacity limit on the buses, but there may be a problem with bus 2 being overfull when servicing two departure flights. The times of bus 5 are not the most convenient, since it arrives 45 minutes before flight 4 leaves. This bus could, at no extra cost, arrive at time 870 and leave at time 890, giving passengers less waiting time at the airport. The model formulation did not impose a condition that a short passenger waiting time is preferred to a long one.

12-13 SENSITIVITY ANALYSIS

In Chapter 4 we discovered the wealth of information the optimal simplex tableau provides for sensitivity analysis. Since integer programming is so akin to linear programming you may ask: What can we say about the sensitivity of the solution in the integer programming situation? The short answer is that we can say very little of practical value. The reason is simply that integer programming involves discrete jumps from solution to solution rather than a continuous change.

If we have used branch and bound as our solution technique (as the case usually will be), we can say almost nothing analytically about sensitivity analysis. The best we can do is to ask the branch and bound algorithm to find the K best solutions to the problem. (See H. Wagner, *Principles of Operations Research*, 2nd Ed., Prentice-Hall, 1975, pages 498–499 for a discussion.) By applying changes of parameters and coefficients to these solutions, some useful but not necessarily conclusive information can be gained. There seems to be no easy way of finding the new optimum when the constraint set is relaxed. The only option is to rerun the branch and bound algorithm using the old integer programming optimum as the new incumbent. When a constraint is tightened, it may be necessary to repeat the whole procedure from scratch.

If Gomory's cutting plane algorithm is being used, ranging of the objective function coefficients can be performed to a limited extent. We can only be confident of the complete accuracy of the cost-ranging if the linear programming constraints derived by the cutting plane are the convex hull of the integer programming problem. Remember, it is likely that the Gomory cutting plane algorithm will have cut away only enough of the feasible region to reveal the optimal integer solution. If this is so, any cost-ranging based on the optimal integer programming tableau underestimates the true cost ranges. Explain why this is so.

Sensitivity analysis of the RHS parameters is no more satisfactory. An important article by R. E. Gomory and W. J. Baumol, ("Integer Programming and Pricing", *Econometrica*, 28, 1960), developed a scheme for finding shadow prices at the optimal integer solution. These prices result from a modification of the optimal linear programming dual variables by correcting for each of the Gomory cuts. Unfortunately, the scheme is far from foolproof, and the prices are not easy to interpret. If we relax a slack constraint in linear programming there is no effect on the optimal solution. This is not necessarily true in integer programming where a constraint may be slack only because of the integer condition on the variable. In linear programming, any change in the solution as the RHS parameter changes is continuous; in integer programming, there is no change in the solution until a superior integer solution becomes feasible. Then, the change is a discrete jump.

Using either technique we can state bounds on the changes in objective function value for a change in a RHS parameter. These bounds come from the optimal linear programming tableau. We can determine with ease the change in the linear programming optimal objective function value for a change in the RHS and we know that the integer programming optimum can have no better value than the linear programming optimum. So the difference between the new linear programming value and the old integer programming value of the objective function is an upper bound on the change in the integer programming value for a relaxation of the RHS, and a lower bound on the change in the integer programming value for a tightening of the RHS that renders the old integer programming optimum infeasible.

EXERCISES

12.1   Formulate the river pollution problem of Section 7-8 as an integer programming problem.

12.2   Show how the following shaded region can be formulated in an integer programming problem.

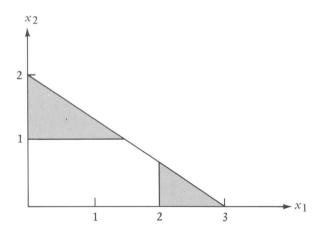

12.3   A company produces three products, requiring 1 machine hour, 1.5 machine hours, and 2 machine hours respectively. There is a limit of 2000 machine hours per week. The following table gives the cost structure for production runs of various lengths.

	Fixed set-up cost ($)	Variable cost ($ per unit)		
		1–100 units	101–500 units	over 500 units
Product 1	100	10	8	5
Product 2	50	20	18	15
Product 3	200	40	30	20

Selling prices per unit are $15, $40, $60 respectively. Formulate the problem as an integer programming problem.

12.4 A company is preparing its 5-year plan for a period commencing a year from now. Part of the plan involves investment in the expansion of facilities. Four projects present themselves as viable. The company wishes to know which of them to implement in the 5-year period, and when to start each of them. The object is to maximize discounted net return from these projects for the 5-year period and the 3 years following. For the 5 years, the company is budgeting the following amounts each year from existing operations,

Year 1	$200,000
Year 2	$100,000
Year 3	$250,000
Year 4	$100,000
Year 5	$200,000

Any amount unused in a period is accumulated for later periods. In addition to this, one-quarter of the positive net returns from any of these projects, once implemented, is available to finance other projects. The following table shows the expected net returns for the years after each of the projects is *commenced*.

	Year 1	Year 2	Year 3	Year 4 onward
Project 1	−100,000	0	100,000	200,000
Project 2	−50,000	−150,000	20,000	100,000
Project 3	−300,000	−100,000	100,000	400,000
Project 4	−400,000	100,000	200,000	400,000

Any implemented project which requires funds after the 5-year planning period must get the funds from amounts accumulated from the budget of the 5-year planning period and created funds from other projects. By their nature, projects 2 and 3 cannot both be implemented since project 3 is a larger scale version of project 2. Formulate the problem as an integer programming problem. Use a discount rate of 0.9.

12.5 Solve problem (12-1) in the text using the opposite order for entering candidate problems, i.e., place the newly created descendant with $x_k > K + 1$ on top first, then $x_k < K$ on top of that, and again choose the candidate problem from the top.

12.6   Solve the problem

$$\text{maximize } z = 10x_1 + 3x_2$$

$$\text{subject to} \qquad 5x_1 + 2x_2 \leqslant 17$$

$$x_1, x_2 \geqslant 0 \text{ and integer}$$

(a) By the branch and bound algorithm.

(b) By Gomory's cutting plane algorithm. (Having worked out the cut constraint in terms of the variables x_1 and x_2, rework the simplex method from scratch.)

12.7   Using the branch and bound algorithm, find the optimum to problem (12-1) of the text when the grant is increased to $3.3 million. The optimum to problem (12-1) can be used as the initial incumbent.   Choose the $x_k \geqslant K+1$ problem first.

12.8   Repeat question 12.7 choosing the candidate problem, $x_k \leqslant K$, first.

12.9   Find the first two Gomory cuts for the problem in question 12.7.

12.10   Solve the following problem by the branch and bound algorithm.   Use a graph to find the solution to the descendant problems.

$$\text{maximize } z = 8x_1 + 4x_2$$

$$\text{subject to} \qquad x_1 + 4x_2 \leqslant 19$$

$$12x_1 + 5x_2 \leqslant 45$$

$$5x_1 + x_2 \leqslant 16$$

$$x_1, x_2 \geqslant 0 \text{ and integer}$$

Construct a graph of the form of Figure 12-4, and a tree of the form of Figure 12-3.

REFERENCES

Texts at a similar level to this chapter, but more extensive are:

Plane, D. R., and C. McMillan. *Discrete Optimization.* Englewood Cliffs, N.J.: Prentice-Hall, 1971. Chapter 2 gives a good series of applications of 0–1 integer programming, Chapter 5 gives further general examples, and Chapter 7 gives a case study. Implicit enumeration techniques for the 0–1 problem are in Chapter 3, and branch and bound and the cutting-plane algorithm are in Chapter 4. In addition, there are computer codes for implicit enumeration of 0–1 problems and a cutting-plane algorithm. This book is a good place to start a more detailed study of integer programming without complicated mathematics.

van de Panne, C. *Linear Programming and Related Techniques.* Amsterdam: North-Holland, 1971. Of particular interest in this text, is the material of Chapters 15 and 16 which expounds more extensively the basic principles of branch and bound methods.

More advanced texts on integer programming include:

Garfinkel, R. S., and G. L. Nemhauser. *Integer Programming.* New York: Wiley, 1972. This is a very comprehensive text on integer programming. It covers a very wide range of techniques skimping neither the theory nor worked examples. This book is suitable for a competent student who wants to study integer programming in depth.

Greenberg, N. *Integer Programming*. New York: Academic Press, 1971. A text for intermediate and advanced students. The theory is tempered with good application and examples.

Hadley, G. *Non-linear and Dynamic Programming*. Reading, Mass.: Addison-Wesley, 1964. For those well equipped mathematically, Chapter 8 has a good series of formulated integer programming problems and a complete treatment of the Gomory cutting-plane theory for both the all-integer and mixed-integer cases.

There are two excellent journal articles that survey integer programming. Both are pitched at a fairly advanced level.

Balinski, M. L. "Integer Programming: Methods, Uses, Computation", *Management Science*, 12, Nov. 1965. Despite its age, this article is still a very important reference in integer programming literature. A thorough reading of the article requires good mathematics and some knowledge of integer programming. However, pages 274–275 give a valuable resume of the success (or otherwise) of integer programming applications. There is a comprehensive list of references up to 1965.

Geoffrion, A. M., and R. E. Marsten. "Integer Programming Algorithms—A Survey", *Management Science*, 18, May 1972. An excellent survey of integer techniques. The approach used in this article greatly influenced our own treatment in this chapter.

Many articles on the application of integer programming have been published. Three recent articles are worth reading.

Forrest, J. J., J. P. H. Hirst, and J. A. Tomlin. "Practical Solution of Large Mixed Integer Programming Problems with UMPIRE", *Management Science*, 20, January 1974. This article is concerned with the computational efficiency of branch and bound methods. It reports success in solving mixed-integer problems using a code called UMPIRE. Many of the finer details necessary for an efficient algorithm are discussed.

Kalvaitis, R., and A. G. Posgay. "An Application of Mixed Integer Programming in the Direct Mail Industry", *Management Science*, 20, January 1974. An application of integer programming to the compilation of mailing lists is discussed in this brief article. It is reported that the company concerned has benefited substantially by the study.

Woolsey, R. E. D. "A Candle to Saint Jude, or Four Real World Applications of Integer Programming", *Interfaces*, 2, Feb. 1972. The article gives potential users of integer programming some rather disconcerting advice to reconsider carefully before using any integer programming code. Maybe some heuristic approach might get almost as good a solution at a fraction of the cost.

13

Nonsimplex Based Nonlinear Programming

In Chapter 11 we concluded that the classical methods of calculus for solving problems involving nonlinear functional relations tend to break down when the number of decision variables goes much beyond two or three. For constrained problems the Lagrangian multiplier approach can handle, in a rather awkward manner, one or two constraints by adding additional variables to the problem, making things even worse. Clearly, what is needed to solve such problems is an iterative approach, based on a powerful algorithm, which explores the feasible set of solutions in an efficient manner and locates the optimum.

In this chapter we will look at two such approaches, namely, *gradient methods* and *penalty and barrier methods*, neither of which is related to the simplex method of linear programming. The next chapter will study approaches to solving similar problems using simplex based techniques. We shall leave aside all the numerous modifications and refinements on these approaches, even though it is they that render these techniques computationally efficient. We shall first take up gradient methods for unconstrained nonlinear programming problems and then for constrained problems, followed by penalty and barrier methods.

Although the mathematical basis needed for this chapter does not go beyond the concepts of first order derivatives and vectors, the reasoning underlying these techniques is considerably more demanding. Usually, nonlinear programming algorithms are viewed as part of the more advanced bag of tools of the operations researcher. As you go along, it will be helpful to periodically pause, recapitulate, and check your understanding.

13-1 AN EXAMPLE OF A NONLINEAR PROGRAMMING PROBLEM

A manufacturer makes three products. The sales volume of each product is dependent on its price, and in one case, product 3, sales volume is also dependent on the price of another product. The market forecasting division estimated the following relationship between monthly sales volume x_j (thousands of units) and unit price p_j for each product:

(13-1)
$$x_1 = 10 - p_1$$
$$x_2 = 16 - p_2$$
$$x_3 = 6 - \tfrac{1}{2}p_3 + \tfrac{1}{4}p_2$$

The variable costs for the three products are \$6, \$7, and \$10 per unit, respectively.

Production is limited by available resources, manpower, and machine time. Each month 1000 machine hours and 2000 man hours are available. Product 1 uses 0.4 machine hour and 0.2 man hour per unit, product 2 uses 0.2 machine hour and 0.4 man hour per unit, and product 3 uses 0.1 hour of each per unit. The manufacturer wishes to find the monthly sales schedule that will maximize profits.

Total profit for each product is equal to total revenue minus total variable cost for the product. For product 1, total revenue is $R_1 = p_1 x_1$. From (13-1), $p_1 = 10 - x_1$, so

$$R_1 = p_1 x_1 = 10x_1 - x_1{}^2$$

Total variable cost for product 1 is $V_1 = 6x_1$. So the total profit for product 1 is

$$\pi_1 = R_1 - V_1 = 10x_1 - x_1{}^2 - 6x_1 = 4x_1 - x_1{}^2$$

Verify that for product 2 the total revenue amounts to $R_2 = p_2 x_2 = 16x_2 - x_2{}^2$, and the total variable cost $V_2 = 7x_2$, with the difference of

$$\pi_2 = R_2 - V_2 = 16x_2 - x_2{}^2 - 7x_2 = 9x_2 - x_2{}^2$$

Product 3 presents a new problem, since x_3 depends on p_2 as well as p_3. Total revenue is

$$R_3 = p_3 x_3 = 2(6 - x_3 + \tfrac{1}{4}p_2)x_3$$

Using $p_2 = 16 - x_2$ from expressions (13-1), we obtain

$$R_3 = 2(6 - x_3 + \tfrac{1}{4}(16 - x_2))x_3 = 20x_3 - 2x_3{}^2 - \tfrac{1}{2}x_2 x_3$$

Variable cost is $V_3 = 10x_3$. Hence total profit for product 3 is

$$\pi_3 = R_3 - V_3 = 20x_3 - 2x_3{}^2 - \tfrac{1}{2}x_2 x_3 - 10x_3$$
$$= 10x_3 - 2x_3{}^2 - \tfrac{1}{2}x_2 x_3$$

Summing π_1, π_2, and π_3, we obtain the total profit function:

(13-2) $\pi = f(x_1, x_2, x_3) = 4x_1 - x_1{}^2 + 9x_2 - x_2{}^2 + 10x_3 - 2x_3{}^2 - \tfrac{1}{2}x_2 x_3$

We want to find values for x_1, x_2, and x_3 that maximize expression (13-2) within the monthly machine time and man hour restrictions imposed:

$$4x_1 + 2x_2 + x_3 \leqslant 10 \qquad \text{(units of 100 machine hours)}$$
$$2x_1 + 4x_2 + x_3 \leqslant 20 \qquad \text{(units of 100 man hours)}$$

Summarizing, we obtain the following programming problem.

$$\text{maximize } f(x_1, x_2, x_3,) = 4x_1 - x_1^2 + 9x_2 - x_2^2 + 10x_3 - 2x_3^2 - \tfrac{1}{2}x_2 x_3$$

(13-3)   subject to $4x_1 + 2x_2 + x_3 \leqslant 10$ (machine time)

$$2x_1 + 4x_2 + x_3 \leqslant 20 \qquad \text{(man hours)}$$

$$x_1 \geqslant 0, \qquad x_2 \geqslant 0, \qquad x_3 \geqslant 0 \qquad \text{(nonnegativity conditions)}$$

Problem (13-3) is a nonlinear programming problem, since some of its functional relationships are nonlinear.

In general, the form of nonlinear programming problems is as follows: Determine values $x_1, x_2, \ldots, x_n$ which

$$\text{maximize } f(x_1, x_2, \ldots, x_n)$$

(13-4)   subject to $g_i(x_1, x_2, \ldots, x_n) \leqslant b_i, \qquad i = 1, \ldots, m,$

$$x_j \geqslant 0, \qquad j = 1, \ldots, n$$

where some or all of the functional relationships of (13-4) are nonlinear.

So as to decrease the writing effort, let $\mathbf{x}$ be a vector with elements $(x_1, x_2, \ldots, x_n)$. Then problem (13-4) can be rewritten more succinctly as

$$\text{maximize } f(\mathbf{x})$$

$$\text{subject to } g_i(\mathbf{x}) \leqslant b_i, \qquad i = 1, \ldots, m,$$

$$\mathbf{x} \geqslant 0$$

While the constraints have been given the specific $\leqslant$ inequality, this does not restrict the general nature of (13-4). Equalities and $\geqslant$ inequalities can easily be converted to this standard form. However, we assume that the first derivatives of all the functions exist and are continuous.

13-2 GRADIENT METHODS FOR UNCONSTRAINED OPTIMIZATION

The general structure of nonlinear programming algorithms is analogous to most algorithmic optimization techniques:

1. Initiate the algorithm at a feasible solution.
2. Find a *direction of movement* away from the current solution which improves the value of the objective function.
3. Determine how far to move away from the current solution in the direction of improvement of the objective function, or, find a *step size*.
4. Repeat steps 2 and 3 using always the last solution found in 3 until no further direction of improvement of the objective function can be found or the improvement in the objective function is less than a specified amount.

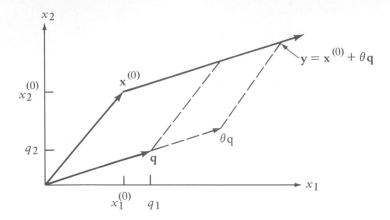

Figure 13-1. *Direction vector.*

It is at steps 2 and 3 that various techniques differ from each other.

The direction of movement from a solution is given by a *direction vector*. An example of such a direction vector is depicted graphically in Figure 13-1. The direction vector, $\mathbf{q} = [q_1, q_2]$ (in two-dimensional space), is the vector that allows us to generate all points along a ray emanating from the current solution, $\mathbf{x}^{(0)} = (x_1^{(0)}, x_2^{(0)})$, in the desired direction. This ray is defined in terms of the direction vector as the set of $\mathbf{y}$ such that $\mathbf{y} = \mathbf{x}^{(0)} + \theta\mathbf{q}$, for all $0 \leqslant \theta < \infty$.

Gradient methods choose the direction of movement from the initial feasible solution at step 2 as the direction defined by the *gradient vector* at that solution. The gradient vector $\mathbf{d}^{(0)}$ at a point $\mathbf{x}^{(0)}$ is the vector whose components (directional numbers) are the first partial derivatives of f evaluated at the point $\mathbf{x}^{(0)}$, i.e.,

$$\mathbf{d}^{(0)} = (\partial f/\partial x_1, \, \partial f/\partial x_2, \, ..., \, \partial f/\partial x_n) \qquad \text{evaluated at } \mathbf{x}^{(0)}$$

The gradient vector gives the greatest rate of increase in the value of the objective in the immediate vicinity of the initial point. It is, therefore, the locally best direction of movement. Geometrically, the gradient vector is the vector at right angles to the tangent plane at $\mathbf{x}^{(0)}$, as shown in Figure 13-2. This technique is sometimes called the *method of steepest ascent*.

A "best" choice for the step size in the gradient direction is to move to the point that gives the largest increase in the objective function value in that direction.

Figure 13-2 graphically depicts the progression toward the optimal solution along gradient vectors starting from an arbitrary point $\mathbf{x}^{(0)}$. This technique finds a solution that is arbitrarily close to the optimal solution (or a local optimum if several optima exist) in a finite number of moves.

Let us maximize expression (13-2) as an unconstrained function. This will give the optimal production levels, ignoring the manpower and machine time constraints. The reduced problem is thus:

$$\text{maximize } f(x) = 4x_1 - x_1^2 + 9x_2 - x_2^2 + 10x_3 - 2x_3^2 - \tfrac{1}{2}x_2 x_3$$

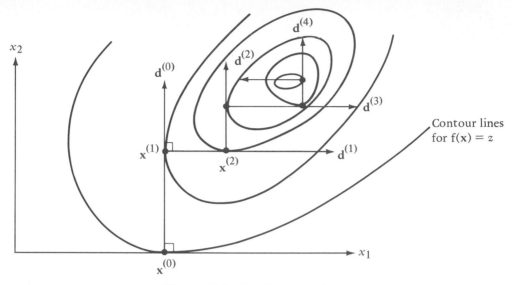

Figure 13-2. *Gradient method.*

The first partial derivatives of $f(\mathbf{x})$ are

(13-5) $\dfrac{\partial f}{\partial x_1} = 4 - 2x_1$, $\dfrac{\partial f}{\partial x_2} = 9 - 2x_2 - \tfrac{1}{2}x_3$, $\dfrac{\partial f}{\partial x_3} = 10 - 4x_3 - \tfrac{1}{2}x_2$

Assume an initial point of $\mathbf{x}^{(0)} = (1, 2, 2)$. Substituting these values for the variables into the three partials of (13-5), we find the gradient vector at $\mathbf{x}^{(0)}$. So

$$\frac{\partial f}{\partial x_1} = 4 - 2(1) = 2, \qquad \frac{\partial f}{\partial x_2} = 9 - 2(2) - \frac{1}{2}(2) = 4,$$

$$\frac{\partial f}{\partial x_3} = 10 - 4(2) - \frac{1}{2}(2) = 1$$

and we obtain

(13-6) $$\mathbf{d}^{(0)} = (2, 4, 1)$$

The next problem is to find a step size in the direction of the gradient vector at $\mathbf{x}^{(0)}$. If we choose the largest improvement of the objective function in the direction of the gradient vector as our criterion, then we want to find a step size θ that yields the point $\mathbf{x}^{(1)}$ defined by

(13-7) $$f(\mathbf{x}^{(1)}) = \underset{0 \leqslant \theta < \infty}{\text{maximum}}\, f(\mathbf{x}^{(0)} + \theta \mathbf{d}^{(0)})$$

where $(\mathbf{x}^{(0)} + \theta \mathbf{d}^{(0)},\ 0 \leqslant \theta < \infty)$ is the line from $\mathbf{x}^{(0)}$ in the direction of $\mathbf{d}^{(0)}$. Expression (13-7) can be solved either by using classical calculus methods to find the optimal value of θ, if that is computationally viable, or by using a one-dimensional search technique on θ. Our example is simple enough for the use of calculus. Since

$\mathbf{x}^{(0)} = (1, 2, 2)$ and $\mathbf{d}^{(0)} = (2, 4, 1)$, the line $\mathbf{x}^{(0)} + \theta \mathbf{d}^{(0)}$, $0 \leqslant \theta < \infty$, is given by

(13-8) $\qquad\qquad (1 + 2\theta, 2 + 4\theta, 2 + \theta), \qquad 0 \leqslant \theta < \infty$

and (13-7) becomes

$$f(\mathbf{x}^{(1)}) = \underset{0 \leqslant \theta < \infty}{\text{maximum}} f(1 + 2\theta, 2 + 4\theta, 2 + \theta)$$

Using the functional relationship (13-2) with $x_1 = 1 + 2\theta$, $x_2 = 2 + 4\theta$, and $x_3 = 2 + \theta$, we have

(13-9)

$$\underset{0 \leqslant \theta < \infty}{\text{maximize}} \ 4(1 + 2\theta) - (1 + 2\theta)^2 + 9(2 + 4\theta) - (2 + 4\theta)^2$$

$$+ 10(2 + \theta) - 2(2 + \theta)^2 - \tfrac{1}{2}(2 + 4\theta)(2 + \theta)$$

$$= \underset{0 \leqslant \theta < \infty}{\text{maximize}} \ (27 + 21\theta - 24\theta^2)$$

The maximum occurs when $(21 - 48\theta) = 0$, i.e., $\theta = 7/16$. By (13-8), with $\theta = 7/16$, we find that $\mathbf{x}^{(1)} = (30/16, 15/4, 39/16)$. This point is now used to find the new direction $\mathbf{d}^{(1)}$ by equations (13-5). The procedure is repeated until it converges arbitrarily close to the optimum, $(2, 4, 2)$, at which point $f(\mathbf{x}) = 32$. Table 13-1 shows the results of the first four iterations. To test your understanding of the method, verify the computations for iterations 2, 3, and 4.

Theoretically, we terminate the algorithm when a point is reached where $\partial f / \partial x_j = 0$ for all j. Unfortunately this technique, like most of the techniques in this chapter and Chapter 14, does not necessarily converge to the optimum in a finite number of iterations. So, in practice, we usually replace the theoretical terminal condition by a convergence criterion which stops the algorithm when the

Table 13-1. *The First Four Iterations of Gradient Method for Unconstrained Maximization.*

Iteration k	$\mathbf{x}^{(k-1)}$	$\mathbf{d}^{(k-1)}$	θ	$\mathbf{x}^{(k)}$	$f(\mathbf{x}^{(k)})$
1	1	2		1.8750	
	2	4	0.4375	3.7500	31.5938
	2	1		2.4375	
2	1.8750	0.2500		1.9420	
	3.7500	0.2813	0.2678	3.8253	31.9663
	2.4375	−1.6250		2.0023	
3	1.9420	0.1161		1.9929	
	3.8253	0.3482	0.4386	3.9781	31.9972
	2.0023	0.0781		2.0366	
4	1.9929	0.0143		1.9967	
	3.9781	0.0256	0.2681	3.9849	31.9989
	2.0366	−0.1353		2.0003	

solution to the *k*th iteration is within a specified tolerance of the solution to the $(k-1)$th iteration. We can express this tolerance either in absolute terms (e.g., as $|x_j^{(k-1)} - x_j^{(k)}| < \varepsilon$ all j, where ε is the tolerance) or in relative terms (e.g., as $|x_j^{(k-1)} - x_j^{(k)}| < \beta |x_j^{(k)}|$ all j). This procedure finds a solution "arbitrarily close" to the optimum provided we can establish that the technique does converge, given enough iterations, to a solution satisfying the terminal condition. We will not prove convergence for the nonlinear programming techniques we discuss. The interested reader should consult a text such as the one by W. I. Zangwill, listed in the references. Note that in our example, if $\varepsilon = 0.05$, the algorithm would terminate at iteration 4.

13-3 GRADIENT METHODS FOR CONSTRAINED OPTIMIZATION

The major difference between unconstrained and constrained optimization using gradient methods is that the direction of movement at any point **x** may be restricted by one or several of the constraints. In order to maintain feasibility of the solution, the direction of movement has to satisfy all constraints. But even for a *feasible direction*, the step size may again be restricted by a constraint. Let us first study the problem of finding a feasible direction and then consider how far to move in that direction.

We will call a direction **r** ($=$ a direction vector) a feasible direction from **x**, if all points along the line $\mathbf{x} + \theta \mathbf{r}$ are feasible points for some positive distance from **x**, i.e., for $0 \leqslant \theta \leqslant \varepsilon$, $\varepsilon > 0$.

The point **x** may either be an interior point, i.e., a point in the interior of the feasible region, or a boundary point of the feasible region. If it is an interior point, then any direction of movement is a feasible direction and the gradient vector may be chosen as for the unconstrained case. If point **x** is a boundary point, it is necessary to ensure that the direction of movement keeps within the feasible region. Figure 13-3 illustrates these two cases.

Point $\mathbf{x}^{(A)}$ is an interior point and the gradient vector $\mathbf{d}^{(A)}$ is a feasible direction. Points $\mathbf{x}^{(B)}$ and $\mathbf{x}^{(C)}$ are boundary points. The feasible directions are restricted to going either along the boundary or into the feasible region. At $\mathbf{x}^{(B)}$, the gradient vector $\mathbf{d}^{(B)}$ is not a feasible direction, whereas at $\mathbf{x}^{(C)}$, $\mathbf{d}^{(C)}$ is feasible.

To decide whether a direction from a boundary point is feasible, it is necessary only to see if it violates the binding constraints at that point. Constraints that are slack at the point will have no effect on which directions are feasible, but they may restrict the step size of the movement in a feasible direction.

To simplify the presentation, we will restrict our attention to problems with linear constraints. So let us return to the constrained production problem (13-3):

$$\text{maximize } f(\mathbf{x}) = 4x_1 - x_1^2 + 9x_2 - x_2^2 + 10x_3 - 2x_3^2 - \tfrac{1}{2}x_2 x_3$$

(13-10)   subject to $4x_1 + 2x_2 + x_3 \leqslant 10$

$$2x_1 + 4x_2 + x_3 \leqslant 20$$

$$x_1, x_2, x_3 \geqslant 0$$

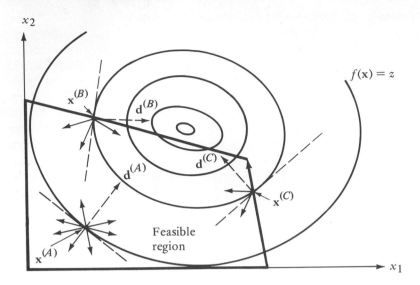

Figure 13-3. *Feasible directions.*

Again take $\mathbf{x}^{(0)} = (1, 2, 2)$ as the starting point. $\mathbf{x}^{(0)}$ lies on the first constraint. The second constraint and the nonnegativity conditions are slack. The feasible directions from $\mathbf{x}^{(0)}$ are those $\mathbf{r}$ that generate points of the form $\mathbf{x} = \mathbf{x}^{(0)} + \mathbf{r}$ such that the first constraint is satisfied, i.e.,

$$4(1 + r_1) + 2(2 + r_2) + (2 + r_3) \leqslant 10$$

where r_1, r_2, and r_3 are the elements of $\mathbf{r}$.

Simplifying, we obtain

(13-11) $$4r_1 + 2r_2 + r_3 \leqslant 0$$

Expression (13-11) defines all feasible directions from $\mathbf{x}^{(0)}$. We now wish to find the best of these directions. We define "best" as that direction which gives the greatest rate of increase in the objective function from $\mathbf{x}^{(0)}$. The rate of change of $f(\mathbf{x})$ in the direction $\mathbf{r}$, i.e., the *directional derivative* at $\mathbf{x}^{(0)}$ is given by

(13-12) $$w = \sum_{j=1}^{3} \frac{\partial f(\mathbf{x}^{(0)})}{\partial x_j} r_j = 2r_1 + 4r_2 + r_3$$

The best direction is the feasible direction that maximizes (13-12), i.e.,

(13-13)
$$\text{maximize } w = 2r_1 + 4r_2 + r_3$$
$$\text{subject to} \quad 4r_1 + 2r_2 + r_3 \leqslant 0$$

This optimization problem is not yet complete, because the length of the vector $\mathbf{r}$ has not been defined. This is needed to make the vector in each direction unique.

Traditionally, **r** is defined as a vector of unit length, i.e.,

(13-14) $$r_1{}^2 + r_2{}^2 + r_3{}^2 = 1$$

Unfortunately, when (13-14) is added to (13-13), the optimization problem becomes a nonlinear one. A satisfactory compromise is to approximate (13-14) by

(13-15) $$-1 \leqslant r_j \leqslant 1, \qquad j = 1, 2, 3$$

In this case, not all vectors that are feasible to (13-13) and (13-15) will be of the same length. Therefore, (13-13) and (13-15) do not necessarily give the best direction, but merely give a good direction that improves the objective function. We will, however, continue to refer to it as the "best" direction.

Before proceeding to determine the step size, let us generalize these ideas for the following problem:

$$\text{maximize } f(\mathbf{x})$$
$$\text{subject to } \sum_{j=1}^{n} a_{ij} x_j \leqslant b_i, \qquad i = 1, 2, \ldots, m,$$
$$\mathbf{x} \geqslant 0$$

GRADIENT METHOD CRITERION FOR "BEST" DIRECTION

At the point $\mathbf{x}^{(k)}$ the "best" direction $\mathbf{r}^{(k)}$ is the solution of the linear programming problem

$$\text{maximize } w = \sum_{j=1}^{n} \frac{\partial f(\mathbf{x}^{(k)})}{\partial x_j} r_j$$

subject to

(13-16)
$$\sum_{j=1}^{n} a_{ij} r_j \leqslant 0 \qquad \text{for binding constraints at } \mathbf{x}^{(k)},$$
$$r_j \geqslant 0 \qquad \text{for all} \quad x_j = 0 \text{ at } \mathbf{x}^{(k)},$$

and

$$-1 \leqslant r_j \leqslant 1, \qquad j = 1, 2, \ldots, n$$

The technique using (13-16) to find the feasible direction is sometimes called *Zoutendijk's method of feasible directions*. There are other methods used to find the feasible direction, e.g., the gradient projection method (that we will not discuss here).

The solution of the linear program given by (13-13) and (13-15) is $\mathbf{r}^{(0)} = (-3/4, 1, 1)$, and $w = 7/2$. This direction is feasible because of the manner in which it was obtained and it will improve the value of the objective function $f(\mathbf{x})$, since $w = 7/2 > 0$.

What happens if the optimal value of (13-16) yields a $w < 0$? This means that no feasible direction exists that can improve the value of the objective function. Therefore we obtain the following stopping rule:

finding the feasible direction.   Zoutendijk's method of feasible directions has met more approval as a nonlinear constraint technique than in the simple form discussed here.

Where gradient methods are applied to linear constraints, greater computational efficiency can be achieved by using a modified form of the simplex method.   A particular example is *Wolfe's reduced gradient method*.

Recent results indicate that two new methods are showing promise.   These are the *generalized reduced gradient method* and the *variable-metric method*.   A description of these techniques is well beyond the scope of this book, and the reader is referred to the relevant papers listed among the references to this chapter.

13-8 INTRODUCTION TO PENALTY AND BARRIER METHODS

In this section and those that follow, we introduce approaches to nonlinear programming quite different from gradient methods.   The two approaches, *penalty methods* and *barrier methods* (also called sequential unconstrained maximization techniques, or SUMT), provide a means of reformulating a constrained nonlinear programming problem as an unconstrained problem.   The resulting unconstrained problem is solved sequentially by an ordinary unconstrained technique, such as a gradient method.

Let us look again at the general nonlinear programming problem (13-4):

$$\text{maximize } f(\mathbf{x})$$

$$\text{subject to } g_i(\mathbf{x}) \leqslant b_i \qquad i = 1, \ldots, m$$

$$\mathbf{x} \geqslant 0$$

So that the $\mathbf{x} \geqslant 0$ constraints are seen as just another set of constraints, we will rewrite $x_j \geqslant 0$ as

(13-24) $$g_{m+j}(\mathbf{x}) = -x_j \leqslant 0 = b_{m+j} \qquad j = 1, \ldots, n$$

Problem (13-4) then becomes

(13-25)
$$\text{maximize } f(\mathbf{x})$$
$$\text{subject to } g_i(\mathbf{x}) \leqslant b_i \qquad i = 1, \ldots, m+n$$

Penalty methods take the objective function f and add to it a *penalty function*—a function that penalizes solutions that do not belong to the feasible region.   Barrier methods add a *barrier function* to f that creates a barrier against movement from feasible points to infeasible points by making points near the boundary of the feasible region carry a heavy penalty.

The details of the two methods are basically similar.

13-9 PENALTY METHODS

Consider the following simple one-variable problem:

$$\text{maximize } f(x) = 10x - x^2$$

(13-26)
$$\text{subject to } g_1(x) = 2x \leqslant 4 = b_1$$

$$g_2(x) = -x \leqslant 0 = b_2$$

We want to replace the constraint $2x \leqslant 4$ by a term in the objective function that penalizes any value of x that violates this constraint and, thus, turn (13-26) into an unconstrained problem. We need a function of the general form:

$$P_1(x) \begin{cases} = 0 & \text{if} \quad 2x \leqslant 4 & \text{(i.e., } g_1(x) \leqslant b_1) \\ < 0 & \text{if} \quad 2x > 4 & \text{(i.e., } g_1(x) \nleqslant b_1) \end{cases}$$

A possible specific form for this function is

$$P_1(x) = -(\text{maximum}[0, 2x - 4])^2$$

Similarly, for $-x \leqslant 0$ (i.e., $g_2(x) \leqslant b_2$) we derive the function

$$P_2(x) = -(\text{maximum}[0, -x])^2$$

Adding these to the objective function we obtain

$$\text{maximize } C(x) = f(x) + P_1(x) + P_2(x)$$

or

(13-27)
$$\text{maximize } C(x) = f(x) + P(x)$$

where $P(x) = -\sum_{i=1}^{2} (\text{maximum}[0, (g_i(x) - b)])^2.$

P is the penalty function. The construction of this function for problem (13-26) is shown in Figure 13-4.

Any x that violates the constraints of (13-26) is penalized in problem (13-27). However, problem (13-27) is not exactly equivalent to (13-26) because it does not place infinite penalty on infeasible points. In many cases this penalty is insufficient to stop an infeasible point from being optimal to (13-27). In fact, from Figure 13-4, we see that the penalty function of (13-27) gives very little penalty to a large range of infeasible points. Clearly, the penalty should be as severe as possible to make the unconstrained problem closely approximate the constrained problem. Rather than define a totally different form of penalty function we can control the severity of the penalty by a parameter λ, and change (13-27) to

(13-28)
$$\text{maximize } C(x, \lambda) = f(x) + \frac{1}{\lambda} P(x)$$

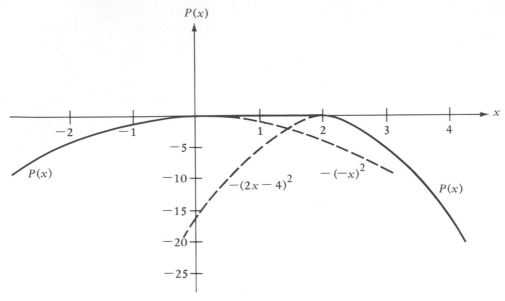

Figure 13-4. *P(x) for problem (13-26).*

As λ decreases, the effect of P on C increases proportionately, and infeasible points become less desirable.   In general:

PENALTY FUNCTION

A penalty function is a function such that

$$P(\mathbf{x}) \begin{cases} = 0 & \text{if } \mathbf{x} \text{ is a feasible solution} \\ < 0 & \text{if } \mathbf{x} \text{ is an infeasible solution} \end{cases}$$

i.e.,

(13-29) $$P(\mathbf{x}) \begin{cases} = 0 & \text{if } g_i(\mathbf{x}) \leqslant b_i \quad \text{for all} \quad i = 1, 2, \ldots, m + n \\ < 0 & \text{otherwise.} \end{cases}$$

As we have seen, a possible and very convenient form of P is

(13-30) $$P(\mathbf{x}) = -\sum_{i=1}^{m+n} \left(\text{maximum} \left[0, (g_i(\mathbf{x}) - b_i) \right] \right)^2$$

This satisfies the definition (13-29) since

$$-\left(\text{maximum} \left[0, (g_i(\mathbf{x}) - b_i) \right] \right)^2 \begin{cases} = 0 & \text{if} \quad g_i(\mathbf{x}) \leqslant b_i \\ < 0 & \text{if} \quad g_i(\mathbf{x}) \nleqslant b_i \end{cases}$$

So:

$$-\sum_{i=1}^{m+n} (\text{maximum}\,[0,(g_i(\mathbf{x})-b_i)])^2 \begin{cases} = 0 & \text{if } g_i(\mathbf{x}) \leqslant b_i & \text{for all } i = 1, \ldots, m+n \\ < 0 & \text{if } g_i(\mathbf{x}) \nleqslant b_i & \text{for any } i \end{cases}$$

Sometimes it is possible to solve (13-28) analytically and give the solution x that results as $\lambda \to 0$. More usually the problem is solved by using a sequence of λ_k, i.e., $\lambda_1, \lambda_2, \lambda_3, \ldots, \lambda_k, \ldots$, where $\lambda_{k+1} < \lambda_k$ and $\lim_{k\to\infty} \lambda_k = 0$. This gives us the sequence of problems of the form

(13-31) $$\underset{\mathbf{x}}{\text{maximize}}\; C(\mathbf{x}, \lambda_k) = f(\mathbf{x}) + \frac{1}{\lambda_k} P(\mathbf{x})$$

and the resultant sequence of solutions $\mathbf{x}^{(1)}, \mathbf{x}^{(2)}, \ldots, \mathbf{x}^{(k)}, \ldots$.

To illustrate this idea we used the sequence

$$\lambda_1 = 1, \quad \lambda_2 = 0.1, \quad \lambda_3 = 0.01, \quad \lambda_4 = 0.001, \ldots$$

on problem (13-26). The sequence of $(1/\lambda_k) P(x)$ functions is shown in Figure 13-5, and the $C(x, \lambda_k)$ functions are shown in Figure 13-6. The point $x^{(0)}$ in Figure 13-6 is the solution to maximize $f(x)$. Clearly, the sequence $x^{(1)}, x^{(2)}, x^{(3)}, \ldots$, is converging to the optimum $x^* = 2$. When the optimum is on the boundary of the feasible region the nature of the penalty methods gives convergence from *outside* the feasible region because, as the penalty becomes more severe, the optimal solutions to (13-31) get closer to feasibility.

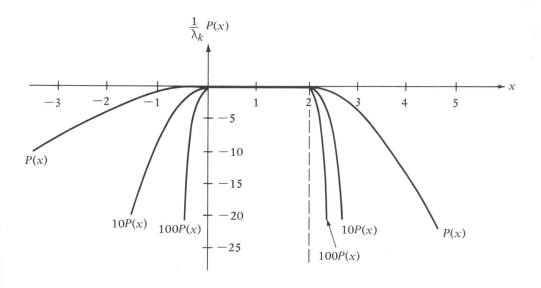

Figure 13-5. $1/\lambda_k P(x)$ *for problem (13-26).*

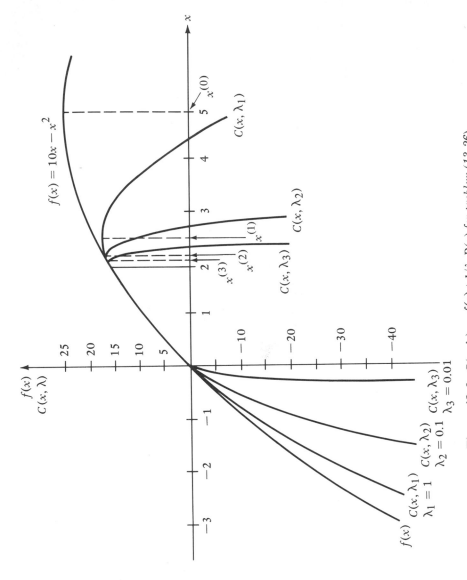

Figure 13-6. $C(x, \lambda_k) = f(x) + 1/\lambda_k P(x)$ *for problem (13-26).*

440

13-10 PENALTY METHODS APPLIED TO PROBLEM (13-3)

Let us now set up and solve problem (13-3) by penalty methods.   Putting it in the form of problem (13-25) we obtain

(13-32)

$$\text{maximize}\quad f(\mathbf{x}) = 4x_1 - x_1{}^2 + 9x_2 - x_2{}^2 + 10x_3 - 2x_3{}^2 - \tfrac{1}{2}x_2 x_3$$

$$\text{subject to } g_1(\mathbf{x}) = \quad 4x_1 + 2x_2 + x_3 \leqslant 10 = b_1$$

$$g_2(\mathbf{x}) = \quad 2x_1 + 4x_2 + x_3 \leqslant 20 = b_2$$

$$g_3(\mathbf{x}) = - \quad x_1 \qquad\qquad \leqslant\ 0 = b_3$$

$$g_4(\mathbf{x}) = \qquad\quad - x_2 \qquad \leqslant\ 0 = b_4$$

$$g_5(\mathbf{x}) = \qquad\qquad\quad - x_3 \leqslant\ 0 = b_5$$

Using the form of the penalty function defined in (13-30), this problem is reduced to the unconstrained approximating problem:

$$\underset{\mathbf{x}}{\text{maximize}}\ C(\mathbf{x}, \lambda) = (4x_1 - x_1{}^2 + 9x_2 - x_2{}^2 + 10x_3 - 2x_3{}^2 - \tfrac{1}{2}x_2 x_3)$$

$$+ \frac{1}{\lambda}\big[-(\text{maximum}\,[0, (4x_1 + 2x_2 + x_3 - 10)])^2$$

(13-33)

$$- (\text{maximum}\,[0, (2x_1 + 4x_2 + x_3 - 20)])^2$$

$$- (\text{maximum}\,[0, -x_1])^2 - (\text{maximum}\,[0, -x_2])^2$$

$$- (\text{maximum}\,[0, -x_3])^2 \big]$$

To find the solution to (13-33) for a small λ, we again consider a sequence of scalars, $\lambda_1, \lambda_2, \ldots, \lambda_k, \ldots$, where $\lambda_{k+1} < \lambda_k$ and $\lim_{k \to \infty} \lambda_k = 0$.   The solution to (13-33) as $k \to \infty$, is the point of convergence of the sequence $\mathbf{x}^{(1)}, \mathbf{x}^{(2)}, \mathbf{x}^{(3)}, \ldots, \mathbf{x}^{(k)}, \ldots$, where $\mathbf{x}^{(k)}$ is the solution of (13-33) for $\lambda = \lambda_k$.   Table 13-3 gives the sequence of solutions to problem (13-33) as λ_k is decreased successively.

Table 13-3. *Sequence of Solutions of Problem (13-33)—Penalty Methods.*

No of iterations

λ_k	$x_1^{(k)}$	$x_2^{(k)}$	$x_3^{(k)}$	$C(\mathbf{x}, \lambda_k)$
1	0.4856	3.2671	1.9021	28.9710
0.1	0.4179	3.2349	1.8981	28.8362
0.01	0.4111	3.2309	1.8977	28.8221
0.001	0.4103	3.2308	1.8974	28.8206
0.0001	0.4103	3.2308	1.8974	28.8205
0.00001	0.4102	3.2308	1.8975	28.8205
True optimum	0.4102	3.2308	1.8975	28.8205

When the problem is solved using a sequence of λ_k, the search for $\mathbf{x}^{(k+1)}$ is initiated at $\mathbf{x}^{(k)}$, since that should be fairly close, particularly when k is large. Such a procedure reduces considerably the time required at each iteration to find the new optimal point. Table 13-3 indicates that the optimum has been reached for $\lambda_k = 0.00001$.

Clearly, we could have started immediately with a small λ, say $\lambda = 0.00001$, instead of using the sequence of λ_k shown. There are two reasons for using the sequence of λ_k. The first is that we can again use the condition for terminating the algorithm: $|x_j^{(k+1)} - x_j^{(k)}| < \varepsilon$ for all j where ε is a predetermined tolerance. Had we set $\varepsilon = 0.0001$ in our example, the algorithm would terminate at $\lambda_k = 0.0001$. Still we may ask what would be lost by setting λ very small at the outset. We tested this possibility (with the benefit of hindsight) for our example using the same computer code. The result was rather surprising. The answers to Table 13-3 were achieved with an iteration limit of 50 for each λ_k, or a total of no more than 300 iterations. Using $\lambda = 0.00001$ directly, the search procedure converged to the same solution in approximately 8000 iterations. The difference in time was considerable. The results of Table 13-3 took under 2 seconds of computation time on a Burroughs B6718, while the solution for $\lambda = 0.00001$ took 45 seconds.

13-11 BARRIER METHODS

Instead of penalizing infeasible points, barrier methods create a *barrier function* which makes it impossible to reach infeasible points. Using a suitable search technique, the search for the optimal solution is started from inside the feasible region. The barrier function prevents any movement across the boundaries of the feasible region.

For barrier methods to be applicable, the feasible region must satisfy the conditions that it is closed and bounded, that it has an interior (as distinct from boundaries), and that every boundary point can be approached from interior points. These conditions are violated, for example, by the existence of equality constraints. As we progress, the significance of these assumptions will become clear.

As in penalty methods, we want to replace the constraints by adding a functional relationship in the objective function, again generating an unconstrained problem. This time the functional relationship, called the barrier function, must penalize so heavily points on and near the boundaries that no search technique would use such points as a solution or ever stray across to infeasible points.

BARRIER FUNCTION

A barrier function, B, is a functional relationship over the interior points of the feasible region which has the properties

(i) $B(\mathbf{x}) \leqslant 0$ for all $\mathbf{x}$

(ii) B is continuous

(iii) $B(\mathbf{x}) \to -\infty$ as $\mathbf{x}$ approaches the boundary of the feasible set.

(Note that an *interior point* is a feasible point that is not a boundary point, i.e., there are other feasible points in *every* direction from that point.)

An example of a suitable barrier function for problem (13-25) is:

$$(13\text{-}34) \qquad\qquad B(\mathbf{x}) = \sum_{i=1}^{m+n} \left[\frac{1}{(g_i(\mathbf{x}) - b_i)} \right]$$

This satisfies the conditions for B. Expression (13-34) is certainly negative, and continuous. It also tends to infinity as the $g_i(\mathbf{x})$ tend to the b_i (the boundaries of the feasible set).

Using (13-34), problem (13-25) is approximated by the problem:

$$(13\text{-}35) \qquad\qquad \underset{\mathbf{x}}{\text{maximize}} \; D(\mathbf{x}, \lambda) = f(\mathbf{x}) + \lambda B(\mathbf{x})$$

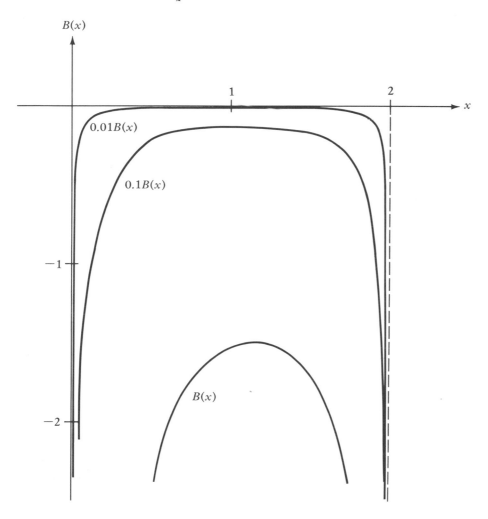

Figure 13-7. $\lambda_k B(x)$ *for problem (13-26).*

where **x** is an interior point of the feasible set, and λ is again used to control the effect of the barrier function. Problem (13-35) is not a true unconstrained problem since **x** is constrained to be an interior point. However, we will see that provided the search for the optimum is initiated at an interior point, no infeasible solution will be found.

Turning again to problem (13-26), the barrier function is

$$(13\text{-}36) \qquad B(\mathbf{x}) = \left[\frac{1}{2x-4} + \frac{1}{-x} \right] = \frac{x-4}{-x(2x-4)} = \frac{x-4}{4x-2x^2}$$

and the "unconstrained" function becomes

$$(13\text{-}37) \qquad \underset{x}{\text{maximize}} \, D(x, \lambda) = 10x - x^2 + \lambda \left(\frac{x-4}{4x-2x^2} \right)$$

As with the penalty methods, this function is solved for λ very small, since the barrier is then close to the boundaries. Again, we use a sequence of λ_k, in the same way as we did for penalty methods.

Figure 13-7 shows the shape of the barrier function (13-36) for various values

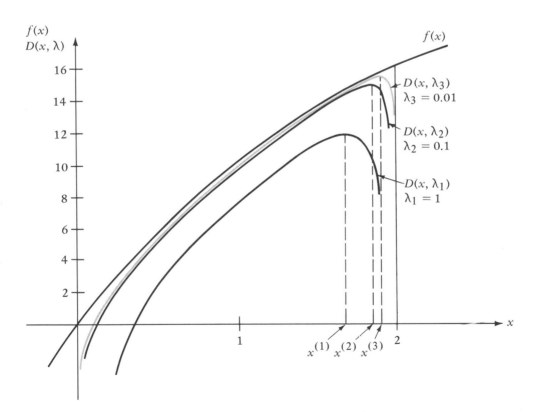

Figure 13-8. $D(x, \lambda_k) = f(x) + \lambda_k B(x)$ *for problem (13-26).*

of λ_k. It is clear that a search for the optimum, starting inside the feasible region, would never go outside it. In fact, not even a boundary point will be attained since only interior points give a finite value to $B(x)$. For this reason the feasible region must have an interior. Figure 13-8 shows the $D(x, \lambda_k)$ functions (13-37), and the optimal $x^{(k)}$, for each λ_k. Once again we see that the sequence, $x^{(1)}, x^{(2)}, x^{(3)}, \ldots$, is converging on $x^* = 2$—this time from *within* the feasible region.

13-12 BARRIER METHODS APPLIED TO PROBLEM (13-3)

Let us apply barrier methods to problem (13-3) as reformulated in (13-32). By (13-34) the barrier function is

(13-38)

$$B(\mathbf{x}) = \left[\frac{1}{(4x_1 + 2x_2 + x_3 - 10)} + \frac{1}{(2x_1 + 4x_2 + x_3 - 20)} + \frac{1}{-x_1} + \frac{1}{-x_2} + \frac{1}{-x_3} \right]$$

and the approximated problem becomes

(13-39)

$$\text{maximize } D(\mathbf{x}, \lambda_k)$$

$$= (4x_1 - x_1^2 + 9x_2 - x_2^2 + 10x_3 - 2x_3^2 - \tfrac{1}{2}x_2 x_3)$$

$$+ \lambda_k \left[\frac{1}{(4x_1 + 2x_2 + x_3 - 10)} + \frac{1}{(2x_1 + 4x_2 + x_3 - 20)} - \frac{1}{x_1} - \frac{1}{x_2} - \frac{1}{x_3} \right]$$

To solve (13-39), we define a sequence of scalars, $\lambda_1, \lambda_2, \lambda_3, \ldots, \lambda_k, \ldots$, such that $\lambda_{k+1} < \lambda_k$ and $\lim_{k \to \infty} \lambda_k = 0$. For each λ_k, the solution to (13-39) is found by using an unconstrained search technique commencing at an interior point of the feasible set. It is usually convenient to start the search for $\mathbf{x}^{(k)}$ at $\mathbf{x}^{(k-1)}$, since they will be close, especially when λ_k becomes small and $\mathbf{x}^{(k-1)}$ is an interior point, as required by the algorithm. There is a practical problem with the use of many unconstrained search techniques for barrier methods. Since they rely on stepping

Table 13-4. *Sequence of Solutions to (13-39)—Barrier Method.*

λ_k	$x_1^{(k)}$	$x_2^{(k)}$	$x_3^{(k)}$	$D(\mathbf{x}, \lambda_k)$
1	0.5562	2.5479	1.8680	23.5715
0.1	0.4071	3.0808	1.8846	27.8795
0.01	0.3945	3.2089	1.8939	28.6054
0.001	0.4082	3.2170	1.8977	28.7604
0.0001	0.4122	3.2207	1.8985	28.8022
0.00001	0.4137	3.2215	1.8988	28.8147
Optimal solution	0.4102	3.2308	1.8975	28.8205

by finite increments, it is important that these increments be small enough to prevent stepping right over the barrier. As λ_k gets smaller and $\mathbf{x}^{(k)}$ gets closer to the boundary, the step size must be made smaller for the unconstrained search to work properly.

Table 13-4 gives the sequence of solutions as λ_k is successively decreased. Convergence to within 0.1 percent of the true optimum is again very fast for this example.

EXERCISES

13.1 Perform two iterations of the unconstrained gradient method technique for each of the following problems. Illustrate the progress of the method.
(a) maximize $f(\mathbf{x}) = 7x_1 - 2x_1^2 + x_1 x_2 - x_2^2$. Commence at $\mathbf{x}^0 = (1,0)$. The optimum is $(2,1)$.
(b) maximize $f(\mathbf{x}) = -x_1^3 + 9x_1^2 - 5x_2^2 + 20x_2$. Commence at $\mathbf{x}^0 = (1,1)$.
(c) Repeat 13.1(b) commencing at $\mathbf{x}^0 = (-1,1)$.
(d) maximize $f(\mathbf{x}) = -x_1^4 + 8x_1^3 - 10x_1^2 - x_2^2 + 2x_2$. Commence at $\mathbf{x}^0 = (0,0)$. The local optima are at $(0,1)$ and $(5,1)$. The global optimum is $(5,1)$.

13.2 Using the constrained gradient method technique, find the first three iterations of the following problems.

(a)
$$\text{maximize } f(\mathbf{x}) = 7x_1 - 2x_1^2 + x_1 x_2 - x_2^2$$
$$\text{subject to} \quad x_1 + x_2 \leq 2$$
$$2x_1 + 4x_2 \leq 6$$
$$x_1, x_2 \geq 0$$
Commence at $\mathbf{x}^0 = (0,0)$.

(b)
$$\text{maximize } f(\mathbf{x}) = 7x_1 - 2x_1^2 + x_1 x_2 - x_2^2$$
$$\text{subject to} \quad x_1 \leq 1$$
$$x_1 + x_2 \geq 1$$
$$x_1, x_2 \geq 0$$
Commence at $\mathbf{x}^0 = (1,0)$.

(c)
$$\text{maximize } f(\mathbf{x}) = \tfrac{1}{}x_1^3 + 9x_1^2 + 5x_2^2 + 20x_2$$
$$\text{subject to} \quad x_1 \leq 3$$
$$x_1 + x_2 \leq 9$$
$$x_1, x_2 \geq 0$$
Commence at $\mathbf{x}^0 = (1,1)$.

(d)
$$\text{maximize } f(\mathbf{x}) = -x_1^4 + 8x_1^3 - 10x_1^2 - x_2^2 + 2x_2$$
$$\text{subject to} \quad x_1 + x_2 \leq 4$$
$$x_1 + 2x_2 \leq 6$$
$$x_1, x_2 \geq 0$$
Commence at $\mathbf{x}^0 = (2,0)$.

13.3 Set up the problems of question 13.2 for solution by penalty methods.

13.4 Set up, where possible, the problems of question 13.2 for solution by barrier methods. Are the suggested commencing points suitable for commencing the barrier methods computations?

13.5 Consider the problem

$$\text{minimize } 5x_1{}^2 - 10x_1 - 10x_2 \log_{10} x_2$$

$$\text{subject to } \quad x_1{}^2 + 2x_2{}^2 \qquad\qquad \leqslant 4$$

$$x_1, x_2 \geqslant 0$$

(Assume $0 \log_{10} 0 = 0$.)
Set up the problem
(a) for solution by penalty methods, and
(b) for solution by barrier methods.

13.6 Why are barrier methods unsuitable for the following problems.

(a)

$$\text{maximize } f(\mathbf{x}) = -x_1{}^2 - 2x_2{}^2$$

$$\text{subject to} \qquad 4x_1 + x_2 \leqslant 6$$

$$x_1 + x_2 = 3$$

$$x_1, x_2 \geqslant 0$$

(b)

$$\text{maximize } f(\mathbf{x}) = -x^2 + 10x$$

$$\text{subject to} \qquad x^2 - 4x \geqslant 0$$

$$x \geqslant 0$$

13.7 A manufacturing company has planned two new products to take up the slack in their production program. They have to decide the selling price, monthly production, and monthly promotional expenses for both of the products. The market analysts predict the following relationships between monthly sales, price, and promotional expenditure.

$$x_1 = 10 - 4\text{p}_1 + 2\text{c}_1$$

$$x_2 = 15 - \tfrac{1}{2}\text{p}_1 - 3\text{p}_2 + \text{c}_2$$

where x_j is monthly sales in thousands of units for product j,
p_j is selling price per unit in dollars for product j, and
c_j is monthly promotional expenses in thousands of dollars for product j.

Only \$7,000 a month is available to spend on promotion. Other expenses are \$3, and \$5 per unit respectively. Product 1 uses 0.2 hour of production capacity per unit, and product 2 uses 0.3 hour per unit. Production capacity is limited to 1000 hours per month.

Set up this problem to find the values of the variables that give maximum total profit per month.

REFERENCES

References for gradient methods:

Hadley, G. *Nonlinear and Dynamic Programming*. Reading, Mass.: Addison-Wesley, 1964. Chapter 9 gives a thorough—although advanced—exposition of gradient methods. Sections 9-1, 9-2, 9-4, and 9-5 cover the material presented in this chapter. Sections 9-6, and 9-7 discuss the gradient projection method, while 9-10 to 9-13 deal with nonlinear constraints.

McMillan, C. *Mathematical Programming*, 2nd Ed. New York: Wiley, 1975. A non-matrix approach to gradient methods is given in Chapter 5. In particular, that chapter discusses the gradient projection method—the mathematics is messy but not difficult.

Wolfe, P. "Methods of Nonlinear Programming", *Nonlinear Programming*, J. Abadie, Ed., Amsterdam: North-Holland, 1967. In this paper, Wolfe summarizes most of the gradient techniques, constrained and unconstrained. The treatment is concise and readable. Pages 121–123 present the reduced gradient method.

Zoutendijk, G. *Methods of Feasible Directions*. Amsterdam: Elsevier Publ. Co., 1960. This is the original work on the method of feasible directions. Chapters 7 to 11 give an exposition of the method including convergence proofs and some comparison with the other methods available at that time.

Recent advances in gradient methods are presented in:

Abadie, J., Ed. *Integer and Nonlinear Programming*. Amsterdam: North-Holland, 1970. Of particular relevance are Chapters 1, 2, 3, 6, 8 and Appendices I, II, and III. They cover the theory and computational experience of such techniques as the generalized reduced gradient (GRG) method and the variable-metric method. This is advanced reading.

References for penalty and barrier methods:

Fiacco, A. V., and G. P. McCormick. *Nonlinear Programming: Sequential Unconstrained Minimization Techniques*. New York: Wiley, 1968. This text is a synthesis of the work done on penalty and barrier methods. It is a complete treatment providing the necessary convergence proofs and discussion of finer computational features. This book is recommended for detailed study of penalty and barrier methods by a mathematically competent reader.

Zangwill, W. I. *Nonlinear Programming: A Unified Approach*. Englewood Cliffs, N.J.: Prentice-Hall, 1969. This book cannot easily be "dipped into," since its structure is tight. For the mathematically very competent reader who is interested in a theoretical development of nonlinear programming—especially related to convergence principles—this book is excellent. The treatment of penalty and barrier methods is particularly good; it is terse but easy to follow.

The continuing progress in refining penalty and barrier methods is reflected in recent journal articles; for example:

Fletcher, R. "An Exact Penalty Function for Nonlinear Programming with Inequalities", *Mathematical Programming*, 5, October 1973.

Lasdon, L. S., R. L. Fox and M. W. Ratner. "An Efficient One-dimensional Search Procedure for Barrier Functions", *Mathematical Programming*, 4, June 1973.

Rockafellar, R. T. "A Dual Approach to Solving Nonlinear Programming Problems by Unconstrained Optimization", *Mathematical Programming*, 5, December 1973.

Applications of nonlinear programming:

Beale, E. M. L., Ed. *Applications of Mathematical Programming Techniques.* London: English Univ. Press, 1970. Applications that result in nonlinear programming problems are described on pages 100–121, 413–420, and 423–451.

Bracken, J., and G. P. McCormick. *Selected Applications of Nonlinear Programming,* New York: Wiley, 1968. Nine case study applications of nonlinear programming are presented in this book. They were all solved using penalty and barrier methods. This is valuable reading.

14

Simplex Based Nonlinear Programming Techniques

Consider again the general form of the nonlinear programming problem. Determine values $x_1, x_2, \ldots, x_n$ which

$$\text{maximize } f(x_1, x_2, \ldots, x_n)$$

(14-1) $\qquad$ subject to $g_i(x_1, x_2, \ldots, x_n) \leqslant b_i, \qquad i = 1, \ldots, m$

$$x_j \geqslant 0, \qquad j = 1, \ldots, n$$

where the objective function or some constraints or both have a nonlinear form.

We have seen that the simplex method is an efficient and robust technique for solving problems of the form (14-1) when all relationships are linear. It happens that the simplex method or slight variations of it are also useful for solving a large class of nonlinear programming problems. In this chapter we will discuss three techniques that have the simplex method as their central computational device.

Since the simplex method is really made for linear systems, any nonlinear programming problem which is to be solved by this method must be reduced, in some way or other, to a linear or almost linear form. The first technique, *separable programming*, deals with a class of nonlinear programming problems where the objective function and the constraints can be reduced to a *linear approximation* of the original problem. The second technique, the *convex simplex method*, is restricted to solving a nonlinear objective function subject to linear constraints. This method approximates the objective function by its tangent line at each iteration. Only if the sufficiency conditions for a global optimum, spelled out in Section 11-11, are satisfied do these two techniques give the global optimum. Otherwise they yield only a local optimum. The third technique studied, *quadratic programming*, guarantees a global optimum of a quadratic objective function with certain properties, subject to linear constraints, by solving the Kuhn-Tucker equations of Section 11-10, which are linear for a quadratic objective function.

14-1 SEPARABLE PROGRAMMING

For separable programming the objective function and constraints of problem (14-1) must be *separable functions*. A function h in the variables $x_1, x_2, ..., x_n$ is separable if it can be expressed as the sum of n functions in one variable each:

(14-2) $$h(x_1, x_2, ..., x_n) = h_1(x_1) + h_2(x_2) + \cdots + h_n(x_n)$$

The function $h(x_1, x_2) = x_1^2 - x_2^3 + x_1 + x_2$ is separable since $h(x_1, x_2) = h_1(x_1) + h_2(x_2)$ with $h_1(x_1) = x_1^2 + x_1$ and $h_2(x_2) = x_2 - x_2^3$. But, $h(x_1, x_2) = x_1^2 - x_2^3 + x_1 x_2$ is not a separable function. However, we can make this function separable by a suitable transformation of variables: Let $y = (x_1 + x_2)$, so $y^2 = x_1^2 + x_2^2 + 2x_1 x_2$. Then the term $x_1 x_2 = \frac{1}{2}(y^2 - x_1^2 - x_2^2)$ and $h(x_1, x_2)$ can be replaced by the system:

$$H(x_1, x_2, y) = \tfrac{1}{2}x_1^2 - x_2^3 - \tfrac{1}{2}x_2^2 + \tfrac{1}{2}y^2$$

$$\text{subject to } y - x_1 - x_2 = 0$$

Many nonseparable functions can be transformed into a separable system. You should consult more advanced texts for further examples.

For separable programming, problem (14-1) can be written as:

Find values $x_1, x_2, ..., x_n$ which

$$\text{maximize } \sum_{j=1}^{n} f_j(x_j)$$

(14-3)

$$\text{subject to } \sum_{j=1}^{n} g_{ij}(x_j) \leqslant b_i, \quad i = 1, ..., m,$$

$$x_j \geqslant 0, \quad j = 1, ..., n$$

To solve problem (14-3) by the simplex method we first have to approximate each nonlinear function in (14-3) by a suitable linearization. The resulting set of linear objective function and linear constraints is referred to as the *approximating problem*. It is this problem that is solved by a somewhat modified version of the simplex method.

Consider the following problem: A cabinet maker is asked by a jeweller to build two display boxes with lids made from a special shatter- and break-proof transparent material. Only 8 square feet of the material are in stock at present, and no more can be procured within the time available to build the boxes. Figure 14-1 shows the dimensions of the two boxes. For box 1, the length has to be 1 foot whereas the width and height are to be of equal but unspecified size x_1. For box 2, the height has to be 1 foot whereas the width and length are to be of equal but unspecified size x_2. The dimensions x_1 and x_2 are to be chosen so as to satisfy the material constraint on the lids of the two boxes. The lid of box 1 requires (length) (width) $= 1x_1$ square feet of the material, and the lid of box 2 requires (length) (width) $= x_2 x_2 = x_2^2$

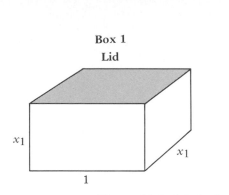
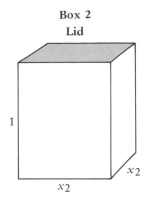

Figure 14-1. *Display box manufacturing problem.*

of the material. The sum of these cannot exceed the amount available, i.e.,

$$x_1 + x_2^2 \leqslant 8$$

The cost for material and labor is \$0.5 per square foot of the outside of each box. For box 1, four of the sides are equal to $1x_1$ square feet and two sides are equal to x_1^2. The total outside area is thus $2x_1^2 + 4x_1$. Similarly, for box 2, four of the sides are equal to $1x_2$ square feet and two sides are equal to x_2^2, summing to $2x_2^2 + 4x_2$. The charge to the customer is proportional to the sum of the three dimensions of the boxes, i.e., width + length + height (\$2 per foot for box 1 and \$2.5 per foot for box 2).

The profit for each box is thus:

$$\text{box 1:} \quad 2(x_1 + x_1 + 1) - 0.5(2x_1^2 + 4x_1) = 2x_1 - x_1^2 + 2,$$
$$\text{box 2:} \quad 2.5(x_2 + x_2 + 1) - 0.5(2x_2^2 + 4x_2) = 3x_2 - x_2^2 + 2.5$$

Total profits for both boxes are

$$2x_1 - x_1^2 + 3x_2 - x_2^2 + 4.5$$

The objective is to determine the dimensions x_1 and x_2 so as to maximize profits, subject to the constraint on the material available. Thus, we get the following nonlinear programming problem, where the constant has been dropped from the objective function:

$$\text{maximize } z = f(x_1, x_2) = 2x_1 + 3x_2 - x_1^2 - x_2^2$$

(14-4) $$\text{subject to } g_1(x_1, x_2) = x_1 + x_2^2 \leqslant 8$$

$$x_1, x_2 \geqslant 0$$

These functions are separable as follows:

(14-5) $$f(x_1, x_2) = f_1(x_1) + f_2(x_2)$$

where $$f_1(x_1) = 2x_1 - x_1^2$$
$$f_2(x_2) = 3x_2 - x_2^2$$

and

(14-6) $$g_1(x_1, x_2) = g_{11}(x_1) + g_{12}(x_2)$$

where $g_{11}(x_1) = x_1$

$g_{12}(x_2) = x_2{}^2$

Our first task is to estimate some lower and upper bounds on the feasible values of x_1 and x_2. This limits the computations involved in linearization. These estimates need not be very accurate, but should be on the generous side. An examination of $g_1(x_1, x_2) \leqslant 8$ shows that x_1 will lie in the range $0 \leqslant x_1 \leqslant 8$, and x_2 will lie in the range $0 \leqslant x_2 \leqslant 3$.

Let us linearize $f_1(x_1)$ and $g_{11}(x_1)$ over each of the intervals $0 \leqslant x_1 \leqslant 2$, $2 \leqslant x_1 \leqslant 4$, $4 \leqslant x_1 \leqslant 6$, $6 \leqslant x_1 \leqslant 8$, and $f_2(x_2)$ and $g_{12}(x_2)$ over each of the intervals $0 \leqslant x_2 \leqslant 1$, $1 \leqslant x_2 \leqslant 2$, $2 \leqslant x_2 \leqslant 3$. The number of intervals for each variable is arbitrary and need not be the same for different variables. We define p_j to be the number of intervals for variable x_j; so $p_1 = 4$ and $p_2 = 3$. The lengths of the intervals for each variable are also arbitrary. Consecutive intervals need not have the same length and should be selected so as to best capture the nonlinearity of the functions approximated. We would obtain a better approximation of $f_1(x_1)$ in our example if we used $x_1 = 1$ as an end point of an interval—the unconstrained optimum of $f_1(x_1)$ is $x_1 = 1$. However, we will not do this so that we can demonstrate some of the weaknesses of separable programming.

Table 14-1. *Data for Linearization of Problem (14-4).*

(1)	(2)	(3)		(4)		(5)	(6)
$x_{01} = 0$		$f_{01} =$	0			$g_{011} = 0$	
$x_{11} = 2$	$\Delta x_{11} = 2$	$f_{11} =$	0	$\Delta f_{11} =$	0	$g_{111} = 2$	$\Delta g_{111} = 2$
$x_{21} = 4$	$\Delta x_{21} = 2$	$f_{21} =$	-8	$\Delta f_{21} =$	-8	$g_{211} = 4$	$\Delta g_{211} = 2$
$x_{31} = 6$	$\Delta x_{31} = 2$	$f_{31} =$	-24	$\Delta f_{31} =$	-16	$g_{311} = 6$	$\Delta g_{311} = 2$
$x_{41} = 8$	$\Delta x_{41} = 2$	$f_{41} =$	-48	$\Delta f_{41} =$	-24	$g_{411} = 8$	$\Delta g_{411} = 2$
$x_{02} = 0$		$f_{02} = 0$				$g_{012} = 0$	
$x_{12} = 1$	$\Delta x_{12} = 1$	$f_{12} = 2$		$\Delta f_{12} =$	2	$g_{112} = 1$	$\Delta g_{112} = 1$
$x_{22} = 2$	$\Delta x_{22} = 1$	$f_{22} = 2$		$\Delta f_{22} =$	0	$g_{212} = 4$	$\Delta g_{212} = 3$
$x_{32} = 3$	$\Delta x_{32} = 1$	$f_{32} = 0$		$\Delta f_{32} =$	-2	$g_{312} = 9$	$\Delta g_{312} = 5$

The points dividing each of the variables into intervals are called *grid points*. So, for example, the grid points for x_1 are $0, 2, 4, 6, 8$. Let us define x_{k1} to be the grid point at the right-hand end of the kth interval for x_1. Similarly, let x_{k2} be the grid point at the right-hand end of the kth interval for x_2. These are shown in the first column of Table 14-1. The length of the kth interval of x_1 is $(x_{k1} - x_{(k-1)1}) = \Delta x_{k1}$, and $\Delta x_{k2} = (x_{k2} - x_{(k-1)2})$ for x_2, shown in the second column of Table 14-1.

Looking at function $f_1(x_1)$, let us define $f_{k1} = f_1(x_{k1})$ as the value of f_1 at the grid point x_{k1}. For $f_2(x_2)$, $f_{k2} = f_2(x_{k2})$. These are shown in the third column of Table 14-1. Similarly, we define $g_{k11} = g_{11}(x_{k1})$ and $g_{k12} = g_{12}(x_{k2})$, as shown in column 5. In Section 14-4 we will also need the differences in the values of functions over each interval, e.g., $(f_{k1} - f_{(k-1)1}) = \Delta f_{k1}$, $(g_{k11} - g_{(k-1)11}) = \Delta g_{k11}$, etc. These are shown in columns 4 and 6 of Table 14-1. For example, $f_{01} = f_1(x_{01}) = f_1(0) = 0$, $f_{11} = f_1(x_{11}) = f_1(2) = 4 - 4 = 0$. So, $\Delta f_{11} = f_{11} - f_{01} = 0$.

We call the functions of linear segments the *approximating functions*. To distinguish between the original and the approximating function, we shall denote the approximating function of f_j by $\hat{f}_j$. Figures 14-2 and 14-3 show the original functions and the approximating functions. We now express the original nonlinear

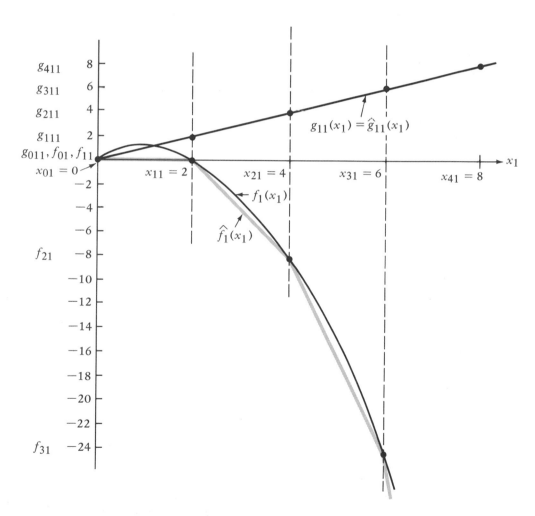

Figure 14-2. *Linearization of $f_1(x_1)$ and $g_{11}(x_1)$.*

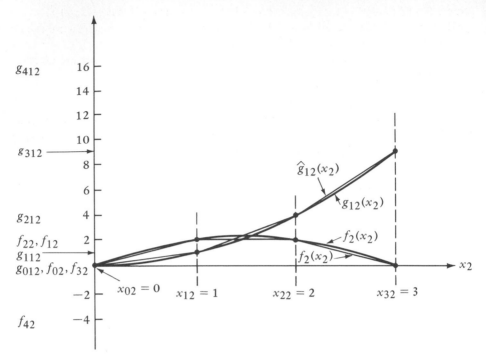

Figure 14-3. *Linearization of $f_2(x_2)$ and $g_{12}(x_2)$.*

programming problem in terms of the approximating functions as follows:

$$\text{maximize } \sum_{j=1}^{2} \hat{f}_j(x_j)$$

(14-7)
$$\text{subject to } \sum_{j=1}^{2} \hat{g}_{1j}(x_j) \leqslant 8$$

$$x_j \geqslant 0, \quad j = 1, 2$$

This is the *approximating problem* that we will manipulate into a form that can be solved by a version of the simplex method.

14-2 THE λ-FORMULATION OF THE APPROXIMATING PROBLEM

We will now look at the problem of formulating the approximating problem explicitly. To do this we will view the values of a variable in the approximating problem in terms of proportions of the grid points of the variable. Let us consider a value of x_1 that lies in the kth interval, i.e., $x_{(k-1)1} \leqslant x_1 \leqslant x_{k1}$. Since x_1 lies on the line segment between $x_{(k-1)1}$ and x_{k1}, it can be expressed as

(14-8)
$$x_1 = \lambda x_{(k-1)1} + (1-\lambda) x_{k1}$$

where $0 \leqslant \lambda \leqslant 1$. The terms, λ and $(1-\lambda)$, give the proportions (or weights) of the grid points defining the kth interval. So, for example, if $x_1 = 5$ (it lies in the 3rd interval), then $x_1 = \frac{1}{2}x_{21} + \frac{1}{2}x_{31}$ (i.e., $5 = \frac{1}{2}(4) + \frac{1}{2}(6)$).

More generally, $x_1 = 5$ can be expressed in terms of all the grid points of x_1, by giving a zero weight to all those grid points other than x_{21} and x_{31}:

$$x_1 = 5 = 0x_{01} + 0x_{11} + \tfrac{1}{2}x_{21} + \tfrac{1}{2}x_{31} + 0x_{41}$$

Since a given interval is defined by only two grid points, at most two grid points can have positive (and nonzero) weights, and those two will always be adjacent. If x_1 has the exact value of the grid point, there will be only one nonzero weight. For example, $x_1 = 2 = 0x_{01} + 1x_{11} + 0x_{21} + 0x_{31} + 0x_{41}$.

We will now generalize this result. Let λ_{uj} be the weight given to the uth grid point of x_j, $(u = 0, ..., p_j)$. Each λ_{uj} must satisfy $0 \leqslant \lambda_{uj} \leqslant 1$; and, since the weights represent proportions of the end points of an interval, we have $\sum_{u=0}^{p_j} \lambda_{uj} = 1$, provided that no more than two weights can be nonzero and they must be adjacent. Then by analogy to (14-8), if x_j is in the kth interval:

(14-9)
$$x_j = \lambda_{(k-1)j} x_{(k-1)j} + \lambda_{kj} x_{kj}$$

with
$$0 \leqslant \lambda_{(k-1)j} \leqslant 1$$

$$0 \leqslant \lambda_{kj} \leqslant 1$$

and
$$\lambda_{(k-1)j} + \lambda_{kj} = 1$$

By including all the other grid points and giving them zero weights, we obtain

(14-10)
$$x_j = \sum_{u=0}^{p_j} \lambda_{uj} x_{uj}$$

with
$$\sum_{u=0}^{p_j} \lambda_{uj} = 1 \qquad \lambda_{uj} \geqslant 0$$

and the usual proviso that for each j, at most two λ_{uj} can be positive and then only if they are adjacent, i.e., for grid points $k-1$ and k. The condition $\lambda_{uj} \leqslant 1$ is made redundant by the constraint $\sum_u \lambda_{uj} = 1$.

What is the value of $\hat{f}_j$ (approximating function of $f_j(x_j)$) for x_j defined by (14-10)? We will look again at $x_1 = 5$. The value of $\hat{f}_1(x_1)$ at $x_1 = 5$ is

$$\hat{f}_1(x_1) = \hat{f}_1(5) = \tfrac{1}{2}f_{21} + \tfrac{1}{2}f_{31} = \tfrac{1}{2}(-8) + \tfrac{1}{2}(-24) = -16$$

You can check this on Figure 14-2. As with x_1, we can write $\hat{f}_1(x_1)$ at $x_1 = 5$, using Table 14-1, as

$$\hat{f}_1(5) = 0f_{01} + 0f_{11} + \tfrac{1}{2}f_{21} + \tfrac{1}{2}f_{31} + 0f_{41}$$

$$= 0(0) + 0(0) + \tfrac{1}{2}(-8) + \tfrac{1}{2}(-24) + 0(-48) = -16$$

This result suggests that, in general terms, for x_j in the kth interval:

(14-11)
$$\hat{f}_j(x_j) = \sum_{u=0}^{p_j} \lambda_{uj} f_{uj}$$

together with the conditions on λ_{uj} given in (14-10.)

Analogous equations can be derived to express the constraint approximating functions $\hat{g}_{11}(x_1)$ and $\hat{g}_{12}(x_2)$:

$$(14\text{-}12) \qquad \hat{g}_{1j}(x_j) = \sum_{u=0}^{p_j} \lambda_{uj} g_{u1j}$$

with the conditions on λ_{uj} given in (14-10).

In expressions (14-10), (14-11), and (14-12), we have derived the *λ-formulation of the approximating problem* (14-7). It is summarized as follows:

$$\text{maximize} \sum_{j=1}^{2} \left(\sum_{u=0}^{p_j} \lambda_{uj} f_{uj} \right)$$

$$(14\text{-}13) \qquad \text{subject to} \sum_{j=1}^{2} \left(\sum_{u=0}^{p_j} \lambda_{uj} g_{u1j} \right) \leqslant 8$$

$$\sum_{u=0}^{p_j} \lambda_{uj} = 1, \qquad j = 1,2$$

$$\lambda_{uj} \geqslant 0 \qquad \text{all } u \text{ and } j$$

with the condition that at most two λ_{uj} can be nonzero for each j, and then only if they are adjacent.

The data in Table 14-1 enable us to write (14-13) in full:

(14-14)

maximize $0\lambda_{01} + 0\lambda_{11} - 8\lambda_{21} - 24\lambda_{31} - 48\lambda_{41} + 0\lambda_{02} + 2\lambda_{12} + 2\lambda_{22} + 0\lambda_{32}$

subject to $0\lambda_{01} + 2\lambda_{11} + 4\lambda_{21} + 6\lambda_{31} + 8\lambda_{41} + 0\lambda_{02} + 1\lambda_{12} + 4\lambda_{22} + 9\lambda_{32} \leqslant 8$

$$\lambda_{01} + \lambda_{11} + \lambda_{21} + \lambda_{31} + \lambda_{41} = 1$$

$$\lambda_{02} + \lambda_{12} + \lambda_{22} + \lambda_{32} = 1$$

$$\lambda_{uj} \geqslant 0 \qquad \text{all } u \text{ and } j$$

with the special condition that at most two λ_{uj} can be nonzero for each j, and then only if they are adjacent.

Problem (14-14) is a linear programming problem with the λ_{uj} as variables. The only snag is the special condition on the variables. However, by superimposing special housekeeping rules on the simplex method that restrict entry of variables into the basis, we can solve the λ-formulation by that powerful algorithm. The major disadvantage of separable programming is that it may expand considerably the number of variables and constraints in the original nonlinear program. In our case, problem (14-4) had 2 variables, x_1 and x_2, and one constraint, while problem (14-14) has 9 variables and 3 constraints. The last two constraints are in a form that can be handled by a generalized upper bounding technique incorporated in most advanced linear programming computer codes.

14-3 ANALYSIS OF THE SOLUTION OF THE λ-FORMULATION

When we solve problem (14-14) we obtain four alternative optimal basic solutions shown in Table 14-2.

The values of the x_j variables can be found from these solutions by equation (14-10) and Table 14-1.   Solution 1 is $x_1 = 0$, $x_2 = 1$; solution 2 is $x_1 = 0$, $x_2 = 2$; solution 3 is $x_1 = 2$, $x_2 = 1$; and solution 4 is $x_1 = 2$, $x_2 = 2$.   In every case, $\hat{f}_1(x_1) = 0$ and $\hat{f}_2(x_2) = 2$, so the objective function value of the approximating problem is 2. These are not the only optimal solutions; every convex combination of them is also optimal to the approximating problem.

In terms of the original problem (14-4) we can show that the four solutions in Table 14-2 also give $z = 2$.   However, they are not optimal.   The optimal solution to (14-4) is $x_1 = 1$, $x_2 = \frac{3}{2}$ and $z = 3\frac{1}{4}$.

Thus, we face a difficulty with separable programming.   There is no reason, in general, to believe that the optimum of the approximating problem is the optimum, or even a good approximation of the optimum, to the original problem.   The accuracy depends on how the variables were segmented.   Usually finer intervals give greater accuracy, but they also lead to a larger approximating problem.

A further difficulty that is not present in this example is the possibility that the problem may have several local optima with different objective function values. Separable programming only guarantees finding a local optimum of the approximating problem, unless the original nonlinear programming problem satisfies the sufficient conditions for a global optimum developed in Section 11-11.

Table 14-2. *Optimal Solutions to Problem (14-14).*

	Solution 1	Solution 2	Solution 3	Solution 4
λ_{01}	1	1	0	0
λ_{11}	0	0	1	1
λ_{21}	0	0	0	0
λ_{31}	0	0	0	0
λ_{41}	0	0	0	0
λ_{02}	0	0	0	0
λ_{12}	1	0	1	0
λ_{22}	0	1	0	1
λ_{32}	0	0	0	0

14-4 SEPARABLE PROGRAMMING—OPTIMUM SATISFIES SUFFICIENCY CONDITIONS

If the sufficiency condition for a global optimum are satisfied by (14-3), i.e., the f_j are concave functions and the g_{ij} are convex functions, then the solution to the approximating problem approximates the global optimum.   Furthermore, under these circumstances it is not necessary to enforce the housekeeping rules restricting entry of the λ_{uj} variables into the basis. These will be satisfied automatically, as we shall see.

Problem (14-4) satisfies the sufficient conditions. From (14-5), $f_1(x_1) = 2x_1 - x_1^2$ is a concave function, and so is $f_2(x_2) = 3x_2 - x_2^2$. Also from (14-6), $g_{11}(x_1) = x_1$ is a convex function as is $g_{12}(x_2) = x_2^2$.

Usually this type of problem is formulated by a simpler method than the λ-formulation—although the results hold for any formulation of the approximating problem. We will first develop this method and then show that the restrictions on the variables can be ignored. In the end we have an ordinary linear programming problem. In fact, this type of problem is sometimes formulated as a linear program without ever considering it as a separable programming problem. Let x_j be split into the variables $\gamma_{1j}, \gamma_{2j}, ..., \gamma_{p_jj}$, i.e., one for each interval, such that

$$(14\text{-}15) \qquad\qquad x_j = \sum_{u=1}^{p_j} \gamma_{uj}$$

The variable γ_{uj} is just that segment of the variable x_j that is in the uth interval, so γ_{uj} is measured in the same units as x_j. However, γ_{uj} is limited by the length of the uth interval (Δx_{uj}), i.e.,

$$(14\text{-}16) \qquad\qquad 0 \leqslant \gamma_{uj} \leqslant \Delta x_{uj}, \qquad u = 1, ..., p_j$$

If x_j lies in the kth interval, then $\gamma_{uj} = \Delta x_{uj}$ for all $u < k$, and $\gamma_{uj} = 0$ for all $u > k$. For example, $x_1 = 5 = \Delta x_{11} + \Delta x_{21} + 1 + 0$, i.e., $\gamma_{11} = \Delta x_{11} = 2$, $\gamma_{21} = \Delta x_{21} = 2$, $\gamma_{31} = 1$, and $\gamma_{41} = 0$. (The values of the Δx_{uj} come from Table 14-1.)

Let us now consider the function $\hat{f}_j(x_j)$. The objective function coefficient for γ_{kj} is the slope of the line segment of $\hat{f}_j(x_j)$ in the kth interval given by $(\Delta f_{kj})/(\Delta x_{kj})$. The value of $\hat{f}_j(x_j)$ for x_j in the kth interval is

$$(14\text{-}17) \qquad \hat{f}_j(x_j) = f_{(k-1)j} + \left(\frac{\Delta f_{kj}}{\Delta x_{kj}}\right)\gamma_{kj} = f_{0j} + \sum_{u=1}^{k-1} \Delta f_{uj} + \left(\frac{\Delta f_{kj}}{\Delta x_{kj}}\right)\gamma_{kj}$$

However, since $\gamma_{uj} = \Delta x_{uj}$ for all $u < k$, and $\gamma_{uj} = 0$ for all $u > k$, this becomes

$$(14\text{-}18) \qquad\qquad \hat{f}_j(x_j) = f_{0j} + \sum_{u=1}^{p_j} \left(\frac{\Delta f_{uj}}{\Delta x_{uj}}\right)\gamma_{uj}$$

Let us apply this to $\hat{f}_1(5)$ of problem (14-7). We obtain

$$\hat{f}_1(5) = 0 + \frac{0}{2}(2) + \frac{-8}{2}(2) + \frac{-16}{2}(1) + \frac{-24}{2}(0) = -16$$

You may want to check this on Figure 14-2.

Similarly, the $\hat{g}_{1j}(x_j)$ are formulated in terms of the slopes of their segments, i.e.,

$$(14\text{-}19) \qquad\qquad \hat{g}_{1j}(x_j) = g_{01j} + \sum_{u=1}^{p_j} \left(\frac{\Delta g_{u1j}}{\Delta x_{uj}}\right)\gamma_{uj}$$

Expressions (14-16), (14-18), and (14-19) give us the formulation (14-20). The f_{0j} terms are omitted from the objective function because they are constants.

$$\text{maximize } \sum_{j=1}^{2} \hat{f}_j(x_j) = \sum_{j=1}^{2} \sum_{u=1}^{p_j} \left(\frac{\Delta f_{uj}}{\Delta x_{uj}}\right)\gamma_{uj}$$

(14-20)

$$\text{subject to } \sum_{j=1}^{2} \hat{g}_{1j}(x_j) = \sum_{j=1}^{2} \sum_{u=1}^{p_j} \left(\frac{\Delta g_{u1j}}{\Delta x_{uj}}\right)\gamma_{uj} \leqslant 8 - \sum_{j=1}^{2} g_{01j}$$

$$0 \leqslant \gamma_{uj} \leqslant \Delta x_{uj}$$

with the special condition that if $\gamma_{kj} > 0$, then $\gamma_{uj} = \Delta x_{uj}$ for all $u < k$.
    Using the data of Table 14-1, problem (14-7) becomes

$$\text{maximize } 0\gamma_{11} - 4\gamma_{21} - 8\gamma_{31} - 12\gamma_{41} + 2\gamma_{12} + 0\gamma_{22} - 2\gamma_{32}$$

(14-21)

$$\text{subject to } \gamma_{11} + \gamma_{21} + \gamma_{31} + \gamma_{41} + \gamma_{12} + 3\gamma_{22} + 5\gamma_{32} \leqslant 8$$

$$0 \leqslant \gamma_{u1} \leqslant 2, \qquad u = 1,...,4$$

$$0 \leqslant \gamma_{u2} \leqslant 1, \qquad u = 1,2,3$$

with the special condition on the variables.
    If we consider problem (14-21), we see that γ_{11} is preferred to γ_{21}, which is preferred to γ_{31}, which in turn is preferred to γ_{41} because their objective function coefficients can be ranked $0 > -4 > -8 > -12$, and in the constraint their coefficients are all unity. Similarly, γ_{12} is preferred to γ_{22}, etc., again because the objective function coefficients are decreasing. But, in this case the preference is reinforced by the increasing values of the constraint coefficients, namely, $1 < 3 < 5$. Hence we can ignore the condition that if $\gamma_{kj} > 0$, then $\gamma_{uj} = \Delta x_{uj}$ for $u < k$. It is automatically satisfied.
    This result holds in general because of the nature of convex and concave functions. For a concave objective function the slope of the approximating function in the first interval is at least as great as the slope in the second interval, and so on. Thus, the coefficients in the approximating problem's objective function decrease for each successive interval of x_j. Hence, in a maximization problem the first interval is preferred to the second, etc. For a convex constraint function, the approximating function has a slope in the first interval no greater than the slope in the second interval, and so on. So the variable for the first interval uses no more of the "resources" than that of the second interval, etc. Since the constraint is a $\leqslant$ constraint, the variable for the first interval is again preferred to that of the second, etc. Hence the approximating problem that satisfies the sufficiency conditions for a global optimum can be solved without forcing the intervals to be selected in ascending order—this is satisfied automatically.

14-5 AN EXAMPLE OF THE CONVEX SIMPLEX METHOD

The *Convex Simplex Method* is a technique designed to solve the problem:

$$\text{maximize } z = f(x_1, \ldots, x_n)$$

(14-22) $$\text{subject to } \sum_{j=1}^{n} a_{ij} x_j = b_i, \qquad i = 1, \ldots, m,$$

$$x_j \geqslant 0, \qquad j = 1, \ldots, n$$

where $f(x_1, \ldots, x_n)$ is a concave differentiable function.

(It got its name because it was posed originally to minimize a convex function. That situation is formally identical to (14-22).) When f is concave, any optimum to (14-22) is a global optimum. However, the convex simplex method can solve (14-22) for any differentiable f, provided a local optimum is an acceptable solution.

The convex simplex method is a true generalization of the simplex method in that if f is linear the mechanics of the convex simplex method are identical to those of the simplex method. However, while the convex simplex method uses the ideas of a basis, basic vectors, and nonbasic vectors, it does not restrict itself to basic solutions because there is no reason to suppose in advance that the optimum to (14-22) will be a basic solution.

The convex simplex method optimizes, at each tableau, the tangent line of the true objective function evaluated at the solution represented by the tableau. Thus, the linear function being optimized will generally vary from tableau to tableau.

Geometrically, the convex simplex method is a hybrid of the simplex method and gradient methods. The direction vector is found in the same way as we find the direction in the simplex method, namely, in the direction of a face or edge of the feasible region. However, instead of going to the next basic feasible solution, we choose the best distance in that direction in the same way as we did in gradient methods, thus, perhaps stopping at a nonbasic solution. This being the case, the convex simplex method generally has a direction vector parallel to the face of the feasible region rather than actually along it, like the simplex method.

Let us go back to problem (13-3) of Chapter 13: adding slack variables we obtain

(14-23)

$$\text{maximize } z = f(x) = 4x_1 - x_1{}^2 + 9x_2 - x_2{}^2 + 10x_3 - 2x_3{}^2 - \tfrac{1}{2}x_2 x_3$$

$$\text{subject to } 4x_1 + 2x_2 + x_3 + x_4 = 10$$

$$2x_1 + 4x_2 + x_3 + x_5 = 20$$

$$x_1, x_2, x_3, x_4, x_5 \geqslant 0$$

Any basic solution to (14-23) is sufficient to initiate the convex simplex method. Normally the two-phase method is used to find the initial basic feasible solution. However, in this case the obvious basic feasible solution is $x_4 = 10$, $x_5 = 20$ with the basis $[\mathbf{a}_4, \mathbf{a}_5]$. The first tableau is based on this first solution which we will call $\mathbf{x}^{(0)}$; $\mathbf{x}^{(0)} = (0, 0, 0, 10, 20)$.

As mentioned earlier, the actual function is replaced by its tangent at this solution. Thus, the c_j values inserted in the tableau for this iteration are given by $c_j = \partial f / \partial x_j$ evaluated at $\mathbf{x}^{(0)}$. The first derivatives are

(14-24)

$$\frac{\partial f}{\partial x_1} = 4 - 2x_1, \qquad \frac{\partial f}{\partial x_2} = 9 - 2x_2 - \frac{1}{2}x_3, \qquad \frac{\partial f}{\partial x_3} = 10 - 4x_3 - \frac{1}{2}x_2$$

Evaluating these at $\mathbf{x}^{(0)}$, we obtain the tangent plane

(14-25)
$$\bar{z} = 4x_1 + 9x_2 + 10x_3 + 0x_4 + 0x_5$$

We derive the first tableau by using the basis $[\mathbf{a}_4, \mathbf{a}_5]$, the solution $\mathbf{x}^{(0)}$, and the objective function (14-25). Table 14-3 gives this tableau. The $(z_j - c_j)$ values are calculated exactly as they were in Chapter 3. For example, $(z_1 - c_1) = (0)(4) + (0)(2) - 4 = -4$.

In this first tableau, the choice of a possible new basic variable is made according to the simplex method criterion:

(14-26)
$$\beta_{1j} = \text{minimum}[(z_j - c_j), \quad \text{all } (z_j - c_j) < 0]$$

This gives x_3.

The next steps in the algorithm are similar, in principle, to gradient methods. We find a feasible direction, a maximum feasible distance in that direction, and then the best objective function value in the feasible direction up to the maximum feasible distance. In the simplex method, the direction of movement and the maximum feasible distance in that direction are found in one step. This is achieved by finding an extreme point in the feasible region which is adjacent to the current solution, i.e., differs from the current solution by one basic vector only. If $\mathbf{x}^{(k)}$ denotes the current solution at iteration k, and $\mathbf{q}^{(k)}$ denotes the new solution, then this immediately defines the direction of movement $\mathbf{r}^{(k)}$ and the maximum feasible distance ε in that direction, because

$$\mathbf{q}^{(k)} = \mathbf{x}^{(k)} + \varepsilon \mathbf{r}^{(k)}.$$

Table 14-3. *First Convex Simplex Method Tableau.*

$\mathbf{x}^{(0)}$		$z = 0$	0	0	0	10	20
$\dfrac{\partial f}{\partial x_j}(\mathbf{x}^{(0)}) = c_j$			4	9	10	0	0
c_j	Vectors / Basis	$\mathbf{b}$	$\mathbf{a}_1$	$\mathbf{a}_2$	$\mathbf{a}_3$	$\mathbf{a}_4$	$\mathbf{a}_5$
0	$\mathbf{a}_4$	10	4	2	1	1	0
0	$\mathbf{a}_5$	20	2	4	1	0	1
$z_j - c_j$			-4	-9	$-10\uparrow$	0	0

Let us now consider how to find $\mathbf{q}^{(0)}$, $\mathbf{r}^{(0)}$, and ε from the current solution, $\mathbf{x}^{(0)} = (0, 0, 0, 10, 20)$, shown in Table 14-3.

Had we been solving a regular linear programming problem, the vector $\mathbf{a}_3$ would enter the basis, and in so doing, x_3 would take the greatest value it feasibly could, i.e., $x_3 = 10$. This value of x_3 just drives x_4 to zero (see Section 3-6 for a detailed discussion). The resulting solution found by applying the simplex transformation rules to Table 14-3, is $\mathbf{q}^{(0)} = (0, 0, 10, 0, 10)$.

The direction vector $\mathbf{r}^{(0)}$ is the change in the solution for a unit increase in x_3. From the definitions of the elements of the simplex tableau, column $\mathbf{a}_3$ expresses the vector $\mathbf{a}_3$ in terms of the basis $[\mathbf{a}_4, \mathbf{a}_5]$, i.e., $\mathbf{a}_3 = 1\mathbf{a}_4 + 1\mathbf{a}_5$. Substituting a unit of the activity of $\mathbf{a}_3$ for the equivalent vector in terms of $\mathbf{a}_4$ and $\mathbf{a}_5$, we find that a unit increase in x_3 results in a decrease of one unit (the value of the element in row $\mathbf{a}_4$ and column $\mathbf{a}_3$) in x_4, and a decrease of one unit (the value of the element in row $\mathbf{a}_5$ and column $\mathbf{a}_3$) in x_5. All other variables remain unchanged because they are nonbasic. So the direction vector is $\mathbf{r}^{(0)} = (0, 0, 1, -1, -1)$.

The maximum feasible distance ε in the direction of $\mathbf{r}^{(0)}$ is given by

$$\mathbf{q}^{(0)} = \mathbf{x}^{(0)} + \varepsilon \mathbf{r}^{(0)} = (0, 0, \varepsilon, 10 - \varepsilon, 20 - \varepsilon),$$

i.e., $\varepsilon = 10$ and $x_4 = 0$.

Like the gradient methods, the convex simplex method now finds the point with the best value of $f(\mathbf{x})$ in the direction of $\mathbf{r}^{(0)}$ from $\mathbf{x}^{(0)}$, i.e., we find $\mathbf{x}^{(1)} = \mathbf{x}^{(0)} + \theta \mathbf{r}^{(0)}$, $0 \leqslant \theta \leqslant \varepsilon = 10$ such that

$$(14\text{-}27) \qquad f(\mathbf{x}^{(1)}) = \underset{0 \leqslant \theta \leqslant 10}{\text{maximum}} f(\mathbf{x}^{(0)} + \theta \mathbf{r}^{(0)})$$

In linear programming this operation is performed implicitly, and the maximum feasible distance ε always gives the best value of θ. This is not always true in the convex simplex method. In terms of problem (14-23), expression (14-27) becomes

$$\underset{0 \leqslant \theta \leqslant 10}{\text{maximize}} [4(0) - (0)^2 + 9(0) - (0)^2 + 10(0 + \theta) - 2(0 + \theta)^2 - \tfrac{1}{2}0(0 + \theta)]$$

or,

$$(14\text{-}28) \qquad \underset{0 \leqslant \theta \leqslant 10}{\text{maximize}} [10\theta - 2\theta^2]$$

The solution to (14-28) is $\theta = 5/2$. So $\mathbf{x}^{(1)} = \mathbf{x}^{(0)} + (5/2) \mathbf{r}^{(0)}$ or

$$(14\text{-}29) \qquad \mathbf{x}^{(1)} = (0, 0, 5/2, 15/2, 35/2)$$

Since $0 < \theta < 10$, $\mathbf{x}^{(1)}$ is not a basic solution; it has three variables greater than zero.

We now take $\mathbf{x}^{(1)}$ as the starting point of the next iteration. To construct a tableau for $\mathbf{x}^{(1)}$ we must have a basis, even though $\mathbf{x}^{(1)}$ is not a basic solution. We arbitrarily take the two largest components of $\mathbf{x}^{(1)}$—in this case $x_4 = 15/2$, and $x_5 = 35/2$, as basic variables. The basis $[\mathbf{a}_4, \mathbf{a}_5]$ for the second tableau is the same as for the first tableau. In a problem with m constraints, the m largest components of $\mathbf{x}^{(1)}$ give the basic variables.

Although x_3 assumes a positive value in this solution, by our criterion for selecting a basis, x_3 does not become a basic variable. Since at the time a nonbasic variable is chosen by (14-26) we do not know whether it will become a basic variable, we shall not use the simplex method terminology *vector to enter the basis*, but rather the term the *nonbasic variable to be changed* at each iteration.

When there are positive nonbasic variables, a situation arises that is never present in ordinary linear programming, namely, if a positive nonbasic variable x_k has $(z_k - c_k) > 0$, the value of the objective function can increase by reducing x_k. This is the reverse of the argument for a nonbasic vector with $(z_j - c_j) < 0$.

Let us consider the product $x_j(z_j - c_j)$ for all nonbasic vectors. When $x_j(z_j - c_j) > 0$, we can increase the value of the objective function by decreasing the value of x_j. To choose just one variable that satisfies this requirement we have the rule:

$$(14\text{-}30) \qquad \beta_{2j} = \underset{j}{\text{maximum}}\,(x_j(z_j - c_j) > 0)$$

Now we have two rules to determine the nonbasic variable to be changed at each iteration, namely, (14-26) and (14-30). They can be combined into the single rule:

$$(14\text{-}31) \qquad \underset{j}{\text{maximum}}\,|\beta_{1j}, \beta_{2j}|$$

Table 14-4 gives the second tableau evaluated at $\mathbf{x}^{(1)}$, including an additional row for the $x_j(z_j - c_j)$ values.

Geometrically, we can view the situation described in Table 14-4 as follows: The constraints that intersect to form the basic solution (x_4, x_5) undergo an imaginary shift parallel to themselves so as to intersect at the point $\mathbf{x}^{(1)}$. However, we allow

Table 14-4. *Second Convex Simplex Method Tableau.*

	$\mathbf{x}^{(1)}$	$\dfrac{25}{2}$	0	0	$\dfrac{5}{2}$	$\dfrac{15}{2}$	$\dfrac{35}{2}$
	$\dfrac{\partial f}{\partial x_j}(\mathbf{x}^{(1)}) = c_j$		4	$\dfrac{31}{4}$	0	0	0
c_j	Vector / Basis	$\mathbf{b}$	$\mathbf{a}_1$	$\mathbf{a}_2$	$\mathbf{a}_3$	$\mathbf{a}_4$	$\mathbf{a}_5$
0	$\mathbf{a}_4$	$\dfrac{15}{2}$	4	2	1	1	0
0	$\mathbf{a}_5$	$\dfrac{35}{2}$	2	4	1	0	1
	$z_j - c_j$		-4	$-\dfrac{31}{4}$	0	0	0
	$x_j(z_j - c_j)$		0	0	0	0	0

the possibility of shifting backward from this solution by letting the positive valued nonbasic variable reduce in value. The directions of movement from $\mathbf{x}^{(1)}$ will be determined by the constraints in their imaginary position.

In performing the next iteration we see that criterion (14-31) is satisfied by $(z_2 - c_2) = -31/4$, so x_2 is the nonbasic vector to be changed. Using the same analysis as we used to find $\mathbf{r}^{(0)}$, we find $\mathbf{r}^{(1)} = (0, 1, 0, -2, -4)$. Since x_2 is the nonbasic vector being changed, $r_2 = 1$, the change in the basic variables is the negative of the elements of column $\mathbf{a}_2$ in the tableau, with $\mathbf{a}_4$ and $\mathbf{a}_5$ in the basis, so $r_4 = -2$, and $r_5 = -4$. The other elements of $\mathbf{r}^{(1)}$ are zero because they correspond to nonbasic variables.

If we perform a simplex transformation on the tableau of Table 14-4, bringing $\mathbf{a}_2$ into the basis, we obtain $\mathbf{q}^{(1)} = (0, 15/4, 5/2, 0, 5/2)$, which is the solution when x_4 goes to zero. Using the formula

$$\mathbf{q}^{(1)} = \mathbf{x}^{(1)} + \varepsilon\mathbf{r}^{(1)} = (0+(0), 0+\varepsilon(1), \tfrac{5}{2}+\varepsilon(0), \tfrac{15}{2}+\varepsilon(-2), \tfrac{35}{2}+\varepsilon(-4))$$

we obtain the value of the maximum feasible distance $\varepsilon = 15/4$. Hence, we find $\mathbf{x}^{(2)}$ from

$$f(\mathbf{x}^{(2)}) = \underset{0 \leqslant \theta \leqslant 15/4}{\text{maximum}} [f(\mathbf{x}^{(1)} + \theta\mathbf{r}^{(1)})]$$

or

$$\underset{0 \leqslant \theta \leqslant 15/4}{\text{maximize}} [4(0) - (0)^2 + 9(0+\theta) - (0+\theta)^2 + 10(\tfrac{5}{2}) - 2(\tfrac{5}{2})^2 - \tfrac{1}{2}(\tfrac{5}{2})(0+\theta)]$$

The unconstrained optimum for θ is $31/8$; but since $0 \leqslant \theta \leqslant 15/4$, the optimal value of $\theta = 15/4$. So

$$\mathbf{x}^{(2)} = (0, 15/4, 5/2, 0, 5/2)$$

We now come to the third tableau. We see from $\mathbf{x}^{(2)}$ that both x_3 and x_5 have the second largest value, so we can arbitrarily choose between them in order to find a basis. We have chosen the basis $[\mathbf{a}_2, \mathbf{a}_5]$. This tableau is shown in the top portion of Table 14-5.

Applying criterion (14-31) to the third tableau, we obtain x_3 as the nonbasic variable to be changed, since $x_3(z_3 - c_3) = 5 > |z_1 - c_1| = |-7/2|$. This means that x_3 must be decreased at this iteration. If we were to increase x_3, the direction of movement would be $\mathbf{r} = (0, -\tfrac{1}{2}, 1, 0, 1)$. With x_3 being decreased, the direction vector is the negative of this, i.e., $\mathbf{r}^{(2)} = (0, \tfrac{1}{2}, -1, 0, -1)$. You should verify this result from Table 14-5.

What is the maximum feasible distance in the direction of $\mathbf{r}^{(2)}$? It will be the value ε that just maintains $\mathbf{q}^{(2)} = \mathbf{x}^{(2)} + \varepsilon\mathbf{r}^{(2)}$ as a feasible solution. This value is found from

$$\mathbf{q}^{(2)} = (0, 3.75 + (\varepsilon/2), 2.5 - \varepsilon, 0, 2.5 - \varepsilon)$$

The largest value ε can assume is $\varepsilon = 5/2$. This is the value that just drives the third and fifth elements of $\mathbf{q}^{(2)}$ to zero. Any $\varepsilon > 5/2$ violates feasibility, hence $\varepsilon = \tfrac{5}{2}$ is the maximum feasible distance.

Table 14-5. *Additional Convex Simplex Method Tableaux.*

c_j	Vector Basis	b	a_1	a_2	a_3	a_4	a_5
	$x^{(2)}$	27.5	0	3.75	2.5	0	2.5
	c_j		4	0.25	−1.875	0	0
0.25	a_2	3.75	2	1	0.5	0.5	0
0	a_5	2.5	−6	0	−1	−2	1
	$z_j - c_j$		−3.5	0	2	0.125	0
	$x_j(z_j - c_j)$		0	0	5	0	0
	$x^{(3)}$	28	0	4	2	0	2
	c_j		4	0	0	0	0
0	a_2	4	2	1	0.5	0.5	0
0	a_5	2	−6	0	−1	−2	1
	$z_j - c_j$		−4	0	0	0	0
	$x_j(z_j - c_j)$		0	0	0	0	0
	$x^{(4)}$	28.8	0.4	3.2	2	0	4.4
	c_j		3.2	1.6	0.4	0	0
1.6	a_2	3.2	2	1	0.5	0.5	0
0	a_5	4.4	−6	0	−1	−2	1
	$z_j - c_j$		0	0	0.4	0.8	0
	$x_j(z_j - c_j)$		0	0	0.8	0	0
	$x^{(5)}$	28.82	0.4	3.25	1.9	0	4.3
	c_j		3.2	1.55	0.775	0	0
1.55	a_2	3.25	2	1	0.5	0.5	0
0	a_5	4.3	−6	0	−1	−2	1
	$z_j - c_j$		−0.1	0	0	0.775	0
	$x_j(z_j - c_j)$		−0.04	0	0	0	0
	$x^{(6)}$	28.8205	0.41	3.23	1.9	0	4.36
	c_j		3.18	1.59	0.785	0	0
1.59	a_2	3.23	2	1	0.5	0.5	0
0	a_5	4.36	−6	0	−1	−2	1
	$z_j - c_j$		0	0	0.01	0.795	0
	$x_j(z_j - c_j)$		0	0	0.019	0	0

So $\mathbf{x}^{(3)}$ is the solution of:

$$f(\mathbf{x}^{(3)}) = \underset{0 \leqslant \theta \leqslant 5/2}{\text{maximum}} [f(\mathbf{x}^{(2)} + \theta \mathbf{r}^{(2)})]$$

which yields $\theta = 1/2$, and $\mathbf{x}^{(3)} = (0, 4, 2, 0, 2)$. Table 14-5 gives the tableau related to $\mathbf{x}^{(3)}$.

The convex simplex method continues in this fashion converging on the optimum, $\mathbf{x}^* = (0.4102, 3.2308, 1.8974, 0, 4.3590)$, $z^* = 28.8205$. We recognize the optimum when criterion (14-31) cannot be satisfied, i.e., $(z_j - c_j) \geqslant 0$ for all nonbasic x_j at zero, and $x_j(z_j - c_j) \leqslant 0$ for all nonbasic $x_j > 0$, or when the tableaux are converging to a solution.

The convergence of this algorithm can be terminated in two ways. Either we can stop when $\mathbf{x}^{(k+1)}$ is arbitrarily close to $\mathbf{x}^{(k)}$, or we can stop when maximum $[\beta_{1j}, \beta_{2j}] < \gamma$, where γ is very small. For this technique the second method is more useful since it is a simple extension of equation (14-31).

As in the ordinary simplex method we have some information for sensitivity analysis. In particular, $(z_4 - c_4)$ gives the imputed value of the first constraint, and $(z_5 - c_5)$ gives the imputed value of the second constraint. Since the objective function is nonlinear, these must be strictly interpreted as marginal values.

14-6 CONVEX SIMPLEX METHOD CRITERIA

Let us now state, in general terms, the convex simplex method criteria developed in the example. Let $\mathbf{x}^{(v)}$ be the solution on which the vth tableau is based.

CSM CRITERION 1: NONBASIC VARIABLE TO BE CHANGED

The nonbasic variable $x_k^{(v)}$ to be changed at the vth iteration is the one that satisfies

$$\underset{j}{\text{maximum}} \left[|(z_j - c_j) < 0|, (x_j(z_j - c_j) > 0) \right]$$

CSM CRITERION 2: CHANGE OF $x_k^{(v)}$

If the nonbasic variable $x_k^{(v)}$ being changed satisfies

(i)
$$\underset{j}{\text{maximum}} \left[|(z_j - c_j) < 0| \right]$$

$x_k^{(v)}$ is increased;

(ii)
$$\underset{j}{\text{maximum}} \left[(x_j(z_j - c_j) > 0) \right]$$

$x_k^{(v)}$ is decreased.

CSM CRITERION 3: DEFINITION OF THE DIRECTION VECTOR $\mathbf{r}^{(v)}$

(a) When $x_k^{(v)}$ is being increased, the elements of the direction vector $\mathbf{r}^{(v)}$ are defined as follows:

    (i) $r_k^{(v)} = 1$,

    (ii) the elements of $\mathbf{r}^{(v)}$ corresponding to basic variables are the negatives of the respective coefficients in the $\mathbf{a}_k$ column,

    (iii) the elements of $\mathbf{r}^{(v)}$ corresponding to all other non-basic variables are zero.

(b) When $x_k^{(v)}$ is being decreased, the vector is the negative of that in case (a).

CSM CRITERION 4: MAXIXUM FEASIBLE DISTANCE

Let $\mathbf{q}^{(v)} = \mathbf{x}^{(v)} + \varepsilon \mathbf{r}^{(v)}$. The maximum feasible distance, ε, is that value that just maintains $\mathbf{q}^{(v)}$ as a feasible solution. Where no limit on ε exists, ε is set to a very large value.

CSM CRITERION 5: FINDING $\mathbf{x}^{(v+1)}$

The solution, $\mathbf{x}^{(v+1)}$, on which the next tableau is to be based, is found from $\mathbf{x}^{(v)}$ by:

$$f(\mathbf{x}^{(v+1)}) = \underset{0 \leqslant \theta \leqslant \varepsilon}{\text{maximum}} [f(\mathbf{x}^{(v)} + \theta \mathbf{r}^{(v)})]$$

CSM CRITERION 6: NEW BASIS

The basis for tableau $(v+1)$ is chosen by taking the m largest components of $\mathbf{x}^{(v+1)}$ as the basic variables, where the basis is of dimension m.

CSM CRITERION 7: TERMINATION OF THE ALGORITHM

The algorithm terminates when

$$[\text{maximum}(|(z_j - c_j) < 0|, x_j(z_j - c_j))] < \gamma$$

where $\gamma > 0$, but very small.

14-7 QUADRATIC PROGRAMMING

Quadratic programming looks at the problem of solving a quadratic objective function subject to linear constraints. Depending on the technique used, restrictions on the nature of the quadratic function are sometimes imposed. We will consider an algorithm suggested by P. Wolfe. This algorithm is restricted to the case of maximizing a concave function.

Since the constraint set is a convex set and the objective function is a concave function, there will be no local optima distinct from the global optimum. We can find this optimum by solving the Kuhn-Tucker conditions for the quadratic programming problem. (Refer to Sections 11-10 and 11-11.) As we will see, these conditions are linear except for a nonlinear restriction on some of the variables. Let us develop the technique using problem (14-23). The Lagrangian function for this problem is

(14-32)

$$L(\mathbf{x}, \lambda) = 4x_1 - x_1{}^2 + 9x_2 - x_2{}^2 + 10x_3 - 2x_3{}^2 - \tfrac{1}{2}x_2 x_3$$
$$+ \lambda_1(10 - 4x_1 - 2x_2 - x_3 - x_4) + \lambda_2(20 - 2x_1 - 4x_2 - x_3 - x_5)$$

From the definition of the Kuhn-Tucker conditions, we can state the necessary conditions for an optimum to expression (14-32):

There exist λ_1 and λ_2 unrestricted in sign, with $x_j \geqslant 0$ ($j = 1, ..., 5$), such that

$$\frac{\partial L}{\partial x_1} = 4 - 2x_1 - 4\lambda_1 - 2\lambda_2 \qquad = -v_1 \leqslant 0 \qquad (1)$$

$$\frac{\partial L}{\partial x_2} = 9 - 2x_2 - \tfrac{1}{2}x_3 - 2\lambda_1 - 4\lambda_2 \quad = -v_2 \leqslant 0 \qquad (2)$$

(14-33)
$$\frac{\partial L}{\partial x_3} = 10 - 4x_3 - \tfrac{1}{2}x_2 - \lambda_1 - \lambda_2 \quad = -v_3 \leqslant 0 \qquad (3)$$

$$\frac{\partial L}{\partial x_4} = \qquad\qquad -\lambda_1 \qquad = -v_4 \leqslant 0 \qquad (4)$$

$$\frac{\partial L}{\partial x_5} = \qquad\qquad -\lambda_2 \quad = -v_5 \leqslant 0 \qquad (5)$$

$$\frac{\partial L}{\partial \lambda_1} = 10 - 4x_1 - 2x_2 - x_3 - x_4 = 0$$

(14-34)
$$\frac{\partial L}{\partial \lambda_2} = 20 - 2x_1 - 4x_2 - x_3 - x_5 = 0$$

and

(14-35)
$$x_j \frac{\partial L}{\partial x_j} = x_j v_j = 0, \qquad j = 1, ..., 5$$

Since λ_1 and λ_2 are unrestricted in sign, to use the simplex method they should be replaced by nonnegative variables. This is normally done as follows:

$$\lambda_1 = \lambda_1{}' - \lambda_1{}'', \qquad \textit{where} \quad \lambda_1{}', \lambda_1{}'' \geqslant 0$$
$$\lambda_2 = \lambda_2{}' - \lambda_2{}'', \qquad \textit{where} \quad \lambda_2{}', \lambda_2{}'' \geqslant 0$$

However, in this example, λ_1 and λ_2 are, in fact, restricted to be nonnegative. By the fourth and fifth equations of (14-33), $\lambda_1 = v_4 \geqslant 0$ and $\lambda_2 = v_5 \geqslant 0$. Restricting λ_1 and λ_2 to being nonnegative enables us to eliminate both these two equations and the variables v_4 and v_5. Hence conditions (14-33) and (14-34) yield the linear system

$$
\begin{aligned}
2x_1 \qquad\qquad\qquad\qquad &+ 4\lambda_1 + 2\lambda_2 - v_1 && = 4 \\
2x_2 + (\tfrac{1}{2})x_3 \qquad\quad &+ 2\lambda_1 + 4\lambda_2 \qquad - v_2 && = 9 \\
(\tfrac{1}{2})x_2 + \; 4x_3 \qquad\quad &+ \;\lambda_1 + \;\lambda_2 \qquad\qquad - v_3 &&= 10 \\
4x_1 + \; 2x_2 + \quad x_3 + x_4 \qquad\qquad\qquad\qquad\quad && = 10 \\
2x_1 + \; 4x_2 + \quad x_3 \qquad + x_5 \qquad\qquad\qquad\qquad && = 20
\end{aligned}
$$

(14-36)

$$x_j \geqslant 0, \qquad \text{all } j$$

$$v_j \geqslant 0, \qquad j = 1,2,3$$

$$\lambda_i \geqslant 0, \qquad i = 1,2$$

In addition, there are the variable restrictions (14-35) that preclude certain combinations of variable values. Having eliminated v_4 and v_5, the restriction $x_4 v_4 = 0$ and $x_5 v_5 = 0$ become $x_4 \lambda_1 = 0$ and $x_5 \lambda_2 = 0$, since $\lambda_1 = v_4$ and $\lambda_2 = v_5$.

If the quadratic function is concave, the Kuhn-Tucker conditions are both necessary and sufficient. So the solution to the system of linear equations (14-36) with the variable restrictions (14-35) will yield the global optimal solution.

In solving (14-36) all we seek is a feasible solution. It is a system of linear simultaneous equations without an objective function; so the use of the simplex method is purely to find this feasible solution. Since no feasible solution can be found by inspection we introduce artificial variables and use the two-phase method. We can tell there is a feasible solution to (14-36) provided there is a feasible solution to the constraints of the original quadratic program. It is convenient to first seek a feasible solution to the original constraints (given by the last two equations of (14-36)), and then, starting with that solution, use the two-phase method on the whole system (14-36). Thus, if there is no feasible solution to the constraint set, there is no need to solve the Kuhn-Tucker equations.

A natural initial basis to choose for the original constraints is $(\mathbf{a}_4, \mathbf{a}_5)$; so $x_4 = 10$ and $x_5 = 20$. We now add artificial variables (u_1, u_2, u_3) to the first three equations of (14-36). The resulting linear program to be solved is shown in Table 14-6. The initial basic solution for the full problem is:

$$u_1 = 4, \qquad u_2 = 9, \qquad u_3 = 10, \qquad x_4 = 10, \qquad x_5 = 20$$

At this basic solution we have the initial tableau shown in Table 14-7 (where vectors $\mathbf{a}_1$ to $\mathbf{a}_5$ are for x_1 to x_5, $\mathbf{a}_6$ and $\mathbf{a}_7$ for λ_1 and λ_2, $\mathbf{a}_8$ to $\mathbf{a}_{10}$ for v_1 to v_3, and $\mathbf{a}_{11}$ to $\mathbf{a}_{13}$ for u_1 to u_3).

Table 14-6. *Linear Program for Solving Quadratic Program.*

maximize $\omega = $ $-u_1 - u_2 - u_3$

subject to

$$
\begin{array}{llllll}
2x_1 & +4\lambda_1 + 2\lambda_2 - v_1 & & +u_1 & & = 4 \\
2x_2 + \tfrac{1}{2}x_3 & +2\lambda_1 + 4\lambda_2 & -v_2 & & +u_2 & = 9 \\
+\tfrac{1}{2}x_2 + 4x_3 & + \lambda_1 + \lambda_2 & & -v_3 & & +u_3 = 10 \\
4x_1 + 2x_2 + x_3 + x_4 & & & & & = 10 \\
2x_1 + 4x_2 + x_3 & +x_5 & & & & = 20 \\
\end{array}
$$

$$
\begin{array}{ll}
x_j \geqslant 0, & j = 1,\ldots,5 \\
v_j, u_j \geqslant 0, & j = 1,2,3 \\
\lambda_i \geqslant 0, & i = 1,2 \\
\end{array}
$$

$$
\text{with restrictions} \quad
\begin{array}{ll}
x_j v_j = 0, & j = 1,2,3 \\
x_4 \lambda_1 = 0 & \\
x_5 \lambda_2 = 0 & \\
\end{array}
$$

Applying the simplex method criterion for the vector to enter the basis gives either $\mathbf{a}_6$ or $\mathbf{a}_7$. However, because of the basis restrictions, $x_4 \lambda_1 = 0$ and $x_5 \lambda_2 = 0$, neither of these is permitted to enter. The next best vector is $\mathbf{a}_3$ which is allowed to enter the basis. Vector $\mathbf{a}_{13}$ leaves the basis. The second tableau of Table 14-7 gives the solution after the first iteration. The optimal solution is reached after four iterations. It can be read from tableau 5 of Table 14-7 as

$$x_1 = 0.4103, \qquad x_2 = 3.2308, \qquad x_3 = 1.8974, \qquad x_5 = 4.3590$$

$$\lambda_1 = 0.795,$$

$$x_4 = \lambda_2 = v_1 = v_2 = v_3 = u_1 = u_2 = u_3 = 0,$$

$$\omega = 0$$

The optimal value of the original objective function to (14-23) is $z = 28.82054$. The values of λ_1 and λ_2 are, of course, the imputed values of constraints 1 and 2, respectively.

Wolfe's algorithm is suitable for solving any quadratic program with a concave objective function and a linear constraint set. (However, to guarantee the convergence of the algorithm to a finite maximum, the objective function must be *strictly concave*. See text by G. Hadley listed in the references, pp. 83–84, 218–220.)

This general quadratic program can be written

$$\text{maximize } z = \sum_{j-1}^{n} \left(c_j x_j + \sum_{k=1}^{n} d_{kj} x_k x_j \right)$$

(14-37) $\text{subject to } \displaystyle\sum_{j=1}^{n} a_{ij} x_j = b_i, \qquad i = 1,\ldots,m$

$$x_j \geqslant 0, \qquad j = 1,\ldots,n$$

Table 14-7. *Simplex Tableaux for Quadratic Program.*

c_j			0	0	0	0	0	0	0	0	0	0	−1	−1	−1
c_j	Basis	$\mathbf{b}$	$\mathbf{a}_1$	$\mathbf{a}_2$	$\mathbf{a}_3$	$\mathbf{a}_4$	$\mathbf{a}_5$	$\mathbf{a}_6$	$\mathbf{a}_7$	$\mathbf{a}_8$	$\mathbf{a}_9$	$\mathbf{a}_{10}$	$\mathbf{a}_{11}$	$\mathbf{a}_{12}$	$\mathbf{a}_{13}$
Initial Tableau															
−1	$\mathbf{a}_{11}$	4	2	0	0	0	0	4	2	−1	0	0	1	0	0
−1	$\mathbf{a}_{12}$	9	0	2	0.5	0	0	2	4	0	−1	0	0	1	0
−1	$\mathbf{a}_{13}$	10	0	0.5	4	0	0	1	1	0	0	−1	0	0	1
0	$\mathbf{a}_4$	10	4	2	1	1	0	0	0	0	0	0	0	0	0
0	$\mathbf{a}_5$	20	2	4	1	0	1	0	0	0	0	0	0	0	0
$z_j - c_j$		−23	−2	−2.5	−4.5	0	0	−7	−7	1	1	1	0	0	0
Tableau 2															
−1	$\mathbf{a}_{11}$	4	2	0	0	0	0	4	2	−1	0	0	1	0	0
−1	$\mathbf{a}_{12}$	7.75	0	1.9375	0	0	0	1.875	3.875	0	−1	0.125	0	1	−0.125
0	$\mathbf{a}_3$	2.5	0	0.125	1	0	0	0.25	0.25	0	0	−0.25	0	0	0.25
0	$\mathbf{a}_4$	7.5	4	1.875	0	1	0	−0.25	−0.25	0	0	0.25	0	0	−0.25
0	$\mathbf{a}_5$	17.5	2	3.875	0	0	1	−0.25	−0.25	0	0	0.25	0	0	−0.25
$z_j - c_j$		−11.75	−2	−1.9375	0	0	0	−5.875	−5.875	1	1	−0.125	0	0	1.125
Tableau 3															
−1	$\mathbf{a}_{11}$	0.25	0	−0.9375	0	−0.5	0	4.125	2.125	−1	0	−0.125	1	0	0.125
−1	$\mathbf{a}_{12}$	7.75	0	1.9375	0	0	0	1.875	3.875	0	−1	0.125	0	1	−0.125
0	$\mathbf{a}_3$	2.5	0	0.125	1	0	0	0.25	0.25	0	0	−0.25	0	0	0.25
0	$\mathbf{a}_1$	1.875	1	0.4688	0	0.25	0	−0.0625	−0.0625	0	0	0.0625	0	0	−0.0625
0	$\mathbf{a}_5$	13.75	0	2.9375	0	−0.5	1	−0.125	−0.125	0	0	0.125	0	0	−0.125
$z_j - c_j$		−8	0	−1	0	0.5	0	−6	−6	1	1	0	0	0	1

Table 14-7—*continued.*

Tableau 4

c_j			0	0	0	0	0	0	0	0	0	0	-1	-1	-1
c_j	Basis	b	a_1	a_2	a_3	a_4	a_5	a_6	a_7	a_8	a_9	a_{10}	a_{11}	a_{12}	a_{13}
0	a_6	0.0606	0	-0.2273	0	-0.1212	0	1	0.5152	-0.2424	0	-0.0303	0.2424	0	0.0303
-1	a_{12}	7.6364	0	2.3636	0	0.2273	0	0	2.9091	0.4545	-1	0.1818	-0.4545	1	-0.1818
0	a_3	2.4848	0	0.1818	1	0.0303	0	0	0.1212	0.0606	0	-0.2424	-0.0606	0	0.2424
0	a_1	1.8788	1	0.4545	0	0.2424	0	0	-0.0303	-0.0152	0	0.0606	0.0152	0	-0.0606
0	a_5	13.7576	0	2.9091	0	-0.5152	1	0	-0.0606	-0.0303	0	0.1212	0.0303	0	-0.1212
$z_j - c_j$		-7.6364	0	-2.3636	0	-0.2273	0	0	-2.9091	-0.4545	1	-0.1818	1.4545	0	1.1818

Tableau 5

c_j	Basis	b	a_1	a_2	a_3	a_4	a_5	a_6	a_7	a_8	a_9	a_{10}	a_{11}	a_{12}	a_{13}
0	a_6	0.79487	0	0	0	-0.0993	0	1	0.795	-0.1987	-0.0962	-0.0128	0.1987	0.0962	0.0128
0	a_2	3.23077	0	1	0	0.0962	0	0	1.2308	0.1923	-0.4231	0.0769	-0.1923	0.4231	-0.0769
0	a_3	1.89744	0	0	1	0.0128	0	0	-0.1026	0.0256	0.0769	-0.2564	-0.0256	-0.0769	-0.2564
0	a_1	0.41026	1	0	0	0.1987	0	0	-0.5897	-0.1026	0.1923	0.0256	0.1026	-0.1923	-0.0256
0	a_5	4.35897	0	0	0	-0.795	1	0	-3.6411	-0.5897	1.2308	-0.1026	0.5897	-1.2308	0.1026
$z_j - c_j$		0	0	0	0	0	0	0	0	0	0	0	1	1	1

We can apply the Kuhn-Tucker conditions in the same manner as we did for problem (14-23):

There exist $\lambda_1, \ldots, \lambda_m$ unrestricted in sign, such that

$$c_j + \sum_{\substack{k=1 \\ j \neq k}}^{n} d_{kj} x_k + 2d_{jj} x_j - \sum_{i=1}^{m} a_{ij} \lambda_i = -v_j \leqslant 0 \qquad j = 1, \ldots, n$$

(14-38)
$$b_i - \sum_{j=1}^{n} a_{ij} x_j = 0 \qquad\qquad i = 1, \ldots, m$$

$$x_j v_j = 0 \qquad\qquad j = 1, \ldots, n$$

There are several other quadratic programming algorithms. The references at the end of this chapter give sources for some of the better known ones. Among those, *Beale's algorithm* is particularly important because of its computational strength. In addition, Beale's algorithm can be applied to a nonconcave objective function. When this is the case, we cannot be sure that the solution obtained is the global optimum; it could be a local optimum or even a saddle point.

There are two areas of application for quadratic programming that are of some interest. Quadratic programming is used in multiple regression where there are inequality constraints on some of the coefficients. This is particularly useful in econometric models where simultaneous equation systems are being estimated. The objective function of the quadratic program is the minimization of the squared deviations from the mean used in least squares estimates. The quadratic programming constraints are any linear constraints that exist on the coefficients. Thus, the quadratic programming optimum is the set of constrained least squares estimates of the coefficients.

A second area of application is in goal programming (see Section 2-14 for a simple example). In goal programming the objective may be to minimize the weighted sum of deviations from target levels for one or several partially or completely conflicting objectives. Rather than penalize deviations linearly, one approach suggested in the literature is to have the penalty proportional to the square of the deviations. This leads to a quadratic programming problem.

EXERCISES

14.1 Give a λ-formulation for the following problems
  (a) The problem in question 13.2(c).
  (b) The problem in question 13.2(d).
  (c) The problem in question 13.5.

14.2 Reformulate the problem in question 13.2(a) so that it is separable. Provide a λ-formulation for it.

14.3 Reformulate question 13.7 so that it is separable. Provide a λ-formulation for it.

14.4 Change the cost structure in question 13.7 so that for product 1 the unit cost for the first 500 units is $3.50, $3 for the next 2000 units, and $2.50 for every unit after that. Give a λ-formulation of this problem.

14.5 Find the first four tableaux of the convex simplex method for the problem in question 13.2(a). Start with the solution $\mathbf{x} = (0, 0)$. Show on a graph the path of the convex simplex method solutions.

14.6 Find the first three tableaux of the convex simplex method for the following problems, and show on a graph the path of the convex simplex method solutions.
(a) The problem in question 13.2(b), starting with $\mathbf{x} = (1, 0)$
(b) The problem in question 13.2(c), starting with $\mathbf{x} = (0, 0)$
(c) The problem in question 13.2(d), starting with $\mathbf{x} = (0, 0)$
(d) The problem in question 13.6(a), starting with $\mathbf{x} = (0, 3)$

14.7 Perform the first two iterations of the quadratic programming algorithm for the following problems:
(a) The problem in question 13.2(a).
(b) The problem in question 13.2(b).

REFERENCES

General texts:

Hadley, G. *Nonlinear and Dynamic Programming*, Reading, Mass.: Addison-Wesley, 1964. Chapter 4 gives a good exposition of separable programming. The λ-formulation is also included along with comprehensive proofs and applications. Chapter 7 develops Wolfe's quadratic programming algorithm in sections 7-1 to 7-6. Definitely an advanced text and by now somewhat outdated.

MacMillan, C. *Mathematical Programming*, 2nd ed. New York: Wiley, 1975. The text gives a tableau-by-tableau solution of the λ-formulation in Chapter 6. Also of particular interest is the FORTRAN program for the λ-formulation in Appendix E, with a worked example on pages 207-216. The average student should have little trouble following the exposition.

Wagner, H. *Principles of Operations Research*, 2nd ed. Englewood Cliffs, N.J.: Prentice-Hall, 1975. The text mentions, if not always lucidly, most of the important nonlinear programming techniques and their variants. Section 14.7 develops the λ-formulation of separable programming, and section 15.10 discusses separable programming when the grid can be refined in the course of the algorithm. The convex simplex method is in section 15.3. Section 15.8 extends the quadratic programming algorithm in our chapter, while section 14.6 presents a different quadratic programming technique.

Zangwill, W. I. *Nonlinear Programming—A Unified Approach*. Englewood Cliffs, N.J.: Prentice-Hall, 1969. Section 8.2 of this text gives a very good exposition of the convex simplex method (which is Zangwill's brain child). A student with average mathematical ability could understand this section provided he/she omitted pages 168-174. In section 8.1, an interesting technique—the Frank-Wolfe algorithm —is presented.

Specialized texts and articles:

Alloin, G. "A Simplex Method for a Class of Nonconvex Separable Problems", *Management Science*, 17, Sept. 1970. Extension of simplex method for separable problems with convex or concave function in the objective, and a convex constraint set. Considerably faster algorithm than λ-formulation for this type of problem.

Beale, E. M. L., "Numerical Methods", *Nonlinear Programming*, J. Abadie, Ed., Amsterdam: North-Holland, 1967. In Sections V and VI of this paper, there is a very interesting introduction to the theory and practical aspects of the λ-formulation —well worth reading. Beale introduces his own quadratic programming technique in Sections II, III, and IV, although much of III and IV is fairly advanced. This quadratic programming technique does not require the objective function to be concave (maximizing problem).

————. "Advanced Algorithmic Features for General Mathematical Programming Systems", *Integer and Nonlinear Programming*, J. Abadie, Ed., Amsterdam: North-Holland, 1970. An up-to-date discussion of separable programming in practice is on pages 130–137.

Boot, J. C. G. *Quadratic Programming*. Amsterdam: North-Holland, 1964. This book is built largely around the Thiel-Van de Panne algorithm for quadratic programming. This method is a geometrically conceived method, interesting but somewhat overshadowed by the algebraic ones of Wolfe and Beale. Chapters 5 and 6 give the basics of the method.

Cottle, R. W. and W. C. Mylander. "Ritter's Cutting Plane Method for Nonconvex Quadratic Programming", *Integer and Nonlinear Programming*, J. Abadie, Ed., Amsterdam: North-Holland, 1970. This is a very technical presentation of Ritter's quadratic programming algorithm which, the authors claim, is "the only *rigorous* procedure we know of for solving the general quadratic programming problem." Only students with good mathematical ability should attempt this article.

Geoffrion, A. M. "Elements of Large-Scale Mathematical Programming, Parts I and II", *Management Science*, 16, July 1970. A two-part survey and unification of techniques for dealing with large-scale problems in mathematical programming —linear and nonlinear. These are important survey articles.

Rutenberg, D. P. "Generalized Networks, Generalized Upper Bounding and Decomposition of the Convex Simplex Method", *Management Science*, 16, January 1970. This paper shows that the convex simplex method can be effectively extended to account for special problem structures.

Zoutendijk, G. "Nonlinear Programming", *Operational Research '72*, M. Ross, Ed., Amsterdam: North-Holland, 1973. A very brief description of the practicality of nonlinear programming.

Selected applications:

Beale, E. M. L., P. J. Coen and A. D. J. Flowerdew. "Separable Programming Applied to an Ore-purchasing problem", *Applied Statistics*, 14, 1965.

Gensch, Dennis H., and Ulf Peter Welam. "An Optimum Budget Allocation Model for Dynamic Interacting Market Segments", *Management Science*, 20, Oct. 1973.

Stolley, H. "Application of Quadratic Programming to the Promotion System of Professional Officers in the German Air Force", *Applications of Mathematical Programming Techniques*, E. M. L. Beale, Ed., London: English University Press, 1970.

15

Simulation

To simulate is to duplicate the dynamic behavior of the essential characteristics of a system, operation, or process over time without attaining reality. Consider an inventory system. To simulate such a system means to trace on paper, step by step, how the daily inventory position for a given product fluctuates over time as customer orders are received and executed and inventory replenishments are scheduled and received. Through simulation, the operations researcher has at his or her disposal a laboratory technique for observation and experimentation which has long been part of the scientific methods in the physical, medical, and biological sciences. The viability of proposed policies for operating a system can be explored and compared within a few minutes of computer time that otherwise would take years to accomplish by real life observations. Simulation often provides the only practical vehicle for experimentation with the dynamic behavior of real or proposed systems.

The basic concepts involved in simulation may look deceptively simple. However, putting them into practice to obtain valid and reliable results is far from simple. Performing simulations is extremely time consuming. Therefore, for all practical purposes, simulations are always performed on high speed electronic computers.

Nowhere in applied operations research does the systems approach appear as naturally and as pure as in simulation. Much of the discussion in Chapter 1 on systems and model building within a systems framework is therefore directly applicable to this chapter. Before embarking into this chapter, it may be a good idea to briefly review the relevant sections of Chapter 1, in particular Sections 1-5, 1-6, 1-7, and 1-8. Later, when we discuss validation of simulation studies in Section 15-6, it may also be helpful to refer to the sections on testing and sensitivity analysis, Sections 1-15 and 1-16.

Since most simulations attempt to study random phenomena, a general knowledge of random variables and their distributions, as well as statistical estimation procedures, is essential to this chapter.

In one short chapter we cannot do justice to as vast a subject as simulation. All we can do is to introduce the basic aspects and demonstrate them with some simple examples. For a detailed treatment, we refer you to the texts listed in the references to this chapter.

15-1 SIMULATION OF AN INVENTORY SYSTEM

The basic principles of simulation will be explored initially by simulating the performance of a proposed inventory control model. As discussed in Chapter 1, such a simulation may be part of testing the theoretical model as to its suitability before proceeding to its implementation. In order to provide some appreciation of the realism possible in simulation in contrast to the simplifications and approximations needed for any theoretical model, we will summarize the mathematical model first. However, there is no need to fully understand its mathematical derivation. This model is discussed in detail in G. Hadley and T. M. Whitin, *Analysis of Inventory Systems* (Prentice-Hall, 1963, pp. 162–175).

A wholesale distributor proposes to use a (Q,r) inventory control model for all the products stocked. This model has the following policy: whenever the inventory on hand (plus any inventory replenishments outstanding) falls to or below a reorder point r a replenishment size Q is placed.

The replenishment lead time varies from a few days to several weeks depending on the product. Customer orders are a random variable and are shipped on the same day that orders are received. Sales are lost if inventory shortages occur. The optimal values of the two control parameters, Q and r, are found for each product by minimizing the relevant expected total annual cost, which consists of ordering costs, holding costs, and the cost of lost sales. For a given product

let R be the average annual demand,

$f(x)$ the probability density function of demand during the lead time,

V the unit value,

c_1 the annual inventory holding cost per dollar,

c_2 the fixed replenishment cost,

c_3 the unit shortage cost.

Then, the expected total annual cost is approximately

(15-1)

$$T(Q,r) = \overbrace{\frac{R}{Q}c_2}^{\substack{\text{annual} \\ \text{ordering} \\ \text{cost}}} + \overbrace{\left(\underbrace{\frac{Q}{2} + \int_0^r (r-x)\,f(x)\,dx}_{\substack{\text{average minimum} \\ \text{inventory}}}\right)c_1 V}^{\text{annual holding cost}}$$

$$+ \underbrace{\frac{R}{Q}c_3 \int_r^\infty (x-r)\,f(x)\,dx}_{\text{annual cost of lost sales}}$$

Using classical methods of calculus, we can determine values for both decision variables, Q and r, that minimize T. (See Chapter 11, Section 11-6.)

Let us use this model for a particular product. From past records of customer orders, the daily demand distribution is

Demand	0	1	2	3	4	5	6	7	8	9	10	11	12	13
Frequency	0.26	0.14	0.12	0.10	0.08	0.07	0.06	0.05	0.04	0.03	0.02	0.01	0.01	0.01

The daily demand distribution is extremely skewed, having an average of 3.2 units per day and a standard deviation of 3.2. Similarly, past records indicate that the replenishment lead time averages about 10 working days, but, in fact, is a random variable with the following approximate frequency distribution:

Lead time	7	8	9	10	11	12	13	14
Frequency	0.07	0.12	0.18	0.25	0.20	0.10	0.05	0.03

These data could be used to derive the lead time demand distribution, $f(x)$, required in (15-1). However, in order to reduce both the cost of data collection and the cost of computations, for most practical applications the lead time demand distribution is approximated by a normal distribution, based on the average lead time of 10. Assuming that demands on consecutive days are independent, this gives a lead time demand distribution with a mean of $10(3.2) = 32$, and a standard deviation of $3.2(\sqrt{10}) = 10$. (See Section B-5 of Appendix B.) Although it is true that for a lead time that is sufficiently long the lead time demand distribution will be approximately normal no matter what the shape of the daily demand distribution, for highly skewed distributions, a lead time of 10 days results in a rather crude approximation, particularly at the tails of the distribution.

For 250 working days per year, $R = 250(3.2) = 800$, and the other cost parameters are $V = \$10.00$, $c_1 = 0.2$, $c_2 = \$4.50$, and $c_3 = \$1.50$. With these simplifications, expression (15-1) assumes a minimum at $Q^* = 60$ and $r^* = 48$, with $T(Q^*, r^*) = \$157.20$.

How will the various approximations made to derive Q and r hold up in practice? Before a firm implements such a model for all its products, it should test the model's performance. Simulation is the tool.

How do we go about this task? Essentially, we follow the same steps as for the construction of any mathematical model. We start by constructing a detailed picture of the document and material flow and the decision points underlying the procedures implied by the model, and then translate this information into diagrammatic form. We have done this in Figure 15-1 for our example. To construct this diagram, we may have to split what in the real world looks like a single operation or decision point into a number of more detailed intermediate steps which, in the simulation,

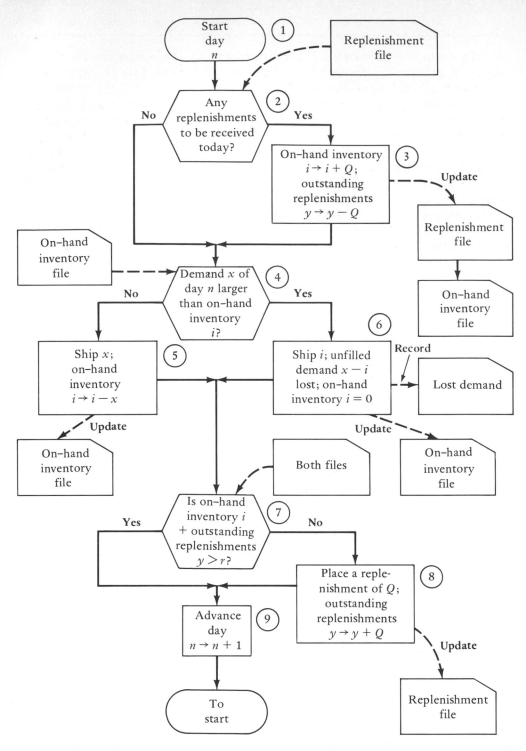

Figure 15-1. *Flow diagram of inventory system.*

482

are followed in a rigid sequence.   The reverse may also happen—a sequence of real life operations are combined into a single step.   Similarly, we may have to introduce steps that have no real counterpart.

In our case, the daily control procedure starts by processing inventory replenishments received on that day (usually received in the morning) and processing incoming customer orders for the day.   The updated inventory file, listing all stock levels and outstanding replenishments, is then reviewed.   If the stock level i plus the outstanding replenishments y for a product have been reduced by sales to the reorder point r, or below, a replenishment of size Q is scheduled.   Translating this sequence of steps into the diagram of Figure 15-1, we arbitrarily assume that replenishments received are added to the inventory prior to processing incoming customer orders (points 2 and 3).   Incoming customer orders are processed next (points 4, 5, and 6), and finally a decision as to whether or not to replenish inventory is made (points 7 and 8).   Since we do not wish to keep track of each individual customer order, all incoming customer orders for the day are processed at the same time.

In order to trace the events in detail over *simulated time*, two files have to be kept and updated as shown in the flow diagram, namely an *on-hand inventory file* and an *outstanding replenishment file*.   If we are given a beginning on-hand inventory balance of size i, a file of outstanding replenishments with their due dates, and a sequence of daily demands—one number for each day—then we can simulate exactly what will happen in this inventory system over time.   On the basis of such a diagram, a detailed computer program can be written to perform the actual simulation. Performance statistics for a simulation run are compiled from the information recorded in the on-hand inventory file, the outstanding replenishment file, and auxiliary files specifically introduced into the computer program to collect status reports on the system.   An example of an auxiliary file is the file of lost demand.

Let us now simulate this system.   Suppose that over a 100-day sequence, daily demands are those shown in column 3 of Table 15-1.   We have a beginning inventory of $i = 60$ (as shown in the on-hand inventory file of columns 1 and 4), and we assume that there are no replenishments outstanding, i.e., $y = 0$ (as shown in the replenishment file of columns 6 through 9).   Starting on day $n = 1$ at point 1 in the flow diagram of Figure 15-1, we leave point 2 via the No branch.   Since $x = 3$ is less than $i = 60$, we proceed from point 4 via point 5 to point 7.   The on-hand inventory, $i = 57$, is larger than the reorder point, $r = 48$, and we advance to 9. At point 9 the *simulated time* is advanced by one day, and we start a new cycle for day $n = 2$ from point 1.   This same path repeats itself through day $n = 6$.   On day $n = 7$, we branch out from point 7 to point 8, since the sum of the on-hand inventory plus the outstanding replenishments ($=47$) is less than the reorder point, $r = 48$. Therefore, a replenishment of size $Q = 60$ is placed on day 7 (point 8).   Let us assume that this replenishment will be received on the morning of day 15 and is available to satisfy demand on that day.   Skipping to day $n = 15$, the process takes the Yes branch from point 2 and the on-hand inventory available is updated from 15 to 75.   After deducting sales of 3 for that day, the ending on-hand inventory is shown as 72.   You should trace this process through for some additional days. Observe what happens on day 93.

Table 15-1. *Simulation of Inventory System.*   (f.) /up)

Period	Beginning on-hand inventory 1	Receipts 2	Demand 3	Ending on-hand inventory 4	Demand lost 5	Replenishments placed 6	lead time 7	date due in 8	on order 9
Start	—			60		—	—	—	0
1	60		3	57					
2	57		0	57					
3	57		0	57					
4	57		1	56					
5	56		6	50					
6	50		1	49					
7	49		2	47		60	8	15	60
8	47		5	42					60
9	42		0	42					60
10	42		4	38					60
11	38		5	33					60
12	33		4	29					60
13	29		4	25					60
14	25		10	15					60
15	15	60	3	72					0
16	72		0	72					
17	72		5	67					
18	67		1	66					
19	66		10	56					
20	56		0	56					
21	56		0	56					
22	56		2	54					
23	54		6	48		60	11	34	60
24	48		6	42					60
25	42		3	39					60
26	39		1	38					60
27	38		3	35					60
28	35		0	35					60
29	35		2	33					60
30	33		2	31					60
31	31		1	30					60
32	30		0	30					60
33	30		0	30					60
34	30	60	2	88					0
35	88		2	86					
36	86		4	82					
37	82		3	79					
38	79		8	71					
39	71		4	67					
40	67		0	67					

Table 15-1.—*continued*

Period	Beginning on-hand inventory 1	Receipts 2	Demand 3	Ending on-hand inventory 4	Demand lost 5	Replenishments placed 6	lead time 7	date due in 8	on order 9
41	67		7	60					
42	60		0	60					
43	60		4	56					
44	56		0	56					
45	56		3	53					
46	53		0	53					
47	53		9	44		60	10	57	60
48	44		12	32					60
49	32		6	26					60
50	26		6	20					60
51	20		6	14					60
52	14		2	12					60
53	12		5	7					60
54	7		0	7					60
55	7		6	1					60
56	1		0	1					60
57	1	60	0	61					0
58	61		11	50					
59	50		0	50					
60	50		2	48		60	8	68	60
61	48		1	47					60
62	47		1	46					60
63	46		3	43					60
64	43		0	43					60
65	43		0	43					60
66	43		0	43					60
67	43		1	42					60
68	42	60	0	102					0
69	102		7	95					
70	95		0	95					
71	95		1	94					
72	94		1	93					
73	93		6	87					
74	87		4	83					
75	83		2	81					
76	81		8	73					
77	73		2	71					
78	71		5	66					
79	66		0	66					
80	66		3	63					
81	63		5	58					

Table 15-1.—*continued*

Period	Beginning on-hand inventory 1	Receipts 2	Demand 3	Ending on-hand inventory 4	Demand lost 5	Replenishments placed 6	lead time 7	date due in 8	on order 9
82	58		5	53					
83	53		5	48		60	11	94	60
84	48		8	40					60
85	40		11	29					60
86	29		7	22					60
87	22		2	20					60
88	20		6	14					60
89	14		5	9					60
90	9		1	8					60
91	8		0	8					60
92	8		3	5					60
93	5		11	0	6				60
94	0	60	8	52					0
95	52		2	50					
96	50		0	50					
97	50		0	50					
98	50		5	45		60	8	106	60
99	45		0	45					60
100	45		10	35					60

The cost of this particular simulation run is obtained as follows:

Ordering cost: 6 replenishments at $4.50	$27.00
Shortage cost: 6 units short at $1.50	$9.00
Holding cost: Average ending inventory 47.55 at 100/250 (0.2) ($10.00)	$38.04
	$74.04
Extrapolated to an annual basis (of 250 working days)	$185.10

The extrapolated annual cost of this simulation differs substantially from the theoretical cost. Let us emphasize that this does not mean that something went wrong in the simulation. It is only one trial, and even a short one. The exact results obtained for this 100-day simulation run are unique to the particular sequence of daily demands and replenishment lead times used. Had we used a different set of demands, we would have found a different set of results. But, if the simulation properly reflects the real-world processes and the input data is representative of the real world, then these results are also representative of the type of answers usually experienced in the real world. However, to be able to draw a valid conclusion, we usually need many more runs covering a sufficient length of time.

Let us now look more formally into the structure of simulation models.

15-2 STRUCTURE OF SIMULATION MODELS

A simulation model describes the dynamic behavior of a system over time. In the terminology of simulation, a system is viewed as a collection of components called *entities* that interact in a well defined environment. Entities have various identifying *attributes* and may belong to *sets* or *files* of entities, which also may have attributes. As simulated time advances, entities and files may change some of their attributes, and entities may change their file membership in prescribed ways, i.e., leave a given file; enter another file; some entities may be cancelled; new ones may be created. These changes in the status of entities and files represent the dynamic behavior of the system and are referred to as *events*. The components of a simulation model are therefore:

(1) entities,
(2) membership relationships or files or sets of entities,
(3) attributes of entities and files,
(4) dynamic phenomena or events that change attributes and file memberships.

To fix ideas, consider the simulation of a car ferry system between two points, A and B, as shown in Figure 15-2.

Cars represent the entities, their length and weight being some of their attributes. The two docks and the ferries represent files; they contain entities (cars) and have attributes, such as the deck space on the ferries. The dynamic phenomena are given by the arrival pattern of various types of cars at the docks; how entities proceed from one file to another, such as how cars take up their place on the ferry decks during loading and leave the ferry during unloading; the operational characteristics of the ferries, such as the traveling speed (which may be a function of their load), and the berthing process. These are represented as events, such as each arrival and departure of a car at the dock side, the change of file membership (a car entering a ferry), or the departure or berthing of the ferry.

Events may be imposed on the simulation from outside, i.e., they are specified in detail by the analyst, such as the timetable of the ferries or the daily demands in

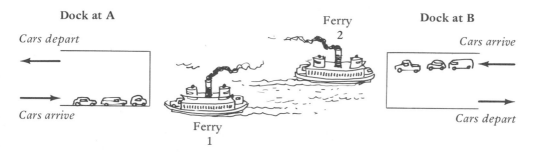

Figure 15-2. *Car ferry system.*

the inventory simulation. Such events are referred to as *exogenous events*. Alternatively, events may be created by the simulation model itself without explicit outside interventions. They are called *endogenous events*. They are either a consequence of exogenous events or of other endogenous events. The loading of cars and trucks on the ferry decks, once unloading has been completed, or the placing of inventory replenishments, as a result of depleting stocks below the reorder point, are examples of endogenous events.

If all events are exogenous, i.e., specified as input into the simulation, then we talk about *deterministic* simulation. For instance, if the sequence of daily demands and lead times used in the preceding section is actually experienced demands and lead times taken from the files of the firm, then the simulation is deterministic. There are some applications of simulation where this is a practical approach, such as simulation of the output mix of a refinery as a function of the input composition and instrument settings at the various units in the refinery.

Most applications of simulation are *stochastic simulations* (also referred to as *Monte-Carlo simulations*). The simulation model has features that allow random events to be generated internally. For instance, rather than specify a sequence of demands and lead times, we use, as input, the probability distribution of daily demands and the probability distribution of lead times and generate "random" demands and lead times as needed during the simulation with the help of *pseudorandom numbers*.

15-3 RANDOM NUMBERS AND OTHER VARIATES

What are random numbers? They are lists of the digits from 0 to 9, that appear to be drawn as completely independent random samples from a uniformly distributed random variable that can assume integer values 0 through 9. Table 15-2 is a short list of 5 digit random numbers.

The most popular methods used to generate random numbers are the *additive* and *multiplicative congruential methods*. To illustrate the general principle, the multiplicative congruential method finds the nth random number r_n, consisting of k digits, from the $(n-1)$th random number r_{n-1} by using the recurrence relation:

$$r_n \equiv pr_{n-1} \,(\text{modulo } m)$$

where p and m are positive integers, $p < m$,

   $m-1$ is a k-digit number, and

   modulo m means that r_n is the remainder when pr_{n-1} is divided by m.

Table 15-2. *Uniform Pseudorandom Numbers.*

59210	33177	29451	67204	65736	86395	57187	13396	01194	28069
79603	75509	41442	90224	50486	65290	65118	62067	04552	19342
98778	18247	75067	91908	97245	01432	36600	71223	29188	51333
27816	54589	46761	16070	73746	48897	84507	97626	25579	78945
00107	21323	95397	91528	89117	16541	61308	91074	83879	03065

Therefore, r_n and pr_{n-1} differ by an integer multiple of m. The first random number r_0, or the *seed*, is specified as an input. This method will generate a sequence of k-digit random numbers with *period $h < m$* at which point the number r_0 occurs again, and hence the sequence repeats itself.

Consider an example. Suppose, $p = 37$, $m = 100$, and $r_0 = 53$. Since $m - 1$ is a two-digit number, this will yield two-digit random numbers:

$$r_1 = pr_0 (\text{modulo } m) = (37)(53)(\text{modulo } 100) = 1961 \ (\text{modulo } 100) = 61$$

$$r_2 = (37)(61)(\text{modulo } 100) = 2257 \ (\text{modulo } 100) = 57$$

$$r_3 = (37)(57)(\text{modulo } 100) = 2109 \ (\text{modulo } 100) = 09$$

and the sequence continues as $(33, 21, 77, 49, 13, 81, 97, 89, \ldots)$. You may wish to verify that the period is 20. Note that the low order digit is far from random, repeating the sequence 3, 1, 7, 9. Therefore, great care has to be taken in the input parameters used. There are certain principles that help in the proper choice of r_0 and p for any given value of m, so as to maximize the period h.

Clearly, the methods commonly used to generate random numbers are not random processes, since the sequence of numbers generated is completely determined by the input data used for the method—hence the term *pseudorandom numbers*.

It is usually convenient to express these uniform random numbers in the form of a fraction between 0 and 1 with a desired degree of precision of k-digits. This is achieved by dividing r_n by m, i.e., $u_n = r_n/m$ is a *uniformly distributed random decimal fraction* between 0 and 1 with at most k significant digits after the decimal point.

Most computer installations provide subroutines in their software packages, called *random number generators*, that will generate uniform random decimal fractions between 0 and 1. Thus, you will hardly ever have to write a computer subroutine to do this.

On the basis of these random decimal fractions, we can generate *random variates* (observations from a statistical population) from any desired probability distribution. This can be seen from Figure 15-3 which shows the cumulative distribution function of some random variable. With each value of the random variable on the x axis, we associate a value of the cumulative distribution function on the y axis. The cumulative distribution function is a transformation of the values of the random variable onto the interval from 0 to 1. In fact, it can be regarded as the transformation of the random variable to a uniformly distributed random variable on the $(0, 1)$ interval.

By taking the *inverse transformation*, we can therefore generate random variates for any desired probability distribution. Consider again the distribution depicted in Figure 15-3. The uniform random decimal fraction 0.7548 is associated with the value x_0 of the random variable.

This inverse transformation can sometimes be done analytically, such as for any arbitrary *uniform*, *triangular*, or *negative exponential distribution*. For instance, for the negative exponential distribution with density function $f(x) = \lambda e^{-\lambda x}$, $x \geqslant 0$, the cumulative distribution function is

$$F(x_0) = \int_0^{x_0} \lambda e^{-\lambda x} \, dx = 1 - e^{-\lambda x_0}$$

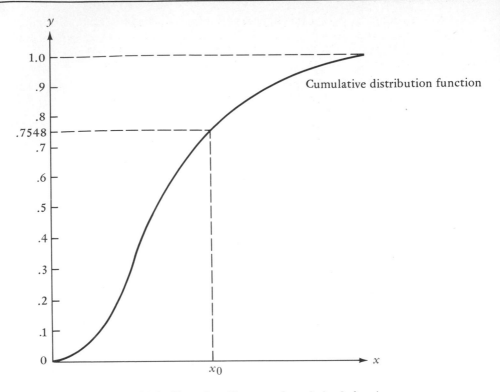

Figure 15-3. *Use of uniform random decimal fractions to generate variates from any arbitrary distribution.*

from which we obtain the inverse transform

$$x_0 = \frac{-\log_e(1 - F(x_0))}{\lambda}$$

where $\log_e$ is the natural logarithm.

Hence, if u_n is a uniform random decimal fraction between 0 and 1, then the exponential variate associated with u_n is

$$x_n = \frac{-\log_e(1 - u_n)}{\lambda}$$

Random variates from *Erlang distributions* of order k or *Gamma distributions* with parameter $a = k$ integer (see Appendix B, Section B-4) can be obtained as the sum of k exponential variates. Random variates from a normal distribution can be generated by taking advantage of the *central limit theorem* (see Appendix B, Section B-5) which states that for large samples the sample mean $\bar{x}$ is approximately normally distributed, regardless of the distribution from which the observations were obtained. Thus, to generate a normal random variate we simply compute the average of a

Table 15-3. *Tabular Method of Inverse Transformation.*

Daily demand, x	Relative frequency	Cumulative frequency, $F(x)$	Associated range of values for u
0	0.26	0.26	0.00 to 0.25
1	0.14	0.40	0.26 0.39
2	0.12	0.52	0.40 0.51
3	0.10	0.62	0.52 0.61
4	0.08	0.70	0.62 0.69
5	0.07	0.77	0.70 0.76
6	0.06	0.83	0.77 0.82
7	0.05	0.88	0.83 0.87
8	0.04	0.92	0.88 0.91
9	0.03	0.95	0.92 0.94
10	0.02	0.97	0.95 0.96
11	0.01	0.98	0.97
12	0.01	0.99	0.98
13	0.01	1.00	0.99

number of uniform random numbers, usually 12 or more, and apply the standardization transformation to it.   This is the approach used by most computer subroutines that generate normal random variates (or deviates) for $N(0, 1)$.

It is always possible to use a *tabular method*.   Let $x-1$ and x be two consecutive values of a discrete random variable X and $F(x-1) = P(X \leqslant x-1)$ and $F(x) = P(X \leqslant x)$ be the corresponding values of the cumulative distribution function. Given a uniform random decimal fraction u, $0 \leqslant u < 1$, the associated random variate is found as that value x such that $F(x-1) \leqslant u < F(x)$.   Thus, with each value of x we associate a range of uniform random decimal fractions of size $P(X = x)$.   If $F(x)$ is specified with up to k significant digits after the decimal point, we use uniform random decimal fractions with k significant digits.   The range of u for each x is $[F(x-1), F(x)-10^{-k}]$, where for $x = 0$, $F(x-1) = 0$ (specified as k zeros).   Consider the daily demand distribution listed in Section 15-1.   Table 15-3 lists the correspondence between the values x and the ranges of two-digit uniform random decimal fractions.

Now, refer to the table of pseudorandom numbers, Table 15-2.   The first two digits of the table yield a random decimal fraction $u_1 = 0.59$.   From Table 15-3 we see that the corresponding variate has a value of $x_1 = 3$.   The second set of two digits in Table 15-2 yields $u_2 = 0.21$, with which we associate a value of $x_2 = 0$. Continuing in this fashion we find

n	3	4	5	6	7
u_n	0.03	0.31	0.77	0.29	0.45
x_n	0	1	6	1	2

These are the demands for the first seven periods shown in Table 15-1. The eighth two-digit set is used to generate a lead time variate of 8 from the lead time distribution. The next 16 sets are again used to generate daily demands, etc. You should check your understanding of the tabular method by verifying the demands and lead times shown.

For a continuous random variable each x gives the endpoint of a suitably chosen interval. The value of the random variate associated with a given u value is found by interpolation between $x-1$ and x.

15-4 STOCHASTIC SIMULATION BY COMPUTER

For a deterministic simulation of the inventory system, where daily demands and lead times are exogenous events and specified in detail as input data to the simulation, the flow diagram of Figure 15-1 is all we need to trace the course of events. In a stochastic simulation, daily demands and lead times are endogenous events generated on the basis of their probability distributions. Prior to creating each endogenous

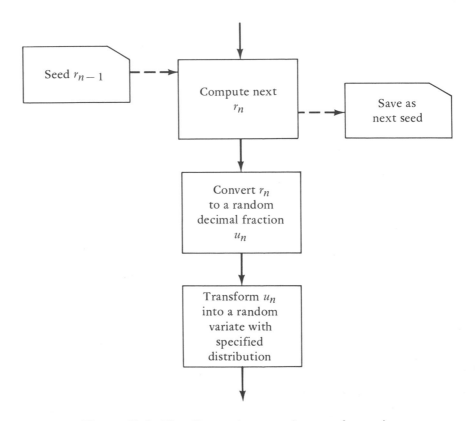

Figure 15-4. *Flow diagram for generating a random variate.*

event, a value of a random variate is determined. This operation consists of three steps.

(1) Using the seed, r_{n-1}, from the preceding computation, generate a new uniform random number, r_n.
(2) Convert r_n into a uniform random decimal fraction, u_n.
(3) Transform u_n into a random variate for the distribution specified (as input).

Steps (1) and (2) are usually combined into one subroutine as part of most computer systems' software packages.

Figure 15-4 is a flow diagram of these three steps, where the uniform random number, r_n, becomes the seed of iteration, $n+1$.

This portion is added to the flow diagram in Figure 15-1 just prior to box 4 to generate a daily demand and just following box 8 to generate a lead time (which is also recorded in the replenishment file for later use). This expanded flow diagram of the events for day n serves as the basis for writing a computer program, either using one of the conventional computer languages, such as FORTRAN, ALGOL, or COBOL, or one of the specialized computer simulation languages, such as GPSS, SIMSCRIPT, or DYNAMO (discussed in Section 15-7).

Table 15-1 is actually a modified computer printout of an inventory simulation program, written in FORTRAN, and listed in the excellent text, *Simulation in Business and Economics*, (Prentice-Hall, 1969) by R. C. Meier, *et al*. As we have seen in Section 15-1, the results of this simulation over 100 working days extrapolated to an annual basis of 250 working days yield a cost of $185.10.

The same problem simulated over 1000 days yields the following summary statistics.

Total demand	3124 units
Average inventory	47.23 units
Number of replenishments	52
Percentage of demand satisfied	99.2%
Total cost	$646.40
Average annual cost	$161.60

This differs from the theoretical expected annual cost of $157.20 by only $4.40, a small difference considering the approximations made in the theoretical model. Without simulation this fact could not have been established. The decision maker would have to take the possibly biased judgment of the operations researcher who claims that the proposed model will stand up in practice.

The outcome of stochastic simulations depends on a large number of randomly generated events. Hence, *a priori*, such simulation results are random variables and each simulation run represents one observation on this random variable. For instance, using different sequences of random numbers yields the following average annual costs (all based on simulation runs over 1000 working days):

	161.00	
154.70	161.60	165.90
154.80	162.10	167.00
	163.20	
Mean		161.30
Standard deviation		4.50

On the basis of these 8 observations, we obtain an estimate of the average annual costs of $161.30. The standard error of this estimate amounts to $4.50/\sqrt{8} = \$1.60$ ($=\sigma/\sqrt{n}$). It can be shown that as the length of the simulation run (the number of periods covered) becomes large the distribution of simulation results approaches a normal distribution. Hence, we may apply standard statistical tools for small sample methods to analyze simulation results. For instance, the sample of 8 observations yields a 99 percent confidence interval for the average annual cost of $155.70 to $166.90 which contains the theoretical cost of $157.20. If the two were substantially different, the analyst should attempt to discover the reason and, if necessary, adjust the model. Analysis of simulation results should always include a measure of the variability of the estimates obtained.

The reliability of the results of simulation runs increases with the length of each simulation run (in our case, with the number of days covered). In other words, the standard error of the statistics derived tends to become smaller as the run length is increased. Therefore, the reliability of simulation results can be increased either by lengthening individual simulation runs or by increasing the number of runs (i.e., the sample size). In both instances, the marginal increase in reliability gained drops off rapidly as these two parameters are increased. A simulation project should always include at least a minimal amount of sensitivity analysis with respect to the best length of the simulation runs.

15-5 EXAMPLE USING EVENT INCREMENTATION

In the inventory control example, simulated time was advanced by equal time increments, each covering one working day. All events that occur during this time interval are considered in a predetermined sequence which remains fixed during the entire simulation. For instance, in the inventory simulation, each day may have one or all of three types of events considered in this sequence: receipt of replenishments, execution of customer orders, and placement of replenishments. All events are assumed to occur at a given point in time during the period. Replenishments are received at the beginning of each day, customer orders are executed by the end of the day, and replenishments are placed at the end of a day. This method of keeping simulated time is referred to as *fixed time incrementation*. It is suitable if some events occur in most periods or if the exact time at which an event occurs within each period does not significantly affect the performance of the operations simulated.

There are many dynamic phenomena where the exact time at which the various events occur is a crucial element of an operation's performance. This is the case for most waiting line problems, or where most periods have no events. Rather than advance simulated time by a constant (often small) time increment, simulated time is advanced, after processing of each event, to the scheduled time of the next most imminent event in the simulation. This type of keeping time is called *event-step incrementation* or *variable time incrementation*.

Consider the following simple assembly line problem. A product is to be assembled on a two-station assembly line, with task A performed at the first station followed by task B at the second station. Each task completes about half of the assembly job, and each consists of a series of individual steps or operations. After completing task A, the operator at station 1 places the partially assembled product on a gravity conveyor belt where it rolls to station 2. Once the operator there has completed the assembly, the finished product is placed on a cart which is periodically taken away to the stock location. The engineer in charge of methods and procedures establishes the following standard times:

	Average time	Standard deviation	Probability distribution
Task A	35 seconds	6 seconds	normal
Task B	38 seconds	5 seconds	normal
Conveyor belt time	6 seconds	zero	constant

We wish to simulate the performance of this assembly line using event-step incrementation. How do we go about this?

For a simulation using fixed time incrementation, such as the inventory simulation, we created a flow chart that contains a path for each possible combination of all events that may happen during each period (one day in our case). Every time the simulation reached the end of a period, simulated time was advanced by one period, and the simulation returned to the first event at the beginning of the flow chart. For a simulation using event-step incrementation we can draw a flow chart that contains a separate sequence of operations for each type of event that can occur in the simulation, as shown in Figure 15-5. The core of this flow chart is the file of scheduled events. During the simulation, at various places events are scheduled to occur at some time in the future. The type of event and the event time are all recorded in a master file of scheduled events.

Suppose that at simulated time $t = 823$ seconds after the start of the simulation, the file contains the following events:

File of Scheduled Events

Event time	Entity	Event type
830	24	completion of task A
847	23	completion of task B

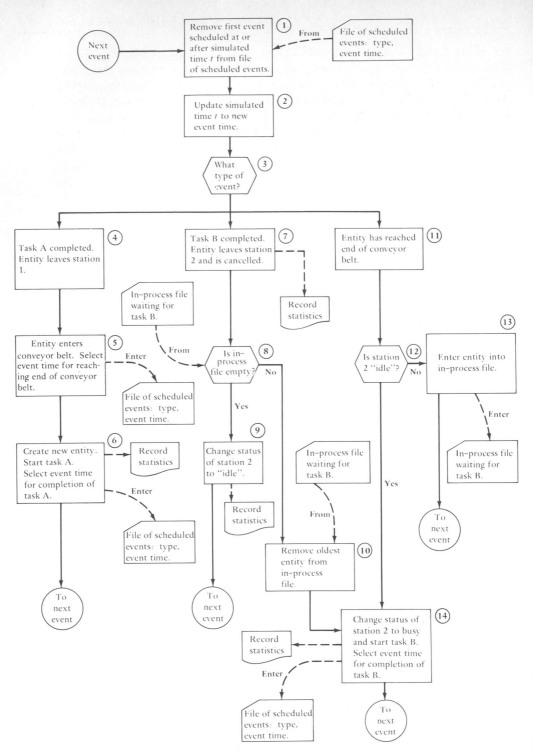

Figure 15-5. *Flow chart for event-step incrementation.*

496

We will now make a new pass through the flow chart. At block 1 we search the file of scheduled events for the first event scheduled to occur at or after simulated time, $t = 823$ seconds. This is entity 24 completing task A at time 830. This event is removed from the file. The current simulated time is updated to $t = 830$ at block 2. The switch at block 3 directs us to block 4. Entity 24 leaves station 1 and enters the conveyor belt (block 5). Since the time taken to roll to the end of the conveyor belt is 6 seconds, entity 24 will reach the end of the conveyor belt at time 836, and we enter a new event into the file of scheduled events.

File of Scheduled Events

Event time	Entity	Event type
847	23	completion of task B
836	24	end of conveyor belt reached

Note that we are still at time $t = 830$, and station 1 is not yet loaded with a new entity. Therefore, we create a new entity at block 6 which starts task A at $t = 830$, and we need to select an event time for the completion of this task. At this point we generate a random variate from a normal distribution with a mean of 35 seconds and standard deviation of 6 seconds. Suppose that this yields a time for completing task A of 29 seconds. This leads to the next entry in the file of scheduled events.

File of Scheduled Events

Event time	Entity	Event type
847	23	completion of task B
836	24	end of conveyor belt reached
859	25	completion of task A

We are now ready for the next scheduled event, and go back to block 1 at simulated time $t = 830$. The next event (in time) removed from the file is entity 24, reaching the end of the conveyor belt at 836 seconds. We update current simulated time to $t = 836$ (block 2) and we are directed from block 3 to block 11. Station 2 is busy working on entity 23 (block 12), and we proceed to block 13, where entity 24 is entered into the file of partially assembled products waiting to be processed by station 2. Assuming that the in-process file was empty just prior to this time, entity 24 is the only entry in this file.

In-process File

End of belt time	Entity
836	24

At the next pass we remove entity 23 from the file of scheduled events, update current simulated time to $t = 847$, cancel entity 23 at block 7, proceed from block 8 to 10, where we remove entity 24 from the in-process file, start a new task B on entity 24, and enter a new event time for completion of task B on entity 24 into the file of scheduled events.

This process is repeated until the simulated time has reached the time set for the end of the simulation run. The statistics collected at strategic points during the simulation, such as at the start or completion of an operation, and when entities are created or cancelled, are then summarized and analyzed.

In a computer program, blocks 1 to 3 would constitute the main program, and each sequence of blocks starting at 4, 7, and 11 would form one or more individual subroutines.

15-6 TACTICAL CONSIDERATION AND VALIDATION OF STOCHASTIC SIMULATION

When simulating dynamic phenomena we are usually interested mainly in their long-run or average behavior after the process has reached a steady state. For Markovian decision processes, we saw that this steady state was independent of the initial state of the process and could be approached as closely as desired by letting the process go over a sufficiently large number of transitions.

The same ideas can be applied in stochastic simulation provided the structure of the system simulated is such that it approaches a steady state. For instance, if we were to observe the inventory system simulated in Section 15-1 repeatedly at random points in time after a very large number of days, then we would expect to observe each inventory level about equally often. In other words, as the length of the simulation run increases, the effects of the initial conditions under which the simulation was started are washed out.

The speed at which this happens depends strongly on the choice of the initial conditions. Therefore, care should be taken to choose initial conditions that are representative for the steady state. Starting a system at an empty state, i.e., with no initial workload, empty queues, etc., may be a rather unfortunate choice, except for dynamic phenomena where the empty state is a natural occurrence at the beginning of every period, such as waiting line situations that go through a daily cycle. For our inventory system, any initial inventory level between the maximum inventory and the reorder point is a representative initial choice.

A convenient way to remove any bias in the simulation results due to the initial conditions chosen is to exclude the initial portion of each simulation run from the analysis and begin accumulating operating statistics only after this initial period. Alternatively, the ending conditions of each run can be used as the initial conditions of the next run.

Many simulation projects involve comparison of several different modes of operation. For example, we want to compare the present inventory policy with the proposed policy, and determine the difference in average annual costs and other operating statistics. In such instances, it is advantageous to use the same sequence of random events, e.g., the same sequence of daily demands and production lead times, or the same sequence of random numbers for all policy configurations analyzed. Since any sequence of random numbers is uniquely determined by the initial seed, this can easily be achieved in computer simulations. Although corresponding runs are no longer independent, this approach reduces the variability of the differences observed. It is a common practice in statistical inference. In such cases, it is usually not desirable to discard the initial period but, rather, to start corresponding runs with the same (representative) initial conditions.

As we have seen in Section 15-4, the outcome of a stochastic simulation run represents one observation on a random variable. If we wish to get sufficiently reliable estimates (in terms of small standard errors), we either need simulation runs covering a long period of simulated time or a large number of smaller simulation runs. There exist a number of techniques to improve the *efficiency of estimators* from simulation, known as *variance reducing techniques*. Although even a cursory discussion of this topic goes beyond the scope of this text, let us at least attempt to impart some of the flavor of one of them referred to as the *antithetic variate method*.

Suppose, the simulation involves generating a sequence of daily demands from a given probability distribution. Rather than generating a total of n independently generated demands, we generate two sequences of $n/2$ demands that exhibit a high negative correlation. This can easily be achieved by using, for the first sequence, the actual random decimal fractions, u_n, generated; and for the second sequence, $(1 - u_n)$, which is also a random decimal fraction. Clearly, whenever u_n produces a demand value above the mean, $(1 - u_n)$ produces a value below the mean and vice versa. As a consequence, the average demand over both sequences tends to be closer to the expected value of the demand than that of a single sequence of n independently generated demands. Such tricks tend to reduce the variability of the simulation results.

Most of these variance reducing techniques were developed for simulations in the physical sciences. The complexity of systems encountered in operations research problems renders their use much more difficult. The improvements gained may often not justify the additional modelling and programming costs incurred. Improvements in reliability of similar magnitude may sometimes be achieved more cheaply by increasing either the length of each simulation run or the number of runs.

As we have seen, simulation models are usually comprised of a number of separate parts (or subroutines) representing the various subsystems of the process simulated. Each of these should be tested separately. However, once these parts have been put together as one interacting package, the model as a whole has to be tested. This validation consists of two steps.

We first determine whether the logical connections between the various parts are correct. This is best done by running the whole simulation model over a number of events, suitably chosen to test the various paths through the simulation logic. The events chosen should include exceptional and extreme circumstances. For a computer simulation, intermediate status reports are printed out at various crucial points in the simulation, such as all decision forks along each path. These status reports are then carefully checked against the results obtained by duplicating the simulation by hand. (Once the internal logic has been checked, these intermediate status report printouts are eliminated from the program.)

The second step is to test whether the model as a whole can properly reproduce the real world process. This part of the validation is considerably more difficult. If the simulation describes an existing real-life process then it can presumably be tested against past data and its performance compared to the results actually experienced.

Many simulation models, however, describe hypothetical or planned future systems for which no past performance data are available. In such instances, the operations researcher has no alternative but to carefully perform the first step of the validation process and then make a value judgment about the reasonableness of the results obtained. The operations researcher will constantly be on the watch for possible anomalies or unusual results, and attempt to find reasonable or satisfactory explanations for any discrepancies until he or she has gained a sufficient degree of confidence in the correctness of the model as a whole.

15-7 SIMULATION COMPUTER LANGUAGES

Simulation and computers go hand in hand. Practically all simulations are executed with the aid of high-speed electronic computers. It is for this reason that we deliberately represented the logic of simulation processes by computer language type flow charts. Nor is it surprising that simulation studies have given rise to a number of specially designed general purpose simulation packages and simulation languages that ease and speed up the writing of simulation computer programs. No matter whether you translate these flow charts into a computer program yourself or have it done by an experienced computer programmer, it is essential that you are familiar with the essential properties, advantages, and drawbacks of these simulation languages. All we can do here though is to give some pointers.

It goes without saying that the conventional computer languages, such as FORTRAN, ALGOL, PL/1, COBOL, and others, may often be the most convenient or the only vehicle available for simulation programs. They are flexible, there is no additional learning cost and no special (and often costly) processing system is needed. Execution time is usually faster than for simulation languages.

On the other hand, simulation languages provide a number of facilities that are used in all simulations, such as random variate generators for many theoretical probability distributions and any desired empirical distribution, automatic updating of files of entities, automatic collection of various statistics, routines to read in various inputs, routines to print out status reports and summary statistics, and the crucial timing routine to update simulated time. These parts usually constitute the major portion of the programming effort. With simulation packages and languages, all that requires programming is the actual logic of the simulation process itself. The remaining parts are done for you.

One of the easiest, though by no means the least powerful, simulation package is the *General Purpose Systems Simulator* (GPSS) developed and maintained by IBM for most of its advanced computer systems. Little or no computer programming knowledge is required for GPSS. The first step is to construct a flow chart of the simulation process using the predefined block types provided by GPSS. Each block type asks for the execution of a given operation, action, or process. The names chosen for the block types are descriptive of the operations. For instance, the block called GENERATE creates entities (called *transactions* in GPSS) spaced according to a specified interarrival time. ENTER allows an entity to occupy space (for example, in a queue). HOLD allows an entity to occupy a service facility for a specified (random) time preventing other entities from entering. ADVANCE represents an operation that takes a (random) time. PICK sends an entity to one of a number of blocks with specified probability, etc. Certain blocks perform the function of accumulating operating statistics. Having drawn the complete block diagram, a separate card is punched for each block. These, together with data cards, such as empirical probability distributions, and control cards form the input deck. GPSS updates time in multiples of a basic time unit specified as input. Simulated time is advanced by event-step incrementation. By the very choice of block types, GPSS seems to be particularly efficient at simulating waiting line problems.

On the other extreme of the scale is SIMSCRIPT, a proper programming language with great flexibility and generality. Although the programming statements resemble English sentence structure, familiarity with FORTRAN and its logic is essential. In SIMSCRIPT, the simulation process is defined in terms of events, entities, sets of entities, and attributes of entities *and* of sets. Entities may be permanent, such as the ferries in the ferry system example, or temporary, such as the cars wanting to use the ferry, created at one point and erased or destroyed at another. Sets are files where entities can be stored. Sets may belong to entities; for instance, the load of cars transported by the ferries belongs to a given entity, namely the ferry. SIMSCRIPT provides facilities for searching these sets and for removing entities with certain attributes from them. For each event type that changes the status of the system, a separate event routine is written. Thus, SIMSCRIPT is an event-oriented language. SIMSCRIPT provides its own event-step incrementation timing routine.

There are a number of other simulation languages with similar features. Of these SIMULA, based on ALGOL, is included in the software packages of advanced Burrough's computer systems.

The only generally available simulation language that is capable of simulating continuous processes is DYNAMO. This language is best known in conjunction with J. W. Forrester's *Industrial Dynamics* (MIT Press, 1961). Events are not considered individually, as for all other simulation languages, but in the aggregate. In industrial dynamics, the basic components of a system are *levels of variables* (or *stocks*) and *rates of flow* (or *rates of change of levels*). Levels may represent stocks of resources, inventories, numbers of people, amounts of information, levels of feeling, levels of activities. Any activity, movement of material or of information, or any decision function in the system that affects level variables give rise to rates of flow.

DYNAMO is best suited for dynamic systems that involve *feedback loops*. A production-inventory-sales system, where the rate of production varies inversely with the inventory level, is an example of a feedback loop. The interrelationships between various level variables and rates of flow are expressed mathematically in the form of difference equations representing time lags of various lengths. Given initial starting conditions, DYNAMO obtains, for each time period, numerical solutions to each difference equation in the sequential order specified by the user. Thus, simulated time is incremented by a constant amount at each iteration. DYNAMO includes facilities for the more common types of functional relations, such as exponential, logarithmic, trigonometric, as well as user specified step and ramp functions. The language has a close resemblance to FORTRAN.

One of the special features of DYNAMO is the option to produce plots of the values of the various variables over simulated time.

DYNAMO has been particularly successful in simulating systems covering the economy or particular industries of an entire region or country. It was used to simulate the various scenarios for the world's economic, social and ecological development reported in *Limits to Growth* (D. H. Meadows and associates, London: Potomac Associates, 1972).

15-8 CONCLUDING REMARKS

Nowhere in applied operations research does the concept of system come forth as naturally as in simulation. Whereas for mathematical optimization tools the complexities of the real world leave the operations researcher little choice but to make abstractions, approximations, and simplifications in his models, in simulation he does not necessarily face the same limitations. The mathematical complexities of simulation seldom go beyond simple numeric computations or logical operations. Hence much more detail and more interactions between the various parts of a system can be taken into account. As a result, simulation models may be fairly true representations of the real world. This is one of the great attractions of simulation over mathematical optimization techniques.

But hand in hand with this advantage go two potentially crippling handicaps. Simulation is not an *a priori* optimizing tool, but rather a tool of analysis, often used for evaluating the performance of decisions derived by other means. Each simulation run just traces through the effects of decision rules that are specified in full detail as part of the input. Attempts at optimization have to be made by a slow process of trial and error. All we can usually strive for is "good" decision rules rather than optimal ones, and even this may be fairly costly in terms of computer time.

In order to be successful, simulation models have to incorporate a large amount of detail. As a consequence, the effort that goes into building a simulation model is usually much larger than for comparable operations research models. Thus, simulation projects turn out to be rather expensive projects.

The uses for simulation are almost unlimited. Some of the better known applications cover such diverse fields as:

- waiting lines—evaluation of alternative proposed facilities or evaluation of alternative modes of operations of existing facilities.
- job shop scheduling—evaluation of alternative dispatch rules and forecasting of workloads at each machine center. Workload forecasts may be used to initiate corrective action such as rescheduling of jobs.
- operation of process plants—the entire operation of a process plant, such as a refinery, is simulated, unit by unit, to determine output composition as a function of input mix and instrument setting (deterministic).
- budget simulations—using the conventional accounting structure, balance sheets, income statements and cash budgets are projected over time (deterministic).
- evaluation of PERT networks to determine more representative completion time distributions.
- entire sectors of a region's economy to explore various industrial and economic policies.
- operational gaming—simulation that allows human intervention is a valuable training tool for all sorts of skills. Business games, mock-up jet airliner cockpits, and simulated space flights are some of the more glamorous applications.

With minor exceptions, such as operational gaming, simulation is best used as a means of last resort only, when all else fails. Where applicable, mathematical tools are, as a rule, much more efficient for evaluating and optimizing a system's performance. Only if mathematical optimization techniques cannot adequately reproduce the complexities of a real system should the operations researcher take refuge in simulation. The apparent simplicity of simulation is deceptive and may lead the unsuspecting analyst into a quagmire that may prove expensive if not disastrous. Before embarking into a simulation project, the objectives of the analysis and the likely outcomes should be clearly spelled out and rough cost estimates obtained. Properly used, simulation can be a very effective tool in the hands of an experienced operations researcher.

EXERCISES

15.1 Use the flow diagram in Figure 15-1 to simulate the performance of an inventory control system, using the same cost parameters as in Section 15-1, for the sequence of daily demands listed below and a sequence of lead times of 11, 8, 10, 13, 7, 9, 14, 10, 9, 11, 10. The beginning inventory is 54 and no replenishments are outstanding. Compute the average inventory level, and the total cost over the 100-day run. Only days with a positive demand are listed.

day	1	3	4	5	7	9	10	14	15	18	20	21	22	23	24	25	27	28	30
demand	1	4	8	2	1	6	3	7	4	2	5	1	3	2	1	1	11	12	4

day	31	32	36	37	39	40	42	43	46	47	48	50	51	52	54	55	56	58	59	60
demand	3	4	1	12	1	1	6	2	4	5	9	4	11	12	8	12	3	1	6	2

day	62	64	65	67	68	69	71	74	75	76	78	79	80	81	83	84	85	87	89	90
demand	2	3	10	4	1	11	6	2	5	3	13	1	1	8	2	10	1	3	8	6

day	91	92	93	95	96	97	98	99	100
demand	5	4	2	11	3	7	6	8	1

15.2   Consider the following port operation. A port has two berths, where ships of various sizes arrive for unloading and loading. The amount of cargo to be unloaded and loaded varies from ship to ship. The maximum number of gangs needed for unloading and loading is a function of the amount of cargo to be moved and the type of ship. The rate of unloading and loading depends on the number of gangs used. The total number of gangs available each day varies and is allocated to the ships by given rules of priority. Only one day shift is worked by the gangs per day and work stops on Saturday and Sunday. Ships vacate berths immediately after loading but remain in port for a variable time prior to departure. Identify entities, files of entities, attributes of entities and files, and events.

15.3   Using the short list of random numbers in Table 15-2 generate 10 random variates for the following frequency distribution.

Value $x =$	0	1	2	3	4	5	6	7	8
Frequency	0.156	0.234	0.208	0.161	0.095	0.064	0.036	0.028	0.018

15.4   Starting (for each distribution) in row 2 of the list of random numbers in Table 15-2, generate 10 random variates from three-digit random numbers for
(a) a uniform distribution with limits $b = 8$, $a = 3$.
(b) a negative exponential distribution with parameter $\lambda = 10$.
(c) a normal distribution with mean, $\mu = 100$, and standard deviation, $\sigma = 20$.
   (Refer to Section B-4 in Appendix B.)

15.5   Using the demand distribution and lead time distribution listed in Section 15-1, simulate the behavior of the inventory system depicted in Figure 15-1 over a 40-day period for the same cost parameter and starting inventory. To obtain random numbers, read Table 15-2 backwards, starting with the last digit (which gives 56030 978...). Find the average inventory and the total cost over this period.

15.6   Using the flow chart of Figure 15-5, simulate the two-station assembly line for the following sequence of time durations of 20 assemblies and a conveyor belt time of 6 seconds.

Assembly	1	2	3	4	5	6	7	8	9	10
Time										
task A	33	38	40	42	36	32	30	35	33	37
task B	36	35	33	38	40	44	40	41	37	39

Assembly	11	12	13	14	15	16	17	18	19	20
Time										
task A	35	34	30	37	31	32	40	42	35	38
task B	44	42	37	40	41	36	38	35	38	40

Both stations are empty at the start, and the operator at station 1 is just ready to start task A for the first assembly. What is the elapsed time to complete all assemblies on both stations? What is the largest number of assemblies waiting on the conveyor belt at any given time? What is the total idle time of the operator at Station 2?

15.7   (a) Using the flowchart of Figure 15-5, simulate the two-station assembly line for a time interval of 10 minutes, starting out with empty stations with the operator at station 1 ready to begin task A on the first assembly. Generate task duration times (rounded to the nearest full second) using the task time probability distribution given in Section 15-5, based on the random numbers listed in Table 15-2. Use 2-digit random numbers to generate the random variates required, and start at the beginning of Table 15-2. Determine the number of assemblies completed, the maximum number of assemblies waiting on the conveyor belt, and the total idle time of the operator at station 2.

   (b) The assembly operations can be regrouped in a way that the average time for task A is increased to 36 seconds, and the average time for task B decreases to 37 seconds, without affecting the standard deviations of the tasks. Redo (a) for this change in data, and compare the two modes of operations. Which one gives a more even work flow?

15.8   Rainfall in the watershed area of a water reservoir is subject to random variations, with rainfalls in consecutive periods highly correlated and dependent on the season as follows:

Season	Rainfall last season	P(Rainfall this season)	
		low	high
summer	high	0.4	0.6
	low	0.7	0.3
winter	high	0.3	0.7
	low	0.6	0.4

The actual water inflow to the reservoir depends on the rainfall in the current and preceding season as follows:

	Seasonal rainfall		$P(\text{Water inflow} = x)$ x			
Season	current	preceding	1	2	3	4 units
summer	high	high	0	0	0.5	0.5
	high	low	0	0.6	0.4	0
	low	high	0.1	0.6	0.3	0
	low	low	0.6	0.4	0	0
winter	high	high	0	0.2	0.5	0.3
	high	low	0	0.4	0.6	0
	low	high	0.2	0.5	0.3	0
	low	low	0.7	0.3	0	0

The reservoir has a maximum capacity of 10 units of water, and the water level cannot be lowered below 5 units of water. The target release for irrigation from the reservoir is 4 units of water in summer and 2 in winter. If the water level in excess of the minimum of 5 plus the water inflow is insufficient to cover the target release, as much as possible is released within the constraints stated. If the reservoir is full, any additional inflow also has to be released. Assume that water inflow and water release occur at the same time, such that only the difference between the two affects the water level of the reservoir. Simulate the operation of the reservoir by fixed time incrementation over a 10-year period, given that the water level at the beginning of the first summer season is 6 and the rainfall in the preceding winter season was high. Construct a flow diagram first. For the simulation, generate random deviates, using 1-digit random numbers starting at the beginning of Table 15-2. Determine the average end-of-season reservoir level, the total amount of shortages, and the total amount of water releases in excess of the target.

15.9 PERT network: Consider the PERT problem discussed in Section 6-5 of Chapter 6. Rather than using the Beta distribution, assume that the duration of each task follows a normal distribution with parameters as shown in Table 6-2. Simulate the project completion time using stochastic simulation. To determine random deviates accurate to 1/10 of a day, use 2-digit random numbers in Table 15-2, starting at the beginning of the table. Simulate 12 separate project completion times, and determine the average and standard deviation of the project completion time and compare it with the theoretical results found in Section 6-5.

15.10 A job shop has three work centers, A, B, and C. Each job has to go through some or all centers in a given sequence. A work center can only work on one job at a time. A job only vacates a work center when all operations to be done at that center have been completed. The present work load in terms of partially completed jobs and jobs on the order list is as follows:

Job	Date received	Date due	Sequence for (Work center—Processing time)
1	01	05	C-2
2	01	04	B-1, C-1
3	01	06	A-2, C-2
4	03	10	A-2, C-2

5	03	10	A-2, C-2
6	04	20	B-2, A-6, B-3
7	06	20	A-1, C-3, B-5
8	06	10	B-2
9	08	16	B-4
10	10	24	C-2
11	10	20	C-2, A-2
12	12	26	B-2, A-3, C-4
13	15	30	A-2, C-4, A-1
14	15	36	B-4
15	18	30	A-5, C-2
16	20	36	B-2, C-6
17	20	40	B-4, A-6
18	24	32	C-2
19	24	40	B-5, A-1, C-4
20	25	38	A-4, B-4

In the last column, the letters identify the work center, the numbers following it the processing times. The work must be done in the sequence of work center shown. Simulate the processing of these jobs, using the following rules for determining priority of jobs waiting at a work center.

(a) The first to arrive at the work center is the first processed.

(b) At each station take first the job ready for processing with the least amount of slack, where slack is determined as:

(due date) − (total processing time left on job) − (simulated time)

Draw a flow diagram first. For each rule find the earliest time that job 20 is completed, find the average lateness of jobs, the total idle time on each center, and compare the two rules in terms of these characteristics.

15.11 Write a computer program in any language you know for the two-station assembly problem in Section 15-6, and determine the average operating characteristics on the basis of 8 simulation runs each covering 4 hours of work, with empty starting conditions. Determine the average ending backlog at station 2.

15.12 Write a computer program in any language you know for the water reservoir simulation problem in exercise 15.8.

REFERENCES

Forrester, Jay W. *Industrial Dynamics*. Cambridge, Mass.: MIT Press, 1969. The classic text on this important simulation tool that has obtained new prominence through its use to predict the future development of this globe as a result of population pressures, incidence of pollution, and scarcity of natural resources. See also *Urban Dynamics*, Cambridge, Mass.: MIT Press, 1969; and *World Dynamics*, Cambridge, Mass.: Wright-Allen Press, 1972, by the same suthor.

Hammersley, J. M., and D. C. Handscomb. *Monte Carlo Methods*. New York: Wiley, 1964. The classic text on variance or error reducing techniques, such as importance sampling, control variates, regression, and antithetic-variate methods and conditional Monte Carlo. An advanced text.

Markowitz, H. M. "Simulating with SIMSCRIPT", *Management Science*, 12, June 1966. A general description of the basic features of SIMSCRIPT, showing copies of coding input sheets and a sample program.

Mattessich, Richard. *Simulation of the Firm Through a Budget Computer Program.* Homewood, Il.: Irwin, 1964. Deterministic simulation of a firm's financial position over time.

Meier, Robert C., William T. Newell, and Harold L. Pazer. *Simulation in Business and Economics.* Englewood Cliffs, N.J.: Prentice-Hall, 1969. An easy, introductory text. Contains a listing of the inventory simulation program used in this chapter. The text has a whole chapter on computer simulation languages, and one on industrial dynamics. Most chapters contain an extensive bibliography on applications reported in the literature up to 1968.

Mihram, G. Arthur. *Simulation—Statistical Foundations and Methodology.* New York: Academic Press, 1972. An advanced text covering the statistical basis of simulation.

Mize, Joe H., and J. Grady Cox. *Essentials of Simulation.* Englewood Cliffs, N.J.: Prentice-Hall, 1968. A text on fundamentals of simulation, such as the basic concepts of probability, sampling of multi-variable random events, and estimation for simulation. Assumes knowledge of FORTRAN programming. Contains a number of simple FORTRAN computer programs for examples discussed in text. A fairly easy text.

Naylor, Thomas H., Joseph L. Balintfy, Donan S. Burdick and Kong Chu. *Computer Simulation Techniques.* New York: Wiley, 1966. A classic text on simulation at an intermediate level.

Naylor, Thomas H. *Computer Simulations Experiments with Models of Economic Systems.* New York: Wiley, 1971. A sequel to *Computer Simulation Techniques* dealing particularly with systems in economics and management science. Statistical methods of validation and design are discussed. The text has a detailed appendix on simulation languages. A fairly demanding text.

Pugh, A. L. *DYNAMO II User's Manual.* Cambridge, Mass.: MIT Press, 1970. Shows how to use the simulation language DYNAMO.

A short list of some recent applications reported in the literature follows:

Eilon, S. and S. Mathewson. "A Simulation Study for the Design of an Air Terminal Building", *IEEE Transactions on Systems, Man, and Cybernetics*, 4, July 1973.

Fairhurst, J. H. and D. Livingston. "A Simulation Model for Product/Inventory Decisions", *Operational Research Quarterly*, 24, June 1973.

Handen, B. M., P. M. Maher, and G. A. Martin. "Forest Fire Detection Systems Design", *Management Science*, 20, Dec. 1973.

Hersley, J. C., W. J. Alermathy, and N. Baloff. "Comparison of Nurse Allocation Policies—A Monte Carlo Model", *Decision Sciences*, 5, Jan. 1974.

Holloway, C. A. and R. T. Nelson. "Job Shop Scheduling with Due Dates and Variable Processing Times", *Management Science*, 20, May 1974.

Kryzanowski, L., P. Lusztig, and B. Schwab. "Monte-Carlo Simulation and Capital Expenditure Decisions—A Case Study", *Engineering Economist*, 18, Feb. 1972.

Kuzdrall, P. J., N. K. Kwak, and H. H. Schmitz. "The Monte Carlo Simulation of Operating-Room and Recovery-Room Usage", *Operations Research*, 22, March-April 1974.

Longley, D. "A Simulation Study of a Traffic Network Control Scheme", *Transportation Research*, 5, April 1971.

Perkins, W. C. and P. E. Paschke. "A Simulation Model of the Higher Educational System of a State", *Decision Sciences*, 4, April 1973.

Sorensen, Eric E., and James F. Gilheany. "A Simulation Model for Harvest Operations Under Stochastic Conditions", *Management Science*, 16, April 1970.

Uyeno, D. H. "Health Manpower Systems: An Application of Simulation to the Design of Primary Health Care Teams", *Management Science*, 20, Feb. 1974.

16

Heuristic Problem Solving

John L. Rodgers

The student of operations research who has mastered the techniques discussed in the previous chapters and has acquired, even if only partially, the skills of problem identification, model construction, and so on, may feel sufficiently well equipped to enter the battle of real world problem solving. However, on entering that formidable arena, he or she will inevitably encounter many problems which cannot be solved by any of the techniques carried in the tool kit of problem solving methods. Heuristic methods provide the operations researcher with an alternative approach. Heuristic problem solving is not a solution method in the sense that the simplex method of linear programming is, but rather it is a philosophy of, or strategy for, seeking out a method or methods which might produce a solution to a particular problem.

Heuristic problem solving involves the development of a set of rules called heuristics (derived from the Greek word *heuriskein* meaning to discover), which hopefully will aid in the discovery of one or more satisfactory solutions to a specific problem. The emphasis is on satisfactory—there is no guarantee of optimality. In many instances, the use of heuristics may reduce the problem space sufficiently so that an analytical or simulation procedure may be applied; sometimes, the heuristics used may, by themselves, be sufficient to produce an acceptable feasible solution.

Whereas analytical procedures are based on deductive reasoning supported by mathematical proofs and known properties, heuristic methods are based on inductive inferences related to human characteristics of problem solving, such as creativity, insight, intuition, and learning. A particular heuristic is followed because it promises, intuitively or from experience, to help in the search for an acceptable solution, and if in the process a better rule is discovered, then the old one is discarded. So while heuristic problem solving involves the use of currently accepted rules, it also involves a search for even better rules to replace them.

Why adopt a heuristic approach to solving a particular problem? We have noted that many real world problems are not amenable to direct analytical solution by known mathematical techniques. But even where it is theoretically possible to apply such methods, if the problem is very large, the task of doing so may be impracticable. A large class of combinatorial problems (such as facility location and production scheduling) fall into this category.

16-1 ILL STRUCTURED PROBLEMS

Problems for which no suitable analytic or algorithmic solution technique is available are often referred to as *ill structured*. An ill structured problem (ISP) is a residual concept in the sense that we can only define what it is not. A problem is an ISP if it is not a well structured problem (WSP). By defining what a WSP is, we effectively have a definition of an ISP. But there is a snag in that it is not possible to provide a precise definition of a well structured problem! We must content ourselves with the following general descriptive characteristics which are possessed in varying degrees by WSPs!

(a) Any knowledge relevant to the problem can be represented in an acceptable model.
(b) An acceptable model should encompass all attainable (feasible) solutions.
(c) There exist definite criteria for judging the validity and acceptability of any solution.
(d) There exists a programmable method for solving an acceptable model.
(e) The solution procedure should involve only practicable amounts of computation.
(f) All information required by the acceptable model should be available within practicable limits of data gathering effort.

The boundary between ISPs and WSPs is vague and fluid. As advances in operations research methodology proceed, new and more sophisticated solution techniques in association with more powerful computers will convert ISPs to WSPs. But considering the state of the art at any given time, certain problems, such as simple linear optimization problems, can definitely be said to be well structured while certain other problems are obvious candidates for the ill structured label, such as chess games, most types of architectural design, and so on. However, many of the problems confronting operations researchers fall into neither of these clearly identified groups. Rather, they occupy the fuzzy in-between area depicted in Figure 16-1.

Bred in an analytical mold, operations researchers have been all too ready to treat such problems as WSPs—an assumption here, a trim there, bend a few facts, overlook a few others, and any fuzzy problem can be made to look respectable. However, models constructed using such an approach can hardly be expected to perform well. Rather than mutilate a problem until it conforms to a model for which an efficient solution technique exists, a more acceptable line of attack is to modify the solution procedure to fit the problem. A heuristic approach may be worth considering in such situations.

WSP   ?   ISP

Figure 16-1. *WSPs, ISPs and in-betweens.*

16-2 HEURISTICS—THE HUMAN APPROACH TO PROBLEM SOLVING

It is obvious that human problem solving abilities, such as *perception, insight, creativity,* and *learning* are involved at all phases of an operations research project in overcoming the inevitable problems that arise as such projects progress. However, our current concern is confined to phase three of the five project phases discussed in Section 1-1 of Chapter 1, namely, deriving a solution to the model.

Many operations research projects involve the application of a standard solution method. As such, the major task of the operations researcher is to construct an acceptable model which is amenable to solution by a known optimizing technique. In a sense, the solution method can be viewed as a black box which, given the correct input, will produce the required output. See Figure 16-2.

In contrast, a heuristic approach might involve a process such as that shown in Figure 16-3. Where are human problem solving capabilities applicable in this process? First, in order to devise the initial rules of search, there must be some perception of the structure of the problem. This perception may come through insight (sudden discovery) or learning (accumulation of experience). In the process of applying the rules, additional information relating to the structure of the problem may be learned, or new insights gained, which allows more intelligent application of

Input   Black Box   Output

Figure 16-2. *Situation where a standard method applies.*

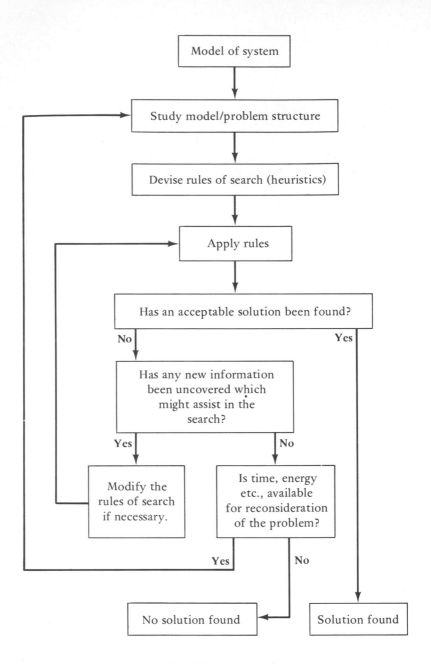

Figure 16-3. *A possible heuristic solution process.*

the rules or possibly a complete redefinition of the search rules. When a search fails to produce either a solution or additional information which may be used to restructure the search procedure, then even such a failure is useful. Given a decision to try again from the beginning, at least one possible avenue of search (namely, the one that failed) can be eliminated. In this way the search for a solution method is narrowed.

The rules of thumb (heuristics) based on accumulated experience are characteristic of human problem solving behavior. Consider a man moving from a rural area, where he has spent all his life, to a large city. There he takes a job as a cab driver. Each time he is hailed he faces the problem of finding a suitable route between two given points in the city. He might begin by using the rule "the shortest distance between two points is a straight line", and plan accordingly. Even after just a few experiences, he might add a further rule "when driving across town, avoid the downtown area". This would probably soon be replaced by "avoid all probable concentrations of traffic", and from personal and communicated experience he would soon learn when and where these might occur. In addition, he would most likely adopt the rule "when in doubt seek advice from radio base regarding such things as traffic conditions, possible routes, and so on". This process of learning continues until the cab driver (the problem solver) has built up a sophisticated set of rules which enable him to plan routes which are (nearly always) satisfactory (probably more often than not near optimal) between any two points in the city at any time of any day of the week.

In the above example, the problem solving procedure was a process of trial and error combined with knowledge accumulation. This resulted in the formation of rules which would be of assistance in future attempts at planning satisfactory routes. However, in human problem solving, the search rules may not be consciously developed, but rather they may form a subconscious backdrop to problem solving behavior.

Often the problem solving activity is guided not so much by rules based on previous experience, but rather on what we might call insight or intuition. To demonstrate what is meant by insight, try the geometrical puzzle, depicted in Figure 16-4, with a one-minute time limit. Rectangle *ABCD* is inscribed inside the quadrant of a circle whose center is *D*. Given the unit of distances indicated, the problem is to determine the exact length of *AC*.

The solution of course lies in recognizing that *AC* is equal in length to diagonal *DB* which is the radius length, i.e., 10 units. Some readers may have observed this immediately while others may have tried alternative methods, for example, trying to determine the length of *CD*. "Suddenness of discovery" would have characterized all the cases where the simple solution method was found. In many cases there would have been a complete absence of overt trial-and-error behavior.

Such examples illustrate two aspects of human problem solving which are not present in the use of analytic techniques. In the first example, we observe a process of trial-and-error search with behavior continually modified in response to accumulated experience. In the second example, we observe a process of sudden discovery, with or without overt search, which we might call "insight."

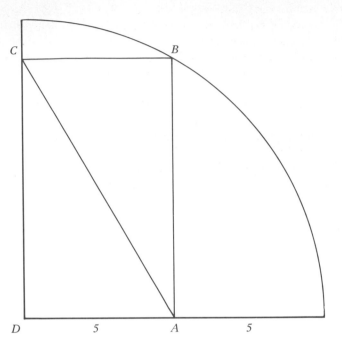

Figure 16-4. *What is the length of* AC?

16-3 AN EXAMPLE OF HEURISTIC PROBLEM SOLVING

Heuristic problem solving behavior is most easily observed in the playing of games and the solving of puzzles. Chess is a classical case. For example, the number of possible combinations of moves in a sequence of five moves is enormous. How do good players decide on a particular move out of all the alternatives available? Rules of thumb (heuristics), based on experience, play a large role in reducing the search for an acceptable move. "How to Play Chess" books usually abound with such rules. For example, aim at weaknesses, never play a move known to be unsound, and search for a sound combination at every move are general rules. Specific rules include: attack weak pawns, never move a pawn without a clear reason, and so on. Sometimes insight (preceded by search behavior) is experienced in chess.

Chess is far too complex to be used as a detailed example of heuristic problem solving. Let us instead analyze a simple guessing game, Cows-and-Bulls, which involves a game controller (usually a computer) and one human player. The controller "thinks" of a four-digit number with all digits different (0 is a legitimate first digit). The player has to guess the number in as few trials as possible. After each guess, which must consist of four different digits, the controller responds by informing the player how many bulls (correct digits in their correct positions) and how many cows (correct digits but not in the correct position), the player has scored.

For example, if the correct number is 8704 and a player submits 9834, the try would score:1ull , 1 b cow; the 4 being the bull, and the 8 the cow.   Note that the player is *not* told which digits are the cows and bulls.

The game can be solved analytically given nine guesses as we shall see later. Using a heuristic search procedure, a player can usually find the solution in six or seven trials.   From repeated playing of the game and observations of the trial-and-error process, the following general heuristics have been constructed.

Rule 1 Extract and record as much information as possible from the outcome of each trial.

Rule 2 Never seek more information than can be obtained with certainty.

Rule 3 Always seek as much information as possible without violating rule 2.

Rule 4 Knowledge of what digits are *not* in the solution is useful in applying rule 2.

This is not the complete set of the heuristics developed for the game, but they suffice for our purpose.   In applying these rules, we shall use a table such as Table 16-1 to record the information obtained as the search for the correct number proceeds.

The following is a record of an actual game with discussion of the search process.

Trial one: 1234;   Score: 2 cows

Thus, two of the digits are in the solution, but not in their correct positions. In Table 16-1 we can therefore place an X against digit 1 in 1st position, indicating an impossible position.   The same holds for 2, 3, and 4.   Also, we can group digits 1, 2, 3, and 4 with a record that two of them are in the solution; that is digits 1 to 4 are bracketed together in the group column of Table 16-1, with a 2 next to the bracket. This has already been done in Table 16-1.

Trial two: 5678;   Score: 1 bull

The outcome of this trial reveals that only one of 5, 6, 7, and 8 is in the number,

Table 16-1. *Table to Record Information in Cows-and-Bulls.*

Digits	1st	2nd	3rd	4th	Groups
		Positions			
1	X				
2		X			
3			X		2
4				X	
5					
6					
7					
8					
9					
0					

Table 16-2. *Record of the Cows-and-Bulls Game after the Second Trial.*

Digits	Positions				Groups
	1st	2nd	3rd	4th	
1	X				
2		X			
3			X		2
4				X	
5		X	X	X	
6	X		X	X	
7	X	X		X	1
8	X	X	X		
9					
0					1

and whichever it is, is in its correct position. We also know that either 9 or 0 is in the solution. In Table 16-2 we have recorded this new information by marking the impossible positions of 5, 6, 7, and 8 with X's and by bracketing off the two new groups. We ask you to update the table from now on.

The first two trials are suggested as standard (unless four hits are scored on the first trial). So far, we have followed only the first heuristic, but now the second can be applied. We know for certain, that one of 5, 6, 7, and 8 is in the solution, so let us narrow the possibilities by including two of them in the next trial leaving them in the same positions as before. At the same time we can also narrow the grouping on the first four digits.

Trial three: 1278 Score: 1 cow

From this result we know that 7 and 8 are not in the solution, otherwise the try would have scored a bull. So, we can completely delete 7 and 8 as possibilities. It also follows that one of 1 and 2 is in the number and, therefore, one of 3 and 4. Record this new grouping.

Using our knowledge that 7 and 8 are not in the solution, we include them in our next try, applying rule 4 to test which of 1 and 2 is in, and which of 5 and 6 is the bull.

Trial four: 1678 Score: 1 bull, 1 cow

The bull must be 6. Delete all other possibilities in 2nd position. So, 5 is out; delete it. The cow must be 1; therefore, 2 is out; delete it. Using the fact that 9 cannot be the second digit, we can definitely determine which of 9 and 0 is in, and also the definite position of 1.

Trial five: 7918; Score 1 cow

Why this arrangement? Had we tried 9718 and scored 1 cow and 1 bull, we would not have known which of 9 and 1 was the bull and which the cow.   A trial of 9718 would have violated rule 2.

From the outcomes of trials one and five we know that 1 cannot be in the first or third position, so it must be in the fourth.   Record this and delete all other possibilities in the fourth position.   Also, 0 must be in the solution for 9 is obviously not.   Delete 9.

We are now so close to the solution that if we do not find it by chance on the next trial, we will, on the basis of that trial, definitely know what the solution is.   The number of possible solutions has been reduced so drastically that the search strategy can be tabulated as follows:

Possible Trial	Outcome	Solution
3601	4 bulls	3601
	3 bulls	4601
	2 bulls, 1 cow	0641
4601	4 bulls	4601
	3 bulls	3601
	2 bulls, 2 cows	0641
0641	4 bulls	0641
	2 bulls, 2 cows	4601
	2 bulls, 1 cow	3601

As there are no grounds for choosing one combination over the other two, let us select the first.

Trial six: 3601   Score: 3 bulls

Therefore, 3 cannot be in the solution because the other three digits definitely are.   The solution must be 4601.   A seventh trial to confirm this is not necessary.

An analytical solution to this problem is possible given 9 trials as follows: Let $x_j, j = 1, ..., 10$, be zero-one variables, representing the presence ($x_j = 1$) or absence ($x_j = 0$) of the jth digit. b_i is the number of hits (cows plus bulls) given by the ith trial.   From the nine trials we can construct nine equations; the tenth equation is of course:

$$(16\text{-}1) \qquad\qquad \sum_{j=1}^{10} x_j = 4$$

Provided that the nine trials and expression (16-1) yield 10 linearly independent equations, a unique solution exists giving the four digits in the solution.   If the arrangements of digits in the nine trials are not repetitive, using the cow/bull score on each trial the exact solution can be determined by a simple comparative search.

Using the heuristic search procedure based on rules derived from accumulated experience, the human player is more efficient than the analytical procedure in a majority of cases.   This is so because the heuristic method uses all information available at each stage of the search in order to formulate a future strategy.   The information to be sought on each successive trial is determined by the information previously obtained; this enables a convergent search for the solution. On the other hand, the analytical method has rigid data requirements, as is the case with most standard operations research techniques.

16-4 SATISFICING

It has been strongly implied throughout the discussion, but until now not explicitly stated, that heuristic problem solving methods are strongly associated with satisficing, as opposed to optimizing, behavior. Heuristic methods do not normally guarantee optimal solutions. This is not necessarily a disadvantage. Many problems with ill structured characteristics do not have optimal solutions in the strict sense. Such problems are essentially solved when one or more acceptable solutions have been identified. In fact, goal satisficing often describes human choice behavior more accurately than does goal optimizing, and it is important that the operations researcher recognizes such situations. In business organizations, goal satisficing is likely to be most prevalent at the higher levels of management. It is there where goal conflicts, calling for trade-offs between opposing goals, are usually most evident.

Two important features of satisficing type problems should be noted. The first concerns the flexible nature of satisficing behavior: What may be regarded as satisfactory at one point in time, may become unsatisfactory when new information comes to light, and vice versa. For example, a manager may regard certain levels of profit, market share, and capital growth as satisfactory. But if it can be pointed out that all these objectives can be substantially and simultaneously increased, the previously acceptable levels may become regarded as unsatisfactory. Alternatively, if it can be adequately demonstrated that the goal levels cannot be simultaneously achieved, he will lower his aspiration level (if he is rational) so that the goals are more consistent.

The second feature of satisficing behavior is of greater consequence. The decision maker may require that an acceptable solution possess some ill defined set of nonquantifiable attributes—nonquantifiable at least in the sense that objective measurement is not attainable by a practicable amount of effort. For example, in a developing country, there may be a set of potential projects of which the government may be able to undertake a small subset. Some of the required attributes of the final selection might be that they should not be unduly disruptive to cultural organization and activity; they should result in an acceptable pattern of income distribution; and they should be seen to contribute substantially to regional development.

One approach which has been suggested as being suitable in such cases is to submit to the decision maker a set of solutions, each possessing the preferred characteristics in varying degrees. The decision maker is then able to select that solution which is found to be "most satisfactory." Using this approach, the operations researcher does not have to make arbitrary assumptions in constructing trade-off functions between conflicting goals, nor does he need to construct artificial constraints containing coefficients estimated on a highly subjective basis.

16-5 HEURISTIC PROCEDURES AND PROGRAMS

The term, *heuristic program*, is used here to mean the computer implementation of a heuristic procedure. Referring to Figure 16-3, most heuristic programs constructed to date involve the writing of computer programs for rule application. Rule formulation and reformulation (subsequent to search failure) is left to the program user. Even so, some of these programs may be very sophisticated in that the rules themselves allow learning behavior by the program and consequent adaptation of the search strategy. At a higher level there are programs which contain built-in rules for automatic heuristic modification based on some form of learning process.

Most heuristic problem solving procedures belong to one or a mixture of four general strategies:

(a) *solution-building strategies*,

(b) *break-make strategies*,

(c) *solution-modification strategies*, and

(d) *search-learning strategies*.

Let us look briefly at each in turn.

Solution-building strategies. In this approach we attempt to construct a solution, one element at a time, according to a set of definite rules. For instance, if the problem involves assigning each of n items to one of m groups (with $n > m$) such that the allocation satisfies some specific criteria, we could start out by first ranking the items by some measure of preference. This measure of preference should reflect the criteria on which the acceptability of the solution will be judged. The second step is to make the assignment in order of preference. For example, suppose we wish to select two evenly matched teams from a group of baseball players in a city neighborhood. Assume that the two best players, Debbie and Gary, are elected as team captains with Debbie having first choice. Let us also assume that both captains have the same perception of the abilities of each player, and that these have been quantified on a 0 to 9 scale as given in Table 16-3.

Suppose, we make the selction on the basis of the arithmetic sum of the ability ratings as given by the total column in Table 16-3. This produces the ranking shown in the last column of Table 16-3. Hence, Debbie's first choice is Archie, who is ranked best after the two captains. Gary's first choice is Irene. Debbie's second choice is Ed, and so on.

However, we may not give each ability an equal weight for the overall ranking of each player. Fielding ability would probably carry a lower weight than the other two abilities. Furthermore, in our example, there are only four players with a pitching rating above 5, while there are 9 batters with this quality. It would seem reasonable to give pitching ability a higher weight so as to reflect the relative scarcity of this desirable trait. A formal heuristic procedure for team selection should include directions on how to weigh the various abilities in calculating the total rating of each player.

Table 16-3. *Ability Ratings of Each Player.*

Player	Batter	Pitcher	Fielder	Total	Ranking
1. Archie	7	9	6	22	3
2. Bud	6	4	5	15	8
3. Chuck	4	4	6	14	9
4. Debbie	8	8	8	24	2
5. Ed	6	9	4	19	5
6. Frank	0	1	2	3	16
7. Gary	9	7	9	25	1
8. Harry	2	2	4	8	14
9. Irene	9	4	8	21	4
10. Gerry	4	3	3	10	12
11. Kate	6	5	7	18	6
12. Larry	2	4	3	9	13
13. Mike	8	5	4	17	7
14. Nancy	7	3	3	13	10
15. Olive	2	3	1	6	15
16. Penny	4	3	5	12	11

The higher the rating, the greater is corresponding ability.

A variation in the ranking procedure involves grouping the items into classes on the basis of relevant characteristics, and then ranking within each class. In our example, the players could be grouped as good all-round players (Archie, Debbie, and Gary), good pitchers (Ed), good batters (Irene, Mike, and Nancy), and run-of-the-mill (the rest). Assignments to each team would then be made from each group separately.

Another variation of this strategy involves a re-evaluation of the rankings after each assignment to reflect the relative desirability of the remaining unassigned items. Hence, in response to Debbie's first choice of Archie, Gary might opt for Ed rather than Irene as his first choice (even though Irene has a higher overall score than Ed) because Ed is the last good pitcher left in the group of unassigned players.

Break-Make Strategies. Here we "break" a complex problem into a number of smaller subproblems. Each subproblem is solved individually or in some hierarchical sequence, where the output of a lower order subproblem is used as input into the next higher order problem, or vice versa, depending on the most appropriate order of solution. The solution to the whole problem is "made" by integrating the solutions to the subproblems into a consistent overall solution. Consider, for instance, the case study in Section 1-9. There the problem involves finding an optimal inventory policy for the entire operation of the lubrication oil division. It might be broken down into a number of subproblems: determining filled stock replenishment sizes, determining filled stock reorder points, and finally, finding empty container replenishment rules. They would be solved in sequence. The results of the subproblem for the filled stock replenishment sizes (namely the number of replenishments per year = number of times shortages may occur) is used as input into the determination of reorder points for each product. Similarly, the size and pattern of filled stock replenishments is used as input into finding good empty container replenishment rules.

Solution-Modification Strategies. An initial solution is modified by applying a specified sequence of heuristics aimed at improving the acceptability of the solution. The initial solution may have been built up by using a solution-building or break-make strategy, or it may have been obtained by an approximation method, such as the use of a standard optimizing technique to a simplified model of the problem. It may be that the starting solution is infeasible and the heuristic modification rules are designed to achieve feasibility and hence acceptability. The facility location solution method described in the next section consists mainly of solution-modification heuristics.

Search-Learning Strategies. This approach involves a directed search of the solution space. As new information is unearthed during the search, it is used to guide the search in new directions. The solution procedure for solving the cows-and-bulls problem falls into this group of strategies, because the outcome of each trial is used to guide the player in eliminating portions of the solution space and formulating trials that will provide further information needed to find the solution. The later phases of the facility location procedure in the next section also rely on this strategy. The analyst uses a *forcing technique* to direct the search for better solutions on the basis of knowledge gained from previous solutions.

A particular heuristic program may involve a combination of two or more of these strategies. For instance, the solution-building or the break-make strategies may provide an initial solution, which is then improved upon by a mixture of the solution-modification and search-learning strategies.

When using a solution-modification or search-learning strategy, we should carefully spell out all conditions for which the procedure should be terminated as successful or abandoned as a failure. For instance, if the procedure involves finding a feasible solution, it is terminated once such a solution has been identified, or it is abandoned if after k trials or m minutes of computer time no feasible solution has been generated. Sometimes, it may be desirable to have an interactive program that allows the analyst to intervene and terminate the procedure at will or at certain points in the search.

Many heuristic programs incorporate optimizing methods during one or several phases of the procedure. For instance, some of the subproblems created in the break-make strategy might be solved by an optimizing technique, such as linear programming. Also, simulation methods may form part of a heuristic program. For instance, a simulation model may be used to test the acceptability of a heuristically derived solution. Alternatively, heuristic rules may be used in conjunction with simulation to speed up the search for good solutions to complex decision problems.

Heuristic programs, like simulation models, tend to be very problem-specific in contrast to, say, linear programming which can be applied to any problem that satisfies the fairly general assumptions of the model. However, the analyst should avoid devising a program that is parameter-specific. A procedure should not be so narrow that its effectiveness in finding acceptable solutions depends on particular or a limited range of parameter values. Should these parameters change (say, over time), the procedure becomes useless. Furthermore, the quality (highly important for heuristic programs) of being able to test the sensitivity of the solution to changes in these parameters, is lost.

Although we have attempted here to give some framework—albeit a fairly loose and not necessarily a completely comprehensive one—for the methodology in heuristic problem solving, it still remains that heuristic problem solving itself falls into the group of ISPs. It is largely the ingenuity of the analyst that makes a particular heuristic program successful.

16-6 SOLVING A FACILITY LOCATION PROBLEM

How can we determine the size and location of processing facilities for a commodity which is available in raw form from a number of sources and is required in processed form at various destinations? If processing of the commodity was not required, the problem would be a simple transportation problem. But if the commodity has to be processed in some way at an intermediate location, the solution procedure is not so straightforward. Processing costs at any particular facility are usually characterized by economies of scale, i.e., the greater the throughput, the lower is the per unit processing cost. The usual criterion for measuring the effectiveness of a solution is total cost which includes assembly cost (source to facility transportation costs), processing costs, and distribution costs (facility to destination transportation costs). A diagrammatic representation of the type of system being discussed is given in Figure 16-5.

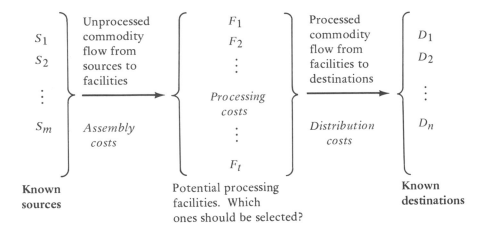

Figure 16-5. *Which facilities involve minimum cost?*

Facility location problems are ideal candidates for heuristic treatment. In addition to cost considerations, there are often qualitative criteria for judging solution acceptability. It is desirable, therefore, to provide the decision maker with a number of feasible low cost solutions so that he can compare the costs of alternative solutions together with their qualitative attributes. The procedure outlined here is an extension of the work of S. H. Logan and G. A. King ("Size and Location Factors Affecting California's Beef Slaughtering Plants," *Hilgardia*, 36, December 1964).

Let us, for a moment, lay aside any consideration of qualitative criteria and multiple solutions, and regard the problem as one of finding a low cost solution. This leaves us with a much simpler problem which can be stated verbally as

$$\text{minimize total cost} = \begin{bmatrix} \text{assembly} \\ \text{costs} \end{bmatrix} + \begin{bmatrix} \text{processing} \\ \text{costs} \end{bmatrix} + \begin{bmatrix} \text{distribution} \\ \text{costs} \end{bmatrix}$$

subject to the supply, facility capacity and demand constraints.
Algebraically the problem is

$$\text{minimize} \sum_{i=1}^{m} \sum_{k=1}^{t} C_{ik} x_{ik} + \sum_{k=1}^{t} \left[P_k \left(\sum_{i=1}^{m} x_{ik} \right) \sum_{i=1}^{m} x_{ik} \right] + \sum_{k=1}^{t} \sum_{j=1}^{n} \hat{C}_{kj} \hat{x}_{kj}$$

where x_{ik} is the quantity transported from the ith source to the kth facility.
$\hat{x}_{kj}$ is the quantity transported from the kth facility to the jth destination.
C_{ik} is the per unit assembly cost from the ith source to the kth facility.
$\hat{C}_{kj}$ is the per unit distribution cost from the kth facility to the jth destination.
$P_k(y)$ is the per unit processing cost at the kth facility given a throughput of y.

subject to:

supply constraints:

$$\sum_{k=1}^{t} x_{ik} = S_i \qquad \text{for} \quad i = 1, 2, ..., m$$

where S_i is the quantity available at the ith source.

processing facility capacity constraints:

$$\sum_{i=1}^{m} x_{ik} \leqslant K_k \qquad \text{for} \quad k = 1, 2, ..., t$$

where K_k is the capacity of the kth facility.

demand constraints:

$$\sum_{k=1}^{t} \hat{x}_{kj} = D_j \qquad \text{for} \quad j = 1, 2, ..., n$$

where D_j is the quantity required at the jth destination.

processing facility input-output relation:

$$\sum_{i=1}^{m} x_{ik} = \sum_{j=1}^{n} \hat{x}_{kj} \quad \text{for} \quad k = 1, 2, ..., t$$

feasibility of total demand and supply

$$\sum_{i=1}^{m} S_i = \sum_{j=1}^{n} D_j \leq \sum_{k=1}^{t} K_k$$

If total supply exceeds total demand, we restore equality by introducing a dummy destination which has a demand equal to the excess supply.

nonnegativity conditions:

$$x_{ij} \geq 0, \quad \hat{x}_{jk} \geq 0 \quad \text{for all } i, k, j$$

If it were not for the complication that per unit throughput cost of each facility is a function of the quantity processed, then the problem would be a simple transshipment problem with the facility locations becoming intermediate transshipment points. (See Section 5-14 of Chapter 5 for a description of basic principles for the transshipment problem). Similarly if the throughput of each facility were known then the problem would also reduce to a transshipment problem.

The last statement provides a clue as to how the problem might be approached.

		Facilities 1 2 ... t	Destinations 1 2 ... n	Supply
Source	1 2 : m	Unit assembly cost from i^{th} source to k^{th} facility + unit processing cost at k^{th} facility.	All cost elements set to prohibitively high level to prevent direct shipment from sources to destinations.	S_1 S_2 : S_m
Facilities	1 2 : t	Cost elements in leading diagonal set to zero, elsewhere set to prohibitively high level.	Unit distribution cost from k^{th} facility to j^{th} destination.	K_1 K_2 : K_t
Demand		$K_1 K_2 ... K_t$	$D_1 D_2 ... D_n$	

Figure 16-6. *Cost/requirements table for the facility location problem.*

Why not assume that each facility is operating at its most efficient throughput level to start with? Then using the associated unit processing cost, it is a simple matter to construct and solve the transshipment model whose cost/requirements table is given in Figure 16-6.

Optimization of this transshipment model will result in the allocation of a throughput to each facility, where throughput of the kth facility is given by $\sum_{i=1}^{m} x_{ik}$. We now have a feasible solution; but almost certainly it can be improved upon. Some potential facilities may have been allocated a relatively small throughput, while others may not have received any at all. For many facilities the actual throughput allocated is different from the most efficient throughput level. Let us now drop unused facilities from the model, and update the processing costs of the remainder on the basis of the throughput allocated by the previous optimization. This gives us a new transshipment model which can be optimized so as to achieve a new solution which is usually an improvement on the previous one. This procedure of dropping unused facilities, updating the processing costs of the remainder, and optimizing is repeated until processing costs are stable and no further opportunity for dropping occurs. The last solution obtained is the solution to the problem. The procedure is more precisely specified in Figure 16-7.

This iterative solution procedure works very well when no potential facility has a significant spatial advantage over any other. For example, if Figure 16-8 represents the spatial situation of a real system under investigation, facility locations F_1 and F_5 both have a spatial advantage over the remaining potential facilities because they are closer to either sources or destinations and are more likely to enter the first solution at a high level of throughput, to the detriment of the other potential facilities.

Such a spatial situation might give rise to a final stable solution with facilities sited at both F_1 and F_5, while a better solution involving only one facility at, say, F_3 would have been missed because F_2, F_3, and F_4 would have been dropped. To overcome such distortion caused by initial spatial advantages, rather than drop unused facilities, let us retain them in the model, leaving the associated processing costs at their previous levels. Thus, we replace heuristic 3 in Figure 16-7 with a new rule:

New Heuristic 3: Any facilities with zero throughput should retain their previous level of unit processing costs.

This modified search procedure in most cases produces final solutions with total costs at least as low as those achieved by the original method, though the number of iterations involved is usually greater. Both search methods yield stable solutions provided that diseconomies associated with larger throughput levels are either absent or are very remote. If diseconomies of scale are significant, thus resulting in unit processing cost functions which have a pronounced U-shape within the range of realistic facility sizes, the solution process may exhibit a cycling or seesaw type behavior. In this case, the problem solver has to intervene in some way so as to ensure that stability is obtained.

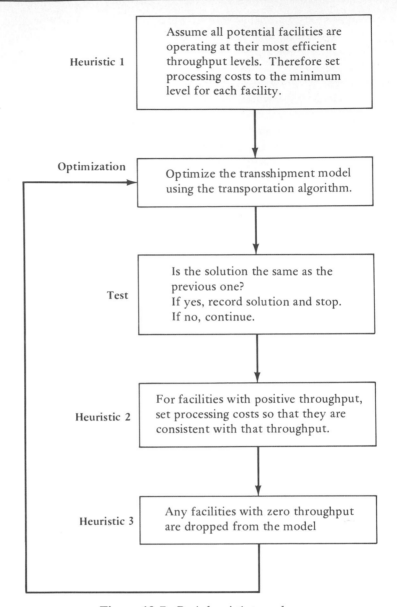

Figure 16-7. *Basic heuristic procedure.*

The procedure does not guarantee a global optimum. Rather, each stable solution is a local optimum, i.e., a small change involving the reallocation of one unit of the commodity would result in a higher cost solution; but there may be other local optima with lower total costs.

Having obtained at least one stable solution, search for more acceptable solutions in terms of both costs and other, possibly qualitative, criteria can be initiated. Even

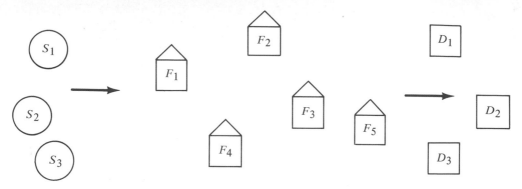

Figure 16-8. *Facilities* F_1 *and* F_5 *have a spatial advantage.*

if the initial solution is acceptable in all aspects, it may be desirable to produce other acceptable alternatives so that the decision maker has a greater range of choice. To this end, a technique known as *forcing* is used.

Forcing entails the artificial manipulation of the unit processing costs so as to encourage a particular facility into the solution or increase its throughput if it is already there, or alternatively force it from a solution or decrease its present throughput. Forcing may be applied at any stage during the iterative search for a stable solution, i.e., before, during, or after. The technique itself is quite simple. Difficulties may arise in determining what facility locations should be forced. This is where heuristics are applied.

Some general rules found useful are:

1. Any location which has been dropped from consideration early in the iterative process is a good candidate for forcing in.
2. Any location which is present in a stable solution, but whose throughput is small is a good candidate for forcing out.
3. If there are two locations present in a stable solution which are geographically close, one of them is a good candidate for forcing out.

Heuristics specific to a particular problem depend on the researcher's knowledge of the system and observation of the solution characteristics during the search procedure. For example, observations of the following type may prove useful in formulating forcing strategies:

1. Good solutions tend to contain facilities which are source (or conversely, destination) biased.
2. Certain pairs of locations tend to enter the same good solution (or conversely, they are never simultaneously present in the same good solution).

A knowledge of at least some preferred qualitative attributes, if any exist, may assist in developing forcing strategies. For instance, if management has a degree of personal preference for establishing facilities in certain locations, then forcing can be used to generate various solutions with the desired characteristics.

Adjustment of the facility capacity constraints can be used as a substitute for or a complement to forcing. Clearly, forcing a facility out by setting its unit processing cost to a prohibitively high level is equivalent to reducing its capacity to zero, which in turn is the same as not including the facility site in the model. Facility capacity adjustments are extremely effective in producing solutions with certain types of preferred attributes. For example, in a military inventory situation, for strategic reasons it may be desirable to have a decentralized system of warehousing, with size limitations on the facilities. But being on a restricted budget, the military planners may wish to know the comparative costs of alternative configurations with varying levels of decentralization and facility size.

To apply the heuristic search approach discussed to problems of a realistic size requires the use of a computer program specifically designed for the task. Initially, the problem is solved using the basic procedure detailed in Figure 16-7. Once a stable solution has been obtained, the analyst is able to begin experimentation with alternative search strategies using forcing and capacity constraint adjustments. Since search plans often evolve and are continually adjusted in response to the outcomes of previous optimization runs, direct access to the computer program via a console keyboard or teletype (i.e., interactive programming) helps to speed up considerably the search for acceptable solutions. Let us apply this approach to a real-life problem—though disguised in a form familiar to all fans of the hobbits.

16-7 MIDDLE EARTH WEED PROCESSING

After the War of the Rings when life had settled back to normal, agricultural scientists found that the legendary tobacco of Middle Earth could be grown in twelve localities in addition to the Shire. Demand for Shireweed—as it has become known—was high and expected to remain so, owing to the discovery that it had no injurious effects on health. In fact, it was beneficial—as evidenced by the longevity of hobbits. Overseas marketing of the weed had become somewhat chaotic with middlemen reaping large profits. So, by royal decree the Weed Marketing Corporation (W.M.C.) was established and made responsible for the processing and marketing of the product for all overseas markets. Apart from weed processed for domestic consumption, all production had to be sold to the W.M.C. In the main, the local inhabitants preferred to process their own weed. "It looses all flavor when processed bulk" was a common dictum.

The W.M.C., not wishing to exploit their monopolistic position, was prepared to sell, for "a reasonable profit," all weed not required for local consumption. They skillfully negotiated long-term trade agreements with the countries to the North, South, East and West, thus ensuring stable markets for all surplus production. The W.M.C. then contracted researchers at the University of Middle Earth (U.M.E.) to investigate the problem determining the size and location for the planned new weed processing factories.

The terms of reference for the research study were that the whole marketing operation should not involve unnecessary costs, but at the same time a view should be kept of "certain political considerations."   For instance, the people of Esgaroth were crying out for some industry in their region, while the inhabitants of Hobbiton were not at all sure that they wanted a large factory in their village.   "It will foul the air and pollute the stream" was the theme of many letters to the *Hobbiton Times*.

The research group (operations researchers, econometricians, engineers—the usual type) gathered the following data:

(a) The expected excess production per annum for each source region and the expected sales to each overseas export region (in accordance with the trade agreements).   (Table 16-4).

(b) Twelve potential plant locations and the scale cost curves applicable for each location.   (Table 16-5).

(c) Per unit transportation costs from source regions to potential locations, from potential facility locations to ports, and from ports to final destinations. (Tables 16-6 to 16-8).

Having decided to use the heuristic search procedure discussed in Section 16-5, the U.M.E. researchers constructed a three-stage transshipment model as shown in Figure 16-9.

The initial solution, obtained by applying the standard heuristic procedure, involves processing facilities at Hobbiton, Tharbad, and Minas Tirith (solution number 2 in Table 16-9).

The U.M.E. investigators were aware of the probable outcry from the environment conscious inhabitants of Hobbiton, and so looked for an alternative site.   The port town of Havens was the obvious candidate; no such problems there!   Producing

Table 16-4. *Supply and Demand Data for Shireweed.*

Source regions	Supply (in bundles)	Destination Regions	Demand (in bundles)
1. Arnor	500		
2. Lhun	600	1. North	2000
3. Shire	1300	2. West	3600
4. Erebor	600	3. South	2400
5. Gladden	650	4. East	1100
6. Hollin	800		
7. Minhiriath	600		
8. Enedhwaith	700		
9. Rohan	700		
10. Nimrias	600		
11. Lebennin	700		
12. Gorgoroth	650		
13. South Gondor	700		

Table 16-5. *Throughput Cost Curves of Potential Plant Locations.*

Location	Throughput cost curve
1. Hobbiton	$P = 2.25 + 1235/Q$
2. Rivendell	$P = 2.25 + 1230/Q$
3. Esgaroth	$P = 2.30 + 1225/Q$
4. Tharbad	$P = 2.35 + 1225/Q$
5. Lorien	$P = 2.40 + 1220/Q$
6. Isengard	$P = 2.35 + 1220/Q$
7. Edoras	$P = 2.30 + 1225/Q$
8. Doom	$P = 2.30 + 1235/Q$
9. Havens	$P = 2.40 + 1235/Q$
10. Lond Daer	$P = 2.40 + 1225/Q$
11. Belfalas	$P = 2.45 + 1225/Q$
12. Minas Tirith	$P = 2.50 + 1300/Q$

P = per unit processing cost in gold pieces
Q = plant throughput in bundles

Table 16-6. *Per Unit Transportation Costs from Sources to Potential Plants.*

	Potential plant locations											
	1	2	3	4	5	6	7	8	9	10	11	12
Source regions	Hobbiton	Rivendell	Esgaroth	Tharbad	Lorien	Isengard	Edoras	Doom	Havens	Lond Daer	Belfalas	Minas Tirith
1. Arnor	140	250	450	300	∞	∞	∞	∞	200	400	∞	∞
2. Lhun	160	280	480	320	∞	∞	∞	∞	100	420	∞	∞
3. Shire	10	200	400	250	∞	∞	∞	∞	65	350	∞	∞
4. Erebor	400	200	40	270	100	320	300	∞	460	370	∞	160
5. Gladden	300	100	180	250	50	260	240	∞	350	350	∞	110
6. Hollin	200	60	220	50	450	200	220	∞	300	150	∞	500
7. Minhiriath	200	250	400	70	600	150	170	∞	300	170	∞	650
8. Enedhwaith	200	250	500	90	600	100	120	∞	350	190	∞	650
9. Rohan	∞	500	450	400	60	80	70	∞	∞	500	∞	100
10. Nimrais	∞	600	∞	350	450	100	90	∞	∞	400	200	150
11. Lebennin	∞	∞	∞	∞	∞	220	100	200	∞	∞	100	50
12. Gorgoroth	∞	∞	∞	∞	∞	270	150	30	∞	∞	200	70
13. South Gondor	∞	∞	∞	∞	∞	270	200	100	∞	∞	200	100

Costs are in silver bits; 100 silver bits = 1 gold piece.

Table 16-7. *Per Unit Transportation Costs from Potential Plants to Ports.*

Ports Plant Locations	1 Havens	2 Lond Daer	3 Belfalas	4 Minas Tirith
1. Hobbiton	50	220	∞	∞
2. Rivendell	270	100	∞	110
3. Esgaroth	420	320	∞	150
4. Tharbad	200	90	500	600
5. Lorien	320	320	600	100
6. Isengard	∞	360	200	80
7. Edoras	∞	450	200	50
8. Doom	∞	∞	180	90
9. Havens	0	∞	∞	∞
10. Lond Daer	∞	0	∞	∞
11. Belfalas	∞	∞	0	110
12. Minas Tirith	∞	∞	110	0

Costs are in silver bits.

the desired solution was an easy matter on their computer at the university. By cost manipulation, Hobbiton was forced from the solution, and Havens was forced into the solution. (The same result could have been achieved by reformulating the model with Hobbiton omitted as a possible location, and then applying the standard method; however, it was computationally faster to work from the previously obtained solution.) The result was pleasing, not only was the new solution more politically acceptable, it also had a lower total cost (see solution 1 in Table 16-9).

What should they look at next? There had been some faint grumbling from Tharbad residents about the social disruption that an influx of factory workers might cause, so the researchers decided to look for further alternatives. Lond Daer and Edoras were possibilities. Tharbad was removed from the solution, and the alternatives were tried in turn. The two new solutions (3 and 4 in Table 16-9) involved only slightly higher costs.

Table 16-8. *Per Unit Transportation Costs from Ports to Final Destinations.*

Ports	Destinations			
	North	West	South	East
1. Havens	400	450	500	650
2. Lond Daer	420	400	480	600
3. Belfalas	600	300	450	400
4. Minas Tirith	640	200	460	520

Costs are in silver bits.

		Facility Locations 1 2 ... 12	Ports 1 ... 4	Destinations 1 ... 4	Supply
Sources	1 2 : 13	Source to facility transport costs & processing costs	Inactive (all cost elements = ∞)	Inactive (all cost elements = ∞)	500 : 700
Facility Locations	1 2 : 12	0 ∞ ∞ 0	Facility to port transport costs	Inactive (all cost elements = ∞)	K K : K
Ports	1 : 4	Inactive (all cost elements = ∞)	0 ∞ ∞ 0	Port to final destination transport costs	K : K
Demand		K K ... K	K ... K	2000 ... 1100	

K is the upper limit on throughput capacity of processing facilities and ports. It can be set to different values for individual transshipment points.

Figure 16-9. *Cost/requirements table for Middle Earth W.M.C. model.*

The government had been recently promising action on regional development, and the W.M.C., wishing to be in accord with government policy, had indicated interest in viewing alternative plans which involved processing factories in at least three towns in addition to Minas Tirith, as well as some which required no factory in Minas Tirith. The W.M.C. was particularly interested in those solutions involving a processing plant at Esgaroth, as had been indicated in the research proposal. Using the forcing technique along with capacity adjustments, the U.M.E. researchers produced a number of solutions meeting these requirements. Solutions 5 to 9 in Table 16-9 are a representative sample. The final aspect to be investigated was not using the port at Minas Tirith, as there had been serious labor problems at the port involving several long strikes in recent times. The W.M.C. was interested in the cost implications of not exporting through this particular port. An answer was easily obtained by setting the throughput capacity of the port to zero. The solution demonstrated the importance of Minas Tirith port, as not using it would result in significantly higher costs. See solution 10 in Table 16-9.

It should be pointed out that some of the solutions presented in Table 16-9 are not local optima in the true sense. For example, to obtain a facility at Esgaroth, the capacity of other potential locations had to be tightly constrained. However,

Table 16-9. *Some Selected Solutions to the W.M.C. Facility Location Problem.*

		Facility and Port Throughput (in bundles)									
	Solution No.	1	2	3	4	5	6	7	8	9	10
Processing Facility Locations	1. Hobbiton										
	2. Rivendell		2400								
	3. Esgaroth					600				600	
	4. Tharbad	2100	2100			2100	2100		1400	800	2100
	5. Lorien						1250	1250	1250	650	
	6. Isengard								700	2600	
	7. Edoras				3400			4050			
	8. Doom										
	9. Havens	2400		2400	2400	2400	2400	2400	2400	2400	2400
	10. Lond Daer			2100							
	11. Belfalas							1400	1100	2050	
	12. Minas Tirith	4600	4600	4600	3300	4000	3350		2250		4600
Ports	1. Havens	2400	2400	2400	2400	2400	2400	2400	2400	2400	2400
	2. Lond Daer	2100	2100	2100		2100	2100		1400	800	2100
	3. Belfalas	1000	1000	1000	1100	1000	1000	1400	1100	2050	4600
	4. Minas Tirith	3600	3600	3600	5600	3600	3600	5300	4200	3850	
	Total cost (in gold pieces)	68990	69175	69305	69550	70306	70608	71541	72135	73843	76450
	Percent above lowest cost		0.3%	0.5%	0.8%	1.9%	2.3%	3.7%	4.6%	7.0%	10.8%

535

given the size and location of the processing factories, the total cost of each solution does represent the minimum cost of transportation.

It is noted that in going from a centralized to a decentralized location pattern, the total cost tends to increase. If the planners have serious intentions concerning decentralization, they might prefer a solution such as solution 9 to the others. The additional cost of this solution is of the order of 7 percent. If only lip service is paid to regional development, solution 5, which involves an additional cost of about 2 percent, might be attractive. There are numerous other solutions within the range covered by the ten results presented.

Postscript. The U.M.E. team selected 20 or so solutions which they considered covered all possible desirable attributes. These were fully documented in the final report which was presented to the W.M.C. A decision is still pending.

EXERCISES

16.1 (a) Ask a friend to write a four-digit number, with all digits different, 0 being a legitimate digit in any position. You are not to be told what the number is. Your task is to find the unknown number in as few guesses as possible. On each guess, your friend is to tell you how many bulls (correct digits in their correct positions) and cows (correct digits but not in their correct positions) you have scored, but you are not to be told which digits are the cows and bulls. While the superficial problem is to find the correct number, the more important and basic problem is to devise a set of rules which will assist you in finding the number. You may wish to start with the heuristics given in Section 16-3, adding your own modifications and refinements, or you may decide to develop a completely new set of rules. Whatever approach you adopt, your rules should be specific, and they should enable you to find the unknown number within seven guesses for most games.

(b) The following is a record of an actual game. Even though it does not look as though the player is doing very well, after the eighth trial he announced to onlookers that he knew the answer. What is it?

No.	Trial	Score
1	1 2 3 4	2 cows
2	5 6 7 8	1 cow
3	5 0 9 4	2 cows
4	9 6 7 8	1 cow
5	0 6 7 8	2 cows
6	1 5 0 4	2 cows
7	9 5 4 2	1 cow
8	9 4 5 8	1 cow

16.2 Nick Dickson, a confirmed gambler, while knowing nothing about politics, enjoys betting on the outcome of elections. For the forthcoming contest, Nick had shopped around and obtained the following odds.

Candidate	Total payout for each $1 bet if candidate wins
Joe Honest	$7
Ted Algood	$10
Bob Friendly	$2
Jack Sincere	$5

"If I place my bets properly, I can't lose," thought Nick. He was able to raise $6600 for the venture. Unfortunately, he made a mistake when placing the bets, so that when Bob Friendly won, Nick came out on the losing end.

Use a heuristic procedure to determine how Nick should have placed his bets so as to ensure a gain whatever the outcome.

16.3 The air force command had received instructions to disrupt the enemy's supply lines so as to slow down their advance. Supplies were being transported along one road on which there were five major bridges. The destruction of any one of these bridges would achieve the desired effect. A problem confronted the air force as they had only a limited number of planes available for the task and a fuel shortage meant that only 1150 thousand liters of fuel could be allocated for this mission.

Relevant data on the available planes are as follows:

Plane	Kilometers per thousand liters of fuel	Number of planes available
B21.5	20	20
F222	30	15

Data concerning the vulnerability of each bridge to attack by each type of plane, and the distance of each bridge from the base are given in the table below.

Bridge	Probability of destruction by a B21.5	by a F222	Distance from base in kilometers
A	0.08	0.06	600
B	0.18	0.18	900
C	0.15	0.13	1100
D	0.28	0.23	1200
E	0.30	out of range	1500

Each plane had to carry sufficient fuel for the round trip (to target and back) plus 10 percent extra as a safety margin. For planning purposes any bomb damage short of complete destruction, is regarded as a miss because the bridge is still usable.

Devise a heuristic procedure which will enable you to allocate planes to targets, so that the probability of success is maximized. In calculating the probability of success for any particular allocation, you will probably find the following method easiest:

Suppose, the allocation decided upon is for all planes to be assigned to bridge A (this allocation is not within the fuel limit). Then:

$$
\begin{aligned}
\text{Probability of success} &= (1-\text{probability of failure}) \\
&= [1-(1-.08)^{20}(1-.06)^{15}] \\
&= [1-(0.1887)(0.3953)] \\
&= 1-0.0746 \\
&= 0.9254
\end{aligned}
$$

16.4 A perennial problem which confronts the administrators in many universities and colleges is that of scheduling classes and examinations. The problem is compounded many times when the number and size of classrooms become limiting factors, when new courses are being introduced, when students are allowed a high degree of latitude in selecting subject combinations, and when student enrolments for individual subjects vary greatly from expected numbers. The problem below is a miniversion of the type of timetabling problem that often has to be solved by college administrators. Examinations for twelve subjects have to be scheduled. Each subject involves two or three courses, each with a three-hour final examination. Because some students are studying more than one subject, examinations in certain subjects cannot be scheduled at the same time. The following table gives the appropriate details.

Subject	Number of courses with 3-hour examinations	Number of students involved	Incompatible subjects
A	2	149	B
B	2	172	A
C	2	198	L
D	3	248	F
E	2	44	K
F	2	139	D
G	3	24	J
H	2	19	I
I	3	49	H
J	2	58	G
K	2	197	E
L	2	19	C

Only three examination rooms are available having the following capacities:

- Room I   200 students
- Room II   230 students
- Room III 300 students

The policy governing the scheduling of examinations is as follows:

(i) Examinations in incompatible subjects cannot be scheduled at the same time.
(ii) There should be at least one full day separating course examinations in the

same subject.   For example if the first course examination in subject A is scheduled for day 1, the next course examination cannot be scheduled until day 3 or later.

(iii) Examinations shall be held between 9:30 AM and 12:30 PM, thus allowing students to prepare for any examinations they might have on the following day.

(iv) All examinations should be completed within 5 days.

(v) Examinations in different subjects may be allocated to the same room on the same day, provided that the capacity of the room is not exceeded.

(vi) There should be no split classes.   That is, all students sitting for the same course examination should be in the same room at the same time.

(vii) Whenever a room is used for an examination, there shall be six supervisors appointed to ensure that the examinations are properly conducted.

Competent supervisors are difficult to find and expensive to pay ($60 per supervisor per examination).   The college administrators wish to minimize the cost of employing supervisors.

(a) Devise a heuristic procedure which can be used to allocate the course examinations to rooms, subject to the stated policy.   Write the procedure as clearly as possible.   Apply it to the given problem and write the solution achieved.

(b) Attempt the following similar problem using the procedure you have written. Details of subject courses, class sizes, and incompatible subjects are given in the following table.

Subject	Number of courses with examinations	Number of students involved	Incompatible subjects
A	3	293	G
B	3	177	H
C	3	369	I
D	2	179	J
E	2	58	K
F	3	109	L
G	2	178	A
H	2	344	B
I	2	223	C
J	2	159	D
K	2	24	E
L	2	107	F

The rooms available are:

- Room I   student capacity, 200
- Room II   student capacity, 250
- Room III   student capacity, 300
- Room IV   student capacity, 400

Room I is not available on days 4 and 5.   The scheduling policy is as for the previous problem.   (Be careful!)

(c) Repeat problem 16.2(b) using the following room availability data.

- Room I   student capacity, 200
- Room II   student capacity, 250
- Room III   student capacity, 300
- Room IV   student capacity, 350
- Room V   student capacity, 400

16.5 Prison authorities were faced with a dilemma. Seven dangerous criminals had to be transferred from the prison at Lokuptown to the high security prison at Tower Hill at the same time. There were only two suitable vans available, each with sufficient capacity for six prisoners, but the chief prison warden did not want the criminals to come into contact with each other because of the possibility of an escape plot. He realized that individual transfer was impossible, and the anxiety this created began to activate his ulcer. The chief discussed the problem with his son, Herbert (who was at the time studying operations research). Herbert suggested that the best course of action would be to allocate the seven criminals to the two vans so that his father's anxiety was minimized. The chief agreed, and enquired how they might determine such an allocation. Herbert thought briefly, and then, by questioning his father, he constructed the following regret matrix.

Regret Matrix

	Alvin	Benny	Chuck	Dick	Edwin	Fred	Garth
Alvin	—	4	1	6	9	3	4
Benny	4	—	7	2	5	6	2
Chuck	1	7	—	8	1	5	3
Dick	6	2	8	—	7	1	4
Edwin	9	5	1	7	—	6	9
Fred	3	6	5	1	6	—	8
Garth	4	2	3	4	9	8	—

Thus, if Alvin and Benny are placed in the same van the chief will feel a regret of 4 (on a regret scale 0 to 9); if Alvin and Chuck are in the same van there will be a regret of 1, and so on. After its meaning had been explained, the chief warden agreed that the regrets were linearly additive. Thus, a straight alphabetical allocation of Alvin, Benny, Chuck, and Dick to van 1 and the others to van 2 would yield a total regret of 51 as follows:

Van 1: Alvin   0   Van 2: Ed   0
        Benny   4   Fred   6
        Chuck   8 $(= 7+1)$ Garth   17 $(= 9+8)$
        Dick   16 $(= 6+2+8)$
                ——   ——
                28   23
                ——   ——

Therefore the total regret is $28 + 23 = 51$. Such an allocation would certainly not sooth the ulcer!

After obtaining the above information, Herbert set to work with pencil and paper. Five minutes later he handed his father two lists of names. "Ah! I'm feeling better already," exclaimed the chief warden.

(a) Devise a heuristic procedure that will yield a solution which might have been equally pleasing to the chief warden. Write the steps of the solution procedure as concisely as possible and the details of the allocation achieved by its application to the prisoner transfer problem.

(b) Apply the heuristic procedure which you have devised to the following problem. Twelve individual tasks have to be allocated between three facilities where each facility has sufficient capacity to handle all tasks. However, there exists the possibility that tasks allocated to the same facility may interfere with each other. The consequences of such interference are reflected in the following regret matrix.

Regret matrix

	A	B	C	D	E	F	G	H	I	J	K	L
A	—	2	4	8	8	9	4	3	9	6	1	6
B	2	—	7	9	6	1	3	8	4	6	7	9
C	4	7	—	1	7	2	4	6	9	4	2	8
D	8	9	1	—	4	1	3	6	9	1	1	4
E	8	6	7	4	—	4	5	1	4	2	3	6
F	9	1	2	1	4	—	8	2	9	4	6	3
G	4	3	4	3	5	8	—	9	8	6	6	9
H	3	8	6	6	1	2	9	—	3	4	8	1
I	9	4	9	9	4	9	8	3	—	2	6	8
J	6	6	4	1	2	4	6	4	2	—	5	6
K	1	7	2	1	3	6	6	8	6	5	—	3
L	6	9	8	4	6	3	9	1	8	6	3	—

The regrets are linearly additive. Allocate the tasks to the three facilities so that the total regret is at a reasonably low level.

16.6 Young Simon thought he could corner the neighborhood lemonade market during the summer school vacation. There were two very productive lemon trees in his home garden, so the only material cost would be for sugar. As the cellar at home was very cool, he decided that he could store the drink there almost indefinitely, if it was properly bottled once it had been made. He estimated that while he would sell only one glass on the first day, as the word about his good lemonade was spread, sales would grow by one glass per day to a total demand of 20 per day on day 20, after which he would have to close the business because he had to return to school. The only drawback in the scheme was that he did not want to do the messy job of making the lemonade. He approached his sister, Mary, with an offer of $2.00 if she would make the batch of 210 glasses of lemonade. Mary agreed. Alfred, Simon's younger brother, wanted to get a part of the action, but Simon replied that Alfred did not possess any resource or skill necessary to the manufacture and marketing of lemonade. Alfred complained to their mother, who, to have some peace and quiet, told Alfred that he could have the rights to the cellar which he could lease to Simon.   Alfred, realizing that Simon had no alternative storage facilities, decided to extract as much of Simon's profit as possible for himself.   He sternly announced to Simon that the storage charge would be 0.5 cents per glass per day and that he expected the $14.35 to be paid in installments at five-day intervals.   Mary was outraged at this as she was only to receive $2.00 for her labor. At first Simon was unhappy as he had planned to sell the lemonade at 10 cents per glass, and the inventory charge would eat well into his profits.   On the other hand, he recognized such costs as legitimate business expenses and realized they could not be avoided if the project went ahead.   "Can they be reduced?" he asked himself.   He attacked the problem with the zeal of a true entrepreneur.   He emerged from his "office" 30 minutes later and announced that so long as Mary was still prepared to accept $2.00 per batch to make the lemonade, he would pay her $6.00 to make three batches, one of x glasses on day A, one of y glasses on day B, and the third batch of z glasses on day C.   Mary joyously agreed.   "In that case, Alfred, I will only have to pay you $$W$!" Simon concluded.

(a) On the assumption that each batch had to be made at least one day before it went on the market, what are the values of x, y, z, A, B, and C which minimize W?   Would two or four batches have been cheaper for Simon?

(b) Devise the heuristic technique which might have been used by Simon to solve his problem.

(c) Apply the procedure to the following problem:

A battery manufacturer receives an order from a light aircraft manufacturer for 6890 special type batteries, to be delivered over a period of 52 weeks as follows:

At the end of week 1,   5 batteries
At the end of week 2,   10 batteries
At the end of week 3,   15 batteries

.
.
.

At the end of week 52, 260 batteries

The cost of carrying inventory is $2.60 per item per year, while the cost to set up a production run is $450 per setup.   How many production runs should be made; when should they be made; and how many items should be produced on each run so as to keep total setup costs plus inventory costs to a minimum?

16.7   Middle Earth is reapportioning its election districts for its high court of wise men. Women with deep voices and mustaches may qualify, too!   The guiding principle of this reapportionment is one person, one vote.   This means that the 22 regions should be assigned to 4 election districts such that each district has about the same population size, say within a margin of 5 percent from either side of the average. No region should be split, i.e., each should be assigned entirely to only one election district.   Furthermore, to avoid gerrymandering, each district should be contiguous, i.e., it should be possible to walk from each region in a district to all other regions in the same district without leaving the district, and compact, i.e., the centers of all regions in a district should be as close together as possible.   In other words, districts that have a circular shape are preferred to districts that have many arms protruding in all directions.   A suitable measure of compactness is given by the ratio of the

Region Number	Name of Region	Population	Area (square miles)
1	Forlindon	1000	16
2	Ered Luin	2000	15
3	Arnor	1100	70
4	Shire	4100	7
5	Harlindon	1500	32
6	Minhiriath	2600	23
7	Enedhwaith	1000	26
8	Dunland	800	14
9	Rhudaur	3000	40
10	Hithaiglin	2000	24
11	Mirkwood	3500	65
12	Brown Lands	1500	22
13	Wold	1900	11
14	Rohan	2700	31
15	Erednimrais	1500	16
16	Anfalas	3800	30
17	Lebennin	2700	31
18	Anorien	4500	13
19	Ithilien	4000	15
20	Gorgoroth	1500	18
21	Nurn	1000	28
22	South Gondor	1500	38

Distances between centers

From \ To	2	3	4	5	6	7	8	9	10	11	12	13	14	15	16	17	18	19	20	21	22
1	4	12	8	7	12	17	18	15	20	24	27	23	22	20	22	28	28	31	33	36	34
2		8	6	7	10	15	15	12	17	21	25	20	20	19	21	26	26	29	31	33	32
3			5	9	9	12	11	5	10	11	18	13	15	16	18	22	20	23	24	27	27
4				4	5	10	10	7	12	16	18	14	14	13	16	20	20	25	25	27	26
5					5	10	11	10	15	18	21	16	16	13	15	21	21	25	27	29	27
6						5	6	7	11	16	16	12	11	8	11	16	16	20	22	24	22
7							4	7	10	14	12	8	6	4	6	10	10	15	18	20	17
8								6	8	1	2	8	9	6	8	11	10	14	15	18	17
9									8	11	14	9	10	11	13	15	14	17	18	21	21
10										4	8	5	8	13	14	14	12	14	15	18	20
11											8	7	10	16	17	15	13	14	13	17	20
12												5	6	12	12	8	5	6	6	10	12
13													3	9	10	9	7	10	11	14	14
14														6	6	7	6	9	11	13	13
15															3	9	10	13	16	18	14
16																7	8	12	15	18	12
17																	3	8	9	9	9
18																		3	6	8	7
19																			3	5	6
20																				4	8
21																					6

sum of the squared distances between the region centers over the total area of the district. A list of populations, areas for each region, and distances between region centers is given on page 543. Find a heuristic procedure for allocating the regions to districts subject to the population constraint, contiguity, and achieving good compactness.

Map of Middle Earth

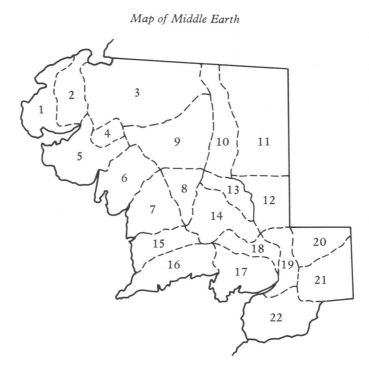

Figure 16-9a.

Region boundaries are based mostly on natural barriers—rivers, mountains, etc., as shown in Tolkien's original map. Region names correspond similarly.

REFERENCES

Ansoff, H. I. "A Quasi-Analytical Method for Long-Range Planning", M. Alexis and C. Wilson, Eds. *Organizational Decision Making.* Englewood Cliffs, N.J.: Prentice-Hall, 1967. An interesting discussion of a problem solving approach which "combines elements of rigor, characteristic of operations research and elements of 'judgemental' insight, typical of the heuristic method". The author ascribes a very narrow meaning to "heuristic method". In the broader sense in which the term is used in the current chapter, the approach which he terms "quasi-analytical" would be classified as heuristic.

Clarkson, G. P. E. "Interactions of Economic Theory and Operations Research", A. R. Oxenfeldt, Ed., *Models of Markets*. New York: Columbia University Press, 1963. Clarkson's contribution is concerned with the theoretical basis for the application of operations research techniques to decision problems of the firm. He advances heuristic techniques involving a satisficing approach as being consistent with behavioral theories of the firm (as opposed to the classical and market theories), and he argues the importance of heuristic methods to operations researchers, particularly in approaching the decision problems of middle management.

Gordon, P. J. "Heuristic Problem Solving", *Business Horizons*, Spring, 1962. The author develops his discussion of heuristic problem solving around a very tricky puzzle and its method of solution. This easy to read article is a must for puzzle addicts.

Hinkle, Charles L., and Alfred A. Kuehn. "Heuristic Models: Mapping the Maze for Management", *California Management Review*, Fall, 1967. A nontechnical introduction to the subject of heuristic problem solving with a brief survey of specific application areas. This article is reprinted in A. Rappaport, Ed., *Information for Decision Making*, Englewood Cliffs, N.J.: Prentice-Hall, 1970. It includes a substantial list of references.

Meier, R. C., W. T. Newell, and H. L. Pazer. *Simulation in Business and Economics*, Englewood Cliffs, N.J.: Prentice-Hall, 1969. Chapter 5 contains an introduction to the nature of heuristic methods along with some detailed examples of the application of the approach. An extensive list of references up to 1968 is included.

Scott, A. J. *Combinatorial Programming, Spatial Analysis and Planning*, London: Methuen and Co., 1971. Chapter 3 contains an exposition of the application of heuristic methods to combinatorial problems. Includes comprehensive reference list.

Simon, H. A. *The New Science of Management Decisions*, New York: Harper and Brothers, 1960. This book contains a series of lectures on the impact of computer technology on managerial decision making. In lecture two, heuristic methods in relation to human problem solving activity are discussed.

———. "The Structure of Ill-Structured Problems", *Artificial Intelligence*, Winter, 1973. The properties of well-structured and ill-structured problems are discussed and the implications of these are examined by use of examples.

For further discussion of heuristic methods and specific applications of the approach the interested reader is referred to the reference lists given by Meier *et al.*, A. J. Scott, and C. L. Hinkle and A. A. Kuehn.

Appendix A

Introduction to Vectors and Simultaneous Equations, and a Matrix Algebra Approach to Linear Programming

The first part of this appendix, Sections A-1 to A-7, briefly develops the concepts of vector analysis and simultaneous equations necessary for the main body of the text. In the second part of the appendix, Section A-8, linear programming is derived in terms of matrices for readers who already have a working knowledge of this type of mathematics. This latter part is not self-contained, it relies on the ideas developed in Chapters 2 and 3. Therefore, it is recommended that those chapters be read before Section A-8 is studied.

A-1 VECTORS

We are familiar with the notion of expressing a point in terms of an origin and co-ordinate axes. This is what most graphical analysis does. Each point in 2 dimensions (*2-space*) uniquely represents an *ordered pair* of real numbers. The pair is *ordered* because it matters which order the numbers are in; e.g., $(0, 1)$ is not the same as $(1, 0)$. Also, each point uniquely represents a line from the origin to the point. This we will call a *vector*. The vector has *direction* (from the origin to the point) and *magnitude* (the length of the line), as illustrated in Figure A-1. Thus, in 2-space there is a unique correspondence between vectors directed from the origin and ordered pairs of real numbers.

These concepts can be generalized to n-space. Every vector in n-space is uniquely represented by an ordered set of n real numbers (the *elements* of the vector). We will write the vector, in terms of its elements, as $(a_1, a_2, a_3, ..., a_n) = \mathbf{a}$.

Vectors are significant in that they facilitate manipulation of points and, thus, ordered sets of real numbers. Take the two points, $\mathbf{a} = (a_1, a_2, ..., a_n)$ and $\mathbf{b} = (b_1, b_2, ..., b_n)$. How do we add these or multiply them? How do we find the distance between them? Geometric ideas in 2-space and 3-space can be generalized to enable algebraic analysis of points in n-space.

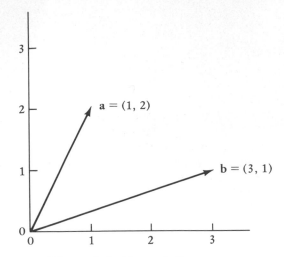

Figure A-1. *Vectors in 2-space.*

A-2 MANIPULATION OF VECTORS

In 2-space, the sum of two vectors, e.g., $(1, 2)$ and $(3, 1)$, is given by the sum of corresponding elements $(1+3, 2+1) = (4, 3)$. This procedure is represented diagrammatically in Figure A-2 by a parallelogram.

When generalizing to n-space, it is necessary to insist that vectors can only be summed if they exist in the same space. For example, the 2-space vector $(2, 1)$ cannot be added to the 4-space vector $(1, 0, 1, 0)$.

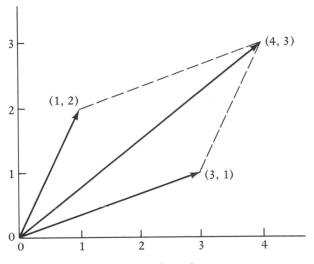

Figure A-2. *Sum of vectors.*

ADDITION OF VECTORS

Given two vectors in n-space, $\mathbf{a} = (a_1, a_2, \ldots, a_n)$ and $\mathbf{b} = (b_1, b_2, \ldots, b_n)$, their sum is $\mathbf{a} + \mathbf{b} = (a_1 + b_1, a_2 + b_2, \ldots, a_n + b_n)$.

Subtraction of vectors follows immediately. If $-\mathbf{b} = (-b_1, -b_2, \ldots, -b_n)$, then $\mathbf{a} - \mathbf{b} = \mathbf{a} + (-\mathbf{b}) = (a_1 - b_1, a_2 - b_2, \ldots, a_n - b_n)$.

Before we discuss multiplication of vectors it will be necessary to distinguish between a *row vector* and a *column vector*. If the elements are written $[g_1, \ldots, g_n]$ it is a row vector, if the elements are written

$$\begin{bmatrix} g_1 \\ \cdot \\ \cdot \\ \cdot \\ g_n \end{bmatrix}$$

it is a column vector. There is no conceptual difference between them; it is purely a matter of usage. In almost every case that we encounter, a vector will be a column vector. So, we will assume that *all vectors are column vectors unless otherwise stated* (and for convenience they will be written as row vectors). If $\mathbf{a}$ is a column vector, we can denote its row vector equivalent as $\mathbf{a}'$.

A useful multiplication of vectors is the *scalar product*. It is called the scalar product because the result of the multiplication is a *scalar* (a real number, not a vector).

SCALAR PRODUCT

If $\mathbf{a}$ and $\mathbf{b}$ are vectors in n-space then the scalar product is

$$\mathbf{a}'\mathbf{b} = \mathbf{b}'\mathbf{a} = \sum_{j=1}^{n} a_j b_j = c$$

where c is the scalar.

An n-dimensional space is called *Euclidean space* (E^n) when the distance between two points $\mathbf{a}$ and $\mathbf{b}$ is measured by the n-dimensional extension of Pythagoras' Theorem. In 2-dimensional Euclidean Space, E^2, the distance between points $\mathbf{a}$ and $\mathbf{b}$ is shown in Figure A-3. The distance γ from $\mathbf{a}$ to $\mathbf{b}$ is the length of the side AB of the triangle ABC. By Pythagoras' Theorem:

$$\gamma^2 = (b_1 - a_1)^2 + (a_2 - b_2)^2 = (a_1 - b_1)^2 + (a_2 - b_2)^2$$

and

$$\gamma = \sqrt{\left[\sum_{j=1}^{2} (a_j - b_j)^2 \right]}$$

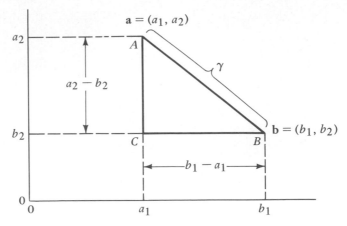

Figure A-3. *Euclidean distance in* E^2.

I.1 n-space, E^n, distance is defined as:

DISTANCE IN EUCLIDEAN SPACE, E^n

The distance between $\mathbf{a} = (a_1, a_2, ..., a_n)$ and $\mathbf{b} = (b_1, b_2, ..., b_n)$ is

$$\sqrt{\left[\sum_{j=1}^{n} (a_j - b_j)^2 \right]}$$

A simple extension of the idea of distance between two points gives the *length of a vector*. The length of a vector is the distance between the origin and the point identifying the vector.

LENGTH OF A VECTOR

The length of a vector $\mathbf{a} = (a_1, a_2, ..., a_n)$ in E^n is

$$\sqrt{\sum_{j=1}^{n} (a_j)^2}$$

Another aspect of vectors which is of importance to us is the multiplication of a vector by a scalar.

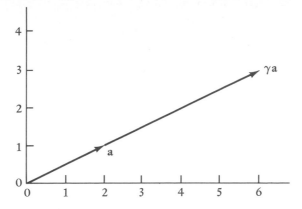

Figure A-4. *Multiplication by a scalar.*

MULTIPLICATION BY A SCALAR

If $\mathbf{a} = (a_1, \ldots, a_n)$ is a vector in E^n and λ is a scalar, then

$$\lambda\mathbf{a} = (\lambda a_1, \lambda a_2, \ldots, \lambda a_n)$$

For example, if $\mathbf{a} = (2, 1)$ and $\lambda = 3$, $\lambda\mathbf{a} = (6, 3)$.   This is illustrated in Figure A-4.

A-3 SPECIAL VECTORS

A number of commonly used vectors are given special names.   All definitions are in Euclidean space, E^n.

NULL VECTOR

The null vector is the vector whose elements are all zero:

$$\mathbf{0} = (0, 0, \ldots, 0)$$

The null vector corresponds to the origin.

SUM VECTOR

The sum vector is the vector whose elements are all unity:

$$\mathbf{1} = (1, 1, \ldots, 1)$$

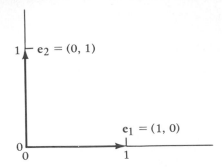

Figure A-5. *Unit vectors in* E^2.

UNIT VECTOR e_i

The unit vector $\mathbf{e}_i$ is the vector with unity as its ith element, and all other elements are zero.

Examples of unit vectors are $\mathbf{e}_1 = (1, 0, ..., 0)$, $\mathbf{e}_2 = (0, 1, 0, ..., 0)$, etc. In 2-space there are 2 unit vectors, and in n-space there are n unit vectors. Geometrically, these vectors lie along the axes of the space and have unit length. Figure A-5 shows the vectors in 2-space.

A-4 REPRESENTING A VECTOR AS A LINEAR COMBINATION OF OTHER VECTORS

If we have a set of vectors in E^n, $\mathbf{a}_1, \mathbf{a}_2, ..., \mathbf{a}_r$, we say that $\mathbf{b}$ is expressed as a *linear combination* of these vectors if for some scalars $\gamma_1, \gamma_2, ..., \gamma_r$:

(A-1) $$\mathbf{b} = \gamma_1 \mathbf{a}_1 + \gamma_2 \mathbf{a}_2 + \gamma_3 \mathbf{a}_3 + \cdots + \gamma_r \mathbf{a}_r$$

Expression (A-1) combines the ideas of vector addition and multiplication by a scalar. We are finding proportions (the γ_i) of the vectors $\mathbf{a}_1, ..., \mathbf{a}_r$ which sum to $\mathbf{b}$.

In Figure A-6 we illustrate this for the case of $\mathbf{a}_1 = (2, 1)$, $\mathbf{a}_2 = (1, 3)$, and $\mathbf{b} = (8, 9)$:

(A-2) $$\mathbf{b} = \gamma_1 \mathbf{a}_1 + \gamma_2 \mathbf{a}_2$$

or

$$\begin{bmatrix} 8 \\ 9 \end{bmatrix} = 3 \begin{bmatrix} 2 \\ 1 \end{bmatrix} + 2 \begin{bmatrix} 1 \\ 3 \end{bmatrix}$$

The proportions are $\gamma_1 = 3$, and $\gamma_2 = 2$, i.e., $\mathbf{b}$ is 3 times $\mathbf{a}_1$ plus 2 times $\mathbf{a}_2$.

A special case of a linear combination is where $\sum_i \gamma_i = 1$, with all $\gamma_i \geqslant 0$. For the two vector case, this defines a vector on the straight line between the vectors (*line segment*).

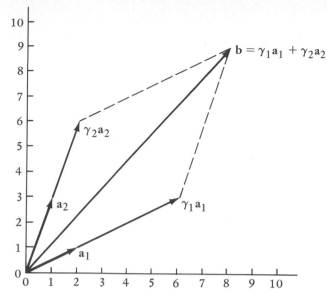

Figure A-6. *Representing* **b** *as a linear combination of* $\mathbf{a}_1, \mathbf{a}_2$.

For example, let $\mathbf{a}_1 = \begin{bmatrix} 12 \\ 9 \end{bmatrix}$, $\mathbf{a}_2 = \begin{bmatrix} 9 \\ 3 \end{bmatrix}$, and let $\gamma_1 = 1/3$, $\gamma_2 = 2/3$. For simplicity, let $\gamma_1 = \gamma = 1/3$, and let $\gamma_2 = (1-\gamma) = 2/3$. We now look at

$$\mathbf{b} = \gamma\mathbf{a}_1 + (1-\gamma)\mathbf{a}_2 = \frac{1}{3}\begin{bmatrix} 12 \\ 9 \end{bmatrix} + \frac{2}{3}\begin{bmatrix} 9 \\ 3 \end{bmatrix} = \begin{bmatrix} 10 \\ 5 \end{bmatrix}$$

This lies on the straight line between $\mathbf{a}_1$ and $\mathbf{a}_2$. In fact, for any $0 \leqslant \gamma \leqslant 1$, the vector $\mathbf{b} = \gamma\mathbf{a}_1 + (1-\gamma)\mathbf{a}_2$ lies γ of the way from $\mathbf{a}_2$ to $\mathbf{a}_1$ on the line segment. Figure A-7 illustrates this.

The concept provides us with a definition of the line segment between two vectors, or points.

LINE SEGMENT BETWEEN $\mathbf{a}_1$ AND $\mathbf{a}_2$

The line segment between two points, $\mathbf{a}_1$ and $\mathbf{a}_2$, is the set of points

$$\mathbf{b} = \gamma\mathbf{a}_1 + (1-\gamma)\mathbf{a}_2,$$

for all γ, $0 \leqslant \gamma \leqslant 1$.

This definition can be extended to any number of points. In its more general form this linear combination is called a *convex combination*, and represents a segment of a plane. The plane segment is called the *convex hull* of the points.

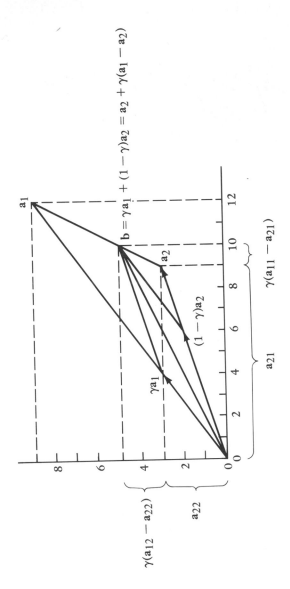

Figure A-7. *Line segment between two vectors.*

554

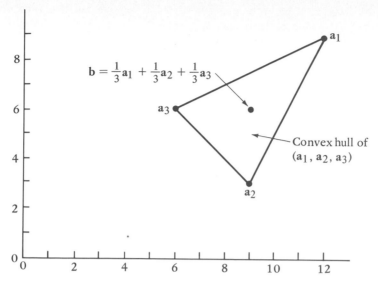

Figure A-8. *Convex hull of three points in* E^2.

CONVEX HULL OF THE POINTS a_1, a_2, ..., a_p IN E^n

The convex hull in E^n, of p points $\mathbf{a}_1, \mathbf{a}_2, \mathbf{a}_3, ..., \mathbf{a}_p$ is the set of points $\mathbf{b} = \sum_{i=1}^{p} \gamma_i \mathbf{a}_i$, for all γ_i, such that $\sum_{i=1}^{p} \gamma_i = 1$, and all $\gamma_i \geqslant 0$.

Consider the points $\mathbf{a}_1 = \begin{bmatrix} 12 \\ 9 \end{bmatrix}$, $\mathbf{a}_2 = \begin{bmatrix} 9 \\ 3 \end{bmatrix}$, $\mathbf{a}_3 = \begin{bmatrix} 6 \\ 6 \end{bmatrix}$.   The convex hull of these points is shown in Figure A-8.   If $\gamma_1 = 1/3$, $\gamma_2 = 1/3$, $\gamma_3 = 1/3$ (so $\sum_{i=1}^{3} \gamma_i = 1$, and all $\gamma_i \geqslant 0$) then

$$\mathbf{b} = \frac{1}{3} \begin{bmatrix} 12 \\ 9 \end{bmatrix} + \frac{1}{3} \begin{bmatrix} 9 \\ 3 \end{bmatrix} + \frac{1}{3} \begin{bmatrix} 6 \\ 6 \end{bmatrix} = \begin{bmatrix} 9 \\ 6 \end{bmatrix}$$

A-5 LINEAR INDEPENDENCE, SPANNING SET, AND BASIS

We now want to define some properties of sets of vectors.   These are crucial for Chapter 3.

If we have a set of vectors in E^n, $\mathbf{a}_1, \mathbf{a}_2, \ldots, \mathbf{a}_r$, we say that they are *linearly independent* if no one of them can be expressed as a linear combination of the remaining ones.

LINEAR INDEPENDENCE

A set of vectors $\mathbf{a}_1, \mathbf{a}_2, \ldots, \mathbf{a}_r$ is linearly independent if $\gamma_1 \mathbf{a}_1 + \gamma_2 \mathbf{a}_2 + \cdots + \gamma_r \mathbf{a}_r = 0$ holds only if $\gamma_1 = \gamma_2 = \cdots = \gamma_r = 0$.

A set of vectors is *linearly dependent* if it is not linearly independent.

Consider the set of vectors $\mathbf{a}_1, \mathbf{a}_2, \mathbf{a}_3, \mathbf{a}_4$ in E^2 where $\mathbf{a}_1 = (2,1)$, $\mathbf{a}_2 = (1,3)$, $\mathbf{a}_3 = (2,3)$, $\mathbf{a}_4 = (4,2)$. These are shown in Figure A-9.

The set $(\mathbf{a}_1, \mathbf{a}_2)$ is linearly independent since neither of the vectors can be expressed in terms of the other. This is clear geometrically from Figure A-9. Algebraically, only $\gamma_1 = \gamma_2 = 0$ will satisfy

$$\gamma_1 \begin{bmatrix} 2 \\ 1 \end{bmatrix} + \gamma_2 \begin{bmatrix} 1 \\ 3 \end{bmatrix} = \begin{bmatrix} 0 \\ 0 \end{bmatrix}$$

There is no finite scalar $(-\gamma_2/\gamma_1)$ such that $\begin{bmatrix} 2 \\ 1 \end{bmatrix} = (-\gamma_2/\gamma_1) \begin{bmatrix} 1 \\ 3 \end{bmatrix}$. However,

the set $(\mathbf{a}_1, \mathbf{a}_2, \mathbf{a}_3)$ is not linearly independent. Geometrically, we see that $\mathbf{a}_3$ can be expressed as a linear combination of $(\mathbf{a}_1, \mathbf{a}_2)$. Algebraically, $\gamma_1 \mathbf{a}_1 + \gamma_2 \mathbf{a}_2 + \gamma_3 \mathbf{a}_3 =$

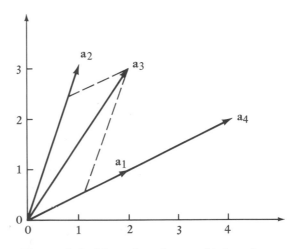

Figure A-9. *Linear dependence and independence.*

0 is satisfied by (at least) $\gamma_1 = 3/5$, $\gamma_2 = 4/5$, $\gamma_3 = -1$. In fact, no set of three vectors in E^2 can be linearly independent. What about the set $(\mathbf{a}_1, \mathbf{a}_4)$? We can write $2\mathbf{a}_1 = \mathbf{a}_4$, so $\gamma_1 = 2$, $\gamma_4 = -1$ gives us $\gamma_1 \mathbf{a}_1 + \gamma_4 \mathbf{a}_4 = 0$. The set is linearly dependent. Is the set $(\mathbf{a}_1)$ linearly independent?

The set of vectors $\mathbf{a}_1, \mathbf{a}_2, ..., \mathbf{a}_r$ in E^n is a *spanning set* of E^n if every vector in E^n can be expressed as a linear combination of the set. From Figure A-9 we can see that no less than two vectors are required to form a spanning set in E^2. So, for example, the set $(\mathbf{a}_1, \mathbf{a}_2)$ is a spanning set and so is $(\mathbf{a}_1, \mathbf{a}_2, \mathbf{a}_3)$. However, the set $(\mathbf{a}_1)$ is not a spanning set, and neither is $(\mathbf{a}_1, \mathbf{a}_4)$, since many vectors in the space cannot be expressed as linear combinations of either of these sets.

A set of vectors $\mathbf{a}_1, \mathbf{a}_2, ..., \mathbf{a}_r$ in E^n is called a *basis* if it is both linearly independent and a spanning set in E^n. Our discussion of linear independence showed us that no set of $r > n$ vectors in E^n could be linearly independent. Similarly, no set of $r < n$ vectors in E^n could span the space. So we conclude that a basis must have exactly n vectors in E^n. Looking at Figure A-9 we see that $(\mathbf{a}_1, \mathbf{a}_2)$ is a basis, and so is $(\mathbf{a}_3, \mathbf{a}_4)$. How many other bases are there? Is $(\mathbf{a}_1, \mathbf{a}_4)$ a basis? Clearly, it is not a basis because it is not linearly independent.

BASIS IN E^n

A set of vectors $\mathbf{a}_1, \mathbf{a}_2, ..., \mathbf{a}_r$ in E^n is a basis if it is a linearly independent spanning set of E^n. If it is a basis then $r = n$.

A-6 MATRICES

Let us look at a few properties of matrices that will be useful in Chapter 8. There are a number of ways of understanding a matrix. We could think of it as a vector of vectors, or as a rectangular array of numbers arranged in rows and columns. Whichever way we perceive it, the result is the same. The following is an example of a matrix:

$$\mathbf{A} = \begin{bmatrix} 2 & 1 & 0 \\ 1 & 3 & 1 \end{bmatrix}$$

The number of rows m and number of columns n of $\mathbf{A}$ define the *dimensions* of $\mathbf{A}$. So $\mathbf{A}$ is a 2×3 (two by three) matrix. If the number of rows and columns are the same it is a *square matrix*. Let $\mathbf{A} = (\mathbf{a}_1, \mathbf{a}_2, ..., \mathbf{a}_n)$ and $\mathbf{B} = (\mathbf{b}_1, \mathbf{b}_2, ..., \mathbf{b}_n)$ be row vectors of column vectors in E^m. The sum of $\mathbf{A}$ and $\mathbf{B}$ follows from the addition of vectors:

$$\mathbf{A} + \mathbf{B} = (\mathbf{a}_1 + \mathbf{b}_1, \mathbf{a}_2 + \mathbf{b}_2, ..., \mathbf{a}_n + \mathbf{b}_n)$$

Expanding this further gives:

ADDITION OF MATRICES

Given two matrices

$$
\mathbf{A} = \begin{bmatrix} a_{11} & a_{12} & \cdots & a_{1n} \\ a_{21} & a_{22} & \cdots & a_{2n} \\ \vdots & \vdots & & \vdots \\ a_{m1} & a_{m2} & \cdots & a_{mn} \end{bmatrix}
\qquad
\mathbf{B} = \begin{bmatrix} b_{11} & b_{12} & \cdots & b_{1n} \\ b_{21} & b_{22} & \cdots & b_{2n} \\ \vdots & \vdots & & \vdots \\ b_{m1} & b_{m2} & \cdots & b_{mn} \end{bmatrix}
$$

their sum is

$$
\mathbf{A} + \mathbf{B} = \begin{bmatrix} a_{11}+b_{11} & a_{12}+b_{12} & \cdots & a_{1n}+b_{1n} \\ a_{21}+b_{21} & a_{22}+b_{22} & \cdots & a_{2n}+b_{2n} \\ \vdots & \vdots & \vdots & \vdots \\ a_{m1}+b_{m1} & a_{m2}+b_{m2} & \cdots & a_{mn}+b_{mn} \end{bmatrix}
$$

The product of matrices is also a generalization of the scalar product of vectors, though it is not as obvious as it is for addition. Let $\mathbf{A}$ be an $m \times r$ matrix, and $\mathbf{B}$ an $r \times n$ matrix. Consider $\mathbf{A}$ as a column vector of m row vectors in E^r, and $\mathbf{B}$ as a row vector of n column vectors in E^r.

$$
\mathbf{A} = \begin{bmatrix} \mathbf{a}_1 \\ \mathbf{a}_2 \\ \vdots \\ \mathbf{a}_m \end{bmatrix}
$$

$$
\mathbf{B} = [\mathbf{b}_1, \mathbf{b}_2, \ldots, \mathbf{b}_n]
$$

PRODUCT OF MATRICES

The product of $\mathbf{A}$ and $\mathbf{B}$ is an $m \times n$ matrix:

$$
\mathbf{AB} = \begin{bmatrix} \mathbf{a}_1\mathbf{b}_1 & \mathbf{a}_1\mathbf{b}_2 & \cdots & \mathbf{a}_1\mathbf{b}_n \\ \mathbf{a}_2\mathbf{b}_1 & \mathbf{a}_2\mathbf{b}_2 & \cdots & \mathbf{a}_2\mathbf{b}_n \\ \vdots & \vdots & & \vdots \\ \mathbf{a}_m\mathbf{b}_1 & \mathbf{a}_m\mathbf{b}_2 & \cdots & \mathbf{a}_m\mathbf{b}_n \end{bmatrix}
$$

where $\quad \mathbf{a}_i\mathbf{b}_j = \sum_{k=1}^{r} a_{ik}b_{kj}$ is the scalar product of the ith row of $\mathbf{A}$ and the jth column of $\mathbf{B}$.

However, note that $\mathbf{BA}$ will only be defined when $m = n$.

If $\mathbf{A}$ is a square matrix of dimension n, we can write $\mathbf{AA}$ as $\mathbf{A}^2$. Let $\mathbf{a}_i$ be the

ith row, and $\mathbf{a}_j$ the jth column of $\mathbf{A}$; the element of $\mathbf{A}^2$ in row i and column j is $\mathbf{a}_i \mathbf{a}_j = \sum_{k=1}^{n} a_{ik} a_{kj}$.   More generally,

$$\mathbf{A}^k = \mathbf{A}\mathbf{A}^{k-1} = \underbrace{\mathbf{A}\mathbf{A}\mathbf{A}\cdots\mathbf{A}}_{k \text{ terms}}$$

It is often convenient for us to view a vector as a matrix with only one row or column. Thus, if $\mathbf{c} = [c_1, c_2, \dots, c_m]$ is a row vector of m elements ($1 \times m$ matrix), and $\mathbf{A}$ is an $m \times n$ matrix, the product $\mathbf{c}\mathbf{A}$ is a row vector of n elements:

$$\mathbf{c}\mathbf{A} = \left[\sum_{i=1}^{m} c_i a_{i1}, \ \sum_{i=1}^{m} c_i a_{i2}, \ \dots, \ \sum_{i=1}^{m} c_i a_{in} \right]$$

A-7 LINEAR SIMULTANEOUS EQUATIONS

Let us consider the problem of finding values of the variables x_1 and x_2 that satisfy simultaneously the linear equations:

(A-3)
$$2x_1 + x_2 = 8$$
$$x_1 + 3x_2 = 9$$

A pair of values for x_1 and x_2 satisfying (A-3) is called a *solution* to the equations. A *unique solution* exists when only one pair (x_1, x_2) will satisfy the equations, and there is *no solution* if no pair of values satisfies the equations.

We see problem (A-3) graphically in Figure A-10.   The problem asks for those x_1 and x_2 that are common to both of the equation lines—in this case a single point, point A.   The solution values are $x_1 = 3$ and $x_2 = 2$.

Consider next the equations:

(A-4)
$$2x_1 + x_2 = 8$$
$$x_1 + 3x_2 = 9$$
$$x_1 + x_2 = 4$$

There is no solution to (A-4).   No pair (x_1, x_2) exists that satisfies all three equations simultaneously.   The equations are *inconsistent*.   This is seen clearly in Figure A-10.   Had the last equation been $x_1 + x_2 = 5$, point A would have provided the unique solution.   In that case any two of the three equations would have generated the solution, so one of the equations is *redundant*.

Let us change the problem again.   Consider the single equation (A-5):

(A-5)
$$2x_1 + x_2 = 8$$

What are the solutions to this equation?   Certainly, $x_1 = 3$, $x_2 = 2$ satisfies the equation, but so does $x_1 = 4$, $x_2 = 0$, and in fact all points on the line $2x_1 + x_2 = 8$. There is an infinite number of solutions.   Some specific solutions can be found by setting one of the variables to some value, e.g., set $x_1 = 0$, then $x_2 = 8$.   We will find some such solutions particularly useful.

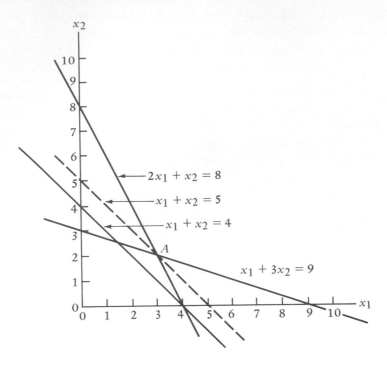

Figure A-10. *Simultaneous equations.*

Let us collect the results we have established for the two-variable case:

(i) Two variables and more than two equations normally have no solution.
(ii) Two variables and two equations normally have a unique solution.
(iii) Two variables and less than two equations normally have an infinite number of solutions,
(iv) Redundant equations may reduce (i) to cases (ii) or (iii), and case (ii) to case (iii).
(v) Inconsistant equations in case (ii) result in no solution.

Provide examples of cases (iv) and (v).

These results generalize to the *n* variable case:

(i) *n* variables and more than *n* equations have no solution unless there are redundant equations (the solution may be unique, or there may be an infinite number of solutions);
(ii) *n* variables and *n* equations have a unique solution unless the equations are inconsistant (there is no solution) or some equations are redundant (there are an infinite number of solutions);
(iii) *n* variables and less than *n* equations have an infinite number of solutions unless there are inconsistant equations (there is no solution).

You may have noticed that (A-3) is the same problem as (A-2). In (A-3) we were solving for x_1 and x_2, while in (A-2) for γ_1 and γ_2, yet the answer was the same. The solution of simultaneous linear equations is synonymous with finding the linear combination of **b** in terms of $\mathbf{a}_1$ and $\mathbf{a}_2$ where **b** is the vector of the parameters on the right-hand side of the equations, and $\mathbf{a}_1$ and $\mathbf{a}_2$ are the vectors of the coefficients of x_1 and x_2, respectively.

For an n variable system with m equations, the solution of the simultaneous equations is the same as finding the linear combination of **b** in terms of $\mathbf{a}_1, \mathbf{a}_2, \ldots, \mathbf{a}_n$. The vectors $\mathbf{b}, \mathbf{a}_1, \mathbf{a}_2, \ldots, \mathbf{a}_n$ are vectors in E^m. When the equations have a unique solution there is only one linear combination of **b** in terms of $\mathbf{a}_1, \mathbf{a}_2, \ldots, \mathbf{a}_n$. When there is an infinite number of solutions, there is an infinite number of linear combinations of **b** in terms of $\mathbf{a}_1, \mathbf{a}_2, \ldots, \mathbf{a}_n$, and when there is no solution then there is no way of constructing the linear combination. For example, in Figure A-11,

(i) **b** in terms of $\mathbf{a}_1$ only, has no solution;
(ii) **b** in terms of $\mathbf{a}_1$ and $\mathbf{a}_2$ has a unique solution;
(iii) **b** in terms of $\mathbf{a}_1, \mathbf{a}_2, \mathbf{a}_3$ has an infinite number of solutions.

These correspond to the equation systems:

(i) $2x_1 = 8$
$\quad x_1 = 9$
(ii) $2x_1 + x_2 = 8$
$\quad x_1 + 3x_2 = 9$
(iii) $2x_1 + x_2 + 3x_3 = 8$
$\quad x_1 + 3x_2 + 3x_3 = 9$

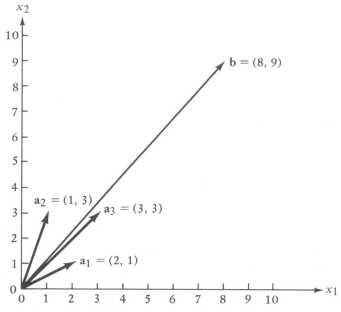

Figure A-11. *Vector representation of simultaneous equations.*

*A-8 LINEAR PROGRAMMING IN MATRIX NOTATION

In this portion we assume that the reader is familiar with the concepts of matrix inversion. We will write the linear program in matrix and vector notation as:

$$\text{maximize } z = \mathbf{cx}$$

(A-6) $$\text{subject to } \mathbf{Ax} = \mathbf{b}$$

$$\mathbf{x} \geqslant 0$$

where z is a scalar
   $\mathbf{x}$ is a column vector in E^n
   $\mathbf{c}$ is a row vector in E^n
   $\mathbf{b}$ is a column vector in E^m
   $\mathbf{A}$ is a $m \times n$ dimensional matrix.

A basic set of columns of $\mathbf{A}$ form a nonsingular matrix $\mathbf{B}$. There is no loss in generality in assuming that the rank of $\mathbf{A}$ is m, and thus $\mathbf{B}$ is an $m \times m$ matrix (we assume that there are no redundant constraints).

The basic solution corresponding to $\mathbf{B}$ is denoted by $\mathbf{x}_B$. If $\mathbf{R}$ is the matrix of nonbasic columns of $\mathbf{A}$, and $\mathbf{x}_R$ is the vector of nonbasic variables, then

(A-7) $$\mathbf{Bx}_B + \mathbf{Rx}_R = \mathbf{b}$$

Since $\mathbf{x}_R = \mathbf{0}$ (by definition):

(A-8) $$\mathbf{Bx}_B = \mathbf{b}$$

and since $\mathbf{B}$ is nonsingular:

(A-9) $$\mathbf{x}_B = \mathbf{B}^{-1}\mathbf{b}$$

where $\mathbf{B}^{-1}$ is the inverse of $\mathbf{B}$.

$\mathbf{x}_B$ is a feasible solution when $\mathbf{B}^{-1}\mathbf{b} \geqslant \mathbf{0}$.

Equation (A-8) expresses $\mathbf{b}$ as a linear combination of the column vectors that form the basic matrix $\mathbf{B}$. We will define the ith column of $\mathbf{B}$ as $\mathbf{b}_i$, and the ith component of $\mathbf{x}_B$ as x_{Bi}, so (A-8) becomes:

(A-10) $$\mathbf{b} = \sum_{i=1}^{m} x_{Bi}\mathbf{b}_i$$

Clearly, the x_{Bi} are the coefficients of linear combination of $\mathbf{b}$ in terms of $\mathbf{B}$.

We will consider now expressing $\mathbf{a}_j$, any column of $\mathbf{A}$, in terms of $\mathbf{B}$. Let y_{ij} be the coefficient of the linear combination of $\mathbf{a}_j$ and $\mathbf{b}_i$, then

$$\mathbf{a}_j = \sum_{i=1}^{m} y_{ij}\mathbf{b}_i$$

or defining y_j as the column vector of the y_{ij}:

(A-11) $$a_j = By_j$$

and

(A-12) $$y_j = B^{-1}a_j$$

The simplex tableau corresponding to the basis **B** consists of x_B and the y_j for all the columns of **A**.

We will call the elements of **c** corresponding to the basic solution by c_B. You will recall that c_j is the objective function value of a_j, and z_j is the objective function value of a_j expressed in terms of the basis, i.e., of By_j. Using logic developed in Chapter 3 we obtain

(A-13) $$z_j = \sum_{i=1}^{m} y_{ij} c_{Bi} = c_B y_j = c_B B^{-1} a_j$$

When the matrix **A** contains an identity matrix **I** within it, and when $b \geqslant 0$ there exists an immediate initial basis, the identity matrix, which provides a basic feasible solution. When **A** does not contain an identity matrix, artificial vectors and variables are used to augment **A** until an **I** exists.

EXERCISES

A.1   (i) Draw the vectors

$$a = \begin{bmatrix} 3 \\ 1 \end{bmatrix}, \qquad b = \begin{bmatrix} 2 \\ 4 \end{bmatrix}, \qquad \text{and} \quad c = \begin{bmatrix} 4 \\ 3 \end{bmatrix}$$

(ii) Show graphically that $a + b = \begin{bmatrix} 5 \\ 5 \end{bmatrix}$.

(iii) Draw $2a + \frac{1}{2}c$, and verify the answer algebraically.

(iv) Find algebraically the distance between **a** and **c**, and find algebraically the length of **b**. Verify these on the graph.

(v) Show where the null vector, sum vector, and unit vectors are on the graph.

A.2   Using the vectors in question 1, express **b** as a linear combination of **a** and **c** both graphically and algebraically. Also, express **a** as a linear combination of **b** and **c**.

A.3   Using the vectors in question 1, find two points on the line segment between **a** and **b**.

A.4   Draw the convex hull of the points

$$a_1 = \begin{bmatrix} 1 \\ 2 \end{bmatrix}, \qquad a_2 = \begin{bmatrix} 4 \\ 1 \end{bmatrix}, \qquad a_3 = \begin{bmatrix} 2 \\ 4 \end{bmatrix}, \qquad \text{and} \quad a_4 = \begin{bmatrix} 6 \\ 4 \end{bmatrix}$$

(i) Find algebraically two points in this convex hull.

(ii) Position the points represented by the following values of the y_i.

(a) $\gamma_1 = 0, \qquad \gamma_2 = 0, \qquad \gamma_3 = \frac{1}{4}, \qquad \gamma_4 = \frac{3}{4}$

(b) $\gamma_1 = \frac{1}{4}, \qquad \gamma_2 = \frac{1}{4}, \qquad \gamma_3 = \frac{1}{2}, \qquad \gamma_4 = 0$

(iii) What are the values of the y_i that give the four corner points of the convex hull.

A.5 Consider the following vectors in E^3: $\mathbf{a}_1 = (1,0,0)$, $\mathbf{a}_2 = (2,1,1)$, $\mathbf{a}_3 = (1,1,1)$, $\mathbf{a}_4 = (0,2,0)$.

  (i) Is the set $(\mathbf{a}_2, \mathbf{a}_3)$ linearly independent?

  (ii) Is the set $(\mathbf{a}_1, \mathbf{a}_2, \mathbf{a}_3)$ a spanning set?

  (iii) Show that the set $(\mathbf{a}_1, \mathbf{a}_3, \mathbf{a}_4)$ is a basis.

A.6 Before solving each of the following sets of simultaneous equations, indicate how many solutions you might expect them to have. How many do they in fact have? Why?

  (i)
$$x_1 + x_2 = 6$$
$$2x_1 + x_2 = 8$$

  (ii)
$$x_1 + x_2 = 6$$
$$2x_1 + x_2 = 10$$
$$3x_1 - 2x_2 = 8$$

  (iii)
$$x_1 + x_2 + x_3 = 5$$
$$4x_1 + 2x_2 + x_3 = 18$$
$$6x_1 + 4x_2 + 3x_3 = 26$$

REFERENCES

Hadley, G. *Linear Algebra*. Reading, Mass.: Addison Wesley, 1961. An excellent text on linear algebra designed as a supplementary text for linear programming courses. Sections 2-1 to 2-6 introduce vectors. Definitions of convex combination and convex hull are in Sections 6-4 and 6-5. These sections are, though, fairly advanced. Similarly Chapter 5 deals with linear simultaneous equations, but assumes a knowledge of matrices. For the reader who wishes to learn matrices, Sections 3-1 to 3-9, 3-21, and 4-1 to 4-3 are very good.

Most texts on linear algebra introduce vectors. Many introductory mathematics texts deal with simultaneous equations at a low level, e.g.:

Kemeny, J. G., A. Schleifer, J. L. Snell, and G. L. Thompson. *Finite Mathematics with Business Applications*. Englewood Cliffs, N.J.: Prentice-Hall, 1962. Pages 229 to 261 cover vectors, matrices, and simultaneous equations.

Appendix B

Elements
of
Probability

This appendix is not intended as a substitute for an in-depth study of probability and statistics. Coverage is restricted to those aspects of probability used in this text; its aim is to serve only as a review.

B-1 RULES OF PROBABILITY

Any experiment whose outcome depends on chance is called a *random experiment*. Any possible outcome of a random experiment that cannot be decomposed into more basic components is called an *elementary event*. The collection of all possible elementary events of a random experiment represents the *sample space S*. For instance, rolling two dice is a random experiment with elementary events: [the number of dots on the first die is i, the number of dots on the second die is j]. Since both i and j may assume any of the integers from 1 to 6, the sample space has 6×6, or 36 elementary events.

Let A be any outcome or *event* of a random experiment. A consists of one or several elementary events. A is thus a subset of S.

AXIOM 1

With each random event A of S there is associated a real number denoted as $P(A)$, called the probability of A, where $P(A) \geqslant 0$.

AXIOM 2

At least one of the possible elementary events has to occur, i.e., $P(S) = 1$.

AXIOM 3: ADDITION RULE

If events $A_1, A_2, ..., A_k$ are pairwise mutually exclusive (i.e., sets of elementary events with no elementary events in common), then the probability of their union is given by:

(B-1) $$P(A_1 \cup A_2 \cup \cdots \cup A_k) = \sum_{i=1}^{k} P(A_i),$$

where $A_i \cup A_j$ denotes the collection of all elementary events that are either in A_i or in A_j or in both.

Define $\overline{A}$ as the set of all elementary events of S not in A. A and $\overline{A}$ are mutually exclusive and their union is equal to S. Hence, it follows from axioms 2 and 3 that $P(\overline{A}) = 1 - P(A)$.

In many physical experiments each elementary event is equally likely. For instance, each elementary event of rolling two dice is equally likely, assuming that the dice are absolutely fair. Let the event $A = $ [the sum of the dots is 6]. Then $P(A)$ is obtained as the ratio of the number of elementary events favorable to A (of which there are 5) over the total number of elementary events, or $P(A) = 5/36$. Similarly, let the event $B = $ [the sum of the dots is 5]. Verify that $P(B) = 4/36$. $A \cup B$ is the event [the sum of the dots is either 5 or 6]. It is the union of events A and B. Since events A and B are *mutually exclusive*, we have, by axiom 3:

$$P(A \cup B) = P(A) + P(B) = 10/36$$

What is the probability that the sum of the dots on the two dice is 6 and at the same time that each die has an even number of dots? If we let event $A = $ [the sum of the dots is 6] and $C = $ [each die shows an even number of dots], then we are asking for the probability of the joint event that both A and C occur, referred to as the intersection of A and C, denoted by $A \cap C$. Only those elementary events that satisfy both A and C simultaneously are considered. Verify that two out of the 36 elementary events have both properties, hence $P(A \cap C) = 2/36$.

What is the probability that the sum of the dots on the two dice is 6 (event A), given that both dice show an even number of dots (event C)? This probability refers to the occurrence of event A, however this time subject to the condition that event C has occurred. Such a probability is appropriately called a *conditional probability* and is denoted by $P(A \mid C)$—read as P of A given C—where C stands for the condition. Note that the condition of event C excludes all those elementary events where either one die or the other or both dice show an odd number of dots. Thus, the essence of conditional probabilities is that we define a new sample space, which is a subset of the original sample space and which contains only those elementary events that satisfy the condition C.

> ## CONDITIONAL PROBABILITY
>
> (B-2) $$P(A \mid C) = \frac{P(A \cap C)}{P(C)}$$
>
> or
>
> (B-3) $$P(A \cap C) = P(A \mid C) P(C)$$

For our example, expression (B-2) yields:

$$P(A \mid C) = \frac{2/36}{9/36} = 2/9$$

Expression (B-3) tells us how to find the probability of the intersection of two dependent events.

If event A is *independent* of event C, then the probability of A is not affected by whether event C has occurred or not, i.e.,

$$P(A \mid C) = P(A \mid \bar{C}) = P(A)$$

It follows that if two events A and C are independent, expression (B-3) simplifies to

(B-4) $$P(A \cap C) = P(A) P(C) \qquad (\textit{Multiplication rule})$$

For instance, referring to one die as the first die and the other as the second die, the events $D =$ [the first die shows an even number of dots] and $E =$ [the second die shows an even number of dots] are clearly independent. The outcome of one does not influence the outcome of the other. Each has a probability of $\frac{1}{2}$. Hence by (B-4):

$$P(C) = P(D \cap E) = P(D) P(E) = (\tfrac{1}{2})(\tfrac{1}{2}) = \tfrac{1}{4}$$

as we have seen earlier.

B-2 RANDOM VARIABLES

Let us associate with each elementary event in S a real number x. This correspondence need not be unique, i.e., several elementary events may map into the same value x. This mapping of the elementary events onto the real line is called a *random variable*, denoted by X. We usually use capital letters to denote the random variable and small letters to denote particular values of the random variable. Note that no probabilities are implied in this mapping.

Example 1:   Let X denote the sum of the dots on the faces up when rolling two dice. X can assume values $2, 3, \ldots, 12$.   Only one elementary event of the experiment maps into the number 2; however, two map into 3, three into 4, etc.

We now redefine the three axioms of probability in terms of random variables.

Define $F(x) = P(X \leqslant x)$ as the *probability distribution function* of the random variable X.   Then

---

AXIOM 1A

$F(x)$ is monotonic nondecreasing in x.   If $a < b$, then $F(a) \leqslant F(b)$

AXIOM 2A

$F(\infty) = 1$ and $F(-\infty) = 0$

AXIOM 3A

(B-5) $P(a < X \leqslant b) = F(b) - F(a)$

This follows immediately if we let event $A = [X \leqslant a]$, $B = [a < X \leqslant b]$, and event $C = A \cup B = [X \leqslant b]$, and use axiom 3.

If the random variable X assumes only discrete values $x_1, x_2, \ldots$, then the probability distribution function is given by:

$$P(X \leqslant x_k) = F(x_k) = \sum_{i=1}^{k} p(x_i), \qquad k = 1, 2, \ldots$$

where $p(x_i)$ is the probability that $X = x_i$.

The function $p(x_i)$ is called the *probability (mass) function*.   Clearly $\sum_{i=1}^{\infty} p(x_i) = 1$. Try to find the probability function for the random variable "the sum of the dots on both dice."

If the random variable X is continuous, i.e., can assume any real value, then the probability distribution function is defined as

$$P(X \leqslant a) = F(a) = \int_{-\infty}^{a} f(x)\, dx$$

where $f(x) = dF(x)/dx$ is called the *probability density function*.
$f(x)\, dx$ is the (approximate) probability that the random variable assumes a value between x and $x + dx$, dx very small.   Again, $\int_{-\infty}^{\infty} f(x)\, dx = 1$.   Figure B-1 depicts some of these concepts.

Let X and Y be two random variables with a *joint* distribution function $P(X \leqslant a, Y \leqslant b) = F(a, b)$.   For continuous random variables the joint distribution

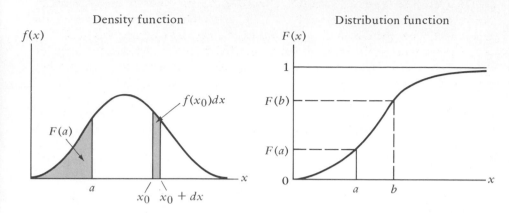

Figure B-1. *Probability distribution and density functions for a continuous random variable.*

function is obtained by integrating the *joint density functions* $f(x, y)$ over both variables:

$$F(a, b) = \int_{-\infty}^{a} \int_{-\infty}^{b} f(x, y)\, dy\, dx$$

If we are interested in the distribution of X or of Y alone, regardless of what value the other random variable assumes, we find the so-called *marginal distribution* of X or of Y. Its density function is defined as

$$g(x) = \int_{-\infty}^{+\infty} f(x, y)\, dy \qquad \text{for } X,$$

or

$$h(y) = \int_{-\infty}^{+\infty} f(x, y)\, dx \qquad \text{for } Y.$$

Two random variables, X and Y, are said to be independent of one another if

$$f(x, y) = g(x)\, h(y)$$

If X and Y are mutually dependent, then the conditional density function of, say, X given $Y = y$ is defined as

$$g(x \mid y) = \frac{f(x, y)}{h(y)}$$

The reader is asked to define the corresponding expressions for discrete random variables.

Often, it is convenient to summarize the information contained in a probability distribution by a few summary measures. The two most important ones are the *expected value* and the *variance* of the random variable. The expected value, denoted by $E(X) = \mu$, is an indication of where the center of mass of the random variable is located. It is defined by

(B-6) $E(X) = \sum\limits_{i=1}^{\infty} x_i\, p(x_i)$ for discrete random variables

and

(B-7) $E(X) = \int_{-\infty}^{\infty} xf(x)\, dx$ for continuous random variables

Thus, for a discrete random variable, $E(X)$ is seen to be the weighted sum of all values that the random variable can assume with the probabilities serving as weights.

The variance, denoted by $VAR(X) = \sigma^2$, is an indication of how dispersed the mass of the random variable is around its expected value μ. It is defined by

(B-8) $VAR(X) = \sum\limits_{i=1}^{\infty} (x_i - \mu)^2 p(x_i)$ for discrete random variables

and

(B-9) $VAR(X) = \int_{-\infty}^{\infty} (x - \mu)^2 f(x)\, dx$ for continuous random variables

The square root of the variance is called the *standard deviation*, denoted by σ.

Example 2:   Let X denote again the sum of the dots when rolling two dice. Then, as you can verify

$X = x_i$	2	3	4	5	6	7	8	9	10	11	12
$p(x_i)$	1/36	2/36	3/36	4/36	5/36	6/36	5/36	4/36	3/36	2/36	1/36

and

$$E(X) = 2(1/36) + 3(2/36) + 4(3/36) + 5(4/36) + 6(5/36) + 7(6/36) + 8(5/36)$$
$$+ 9(4/36) + 10(3/36) + 11(2/36) + 12(1/36) = 7$$
$$VAR(X) = (2-7)^2(1/36) + (3-7)^2(2/36) + (4-7)^2(3/36) + (5-7)^2(4/36)$$
$$+ (6-7)^2(5/36) + (7-7)^2(6/36) + (8-7)^2(5/36)$$
$$+ (9-7)^2(4/36) + (10-7)^2(3/36) + (11-7)^2(2/36)$$
$$+ (12-7)^2(1/36) = 5\tfrac{5}{6}$$

and

$$\sigma = \sqrt{5\tfrac{5}{6}} = 2.415$$

Other measures of central location are the *mode* (value of X for the highest point in the probability mass or density function) and the *median* (value of X that divides the entire mass or density function into two equal parts, i.e., the number M such that $P(X \leqslant M) = P(X \geqslant M) = \tfrac{1}{2}$).

PROPERTIES OF *E(X)*

1. Let $Y = cX$, c constant, then

(B-10) $$E(Y) = E(cX) = cE(X)$$

2. Let $Y = X + c$, c constant, then,

(B-11) $$E(Y) = E(X + c) = E(X) + c$$

3. Let $Y = \sum_{j=1}^{k} X_j$, *where* each X_j is a random variable. Then

(B-12) $$E(Y) = E(X_1 + X_2 + \cdots + X_k) = \sum_{j=1}^{k} E(X_j)$$

PROPERTIES OF *VAR(X)*

1. Let $Y = cX$, c constant, then

(B-13) $$VAR(Y) = VAR(cX) = c^2 VAR(X)$$

2. Let $Y = X + c$, c constant, then

(B-14) $$VAR(Y) = VAR(X + c) = VAR(X)$$

3. Let $Y = \sum_{i=1}^{k} X_j$ where the X_j form a set of mutually independent random variables. Then

(B-15) $$VAR(Y) = VAR(X_1 + X_2 + \cdots + X_k) = \sum_{j=1}^{k} VAR(X_j)$$

Note that property 3 of $VAR(X)$ requires the random variables to be mutually independent.

Example 3. (a) Let X denote the random variable for monthly sales (in units sold) for a given product. Assume that X has the following probability function:

x_i	1	2	3	4
$p(x_i)$	0.4	0.3	0.2	0.1

Verify that $E(X) = 2$ and $VAR(X) = 1$.

Each unit sold brings in a revenue of \$4.00. Let Y denote the revenue in dollars generated by this product per month; $Y = 4X$ is also a random variable. If $c = 4$, then by (B-10) $E(Y) = 4E(X) = 4(2) = 8$, and by (B-13) $VAR(Y) = 4^2 E(X) = 4^2(2) = 32$.

(b) Consider now sales over 6 months. Each month's sales follow the same probability distribution as for (a). Let X_i be the random variable for sales in month i, and Y be sales over six months. $Y = \sum_{i=1}^{6} X_i$. Then, the expected sales over six months are

$$E(Y) = \sum_{i=1}^{6} E(X_i) = 2 + 2 + 2 + 2 + 2 + 2 = 12$$

by (B-12)

and the variance of sales over six months is

$$VAR(Y) = \sum_{i=1}^{6} VAR(X_i) = 1 + 1 + 1 + 1 + 1 + 1 = 6$$

by (B-15)

assuming sales in consecutive months are independent.

B-3 DISCRETE PROBABILITY DISTRIBUTIONS

Binominal Distribution

Consider a random experiment that consists of n independent trials. Each trial has only two outcomes, such as *success* or *failure*, where $P(Success) = p$ and $P(Failure) = 1 - p$. Then, the random variable X denoting the number of successes in n trials has a binomial distribution with the probability function defined by

(B-16) $$p(x) = \frac{n!}{x!(n-x)!} p^x (1-p)^{n-x}, \qquad x = 0, 1, \ldots, n,$$

with

(B-17) $$E(X) = np$$

(B-18) $$VAR(X) = np(1-p)$$

Binomial distributions are important for attribute sampling, where the state of each observation is either "on" or "off" (i.e., either 1 or 0).

As n gets large, the binomial distribution approaches a *normal distribution* with $\mu = np$ and $\sigma^2 = np(1-p)$. For $np > 5$ the normal approximation is satisfactory. If $p \leqslant 0.01$, the Poisson distribution provides a good approximation for $n \geqslant 50$.

Poisson Distribution

A random variable has a Poisson distribution with parameter λt, if its probability function is defined by

(B-19) $$p(x) = \frac{(\lambda t)^x e^{-\lambda t}}{x!}, \qquad x = 0, 1, 2, \ldots,$$

with

(B-20) $$E(X) = \lambda t$$

(B-21) $$VAR(X) = \lambda t$$

For the Poisson distribution, λ represents the rate per unit time ($t = 1$) at which the events of the chance phenomenon occur.   For instance, if the random variable X represents the number of customers that each demand one unit of a given product over a length of time t, then λ is the average rate of customer arrivals (or the average rate of demand) per unit time $t = 1$.   Note the interesting fact that the form of the distribution remains Poisson as the length of time t considered changes.

The Poisson distribution is particularly suitable for depicting the random behavior of individual events that occur relatively infrequently within the time span considered, such as the demand for indivudal spare parts or the number of individual arrivals at a service counter.   For $\lambda t > 20$, the normal distribution provides a good approximation, except at the extreme tails.

There are extensive tables available in handbooks on statistics for both the binomial and the Poisson distributions.

B-4 CONTINUOUS PROBABILITY DISTRIBUTIONS

Uniform Distribution (Rectangular Distribution)

A random variable X defined over the interval from a to b has a uniform probability distribution if its density function has the form

(B-22)
$$f(x) = \begin{cases} \dfrac{1}{b-a} & \text{for} \quad a \leqslant x \leqslant b \\ 0 & \text{otherwise} \end{cases}$$

with

(B-23)
$$E(X) = \frac{a+b}{2}$$

(B-24)
$$VAR(X) = \frac{(b-a)^2}{12}$$

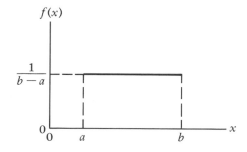

Figure B-2. *Uniform distribution.*

Exponential Distribution (Negative Exponential Distribution)

A random variable X defined for all nonnegative values has an exponential probability distribution if its density function has the form

(B-25)
$$f(x) = \begin{cases} \lambda e^{-\lambda x} & \text{for } x \geqslant 0 \\ 0 & \text{otherwise} \end{cases}$$

with

(B-26)
$$E(X) = 1/\lambda$$

(B-27)
$$VAR(X) = 1/\lambda^2$$

and

(B-28)
$$F(x) = 1 - e^{-\lambda x}$$

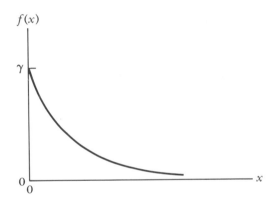

Figure B-3. *Exponential distribution.*

The exponential distribution is often used to depict the random behavior of the time interval between the occurrence of two consecutive events, such as the time between two consecutive arrivals or the time to the next breakdown of a machine. This distribution has the often overlooked implication that the probability of, say, a breakdown occurring within the next 20 hours of operation does not depend on when the last breakdown occurred.

Normal Distribution

The normal distribution is the most important probability distribution. For numerous random phenomena in all fields of knowledge the value of the random variable is the cumulative result of a large number of individually small random effects. Such phenomena tend to follow a normal distribution. Furthermore, the limiting form of a number of other distributions (binomial, Poisson, Gamma, chi-square) is normal. The normal distribution is completely determined by two parameters, the expected value or mean, μ, and the variance, σ^2, of the random variable. The expression for the normal density function cannot be integrated analytically. However, any normal random variable X with mean μ and variance σ^2 can be expressed in terms of the standardized normal random variable Z with mean 0 and variance 1 for which extensive tables exist. We use the following transformation:

$$x = \mu + z\sigma$$

or

$$z = \frac{x - \mu}{\sigma}$$

and

(B-30)
$$P(X \leqslant a) = P\left(Z \leqslant \frac{a - \mu}{\sigma}\right)$$

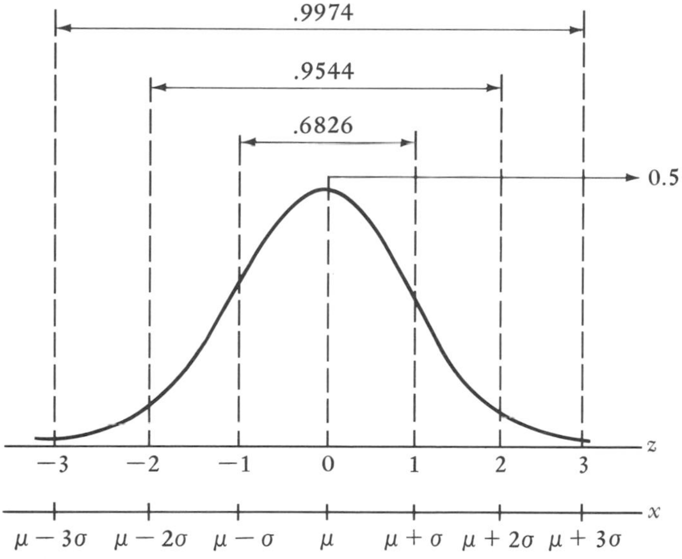

Figure B-4. *Normal curve.*

Gamma Distribution

The Gamma distribution depends on two nonnegative parameters a and b. Its probability density function is given by

(B-31)
$$f(x) = \begin{cases} \dfrac{b^a}{\Gamma(a)} x^{a-1} e^{-bx} & \text{for } x > 0 \\ 0 & \text{otherwise} \end{cases}$$

where $\Gamma(a) = \int_0^\infty t^{a-1} e^{-t} dt$ *is the* gamma function. For a integer, $\Gamma(a) = (a-1)!$

(B-32)
$$E(X) = \frac{a}{b}$$

(B-33)
$$VAR(X) = \frac{a}{b^2}$$

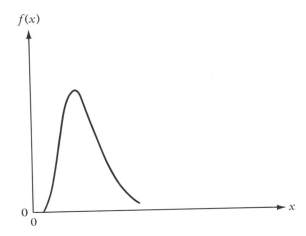

Figure B-5. *Gamma distribution.*

For $a = 1$, the gamma distribution reduces to an exponential distribution with parameter $\lambda = b$.

For large a the gamma distribution approaches a normal distribution.

Beta Distribution

The Beta distribution depends on two nonnegative parameters, α and β. Its probability density function is given by

$$(B\text{-}34) \qquad f(x) = \begin{cases} \dfrac{\Gamma(\alpha+\beta)}{\Gamma(\alpha)\Gamma(\beta)} x^{\alpha-1}(1-x)^{\beta-1} & \text{for} \quad 0 < x < 1 \\ 0 & \text{otherwise} \end{cases}$$

where $\Gamma(s)$ is the gamma function (see gamma distribution), and

$$(B\text{-}35) \qquad\qquad\qquad E(X) = \frac{\alpha}{\alpha+\beta}$$

$$(B\text{-}36) \qquad\qquad\qquad VAR(X) = \frac{\alpha\beta}{(\alpha+\beta)^2(\alpha+\beta+1)}$$

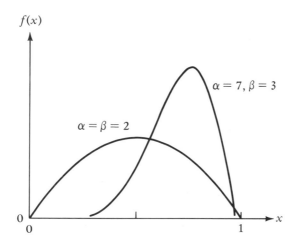

Figure B-6. *Beta distribution.*

For the PERT model in Chapter 6 we used the following transformation:

$$T = a + (b-a)X$$

with

$$E(T) = a + (b-a)\left[\frac{\alpha}{\alpha+\beta}\right]$$

and

$$VAR(T) = (b-a)^2 \frac{\alpha\beta}{(\alpha+\beta)^2(\alpha+\beta+1)}$$

The mode of the distribution of T occurs at

$$m = \frac{a(\beta-1)+b(\alpha-1)}{(\alpha+\beta-2)}$$

Setting $\alpha = 3+\sqrt{2}$ and $\beta = 3-\sqrt{2}$, the expected value and variance of T simplify to

$$E(T) = \frac{a+b+(\alpha+\beta-2)m}{\alpha+\beta} = \frac{a+b+4m}{6}$$

and

$$VAR(T) = \left[\frac{a-b}{6}\right]^2$$

which are the expressions used in Section 6-5.

The beta distribution is often suitable if the random variable is a proportion.

B-5 DISTRIBUTIONS OF FUNCTIONS OF RANDOM VARIABLES

In operations research we quite often deal with functions of random variables, such as benefit or cost functions that involve random variables or sums of random variables.

Let $Y = g(X)$ be a single-valued function of a discrete random variable. Then

(B-37) $$P(Y=y_i) = P(Y=g(x_i)) = p(x_i)$$

and

(B-38) $$E(Y) = E(g(X)) = \sum_{\text{all } i} g(x_i)\, p(x_i)$$

(B-39) $$VAR(Y) = VAR(g(X)) = \sum_{\text{all } i} [g(x_i)-E(g(X))]^2 p(x_i)$$

Example 4. Let X be the random variable for the monthly demand with probability function $p(x)$ as listed in Example 3(a). Assume that at the beginning of a given month there are two units left for sale. New units would only become available at the beginning of next month. If more than 2 units are demanded, some sales would be lost. What is the probability distribution of lost sales for that month? If Y denotes lost sales, then

$$Y = g(X) = \begin{cases} 0 & \text{for } X \leq 2 \quad \text{with } p(Y=0) = p(X=1)+p(X=2) \\ X-2 & \text{for } X=x > 2 \text{ with } p(Y=x-2) = p(x) \end{cases}$$

The expected value of lost sales is

$$E(Y) = 0\,(p(X=1)+p(X=2)) + (3-2)\,p(X=3) + (4-2)\,p(X=4)$$
$$= 0\,(0.4+0.3) \qquad\qquad + 1\,(0.2) \qquad\qquad + 2\,(0.1)$$
$$= 0.4 \text{ units.}$$

Similarly, for continuous random variables, if X has a density function $f(x)$, then $Y = g(X)$ has the density function

(B-40) $$h(y) = f(\psi(y))\left|\frac{d\psi(y)}{dy}\right|$$

where $x = \psi(y)$ is the unique inverse function of $y = g(x)$. All other properties can now be obtained from $h(y)$.

Example 5. Let $Y = a + bX$. Then the inverse function is given by $X = (Y-a)/b$ with derivative $1/b$. The density function of Y becomes

(B-41) $$h(y) = f((y-a)/b)\left|\frac{1}{b}\right|$$

If X is normally distributed, then $Y = a + bX$ will also be normal with $\mu = E(Y) = a + bE(X)$ and $\sigma^2 = VAR(Y) = b^2 VAR(X)$.

Next, we consider the distribution of a sum of independent random variables, often referred to as the *convolution* of their probability distributions. We shall demonstrate the concept by looking at the sum of two independent random variables. The generalization follows immediately by repeated application of the same argument.

Let X and Y be two discrete random variables with probability functions $p(x)$ and $r(y)$ for $x = 0, 1, 2, ...$, and $y = 0, 1, 2, ...$. Let $Z = X + Y$ and $h(z)$ be the probability function. Then Z can assume values $z = 0, 1, 2, ...$. $Z = 0$ if both $X = 0$ and $Y = 0$. Given that X and Y are independent, the probability that they are both 0 and hence $Z = 0$ is $h(0) = p(0)r(0)$ by (B-2). Similarly, $Z = 1$ if either $X = 0$ and $Y = 1$, or $X = 1$ and $Y = 0$. Hence $h(1) = p(0)r(1) + p(1)r(0)$ by (B-2) and (B-1). Using the same principle, we get

(B-42) $$h(z) = \sum_{x=0}^{z} p(x)r(z-x), \qquad z = 0, 1, 2, ...$$

Example 6. Consider again the demand distribution in Example 3(a). What is the demand distribution over two months, assuming sales on consecutive months are independent?

Let X_1 be the demand for month 1 and X_2 for month 2 and let $Z = X_1 + X_2$. Then

$$p(Z = 2) = p(X_1 = 1)\,p(X_2 = 2-1) = (0.4)(0.4) = 0.16$$

$$p(Z = 3) = p(X_1 = 1)\,p(X_2 = 3-1) + p(X_1 = 2)\,p(X_2 = 3-2)$$
$$= (0.4)(0.3) + (0.3)(0.4) = 0.24$$

$$p(Z = 4) = p(X_1 = 1)\,p(X_2 = 4-1) + p(X_1 = 2)\,p(X_2 = 4-2)$$
$$+ p(X_1 = 3)\,p(X_2 = 4-3)$$
$$= (0.4)(0.2) + (0.3)(0.3) + (0.2)(0.4) = 0.25$$

$$p(Z = 5) = p(X_1 = 1)\, p(X_2 = 5-1) + p(X_1 = 2)\, p(X_2 = 5-2)$$
$$+ p(X_1 = 3)\, p(X_2 = 5-3) + p(X_1 = 4)\, p(X_2 = 5-4)$$
$$= 0.04 + 0.06 + 0.06 + 0.04 = 0.20,\ \text{etc.}$$

Verify that $p(Z = 6) = 0.10$, $p(Z = 7) = 0.04$, $p(Z = 8) = 0.01$ and, as required, their sum is 1.

If X and Y have binomial distributions with parameters, n_1 and n_2, but the same value of p (probability of *success*), then Z also has a binomial distribution with parameters $n = n_1 + n_2$ and p. Similarly, if X and Y are Poisson variables, both with parameter λ, then Z will also have a Poisson distribution with parameter 2λ.

For two independent continuous random variables with density functions $f(x)$ and $r(y)$, the density function of $Z = X + Y$ is

(B-43)
$$h(z) = \int_{-\infty}^{\infty} f(x)\, r(z-x)\, dx$$

If X and Y are normally distributed random variables, then Z will also be normally distributed with parameters $\mu = \mu_X + \mu_Y$ and $\sigma^2 = \sigma_X^2 + \sigma_Y^2$, where μ_X, σ_X^2 and μ_Y, σ_Y^2 are the parameters of X and Y. If X and Y are exponentially distributed, both with parameter λ, then Z has a gamma distribution with $a = 2$, and $b = \lambda$. Both of these results extend to more than 2 independent random variables.

We have seen that the normal distribution describes the limiting behavior of a number of theoretical probability distributions. It turns out that the normal distribution also provides an approximation for the probability distribution of the sum of n independent random variables for n sufficiently large. By (B-12) and (B-15) the parameters of the normal approximating distribution are

$$\mu = \sum_{i=1}^{n} \mu_{X_i}$$

$$\sigma^2 = \sum_{i=1}^{n} \sigma_{X_i}^2$$

where μ_{X_i} and $\sigma_{X_i}^2$ are the expected value and variance of random variable X_i.

If the individual distributions are not highly skewed and none of the random variables dominates all others in terms of the relative size of its parameters, the normal approximation may already be satisfactory for the sum of as few as $n = 10$ random variables.

This is one version of the famous *central limit theorem*. Another version asserts that the distribution of the average value or sample mean $\bar{x} = \sum_{i=1}^{n} x^{(i)}/n$ of n independent observations $x^{(1)}, x^{(2)}, x^{(3)}, \ldots, x^{(n)}$ on an arbitrarily distributed random variable X also tends to be normally distributed as n gets large with parameters $\mu_{\bar{x}} = \mu_X$ and $\sigma_{\bar{x}}^2 = \sigma_X^2/n$.

EXERCISES

B.1   Consider an urn that contains 5 balls numbered 0, 1, 2, 3 and 4. Balls numbered 0 and 3 are black, the other 3 balls are white.

(a) You draw one ball at random from the urn and record its number. It is then replaced and a second ball is drawn at random from the urn and its number recorded. Define the sample space for this experiment.

(b) What is the probability of event $A_i = $ [the sum of the numbers is i], for $i = 6$, 7, and 8. What is the probability of event $B = $ [the sum is at least 6]? event $C = $ [the sum is no more than 5]?

(c) What is P (the sum is at least 6 and at least one ball is black)?

(d) What is the conditional probability that the sum is at least 6, given that at least one ball drawn is black? First use the definition (B-2) and then verify the result directly from the reduced sample space.

(e) What is the probability that at least one ball is black, given that the sum is at least 6?

(f) Consider drawing of each ball as a separate experiment. Let event $A = $ [first ball is black] and event $B = $ [second ball is black]. Are A and B independent events? If so, find $P(C)$, where $C = A \cap B$, using the multiplication rule.

(g) Two balls are drawn consecutively without replacement. Find the probability that both balls are black.

B.2 The firm XYZ considers submitting a bid as a subcontractor for a large computer system. It is known that three major computer manufacturers, A, B, and C, compete for the main contract. Firm XYZ has previously been subcontractor for A and B. The president of XYZ estimates that A has a 15 percent chance and B a 30 percent chance of getting the contract. If A gets the contract, XYZ has an 80 percent chance of being the subcontractor, whereas if B gets the contract, XYZ's chance is only 50 percent. It is only profitable for XYZ to prepare a bid if its chances of being chosen as subcontractors are at least 25 percent.

(a) Should XYZ prepare a bid? Why?

(b) Find the conditional probability that XYZ is chosen as subcontractor, given that it is known that either A or B has been given the contract.

(c) Find the conditional probability that A got the main contract, given that XYZ is the subcontractor.

B.3 Consider again the sample space of question 1 (a). Let X denote the random variable for the sum of the two numbers on the balls drawn.

(a) Determine the mapping of the sample space onto x, where x stands for the values that X can assume and find the probability mass function.

(b) Find $P(X \leqslant 3)$, $P(X \leqslant 4)$, $P(X \geqslant 4)$.

(c) Find $E(X)$, $VAR(X)$, and the standard deviation of X.

(d) Let X denote sales per week for a given product sold at \$5 per unit where X has the distribution defined in (a). What is the expected value of the sales revenue per week? the variance of the sales revenue per week?

(e) Consider sales over two separate weeks. What is the expected value of the sum of sales for the two weeks? What is the variance of this sum? What is the expected value of the revenue of this sum?

B.4 Consider a random variable that assumes the value 1 with probability p and 0 with probability $1 - p$ (known as a *Bernoulli variable*). Find the expected value and the variance and standard deviation of this variable. (Note that a binomial variable is given as the sum of n Bernoulli variables. Verify expressions (B-17) and (B-18) using the properties of $E(X)$ and $VAR(X)$ for the sum of independent variables.)

B.5 A product has the following probability density function for its daily sales:

$f(x) = 0.1 - 0.005x$ for $0 \leqslant x \leqslant 20$ and $f(x) = 0$ elsewhere. (Triangular distribution)
(a) Find $P(X \leqslant 10)$, $P(X > 10)$.
(b) Find $E(X)$ and $VAR(X)$.
Note: requires integration.

B.6   The monthly demand for a given spare part has a normal distribution. It is known that chances are 50 percent that the demand is at most 200 and that approximately 9 out of 10 weeks sales lie between 140 and 260 units.
(a) Determine the two parameters of the corresponding normal distribution. Use the following approximation: For the standard normal distribution $P(-1.67 < Z \leqslant +1.67)$ equals about 0.9.
(b) What is the probability that monthly sales exceed 280?

B.7   Consider the following weekly demand distribution:

x	0	1	2	3	4	5	6	7	8
$p(x)$	0.10	0.20	0.25	0.20	0.12	0.06	0.04	0.02	0.01

The stock on hand at the beginning of a given week is 4.
(a) Find the probability distribution for the amount short.
(b) If each unit sold brings in a profit of $2.50, find the expected value of profits lost due to shortages.

B.8   Consider the probability distribution of question 7. Assuming that sales in consecutive weeks are independent, find the probability distribution of sales over a two-week period.

B.9   Consider the distribution given in question 5. Assume that stocks on hand at the beginning of the day amount to 15.
(a) Determine the probability density function of lost sales.
(b) If each unit brings in a profit of $3, what is the expected value of the daily profits lost due to shortages?

B.10   Find the approximate probability distribution for sales over 30 days for the distribution defined in question 5. Assume that each week has the same distribution and that sales between weeks are independent.

REFERENCES

Ackoff, Russell L. *The Design of Social Research*. Chicago: University of Chicago Press, 1953. An easy text covering design aspects as well as statistical tests with a cookbook approach.

Burington, R. S., and D. C. May. *Handbook of Probability and Statistics with Tables*, Sandusky, Ohio: Handbook Publishers, A reference book of this sort with tables of the Binomial, Poisson, Normal and exponential distributions is part of every operations researcher's library.

Kendall, M. G., and A. Stuart. *The Advanced Theory of Statistics* (3 volumes), London: Griffin, 1967-69. For those with a taste of rigor right from Mr. Statistics himself. No doubt the most authoritative text in the field.

Mendenhall, W., and L. Ott and R. L. Schaeffer. *Elementary Survey Sampling,* Belmont, Cal: Wadsworth, 1971.

Mosteller, F., R. E. K. Rourke, and G. B. Thomas. *Probability with Statistical Applications.* Reading, Mass.: Addison Wesley, 1969. A good introductory text for a thorough review.

Siegel, Sidney. *Nonparametric Statistics for the Behavioral Sciences.* New York: McGraw-Hill, 1956.

Snedecor, George W., and William G. Cochran. *Statistical Methods.* Ames, Iowa: Iowa State University Press, 1967. An excellent text for the practitioner or those who have to use statistical tools without wanting to learn all the mathematical bases and proofs. Very thorough coverage of most tools with lots of good examples and useful pointers. Highly recommended as a reference text.

Bibliography

OPERATIONS RESEARCH BIBLIOGRAPHIES

Batchelor, James H., *Operations Research: An Annotated Bibliography*, Saint Louis University Press, Saint Louis, Vol 1—1959, Vol. 2—1962, Vol. 3—1963, Vol. 4—1964.

A Comprehensive Bibliography on Operations Research, Operations Research Group, Case Institute of Technology, Publication in Operations Research Series No. 4, published by Wiley and Sons under the Sponsorship of ORSA, 1959.

International Abstracts In Operations Research, published for IFORS by North-Holland, P.O. Box 211, Amsterdam, The Netherlands (since 1961).

Operations Research/Management Science, (International literature digest periodical), published monthly by Executive Science Institute, Inc., Whippany, N.J. 07981 (since 1961).

SELECTED TECHNICAL AND PROFESSIONAL JOURNALS IN OPERATIONS RESEARCH IN ENGLISH

Computers and Operations Research, a quarterly journal published by Pergamon Press, Inc. Maxwell House, Fairview Park, Elmsford, New York 10523.

Decision Sciences (U.S.): published by the American Institute for Decision Sciences, Kanawha Valley Graduate Center, Box 547, W. Nitro., W. Virg. 25143

European Journal of Operational Research: sponsored by the Association of European Operational Research Societies, published six times per year by North-Holland Publishing Company, P.O. Box 103, Amsterdam, The Netherlands.

INFOR (Canadian Journal of Operational Research & Information Processing) (Canada): published 3 times per year by INFOR Journal, P.O. Box 2225, Station D, Ottawa, Canada.

Interfaces (U.S.): published quarterly jointly by TIMS and ORSA. Dealing with practice in O.R. and management science. See *Management Science* and *Operations Research* for details.

The International Journal of Production Research (U.K.): published bi-monthly by Taylor & Francis Ltd., 10-14 Macklin Street, London WC2B 5NF, England.

Management Science (U.S.): Journal of the Institute of Management Sciences, 146 Westminster Street, Providence, R.I. 02903, (TIMS); published monthly.

Mathematical Programming: published bi-monthly by North-Holland, P.O. Box 211, Amsterdam, The Netherlands.

Mathematics of Operations Research (U.S.): quarterly published jointly by ORSA and TIMS; subscriptions through either society. See *Management Science* and *Operations Research* for details.

Naval Research Logistics Quarterly (U.S.): published by the Office of Naval Research, Managing Editor NRLQ, Arlington, Va. 22217.

New Zealand Operational Research (N.Z.): published twice per year by the Operational Research Society of N.Z., P.O. Box 904, Wellington, New Zealand.

OMEGA (U.K.): an international journal of management science, published bi-monthly by Pergamon Press Ltd., Headington Hill Hall, Oxford, OX3 0BW, England.

Operational Research Quarterly (U.K.): published quarterly for the Operational Research Society Ltd. by Pergamon Press, Headington Hill Hall, Oxford, OX3 0BW, England.

Operations Research (U.S.): Journal of the Operations Research Society of America. 428 East Preston Street, Baltimore, Maryland 21202, (ORSA); published bi-monthly.

OPSEARCH (India): (Editor, N. K. Jaiswal) c/o Institute for Defence Studies and Analyses, Sapru House, Barakhamba Road, New Delhi—1, India.

SIAM Journal on Applied Mathematics (U.S.): published 8 times per year by the Society for Industrial and Applied Mathematics, 33 South 17th Street, Philadelphia, Penn. 19103.

Transportation Research (U.S.): published quarterly by Pergamon Press Ltd, Headington Hill Hall, OX3 0BW, England.

Transportation Science (U.S.): published quarterly by the Operations Research Society of America, 428 East Preston Street, Baltimore, Maryland 21202.

For a list of non-English language journals see International Abstracts in Operations Rescarch. It goes without saying that many articles dealing with operations research problems have appeared in other journals, particularly in the field of

Economics, Finance, Marketing Research, Business Administration, Industrial and Electrical Engineering, Statistics and Mathematics.

LIST OF GENERAL TEXTS IN OPERATIONS RESEARCH

Baumol, W. J., *Economic Theory and Operations Analysis*, Prentice-Hall, Englewood Cliffs, N.J., 1972. Operations Research as tools of economic analysis and their place in economic theory as viewed from the vantage point of an economist. This is not really a text for future operations researchers, but for economists who wish to obtain some background in operations research use within their own field of knowledge. A succesful text that has gone through numerous revisions.

Buffa, Elwood S., and James S. Dyer, *Management Science/Operations Research*, A Wiley/Hamilton Publication, Wiley, New York, 1977. An interesting elementary text with a different flavor, directed at the future manager to enable him or her to recognize potential operations research problems, have a fruitful two-way communication with operations research specialists, and properly implement and use the result of such studies.

Hillier, Frederick S., and Gerald J. Lieberman, *Introduction to Operations Research*, Holden Day, San Francisco, 1974. One of the better more advanced operations research texts. Techniques oriented with numerous examples of potential (by necessity simplified) applications.

Kaufmann, A., *Introduction to Operations Research*, Academic Press, New York, 1968. A delightful series of stories, each dealing with the use of an operations research tool at an elementary level.

McMillan, C., *Mathematical Programming*, Wiley & Sons, New York, 1975. Fairly elementary coverage of deterministic mathematical programming techniques.

Taha, H. A., *Introduction to Operations Research*, Macmillan, New York, 1971. Not really an introduction to operations research, but rather to operations research techniques. Coverage of techniques uneven, with strong bias toward linear programming and extensions. Sequence of topics poorly organized.

Teichroew, Daniel, *An Introduction to Management Science: Deterministic Models*, Wiley & Sons, New York, 1964. One of the few texts that recognizes the importance of the methods of classical optimization in operations research. More than half of the text is devoted to this topic. Tends to belabor each point and should be read with generous skipping. Non-calculus portion somewhat weak.

Thierauf, R. J., and R. C. Klekamp, *Decision Making through Operations Research*, Wiley & Sons, New York, 1975. Fairly elementary coverage of most operations research techniques using a cookbook method approach.

Wagner, Harvey M., *Principles of Operations Research*, Prentice-Hall, Englewood Cliffs, N.J., 1975. Over a thousand pages long with more than 1000 exercises, this is an attempt to co r the present state of the art in operations research in sufficient depth, inclu ig many refinements. Style of writing is delightful. Intersperses more advanced and optional material within main line of thought. This makes reading often somewhat disruptive and hard to follow. This text should however be on the bookshelf of any operations researcher.

CASE BOOKS IN OPERATIONS RESEARCH

Haehling von Lanzenauer, C., *Cases in Operations Research*, Research and Publication Division, School of Business Administration, University of Western Ontario, London, Canada N64 3K7, 1975. Contains twenty-five comprehensive real cases in operations research, some of which originate at Harvard, Stanford, and IMEDE (Switzerland). An ideal companion book to this text. A detailed *Instructor's Manual* is available from the publishers to bona fide course instructors.

Martin, M. J. C., and R. A. Denison, eds., *Case Exercises in Operations Research*, London: Wiley-Interscience, 1971. Contains fifteen comprehensive real cases in operations research, cost benefit analysis, and Bayesian statistical decision theory. Except for the last three, the cases are British. A detailed *Tutor's Guide* is available to instructors.

Index

Page numbers in *italics* refer to exercises or references.